I0028230

THE COLLECTED WORKS OF
J. G. FRAZER

.

THE COLLECTED WORKS OF
J.G. FRAZER

VOLUME XX

Garnered Sheaves

Essays, Addresses and Reviews

HON-NO
TOMOSHA

Routledge
Taylor & Francis Group

LONDON AND NEW YORK

First published 1994 by Curzon Press
Co-published in 1994 by Hon-no-Tomosha Ltd.

Published 2018 by Routledge
2 Park Square, Milton Park, Abingdon, Oxon OX14 4RN
52 Vanderbilt Avenue, New York, NY 10017

First issued in paperback 2018

*Routledge is an imprint of the Taylor & Francis Group,
an informa business*

Copyright © by 1994 Taylor & Francis

All rights reserved. No part of this book may be reprinted or
reproduced or utilised in any form or by any electronic,
mechanical, or other means, now known or hereafter invented,
including photocopying and recording, or in any information
storage or retrieval system, without permission in writing from
the publishers.

Notice:
Product or corporate names may be trademarks or registered
trademarks, and are used only for identification and
explanation without intent to infringe.

British Library Cataloguing-in-Publication Data
A CIP record for this title is
available from the British Library

The Collected Works of J.G. Frazer : 28 Volumes

ISBN 13: 978-1-138-99185-9 (pbk)
ISBN 13: 978-0-7007-1439-1 (hbk)

PREFACE

MOST of the pieces included in this volume have seen the light before in one or other of a variety of publications in which till now they have lain scattered. I have ventured to collect these *disjecta membra* and submit them afresh to the reader, to whom they might otherwise not be easy of access, in the hope that he may find at least some of them to be of more than ephemeral interest. Apart from a few necessary corrections I have allowed them to stand in their original form without attempting to trim or prune them, though some of the sheaves tied up in this bundle were reaped in harvests long years ago. On the whole I have not seen reason to change my views on any essential point dealt with in these pages. Such supplementary observations as I have thought it worth while to make are printed together in the Notes at the end of the volume.

The essay " On certain Burial Customs as illustrative of the Primitive Theory of the Soul " was my first serious incursion into the wide field of Comparative Anthropology. On the subject of which it treats I have since collected a good deal of fresh evidence which I hope hereafter to embody in a separate work on that fear of the dead which has influenced profoundly the growth of religion.

The essay on Taboo was contributed as an article to the Ninth Edition of the *Encyclopaedia Britannica*. When I undertook to write it I supposed that taboo was a system peculiar to Polynesia ; it was only in studying the evidence that I came to perceive that the Polynesian system is only a particularly well-developed instance of a social phenomenon which is world-wide. Hence my old essay, tentative and slight as it is, may be thought to possess a certain historical interest as an early, perhaps the earliest, recognition of the great part which taboo and systems like it have played in the evolution of society and morality. My ever lamented friend, William Robertson Smith, was one of the first to accept the new view of taboo as a prime factor in moulding human history, and he gave it a wide currency in his famous *Lectures on the Religion of the Semites.* It has since become a commonplace of anthropology.

The essay on " The Scope and Method of Mental Anthropology " was written as a General Introduction to a special course of lectures delivered, by invitation of the College Council, at Trinity College, Cambridge. The lectures were subsequently published, but without the Introduction, which is here reprinted from *Science Progress.*

The only substantial addition which I have made to my old essays is a Note dealing with a particular story of the Language of Animals which is notable because it illustrates the wide diffusion a popular tale may enjoy, until, after starting from a single point, it has spread over three-quarters of the globe. For the evidence of that diffusion in this particular case I am indebted in large measure to the labours of my learned predecessors, the German orientalist Theodor Benfey, and the Finnish scholar Antti Aarne, each of whom has devoted an erudite monograph to the theme.

It only remains to thank the publishers, editors, and authors who have kindly allowed me to reprint the great bulk of the pieces included in this volume. I have to thank The Times Publishing Company for leave to reprint all the reviews included in Part III., together with the obituary notices of Sir Baldwin Spencer and Mr. William Wyse ; the Encyclopaedia Britannica Company for permission to reprint the essay " Taboo " from the Ninth Edition of the *Encyclopaedia Britannica* ; the Royal Anthropological Institute for leave to reprint the essay " On certain Burial Customs as illustrative of the Primitive Theory of the Soul " from the *Journal* of the Institute ; the Folk-lore Society for permission to reprint several articles from *Folk-lore, The Folk-lore Journal,* and *The Archaeological Review*; the Editors of *The Classical Review* for leave to reprint nine articles ; the Editor of *The Fortnightly Review* for leave to reprint the essay " A Suggestion as to the Origin of Gender in Language "; the Editor of *Science Progress* for leave to reprint " The Scope and Method of Mental Anthropology "; Mr. C. W. Hobley for leave to reprint the introduction to his book *Bantu Beliefs and Magic* ; Messrs. George Routledge & Sons for leave to reprint the preface to Dr. B. Malinowski's book *Argonauts of the Western Pacific* ; the Clarendon Press, Oxford, for permission to reprint the preface to Professor Martin P. Nilsson's book *A History of Greek Religion* ; the Australian and New Zealand Association for the Advancement of Science for permission to reprint from its *Proceedings* the article entitled " On some Ceremonies of the Central Australian Tribes "; and the Society for the Promotion of Hellenic Studies for leave to reprint from its *Journal* an Address delivered at the Jubilee celebration of the Society. To all these I here tender my grateful thanks for their courtesy.

J. G. FRAZER

18th February 1931

CONTENTS

PART II

ADDRESSES

PART III

REVIEWS

PART IV

NOTES

PART I

ESSAYS

B

I

ON CERTAIN BURIAL CUSTOMS AS ILLUSTRATIVE OF THE PRIMITIVE THEORY OF THE SOUL [1]

IN his *Roman Questions*,[2] that delightful storehouse of old-world lore, Plutarch asks—" When a man who has been falsely reported to have died abroad, returns home alive, why is he not admitted by the door, but gets up on the tiles and so lets himself down into the house ? " The curious custom to which Plutarch here refers prevails in modern Persia, for we read in *Hajji Baba* (c. 18) of the man who went through " the ceremony of making his entrance over the roof, instead of through the door ; for such is the custom when a man who has been thought dead returns home alive ". From a passage in Agathias we may perhaps infer that the custom is at least as old as the sixth century of our era.[3] A custom so remote from our modern ways must necessarily have its roots far back in the history of our race. Imagine a modern Englishman, whom his friends had given up for dead, rejoining the home circle by coming down the chimney,

[1] This paper was read before the Anthropological Institute of Great Britain and Ireland at London, March 10th, 1885. Mr. (afterwards Sir) Francis Galton, the President, was in the chair. The paper was printed, with some additions, in *The Journal of the Anthropological Institute*, vol. xv. (1886), pp. 64 *sqq.*, from which it is here reprinted with a few corrections.

[2] No. 5. It is to be observed that the explanations which I give of many of the following customs are not the explanations offered by the people who practise these customs. Some-times people give no explanation of their customs, sometimes (much oftener than not) a wrong one. The reader is therefore to understand that the authorities referred to are quoted for the fact of the customs, not for their explanation.

[3] Agathias, ii. 23. A man grievously sick was exposed in a desert place, and if he recovered and came home he was shunned as a ghost by everyone till he had been purified by the Magi, and had, as it were, come back to life (οἶον ἀνταπολάβοι τὸ αὖθις βιῶναι).

3

instead of entering by the front door. In this paper I propose to show that the custom originated in certain primitive beliefs and observances touching the dead—beliefs and observances by no means confined to Greece and Rome, but occurring in similar if not identical forms in many parts of the world.

The importance attached by the Romans in common with most other nations to the due performance of burial rites is well known, and need not be insisted upon. For the sake of my argument, however, it is necessary to point out that the attentions bestowed on the dead sprang not so much from the affection as from the fear of the survivors. For, as everyone knows, ghosts of the unburied dead haunt the earth and make themselves exceedingly disagreeable, especially to their undutiful relatives. Instances would be superfluous; it is the way of ghosts all the world over, from Brittany to Samoa.[1] But burial by itself was by no means a sufficient safeguard against the return of the ghost; many other precautions were taken by primitive man for the purpose of excluding or barring the importunate dead. Some of these precautions I will now enumerate. They exhibit an ingenuity and fertility of resource worthy of a better cause.

In the first place an appeal was made to the better feelings of the ghost. He was requested to go quietly to the grave, and at the grave he was requested to stay there.[2]

But to meet the possible case of hardened ghosts, upon whom moral persuasion would be thrown away, more energetic measures were resorted to. Thus, among the South Slavonians and Bohemians, the bereaved family, returning from the grave, pelted the ghost of their deceased relative with sticks, stones, and hot coals.[3] The Chuwash, a tribe

---

[1] P. Sebillot, *Traditions et Superstitions de la Haute-Bretagne*, i. p. 238; G. Turner, *Samoa*, p. 150. The Annamese and Hindoos particularly dread the ghosts of the unburied dead (J. G. Scott, *France and Tongking*, p. 99; Monier Williams, *Religious Thought and Life in India*, p. 239 *sqq.*).

[2] J. H. Gray, *China*, i. pp. 300, 304. Similarly, the Dacotahs address the ghost begging him to remain in his own place and not disturb his friends (H. R. Schoolcraft, *Indian Tribes*, v. p. 65). The Karieng address their dead in like manner (Pallegoix, *Description du royaume Thai ou Siam*, i. p. 58).

[3] W. R. S. Ralston, *Songs of the Russian People*, p. 319; A. Bastian, *Der Mensch in der Geschichte*, ii. p. 329. Compare K. Schwenk, *Slawische Mythologie*, p. 325.

of the Finnish stock in Russia, had not even the decency to wait till he was fairly in the grave, but opened fire on him as soon as the coffin was outside the house.[1] The Jewish missiles are potsherds before, and clods after, the burial.[2] Again, heavy stones were piled on his grave to keep him down, on the principle of " sit tibi terra *gravis* ". This is the origin of funeral cairns and tombstones. As the ghosts of murderers and their victims are especially restless, everyone who passes their graves in Arabia, in Germany, and in Spain is bound to add a stone to the pile. In Oldenburg (and no doubt elsewhere), if the grave is shallow, the ghost will certainly walk.[3]

One of the most striking ways of keeping down the dead man is to divert the course of a river, bury him in its bed, and then allow the river to resume its course. It was thus that Alaric was buried, and Commander Cameron found the same mode of burial still in vogue for chiefs amongst a tribe of Central Africa. Du Chaillu was informed that the Obongos, a dwarf tribe of negroes on the Equator, sometimes bury their dead thus.[4]

The expedient of enclosing the grave with a fence too high for the ghost to " take " it, especially without a run, is common to the Finnlanders and the Dyaks.[5]

Another simple but effectual plan is to nail the dead man to the coffin (the Chuwash again)[6] or to tie his feet together (among the Arabs), or his hands together (in Voigtland),[7] or his neck to his legs (among the Troglodytes, Damaras,

[1] M. A. Castren, *Vorlesungen über die finnische Mythologie*, p. 120.

[2] J. Buxtorf, *Synagoga Judaica*, p. 701 *sqq.*; J. C. G. Bodenschatz, *Kirchliche Verfassung der heutigen Juden*, iv. pp. 173, 175.

[3] W. Sonntag, *Todtenbestattung*, p. 197 ; J. Brand, *Popular Antiquities*, ii. p. 309; A. Wuttke, *Der deutsche Volksaberglaube*, § 754, compare 739, 748, 756, 758, 761; G. F. Klemm, *Culturgeschichte*, ii. p. 225; Th. Waitz, *Anthropologie der Naturvölker*, ii. pp. 195, 324, 325, 524; *id.* iii. p. 202 ; Fr. Ratzel, *Völkerkunde*, i. p. 74 ; K. Weinhold, *Altnordisches Leben*, p. 488 ; L. Strackerjan, *Aber-glaube und Sagen aus dem Herzogthum Oldenburg*, i. p. 154.

[4] Jordanes, *Getica*, c. xxx. § 158 ; V. L. Cameron, *Across Africa*, i. p. 110 ; Du Chaillu, *A Journey to Ashangoland*, p. 321.

[5] M. A. Castren, *op. cit.* p. 121 ; A. Bastian, *Mensch*, ii. p. 368.

[6] A. Bastian, *ib.* p. 337 ; likewise the Cheremiss (*ib.* p. 365). The modern Greeks sometimes resort to this practice, but only after a ghost has proved himself troublesome (B. Schmidt, *Das Volksleben der Neugriechen*, p. 167 *sq.*).

[7] J. A. E. Köhler, *Volksbrauch im Voigtlande*, p. 251.

and New Zealanders).[1] The Wallachians drive a long nail through the skull and lay the thorny stem of a wild rose bush on the shroud.[2] The Californians and Damaras clinched matters by breaking his spine.[3] The corpses of suicides and vampires had stakes run through them.[4] Sometimes the heads of vampires are cut off,[5] or their hearts torn out and hacked in pieces, and their bodies burned,[6] or boiling water and vinegar are poured on their graves.[7]

Other mutilations of the dead were intended not so much to keep the dead man in his grave as to render his ghost harmless. Thus the Australians cut off the right thumb of a slain enemy, that his ghost might not be able to throw the spear,[8] and Greek murderers used to hack off the extremities of their victims with a similar object.[9]

Again, various steps are taken to chase away the lingering ghost from the home he loves too well. Thus, the New Zealanders thrash the corpse in order to hasten the departure of the soul ; [10] the Algonkins beat the walls of the death-chamber with sticks to drive out the ghost ; [11] the Chinese knock on the floor with a hammer ; [12] and the Germans wave towels about or sweep the ghost out with a besom,[13] just as in old Rome the heir solemnly swept out the ghost of his predecessor with a broom made specially for the purpose.[14]

---

[1] Strabo, xvi. 4. 17 ; Diodorus Siculus, iii. 33 ; J. G. Wood, *Natural History of Man,* i. p. 348 ; W. Yate, *New Zealand,* p. 136. The Burmese tie together the two big toes, and usually also the two thumbs of the corpse (*The Burman: his Life and Notions,* by Shway Yoe [J. G. Scott], ii. p. 338 ; C. J. F. S. Forbes, *British Burma,* p. 93).

[2] A. und A. Schott, *Walachische Maehrchen,* p. 298 ; H. F. Tozer, *Researches in the Highlands of Turkey,* ii. p. 92.

[3] A. Bastian, *Mensch,* ii. p. 331 ; C. J. Andersson, *Lake Ngami,* p. 226.

[4] A. Bastian, *Mensch,* ii. p. 365 ; Ralston, *Songs of the Russian People,* p. 413.

[5] Tettau und Temme, *Die Volkssagen Ostpreussens, Litthauens und Westpreussens,* p. 275 *sq.* ; A. Wuttke,

Deutscher Aberglaube, § 765 ; M. Toeppen, *Aberglauben aus Masuren,* p. 114.

[6] B. Schmidt, *loc. cit.*

[7] J. T. Bent, *The Cyclades,* p. 45.

[8] E. B. Tylor, *Primitive Culture,* i. p. 451.

[9] Suidas, *s.v.* μασχαλισθῆναι, μασχαλίσματα.

[10] W. Yate, *New Zealand,* p. 136 ; J. S. Polack, *Manners and Customs of the New Zealanders,* i. p. 69.

[11] D. G. Brinton, *Myths of the New World,* p. 255 ; *Relations des Jésuites,* 1634, p. 23 (Canadian reprint).

[12] J. H. Gray, *China,* i. p. 280.

[13] Wuttke, *Deutscher Aberglaube,* §§ 725, 737 ; F. Schmidt, *Sitten und Gebräuche bei Hochzeiten, Taufen und Begräbnissen in Thüringen,* p. 85; J. A. E. Köhler, *Volksbrauch im Voigtlande,* p. 254.

[14] Festus, *s.v. everriator.*

Amongst the Battas in Sumatra the priest officiates as ghost-sweeper, and he is helped by the female mourners.[1]   In modern Greece, as soon as the corpse is out of the house, the whole house is scoured.[2]   In Madagascar when it rains heavily the people beat the walls of their houses violently, in order to drive out the ghosts who may be taking shelter from the inclemency of the weather.[3]   In Scotland and Germany, when the coffin was lifted up, the chairs on which it had rested were carefully turned upside-down, in case the ghost might be sitting on them.[4]   The Kakhyens in Northern Burma, on the Chinese frontier, dance the ghost out of the house, accelerating his departure by a liberal application of stick.[5]   In ancient Mexico certain professional men were employed, who searched the house diligently till they found the lurking ghost of the late proprietor, whom they there and then summarily ejected.[6]   In Siberia they give the ghost forty days' " law " ; after which, if he is still hanging about, the shaman (medicine-man) hunts him out and drums him down to hell.   To prevent the possibility of a mistake the shaman conducts the lost soul personally to the lower regions and secures him a favourable reception by standing brandy to the devils all round.[7]

In North Germany, if a ghost persistently intrudes on your premises, you can get rid of him very simply.   You have only to throw a sack over him, and having thus bagged him to walk off with your sack to some other place and there empty it out, having first clearly explained to the ghost the exact bounds which you wish him to keep.   Of course no sooner is your back turned than the ghost starts for home too.   His

[1] W. Marsden, *History of Sumatra*, p. 388.
[2] C. Wachsmuth, *Das alte Griechenland im neuen*, p. 120 ; J. T. Bent, *The Cyclades*, p. 45.
[3] H. W. Little, *Madagascar, its History and People*, p. 84.
[4] *Folk-lore Record*, ii. p. 214; Wuttke, *Deutscher Aberglaube*, § 737 ; Köhler, *loc. cit.* ; F. Schmidt, *Sitten und Gebräuche*, etc., p. 92 ; A. Kuhn und W. Schwartz, *Norddeutsche Sagen, Märchen und Gebräuche*, p. 435 *sq.*
[5] J. Anderson, *Mandalay to Momien*, p. 77 *sq.*   This death-

dance was witnessed by Dr. Anderson and his companion, Col. Sladen.   Indeed, by special invitation the learned doctor and the gallant colonel joined in the lugubrious dance and exerted themselves to such good purpose that after two turns the ghost fairly took to his heels and bolted out of the house, hotly pursued by the *premier danseur* with a stick.
[6] H. H. Bancroft, *Native Races of the Pacific States of North America*, i. p. 641.
[7] W. Radloff, *Aus Sibirien*, ii. p. 52 *sqq.*

plan is to jump on the back of the first person he sees and ride him in, but when he comes to the boundary, off he falls ; and so it goes on, the ghost falling off and jumping on again most gamely, to all eternity. I nearly forgot to say that you had better not try to sack a ghost unless you have been born on a Sunday night between eleven and twelve o'clock.[1]

The favourite haunt of the ghost is usually the spot where he died. Hence in order to keep him at least from the house it has been a common practice to carry dying persons to lonely places and leave them there ; but if the man dies in the house it is deserted and left to its ghostly tenant. Thus the Kaffirs carry a sick man out into the open air to die, and the Maoris and Esquimaux remove their sick into special sheds or huts. If a Kaffir or Maori dies before he can be carried out, the house is tabooed and deserted. If an Esquimaux is present at the death of a relative, he has to throw away his clothes and never use them again.[2] The Bakalai in Equatorial Africa drive sick people from the village, but if several people should happen to die in the village it is deserted.[3] Amongst the Balondas, when a chief or his principal wife dies, the village is deserted ; but when an ordinary man dies it is only his house which is abandoned.[4] In England up to the end of the eighteenth century it was a common practice to shut up a room in which a member of the family had died.[5] Amongst the Damaras, when a chief dies, the tribe deserts the neighbourhood ; but after a time they return, the new chief offers sacrifice at the grave of his predecessor, and the village is occupied as before.[6] After a death the Andaman Islanders migrate temporarily to a new camping ground.[7] The Altaians in Siberia make a practical distinction between a hut which is portable (a

[1] A. Kuhn und W. Schwartz, *Norddeutsche Sagen, Märchen und Gebräuche*, p. 120.
[2] Lichtenstein, *Travels in Southern Africa*, i. pp. 258, 259 ; J. Campbell, *Travels in South Africa*, p. 515 *sq.* ; G. Fritsch, *Die Eingeborenen Süd-Afrika's*, p. 116; R. Taylor, *Te Ika A Maui ; or, New Zealand and its Inhabitants*, p. 170; W. Yate, *New Zealand*, p. 86 ; J. G. Wood, *Natural History of Man*, ii. p. 719.

[3] Du Chaillu, *Explorations and Adventures in Equatorial Africa*, pp. 384, 385. So with the Ashira, *ib.* p. 413.
[4] J. G. Wood, *Natural History of Man*, i. p. 419.
[5] T. F. Thiselton Dyer, *English Folk-lore*, p. 231.
[6] G. Fritsch, *Die Eingeborenen Süd-Afrika's*, p. 236; J. G. Wood, *Natural History of Man*, i. p. 349.
[7] E. H. Man, *Aboriginal Inhabitants of the Andaman Islands*, pp. 74, 77.

felt hut) and one which is not so (a hut of bark or wood). After a death they abandon the latter, but carry the former away with them after it has been purified by the shaman.[1]   In Panama and Darien they send the sick into the woods, just as in Persia they sent them into the wilderness, to die.[2] In Madagascar no one except the sovereign is allowed if ill to stay within the palace.[3] There are traces in Greece, Rome, China, and Corea of this custom of carrying dying persons out of the house.[4]

But in case the ghost should, despite of all precautions, make his way back from the grave, steps were taken to barricade the house against him.   Thus in some parts of Russia and East Prussia an axe or a lock is laid on the threshold, or a knife is hung over the door,[5] and in Germany as soon as the coffin is carried out of the house all the doors and windows are shut, whereas so long as the body is still in the house the windows (and sometimes the doors) are left open to allow the soul to escape.[6] In some parts of England every bolt and lock in the house is unfastened, that the ghost of the dying man may fly freely away.[7]

[1] W. Radloff, *Aus Siberien*, i. p. 321.   Compare G. F. Klemm, *Cultur-geschichte*, iii. p. 174.   On the huts, see Radloff, *op. cit.* p. 267 *sqq.*

[2] H. H. Bancroft, *Native Races of the Pacific States*, i. p. 781; Agathias, ii. 23.

[3] W. Ellis, *History of Madagascar*, i. p. 242.

[4] Euripides, *Alcestis*, 234 *sqq.*, compare 205 ; Scholiast on Aristophanes, *Lysistrata*, 611; Seneca, *Epist.* i. xii. 3 ; Gray, *China*, i. p. 279.   In modern Greece the corpse is laid out in the entrance hall (C. Wachsmuth, *Das alte Griechenland im neuen*, p. 108).   In Corea no one is allowed to die on the *kang* (ordinary sleeping place), but is placed on a board (J. Ross, *History of Corea*, p. 321.)

[5] Ralston, *Songs of the Russian People*, p. 318; Wuttke, *Der deutsche Aberglaube*, §§ 736, 766 ; Toeppen, *Aberglauben aus Masuren*, p. 108.

[6] Rochholz *Deutscher Glaube und Brauch*, i. p. 171 ; Schleicher, *Volks-thümliches aus Sonnenberg*, p. 152 ; Sonntag, *Todtenbestattung*, p. 169 ;

Wuttke, *op. cit.* §§ 737, 725 ; Gubernatis, *Storia comparata degli usi funebri in Italia e presso gli altri popoli Indo-Europei*, p. 47 ; G. Lammert, *Volks-medizin und medizinischer Aber-glaube in Bayern*, pp. 103, 105, 106 ; F. Schmidt, *Sitten und Gebräuche*, pp. 85, 92 ; Strackerjan, *Aberglaube und Sagen aus dem Herzogthum Olden-burg*, ii. p. 129 ; Tettau und Temme, *Volkssagen*, p. 285 ; A. Kuhn, *Mär-kische Sagen und Märchen*, p. 367 ; Nork, *Die Sitten und Gebräuche der Deutschen und ihrer Nachbarvölker*, pp. 479, 482 ; Köhler, *op. cit.* pp. 251, 254 ; F. Panzer, *Beitrag zur deut-schen Mythologie*, i. p. 263 ; A. Kuhn und W. Schwartz, *op. cit.* p. 435.   In Masuren, on the other hand, the doors and windows are left open for some time after the corpse has been carried out in case the ghost may be lingering in the house (Toeppen, *Aberglauben aus Masuren*, p. 108).

[7] T. F. Thiselton Dyer, *English Folk-lore*, p. 230; J. Brand, *Popular Antiquities*, ii. p. 231.   Compare W. Henderson, *Folk-lore of the Northern Counties*, pp. 53, 56 *sq.*

But if primitive man knew how to bully he also knew how to outwit the ghost. For example, a ghost can only find his way back to the house by the way by which he left it.[1] This little weakness did not escape the vigilance of our ancestors, and they took their measures accordingly. The coffin was carried out of the house, not by the door, but by a hole made for the purpose in the wall, and this hole was carefully stopped up as soon as the body had been passed through ; so that when the ghost strolled quietly back from the grave he found, to his surprise, that there was no thoroughfare. The credit of this ingenious device is shared by Greenlanders, Norsemen, Hottentots, Bechuanas, Samoieds, Ojebways, Algonkins, Laosians, Hindoos, Tibetans, Siamese, Chinese, Balinese, and Fijians. These special openings, or " doors of the dead ", are still to be seen in a village near Amsterdam, and they were common in some towns of Central Italy, as Perugia and Assisi.[2] In Lao this mode of exit is reserved for the bodies of women dying in childbirth,[3] the reason for which is apparent from the belief of the neighbouring Kakhyens that the ghosts of such women are

---

[1] For a similar reason you should never move a sleeper's body, for if you do the absent soul on its return will not be able to find its way back into the body and the sleeper will wake no more. See L. Strackerjan, *Aberglaube und Sagen aus dem Herzogthum Oldenburg*, i. p. 378 ; *id.* ii. p. 114; Wuttke, *Deutscher Aberglaube*, § 60 ; Köhler, *Volksbrauch im Voigtlande*, p. 501 ; J. V. Grohmann, *Aberglauben und Gebräuche aus Böhmen und Mähren*, p. 60.
[2] H. Yule on Marco Polo, i. p. 188; D. Crantz, *Greenland*, i. p. 237 ; Weinhold, *Altnordisches Leben*, p. 476 ; Tylor, *Prim. Cult.*, ii. p. 26 ; Waitz, *Anthropologie*, iii. p. 199; Fritsch, *Die Eingeborenen Süd-Afrika's*, p. 335 ; Thunberg's " Account of the Cape of Good Hope," in Pinkerton's *Voyages and Travels*, xvi. p. 142 ; Moffat, in Gardner, *Faiths of the World*, i. p. 939; Bastian, *Mensch*, ii. p. 322 ; Klemm, *Culturgeschichte*, ii. pp. 221, 225 ; *id.* iii. p. 293 ; Sonntag, *Todtenbestattung*, p. 51 ; *Relations des Jésuites*, 1634, p.

23 ; Brinton, *Myths of the New World*, p. 255 ; T. Williams, *Fiji and the Fijians*, i. p. 197 (ed. 1860) ; C. J. Andersson, *Lake Ngami*, p. 466 ; Gubernatis, *Usi funebri*, p. 52 ; C. Bock, *Temples and Elephants*, p. 262 ; Pallegoix, *Description du royaume Thai ou Siam*, i. p. 245 ; J. Bowring, *Kingdom and People of Siam*, i. p. 222 ; J. Crawfurd, *History of the Indian Archipelago*, ii. p. 245 ; Lafitau, *Mœurs des Sauvages Amériquains*, ii. p. 401. An extraordinary variation of this custom is seen amongst the Jolloffs on the Gambia, who break down the whole fence before they carry the dead out of the house (A. B. Ellis, *The Land of Fetish*, p. 13). A dead Pope is carried out by a special door, which is then blocked up till the next Pope dies.
[3] C. Bock, *loc. cit.* Strictly speaking the body is taken out through a hole in the floor, for houses in Lao are built on posts at a height of five to eight feet from the ground (Bock, *op. cit.* p. 304).

changed into fearful vampires [1]—a villainous conceit very different from the knightly courtesy of the Aztecs, who allowed the souls of women who died in childbed to take their places side by side with the brave who died in battle in the better land.[2] A trace of the same custom survives in Thüringen, where it is thought that the ghost of a man who has been hanged will return to the house if the body be not taken out by a window instead of the door.[3] In Burma the dead are carried out of a town by a gate reserved for the purpose.[4] The Siamese, not content with carrying the dead man out by a special opening, endeavour to make assurance doubly sure by hurrying him three times round the house at full speed—a proceeding well calculated to bewilder the poor soul in the coffin.[5]

The Araucanians adopt the plan of strewing ashes behind the coffin as it is being borne to the grave, in order that the ghost may not be able to find his way back.[6] With a like intent the Kakhyens returning from the grave scatter rice along the path.[7] The Tonga Islanders strewed sand about the grave.[8]

The very general practice of closing the eyes of the dead appears to have originated with a similar object ; it was a mode of blindfolding the dead, that he might not see the way by which he was carried to his last home. At the grave, where he was to rest for ever, there was of course no motive for concealment ; hence the Romans,[9] and apparently the Siamese,[10] opened the eyes of the dead man at the funeral

[1] J. Anderson, *Mandalay to Momien*, p. 145.

[2] D. G. Brinton, *Myths of the New World*, p. 263; H. H. Bancroft, *Native Races of the Pacific States*, iii. p. 533.

[3] Wuttke, *op. cit.* § 756; Schleicher, *op. cit.* p. 152. It was an old German law that the corpses of criminals and suicides should be carried out through a hole under the threshold (Grimm, *Deutsche Rechtsalterthümer*, p. 726 *sqq.*).

[4] *The Burman*, by Shway Yoe, ii. p. 342.

[5] Pallegoix and Bowring as above. In some parts of Scotland and Germany the corpse used to be carried three times round the church (C. Rogers, *Social Life in Scotland*, i. p.

167 ; Rochholz, *Deutscher Glaube und Brauch*, i. p. 198).

[6] G. F. Klemm, *Culturgeschichte*, v. p. 51 ; J. G. Wood, *Natural History of Man*, ii. p. 565.

[7] J. Anderson, *Mandalay to Momien*, p. 144.

[8] W. Mariner, *Tonga Islands*, i. p. 392.

[9] Pliny, *Natural History*, xi. § 150. The reason assigned by Pliny is that the dead should be seen for the last time not by man but by heaven.

[10] C. Bock saw that the eyes of a dead man at the pyre were open (in Siam), and he says that in Lao (in Northern Siam) it is the custom to close the eyes of the corpse (*Temples and Elephants*, pp. 58, 261).

pyre, just as we should unbandage the eyes of an enemy after conducting him to his destination. In Nuremberg the eyes of the corpse were actually bandaged with a wet cloth.[1] In Corea they put blinkers, or rather blinders, on his eyes ; they are made of black silk, and are tied with strings at the back of his head.[2] The Jews put a potsherd and the Russians coins on each of his eyes.[3] The notion that if the eyes of the dead be not closed his ghost will return to fetch away another of the household still exists in Bohemia, Germany, and England.[4]

With a similar object, the corpse is carried out of the house feet foremost, for if he were carried out head foremost his eyes would be towards the door and he might find his way back. This custom is observed and this reason is assigned for it in many parts of Germany and among the Indians of Chile.[5] Conversely in Persia when a man is setting out on a journey he steps out of the house with his face turned towards the door, hoping thereby to secure a safe return.[6] In Thüringen and some parts of the North of England it used to be the custom to carry the body to the grave by a roundabout way.[7] In Voigtland there are special "church roads" for carrying the dead to the graveyard ; a corpse is never carried along the high road.[8] In Madagascar no corpse is allowed to be carried along the high road or chief thoroughfare of the capital.[9] In Burma a corpse is never carried towards the centre of a town, much less taken into it ; if a man dies in the jungle and the funeral has to pass a village it skirts the outside of it.[10] The Chinese

[1] G. Lammert, *Volksmedizin*, p. 103.

[2] J. Ross, *History of Corea*, p. 325.

[3] J. C. G. Bodenschatz, *Kirchliche Verfassung der heutigen Juden*, iv. p. 174 ; A. de Gubernatis, *Usi funebri*, p. 50 ; Ralston, *Songs of the Russian People*, p. 316.

[4] J. V. Grohmann, *Aberglaube*, etc., p. 188 ; Lammert, *Volksmedizin*, p. 106; A. Wuttke, *op. cit.* § 725; Dyer, *English Folk-lore*, p. 230 ; Schleicher, *Volksthümliches aus Sonnenberg*, p. 152; C. L. Rochholz, *Deutscher Glaube und Brauch*, i. p. 196.

[5] A. Wuttke, *Deutscher Aberglaube*, § 736 ; Klemm, *Culturgeschichte*, ii.

p. 101. On the other hand, in modern Egypt the corpse is carried out head foremost (E. W. Lane, *Manners and Customs of the Modern Egyptians*, ii. p. 291, ed. 1836).

[6] Monier's *Hajji Baba*, c. i. *fin.*

[7] F. Schmidt, *Sitten und Gebräuche in Thüringen*, p. 94. The English custom was verbally communicated to me.

[8] J. A. E. Köhler, *Volksbrauch im Voigtlande*, p. 258.

[9] W. Ellis, *History of Madagascar*, i. p. 241.

[10] *The Burman : his Life and Notions*, by Shway Yoe, ii. p. 342 *sq.*

are not allowed to carry a corpse within the gates of a walled city.[1]

I venture to conjecture that the old Hawaiian, Roman, German, and Mandingo practice of burying by night [2] or in the dusk may have originally been intended, like the customs I have mentioned, to keep the way to the grave a secret from the dead man, and it is possible that the same idea gave rise to the practice of masking the dead—a practice common to the prehistoric inhabitants of Greece and to the Aleutian Islanders.[3] The Aztecs masked their dead kings, and the Siamese do so still.[4] Among the Shans the face of a dead chief is invariably covered with a mask of gold or silver.[5]

To a desire to deceive the dead man I would also refer the curious custom amongst the Bohemians of putting on masks and behaving in a strange way as they returned from a burial.[6] They hoped, in fact, so to disguise themselves that the dead man might not know and therefore might not follow them. Whether the widespread mourning customs of smearing the body with ashes, mud, or paint, mutilating it by gashes, cutting off the hair or letting it grow, and putting on beggarly attire or clothes of an unusual colour (black, white, or otherwise), may not also have originated in the desire to disguise and therefore protect the living from the dead, I cannot here attempt to determine.[7] This much is certain, that mourning customs are always as far as possible the reverse of those of ordinary life. Thus at a Roman funeral the sons of the deceased walked with their heads covered, the daughters with their heads uncovered,

[1] J. H. Gray, *China*, i. p. 323.

[2] W. Ellis, *Polynesian Researches*, iv. p. 361 (compare Cook's *Voyages*, vii. p. 149 *sqq.*, ed. 1809); Servius on Virgil, *Aen.* i. p. 186 ; F. Schmidt, *loc. cit.* ; Mungo Park, *Travels in the Interior Districts of Africa*, p. 414. Night burial was sometimes practised in Scotland (C. Rogers, *Social Life in Scotland*, i. p. 161). In Benguela (West Africa) the corpse is burned at sundown (Waitz, *Anthropologie*, ii. p. 196).

[3] Schliemann, *Mycenae*, pp. 198, 219-223, 311 *sq.* ; Bancroft, *Native Races of the Pacific States*, i. p. 93. Compare Miss A. W. Buckland in *Journal of the Anthropological Institute*, xiv. p. 229. I regret that I have not seen the standard work of Bendorf, *Antike Gesichtshelme und Sepulcralmasken* (Wien, 1878).

[4] H. H. Bancroft, *Native Races of the Pacific States*, ii. p. 606 ; Pallegoix, *Siam*, i. p. 247.

[5] A. S. Colquhoun, *Amongst the Shans*, p. 279.

[6] A. Bastian, *Der Mensch in der Geschichte*, ii. p. 328.

[7] See note I. at end, pp. 42-46.

thus exactly reversing the ordinary usage, which was that women wore coverings on their heads while men did not. Plutarch, who notes this, observes that similarly in Greece men and women during a period of mourning exactly inverted their usual habits of wearing the hair—the ordinary practice of men being to cut it short, that of women to wear it long.[1]

The objection, deeply rooted in many races, to utter the names of deceased persons,[2] sprang no doubt from a fear that the dead might hear and answer to his name. In East Prussia if the deceased is called thrice by his name he appears.[3] This reluctance to mention the names of the dead has modified whole languages. Thus among the Australians, Tasmanians, and Abipones, if the name of a deceased person happened to be a common name, for instance the name of an animal or plant, this name was abolished and a new one substituted for it.[4] During the residence of the Jesuit missionary Dobrizhoffer amongst the Abipones, the name for tiger was thus changed three times.[5] Amongst the Indians of Columbia near relatives of the deceased often change their names, in the belief that the ghost will return if he hears the familiar names.[6]

While no pains were spared to prevent the dead man from returning from the grave, on the other hand precautions were taken that he should not miss the way to it. The kings of Michoacan were buried at dead of night, but the funeral train was attended by torch-bearers and preceded by men who swept the road, crying, " Lord, here thou hast to pass, see that thou dost not miss the way." [7]   In many

[1] Plutarch, *Quaestiones Romanae*, 14.
[2] E. B. Tylor, *Early History of Mankind*, p. 142. Amongst some Indian tribes of North America whoever mentions a dead man's name may be compelled to pay a heavy fine to the relatives (H. H. Bancroft, *Native Races of the Pacific States*, i. p. 357, note).
[3] A. Wuttke, *Deutscher Aberglaube*, § 754.
[4] E. B. Tylor, *op. cit.* p. 144 *sqq.*
[5] Klemm, *Culturgeschichte*, ii. p.

99; M. Dobrizhoffer, *The Abipones*, ii. p. 208 *sqq.*
[6] H. H. Bancroft, *Native Races*, i. p. 248. Compare Waitz, *Anthropologie*, vi. p. 811. When a survivor bears the same name as the deceased he drops it during the time of mourning (Charlevoix, *Journal Historique d'un Voyage dans l'Amérique septentrionale*, ii. p. 109; Lafitau, *Mœurs des Sauvages Ameriquains*, ii. p. 434).
[7] H. H. Bancroft, *Native Races*, ii. p. 621. Compare Charlevoix, *op. cit.* p. 107.

Wallachian villages no burial takes place before midday, because the people believe that, if the body were buried before noon, the soul might lose its way and never reach its place of rest. But if it is buried in the afternoon they think that the sun, descending to his rest, will guide the tired spirit to its narrow bed.[1]

> " *Soles occidere et redire possunt :*
> *Nobis cum semel occidit brevis lux,*
> *Nox est perpetua una dormienda.*"

I must pass lightly over the kindlier modes of barring the dead by providing for the personal comforts of the poor ghost in his long home. That the dead still think and feel in the grave is a very old opinion, the existence of which is attested by many customs as well as by the evidence of the poets, those lovers of the past, and by no poet more vividly than by Heine, where he tells us how the French grenadier lies in his quiet grave, listening, listening, till his ear catches the far-off thunder of the guns, and with a clatter of horse-hoofs and clash of steel the cavalry rides over his grave. Hades, or the common abode of all the dead, whether beneath the earth or in a far island of the sea, is probably the later dream of some barbaric philosopher, some forgotten Plato ; and the partition of Hades into heaven and hell is certainly the latest, as it is possibly the last, development of the belief in a life hereafter.[2]

The nearly universal practice of leaving food on the tomb or of actually passing it into the grave by means of an aperture or tube is too well known to need illustration. Like the habit of dressing the dead in his best clothes,[3] it

[1] Schott, *Walachische Maehrchen*, p. 302. The custom is perhaps a relic of night burial. The reason assigned for it is too beautiful to be old. In Russia also the sun is regarded as ψυχοπομπός; but it is apparently enough if the burial takes place by daylight (Ralston, *Songs of the Russian People*, p. 319).

[2] It is interesting to find the three strata of belief still clearly existing side by side in modern Greece. See B. Schmidt, *Das Volksleben der Neugriechen*, p. 235 *sqq.*

[3] Charlevoix, *Journal Historique*, ii. p. 107 ; W. Radloff, *Aus Siberien*, i. pp. 321, 379 ; Spenser St. John, *Life in the Forests of the Far East*, i. p. 57 ; Klemm, *Culturgeschichte*, ii. pp. 104, 225 ; *id.* iv. p. 38 ; J. G. Scott, *France and Tongking*, p. 97 ; Schoolcraft, *Indian Tribes*, ii. p. 68 ; *id.* iv. 54 ; Wood, *Natural History of Man*, i. p. 562 ; *id.* ii. 190, 512, 542 ; H. H. Bancroft, *Native Races*, i. p. 86 ; *The Burman*, by Shway Yoe, ii. p. 338 ; P. Bouche, *La Côte des Esclaves*, p. 213 ; Lafitau, *Mœurs des Sauvages*

probably originated in the selfish but not unkindly desire to induce the perturbed spirit to rest in the grave and not come plaguing the living for food and raiment.[1] One instance, however, of the minute care with which the survivors will provide for the wants of the departed, in order that he may have no possible excuse for returning, I cannot refrain from mentioning. In the Saxon district of Voigtland, with its inclement sky, people have been known to place in the coffin an umbrella and a pair of goloshes.[2] Whether these utensils are meant for use in heaven or elsewhere is a question which I must leave to theologians.

A pathetic example is furnished by some Indian tribes of New Mexico, who drop milk from the mother's breast on the lips of her dead babe.[3] Similarly in Africa we hear of a Myoro woman who bore twins that died ; so she kept two little pots to represent the children, and every evening she dropped milk from her own breast into them, lest the spirits of the dead babes should torment her.[4]

Ameriquains, ii. p. 389 ; A. und A. Schott, *Walachische Maehrchen*, p. 302 ; Wachsmuth, *op. cit.* p. 108 ; R. Taylor, *New Zealand*, p. 218 ; Köhler, *Volksbrauch im Voigtlande*, p. 252 ; Baron's " Description of the Kingdom of Tonqueen", in Pinkerton's *Voyages and Travels*, ix. pp. 698, 700, 730. In modern Greece the corpse is arrayed in its best clothes, but at the grave these are entirely destroyed, or at least rendered valueless, by being snipped with scissors or saturated with oil (*Folk-lore Journal*, ii. p. 168 *sq.*). This may be (as the writer half suggests) a modern precaution against thieves. On the destruction of the property of the dead, see next note.
[1] The fear of the dead, which underlies all these burial customs, may have sprung from the idea that they were angry with the living for dispossessing them. Hence, rather than use the property of the deceased and thereby incur the anger of his ghost, men destroyed it. The ghost would then have no motive for returning to his desolated home. Thus we are told by the careful observer, Mr. G. M. Sproat, that the Ahts of Vancouver's

Island " bury a man's personal effects with him, and burn his house, in the fear that if these were used, the ghost would appear and some ill consequences would follow ". He adds : " I have not found that any articles are deposited in burying grounds with the notion that they would be useful to the deceased in an after time, with the exception of blankets " (*Scenes and Studies of Savage Life*, p. 260). The idea that the souls of the things thus destroyed are despatched to the spiritland (see Tylor, *Primitive Culture*, i. p. 480 *sqq.* ; and for an additional example of " killing " the things placed in the grave, see H. H. Johnston, *The River Congo*, p. 246) is less simple and therefore probably later. For in the evolution of thought as of matter the simplest is the earliest.
[2] Köhler, *Volksbrauch im Voigtlande*, p. 441 ; Wuttke, *Der deutsche Volksaberglaube*, § 734.
[3] H. H. Bancroft, *Native Races of the Pacific States*, i. p. 360 ; compare *id*. iii. 543.
[4] J. H. Speke, *Journal of the Discovery of the Source of the Nile*, p. 541.

In the Mili Islands, in the Pacific, after they have committed the body to the earth, they lade a small canoe with coco-nuts, hoist a sail, and send it out to sea, hoping that the soul will sail away with the frail bark and return no more.[1]

Merely mentioning the customs of building a little hut for the accommodation of the soul, either on the grave or on the way to it,[2] and of leaving straw on the road, in the hope that the weary ghost will sit down on it and never get as far as the house,[3] I now come to two modes of barring the ghost which, from their importance, I have reserved to the last, I mean the methods of barring the ghost by fire and water.

First, by fire. After a funeral certain heathen Siberians, who greatly fear the dead, seek to get rid of the ghost of the departed by leaping over a fire.[4] Similarly, at Rome, mourners returning from a funeral stepped over fire,[5] and in China they sometimes do so to this day.[6] Taken in connexion with the Siberian custom, the original intention of this ceremony of stepping over fire at Rome and in China can hardly have been other than that of placing a barrier of fire between the living and the dead. But, as has been the case with so many other ceremonies, this particular ceremony may well have been practised long after its original

---

[1] Waitz, *Anthropologie*, v. ii. p. 152 *sq.* Gerland remarks that this is a remnant of the Polynesian custom of sending the body (as well as the soul) out to sea. Compare G. Turner, *Samoa*, p. 306. The Norsemen sometimes disposed of their dead thus (Grimm, *Deutsche Mythologie*, ii. p. 692 *sq.* ; Weinhold, *op. cit.* pp. 479, 483 *sq.* ; Rochholz, *op. cit.* i. p. 174). The custom of burying the corpse in a canoe or boat is common to the Norsemen, Slavonians, Ostiaks, Indians of the Columbia River, and Polynesians (Grimm, *loc. cit.* ; Weinhold, *op. cit.* p. 495 *sqq.*; Ralston, *op. cit.* p. 108 ; Brinton, *Myths of the New World*, p. 265 ; A. Bastian, *Mensch*, ii. p. 331 ; Waitz, *loc. cit.* and vi. pp. 401, 405, 411).

[2] J. Chalmers and W. W. Gill, *Work and Adventure in New Guinea*, p. 56 ;

Klemm, *Culturgeschichte*, ii. p. 297 ; A. Bastian, *Mensch*, ii. p. 328 ; Waitz, *Anthropologie*, ii. p. 195 ; *id.* iii. p. 202 ; *id.* v. ii. p. 153 ; *id.* vi. pp. 686, 806, 807 ; Wood, *Natural History of Man*, i. p. 574 ; Cook's *Voyages*, iv. p. 62 *sq.* (ed. 1809) ; *id.* i. p. 93 *sq.*; Bosman's " Guinea " in Pinkerton's *Voyages and Travels*, xvi. p. 431 ; J. Leighton Wilson, *Western Africa*, p. 231 ; J. Anderson, *Mandalay to Momien*, p. 144 ; V. L. Cameron, *Across Africa*, i. p. 49 ; Marco Polo, i. c. 40.

[3] Wuttke, *Deutscher Aberglaube*, § 739 ; M. Toeppen, *Aberglauben aus Masuren*, p. 109.

[4] C. Meiners, *Geschichte der Religionen*, ii. p. 303.

[5] Festus, *s.v. aqua et igne.*

[6] J. H. Gray, *China*, i. pp. 287, 305.

intention was forgotten. For customs often live on for ages after the circumstances and modes of thought which gave rise to them have disappeared, and in their new environment new motives are invented to explain them. As might have been expected, the custom itself of stepping over fire often dwindled into a mere shadow of its former self. Thus the South Slavonians returning from a funeral are met by an old woman carrying a vessel of live coals. On these they pour water, or else they take a live coal from the hearth and fling it over their heads.[1] The Brahmans contented themselves with simply touching fire,[2] and in Ruthenia the mourners merely look steadfastly at the stove or place their hands on it.[3] The Arabs of old, it may be noted, adopted much the same means to prevent the return of a living man whom they disliked ; when he departed they lit a fire behind his back and cursed him.[4]

So much for the barrier by fire. Next for the barrier by water. The Wends of Geislitz make a point of passing through running water as they return from a burial ; in winter, if the river is frozen, they break the ice in order to wade through the water.[5] In modern Mytilini and Crete, if a man will not rest in his grave, they dig up the body, ferry it across to a little island, and bury it there.[6] The Kythniotes in the Archipelago have a similar custom, except that they do not take the trouble to bury the body a second time, but simply tumble the bones out of a bag and leave them to bleach on the rocks, trusting to the " silver streak " of sea to imprison the ghost.[7] In many parts of Germany, in modern Greece, and in Cyprus, water is poured out behind the corpse as it is being carried from the house, in the belief that, if the ghost returns, he will not be able to cross it.[8]

[1] W. R. S. Ralston, *Songs of the Russian People*, p. 320.
[2] Monier Williams, *Religious Life and Thought in India*, pp. 283, 288.
[3] Ralston, *loc. cit.*
[4] D. J. Lassen Rasmussen, *Additamenta ad historiam Arabum ante Islamismum*, p. 67.
[5] K. Haupt, *Sagenbuch der Lausitz*, i. p. 254.
[6] B. Schmidt, *Das Volksleben der Neugriechen*, p. 168.

[7] J. T. Bent, *The Cyclades*, p. 441 *sq.*
[8] A. Kuhn, *Märkische Sagen*, p. 368 ; J. D. H. Temme, *Volkssagen der Altmark*, p. 77 ; Nork, *Sitten und Gebräuche der Deutschen und ihrer Nachbarvölker*, p. 479 ; Wuttke, *Deutscher Aberglaube*, § 737 ; Rochholz, *op. cit.* i. p. 177 ; Lammert, *Volksmedizin*, p. 105 ; Toeppen, *Aberglauben aus Masuren*, p. 108 ; Panzer, *Beitrag zur deutschen Mythologie*, i.

Sometimes, by night, the Germans pour holy water before the door ; the ghost is then thought to stand and whimper on the further side.[1] The inability of spirits to cross water might be further illustrated by the Bagman's ghastly story in Apuleius, the Goblin Page in the *Lay of the Last Minstrel*, the witch in *Tam o' Shanter*, and other instances.[2]

p. 257 ; *Folk-lore Journal*, ii. p. 170 ; C. Wachsmuth, *Das alte Griechenland im neuen*, p. 119; compare Tettau und Temme, *Die Volkssagen Ostpreussens, Litthauens und Westpreussens*, p. 286.

[1] Wuttke, *Deutscher Aberglaube*, § 748 ; Rochholz, *Deutscher Glaube und Brauch*, i. p. 186.

[2] Apuleius, *Metam.* i. 19, compare 13 ; *Lay of the Last Minstrel*, iii. 13. Compare Giraldus Cambrensis, *Topographie of Ireland*, c. 19 ; J. Grimm, *Deutsche Mythologie*, iii. p. 434; Theocritus, xxiv. 92 ; Homer, *Odyss.* xi. 26 *sqq.*; W. Henderson, *Folk-lore of the Northern Counties*, p. 212. Observe that the inability of spirits to cross water is not absolute, but is strictly analogous to that of living men. The souls, like the bodies of men, can cross water by a boat or bridge, or by swimming. For instances of the soul of the sleeper leaving his body and crossing a brook by means of a sword laid across it, see Paulus, *Historia Langobardorum*, iii. 34 ; J. Grimm, *Deutsche Sagen*, 461. Again the souls of the dead regularly pass by bridge or boat the River of Death, that sombre stream which has flowed in the imagination of so many nations of the world. For evidence see Grimm, *Deutsche Mythologie*, p. 692 *sqq.*; K. Simrock, *Handbuch der deutschen Mythologie*, p. 255 *sqq.* ; Rochholz, *Deutscher Glaube und Brauch*, i. p. 173 *sqq.* ; Tylor, *Primitive Culture*, ii. p. 94 ; Brinton, *Myths of the New World*, p. 265 *sqq.* ; B. Schmidt, *Das Volksleben der Neugriechen*, p. 236 *sqq.*; W. Sonntag, *Todtenbestattung*, p. 164 ; Bancroft, *Native Races*, iii. pp. 519, 538, 543 ; Ralston, *Songs of the Russian People*, p. 107 ; Monier Williams, *Religious Thought and Life in India*, p. 290 ; N. B. Dennys, *Folk-lore of China*, p. 24.

Amongst the Kasi Indians, when the funeral happens to pass a puddle, they lay a straw over it for the soul of the dead man to use as a bridge (Dennys, *loc. cit.*). Polynesian ghosts can swim (A. Bastian, *Die heilige Sage der Polynesier*, p. 52 ; G. Turner, *Nineteen Years in Polynesia*, p. 235). On the other hand, the idea of a journey by land appears in the Norse, German, Prussian, and Californian custom of shoeing the dead (Grimm, *Deutsche Mythologie*, ii. p. 697; K. Simrock, *op. cit.* p. 127; K. Weinhold, *Altnordisches Leben*, p. 494; G. W. Dasent, *Burnt Njal*, i. p. cxxii; Rochholz, *op. cit.* i. p. 186; Sonntag, *Todtenbestattung*, p. 171; Toeppen, *Aberglauben aus Masuren*, p. 107 ; Bancroft, *Native Races*, i. p. 569 ; Brinton, *Myths of the New World*, p. 250). In Bohemia, on the contrary, no shoes are put in the grave, because, if they were, the ghost would be obliged to walk the earth till they were worn out (Grohmann, *Aberglauben*, etc., p. 197). The custom of placing a coin in the mouth of the corpse has prevailed in ancient Greece (Lucian, *De Luctu*, 10), ancient Italy (Marquardt, *Das Privatleben der Römer*, i. p. 338 *sq.*), amongst the Franks (K. Weinhold, *Altnordisches Leben*, p. 493), in modern Greece, Thessaly, Macedonia, and Asia Minor (Wachsmuth, *Das alte Griechenland im neuen*, p. 117 *sqq.*; B. Schmidt, *Das Volksleben der Neugriechen*, p. 236 *sqq.*), Albania (Hahn, *Albanesische Studien*, i. p. 151), France (Vréto, *Mélanges néohelléniques*, p. 30, referred to by B. Schmidt, *loc. cit.*), Germany (Grimm, *Deutsche Mythologie*, ii. p. 694, *id.* iii. p. 441 ; Wuttke, *Deutscher Aberglaube*, § 734 ; F. Schmidt, *Sitten und Gebräuche in Thüringen*, p. 91; Rochholz, *op. cit.* i. 189 *sqq.*), Burma (Forbes, *British*

Another way of enforcing the water barrier is to plunge into a stream, in the hope of drowning, or, at least, washing off, the ghost. Thus among the Matamba negroes a widow is bound hand and foot by the priest, who flings her into the water several times over, with the intention of drowning her husband's ghost, who may be supposed to be clinging to his unfeeling spouse.[1] In Angola, for a similar purpose, widows adopt the less inconvenient practice of ducking

---

Burma, p. 93; *The Burman*, by Shway Yoe, ii. p. 338), Lao (C. Bock, *Temples and Elephants*, p. 361), among the Kakhyens (J. Anderson, *Mandalay to Momien*, p. 143), in China (Gray, *China*, i. p. 281), among the Hindoos (Monier Williams, *Religious Thought and Life*, p. 296), Madagas of Southern India (W. E. Marshall, *Travels among the Todas*, p. 172), and in Yucatan (Bancroft, *Native Races*, ii. p. 800). The idea that this money in the dead man's mouth is to pay the ferry across the River of Death occurs in Italy, Greece, Asia Minor, Germany, Burma, among the Kakhyens, and in Yucatan. In Asia Minor the money is called περατίκιον, in Burma *Kádô dkáh*, both meaning "ferry-money", like the old Greek ναῦλον, πορθμήιον. At Komiakè in Naxos the old name ναῦλον is still retained, but it is applied, not to a coin, but to a little wax cross placed on the lips of the corpse (Bent, *The Cyclades*, p. 363). At Arachoba on Parnassus it is thought to be a bridge-toll, an idea probably imported into Greece by the Turks, as Schmidt suggests. In some parts of Germany the notion is that, if the deceased has hidden a treasure, the coin in his mouth will prevent him returning. In Lao it is to pay a fine in the spirit-world. The Hindoos suppose that it keeps at bay the ghostly ministers of death; hence it is inserted in the mouth of the dying, and to make sure of having it in the hour of need a Hindoo in good health will have gold inserted in his teeth. In Corea the mouth of the dead is filled with boiled *whangmi*, three holeless pearls, and a piece of jade (J. Ross, *History of Corea*, p. 324 *sq.*). In Tonquin the

common people put three grains of rice in the mouth of the corpse; wealthy families put one or more precious stones (J. G. Scott, *France and Tongking*, p. 97); Baron tells us that persons of quality put small pieces of gold and silver together with seed pearls, in the belief that this would secure the spirit respect in the other world and save him from want ("Description of the Kingdom of Tonqueen" in Pinkerton's *Voyages and Travels*, ix. p. 698). In China the things inserted in the mouth vary in value with the rank of the deceased; grains of paddy or seeds of three different kinds are sometimes inserted. In Yucatan corn as well as money is put in the mouth. In Wallachia the coin is placed in the hand of the corpse (Schott, *Walachische Maehrchen*, p. 302); and so in Masuren, where the dead is at the same time addressed in these words, "Now you have got your pay, so don't come back again" (Toeppen, *Aberglauben aus Masuren*, p. 108). The Slavonians used to put money in the grave to pay the passage of the spirit across the Sea of Death, and Russian peasants at a funeral still throw small coins into the grave (Ralston, *Songs of the Russian People*, p. 107 *sq.*); the coin is sometimes put in the hand of the corpse (*ib.* p. 315). The Norsemen also put a piece of money in the grave (Weinhold, *loc. cit.*). The original custom may have been that of placing food in the mouth, for which in after times valuables (money or otherwise) were substituted, that the dead might buy his own food.

[1] W. Sonntag, *Todtenbestattung*, p. 113.

their late husbands.[1] In New Zealand all who have attended a funeral betake themselves to the nearest stream and plunge several times, head under, in the water.[2] In Fiji the sextons always washed themselves after a burial.[3] In Tahiti all who had assisted at a burial fled precipitately and plunged into the sea, casting also in the sea the garments they had worn.[4] All who had helped to bury a king of Michoacan bathed afterwards.[5] Amongst the Mosquito Indians all persons returning from a funeral undergo a lustration in the river.[6] In Madagascar the chief mourner returning from the funeral immediately washes himself.[7] In North Guinea, after a corpse has been buried, the bearers rush to the water and wash themselves thoroughly before they return to the town.[8]

But the barrier by water, like the barrier by fire, often dwindled into a mere stunted survival. Thus, after a Roman funeral it was enough to carry water three times round the persons who had been engaged in it and to sprinkle them with the water.[9] Modern Jews, as they leave the graveyard, wash their hands in a can of water placed at the gate ; before they have done so they may not touch anything, nor may they return to their houses.[10] In modern Greece, Cappadocia, and Crete, persons returning from a funeral wash their hands.[11] In Samoa they wash their faces and hands with hot water.[12] In ancient India it was enough merely to touch water.[13] In China, on the fifth day after a death, the mourners wash their eyes and sprinkle their faces three times with water.[14] In ancient Greece, so long as a corpse was in the house a vessel of water stood before the street-door, that all who left the house might sprinkle themselves with it.[15] Note

[1] W. Sonntag, op. cit. p. 115.
[2] W. Yate, New Zealand, p. 137 ; R. Taylor, New Zealand and its Inhabitants, p. 224.
[3] T. Williams, Fiji and the Fijians, i. p. 191.
[4] W. Ellis, Polynesian Researches, i. p. 403.
[5] H. H. Bancroft, Native Races of the Pacific States, ii. p. 621.
[6] H. H. Bancroft, op. cit. i. p. 744.
[7] W. Ellis, History of Madagascar, i. p. 238.
[8] J. L. Wilson, Western Africa, p. 231.
[9] Virgil, Aeneid, vi. 228. Servius

on this passage speaks of carrying fire round similarly.
[10] J. C. G. Bodenschatz, Kirchliche Verfassung der heutigen Juden, iv. p. 175.
[11] C. Wachsmuth, Das alte Griechenland im neuen, p. 120; J. T. Bent, The Cyclades, p. 221.
[12] G. Turner, Samoa, p. 145.
[13] Monier Williams, Religious Life and Thought in India, pp. 283, 288.
[14] J. H. Gray, China, i. p. 305.
[15] Pollux, viii. 65 ; Hesychius and Suidas, s.v. ἀρδάνιον ; compare C. Wachsmuth, op. cit. p. 109.

that in this case the water had to be fetched from another house; water taken from the house in which the corpse lay would not do. The significance of this fact I shall have occasion to point out presently.

When considered along with the facts I have mentioned, it can hardly be doubted that the original intention of this sprinkling with water was to wash off the ghost who might be following from the house of death ; and, in general, I think we may lay down the rule that wherever we find a so-called purification by fire or water from pollution contracted by contact with the dead, we may assume with much probability that the original intention was to place a physical barrier of fire or water between the living and the dead, and that the conceptions of pollution and purification are merely the fictions of a later age, invented to explain the purpose of a ceremony of which the original intention was forgotten. The discussion of the wider question, whether all forms of so-called purification may not admit of an analogous explanation, must be reserved for another occasion. Here I will merely point to two kinds of purification which are most obviously explicable on the hypothesis that they are modes of barring spirits. The first of these is the purification for manslaughter. The intention of this ceremony was probably to rid the slayer of the vengeful spirit of the slain, the ghosts of all persons who come by a violent end being especially vicious. In accordance with this view we find purification exacted when the slain man was an enemy of the tribe as well as when he was a member of it. Thus when a Pima Indian slays an Apache, he has to undergo a strict and solitary purification in the woods for sixteen days.[1] Similarly, Bechuana warriors returning from battle wash themselves and their weapons with solemn ceremony.[2] Again, since the savage has no hesitation in deciding affirmatively the question whether animals have souls, purification is found to be practised for the slaughter of beasts as well as of men. Thus a Damara hunter, returning successful from the chase, takes water in his mouth and ejects it three times over his feet

[1] Bancroft, *Native Races*, i. p. 553. For the enmity of the Pimas and Apaches, see *id.* p. 542.

[2] G. Fritsch, *Die Eingeborenen Süd-Afrika's*, p. 201.

and also in the fire of his own hearth.[1] Amongst the Koossa
Kaffirs the first man who receives a wound in a fight with a
lion is made " unclean " by it, though at the same time he
is regarded as a hero. The idea plainly is that by wounding
this man first the lion showed that he had an especial grudge
at him, and this grudge the lion's ghost will not be likely to
forget. Hence, following the usual Kaffir mode of purification, the man is shut up in a small hut, away from everyone
else for four days, after which he is purified ; and, having
now given the slip to the ghost, he is marched back to the
village, surrounded by a guard of honour.[2] My interpretation of this custom will not seem extravagant when we
remember the punctilious politeness with which a savage
treats the spirits of the beasts he has killed.[3] The second
kind of purification to which I will here refer is the passing
of men and cattle through the need-fire during the prevalence
of a plague. This custom is explained most simply by
supposing that people thereby intended to interpose a barrier
between themselves and their cattle on the one side and the
maleficent spirits of the plague on the other.[4] One more
kind of purification—that of women after childbirth—will be
referred to in the course of this paper.

Such, then, are some of the modes of excluding or barring
the ghost. Before quitting the subject, however, I wish to
observe that as the essence of these proceedings was simply
the erection of a barrier against the disembodied spirit, they
might be, and actually were, employed for barring spirits
in other connexions. Thus, for example, since to early man
death means the departure of the soul out of the body, it is
obvious that the very same proceedings which serve to exclude
the soul after it has left the body, that is, to bar the ghost,
may equally well be employed to bar the soul *in* the body,
that is, to prevent its escaping ; in other words, they may be
employed to prevent a sick man from dying, in fact they

[1] C. J. Andersson, *Lake Ngami*, p.
224.
[2] H. Lichtenstein, *Travels in
Southern Africa*, i. p. 257 *sq.*
[3] E. B. Tylor, *Primitive Culture*,
i. p. 468 *sq.*
[4] See J. Grimm, *Deutsche Mytho-*

logie, p. 503 *sqq.*; E. B. Tylor, *Early
History of Mankind*, p. 256 *sq.*;
W. Mannhardt, *Der Baumkultus der
Germanen und ihrer Nachbarstämme*,
p. 518 *sqq.*; U. Jahn, *Die deutschen
Opfergebräuche bei Ackerbau und
Viehzucht*, p. 26 *sqq.*

may be used as cures. Thus the Chinese attempt to frighten back the soul of a dying man into his body by the utterance of wild cries and the explosion of crackers, while they rush about with extended arms to arrest its progress.[1] The use of water as a cure is perhaps best illustrated by the Circassian treatment of the sick. It is well known that according to primitive man the soul of a sleeper departs from his body to wander far away in dreamland; indeed, the only distinction which early man makes between sleep and death is that sleep is a temporary, while death is a permanent, absence of the soul. Obviously then, on this view, sleep is highly dangerous to a sick man, for if in sleep his soul departs, how can we be sure that it will come back again ? Hence in order to ensure the recovery of a sick man one of the first requisites is to keep him from sleeping. With this intention the Circassians will dance, sing, play, and tell stories to a sick man by the hour. Fifteen to twenty young fellows, naturally selected for the strength of their lungs, will seat themselves round his bed, and make night hideous by singing in chorus at the top of their voices, while from time to time one of them will create an agreeable variety by banging with a hammer on a ploughshare which has been thoughtfully placed for the purpose by the sick man's bed. But if, in spite of these unremitting attentions, the sick man should have the misfortune to fall asleep—mark what follows —they immediately dash water over his face.[2] The intention of this latter proceeding can hardly be doubtful : it is a last effort to stop the soul about to take flight for ever.[3] So

[1] Huc, *L'Empire chinois*, ii. p. 241 *sqq.*

[2] Klemm, *Culturgeschichte*, iv. p. 34 *sq.*

[3] The reason for throwing water on the face is that the soul is usually thought to issue either by the mouth or the nose. The Romans, Franks, Germans, English, Slavonians, Mexicans, and Quichés believed that it issued through the mouth (Ovid, *Met.* xii. 424 *sq.*, where the man is dying of a wound in the breast; Paulus, *Historia Langobardorum*, iii. 34 ; Wuttke, *Deutscher Aberglaube*, § 60; J. Grimm, *Deutsche Mythologie*,

p. 690 *sq.*; *id., Deutsche Sagen*, 461 ; Dyer, *English Folk-lore*, p. 214; Grohmann, *Aberglauben und Gebräuche aus Böhmen und Mähren*, pp. 60, 194 ; Tylor, *Primitive Culture*, ii. p. 29 ; Bancroft, *Native Races*, iii. p. 315, compare ii. p. 799). The ancient Greeks believed that the soul issued through the mouth or through a gaping wound (Homer, *Iliad*, ix. 409 ; xiv. 518; xvi. 505; compare E. Buchholz, *Die homerischen Realien*, II. ii. 284 *sqq.*). The modern Greeks believe that Charos, the Death - god, draws the soul out of the mouth ; but if the man is wicked or resists his fate, Charos

among the Abipones, a dying man is surrounded by a crowd
of old crones brandishing rattles, stamping and yelling, while
every now and then one of them flings water over his face

(so say the Arachobites) cuts open his
breast with a sword, for the soul has
its seat under the left breast (B.
Schmidt, *Das Volksleben der Neugriechen*, p. 228 *sq*.). The Jews, Arabs,
and Battas of Sumatra believe that the
soul issues through the nostrils
(Bastian, *Mensch*, ii. p. 322; *id.*, *Die
Seele*, p. 52; W. Marsden, *History of
Sumatra*, p. 386); but if a man dies
of a wound, the Arabs (like the
Homeric Greeks) believe that the soul
escapes through the wound (communicated by Professor Robertson
Smith). The Tonquinese used to
throw a handkerchief over the face
of the dying in order to catch his soul
(Richard's "History of Tonquin", in
Pinkerton's *Voyages and Travels*, ix.
p. 730). The modern Tonquinese
hang a film of cotton before the
nostrils by a silken thread (J. G. Scott,
France and Tonking, p. 96; Mr. Scott
supposes that this is to verify the fact
of death; it is possible that the old
custom may have been thus rational-
ized). The inhabitants of the Marquesas Islands are apparently of
opinion that the soul may pass out
indifferently either by the nose or the
mouth, for when a man is at his last
gasp the nearest relative holds both
the nose and the mouth of the dying
man with the kind intention of preventing the escape of the soul (Waitz,
Anthropologie, vi. p. 397). Among
the Seminoles of Florida, when a
mother died in childbirth, the baby
was held over her face to receive her
parting spirit (Brinton, *Myths of the
New World*, p. 271). But the soul
has other gateways or posterns. The
Chuwash think that it goes out at the
back of the head (Bastian, *Mensch*, ii.
p. 322). The Tibetans believe that it
issues by the top of the head, but its
escape has to be facilitated by cutting
off a lock of hair from the crown of the
head; this is done by a lama (Orazio
della Penna di Billi, "Brief Account of
the Kingdom of Tibet", in Bogle and

Manning's *Tibet*, p. 338 *sq.*; compare
C. Meiners, *Geschichte der Religionen*,
ii. p. 726 *sq.*). A similar theory is
revealed by the practice of the Káni-
kárs (a hill tribe of Travancore); when
a man is sick to death, his top-knot
is cut off by the headman of the
village, and his friends then take their
last farewell of him (Samuel Mateer,
Native Life in Travancore, p. 68).
The Greeks and Romans appear to
have had at one time the same belief
and custom (Euripides, *Alcestis*, 74
sqq., 101 *sq.*; Virgil, *Aeneid*, iv. 698
sqq.; compare Macrobius, *Saturn.* v.
19. The lock so cut off may be that
referred to in *Etymologicon Magnum*,
s.v. ἀπεσκολυμμένος. κολλὺς γὰρ ἡ θρὶξ
ἡ ἐπὶ τοῦ ἄκρου, ἣν ἐφύλαττον ἀκού-
ρευτον, θεοῖς ἀνατιθέντες), and we
may perhaps say the same of the
Canadian Indians, for when one of
them died a lock from his head was
cut off and presented to the nearest
relative (*Relations des Jésuites*, 1634,
p. 24; compare Lafitau, *Mœurs des
Sauvages Americquains*, ii.p.409). This
lock may have been the scalp-lock
which it was a point of honour to
leave unshorn that the conqueror
might cut it off as a trophy (Catlin,
North American Indians, ii. p. 24).
The Tahitians believed that at death
the soul was drawn out of the head
by a god (Ellis, *Polynesian Researches*,
i. p. 396—the part of the head is not
specified). Amongst the Kalmucks an
incision is sometimes made in the skin
to enable the soul to escape (Bastian,
Mensch, ii. p. 342, compare 343). In
Macassar for a similar purpose the
priest rubs the middle finger of the
dying man, because the soul has its
seat there (*ib.* p. 322). The Hindoo
belief (as set forth in the *Garuda-
purāna*) is that the soul of a bad man
goes downwards and emerges like the
excreta, but that the soul of a good
man issues through a suture at the
top of the skull. Hence the skull of
the corpse is cracked with a coco-nut

so long as there is breath left in his body.[1] The same practice
of throwing water over or washing the sick is observed also
in China, Siam, Siberia, Hungary, Ruthenia, Carniola, and
amongst the Koossas of South Africa.[2]

By analogy, the origin of the Kaffir custom of kindling a
fire beside a sick person,[3] the Russian practice of fumigating
him,[4] and the Persian practice of lighting a fire on the roof
of a house where anyone is ill,[5] may perhaps be found in
the intention of interposing a barrier of fire to prevent the
escape of the soul. For with regard to the custom of lighting
a fire on the roof, it is a common belief that spirits pass out
and in through a hole in the roof.[6] In the same way I would

or a piece of sacred wood to let out
the soul. Professor Monier Williams
heard of a sorcerer at Lahore who made
it his business to collect skulls which
had not been properly cracked and so
retained the souls of the deceased
inside (Monier Williams, *Religious
Thought and Life in India*, pp. 291,
297, 299; A. Bastian, *Die Seele*, p. 30).
The Nasairiens believe that when a
man is hanged his soul cannot pass
out through the mouth; hence they
will give the Turks large sums for the
privilege of being impaled instead of
hung (Bastian, *Mensch*, ii. p. 322).
On the belly of an old Esquimaux,
Ross remarked an incision which had
been clearly made after death, but the
reason of which he could not ascertain
(Klemm, *Culturgeschichte*, ii. p. 225);
it may have been made to allow the
soul to escape. For the soul is sometimes represented as lodged in the
belly; so at Smyrna they say "My
soul aches", meaning their belly
aches, and a stomach plaster is digni-
fied by the name of ἀντίψυχο (B.
Schmidt, *Das Volksleben der Neugriechen*, p. 229).

[1] M. Dobrizhoffer, *Account of the
Abipones*, ii. p. 266. Amongst the
Indians of California, if a sick man
falls asleep they knock him about the
head till he wakes, with the sincere
intention of saving his life (Bancroft,
Native Races, i. p. 569). Kaffirs,
when circumcised at the age of fourteen, are not allowed to sleep till the
wound has healed (Campbell, *Travels

in South Africa*, p. 514). In Venice,
when a woman has given birth to a
child, a female attendant stays by her
for some hours in order to keep her
from sleeping, and to drive off a
certain witch called Pagana (Gubernatis, *Storia comparata degli usi
natalizi in Italia e presso gli altri
popoli Indo-Europei*, p. 147).

[2] Gray, *China*, i. p. 278; Pallegoix,
Siam, i. p. 294; J. Bowring, *Siam*, i. p.
121; Klemm, *Culturgeschichte*, x. p.
254; *Folk-lore Journal*, ii. p. 102;
Ralston, *Songs of the Russian People*,
p. 315; Wood, *Natural History of
Man*, i. p. 189; H. Lichtenstein, *Travels
in Southern Africa*, i. p. 258. In the
Tiree a wet shirt is put on the patient
(*Folk-lore Journal*, i. p. 167).

[3] H. Lichtenstein, *loc. cit.*

[4] Ralston, *Songs of the Russian
People*, p. 380.

[5] Klemm, *Culturgeschichte*, vii. p.
142.

[6] Rochholz, *Deutscher Glaube und
Brauch*, i. p. 172; Wuttke, *Deutscher
Aberglaube*, §§ 725, 755; A. Bastian,
Mensch, ii. pp. 319, 323; *id.*, *Die
Seele*, p. 15; Ralston, *Songs of the
Russian People*, p. 314; J. T. Bent,
The Cyclades, p. 437; Dennys, *Folk-
lore of China*, p. 22; Lammert,
Volksmedizin, p. 103; B. Schmidt,
Das Volksleben der Neugriechen, p.
149; *Relations des Jésuites*, 1634, p.
23. On the Slave Coast, the roof of
the house is often taken off after a
death (P. Bouche, *La Côte des Esclaves*,
p. 214).

explain the extraordinary custom in Lao and Siam of surrounding a mother after childbirth with a blazing fire, within or beside which she has regularly to stay for weeks after the birth of the child.[1] The object, I take it, is to hem in the fluttering soul at this critical period with an impassable girdle of fire. In Abyssinia immediately after the birth the woman is laid on a wooden bed, which is surrounded by blazing herbs, and here she is held fast by stout young fellows.[2]

Conversely, among the Kaffirs a widow must stay by herself beside a blazing fire for a month after her husband's death, no doubt in order to get rid of his ghost.[3] If any

[1] Carl Bock, *Temples and Elephants*, p. 259 *sq.*; Pallegoix, *Siam*, i. p. 223; Bowring, *Siam*, i. p. 120. In Burma a similar custom prevails, but the time is shorter, about seven days (Forbes, *British Burma*, p. 66; *The Burman*, by Shway Yoe, i. p. 1 *sq.*). Amongst the modern Parsis a fire should be kept up three days and nights after the birth of the child (J. Darmesteter, *Zend-Avesta*, i. p. xciii). In Madagascar a fire is kept up in the room day and night frequently for a week after the birth (Ellis, *History of Madagascar*, i. p. 151, compare p. 149). It appears that it is only in Lao and Abyssinia that the fire actually surrounds the bed, and in Lao it is not kept up constantly, but is repeated day after day. But putting the intermittent circular fire of Lao beside the continued side fire of Siam and Burma, and taking into account the Malagasy, Abyssinian, Scottish, and Albanian practices (see below), we are perhaps justified in inferring that the original form of the custom was a continual and continuous circle of fire. A survival of this custom is seen in the old Scottish practices of whirling a fir-candle three times round the bed on which the mother and child lay (C. Rogers, *Social Life in Scotland*, i. p. 135), and of carrying fire morning and night round the mother till she was churched, and the child till it was christened (Martin's "Description of the Western Islands of Scotland", in Pinkerton's *Voyages and Travels*, iii.

p. 612). In Sonnenberg a light must be kept constantly burning after the birth, or the witches will carry off the child (A. Schleicher, *Volksthümliches aus Sonnenberg*, p. 144). Amongst the Albanians a fire is kept constantly burning in the room for forty days after the birth; the mother is not allowed to leave the house all this time, and at night she may not leave the room; and anyone during this time who enters the house by night is obliged to leap over a burning brand (Hahn, *Albanesische Studien*, i. p. 149). In the Cyclades no one is allowed to enter the house after sunset for many days after birth (Bent, *The Cyclades*, p. 181), and in modern Greece generally the woman may not enter the church for forty days after the birth (C. Wachsmuth, *Das alte Griechenland im neuen*, p. 73 *sq.*; Bent, *op. cit.* p. 180), just as in ancient Greece she might not enter a temple during the same period (Censorinus, *De die natali*, xi. 7). For similar restrictions in many parts of the world, see Gubernatis, *Usi natalizi*, c. 14, and especially H. Ploss, *Das Kind in Brauch und Sitte der Völker*, i. p. 49 *sqq.*; *id.*, *Das Weib in der Natur- und Völkerkunde*, ii. p. 434 *sqq.*

[2] H. Ploss, *Das Weib*, ii. p. 434.

[3] Lichtenstein, *Travels in Southern Africa*, i. p. 259. This too is probably the object of the dreadful ordeal through which widows among the Minas on the Slave Coast have to pass. After being shut up for six months

confirmation of this interpretation of the Siamese practice were needed, it would seem to be found in the fact that, during her imprisonment within the fiery circle, the woman washes herself daily for a week with a mixture of salt and water,[1] for salt, or salt and water, is a regular specific against spirits.[2]

Another of these two-edged weapons which can be used either to save the soul of the dying or to repel the ghost of the dead is fine clothes. We saw that the corpse is dressed in his best clothes in order to save the ghost the trouble of coming to fetch them. Conversely, when a Mongol is sick and like to die, all his finery is spread round about him in the hope of tempting the truant soul back to its deserted tabernacle, while a priest in full canonicals reads aloud a list of the pains and penalties of hell and of the risks run by souls which wilfully absent themselves from their bodies.[3] Thus, placed on the dying, fine clothes are a bait to lure the soul back ; placed on the dead, they are a bribe to it to stay away. The same custom of dressing a dying person in fine clothes is observed by the Chinese, the Todas of Southern India, and the Greenlanders.[4]

Of course it is possible that the fiery barriers described above may also be intended to keep off evil spirits, and this is the second supplementary use to which the proceedings for barring ghosts may be turned. This would appear to have been the object with which, in Siberia, women after childbirth leaped several times over a fire,[5] exactly as we

in the room where their husband is buried, they receive a severe beating and undergo an agonizing fumigation, after which they bathe in the sea (P. Bouche, *La Côte des Esclaves*, p. 218 *sq*.).

[1] C. Bock, *Temples and Elephants*, p. 260.

[2] Amongst the Moors of Morocco when a person goes from one room to another in the dark he carries salt in his hand as a protection against ghosts (A. Leared, *Morocco and the Moors*, p. 275). For other " spiritual " uses of salt, see W. G. Black, *Folk-Medicine*, p. 131 ; W. Henderson, *Folk-lore of the Northern Counties*, p. 53 ; J. Brand, *Popular Antiquities*, ii. p. 234 *sq*. ; Wuttke, *Deutscher Aberglaube*, §§ 118,

733 ; Rochholz, *Deutscher Glaube und Brauch*, i. p. 186 ; Strackerjan, *Aberglaube und Sagen aus dem Herzogthum Oldenburg*, § 232 ; Theocritus, xxiv. 95 *sq*. Salt is said to be particularly distasteful to the Devil (Moresin and Reginald Scott, quoted by J. Brand, *loc. cit.*).

[3] A. Bastian, *Die Seele*, p. 36.

[4] J. H. Gray, *China*, i. p. 278 ; W. E. Marshall, *Travels among the Todas*, p. 171 ; D. Crantz, *History of Greenland*, i. p. 237.

[5] C. Meiners, *Geschichte der Religionen*, ii. p. 107. Women before and after childbirth are thought to be especially exposed to the influence of malignant spirits.

saw that in Siberia mourners returning from a funeral leap over a fire for the express purpose of shaking off the spirit of the dead.

In China, the streets along which a funeral is to pass are previously sprinkled with holy water, and even the houses and warehouses along the street come in for their share, in case some artful demon might be lurking in a shop, ready to pounce out on the dead man as he passed.[1] Special precautions are also taken by the Chinese during the actual passage of the funeral; in addition to the usual banging of gongs and popping of crackers, an attempt is made to work on the cupidity of the demons. With this view, bank-notes are scattered, regardless of expense, all along the road to the grave. The notes, I need hardly observe, are bad, but they serve the purpose, and while the ingenuous demons are engaged in the pursuit of these deceitful riches, the soul of the dead man, profiting by their distraction, pursues his way tranquilly behind the coffin to the grave.[2]

A similar custom is observed in Corea.[3]

In Annam it is the restless spirits of the unburied dead (Co-hon) who lie in wait for funerals. To appease them sham gold and silver leaf are strewed about the road to the grave, and occasionally sheets of paper are burned containing

---

[1] J. H. Gray, *China*, i. p. 299. The custom of closing the houses and shops before which a funeral passes (such as prevails in modern Greece, Wachsmuth, *Das alte Griechenland im neuen*, p. 120) may have originally been meant to exclude the ghost.

[2] Huc, *L'Empire chinois*, ii. p. 249 *sq.*; J. H. Gray, *loc. cit.*; J. Doolittle, *Social Life of the Chinese*, p. 153 (ed. Paxton Hood). There is a popular impression that the ghost is always in the coffin. This, however, is an error. Huron ghosts, broadly speaking, walk in front of the coffin (*Relations des Jésuites*, 1636, p. 104), Chinese ghosts (as we have just seen) walk behind it, while some Prussian ghosts exhibit a marked preference for riding on the top of it (Toeppen, *Aberglauben aus Masuren*, p. 108; on the next page we read of the ghost following the corpse). The Coreans

place a chair beside the corpse for the ghost to sit on (J. Ross, *History of Corea*, p. 326). In Wallendorf, when the father of the family dies and the corpse is being carried out of the house, they place a chair and a towel for the convenience of the ghost (Toeppen, *op. cit.* p. 111). Some Negro ghosts in North Guinea are undoubtedly in the coffin, for they struggle in it as they are being carried to the grave, and the bearers have the greatest difficulty in running them in (J. L. Wilson, *Western Africa*, p. 231). Can this be the origin of the custom which the Burmese have of dancing with the coffin on their shoulders every now and then on the way to the grave? (Forbes, *British Burma*, p. 95 *sq.*; *The Burman*, by Shway Yoe, ii. p. 342).

[3] J. Ross, *History of Corea*, p. 319.

pictures of everything that the most exacting ghost could
desire, coats, boots, and so forth, together with prayers to
the saints that they would be pleased in mercy to take
away these weary wanderers of earth to the eternal peace of
heaven.[1]

In the Hervey Islands, in the South Pacific, after a death
the ghosts or demons are fought and soundly pummelled by
bodies of armed men, just as the Samogitians and old
Prussians used to repel the ghostly squadrons by sword-
cuts in the air.[2] New weapons, again, may be turned to
old purposes, as when a Kakhyen is borne to his last resting-
place amid a rolling fire of musketry.[3]

In Christian times bells have been used to repel evil
spirits ; this, of course, was the intention of the passing bell.[4]
In Scotland funerals used to be preceded by a man ringing a
bell.[5] The idea that the sound of brass or iron has power
to put spirits to flight prevailed also in classical antiquity,
from which it may have been inherited by mediaeval
Christianity.[6] We may perhaps see the germ of the passing
bell in the kettle which the Spartan women beat up and down
the streets on the death of a king.[7] The Moquis of Arizona

[1] J. G. Scott, *France and Tonking*,
pp. 99, 101 *sqq.* If the " prowling
devils " for whose special benefit the
funeral is preceded by men with sticks
are identical with the Co-hon, it would
appear that the Annamese have not a
robust faith in the unassisted efficacy
of prayer.

[2] W. W. Gill, *Myths and Songs
from the South Pacific*, p. 269; A.
Bastian, *Mensch*, ii. p. 341.

[3] J. Anderson, *Mandalay to Momien*, p. 143. In Tonquin a great
army used annually to muster and
open a terrific fire of artillery and
small arms on the ghosts (Baron's
"Description of the Kingdom of Tonqueen", in Pinkerton's *Voyages and
Travels*, ix. p. 696).

[4] J. Brand, *Popular Antiquities*,
ii. p. 202; Forbes Leslie, *Early Races
of Scotland*, ii. p. 503. In Neusohl
(North Hungary) the use of the bell is
somewhat peculiar. When a sick man
is near his end, they ring a little bell at
his head, that the parting soul may

linger a little to listen to the chime.
When the man is dead, they still ring
the bell, but go farther and farther
off, then out of the door, and round
about the house, still ringing the bell.
A message is then sent that the church
bell may begin to toll (Th. Vernaleken, *Mythen und Sagen des Volkes
in Österreich*, p. 311). There is or
was a similar custom in Bohemia
(C. L. Rochholz, *Deutscher Glaube und
Brauch*, i. p. 179). The object appears
to be to drive the ghost out of the house,
just as at the *Lemuria* a Roman householder ejected the ghosts by the tinkling
of brass (Ovid, *Fasti*, v. 441 *sqq.*).

[5] Ch. Rogers, *Social Life in Scotland*, i. p. 163 ; E. J. Guthrie, *Old
Scottish Customs*, p. 140.

[6] Lucian, *Philopseudes*, 15 ; Ovid,
loc. cit. Compare Fritsche on Theocritus, ii. 36 ; Prof. Robertson Smith
in the *Journal of Philology*, vol. xiii.
No. 26, p. 283, *note*.

[7] Herodotus, vi. 58.

exorcize evil spirits by the ringing of bells;[1] and at Port Moresby, in New Guinea, when the church bell was first used, the natives returned thanks to the missionaries for having driven away the ghosts.[2]

I have still one observation to make on the means employed to bar ghosts, and it is this. The very same proceedings which were resorted to *after* the burial for the purpose of barring the ghost were *avoided* so long as the corpse was in the house, from fear, no doubt, of hurting and offending the ghost. Thus we saw that an axe laid on the threshold or a knife hung over the door has power, after the coffin has been carried out, to exclude the ghost, who could not enter without cutting himself. Conversely, so long as the corpse is still in the house, the use of sharp-edged instruments should be avoided in case they might wound the ghost. Thus for seven days after a death, the corpse being still in the house, the Chinese refrain from the use of knives and needles, and even of chopsticks, eating their food with their fingers.[3] So at the memorial feasts to which they invited the dead, the Russians ate without using knives.[4] In Germany and Bohemia a knife should not be left edge upward, lest it hurt the ghosts or the angels.[5] They even say that if you see a knife on its back and a child in the fire, you should run to the knife before the child.[6] Again, we saw that the Romans and Germans swept the ghost, without more ado, out of his own house. On the other hand, the negroes on the Congo considerately abstain for a whole year from sweeping the house where a man has died, lest the dust should annoy the ghost.[7] On the day of the funeral the Albanians refrain from sweeping the place where the corpse lay, though by a curious contradiction someone regularly sits down three times on the spot.[8] Again, we have seen the repugnance of ghosts to water. Hence when a

[1] J. G. Bourke, *The Snake Dance of the Moquis of Arizona*, p. 258.

[2] J. Chalmers and W. W. Gill, *Work and Adventure in New Guinea*, p. 260.

[3] J. H. Gray, *China*, i. p. 288.

[4] W. R. S. Ralston, *Songs of the Russian People*, p. 321.

[5] J. Grimm, *Deutsche Mythologie*, iii. pp. 441, 454; Tettau und Temme, *Volkssagen Ostpreussens, Litthauens und Westpreussens*, p. 285; J. V. Grohmann, *Aberglauben*, etc., p. 198.

[6] J. Grimm, *op. cit.* p. 469.

[7] A. Bastian, *Mensch*, ii. p. 323.

[8] J. G. von Hahn, *Albanesische Studien*, i. p. 152.

death took place the Jews used to empty all the water in the house into the street, lest the ghost should fall in and be drowned.[1] Similarly in some parts of Calabria (Castrovillari and Nocara) and Germany all the water vessels are emptied at death.[2] In Burma, when the coffin is being carried out, every vessel in the house that contains water is emptied.[3] In some parts of Bohemia, after a death, the water-butt is emptied, because if the ghost happened to bathe in it, and anyone drank of it afterwards, he would be a dead man within the year.[4] We can now appreciate the significance of the fact mentioned above, that in Greece the lustral water before the door of a house where a dead body lay had always to be fetched from a neighbouring house.[5] For if the water had been taken from the house of death, who could tell but that the ghost might be disporting himself in it ?[6] Hence among the Jews all open vessels in the chamber of death were "unclean".[7] In Pomerania, even *after* a burial, no washing is done in the house for some time lest the dead man should be wet in his grave.[8] Amongst the old Iranians no moisture was allowed to rest on the

---

[1] J. Buxtorf, *Synagoga Judaica*, pp. 699, 712 (ed. 1712) ; J. C. G. Bodenschatz, *Kirchliche Verfassung der heutigen Juden*, iv. p. 178 ; J. Allen, *Modern Judaism*, p. 435 (ed. 1830) ; Gardner, *Faiths of the World*, i. p. 676. The reason assigned for this custom by the most learned Talmudists is that the water is unclean because the Angel of Death has washed his dripping sword in it. Contrast the vivid spiritualism of this explanation with the vapid rationalism of the view that the emptying of the water is a means of announcing the death. Truly it is vain to bottle the new wine of reason in old customs.

[2] Vincenzo Dorsa, *La Tradizione Greco-Latina negli usi e nelle credenze popolari della Calabria Citeriore*, p. 93 ; Rochholz, *Deutscher Glaube und Brauch*, i. p. 176. On the other hand at San Pietro in Calabria, when a man is dying, all the vessels in the house are filled with water, for the benefit of the thirsty souls of deceased relations who are supposed to gather in the house in order to accompany the spirit of the dying man to the other world (Dorsa, *op. cit.* p. 92 *sqq.*).

[3] C. J. F. S. Forbes, *British Burma*, p. 95.

[4] J. V. Grohmann, *Aberglauben und Gebräuche aus Böhmen und Mähren*, p. 193.

[5] In modern Greece a vessel with water stands beside the corpse, and all who approach it sprinkle themselves, but the refinements of bringing the water from another house and placing it outside the door appear to be forgotten (C. Wachsmuth, *Das alte Griechenland im neuen*, p. 109).

[6] In a similar way we may explain the rule in East Prussia, Schleswig, Lausitz, and Voigtland, that while the corpse is in the house nothing should be lent or given out of it (Wuttke, *Deutscher Aberglaube*, § 730; J. A. E. Köhler, *Volksbrauch im Voigtlande*, p. 441).

[7] Numbers xix. 15.

[8] Wuttke, *Deutscher Aberglaube*, § 737.

bread offered to the dead, for of course if the bread was damp the ghost could not get at it.[1] Once more, we saw that fire was a great stumbling-block to ghosts. Hence in Calabria and Burma the fires in the house are extinguished when a death takes place, doubtless (originally) in case they should burn the ghost.[2] The same custom used to be observed in the Highlands of Scotland, in Germany, and apparently in Rome.[3] So in old Iran, no fire was allowed to be used in the house for nine days (in summer for a month) after a death,[4] and in later times every fire in the Persian empire was extinguished in the interval between the death and burial of a king.[5]

[1] Fr. Spiegel, *Erânische Alterthumskunde*, iii. p. 705.

[2] Vincenzo Dorsa, *La Tradizione Greco-Latina negli usi e nelle credenze popolari della Calabria Citeriore*, pp. 20, 88 ; Forbes, *British Burma*, p. 94.

[3] J. Brand, *Popular Antiquities*, ii. p. 235 ; James Logan, *The Scottish Gaël*, ii. p. 387 ; L. Preller, *Römische Mythologie*, ii. p. 159 ; Apuleius, *Metam.* ii. 24 ; Juvenal, iii. 214, " *tunc odimus ignem* ". In North Germany there is no baking in the house on the day of a death (Kuhn und Schwartz, *Norddeutsche Sagen, Märchen, und Gebräuche*, p. 435). The reason of the custom appears to be forgotten in Oldenburg, where the fire is only extinguished when the corpse is carried out (Strackerjan, *Aberglaube und Sagen aus dem Herzogthum Oldenburg*, i. p. 154 ; Wuttke, *Deutscher Aberglaube*, § 609).

[4] *Vendîdâd*, v. 39 *sqq.*; Fr. Spiegel, *Erânische Alterthumskunde*, iii. p. 706 ; W. Geiger, *Ostiranische Kultur im Alterthum*, p. 258.

[5] Diodorus, xvii. 114. On the other hand it has been a common practice to place a light beside the corpse for the convenience of the ghost. But it would appear that people have been somewhat puzzled how to light and warm the ghost without burning him. Thus some modern Jews place a burning candle beside the corpse in order to light the soul ; but others maintain that a lighted candle near the body causes acute pain to the disembodied spirit (Gardner, *Faiths of the World*, p. 677 ; Buxtorf, *Synagoga Judaica*, p. 699 ; Bodenschatz, *Kirchliche Verfassung der heutigen Juden*, iv. p. 171). In Germany, so long as the body is above ground a light must be kept constantly burning beside it, for which the reason assigned in Voigtland is that the soul may not walk in darkness (Wuttke, *Deutscher Aberglaube*, § 729 ; Köhler, *Volksbrauch im Voigtlande*, p. 442 ; A. Birlinger, *Volksthümliches aus Schwaben*, p. 404 ; F. Schmidt, *Sitten und Gebräuche in Thüringen*, p. 87). In England candles used to be burned, beside or on the corpse (Brand, *Popular Antiquities*, ii. p. 234; Henderson, *Folk-lore of the Northern Counties*, p. 54). In Russia a lighted candle is usually placed beside the corpse or in its hand (Ralston, *Songs of the Russian People*, p. 314). In modern Greece when a death takes place candles or lamps are immediately lighted and kept burning three days and three nights, for during that time the soul of the deceased is supposed to linger in or to return to the house (*Folk-lore Journal*, ii. p. 168; Bent, *The Cyclades*, p. 221. Compare Wachsmuth, *Das alte Griechenland im neuen*, pp. 107, 108, 119). In China candles are kept burning round the coffin " to light the spirit of the dead on his way ", or " to give light to the spirit which remains with the corpse " (Doolittle, *Social Life of the Chinese*, p. 126 ; Dennys, *Folk-lore of China*, p. 21 ;

This leads me to speak of the custom of fasting after a death. The Jews may eat no flesh and drink no wine so long as the corpse is in the house ; they may not eat at all

Gray, *China*, i. p. 285). In Corea, when an offering is made by night to the corpse lying in the house, a candle is lit that the ghost may see what he is getting (J. Ross, *History of Corea*, p. 324 ; on page 319 it is said that candles are kept burning beside the corpse day and night). Again we hear of fires being lit (generally on the grave) either to warm the ghost or to light him on his way to the spirit world. Thus in the island of Ruk and in some parts of Australia a fire is kept burning on the grave for some time "that the soul may warm himself" (Waitz, *Anthropologie*, vi. pp. 686, 807. Compare Tylor, *Primitive Culture*, i. p. 484 *note*). In Western Africa the Krumen keep up a fire before the house of the deceased " that his spirit may warm itself " (Wood, *Natural History of Man*, i. p. 616). In Ashira-land a fire is kept up in the cemetery beside the corpse of a chief for weeks (Du Chaillu, *Journey to Ashango-land*, p. 133). The Winnebagoes, Algonkins, and Mexicans kept up a fire on the grave for four nights in order to light the spirit to the other world (Schoolcraft, *Indian Tribes*, iv. p. 55; Brinton, *Myths of the New World*, p. 257 ; Longfellow, *Hiawatha*, xx.). The Mintira kindle a fire on the grave that the ghost may not be cold (Bastian, *Die Seele*, p. 110). Those of the Indians near the mouth of the Russian River who bury their dead keep up fires on the grave and make great noises, in order to ward off the evil spirit who lies in wait for the soul (Bancroft, *Native Races*, iii. p. 523). Some Californian Indians keep a fire burning near the grave for several nights, for which one reason assigned is that it scares away the devil, and another is that it helps to light the ghost in its precarious passage across a greasy pole to heaven (Bancroft, *op. cit.* i. p. 357). The maidservants maintained a fire on the grave of Hruba for three days (K. Schwenk, *Slawische Mytho-*

logie, p. 325). The Caribs made a great fire round the grave and sat there addressing speeches to the dead (Rochefort, *Histoire naturelle et morale des Isles Antilles*, Rotterdam, 1665, p. 567). The Indians of Guiana make a fire on the grave and celebrate a feast there (Im Thurn, *Among the Indians of Guiana*, p. 225). The Andaman Islanders make a fire on the grave and leave beside it a shell with water and some article that belonged to the deceased (E. H. Man, *The Aboriginal Inhabitants of the Andaman Islands*, p. 76). On Pitt Island, Kingsmill group, in the Pacific, a fire was kept continually burning in the house during all the time (four months to two years) that the corpse was in it (Waitz, *Anthropologie*, v. ii. p. 155 ; Wood, *Natural History of Man*, ii. p. 382). In Vate or Efat (one of the New Hebrides) a fire was kindled on the grave to enable the soul to rise to the sun ; if this was not done, the soul went to the dreary lower regions of Pakasia (G. Turner, *Samoa*, p. 335). In Samoa a number of fires were kept up on the grave of a great chief during the night for ten days after the funeral ; in the house where he lay or out in front of it fires were kept up all night. " The common people had a similar custom. After burial they kept a fire blazing in the house all night, and had the space between the house and the grave so cleared that a stream of light went forth all night from the fire to the grave " (G. Turner, *ib.* p. 149). The last-mentioned custom may have been meant to show the ghost the way either to or from the grave. To this I shall have to recur shortly. The Aztecs burned the clothing, weapons, and some of the furniture of the deceased, in order that the heat of the fire might protect him against the bitter cutting wind that met him on his way to the land of souls (Klemm, *Cultur-geschichte*, v. p. 50).

in the same room with the corpse, but if there is only one room in the house they may eat in it if they interpose a screen, so that in eating they do not see the corpse.[1] The Kaffirs are bound to fast from the time of the death till after the burial,[2] and the same rule is or was observed by certain tribes of North American Indians.[3] The negroes of the Gold Coast fast long and severely after a death.[4] There is a German belief that, if anyone eats bread while a corpse is in the house, his teeth will fall out.[5] In modern Persia a fast of eight days is observed after a death.[6] In India a son is allowed only one meal a day during the mourning for his father ; a Brahman must continue this fasting for ten days.[7] According to another authority, a Hindoo family is not allowed to eat so long as a corpse is in the house.[8] In Corea during the first day of mourning no food is eaten by the family mourners ; sons and grandsons of the deceased eat nothing for three, less near relations for two, days.[9] During the mourning for the Kings of Michoacan no corn was ground, no fires lighted, no business transacted ; all the people remained at home and fasted.[10] When a chief died among the Guaycurus (an Indian tribe of Paraguay), the tribe abstained from eating fish, their principal dainty.[11] Amongst the Mbayas, another South American tribe, the women and slaves refrained from flesh and observed deep silence during mourning.[12] The Samoans commonly fasted during mourning ; they ate nothing during the day, but had a meal at night.[13] So amongst the Jews the chivalrous David

[1] J. C. G. Bodenschatz, *Kirchliche Verfassung der heutigen Juden*, iv. p. 177. The Jewish rule is to bury a man the day he dies (*ib.* p. 172 ; J. Buxtorf, *Synagoga Judaica*, p. 703). From Buxtorf (*op. cit.* p. 706) it appears that the prohibition to eat flesh and drink wine extends for seven days after the death. Another authority speaks of a fast from the moment of death till after the burial (J. Allen, *Modern Judaism*, p. 439).
[2] J. G. Wood, *Natural History of Man*, p. 220.
[3] Charlevoix, *Journal historique*, ii. p. 108 ; Th. Waitz, *Anthropologie*, iii. p. 196.
[4] Th. Waitz, *Anthropologie*, ii. p. 194.

[5] Wuttke, *Deutscher Aberglaube*, § 735, compare 740.
[6] C. Meiners, *Geschichte der Religionen*, ii. p. 702.
[7] S. C. Bose, *The Hindoos as they are*, p. 254.
[8] Sonnerat, *Reise*, i. pp. 74, 79, referred to by Knobel on Numbers xix.
[9] J. Ross, *History of Corea*, p. 322.
[10] H. H. Bancroft, *Native Races of the Pacific States*, ii. p. 622.
[11] Charlevoix, *Histoire du Paraguay*, i. p. 73.
[12] G. F. Klemm, *Culturgeschichte*, ii. p. 101.
[13] G. Turner, *Nineteen Years in Polynesia*, p. 228 ; *id.*, *Samoa*, p. 145.

fasted till evening in honour of his gallant enemy Abner [1]
—an ancient parallel to the minute guns which in the War
of Independence the Americans fired at the close of a
desperate battle, when an English General was buried on
the field, just as the French guns paid funeral honours to
Sir John Moore on the battlefield of Coruña.[2]

It might, perhaps, be supposed that this practice of
fasting was a direct consequence of the extinction of fires,
which, as we have seen, sometimes took place after a death,
and there are facts which seem at first sight to favour this
supposition. Thus the Chinese, though they are not allowed
to cook in the house for seven days after a death, are not
prohibited from eating food which has been prepared elsewhere ; indeed during this time of mourning their wants
are regularly supplied by their neighbours.[3] In Florida the
family was thus supplied by friends for three months.[4]
On the evening of mourning (which is usually also the evening
of the burial, the burial taking place on the day of death) a
Jew may not eat his own food, but is supplied with food by
his friends.[5] Amongst the Albanians there is no cooking
in the house for three days after a death, and the family is
fed by friends.[6] The Greeks of the Cyclades consider it
wrong to cook or perform household offices in the house of
mourning, so friends and relatives bring food and lay the
" bitter table ", as it is called.[7] But this explanation will not
suit the German superstition that while the passing bell is
tolling no one within hearing should eat.[8] For here the
prohibition evidently extends to all the food in the neighbourhood. The key to the solution of this problem will perhaps

[1] 2 Samuel iii. 35.
[2] Napier, *History of the Peninsular War*, i. p. 500.
[3] J. H. Gray, *China*, i. p. 287 *sqq.*
[4] Waitz, *Anthropologie*, iii. p. 196.
[5] J. Buxtorf, *Synagoga Judaica*, p. 707 ; J. C. G. Bodenschatz, *Kirchliche Verfassung der heutigen Juden*, iv. p. 178.
[6] J. G. von Hahn, *Albanesische Studien*, i. p. 151. Hahn forgot to inquire whether the fires in the house are extinguished, but he inclines to think that they are (*ib.* p. 199).

[7] T. H. Bent, *The Cyclades*, pp. 197, 221.
[8] W. Sonntag, *Todtenbestattung*, p. 176. In its present form the super-stition applies to the bell which rings for the funeral, but it seems hardly rash to assume that it originally applied to the passing bell. The same belief exists in New England (*Folklore Journal*, ii. p. 24). The reason assigned for the rule in Germany is that if you eat, your teeth will be hollow, in New England that you will have toothache. See next note.

be found in the Samoan usage. We are told that in Samoa, " while a dead body was in the house, no food was eaten under the same roof ; the family had their meals outside, or in another house. Those who attended the deceased were most careful not to handle food, and for days were fed by others as if they were helpless infants."[1] Observe here, firstly, that the objection is not to all eating, but only to eating under the same roof with the dead ; and, secondly, that those who have been in contact with the dead may eat, but may not touch their food. Now considering that the ghost could be cut, burned, drowned, bruised with stones, and squeezed in a door (for it is a rule in Germany not to slam a door on Saturday for fear of jamming a ghost),[2] it seems not unreasonable to suppose that a ghost could be eaten, and if we make this supposition I venture to think we have a clue to the origin of fasting after a death. People, in fact, originally refrained from eating just in those circumstances in which they considered that they might possibly in eating have devoured a ghost. This supposition explains why, so long as the corpse is in the house, the mourners may eat outside of the house, but not in it. Again, it explains why those who have been in contact with the dead and have not yet purified themselves (that is, have not yet placed a barrier between themselves and the ghost) are not allowed to touch the food they eat ; obviously the ghost might be clinging to them and might be transferred from their person to the food, and so eaten.[3]

[1] G. Turner, *Samoa*, p. 145. The punishment inflicted by the household god for a violation of this rule was supposed to be baldness and the loss of teeth—a curious coincidence with the reason assigned for the corresponding German and New England rule. The prohibition laid on those who had been in contact with the dead to touch food with their hands was a regular taboo in Polynesia and New Zealand. See W. Ellis, *Polynesian Researches*, i. p. 403 ; W. Mariner, *Tonga Islands*, i. p. 142 *note* ; J. S. Polack, *Manners and Customs of the New Zealanders*, i. p. 66 *sqq.* ; R. Taylor, *New Zealand*, p. 163 ; *Old New Zealand*, by a Pakeha Maori, p.

124 *sqq.* (p. 105 *sqq.*, ed. 1884) ; W. Yate, *New Zealand*, p. 85. The same rule seems to have prevailed amongst the Aleutian Islanders and the Jews, except that amongst the former it applied only to widows (Waitz, *Anthropologie*, iii. p. 316; A. Bastian, *Mensch*, iii. p. 81 ; Jeremiah xvi. 7, " Neither shall men break bread for them in mourning ", which is the reading of the Revised Version, but the marginal reading of the Authorized).

[2] A. Wuttke, *Der deutsche Aberglaube*, § 752.

[3] The probability of this explanation is at first sight somewhat diminished when we find that the prohibition to partake of food indoors was not

This theory further explains the German superstition mentioned above, that no one within hearing should eat while the passing bell is tolling. For the passing bell is rung when a soul is issuing for the last time from its mortal tabernacle, and if anyone in the neighbourhood were at this moment to eat, who knows but that his teeth might close on the passing soul? This explanation is confirmed by the companion superstition that no one should sleep while the passing bell is tolling, else will his sleep be the sleep of death.[1] Put into primitive language, this means

confined to cases where there was a corpse in the house, but applied to all persons who, from whatever cause, were under a taboo. Hence a chief, who was always taboo (*Old New Zealand*, p. 94), never under any circumstances ate in his house (Short-land, *Maori Religion and Mythology*, p. 28; R. Taylor, *New Zealand*, pp. 165, 168; W. Yate, *New Zealand*, p. 87). A discussion of the ideas at the root of the taboo system would lead me too far, but I may indicate a line of argument by which the presumption raised by the fact just stated against the theory in the text may perhaps be rebutted, if not a contrary presumption raised in its favour. The infringement of a taboo was supposed to bring sickness and death on the guilty person (*Old New Zealand*, p. 95 *sqq.*; Shortland, *op. cit.* p. 31; W. Mariner, *Tonga Islands*, i. pp. 142 *note*, 194; Klemm, *Culturgeschichte*, iii. p. 373). But sickness, according to the Maoris, was produced by an *atua* slipping down the throat of a man and devouring his vitals, and the aim of the medicine-man was therefore to expel the *atua* (R. Taylor, *New Zealand*, p. 135, compare pp. 137, 170; Polack, *Manners and Customs of the New Zealanders*, i. p. 263 *sq.*, compare p. 234; Shortland, *loc. cit.*). Now the *atuas* were ancestral spirits of chiefs (Polack, i. p. 51; compare Taylor, p. 135 *sqq.*), and would, when they visited the earth, naturally stay in the chief's house, who was himself an *atua* (Taylor, p. 352); hence anyone who ate in the chief's house would run the risk of swallowing

an *atua*, and thereby of falling sick and dying, which was exactly the effect supposed to be produced by the violation of a taboo. Consistency, however, is as little characteristic of savage as of civilized man; hence we need not be surprised to find that with this theory of sickness a Maori warrior would nevertheless gouge out and swallow the eyes of a chief whom he had slain, hoping thus to appropriate his *atua*, which resided in the eyes (Taylor, *loc. cit.*). When a Natchez had killed his first foe or made his first prisoner, he ate no flesh for six months, lest the ghost of his slain enemy should kill him (C. Meiners, *Geschichte der Religionen*, ii. p. 150 *sq.*). Part of the purification undergone by a Pima, after killing an Apache, was a fast of sixteen days; only after the fourth day was he allowed to drink a little pinole (Bancroft, *Native Races*, i. p. 553, referred to above, p. 22). The Caribs are said to have fasted rigorously *after* the body had been buried (Rochefort, *Histoire naturelle et morale des Isles Antilles*, p. 569, ed. 1665). Why they did not do so before, it is not easy to see.

[1] W. Sonntag, *Todtenbestattung*, p. 176, who says *sonst stirbt man bald*, but I cannot doubt that the original belief was as stated in the text, for it is a common belief in Germany that when a death takes place all sleepers in the house should be immediately roused or they will never wake again (Wuttke, *Deutscher Aberglaube*, § 726). This again confirms my view that the bell, during the ringing of which no

that as the soul quits the body in sleep, if it chanced in this its temporary absence to fall in with a soul that was taking its eternal flight, it might, perhaps, be coaxed or bullied into accompanying it, and might thus convert what had been intended to be merely a ramble into a journey to that bourne from which no traveller returns.

All this time, however, Plutarch has been waiting for his answer, but, perhaps, as he has already waited two thousand years, he will not object to be kept in suspense for a very few more minutes. I have already detained you too long, and for the sake of brevity in what remains I will omit all mention of the particular usages on a comparison of which my answer is based, and will confine myself to stating in the briefest way their general result.

We have seen the various devices which the ingenuity of early man struck out for the purpose of giving an " iron welcome to the dead ". In all of them, however, it was pre-supposed that the body was in the hands of the survivors and had been by them securely buried ; that was the first and most essential condition, and if it was not fulfilled no amount of secondary precautions would avail to bar the ghost.

But what happened when the body could not be found, as when the man died at sea or abroad ? Here the all-important question was, What could be done to lay the wandering ghost ? For wander he would, till his body was safe under the sod, and by supposition his body was not to be found. The case was a difficult one, but early man was equal to it. He buried the missing man in effigy,[1] and accord-

---

one must eat or sleep, was originally not the funeral, but the passing bell. The very cattle in the stalls and the bees in the hives are wakened after a death or they too will die (Wuttke, *loc. cit.*; Fr. Panzer, *Beitrag zur deutschen Mythologie*, ii. p. 293). In Scotland it was an old custom to allow no one in a house to sleep when a sick man was near his end (C. Rogers, *Social Life in Scotland*, i. p. 152).

[1] The practice of burying in effigy prevailed in ancient Greece (and apparently ancient Italy), Mexico, and Samoa, and it is still preserved in more

or less perfect forms in modern Greece, Italy, Albania, India, China, and Vancouver's Island. (1) In Chariton, iv. 1, an effigy of a missing man is carried on a bier, and it is said that it was an ancient Greek custom to give rites of sepulture to those whose bodies were not to be found (καὶ τοὺς ἀφανεῖς τάφοις κοσμεῖν). Euripides tells us that when a man had been drowned at sea his friends at home buried him κενοῖσιν ἐν πέπλων ὑφάσμασιν (Euripides, *Helene*, 1243), which seems to mean that an image of him was made up with clothes ; this was laid on a bier, and taken out to sea,

ing to all the laws of primitive logic an effigy is every bit as

where, along with offerings, it was thrown overboard. But it is not easy to say whether this was really a Greek custom or only a dramatic stratagem. (2) In Rome, burial of the absent took place according to certain solemn rites (Servius on Virgil, *Aeneid*, vi. 366). Compare Apuleius, *Metamorphos.* i. 6, "*At vero domi tuae iam defletus et conclamatus es ; liberis tuis tutores iuridici provincialis decreto dati ; uxor persolutis feralibus officiis luctu et maerore diuturno deformata*", etc. (3) In ancient Mexico, when a trader died in a far country the relations at home made a puppet of candlewood, adorned it with the usual paper ornaments, mourned over it, burned it, and buried the ashes in the usual way. Similarly soldiers who fell in battle were buried in effigy (H. H. Bancroft, *Native Races*, ii. p. 616 *sq.*). (4) In Samoa the relations spread out a sheet on the beach near where the man had been drowned, or on the battlefield where he had fallen ; then they prayed, and the first thing that lighted on the sheet (grasshopper, butterfly, or whatever it might be) was supposed to contain the soul of the deceased and was buried with all due ceremony (G. Turner, *Samoa*, p. 150 *sq.*). (5) In modern Greece, when a man dies abroad, a puppet is made in his likeness, and dressed in his clothes ; it is laid on the bed, and mourning is made over it (C. Wachsmuth, *Das alte Griechenland im neuen*, p. 113). It is not, however, said that this puppet is actually buried. Mr. T. H. Bent witnessed at Mykonos a formal lamentation for an absent dead man, but where the bier would have stood there was an empty space (T. H. Bent, *The Cyclades*, p. 222 *sqq.*). (6) A similar custom of mourning over an effigy is observed in some parts of Calabria (Vincenzo Dorsa, *La Tradizione Greco-Latina negli usi e nelle credenze popolari della Calabria Citeriore*, p. 93). (7) In Albania, when a man dies abroad all the usual lamentations are made at home as if the body were present ; the funeral

procession goes to the church, but in place of the bier a boy walks carrying a dish on which a cracknel is placed over some boiled wheat. This dish is set in the middle of the church, and the funeral service is held over it ; it is not, however, buried, but the women go and weep at the grave of the relation who died last (J. G. von Hahn, *Albanesische Studien*, i. p. 152). (8) The *Garuḍa-purāna* (the best authority on modern Hindoo beliefs and ceremonies relating to the dead) directs that " if a man dies in a remote place, or is killed by robbers in a forest, and his body is not found, his son should make an effigy of the deceased with Kusi grass, and then burn it on a funeral pile " with the usual ceremonies (Monier Williams, *Religious Thought and Life in India*, p. 300). (9) In China, " during the reign of the Emperor Chan-tuk, in the first century of the Christian era, it was enacted that if the bodies of soldiers who fall in battle, or those of sailors who fall in naval engagements, cannot be recovered, the spirits of such men shall be called back by prayers and incantations, and that figures shall be made either of paper or of wood for their reception, and be burned with all the ordinary rites. . . . The custom is now universally observed" (J. H. Gray, *China*, i. p. 295 *sq.*). " In case the corpse is not brought home to be buried, a letter, or some of the clothing recently worn by the deceased, or his shoes, or part of his baggage, is often sent home instead. The white cock and the mourners go forth to meet the letter or relic of the departed just as they would go to meet the corpse. On meeting the letter or the relic, the spirit passes as readily into the fowl as it would pass into it were the corpse itself met, and the spirit is conducted home just as surely" (J. Doolittle, *Social Life of the Chinese*, p. 164, ed. Paxton Hood). (10) In Vancouver's Island, when a man was drowned and his body could not be found, the mourning took place in the usual way, and to the grave were carried two

good as its original.[1] Therefore when a man is buried in
effigy with all due formality, that man is dead and buried
beyond a doubt, and his ghost is as harmless as it is in the
nature of ghosts to be.

But it occasionally happened that this burial by proxy
was premature, that in fact the man was not really dead, and
if he came home in person and positively declined to consider
himself as dead, the question naturally arose, was he alive
or was he dead ? It was a delicate question, and the solution
was ingenious   The man was dead, certainly—that was past
praying for. But then he might be born again ; he might
take a new lease of life. And so it was ; he was put out to
nurse, he was dressed in long clothes ; in short, he went
through all the stages of a second childhood.[2] But before
he was eligible even for this pleasing experience he had to
overcome the initial difficulty of getting into his own house.
For the door was as ghost-proof as fire and water could make
it, and *he* was a ghost. As such, he had to do as ghosts do ;
in fact, not to put too fine a point on it, he had to come down
the chimney.[3] And down the chimney he came—and this
is an English answer to a Roman question.

cedar boards, on " one of which was a
small porpoise, over which the other
board was placed, which bore the
roughly traced representation of a
man " (G. M. Sproat, *Scenes and
Studies of Savage Life*, p. 263).

In Madagascar cenotaphs are
erected for those whose bodies cannot
be found and their ghosts are supposed
to be allured thither (W. Ellis, *History of Madagascar*, i. p. 255). In New
Zealand " when a chief was killed in
battle, and eaten, his spirit was supposed to enter the stones of the oven,
with which his body had been cooked,
which retained their heat so long as it
remained in them ; his friends repeated their most powerful spells to
draw his spirit out of the stones, and
bring it within the wahi tapu [sacred
grove], for it was thought otherwise it
could not rest, but would wander about
inflicting injury on the living, all
spirits being considered maliciously
inclined towards them ; so when any
were slain in battle, if the body

could not be obtained, the friends
endeavoured to procure some of the
blood, or fragments of their garments,
over which they uttered a karakia
[spell], and thus brought the wandering
soul into the spiritual fold " (R.
Taylor, *Te Ika a Maui or New
Zealand and its Inhabitants*, p. 221).

[1] For evidence see E. B. Tylor's *Researches into the Early History of Man*,
p. 116 *sqq.*

[2] Plutarch, *Rom. Quaest.* 5 ; Hesychius, *s.v.* δευτερόποτμος: According
to Hesychius, the supposed dead man
had to imitate the act of birth by passing through the bosom of a woman's
robe (διὰ γυναικείου κόλπου διαδύς) ;
this was especially an Athenian custom.
The ritual described by Plutarch and
Hesychius was Greek, but Plutarch
was probably right in thinking that a
similar ritual lay at the base of the
Roman custom discussed by him.

[3] See the passages cited in note 6
on p. 26. In classical times, when
Plutarch wrote, the man probably

APPENDIX

NOTE I.—MOURNING COSTUMES

IT has been said above (p. 13) that mourning costume is usually the reverse of that of ordinary life. Thus we find that savages who ordinarily paint themselves sometimes refrain from doing so after a death.[1] Again, in similar circumstances, tribes which usually go naked put on certain articles of dress. Thus in some parts of New Guinea, where the men go naked and the women wear only a short grass petticoat, women in mourning wear a net over the shoulders and breast.[2] Elsewhere in New Guinea men also wear netted vests,[3] and in another place " when in deep mourning they envelop themselves with a very tight kind of wicker-work dress, extending from the neck to the knees in such a way that they are not able to walk well ".[4] On the other hand, when the Mpongwés in Western Africa are in mourning, a woman wears as few clothes as possible, and a man wears none at all,[5] though the tribe is very fond of dress, the usual garb of a man being a shirt, a square cloth falling to the ankles, and a straw hat.[6] The Lycians in mourning dressed as women.[7]

Whether or not these peculiar costumes (or absence of costume) were meant to disguise the wearers of them from the ghost of the deceased, certain it is that disguises have been assumed as a means of bilking spirits. Thus the Mosquito Indians believe that the devil (Wulasha) tries to get possession of the corpse ; so after they have lulled him to sleep with sweet music " four naked men *who have disguised themselves with paint,* so as not to be recognised and punished by Wulasha, rush out from a neighbouring hut " and drag the body to the grave.[8] At the feast held on the anniversary of the death these same Indians wear cloaks fantastically

descended through the *compluvium* (or *impluvium*, as it was less strictly called), an opening in the roof of the *atrium* or principal apartment. (See J. Marquardt, *Privatleben der Römer*, i. p. 231 *sqq.*) It is through this opening that Terence represents Jupiter as descending to Danaë (*Eunuchus*, ii. 5, 40) ; and if anyone was carried bound into the house of the Flamen Dialis, the ropes with which he had been tied had to be drawn up through the *compluvium*, and thence let down into the street (Aulus Gellius, x. 15, 8). But the *atrium* was originally dining-room and kitchen in one (Servius on Virgil, *Aeneid*, i. 726) ; hence the *compluvium* was probably the smoke-hole or chimney of the primitive house.

[1] P. F. X. de Charlevoix, *Histoire du Paraguay*, i. p. 73.
[2] J. Chalmers and W. W. Gill, *Work and Adventure in New Guinea*, p. 35.
[3] *Ib.* p. 130.
[4] *Ib.* p. 149.
[5] J. G. Wood, *Natural History of Man*, i. p. 586.
[6] Du Chaillu, *Equatorial Africa*, p. 9 ; compare J. Leighton Wilson, *Western Africa*, p. 262.
[7] Valerius Maximus, ii. 6. 13 ; Plutarch, *Consol. ad Apoll.* 22.
[8] H. H. Bancroft, *Native Races*, i. p. 744, *sq.*

painted black and white, while their faces are correspondingly streaked with red and yellow, perhaps to deceive the devil. Again in Siberia, when a Shaman accompanies a soul to the under world,[1] he often paints his face red, expressly that he may not be recognized by the devils.[2] In South Guinea, when a woman is sick she is dressed in a fantastic costume ; her face, breast, arms, and legs are painted with streaks of white and red chalk, and her head is decorated with red feathers. Thus arrayed she struts about before the door of the hut brandishing a sword.[3] The intention is doubtless to deceive or intimidate the spirit which is causing the disease. To deceive the demon of disease modern Jews will formally change the sick man's name.[4] In Guinea, women in their pregnancy also assume a peculiar attire ; they leave off ornaments, allow their hair to grow, cease to paint themselves, wear peculiar bracelets, anklets, etc., and in the last eight days their heads are thickly plastered with red clay, which they may not leave off till the child is born.[5] This is probably to disguise them from the demons, who lie in wait for women at these periods. And it may be the same idea which caused the Kaffirs to paint the child after birth,[6] for new-born children are apt to be carried off by spirits. Hence the Laosians tie strings round the wrists of the baby on the first night after its birth.[7] Australian widows near the north-west bend of the Murray shave their heads and plaster them with pipe-clay, which, when dry, forms a close-fitting skull-cap, about an inch thick.[8] In Ceylon the Kattadias dance in masks, in order to heal diseases caused by demons.[9] At the funeral of a high official in Corea there is a man with a hideous mask to frighten away the spirits.[10] If my explanation of the cere-mony of passing through the fire[11] is correct, the custom which the people had of blackening each other on these occasions and wearing the smut on their faces for long afterwards was probably intended as an additional precaution against the demons of the plague.[12]

The customs of blackening the face or body and of cutting the hair short after a death are very widespread. But when we find these customs observed after the death, not of a friend, but of a slain enemy,[13] no one will pretend that they are intended as marks of sorrow, and the explanation that they are intended to disguise the

[1] See above, p. 7.
[2] W. Radloff, *Aus Sibirien*, ii. p. 55.
[3] J. L. Wilson, *Western Africa*, p. 389.
[4] J. Buxtorf, *Synagoga Judaica*, p. 696 ; J. C. G. Bodenschatz, *Kirch-liche Verfassung der heutigen Juden*, iv. p. 168 ; J. Allen, *Modern Judaism*, p. 434, ed. 1830.
[5] G. F. Klemm, *Culturgeschichte*, iii. p. 284 *sq.*   [6] *Ib.* p. 285.

[7] C. Bock, *Temples and Elephants*, p. 259.
[8] J. G. Wood, *Natural History of Man*, ii. p. 92.
[9] A. Bastian, *Die Seele*, p. 102.
[10] W. E. Griffis, *Corea, the Hermit Nation*, p. 278.   [11] Above, p. 23.
[12] J. Grimm, *Deutsche Mythologie*, ii. p. 504.
[13] H. H. Bancroft, *Native Races of the Pacific States*, i. p. 764.

slayer from the angry ghost of the slain may be allowed to stand till a better is suggested. These disguises are meant to serve the same purpose as the so-called purifications of slayers of men and beasts.[1] In fact, " mourning " and " purification " run into each other ; this " mourning " is not mourning, and this " purification " is not purification. Both are simply pieces of spiritual armour, defences against ghosts or demons. In regard to " mourning " costume this appears clearly in the Myoro custom ; when the child of a Myoro woman dies, she smears herself with butter and ashes and runs frantically about, while the men abuse her in foul language, for the express purpose of frightening away the demons who have carried off the child.[2] If the curses are meant to frighten, are not the ashes meant to deceive the demon ? Here the disguise is adopted as a protection, not against the spirit of the dead, but against the devils which carried it off, and it is possible that the same may be true of " mourning " costume in other cases ; but considering the general vicious and dangerous nature of ghosts, it is probable that " mourning " costume was usually a protection against them rather than against devils. The custom of blackening the body in mourning by means of ashes, soot, and so forth is common.[3] The Andaman Islanders smear themselves with clay ;[4] the Egyptians threw mud on their heads,[5] and they sometimes do so still.[6] The custom of cutting the hair short in mourning is very common all over the world ; examples would be endless. I may mention, however, that the Greek and Persian custom of cutting off the manes of their horses in extreme mourning is also observed by the Comanche Indians of North America.[7] The opposite custom of

---

[1] See above, pp. 22 sq.
[2] J. H. Speke, *Journal of the Discovery of the Source of the Nile*, p. 542.
[3] See Jonathan Carver, *Travels through the Interior Parts of North America*, p. 407; H. H. Bancroft, *Native Races*, i. pp. 86, 134, 173, 180, 206, 288, 370 ; *id.* ii. p. 618; H. H. Johnston, *The River Congo*, p. 426 ; J. Chalmers and W. W. Gill, *Work and Adventure in New Guinea*, pp. 36, 37, 149, 266, 286 ; H. R. Schoolcraft, *Indian Tribes*, ii. p. 68 ; *id.* iv. pp. 55, 66 ; Cook's *First Voyage*, Bk. i. c. 14 ; Charlevoix, *Journal Historique*, ii. p. 111 ; Du Chaillu, *Journey to Ashangoland*, p. 133 ; G. Turner, *Samoa*, p. 308 (*id.*, *Nineteen Years in Polynesia*, p. 322) ; Th. Waitz, *Anthropologie*, iii. p. 196; *id.* vi. p. 403 ; J. G. Wood, *Natural History of Man*, i. p. 580 ; G. M. Sproat, *Scenes and Studies of*

Savage Life, p. 259 ; Smith's " Virginia ", in J. Pinkerton's *Voyages and Travels*, xiii. p. 39.
[4] E. H. Man, *Aboriginal Inhabitants of the Andaman Islands*, pp. 73, 77, 78.
[5] Herodotus, ii. 85 ; Diodorus Siculus, i. 72.
[6] Sir J. G. Wilkinson, *Manners and Customs of the Ancient Egyptians*, iii. p. 442.
[7] Euripides, *Alcestis*, 429 ; Plutarch, *Pelopidas*, 33 ; *id.*, *Alexander*, 72 ; *id.*, *Aristides*, 14 ; Herodotus, ix. 24 ; H. H. Bancroft, *Native Races*, i. 523 ; the Comanches cut off the tails as well as the manes ; possibly the Greeks and Persians did so too, but it is only said that they " shaved " their horses, except in Euripides, where the shaving is distinctly confined to the manes.

letting the hair grow long in mourning is much rarer; it has been practised by the Egyptians,[1] Jews,[2] Chinese,[3] widows on the Slave Coast,[4] and Hindoo sons in mourning for a parent.[5]   The practice of wounding or mutilating the body has also been very general.   The case of the Koossa widow in South Africa is instructive in various ways.   She had to stay by herself in a solitary place beside a blazing fire for a month (as we saw above, p. 27); by night she came secretly to the hut where she had lived with her husband, and burned it down, after which she returned to her solitude.   At the end of the month she *threw away her clothes, washed her whole body, scratched her breasts, arms, and thighs with sharp stones, girded her body round with rushes twisted together, and at sunset* returned to the kraal.[6]   Now when we remember the pains taken by widows in other parts of Africa to get rid of their husbands' ghosts (see above, pp. 20 *sq.*), we can hardly doubt that the precautions taken by the Koossa widow had a similar object in view; that, in fact, by scratching her person, assuming a peculiar garb, and returning at dusk to her home, she was trying to throw the ghost off the scent. Some peoples (as the Sacae), after a death, went down into the pits and hid themselves for days from the light of the sun.[7]   At sunset Calabrian women cease from their wild lamentations and doff the black veils which they donned at the moment of death.[8]   On my hypothesis the explanation of this interesting custom is that disguise is superfluous in the dark.   At the same time it is curious to find the contrary custom (strict silence by day, loud lamentations by night) in places so widely apart as Madagascar and Yucatan.[9] In Corea, sons in mourning for their parents wear a peaked hat, which covers the face as well as the head; the Jesuits in Corea have successfully availed themselves of this costume as a disguise.[10]

A few words may be added on mourning colours, though the subject does not concern us here very closely.   Black dress (developed out of the habit of blackening the body with ashes, etc.) was, or is still, the usual mourning in ancient Greece,[11] Rome,[12] modern Greece,[13]

[1] Herodotus, ii. 36.
[2] Buxtorf, *op. cit.* p. 706; Bodenschatz, *op. cit.* iv. p. 179.
[3] J. H. Gray, *China*, i. p. 286.
[4] P. Bouche, *La Côte des Esclaves*, p. 218 *sq.*
[5] S. C. Bose, *The Hindoos as they are*, p. 254.
[6] H. Lichtenstein, *Travels in South Africa*, i. p. 259.
[7] Plutarch, *Consol. ad Apoll.* 22; Aelian, *Var. hist.* xii. 38.
[8] V. Dorsa, *La Tradizione Greco-Latina negli usi e nelle credenze popolari della Calabria Citeriore*, p. 91.

[9] W. Ellis, *History of Madagascar*, i. p. 233; H. H. Bancroft, *Native Races*, ii. p. 801.
[10] W. E. Griffis, *Corea, the Hermit Nation*, p. 279; É. Reclus, *Nouvelle Géographie Universelle*, vii. p. 675.
[11] Homer, *Iliad*, xxiv. 94; Artemidorus, *Onirocrit.* ii. 3; Euripides, *Alcestis*, 427; Plutarch, *Pericles*, 38; Xenophon, *Hellen.* i. 7. 8; etc.
[12] J. Marquardt, *Privatleben der Römer*, i. p. 346.
[13] C. Wachsmuth, *Das alte Griechenland im neuen*, p. 109.

and among widows on the Slave Coast.[1] The Omahas in North America painted themselves white,[2] and white dress is (or was) mourning in Corea,[3] China,[4] Tonquin,[5] Siam,[6] among the Mussas,[7] in ancient Argos,[8] among Roman women, in Imperial times at least,[9] in Voigtland [10] and in Saterland in Oldenburg.[11] In England the scarfs, hatbands, and gloves worn at the funerals of unmarried persons and infants used always to be white,[12] and they are so still at the funerals of young persons in Scotland. When Sophocles heard of the death of Euripides he put on gray or dark blue,[13] and gray (with the alternative of white) was mourning among the Γαμβρείωται.[14] Blue is the mourning colour for women in some parts of Germany.[15] A strip of blue is worn round the head by modern Egyptian women at a funeral, and from the monuments this appears to have been an ancient custom.[16] Blue is said also to be the Syrian, Cappadocian, and Armenian colour,[17] and dark blue may be used as an alternative to black by widows on the Slave Coast.[18] In Guatemala a widower dyed himself yellow,[19] and it is said that Anne Boleyn wore yellow for Catherine of Aragon.[20]

Note II.—The Golden Welcome

If the spirit of the dead usually receives a grim or iron he occasionally receives a loving or golden welcome from his friends. The Coreans seek to recall the departed soul. A servant takes a

[1] P. Bouche, *La Côte des Esclaves,* p. 218.

[2] Th. Waitz, *Anthropologie,*i ii. p. 196.

[3] J. Ross, *History of Corea,* p. 318; compare Ch. Dallet, *Histoire de l'Église de Corée,* i. p. 29.

[4] N. B. Dennys, *Folklore of China,* p. 25; but for a more exact statement, see J. Doolittle, *Social Life of the Chinese,* p. 138.

[5] J. G. Scott, *France and Tongking,* p. 98; Baron, however, describes it as ash-coloured, " Description of the Kingdom of Tonqueen ", in J. Pinkerton's *Voyages and Travels,* ix. p. 698; Richard—in Pinkerton, *ib.* p. 708—agrees with Scott.

[6] Pallegoix, *Siam,* i. p. 246; C. Bock, *Temples and Elephants,* p. 246.

[7] C. Bock, *op. cit.* p. 310.

[8] Plutarch, *Quaest. Rom.* 26.

[9] Plutarch, *ib.*; Herodian, iv. 2.

[10] J. A. E. Köhler, *Volksbrauch im Voigtlande,* p. 257, but the custom has nearly, if not quite, died out.

[11] L. Strackerjan, *Aberglaube und Sagen aus dem Herzogthum Oldenburg,* ii. p. 132.

[12] J. Brand, *Popular Antiquities,* ii. p. 283.

[13] 'Ιματίῳ φαιῷ ἤτοι πορφυρῷ, A Westermann's *Biographi Graeci,* p. 135.

[14] *Corp. Inscript. Graec.* ii. n. 3562, quoted by K. F. Hermann, *Lehrbuch der griechischen Privatalterthümer,* p. 370, 3te Aufl.

[15] C. L. Rochholz, *Deutscher Glaube und Brauch,* i. p. 198.

[16] E. W. Lane, *Manners and Customs of the Modern Egyptians,* ii. p. 257.

[17] J. Brand, *Popular Antiquities,* ii. p. 282.

[18] P. Bouche, *loc. cit.*

[19] H. H. Bancroft, *Native Races,* ii. p. 802.

[20] J. Brand, *op. cit.* ii. p. 283.

garment once worn by the deceased, ascends to the top of the house, and, looking northward (whither the spirits flee), he calls aloud thrice the name of the deceased.[1] The loud cry (*conclamatio*) raised by the Romans at death may have had the same object.[2] In Masuren on the evening of the funeral day they place a chair in the chamber of death and hang a towel on the door, for on that evening the ghost comes back from the grave, seats himself on the chair, weeps bitterly, dries his tears with the towel, and goes away for ever.[3] The Jews keep a lamp burning for seven days at the head of the bed where the man died, because the ghost returns thither to weep ; [4] beside this light were placed a glass of water and a towel.[5] In some parts of Calabria they place bread and water in the room for three nights, because the ghost returns at midnight to eat and drink.[6] The Samoan custom of keeping up a stream of light between the house and the grave may have been intended (as we saw, p. 34 note) to show the ghost the way back to the house. With this object, apparently, some Central American tribes extend a thread from the house to the grave, carrying it in a straight line over every obstacle.[7] In some parts of Germany the funeral always goes by the high road, in order that the ghost may be able to find his way home.[8] In the Mariana Islands when a man was dying they placed a basket beside him and begged the soul at its departure to go into the basket, and to take up its quarters there on any future visits to the house.[9] In some Russian villages from time to time all the dead are feasted in a house and are then let down through the window by a shroud into the street and go their way.[10]

DISCUSSION

The PRESIDENT (Mr. Francis Galton) thought it a fair topic of discussion whether it was likely that any widely prevalent and long enduring custom sprang from a single root, and whether, on the other hand, its existence and persistence under very varied conditions was not some evidence of its origin in many roots, and of

[1] J. Ross, *History of Corea*, p. 321.
[2] W. A. Becker, *Gallus*, p. 506.
[3] M. Toeppen, *Aberglauben aus Masuren*, p. 111.
[4] J. Buxtorf, *Synagoga Judaica*, p. 711.
[5] J. C. G. Bodenschatz, *Kirchliche Verfassung der heutigen Juden*, iv. p. 178. The reason here assigned is that the Angel of Death may wash his sword in the water and wipe it with the towel, but probably the water and the towel were originally intended, like

the light, for the convenience of the ghost.
[6] V. Dorsa, *La Tradizione Greco-Latina negli usi e nelle credenze popolari della Calabria Citeriore*, p. 92.
[7] H. H. Bancroft, *Native Races*, i. p. 745.
[8] W. Sonntag, *Todtenbestattung*, p. 175.
[9] Th. Waitz, *Anthropologie*, v. ii. p. 151.
[10] W. R. S. Ralston, *Songs of the Russian People*, p. 321 *sq.*

its being sustained by a concurrence of motives. He would instance
the prevalent custom in society of avoiding the name of a recently
deceased person when speaking to his or her very near relatives.
For his own part he felt the disinclination very strongly, on the
ground that it was too direct under the circumstances, and that a
euphemism was more appropriate. Probably others felt the same,
and he and they followed a savage custom for totally different
reasons to that by which the savage was principally governed.

Dr. E. B. TYLOR remarked that Mr. Frazer's original and ingenious treatment of the evidence must materially advance the
study of animistic funeral customs. His theory of the connexion
of purification by water or fire with attempts to bar the return of
ghosts deserved, and would doubtless receive, the careful consideration of anthropologists. Dr. Tylor adduced from Mr. Yarrow's
paper on Mortuary Customs a case of water burial carried out for
the purpose of preventing the return of harmful ghosts. With
regard to the entrance of the person supposed dead by the roof, he
called attention to the fact that such entrance is adopted in some
districts as a symbolic rite, perhaps indicating descent from heaven,
which might possibly be the explanation of the Roman practice.
Dr. Tylor concluded by expressing his satisfaction at the excellent
results of Mr. Frazer's study of classical authors, not as mere
ancient texts, but as repertories of real facts full of anthropological
value.

Mr. F. T. HALL suggested that the idea of water as a barrier
between the dead and the living might have originated with the
primitive and indeed general belief that the souls of the departed
are not at rest until they have passed to the other side of some great
water, now referred to as " the river of death ". The Chaldeans
made their dead cross a mysterious sea, the Egyptian dead navi-
gated across the infernal Nile ; the Greeks and Romans had their
Styx, over which the soul could not be ferried until proper funeral
rites had been performed with the body, the unburied wandering
on this side of these waters for twelve months before being allowed
to cross. Even the waters of the firmament were considered to be
interposed between earth and heaven. The general idea was that
the earth, the abode of the living, was encompassed by water over
which the dead souls had to pass before they reached the place of
rest, and that until water was interposed between the dead and the
living the soul could not be at rest and was apt to wander through
the earth.

Mr. BEAUFORT observed that there was at all events one modern
nation where water was not supposed to restrict the movements of
ghosts, namely, Japan. On the evening that the speaker entered
Nagasaki the Japanese were celebrating the annual return of the
dead to visit the living. All the tombs were lighted by pretty

coloured lanterns, and food was placed there for the use of the spirits. On the third day hundreds of miniature vessels were sent to sea freighted with food for the spirits on their return voyage. Thus the spirits make two voyages every year.

Mr. HYDE CLARKE said that in the consideration of the re-entry to the house it must be taken into account that in the Persian example, as in many others, the house would be terraced on the top, with an approach from below. In most cases the houses are isolated, and as there is no exit elsewhere from the terrace it is naturally suggestive as an entry for the ghost. With regard to not mentioning the name of the dead, it must be borne in mind there is equal superstition as to mentioning the name of the living, as of a husband. So also the sacred name of a city. The name is the spiritual essence of the ghost and the Ka. A character for name is the round or circle, and this is perhaps the origin of the cartouche encircling names in hieroglyphics, etc. He might mention one legend as to the connexion of the dead and the living in Slav countries, which he had learned from a Servian friend, in whose family an example had happened, and which he believed was included in the MSS. of the folk-lore of Servia prepared for the press by Madame Mijatovich. There is a superstition of a mysterious connexion between those members of a family born in the same month, who are denoted in Slav as " Same month ", and of whom of course there are many examples, as we may observe that even in a family of six the births will be severally in three or four months, and not in separate months for each. On a child dying there was great fear for the sister of the " same month," and it was considered necessary to preserve her from the danger or certainty of a similar premature death. A hobble was got in with which horses of the herd are hobbled on the plain, and the living was hobbled by the leg to the dead. An exorcist then repeated the necessary formula, and to him was handed a piece of silver money (about a shilling) which had been given or begged. The child lived, which is a testimony, and of course a confirmation, of the efficacy of the process.

Mr. FRAZER, in reply, expressed his deep gratification at the interest which Mr. Tylor had expressed in his paper. It was the writings of Mr. Tylor which had first interested him in anthropology, and the perusal of them had marked an epoch in his life. He fully agreed with an observation of the President, that it would be hazardous to assume that when in modern times a man dresses very carefully on such momentous occasions as going into battle (as General Skobeleff used to do), we had here a relic of the old feeling which prompted people to dress a dying man in his best clothes. On the other hand, he was inclined to think that in the modern reluctance to mention the name of a person recently deceased we had a relic (of course quite unconscious) of the old belief that a dead man will hear

E

and answer to his name ; there was a large substratum of savagery underlying all our civilization. Replying to Mr. Tylor, he said that he (Mr. Tylor) had laid his finger on the apparent inconsistency of the facts that ghosts could bathe in water, yet not cross it ; but the author pointed out that men were exactly in the same predicament —that, in fact, in dealing with primitive ghosts we always had to regard them as being as nearly as possible the exact counterpart (only visible) of men, and hence that though ghosts had the same difficulty which men had in crossing water, yet the difficulty was not insuperable for ghosts any more than for men. Thus Mr. Beaufort had informed them that Japanese ghosts could cross water in boats, and the author referred to the well-known story of King Gunthram, whose soul was seen to depart from him in sleep and to seek in vain to cross a stream till someone laid a sword across it, on which the soul immediately crossed over to the other side. With regard to the interesting Slavonic superstition mentioned by Mr. Hyde Clarke, that a child born in the same month with a child that had died was especially likely to die, and that special precautions had to be taken to save it, the author suggested that we might get some light by comparing the Laosian beliefs with regard to children. The Laosians think that an infant is the child, not of its parents, but of the demons ; and hence they call on the demons to carry off their child within four and twenty hours after birth or else to leave it for ever. Moreover, they give the child a hideous name by way of frightening away the demon, and they sell it for a nominal price to a friend, under the impression that the demons are too honest to carry off what has been actually bought and paid for. Now if the demons had carried off a child born in a particular month, it might be thought that this gave them a special power over another child born in the same month, and that therefore special precautions were needed to prevent its dying. One of the speakers had suggested that in Persia the supposed dead man might have returned through a door in a terraced roof. In reply, Mr. Frazer said that there was evidence to show that in the Roman case in question the entrance was made through the *compluvium*, an opening in the *atrium* or principal apartment of the house. Now as this *atrium* was distinctly stated by the ancients to have been originally sitting-room and kitchen in one, it is not unreasonable to infer that it represented the single apartment of the primitive house, and that the aperture in the roof (afterwards known as the *compluvium*) was originally the smoke-hole or chimney.

II

THE PRYTANEUM, THE TEMPLE OF VESTA, THE VESTALS, PERPETUAL FIRES[1]

THE object of this paper is to prove the common origin of the Greek prytaneum and the Italian temple of Vesta,[2] and to suggest an explanation of the origin of the order of the Vestals as well as of the custom of maintaining perpetual fires.

Every Greek state had its prytaneum which may be described as the town-hall of the capital. None but capital cities had a prytaneum. Hence when the king of Athens extended his sway over the whole of Attica, each petty town, hitherto independent, had to abolish its prytaneum, and for the future the prytaneum of Athens was the prytaneum of Attica.[3] The essential feature of the prytaneum was its hearth (ἑστία) which differed from other hearths only in this, that it was pre-eminently the hearth of the city, the common hearth.[4] On this hearth there burned a perpetual fire.[5] The

[1] Reprinted, with a few corrections, from *The Journal of Philology*, vol. xiv. (1885).

[2] To a minute comparison of Hestia and Vesta Mr. August Preuner has devoted five hundred laborious pages which it would be rude to characterize as dull and inaccurate to describe as lively. That Mr. Preuner has not anticipated the conclusions reached in this paper will appear from the following passage, which I extract from the two hundred and sixty-sixth page of his learned work : " *In der That weder die Hestia im griechischen Königshaus entspricht der in der Aedes Vestae zu Rom, noch das Prytaneon der republi-* *canischen Zeit in Hellas der Regia mit dem Vestaheiligthum, und zwar wiederum weder in der republicanischen noch in der königlichen Zeit. Und die Unterschiede bestehen nicht etwa in blossen Modificationen wie sie auch bei Entlehnung statt finden können, es sind generelle Unterschiede* " (*Hestia-Vesta*, Tübingen, 1864).

[3] Thucydides, ii. 15; Plutarch, *Theseus*, 24.

[4] Pollux, i. 7 ; *id.* ix. 40 ; κοινὴ ἑστία, Aristotle, *Pol.* 1322 b 28.

[5] Casaubon on Athenaeus 700 D (vol. iii. p. 279 of the separate reprint of his commentary) was of opinion that the fire in the prytaneum was

prytaneum was sacred to Hestia,[1] the personified goddess of
the hearth.[2]   In the prytaneum ambassadors were entertained
and distinguished citizens maintained at the public expense,
and it was the headquarters of the officials known as prytanes.[3]
Now considering (1) that the name prytanis is nearly equivalent to king,[4] (2) that in some states, as Rhodes,[5] the prytanes always continued to be the chief magistrates, (3) that
the prytanes had their headquarters in the prytaneum, (4)
that the prytaneum was the mark of a capital city, (5) that
at Athens it was the seat of the most ancient law court,[6] and

merely a lamp, and he is supported by
Theocritus, xxi. 36 *sq.*, as well as
by the passage in Athenaeus on which
he comments.   It is quite possible
that in some places the original fire
on the hearth may have dwindled into
the "rudimentary organ" of a simple
lamp (see below, pp. 74 *sq.*), but that this
was not universally the case appears
from Pausanias' description of the fire
in the prytaneum of Olympia (v. 15. 9).
    [1] Pindar, *Nem.* xi. 1, with the scho-
liast.   For the statement that the
Athenian prytaneum was sacred to
Pallas there is no better authority
than that of the scholiast on Aristides,
Panath. p. 103 ed. Jebb (vol. iii. p. 48
ed. Dindorf), the doubtfulness of whose
testimony is sufficiently revealed by
the hesitation with which he speaks :
τὸ δὲ πρυτανεῖον τόπον εἶναι λέγουσιν
τῆς Παλλάδος ἱερόν κτλ.   In his day the
prytaneum clearly lived only in tradition.   Weighed against the statements of Pindar and his old scholiast
as well as the silence of Pausanias,
and the fact that the Athenian prytaneum contained an image of Hestia,
the testimony of this feather-weight
scholiast kicks the beam.
    [2] The Athenian prytaneum con-
tained an image of Hestia (Pausanias,
i. 18. 3).   Whether other prytanea had
images of her, we cannot tell.
    [3] For the apparent exception to this
rule at Athens, see below.
    [4] Hesychius πρύτανις· βασιλεύς, ἄρ-
χων, χορηγός, ταμίας, διοικητής; Suidas
πρύτανις· διοικητής, προστάτης, φύλαξ,
βασιλεύς, ἄρχων, ταμίας, ἔξαρχος; *Etym.*
Magnum πρυτανεῦσαι· διοικῆσαι, προ-

στατεῦσαι, φυλάξαι, βασιλεῦσαι, ταμιεῦ-
σαι.   The officials known at Athens
and elsewhere as prytanes were known
in some states as ἄρχοντες, in others
as βασιλεῖς (Aristotle, *Pol.* 1322 b 28).
In Aeschylus (a poet especially con-
servative of ancient usages) we find
the king of Argos thus addressed :
πρύτανις ἄκριτος ὢν | κρατύνεις βωμὸν
ἑστίαν χθονός (note that the ἑστία of
the king or prytanis is the ἑστία of
the state) (*Suppl.* 370 *sq.*).   Again in
Prom. 169 Zeus is spoken of as μακά-
ρων πρύτανις.   The old historian Charon of Lampsacus wrote a work on
the Spartan kings, whom he called
prytanes (Suidas, *s.v.* Χάρων) ; see
Müller's *Fragmenta Historicorum*
Graecorum, vol. i. p. xvi *sqq.*
    [5] Livy, xlii. 45; Appian, *Bell. Civ.*
iv. 66 ; Plutarch, *Praec. ger. reip.*
xvii.3. Compare Polybius, xiii. 5, xv.23,
xxvii. 6, xxix. 4. Dionysius Halicarnasensis even says τά γέ τοι καλούμενα
πρυτανεῖα παρ' αὐτοῖς [the Greeks in
general] ἐστιν ἱερά καὶ θεραπεύεται πρὸς
τῶν ἐχόντων τὸ μέγιστον ἐν ταῖς πόλεσι
κράτος (*Antiq. Rom.* ii. 65).
    [6] This seems proved by the legal
use of the term πρυτανεῖα as well as
by the nature of the cases which in
historical times were tried in the
court of the prytaneum (Demosthenes,
Aristocr. 644 ; Pollux, viii. 120 ; Pausanias, i. 28. 10).   Indeed, among the
innumerable relics of ancient thought
and custom preserved, as in a museum,
by the law, there can be few if any
that bear the marks of a hoarier
antiquity than the court of the prytaneum.

(6) that its essential feature was a hearth such as every house possessed, we can hardly help concluding that the prytanis was anciently the king or perhaps rather the chief or headman of a petty independent town, and that the prytaneum was his house.[1] The king proper (βασιλεύς) was the powerful chief who put down the petty chieftains round about, added their territories to his own, and welded the whole into a single state. The memory of this political revolution was clearly preserved in Attica,[2] where down to the time of Pausanias some of the small towns still cherished traditions of the days when they had been ruled by kings of their own.[3]

This general conclusion is confirmed and illustrated by the history of the prytaneum at Athens. The situation of the Athenian prytaneum in the time of Pausanias is not doubtful. It stood on high ground at the foot of the northern declivity of the Acropolis. This situation, indicated by inscriptions and harmonizing with the narrative of Pausanias, is accepted by all modern inquirers.[4] But it is equally certain that in the time of Pausanias the prytanes sacrificed and dined, not in the prytaneum, but in the Round-house (Tholus, a circular building in a different part of Athens).[5] Persons maintained for honour's sake at the expense of the State always received their allowances in the prytaneum, and that the prytanes did so originally there can be no doubt. Why did they not continue to do so ? A glance at the topography

---

[1] Observe that the hearth in the prytaneum appears to have had the same privilege of sanctuary as the hearth in the king's house (Plutarch, *De mul. virt.* 17 compared with Thucydides, i. 136). The identity of the prytaneum with the king's house had already been assumed by Duncker (*Geschichte des Alterthums*, 3rd ed. 1881, vol. v. pp. 83, 467, 470), and (more ambiguously) by Preller (*Griechische Mythologie*, 3rd ed. 1872, i. p. 345).

[2] Thucydides, ii. 15 ; Plutarch, *Thes.* cc. 24, 32.

[3] Pausanias, i. cc. 14, 31, 38.

[4] W. M. Leake, *Topography of Athens*, i. pp. 8, 252, 269 ; E. Curtius,

Attische Studien, ii. p. 62 ; *id.*, *Erläuternder Text der sieben Karten zur Topographie von Athen*, pp. 45 *sq.*, 53 ; *id.*, *Atlas von Athen*, p. 12 ; *id.*, *Karten von Attika, Erläuternder Text*, p. 6 ; C. Wachsmuth, *Die Stadt Athen im Alterthum*, i. p. 221 ; C. Bursian, *Geographie von Griechenland*, i. p. 295 ; T. H. Dyer, *Ancient Athens*, p. 263 ; Baedeker, *Griechenland*, p. 27 (on p. 77 the author has confused the tholus with the prytaneum); A. Milchhöffer in Baumeister's *Denkmäler des klassichen Alterthums s.* Athen, i. p. 172 ; G. F. Hertzberg, *Athen*, p. 26.

[5] Pausanias, i. 5. 1 ; Pollux, viii. 155 ; Suidas, Harpocration, Timaeus, *Lex. Plat., s.v.* θόλος; Bekker, *Anecdota Graeca*, i. p. 264.

of Athens will supply the answer. In historical times the
government offices [1] stood in the inner Ceramicus, the busy
centre of Athenian city life.[2] That the Ceramicus was not
the oldest quarter of the city may be inferred from its situation on the low ground to the north-west of the Acropolis,
and follows from the express statement of Thucydides.[3] If
then the Ceramicus was a comparatively new quarter, we can
understand why it never contained the prytaneum.[4] For the
prytaneum no doubt stood in the oldest part of the town, and
there would always be a strong sentimental and religious
feeling against shifting this ancient hearth of the city to the
newer quarters. Hence when the government offices were
transferred for the sake of convenience to the bustling new
town, the prytaneum would be left to slumber, with other
venerable relics of the past,[5] in the quiet back streets of the
sleepy old town. The Council Chamber [6] formed one of the
group of public offices in the new town, and as the prytanes
were the committee for the time being of the Council their
presence was of course required in the Ceramicus. Thus it
would have been obviously inconvenient for them to go up
for lunch or an early dinner to the prytaneum.[7] To toil up

---

[1] τὰ ἀρχεῖα, Bekker, *An. Gr. loc. cit.*;
W. M. Leake, *Topography of Athens*,
i. p. 243.

[2] For a vivid picture of this quarter
of the city with its motley life see
E. Curtius, *Attische Studien*, ii. p.
42 *sqq.*

[3] ii. 15 τὸ δὲ πρὸ τούτου ἡ ἀκρόπολις
ἡ νῦν οὖσα πόλις ἦν καὶ τὸ ὑπ' αὐτὴν
πρὸς νότον μάλιστα τετραμμένον.

[4] When the scholiast on Aristophanes (*Peace*, 1183) says that the
statues of the Eponymi stood near
the prytaneum, he confuses the Tholus with the prytaneum. The Eponymi stood over above the Tholus
(Pausanias, i. 5. 1), that is, on the
northern slope of the Areopagus overlooking the Ceramicus.

[5] The Agraulium (Pausanias, i. 18),
the Bucoleum (Suidas *s.v.* ἄρχων;
Bekker, *Anecd. Gr.* i. 449, 20), and
the Basileum (Pollux, viii. 111).

[6] βουλευτήριον, Pausanias, i. 3. 5.

[7] The prytaneum lay (as mentioned
above) at the foot of the northern

declivity of the Acropolis between
what are now known as the chapel of
the Saviour (Sotir) and the chapel of
Simeon (Wachsmuth and Milchhöffer,
ll. cc.). The height of the chapel of the
Saviour above the sea is 110·09 metres
(Curtius, *Atlas von Athen*, p. 10), that
of the site of the στοὰ βασίλειος (near
which was the Council Chamber, Pausanias, i. 3. 1 and 5. 1) 62·5 metres
(*Atlas von Athen*, Bl. iii.). I follow,
without attempting to pass judgement
on, the usual hypothesis that the prytaneum of Pausanias' time was the
old prytaneum and not (as Curtius
supposes) a structure of Roman times.
But my argument would only be
strengthened if we could accept the
theory (put forward by Curtius with
more of ingenuity than proof in the
second part of his *Attische Studien*)
that the Old Market of Athens, and
with it the old prytaneum, lay on the
southern side of the Acropolis. For
in that case the prytanes would have
had a much longer and wearier way

the steep and dusty street in the sweltering heat of a southern noon would have been trying to elderly gentlemen (of whom there was no doubt a fair sprinkling among the fifty prytanes) and to hurry down to their office immediately after lunch would have been exceedingly bad for their digestion. It was natural therefore that a building should be put up for their convenience in the neighbourhood of the Council Chamber where they could dine and sacrifice without the expenditure of time and energy which daily visits to the prytaneum during business hours would have entailed. This building was the Tholus or Round-house.[1] On the other hand the distinguished persons whom Athens delighted to honour by providing them with a free breakfast, lunch, and dinner every day of their lives, as they had no business to take them down to the Ceramicus, had also no need to shift their quarters there, and they continued to take their meals regularly up at the prytaneum.[2] The Tholus where the prytanes dined was a round building with a pointed, umbrella-shaped roof.[3] So unusual a shape of building was probably adopted for some special reason, and this reason could hardly be other than that this was the shape of the prytaneum itself, of which the Round-house was in some respects the representative. When with the growth of the city in a new direction it was found

to trudge from the New Market (in the Ceramicus) to the Old. They would have been obliged to cross the saddle between the Acropolis and the Areopagus and skirt the southern face of the Acropolis, without so much as the shadow of the great rock to screen them from the fierce glare of the sun. Dr. Dyer, doing battle with Curtius, makes Plutarch (*Theseus*, 24) assert roundly that the prytaneum of his day stood where it had stood since the time of Theseus (*Ancient Athens*, p. 264). All that Plutarch does say is that the prytaneum of Theseus stood " where the city (τὸ ἄστυ) now stands "—a sufficiently vague expression. Dr. Dyer may be right in crossing swords with Curtius on this question, but if he is to vanquish so redoubtable a *sabreur* he would need sharper weapons than a misplaced comma and a little bad Greek.

[1] Pausanias, i. 5. 1.

[2] On the separation of the two sets of meals, see Curtius, *Attische Studien*, ii. p. 63 *sqq.* and Westermann in Pauly's *Real-Encyclopädie, s.v. σίτησις.* The ground about the prytaneum was found littered with lists of the prytanes and state-pensioners (ἀείσιτοι) (A. Milchhöffer, *loc. cit.*). In the " Field of Famine " (Λιμοῦ πεδίον), which adjoined the prytaneum, we may perhaps detect a sarcastic reference to the persons who fared sumptuously every day at the expense of their less fortunate fellow-citizens, or perhaps rather a feeling allusion to the numerous lazzaroni (familiar to every visitor to the south of Europe) who sat (and still sit) at the gates of the rich.

[3] Hesychius, Harpocration, Suidas, Timaeus, *Lex. Plat., s.v. θόλος* ; *Etym. Magnum, s.v. σκιάι.*

necessary to strip the prytaneum of some of its functions and transfer them to a new building in a more convenient site, it was but natural, considering the sacred and venerable character of the building, that the new structure should be a close copy of the old ; if the new was round, so probably was the old. Recollecting that the Italian temples of Vesta (the correspondence of which to the Greek prytanea will be shown on independent grounds) were round,[1] we may perhaps venture to generalize the conclusion arrived at for the prytaneum of Athens and say that originally the prytanea of Greece were round.[2]

If the prytaneum was originally the house of the chief (prytanis), we should expect to find it forming part of, or at least adjoining, the king's palace ($\beta a\sigma i\lambda\epsilon\iota o\nu$) at Athens. When the $\pi\rho\upsilon\tau a\nu\iota s$ of Athens rose to be $\beta a\sigma\iota\lambda\epsilon\upsilon s$ of Attica, his increase of dignity would be marked by an increase in the splendour of his house—his $\pi\rho\upsilon\tau a\nu\epsilon\hat{\iota}o\nu$ became a $\beta a\sigma i$-$\lambda\epsilon\iota o\nu$. In point of fact the prytaneum did stand near (how near we cannot say) to the palace.[3] The latter was the headquarters of the tribal kings, four in number, one for each of the ancient Attic tribes.[4] In historical times these tribal kings were still men of the old blue blood ; their functions were largely sacerdotal, but they also presided in the ancient criminal court of the prytaneum. What their original

---

[1] The very word tholus is used of the temple of Vesta by Ovid (*Fasti*, vi. 282, 296). Compare Servius on Virgil, *Aen.* ix. 408 : *Alii tholum aedium sacrarum dicunt genus "fabricae Vestae et "Panthaere . . . Aedes autem rotundas tribus deis dicunt fieri debere, Vestae Dianae, vel Herculi vel Mercurio."*

[2] The excavations at Olympia have raised a presumption that the prytaneum there was square (Curtius und Adler, *Olympia und Umgegend*, p. 35). But owing to the superposition of later buildings the excavation of the prytaneum was very laborious and its results uncertain. Even if it were proved to have been square, we should hardly be surprised that in this splendid centre of Greek life the antiquated prytaneum should have made way for

a new and grander structure in the fashionable style of the day. In the common meeting ground of all Greeks architectural conservatism could hardly maintain so firm a footing as in individual states.

It would be unsafe to lay much weight on the evidence of Suidas (who defines $\pi\rho\upsilon\tau a\nu\epsilon\hat{\iota}o\nu$ by $\theta\delta\lambda os$ and $\theta\delta\lambda os$ by $\pi\rho\upsilon\tau a\nu\epsilon\hat{\iota}o\nu$) because, like the scholiast on Aristophanes referred to above, he may have confused these two buildings at Athens. But this confusion would be all the more likely to arise if the buildings were of similar shape.

[3] The $\beta a\sigma i\lambda\epsilon\iota o\nu$ was near the $\beta o\upsilon\kappa o$-$\lambda\epsilon\hat{\iota}o\nu$ (Pollux, viii. 111) and the $\beta o\upsilon\kappa o$-$\lambda\epsilon\hat{\iota}o\nu$ was near the $\pi\rho\upsilon\tau a\nu\epsilon\hat{\iota}o\nu$ (Suidas, *s.v.* $\check{a}\rho\chi\omega\nu$; Bekker, *An. Gr.* 449. 20).

[4] Pollux, viii. 111, 120.

relations were to the kings of Attica cannot now be determined ; but their titles, their residence in the palace, their
analogy (as priests and titular kings) to the *rex sacrificulus*
at Rome (whom we know to have been a representative of
the old kings), all point to the conclusion that they were the
representatives of the ancient tribal chieftains. And when
we consider that their headquarters adjoined the prytaneum,
that they presided in the criminal court of the prytaneum,
and that they themselves are spoken of by Plutarch [1] in the
same chapter as kings and prytanes indifferently, we have
fresh reason for confidence in the view that the prytanis was
originally the chief and the prytaneum his house.

The history of the palace at Athens resembled that of the
prytaneum. As some of the functions of the latter were
transferred to a building more conveniently situated for the
transaction of public business, while the old building retained
the title, together with the less pressing business, of the
prytaneum, so some of the duties previously no doubt discharged by the king (βασιλεύς) in the palace (βασίλειον)
were for similar reasons transferred to the Royal Portico
(στοὰ βασίλειος),[2] the office of the King Archon (ἄρχων
βασιλεύς) in the Ceramicus. But like the prytaneum the
older building retained its title : it was still the palace
(βασίλειον), while the office in the Ceramicus was only the
Royal Portico (στοὰ βασίλειος).

To sum up : the prytaneum, a round building with a
pointed, umbrella-shaped roof, was originally the house of
the king, chief, or headman (prytanis) of an independent
village or town, and it contained a fire which was kept constantly burning. It is only necessary to add that when a
colony was sent out, the fire for the chief's house (prytaneum)
in the new village was taken from that in the chief's house of
the old village.[3]

Turning to Italy we at once identify the Latin Vesta with
the Greek Hestia [4] (to whom the prytaneum was sacred). But
while in Greece the original identity of the goddess with the
domestic hearth was still shown by the identity of their

[1] *Solon*, 19.
[2] Pausanias, i. 3. 1.
[3] *Etym. Magnum*, 694. 28 ; Schol.
on Aristides, *Panath.* p. 103, ed. Jebb.

[4] G. Curtius, *Greek Etymology*, p.
400 ; H. Jordan in Preller's *Römische
Mythologie*, 3rd ed. ii. p. 155 note 3.

names, in Italy their relationship was so far obscured that the hearth had resigned its old name to the goddess (who had really much less claim to it) and was content to be known by the modest title of *focus*. But the origin of the goddess, if obscured, was not forgotten,[1] and in that " twilight of the gods " when Vesta too paled her ineffectual fires, her humble birth was dragged to light and all her little peccadilloes held up to scorn by the pitiless logic of a great Christian divine.[2] Vesta, then, like Hestia, was originally the fire on the hearth, and hence the main feature in her sanctuary, as in the prytaneum, was an ever-burning fire. To complete the resemblance it is needful to show that the so-called Temple of Vesta was originally not a temple but the king's house.

In the first place, her so-called temple never was, strictly speaking, a temple at all. This fact we have on the authority of Varro himself.[3] Adjoining the temple or house of Vesta were two buildings, the one known as the Atrium Vestae, the other as the Regia, and tradition asserted that on the site of one or other of these buildings or on that of the temple itself once stood the Palace of Numa.[4] Now as the Regia was officially associated, in republican times, with the Pontifex Maximus [5] and Rex Sacrificulus,[6] both of whom succeeded to the priestly functions of the king, there is little room to doubt that the temple of Vesta was once part of the king's house, and since its essential feature was its hearth, we may reasonably conclude that this hearth was originally the hearth of the king's house. The Lares and Penates, which were worshipped here [7] as in every private house, were no doubt originally the Lares and Penates of the king. In fact the public hearth with its gods was a simple repetition of

[1] Ovid, *Fasti*, vi. 291 : " *Nec tu aliud Vestam quam vivam intellige flammam.*"

[2] Augustine, *De civ. Dei*, iv. 10. Even before Augustine, Firmicus Maternus had taken up his parable and suggested that, as Vesta was after all only the kitchen fire, she should have cooks to look after her and not virgin priestesses, who were often no better than they should be (*De errore profanarum religionum*, 14. 3).

[3] Aulus Gellius, xiv. 7. 7 : " *Inter quae id quoque scriptum reliquit [Var-*

ro] non omnes aedes sacras templa esse ac ne aedem quidem Vestae templum esse." Compare Servius on Virgil, *Aen.* vii. 152, ix. 4.

[4] Ovid, *Fasti*, vi. 263 *sq.*; *id., Trist.* iii. 1, 28 *sqq.*; Solinus, i. 21. Compare Servius on Virgil, *Aen.* viii. 363.

[5] R. Burn, *Rome and the Campagna*, p. 78.

[6] Servius, *l.c.*; Varro, *De lingua Latina*, vi. 12.

[7] J. Marquardt, *Römische Staatsverwaltung*, iii. p. 244 *sq.*

what was to be seen in every Roman house: the only difference was that here the householder (the king) had departed.[1]

Two more points of resemblance to the prytaneum may be noted. In the first place the traditions which connected the Vesta and Penates of Rome with those of Alba and Lavinium point clearly to the custom of colonies lighting their perpetual fires at the ever-burning hearth of the mother town, for there can be little doubt that Alba was the earliest seat of the Latin race in Latium.

In the second place the Italian temple of Vesta, like the Greek prytaneum, was a round building. In regard to the Roman temple of Vesta tradition preserved the memory of the time when its walls were made of wattled osiers and the roof was of thatch;[2] indeed, with that peculiar clinging to the forms of the past which is characteristic of royalty and religion, the inmost shrine continued down even to late times to be formed of the same simple materials.[3] Thus looking back into the dim past, as our eyes get accustomed to the gloom, we descry the chiefs of the old Graeco-Italian clans dwelling in round huts of wattled osiers with peaked roofs of thatch. And through the open door of the hut we see a fire burning on the hearth. Who tended the fire?

No doubt the chief himself saw to it that the fire was kept constantly burning,[4] but the actual gathering of sticks and putting them on the fire probably fell on those maids-of-

---

[1] The resemblance of the Italian temple of Vesta to the Greek prytaneum did not escape Dionysius Halicarnasensis, and he explained it by supposing that the former was a direct imitation of the latter (*Ant. Rom.* ii. 65). Mommsen also notes the resemblance, and appears to account for it in the same way (*History of Rome*, i. p. 125). The parallels which I shall presently cite make it much more probable that the prytaneum and the temple of Vesta were independent developments from a common original type. Mommsen, however, has approached, if not quite grasped, the idea that the hearth of Vesta was of old neither more nor less than the hearth of the king (i. pp. 70, 124).

A distinct tradition of the time when each head of a clan was at the same time priest of Vesta for his people, is preserved in Dionysius Halicarnasensis, *loc. cit.* Examples of the king acting as priest for his people need not be multiplied; I will cite only one: the Eastern Slavonians had no regular class of priests; "the chief of the *Rod* [clan] exercised the functions of priest, king, and judge" (W. R. S. Ralston, *Songs of the Russian People*, p. 83).

[2] Ovid, *Fasti*, vi. 261 *sq.*

[3] Festus, *s.v. penus.*

[4] See the reference to Dionysius Halicarnasensis on p. 60, note 3, and compare p. 63, note 1.

all-work in early households—the wife and daughters.
Afterwards the fire in the hut which royalty had relinquished
to religion was tended by maidens, four, later six in number,
who entered on the service in childhood (between the years
of six and ten) and continued in it for thirty years, when they
were free to return to the world.[1] These vestal virgins appear
to have been under the *patria potestas* of the king, and, under
the republic, of his successor the Pontifex Maximus.[2] But
if they were under the *patria potestas* of the king, they
must have been either his wives or daughters ; their rule of
celibacy excludes the former supposition ; it remains therefore that they were his daughters.[3] Various circumstances
confirm this view. Down to the time of Augustus the *rex
sacrificulus* (one of the representatives of the old king) continued to officiate in the Regia adjoining the temple of Vesta,
and the Vestals lived in a house abutting on the Regia.[4] It
appears that originally they had to be of patrician birth.[5]
They were treated with marks of respect usually accorded to
royalty : thus on the streets they were preceded by a lictor
and the highest magistrates made way for them ; they
sometimes enjoyed the exceptional privilege of riding in a
carriage ; at public games a place of honour was assigned
to them ; and after death they, like the Imperators, were
allowed to be buried within the city walls " because they
were above the laws ".[6] Again they enjoyed the royal
privilege of mercy, for if they met a criminal on the way to

[1] Dionysius Halicarnasensis, *Ant.
Rom.* ii. 67 ; Aulus Gellius, i. 12.
Compare J. Marquardt, *Römische
Staatsverwaltung*, iii. p. 323 *sqq.*
[2] J. Marquardt, *op. cit.* p. 341.
[3] The number of the Vestals perhaps
points to a union of tribes and their
chiefs. Festus (p. 468 ed. Lindsay)
thought that they represented the
" first and second Titienses, Ramnes
and Luceres ", and there was a tradition of the time when there was as yet
no common hearth for the whole
people, but only a common hearth for
each *curia* on which the headman of
the *curia* offered sacrifice (Dionys.
Halic. *Ant. Rom.* ii. 65)—a state of
things corresponding perhaps to the
condition of Attica before the συν-

οικισμός, when each village had as yet
its own prytaneum.
[4] Dion Cassius (liv. 27) says that
Augustus gave up the Regia to the
Vestals : τὴν μέντοι τοῦ βασιλέως τῶν
ἱερῶν (οἰκίαν) ταῖς ἀειπαρθένοις ἔδωκεν,
ἐπειδὴ ὁμότοιχος ταῖς οἰκήσεσιν αὐτῶν ἦν.
The foundations of the temple of Vesta
were discovered in 1874 and the house of
the Vestals in 1884 (H. Jordan, "Der
Tempel der Vesta, die Vestalinnen,
und ihr Haus ", in the *Historische und
philologische Aufsätze* published in
honour of E. Curtius' seventieth birth-
day, Berlin, 1884).
[5] J. Marquardt, *op. cit.* p. 325.
[6] " *Quia legibus non tenentur* ",
Servius on Virgil, *Aen.* xi. 204.

execution, his life was spared, just as in Madagascar " if a criminal can obtain sight of the sovereign, he is pardoned whether before or after conviction. . . . Even criminals at work on the highroad, if they can catch sight of the monarch as he passes by, may claim their pardon. Hence, by a sort of anomaly in this singular law, they are ordered to withdraw from the road when the sovereign is known to be coming by." [1] The custom seems to have its root in the very common unwillingness of the sovereign to be reminded of death. [2] If this explanation is correct we may be sure that no such " march past " took place in regal as was often witnessed in imperial Rome : *morituri te salutant.*

The functions of the Vestals [3] consisted of those simple household duties which naturally fell to the women even of a chief's family in the olden time. They looked after the fire, fetched water from the spring, [4] mopped the house, and baked

---

[1] W. Ellis, *History of Madagascar*, i. p. 376.

[2] For an example of this, see J. G. Wood's *Natural History of Man*, i. p. 72.

[3] J. Marquardt, *op. cit.* p. 329.

[4] Down to the latest times this water had to be fetched, as it was fetched in the beginning, from a natural source (springs or rivers), in Rome from the spring of Egeria or the Camenae. This piece of religious conservatism was pathetically illustrated when the excavations at Rome revealed the fact that water was never "laid on " the house of the Vestals : the benefit of those great aqueducts which brought water from the Alban hills to the rest of Rome was denied to the Vestals alone (H. Jordan, *Der Tempel der Vesta*, p. 215 *sq.*). When water-pipes were first introduced at Rome, they were no doubt condemned as irreligious, and pious people would have nothing to do with them. Similarly, bridges at Rome and elsewhere were long regarded with suspicion and existed only in a deprecatory manner under the scowl of a justly offended god. For is it not an injury to the river god to rob him of his food by carrying dryshod over his head the people who in the course of nature would have been drowned at the ford ? Clearly it is but common justice to give him " compensation for disturbance" in the shape of a toll of human blood. At Rome Father Tiber kindly agreed to waive all proprietary rights for an annual consideration of two dozen persons flung from the old wooden bridge into his yellow stream. Thus to reconcile science and religion was the special business of the Big Bridge-maker—*Pontifex Maximus*—a cross between a theologian and a civil engineer. In Germany, when a man is drowning in a river, they say " The spirit of the stream is getting his yearly victim " (J. Grimm, *Deutsche Mythologie*, p. 409). In England, the spirit of the Ribble (known as Peg o' Nell) was content with a life every seven years (W. Henderson, *Folklore of the Northern Counties*, p. 265). When a new bridge was built at Halle in 1843 the people thought that a child should have been built into it (Grimm, *D.M.*956). When the Hooghly bridge was being built at Calcutta, the natives " got hold of the idea that Mother Ganges, indignant at being bridged, had at last consented to submit to the insult on the condition that each pier of the structure was founded

cakes of meal. We are reminded of the princess Nausicaa in the *Odyssey* washing the family linen, and of those royal damsels who, going forth to draw water, found Demeter

on a layer of children's heads"
(*Times* correspondent at Calcutta, 1st
August 1880, quoted in L. Gomme's
Folk-lore Relics of Early Village Life,
p. 29). In Albania there is a general
tradition that human sacrifices were
offered when a bridge was built. When
a new bridge was built over the Arcen
twelve sheep were killed and their
heads placed under the foundations
of the pillars (J. G. von Hahn,
Albanesische Studien, i. p. 161). Traditions of human sacrifices at the
building of bridges are current also in
Greece, and it is even said that in
Zacynthus the people would still offer
such sacrifices if they did not fear
the law (B. Schmidt, *Das Volksleben
der Neugriechen*, p. 197 *sq.*). For less
precious sacrifices still offered annually
in Austria and Germany to water
spirits see Th. Vernaleken, *Mythen
und Bräuche des Volkes in Österreich*,
p. 168; A. Wuttke, *Der deutsche
Volksaberglaube*, § 429. Compare
J. H. Gray, *China*, ii. p. 34 *sqq.* Formerly in Germany bridges were often
built by the devil (Grimm, *D.M.* 853).
In Herzegovina the Moslems regard
the office of engineer with pious horror
and curse a new bridge when they
pass it as the devil's own handiwork
(A. J. Evans, *Through Bosnia and
Herzegovina*, p. 314).
We can now understand why no
iron was allowed to be used either in
the construction or repair of the old
wooden bridge over the Tiber (see
the passages quoted in H. Jordan's
*Topographie der Stadt Rom im Alter-
thum*, I. i. p. 396). The reason was
not, as Mommsen appears to suppose,
political (viz. in order that the bridge
might the more easily be broken down
at the approach of an enemy), but
religious. In the history of man iron
is a modern innovation as compared
to bronze and still more to wood and
stone; therefore like every innovation
it is offensive to the gods. Hence no
iron was used in making the old Tiber

bridge, just as amongst the Jews no
iron tool was used in building the
temple at Jerusalem (1 Kings vi. 7)
or in making an altar (Exodus xx.
25). (The latter may be a consequence
of the fact that the original altar was
of natural unhewn stones, but the
analogy of the temple makes the other
way.) Arrian found an altar of unhewn stone at Trebizond and kindly
"restored" it, little wotting of the
impiety he was guilty of (*Periplus
Ponti Euxini*, § 2). In making the
clavie (one of the usual Yuletide
firewheels) at Burghead in Scotland,
no hammer was allowed to be used;
the hammering had to be done with
a stone (E. J. Guthrie, *Old Scottish
Customs*, London and Glasgow, 1885,
p. 223). Again, the men who made
the need-fire in Scotland had to divest
themselves of all metal (Grimm, *D.M.*
507). In Cappadocia it was not
allowed to slay the victim with a
knife; it had to be beaten to death
with a club (Strabo, xv. 3. 15). The
implements employed by the Roman
priests were of bronze (Macrobius,
Saturn. v. 19. 11 *sqq.*; Servius on
Virgil, *Aen.* i. 448; Joannes Lydus,
De mensibus, i. 31). It is this dislike
of the old deities to iron which makes
it so effective a charm against them;
iron keeps off angry spirits as a fire
does wild beasts. Thus when Scottish
fishermen were at sea and one of them
happened to take the name of God in
vain, the first man who heard him
called out "Cauld airn", at which
every man of the crew grasped the
nearest bit of iron and held it fast for a
while (Guthrie, *op. cit.* p. 149). With a
similar intention the Moors of Morocco
put a knife or dagger under a sick
man's pillow (A. Leared, *Morocco and
the Moors*, p. 273). For more examples see L. Strackerjan, *Aberglaube
und Sagen aus dem Herzogthum
Oldenburg*, § 233; A. Wuttke, *Der
deutsche Volksaberglaube*, §§ 414 *sq.*;
Tylor, *Primitive Culture*, i. p. 140.

sitting sad and weary under the shadow of an olive tree by
the Maiden's Well. In short, in those early times the daughters
were the servants of the house, a daughter married out of
the house was a servant lost, and hence it would be natural
that the father should seek to keep at least one daughter at
home to do housemaid's work. From this simple origin, I
venture to conjecture, arose the order of the Vestals. They
were the unmarried daughters whom the chief kept at home
to mind the house, their special duties being to fetch water
and attend to the fire. These duties would naturally be
discharged first by the elder, and after their marriage, by
the younger daughters, and in time it would come to be an
obligation binding on one at least of the daughters (probably
the youngest) not to marry out of the house in her parents'
life. Hence the obligation of temporary celibacy ; and it is
to be observed that at Rome the vow of the Vestals was
only for thirty years, so that every Vestal was free to marry
at the age of thirty-six or forty at the latest—a rule which
tallies perfectly with the above theory of the origin of the
obligation of celibacy, for by that time the daughter's services
would probably be no longer needed in the house of her
parents. Why this long service at home, and with it the
obligation of celibacy, was binding on the daughters of chiefs
more than on those of common men will appear presently.[1]
That a religious order of so much dignity and importance as
that of the Vestals should have arisen from so humble a
beginning need surprise no one. From the unthinking
majority of mankind long-established customs receive a
blind homage approaching or equalling that which they
pay to the unchanging laws of nature ; time elevates the
mean and sanctifies the commonplace, till men may end
by believing, as they did believe at Rome, that the safety

As was to be expected, the dislike of
gods to iron is shared by kings. The
king of Corea " is hedged round with
a divinity that has an antipathy to
iron. This metal must never touch
his august body" (W. E. Griffis,
Corea, the Hermit Nation, London,
1882, p. 219).

[1] A reminiscence of the time when
the ultimate responsibility for the
maintenance of the fire rested with
the king, though the immediate super-
intendence fell to his daughter, may
perhaps be found in a ceremony
regularly performed by the Vestals :
on a certain day they went to the *rex
sacrorum* (the representative of the old
king) and said, " Watchest thou O
King ? Watch " (Servius on Virgil,
Aen. x. 228).

of a great empire hangs on the twirling of a housemaid's mop.[1]

The question still remains, why was so much importance attached to the maintenance of a perpetual fire? The extinction of this fire at Rome was regarded as the greatest misfortune that could befall the State ; it was thought to portend the destruction of the empire, and expiatory sacrifices were offered and ceremonies performed in order to avert the evil omen.[2] Of course, on the principle just stated, once the custom of maintaining a perpetual fire was started its final canonization, so to speak, was almost inevitable. But what started the custom? That its history goes back to the embryo state of human civilization seems proved by the fact that when the fire chanced to go out it was formally rekindled by the most primitive of all modes of lighting a fire, that of rubbing two sticks against each other.[3] It is probable therefore that some light may be thrown on the Roman custom by comparing it with the customs of peoples in earlier stages of civilization.[4]

Turning to South Africa, we are told by a distinguished traveller that amongst the Damaras the chief's daughter " is

[1] The question naturally suggests itself : if the temple of Vesta and the prytaneum both sprang from the chief's house and if the Vestals were originally his daughters, why was there not developed an order of Vestals in Greece, to attend to the perpetual fire in the prytaneum? To this we can only reply that many circumstances may have occurred to prevent the custom developing in the particular line which it followed in Italy. The chief, *e.g.*, may have had no daughters, or if he had he may have preferred to leave the household duties to slaves. In classical times the fire in the prytaneum was attended to by elderly widows (γυναῖκες πεπαυμέναι γάμων, Plutarch, *Numa*, 9). It is possible, as Thomas Hyde suggested, that the Greeks had tried the system of vestal virgins and found it wanting (*Historia religionis veterum Persarum*, p. 142).
[2] Dionysius Halic. *Ant. Rom.* ii. 67 ; Livy, xxviii. 11.
[3] Festus, *s.v.* *ignis*, p. 94, ed. Lind-

say. Compare E. B. Tylor, *Researches into the Early History of Mankind*, p. 237 *sqq.* ; G. F. Klemm, *Culturwissenschaft, Das Feuer*, p. 67 ; A. Kuhn, *Die Herabkunft des Feuers*, p. 12 *sqq.*
[4] A section of Mr. Preuner's learned work bears the heading " Über arische Parallelen " (*Hestia - Vesta*, p. 416). This looks promising, and we start off in gallant style with a comparison of Vesta to the Indian Agni. But the audacity of this comparison appears to have taken Mr. Preuner's breath away, for after making it he stops as dead as if he had been shot : "*Allein wir bleiben hiebei stehen.*" Here then we will let Mr. Preuner stand and get his wind, while we venture a little way from the weary highroad of Greece and Rome into the virgin forest of comparative custom and religion. It is true that there are certain conspicuous " Notices to trespassers " warning us back, but nobody minds them.

to the Damaras what the Vestal was amongst the ancient Romans ; for, besides attending to the sacrifices, it is her duty to keep up the ' holy fire '. Outside the chief's hut, where he is accustomed to sit in the day-time, a fire is always kept burning ; but, in case of rain or bad weather, it is transferred to the hut of the priestess, who, should it be deemed advisable to change the site of the village, precedes the oxen with a portion of this consecrated fire, every possible care being taken to prevent it being extinguished. Should, however, this calamity happen, the whole tribe is immediately assembled, and large expiatory offerings of cattle are made ; after which the fire is re-lit in the primitive way—namely by friction. . . . A portion of such fire is also given to the head man of a Kraal, when about to remove from that of the chief. The duties of a Vestal then devolve on the daughter of the emigrant."[1] Observe that " the hut of the priestess " here mentioned is the chief's hut, for the priestess is his daughter and the chief has as many houses as wives. The daughter who acts as priestess is probably (according to Mr. Andersson) the daughter of the chief or favourite wife.[2] To complete the resemblance between these African chieftains and the old Graeco-Italian kings, it is only needful to add that the Damara huts are circular and are constructed of pliant sticks lashed together, so as to form a pointed umbrella-shaped roof, brushwood being inwoven between the ribs and mud plastered over the brushwood.[3]

Mark the complete correspondence between Damaraland and ancient Italy. In both we see the chief's round hut, formed of wattled osiers, with its umbrella-like roof. In the hut (or outside of it in fine weather) burns a perpetual fire tended by the vestal, his daughter ; its extinction is regarded as a great calamity, to be expiated by sacrifices ; it is re-

[1] C. J. Andersson, *Lake Ngami*, pp. 223, 224.
[2] That the daughter who acts as priestess is unmarried is not stated in my authorities (C. J. Andersson, *op. cit.* ; Th. Waitz, *Anthropologie der Naturvölker*, ii. p. 416 ; J. G. Wood, *Natural History of Man*, i. p. 348 ; G. Fritsch, *Die Eingeborenen Süd-Afrika's*, p. 233 ; A. Bastian, *Der Papua des dunkeln Inselnreichs*, p. 257 *sq.*) but seems a natural inference from the nature of her duties. See the Note at the end of this volume.
[3] F. Galton, *Tropical South Africa*, p. 181 ; J. G. Wood, *op. cit.* i. p. 343 *sq.* Andersson (*op. cit.* p. 225) says that the huts are semi-circular, but he means hemispherical.

kindled by friction ; and when a new village is founded (or colony sent out) fire from the old sacred fire is taken to be the sacred fire of the new village.[1]

When we have thus tracked the custom of maintaining a perpetual fire to a savage tribe in Africa, a simple explanation of its origin is not far to seek. Savages are commonly obliged to make fire by rubbing two sticks against each other, in the form either of the fire-drill or of the stick-and-groove.[2] The process is laborious at the best of times, and it is especially so in wet weather. Hence it is convenient to keep a fire constantly burning from which other fires may be kindled as they are needed.[3] This convenience rises to necessity in the case of savages who do not know how to make fire. Thus the Andaman Islanders, according to Mr. E. H. Man (whom an eleven years' residence in the Islands and an intimate acquaintance with the people entitle to speak with authority), have always been ignorant of the art of producing fire, and hence they take the utmost pains to prevent its extinction. " When they all leave an encampment with the intention of returning in a few days, besides taking with them one or more smouldering logs, wrapped in leaves if the weather be wet, they place a large burning log or faggot in some sheltered spot, where, owing to the character and condition of the wood invariably selected on these occasions, it smoulders for several days, and can easily be rekindled when required." [4]   Here we see the perpetual fire,

---

[1] The same applies to Greece, except that in Greece there is no evidence that the fire was tended by the chief's daughter.

[2] See E. B. Tylor, *loc. cit.*

[3] This obvious explanation of the origin of perpetual fires is given by Dr. Gustav Fritsch in his valuable work *Die Eingeborenen Süd-Afrika's* (Breslau, 1872), p. 232. It had occurred to me independently. Compare also R. Taylor, *Te Ika a Maui, or New Zealand and its Inhabitants* (London, 1870), p. 368, and Sir John Lubbock, *Origin of Civilisation*, p. 312.

[4] E. H. Man, *Aboriginal Inhabitants of the Andaman Islands*, Trübner and Co. (1885), p. 82. How the Andamanese (or mankind in general) got fire originally is a question which does not here concern us. That fire was first procured from a tree struck by lightning is unlikely, though the peculiar sanctity which the Parsis ascribe to such fire and the pains they take to procure it might put us on this scent. See D. J. Karaka, *History of the Modern Parsis*, London, 1884, ii. p. 213. Mr. Man inclines to think that the Andamanese got their fire from one or other of the two volcanos (one of them now extinct) in the Islands. This so far confirms Oscar Peschel's view of the origin of fire among men (*Völkerkunde*, 6te Aufl. 1885, p. 138). On this view the heaven from which Prometheus stole his fire was the "skyish head" of some great volcano.

pure and simple, the maintenance of which is a mere matter of practical necessity and has not yet been elevated into a religious obligation; for we are assured by the same excellent authority that the Andamanese do not hold fire sacred and have no superstitious beliefs in reference to its extinction.[1] Again, the Tasmanians, we are positively assured, never remembered a time when they were obliged to make fire; even the method of kindling fire by friction was unknown to them. Hence they never allowed the fire to die out; when they migrated, fire-brands were carried by the women, one of whose duties it was to keep up the perpetual fire.[2]

In a village the perpetual fire would be most likely to be maintained in the chief's house, and the persons who would most naturally look after it would be the chief's wife or daughters. Amongst the Damaras and old Italians this duty devolved on the daughters, and that this was often the case may perhaps be inferred from the fact that we find perpetual fires tended by virgins in other parts of the world.[3] Thus in Lithuania the holy fire was maintained in the temple of Prauronia by maidens who had taken a vow of chastity.[4] At Kildare in Ireland the perpetual fire sacred to St. Bridget was tended by holy virgins.[5] Amongst the Iroquois there

---

[1] E. H. Man, *op. cit.* p. 83. Mr. Man further informs us that "while it is the women's business to collect the wood, the duty of maintaining the fires, whether at home or while travelling by land or sea, is not confined to them, but is undertaken by those of either sex who have most leisure or are least burdened".

[2] The Rev. Mr. Dove, quoted by James Bonwick, *Daily Life and Origin of the Tasmanians,* p. 20. On the other hand, Mr. Bonwick, standing up for his ill-starred protegés, stoutly asserts that there is plenty of evidence that they knew how to make fire. But the only evidence he adduces is that of a respectable bushranger. See also E. B. Tylor's *Researches into the Early History of Mankind,* p. 235 *sq.*

[3] P. II. Mallet (*Northern Antiquities,* i. p. 120, ed. 1809) says: "The goddess Frigga was usually served by

King's daughters, whom they called prophetesses and goddesses; these pronounced oracles, devoted themselves to perpetual virginity, and kept up the sacred fire in her temples." But there appears to be no good authority for this statement, which is omitted in the revised edition of Mallet by J. A. Blackwell.

[4] A. Bastian, *Der Mensch in der Geschichte,* iii. p. 215.

[5] W. Camden, *Britannia,* p. 747 (ed. 1607). Amongst the Celts virgin priestesses had charge of the sacred fire (Gardner, *Faiths of the World,* i. p. 899). Solinus speaks of the sacred fires amongst the ancient Britons (p. 115, ed. Mommsen). On the sacredness of fire amongst the Irish, compare Spenser, *A View of the Present State of Ireland,* p. 634 (Globe ed.): "Likewise at the kindling of the fire, and lighting of candells, they say

68 GARNERED SHEAVES PART I

was a class of virgins whom Lafitau compares to the Vestals, but of their functions he had no very definite information.[1] The Iroquois certainly maintained a perpetual fire, the extinction of which would have been thought to portend their national destruction.[2] In Peru the Virgins of the Sun preserved the sacred fire, and it was an evil omen if they let it go out. This holy fire was annually kindled by the sun's rays reflected from a concave mirror ; in bad weather, when there was no sun (as indeed must have been often the case at Cuzco, where, according to the proverb, they have thirteen months of rain in the year [3]) the fire was lit by the friction of two sticks. An unfaithful virgin, like a Vestal at Rome, was punished by being buried alive.[4] At Cuzco these virgins were the daughters of the Inca and his relations ; in the provinces they might be the daughters of distinguished chiefs, but the lady superior was usually of the blood royal.[5] A

certayne prayers, or use some other superstitious rites, which sheweth that they honour the fire and the light."

[1] J. F. Lafitau, Mœurs des sauvages Ameriquains (Paris, 1724), i. p. 173.

[2] D. G. Brinton, Myths of the New World, p. 151.

[3] Fr. von Hellwald, Die Erde und ihre Völker, Berlin und Stuttgart, 1884, p. 204.

[4] Garcilasso de la Vega, Royal Commentaries of the Yncas, i. p. 298, ii. p. 163, Markham's translation. The other duties of the virgins were to make the Inca's clothes, to bake the bread for the great sacrifices, and brew the liquor which the Inca and his family drank on these occasions (Garcilasso, op. cit. i. p. 296 sqq.). It is possible that Garcilasso may, as Mr. Tylor suggests (Early History of Mankind, p. 252), have touched up the picture of these virgins in order to complete the resemblance between them and the Vestals, but that he, the son of an Inca princess and born about ten years after the conquest of Peru by the Spaniards, should have invented the whole story is of course incredible and is not intended to be insinuated by Mr. Tylor. For references to the other Spanish authorities who treat of these Virgins of the Sun, see

J. G. Müller, Geschichte der amerikanischen Urreligionen, Basel, 1867, p. 388 ; Th. Waitz, Anthropologie, iv. p. 464. M. Albert Reville suggests that the intention of burying an unchaste virgin was to hide his faithless priestess from the sight of the sun she had dishonoured (Les Religions du Mexique, de l'Amérique centrale et du Pérou, Paris, 1885, p. 367), but the real reason (as pointed out to me by Prof. Robertson Smith) is the reluctance to shed tribal blood. In early times when the blood-feud is in full force, to shed the blood of a fellow-tribesman, from whatever cause, is an inexpiable offence. Hence modes of execution are adopted which do not involve the actual spilling of blood. Such modes are drowning (the penalty of a parricidium in old Rome) and burying alive. Both penalties occur in old German law (Grimm, Deutsche Rechtsalterthümer, p.694 sqq.) In mediaeval Italy assassins were buried alive (comment. on Dante, Inferno, xix. 49). The fact that such a penalty was adopted for the Virgins of the Sun and for the Vestals seems to prove that both were originally tribal, not national, priestesses.

[5] Garcilasso de la Vega, op. cit. i. pp. 294, 299 ; R. B. Brehm, Das

fugitive from the emissaries of justice who succeeded in throwing himself at the feet of these virgins as they marched in solemn procession through the streets was saved.[1] In the great temple at Mexico before each chapel stood a stone hearth, on which a fire was kept constantly burning by the virgins and priests, and dreadful misfortunes were supposed to follow its accidental extinction.[2] Girls were sometimes devoted from infancy to the service of the god ; some took a vow of perpetual virginity, some entered the service only for a term of years. A broom and a censer were their emblems. Death was the penalty for incontinence.[3] That the fire-worship of Mexico, for all its gorgeous and awful pageantry, sprang from the fire on the domestic hearth may be inferred from the Mexican custom (like the old Italian, Greek, Slavonian, and modern Hindoo custom) of throwing food and drink into the fire before a meal.[4] The same primitive offering to the fire was common amongst the savage Redskins who never developed an elaborate religious ritual like that of barbarous Mexico.[5] In Yucatan there was an order of Vestals instituted by a princess who acted as lady superior. The members were volunteers who enrolled themselves either for a fixed time or for life. Their duty was to tend the sacred fire ; those who broke their vow of chastity were shot to death with arrows.[6]

Next to the Peruvians and Mexicans, the American tribes which had the most marked fire-worship were those of Louisiana, and though they had no order of Vestals, we may

Inka-reich, Jena, 1885, p. 139 ; J. G. Müller, *op. cit.* p. 387. Compare Prescott, *History of the Conquest of Peru*, Bk. I. ch. 3
[1] R. B. Brehm, *op. cit.* p. 141.
[2] H. H. Bancroft, *Native Races of the Pacific States*, ii. p. 583.
[3] H. H. Bancroft, *op. cit.* ii. p. 204 *sqq.*, compare 245 and iii. p. 435.
[4] For Mexico, see Bancroft, iii. 393; for Italy, Servius on Virgil, *Aen.* i. 729 and L. Preller, *Römische Mythologie*, 3te Aufl. (1883,) ii. 107 *sq.*; for Greece, E. Buchholz, *Die homerische Realien*, II. ii. p. 213 *sqq.* and Merry on *Odyssey*, ix. 231 ; for India, Monier

Williams, *Religious Thought and Life in India* (London, 1883), p. 416 *sqq.* ; for the Slavonian custom, J. V. Grohmann, *Aberglauben und Gebräuche aus Böhmen und Mähren*, p. 41.
[5] Th. Waitz, *Anthropologie*, iii. p. 208. To this day no well-bred Moqui, Zuni, or other Pueblo Indian will eat of food without throwing a scrap into the fire (J. G. Bourke, *The Snake-dance of the Moquis of Arizona*, London, 1884, p. 255).
[6] H. H. Bancroft, *op. cit.* iii. p. 473. That fire-worship is still practised by the Indians of Yucatan appears from a native calendar for 1841–2. See the *Folk-lore Journal*, i. p. 248.

glance at their customs before we return to the Old World.
Amongst the Natchez the temple, containing an ever-burning
fire, stood beside the chief's hut. According to early travellers
the temple was round, with a dome-like roof, and contained
the bones of chiefs, but when Charlevoix visited the tribe in
1721, though the perpetual fire was maintained, the temple
was not round but oblong, and the few old bones he saw
about would not have furnished forth half a human skeleton.[1]
Of the Assinais or Ainais we are told [2] that they had in common
with the Naichas (probably the Natchez) a house of sacred,
ever-burning fire. It stood midway between the tribes, was
round and built of straw, and served as council- and assembly-
house. The resemblance to the prytaneum is obvious, especially to that which Theseus established at Athens as the
centre and symbol of united Attica. From Louisiana it is
(to the anthropologist) a mere step to New Mexico, where
the Pueblo Indians watch over the eternal fire in the estufa,
a large subterranean chamber, serving as bath-room, town-
house, council-chamber, club-room, and church.[3]

It is a necessary consequence of the practice of maintaining a perpetual fire that when the tribe is migratory the fire
is carried with it. Thus we saw that when the Damaras shift
their kraal, the fire is solemnly carried before the cattle by
the chief's daughter. Similarly the Israelites carried their
fire before them on the march.[4] A survival of this practice
is seen in a custom of Russian peasants. When they move

[1] Charlevoix, *Histoire de la Nouvelle France*, vi. p. 173 *sqq.* ; Lafitau,
Mœurs des sauvages Ameriquains,
i. p. 167 ; Chateaubriand, *Voyage en
Amérique*, p. 227 *sqq.* (ed. 12mo,
Michael Levy); H. R. Schoolcraft,*Information respecting the History, Condition and Prospects of the Indian
Tribes of the United States*, v. p. 68 ;
Waitz, *Anthropologie*, iii. p. 217 *sqq.*
[2] By Espinosa in Waitz, iii. 221.
[3] H. H. Bancroft, *op. cit.* i. pp.
537, 554. Since the conversion of these
Indians to Christianity the maintenance of the perpetual fire in the estufa
has become exceptional (W. A. Bell,
New Tracks in North America, p.
161). There was no fire burning in the
estufa from which Captain Bourke was
so summarily ejected (J. G. Bourke, *op.
cit.* p. 22 *sqq.*). The estufa is in the chief
house in the village, but as the office
of chief is elective it does not follow
that the chief house is the house of the
chief (W. A. Bell, *loc. cit.*).
[4] Exodus xiii. 21. Different from
this are the cases (referred to by
Knobel on Exodus, *loc. cit.*) where the
fire is carried as a signal at the head
of a column marching by night, as
is still done by caravans in Arabia,
and as Thrasybulus did when he led
the exiles home to Athens by wild
mountain-paths on a moonless night
(Clemens Alexand., *Strom.*, i. 24,
§ 163 (p. 150 Sylb.).

from one house to another they rake the fire out of the old stove into a jar and solemnly carry it to the new one, greeting it with the words " Welcome, grandfather, to the new home." [1]

Again, when, the old village remaining stationary, a new one was founded, it was natural that the fire for the new village should be taken from the common fire of the old. This is done by the Damaras and used to be done by the old Greeks and Romans and apparently also by some North American Redskins, for we hear of one of these tribes having received its fire from another kindred tribe.[2] Similarly Phoenician colonists setting out from Tyre took fire with them from the altar of Hercules (Melqart).[3]

As the common fire of the village was that in the chief's house, it was natural that in course of time fire should be regarded as the outward symbol of a king and should be carried before him, as it used to be carried before his predecessor, the chief of a nomadic tribe, in days of old. The fire was carried before Asiatic kings,[4] and from them the

[1] W. R. S. Ralston, *Songs of the Russian People*, p. 120 *sq*. See the ceremony described at length, *ib.* 137-139. A trace of the same custom appears in the old Norse mode of taking possession of land. When a Norseman landed in Iceland, he took possession of as much land as he could march round from six in the morning till six at night, and where his march began and ended he lit a fire ; this was called " marching round the land with fire" (Grimm, *Deutsche Rechts-alterthümer*, 3rd ed. 1881, p. 195). The rule here mentioned by Grimm was itself a limitation (introduced when unoccupied land in Iceland was growing scarce) of the old custom which allowed a man to take possession of as much land as he could march round carrying fire ; see K. Maurer, *Island von seiner ersten Entdeckung bis zum Untergang des Freistaats* (München, 1874), p. 36 *sq.* For other (perhaps derivative) forms of this Norse mode of taking possession by fire see J. C. Poestion, *Island, das Land und seine Bewohner* (Wien, 1885), p. 296. It is possible that the old custom in Lewis of carrying fire round the homestead may be derived from this Norse custom (Martin's " Description of the Western Islands of Scotland ", in Pinkerton's *Voyages and Travels*, vol. iii. p. 612). But taken in connexion with the other forms of *dessil* (as it was called) which prevailed there, it is much more likely that this was a mode of so-called purification. It is a question whether the Norse custom itself may not best be explained in this way. Carrying fire round was a Roman mode of purification (Servius on Virgil, *Aen.* vi. 229). See J. Lomeier, *De veterum gentilium lustrationibus*, c. xxxv.

[2] Th. Waitz, *Anthropologie*, iii. 208.

[3] A. Bastian, *Der Mensch*, iii. p. 218. Compare F. C. Movers, *Das phönizische Alterthum*, i. pp. 48, 101. Movers (p. 404) believes that the priestesses of Melqart were virgins, and he points to the virgin priestesses of Hercules at Thespiae in Boeotia (Pausanias, ix. 27. 7).

[4] Xenophon, *Cyropaedia*, viii. 3. 12; Ammianus Marcellinus, xxiii. 6. 34 ; Quintus Curtius, iii. 3. 7.

practice was borrowed by later Roman emperors.[1] High
above the tent of Alexander the Great hung a fiery cresset,
and " the flame of it was seen by night and the smoke by
day ".[2] When a Spartan king marched to war, fire from
the altar in his house was carried before him and might not
be quenched.[3]

Finally, if the religious duty of maintaining a sacred fire
sprang simply from the convenience of keeping up a constant
fire in ages when the kindling of fresh fire was difficult, it
might be expected that, though the maintenance of a perpetual fire was obligatory as a public duty on the chief,
every individual householder would have found it a practical
convenience to keep up such a fire for his own use. And
this appears to have been a widespread custom. The native
Australian always has (or had, before he was corrupted by
lucifer-matches) his fire-stick with him, and if his wife lets it
out, so much the worse for her.[4] Similarly the Fuegians,
though they know how to make fire by means of iron pyrites,
never use it except when forced to do so, preferring to keep
a fire always burning and to take a fire-stick with them when
they travel.[5] Amongst the Indians of Guiana we are told
that " fire has very seldom to be made afresh; for it is continually kept burning in every house, and even on long
canoe-journeys a large piece of smouldering timber is usually
carried. Even when walking across the savannah an Indian

[1] Dio Cassius, lxxi. 35; Herodian, i. 8. 4; i. 16. 4; ii. 3. 2; ii.
8. 6; vii. 1. 9; vii. 6. 2; C. Meiners,
Geschichte der Religionen, i. p.
237. Compare De Quincey, *Confes-
sions of an English Opium-eater*, p.
151.

[2] Q. Curtius, v. 2. 7: "*Observabatur
ignis noctu, fumus interdu.*" Curtius
represents this as an innovation introduced by Alexander from purely
military motives, because the sound
of the bugle was lost in the trampling
and hum of the great multitude. But
this looks like a rationalizing explanation of the historian.

[3] Xenophon, *Respub. Laced.* 13;
Nicolaus Damascenus in Stobaeus,
Florilegium, xliv. 41.

[4] R. Taylor, *Te Ika a Maui, or
New Zealand and its Inhabitants*,
p. 367, " On the western coast the
best way which the Australian native
has of preserving this element so
essential to his comfort is to collect
the seed stems or stalks of the Bank-
sias, or rather the abortive ones. These
are denuded of their outer coverings,
leaving a dark-brown velvety looking
centre, which is very retentive of fire,
and burns slowly, so that one of those
fire-sticks, which is only eight inches
long, will last for a considerable time,
a bag of them will suffice for an entire
day."
Here we have the νάρθηξ of Prometheus.

[5] J. G. Wood, *Natural History of
Man*, ii. p. 522.

sometimes carries a fire-brand." [1] In New Zealand the ridge-pole of the roof is supported in the middle of the house by a pillar, the bottom of which is carved in the likeness of a human being supposed to represent the founder of the family, and on the fireplace immediately before this ancestral figure the fire burns perpetually.[2] (Here we see Vesta and the Lar together.) We have M. François Lenormant's word for it that the Accadians recognized as a god the flame that burned on the domestic hearth.[3] It is therefore only charitable to suppose that they did not suffer the deity to die for simple lack of dry sticks. In a Laplander's hut the fire burns continually summer and winter.[4] The lamps in the houses of the Arctic Highlanders are never allowed to go out.[5] In Corea great pains are taken to maintain the house-fire unextinguished from generation to generation ; its extinction is regarded as the prognostic and cause of the greatest misfortunes to the family.[6] The custom of maintaining a perpetual fire on every family hearth appears to have been Indo-European,[7] for it is to be found amongst almost all the peoples of our widespread race from Hindoostan to Scotland. At Benares and other strongholds of Brahmanism a certain number of orthodox Brahmans still maintain sacred fires in their houses.[8] Amongst the old Iranians the fire on the domestic hearth was kept constantly burning.[9] Amongst the South Slavonians

[1] E. F. Im Thurn, *Among the Indians of Guiana*, London, 1883, p. 257.
[2] R. Taylor, *op. cit.* p. 501. Compare J. S. Polack, *Manners and Customs of the New Zealanders*, i. p. 165, who, however, only says that the fires are rarely wholly extinguished in a village.
[3] *La Magie chez les Chaldéens et les origines Accadiennes*, p. 171.
[4] Regnard's "Journey to Lapland", in Pinkerton's *Voyages and Travels*, i. p. 177.
[5] Sir John Ross, *Voyage of Discovery*, p. 130.
[6] Ch. Dallet, *Histoire de l'Église de Corée* (Paris, 1874), i. p. cxlvii.
[7] Compare Max Müller, *Lectures on the Science of Religion*, p. 153 ; W. E. Hearn, *The Aryan Household* (London

and Melbourne, 1879), p. 49 *sqq.* ; G. L. Gomme, *Folklore Relics of Early Village Life* (London, 1883), p. 85 *sqq.*; E. Meyer, *Geschichte des Alterthums* (Stuttgart, 1884), § 428.
[8] Monier Williams, *Religious Thought and Life in India*, p. 392 ; compare *id.* p. 364. Compare *Ordinances of Manu*, ii. 230, 231, 232, 248 ; *id.* iii. 84; *Institutes of Vishnu*, lix. 1, 2; *Âpastamba*, II. ii. iii. 15 (with Bühler's note, *Sacred Books of the East*, vol. ii. p. 105) ; *Gautama*, v. 7 *sqq.*, ; *Baudhâyana*, II. ii. iv. 22. On reverence for the fire in Vedic times see Duncker, *Geschichte des Alterthums*, iii. p. 31.
[9] W. Geiger, *Ostiranische Kultur im Altertum* (Erlangen, 1882), p. 254; Fr. Spiegel, *Eranische Alterthumskunde*, iii. p. 693. In every settlement of Parsis an everlasting fire is kept burn-

to this day the fire on the hearth of a peasant's house is never allowed to die out ; its extinction would be the sign of the extinction of the family.[1] In the cottage of a German (especially North German) peasant the fire was never allowed to die out except on the death of the head of the house.[2] In the Isle of Man " not a family in the whole island, of natives, but keeps a fire constantly burning ; no one daring to depend on his neighbour's vigilance in a thing which he imagines is of so much consequence ; and every one firmly believing that if it should ever happen that no fires were to be found throughout the island, the most terrible revolutions and mischiefs would immediately ensue ".[3] At Burghead in Scotland the cottage fires used to be lit from a common fire on the 12th of January, and it was lucky to preserve this fire throughout the year.[4] Lastly (for the shadows in the forest are growing long and it is time to return to the high road) we find the custom, or clear traces of it, in modern Greece and Italy and may therefore fairly suppose that it existed there of old, though direct proof of this seems wanting.[5] In modern Greece the old custom survives in the practice of

ing, the Bahrâm fire, " preserved by a more than Vestal care " (J. Darmesteter, *Zend-Avesta*, i. p. lxxxix). Compare D. J. Karaka, *History of the Modern Parsis* (London, 1884), ii. p. 213 *sqq.*
[1] F. S. Krauss, *Sitte und Brauch der Südslaven* (Wien, 1885), p. 592. The religious importance attached by the South Slavonians to the fire on the domestic hearth is further shown by the conspicuous part which it plays in their marriage ceremonies; see Krauss, *op. cit.* pp. 386, 399, 400, 430, 431, 436. Compare A. Kuhn und W. Schwartz, *Norddeutsche Sagen, Märchen und Gebräuche*, p. 522. The Slavonic worship of ancestral spirits was clearly connected with the fire on the hearth (Ralston, *Songs of the Russian People*, p. 84, compare pp. 86, 119, 120). For traces in Bohemia of Slavonic reverence for fire see J. V. Grohmann, *Aberglauben und Gebräuche aus Böhmen und Mähren*, pp. 41 *sq.*
With regard to the Lithuanians we know that they worshipped fire (Olaus

Magnus, *Gentium Septentrionalium hist. brev.* iii. 1) and maintained perpetual fires in honour of Perkunas (K. Schwenk, *Die Mythologie der Slawen*, pp. 73, 75) and of Curcho (*id* p. 92), and they appear to have worshipped the fire on the domestic hearth, for in some places they adored a domestic god called Dinstipan, *i.e.* the director of the smoke or chimneys (L. Gomme, *Folklore Relics of Early Village Life*, p. 90, note).
[2] A. Wuttke, *op. cit.* § 609; L. Preller, *Römische Mythologie*, ii. p. 159.
[3] Waldron's *Description of the Isle of Man*, folio 101, quoted by Joseph Train; *Historical and Statistical Account of the Isle of Man* (Douglas, Isle of Man, 1845), vol. i. p. 316.
[4] L. Gomme, *op. cit.* p. 98 ; compare T. F. Thiselton Dyer, *Popular British Customs*, p. 507 *sq.*; E. J. Guthrie, *Old Scottish Customs*, p. 223 *sqq.*
[5] The passages of ancient authors referred to by M. Fustel de Coulanges (*La cité antique*, 11ème éd. Paris, 1885, p. 21) seem inconclusive.

keeping a lamp always burning before the holy pictures. The chief picture is usually that of the Virgin or of the saint whose name the householder bears, but that these holy pictures represent the old household gods and that the lamp represents the domestic fire there can hardly be a doubt.[1] If the lamp dies out, it is an evil portent ; and when the family moves to a new house, they carefully carry the burning lamp with them,[2] thus keeping up the custom of carrying the fire to the new home which we have seen practised by the Damaras in South Africa, by the Israelites in the Desert, and by the ancestors of these same Greeks more than two thousand years ago. But it is to Calabria that we must look for the most perfect survival of the primitive custom. At the present day the fire on the hearth of a Calabrian peasant's house is never (except after a death) allowed to die quite out, even in the heat of summer. It is a bad omen if it should chance to be extinguished, and the girls of the house, whose special care it is to keep at least a single brand burning on the hearth, are sadly dismayed at such a mishap.[3] Here we

[1] The differentiation of the single original house-fire into a fire for ordinary purposes and a sacred fire (lamp or otherwise) before the images of the gods, naturally takes place when the original single room is differentiated into a kitchen and parlour. Amongst the Romans it took place in antiquity. The atrium was originally dining-room and kitchen in one (Servius on Virgil, *Aen.* i. 726), and in it stood the images of the household gods beside the fire (Horace, *Epod.* ii. 66 ; Martial, iii. 58, 22 *sq.*). But when the kitchen was removed to the back of the house, the gods sometimes remained in the parlour, and sometimes followed the kitchen. In the later empire their shrine stood at the entrance of the house and before it burned a perpetual lamp (Marquardt, *Römische Staats-verwaltung*, iii. p. 123 ; Overbeck und Mau, *Pompeji*, 4te Aufl. (1884), p. 268 *sq.*). A similar separation appears to have taken place in ancient Greece. See K. F. Hermann, *Lehrbuch der griechischen Privatalterthümer*, 3te Aufl. (1882), p. 151.

[2] B. Schmidt, *Das Volksleben der Neugriechen und das hellenische Alter-thum* (Leipzig, 1871), p. 54 ; J. T. Bent, *The Cyclades* (London, 1885), p. 43 ; W. M. Leake, *Travels in Northern Greece*, iv. p. 145. In a Greek folk-tale we read of a poor man who sold his son that he might have where-withal to buy oil for the holy lamp (J. G. von Hahn, *Griechische und albanesische Märchen*, i. p. 288). In ancient Greece it was an evil omen to dream of extinguishing the fire on the hearth (Artemidorus, *Onirocr.* ii. 10).

[3] Vincenzo Dorsa, *La Tradizione Greco-Latina negli usi e nelle credenze popolari della Calabria Citeriore* (Cosenza, 1884), p. 20. In some districts on winter nights, when the family is retiring to rest, the mother makes the sign of the cross over the fire and blesses it. A Calabrian form of oath is to nip a flame between the fingers and swear, saying, " By this light of God " (*ib.* p. 21). The custom, still observed in Calabria, of ex-tinguishing fires after a death appears to have existed in ancient Greece and

have embryo Vestals and a fairly developed Vesta. Here too, as in the Aryan family, the father acts as household priest when he blesses the Yule log and calls upon his children to pay it reverence.[1]

So much for perpetual fires. The further and closely related question of the meaning of new fires, that is, the formal extinction and rekindling of fires at fixed periods (especially at the solstices and at the beginning of summer and of winter) cannot be treated of here.[2] Suffice it to say that a careful examination of the many different forms of this custom—ranging from the homely Scottish mode of making the yearly fire to the stately Mexican rite of rekindling the fires at the close of every cycle of fifty-two years (one of the most striking ceremonies the world has ever witnessed)—will probably show that, however widely they diverged from the parent type, they, like the custom of maintaining perpetual fires, owed their origin not to any profound theory of the relation of the life of man to the courses of the heavens, but to the elementary difficulty of lighting the kitchen fire by rubbing two sticks against each other.[3]

NOTE ON THE EARLY ITALIAN HUTS[4]

SINCE writing my paper on the Prytaneum, etc., which appeared in Number XXVIII. of the *Journal of Philology*, I have learned from Helbig's able book[5] that the views which I ventured to put forward in that paper on the shape and materials of the early

Rome (compare Apuleius, *Met.* ii. 24), and this is perhaps the true explanation of "*tunc odimus ignem*" in Juvenal, iii. 214, about which the commentators σεμνῶς πάνυ σιγῶσι. For an explanation of the custom see above, p. 33.

[1] Vincenzo Dorsa, *op. cit.* p. 20.

[2] Still less can I discuss the extinction and renewal of fire on special occasions, as during an epidemic or after a death (see last note but one). For this class of cases appears to rest on other trains of thought than the class referred to in the text.

[3] I am painfully conscious of the lameness and impotence of this con-

clusion when I contrast it with the gorgeous passage in which Mr. Preuner takes leave of his readers. The rocket (for fired by his eloquence I feel that I am soaring into metaphor) begins to rise on p. 449 and culminates on p. 464, bursting into a dazzling effulgence of rhetoric, in which "unity", "nationality", "freedom", "religion", etc., are seen circling in more than rainbow brilliance round the Idea, their centre and sun.

[4] Reprinted from *The Journal of Philology*, vol. xv. (1886).

[5] Wolfgang Helbig, *Die Italiker in der Poebene* (Leipzig, 1879).

Italian huts [1] had been strongly confirmed, if not fully established, by the result of excavations in Italy made some years ago. I have Prof. Helbig's leave to give a brief summary of his facts and conclusions in so far as they bear on the points raised in my paper. A considerable number of prehistoric villages have been disinterred within late years in the Emilia and Lombardy. They are built on piles by the banks of rivers and streams, and usually on the same site there are remains of three such villages, one above the other ; the lower villages exhibiting traces of fire. From the remains found in them it appears that the inhabitants belonged to the stone and bronze ages, or rather to a period in the bronze age at which stone implements were still not only employed but manufactured ; the villages in the Emilia exhibit a preponderance of bronze, those in Lombardy of stone, utensils. Different views have been held as to the race which built these villages. Helbig decides against the Celts on the ground that the bronze utensils found in the villages are much inferior to those of the countries north of the Alps from which the Celts migrated,[2] and also because the objects which tradition regards as especially characteristic of the Celts (the long iron sword, the necklace, the gold ornaments) are all absent from the villages. Besides over some of the villages have been found remains of Etruscan settlements. But as the Celts are known to have invaded and conquered the Etruscans, to attribute the lower and older remains to the conquerors would be preposterous. Again the people could not have been Ligurians ; for though the Ligurians appear at a remote date to have occupied a great part of Italy, and to be indeed the oldest race in the peninsula, they were found as late as about 104 B.C. by the philosopher Posidonius, who visited them on that lovely coast now familiar to us as the Riviera, to be in a state of barbarism or savagery much lower than that of the inhabitants of the pile-villages. Posidonius describes the Ligurians as wild huntsmen, almost ignorant of agriculture, clad in skins, and dwelling mostly in the clefts of the rocks. Helbig concludes that the people who built these pile-villages were the forefathers of the Italians who made a long halt in the valley of the Po before they resumed their southward march.

Out of 175 huts (or rather foundations of huts) found in the neighbourhood of Bologna, all but three were round and appear from the remaining fragments of the walls to have been constructed

---

[1] I described them as "round huts of wattled osiers with peaked roofs of thatch ".

[2] Some archaeologists, however, now hold that the great majority of bronze objects which have been found in central Europe are not of Celtic but Italian manufacture. See J. N. von Sadowski, *Die Handelstrassen der Griechen und Römer durch das Flussgebiet der Oder, Weichsel, des Dniepr und Niemen an die Gestade des Baltischen Meeres* (Jena, 1877), ch. iv.

of clay and brushwood. In the Emilia and the valley of the Vibrata several hundreds of such foundations were found, all of them round and corresponding in size and arrangement to those of Bologna. This primitive sort of hut appears to have persisted down to the end of the fifth century B.C. on the east side of the Apennines, where the Greek influence was less felt ; for to the Greeks the " restless Adriatic " seems to have been almost a closed sea, at least on its western shores.

For an insight into the primitive mode of hut-building to the west of the Apennines, a clue is afforded us by the older portion of the cemetery of Alba Longa. Here the ashes of the dead are deposited in earthen vessels which are obviously copies of the dwellings of the living. The urns represent round huts, of which the walls (says Helbig) must be supposed to have been constructed of clay, brushwood, or other perishable stuff. The roof appears to have been made of layers of straw or reeds, held together by wooden ribs. There was no regular opening in the roof corresponding to the later *compluvium*, the door in primitive fashion doing duty also as window and chimney ; though some of the urns have a small triangular hole on the front or back slope of the roof. The actual huts, of which remains were discovered on the Esquiline and not far from Marino, appear to have corresponded to those miniature huts. For evidence of the materials of the early Latin huts, Helbig next points to the Hut of Romulus, as it was called, a structure of reeds and straw on the Palatine, and to a similar structure in the temple of Jupiter on the Capitol, which was kept in constant repair by the addition of fresh brushwood.[1] For evidence of the shape of the huts, he remarks that when an artist had to depict scenes from the early history of Latium with buildings in the background, these buildings were always round. From all this he infers that at the time when the Latin race settled on the Alban Mountain to spread thence over the Campagna, they still retained the primitive kind of hut which had housed their ancestors in the forest-clearings by the rivers of North Italy.

Applying these results to the temple of Vesta, Helbig concludes that its round shape was a survival of the old Italian hut ; and he finds the origin of the perpetual holy fire of Vesta in the practical need of keeping up a fire from which the villagers could at any time get a light. Lastly, from the etymological connexion of Ἑστία and Vesta, he draws the inference that the custom of keeping up a public fire for the benefit of the village may date from Graeco-Italian times. That we should have reached the same conclusion independently and by different roads is a strong presumption in favour of its truth.[2]

[1] Conon, *Narrationes*, 48, in Photius, *Bibliotheca*, p. 141, ed. Bekker.
[2] In a note to my former paper I referred to the religious aversion of Roman priests to iron, but omitted to notice what is perhaps the most strik-

As to Greek houses, Mr. C. D. Tsountas in a paper on the pre-historic graves of Greece[1] supposes that the round shape of the beehive tombs at Mycenae, Orchomenus, etc., was a survival of the earliest form of Greek dwelling ; and he thinks that the mysterious Homeric θόλος may have been a primitive round hut preserved in later architecture, like the round temple of Vesta or the Hut of Romulus on the Palatine. As he mentions the widespread custom of burying the dead in the house and then deserting it, he would seem to suggest that the custom of building these beehive tombs grew out of such an earlier custom. House-burial is certainly stated by the ancients themselves to have been the original custom both of Greeks and Latins.[2] But after all it is to be remembered that the motive to build tombs and dwellings of this shape in stone may have been simply a constructional one (for they are easiest to build), and not a desire to imitate earlier huts of this form built of wood and other perishable materials.

ing example of it, namely the obliga-tion laid on the Arval Brothers to offer an expiatory sacrifice of a lamb and a pig whenever they used an iron tool in their sacred grove (J. Marquardt, *Rö-mische Staatsverwaltung*,[2] iii. p. 459).

The sceptical Nissen whispers in a note to his *Italische Landeskunde* (vol. i. p. 447) that the idyllic inhabitants of the pile-villages may have been mere prosaic Roman backwoodsmen of the second century B.C. His suspicions are roused by the fact that wheat has been found in the pile-villages, whereas accor-ding to Verrius Flaccus (in Pliny, *Nat. Hist.* xviii. 63) wheat was unknown to the Romans up to 454 B.C. But Helbig with apparent justice thinks it incredible that the Romans should have

been ignorant of wheat at a time when the Greek cities of Southern Italy and Sicily appear to have not only cultivated but exported it, and he ingeniously ex-plains away the statement of Verrius Flaccus (p. 65 *sq*.). Besides, wheat was found in the earliest lake-dwellings of Western Switzerland (A. de Candolle, *Origin of Cultivated Plants*, p. 355). Finally Professor Middleton assures me that the objects found in these Italian pile-villages (at least those pre-served at Rome) are beyond doubt prehistoric ; the pottery in particular is of the rudest and most archaic type.

[1] Ἐφημερὶς ἀρχαιολογική, No. 1, 1885.

[2] Plato, *Minos*, p. 315 D ; Servius on Virgil, *Aen.* v. 64, vi. 152.

III

TABOO [1]

TABOO (also written " Tabu " and " Tapu ") is the name given to a system of religious prohibitions which attained its fullest development in Polynesia (from Hawaii to New Zealand), but of which under different names traces may be discovered in most parts of the world.

The word " taboo " is common to the different dialects of Polynesia, and is perhaps derived from *ta*, " to mark ", and *pu*, an adverb of intensity. The compound word "taboo" (tapu) would thus originally mean " marked thoroughly ". Its ordinary sense is " sacred ". It does not, however, imply any moral quality, but only " a connexion with the gods or a separation from ordinary purposes and exclusive appropriation to persons or things considered sacred ; sometimes it means devoted as by a vow ". Chiefs who trace their lineage to the gods are called *arii tabu*, " chiefs sacred ", and a temple is called a *wahi tabu*, " place sacred ". The converse of taboo is *noa* (in Tonga *gnofoóa*), which means " general " or " common ". Thus the rule which forbade women to eat with men, as well as, except on special occasions, to eat any fruits or animals offered in sacrifice to the gods, was called *ai tabu*, " eating sacred " ; while the present relaxation of the rule is called *ai noa*, eating generally, or having food in common. Although it was employed for civil as well as religious purposes, the taboo was essentially a religious observance. In Hawaii it could be imposed only by priests ; but elsewhere in Polynesia kings and chiefs, and even to a certain extent ordinary individuals, exercised the same power.

[1] Reprinted, with the permission of the Encyclopaedia Britannica Company, from the *Encyclopædia Britannica*, 9th edition, vol. xxiii. (1888), pp. 15-18.

The strictness with which the taboo was observed depended largely on the influence of the person who imposed it : if he was a great chief it would not be broken ; but a powerful man often set at nought the taboo of an inferior.

A taboo might be general or particular, permanent or temporary. A general taboo applied, for example, to a whole class of animals ; a particular taboo was confined to one or more individuals of the class. Idols, temples, the persons and names of kings and of members of the royal family, the persons of chiefs and priests, and the property (canoes, houses, clothes, etc.) of all these classes of persons, were always taboo or sacred. By a somewhat arbitrary extension of this principle a chief could render taboo to (that is, in favour of) himself anything which took his fancy by merely calling it by the name of a part of his person. Thus, if he said " That axe is my backbone," or " is my head," the axe was his ; if he roared out " That canoe ! my skull shall be the baler to bale it out," the canoe was his likewise. The names of chiefs and still more of kings were taboo, and could not be uttered. If the name of a king of Tahiti was a common word or even resembled a common word, that word dropped out of use and a new name was substituted for it. Thus in course of time most of the common words in the language underwent considerable modifications or were entirely changed.

Certain foods were permanently taboo to (that is, in favour of or for the use of) gods and men, but were forbidden to women. Thus in Hawaii the flesh of hogs, fowls, turtle, and several kinds of fish, coco-nuts, and nearly everything offered in sacrifice were reserved for gods and men, and could not, except in special cases, be consumed by women. In the Marquesas Islands human flesh was tabooed from women. Sometimes certain fruits, animals, and fish were taboo for months together from both men and women. In the Marquesas houses were tabooed against water : nothing was washed in them ; no drop of water might be spilled in them. If an island or a district was tabooed, no canoe or person might approach it while the taboo lasted ; if a path was tabooed, no man might walk on it. Seasons generally kept taboo were the approach of a great religious ceremony, the time of preparation for war, and the sickness of chiefs. The

time during which they lasted varied from years to months
or days. In Hawaii there was a tradition of one that lasted
thirty years, during which men might not trim their beards,
etc. A common period was forty days. A taboo was either
common or strict. During a common taboo the men were
only required to abstain from their ordinary occupations and
to attend morning and evening prayers. But during a strict
taboo every fire and light on the island or in the district was
extinguished ; no canoe was launched ; no person bathed ;
no one, except those who had to attend at the temple, was
allowed to be seen out of doors ; no dog might bark, no pig
grunt, no cock crow. Hence at these seasons they tied up
the mouths of dogs and pigs, and put fowls under a calabash
or bandaged their eyes. The taboo was imposed either by
proclamation or by fixing certain marks (a pole with a bunch
of bamboo leaves, a white cloth, etc.) on the places or things
tabooed.

The penalty for the violation of a taboo was either religious
or civil. The religious penalty inflicted by the offended *atuas*
or spirits generally took the form of a disease : the offender
swelled up and died, the notion being that the *atua* or his
emissary (often an infant spirit) had entered into him and
devoured his vitals. Cases are on record in which persons
who had unwittingly broken a taboo actually died of terror
on discovering their fatal error. Chiefs and priests, however,
could in the case of involuntary transgressions perform certain mystical ceremonies which prevented this penalty from
taking effect. The civil penalty for breaking a taboo varied
in severity. In Hawaii there were police officers appointed
by the king to see that the taboo was observed, and every
breach of it was punished with death, unless the offender had
powerful friends in the persons of priests or chiefs. Elsewhere
the punishment was milder ; in Fiji (which, however, is
Melanesian) death was rarely inflicted, but the delinquent
was robbed and his gardens despoiled. In New Zealand
this judicial robbery was reduced to a system. No sooner
was it known that a man had broken a taboo than all his
friends and acquaintances swarmed down on him and carried
off whatever they could lay hands on. Under this system
(known as *muru*) property circulated with great rapidity.

If, for instance, a child fell into the fire, the father was robbed of nearly all he possessed.[1]

Besides the permanent and the artificially created taboos there were others which arose spontaneously as a result of circumstances. Thus all persons dangerously ill were taboo and were removed from their houses to sheds in the bush ; if they remained in the house and died there the house was tabooed and deserted. Mothers after childbirth were taboo, and so were their new-born children. Women before marriage were *noa*, and could have as many lovers as they chose ; but after marriage they were strictly tabooed to their husbands and from everyone else. One of the strictest taboos was incurred by all persons who handled the body or bones of a dead person or assisted at his funeral. In Tonga a common person who touched a dead chief was tabooed for ten lunar months ; a chief who touched a dead chief was tabooed for from three to five months according to the rank of the deceased. Burial grounds were taboo ; and in New Zealand a canoe which had carried a corpse was never afterwards used, but was drawn on shore and painted red. Red was the taboo colour in New Zealand ; in Hawaii, Tahiti, Tonga, and Samoa it was white. In the Marquesas a man who had slain an enemy was taboo for ten days : he might have no intercourse with his wife and might not meddle with fire ; he had to get someone else to cook for him. A woman engaged in the preparation of coco-nut oil was taboo for five days or more, during which she might have no intercourse with men. A tabooed person might not eat his food with his hands, but was fed by another person ; if he could get no one to feed him, he had to go down on his knees and pick up his food with his mouth, holding his hands behind him. A chief who was permanently taboo never ate in his own house but always in the open air, being fed by one of his wives or taking his food with the help of a fern stalk so as not to touch his head with his hands ; food left by him was kept for him in a sacred

---

[1] The origin of this custom may perhaps be discerned in a custom of the Dieri tribe, South Australia. Among them, if a child meets with an accident, all its relations immediately get their heads broken with sticks or boomerangs till the blood flows down their faces, this surgical operation being supposed to ease the child's pain. See J. D. Woods, *Native Tribes of South Australia* (Adelaide, 1879), p. 280.

place ; any other person eating of it was supposed to die immediately. A man of any standing could not carry provisions on his back ; if he did so they became taboo and were useless to anyone but himself. For the taboo was communicated as it were by infection to whatever a tabooed person or thing touched. This rule applied in its fullest force to the king and queen of Tahiti. The ground they trod on became sacred ; if they entered a house, it became taboo to them and had to be abandoned to them by its owner. Hence special houses were set apart for them on their travels, and, except in their hereditary districts, they were always carried on men's shoulders to prevent them touching the ground. Elsewhere, as in New Zealand, this rule was not carried out so strictly. But even in New Zealand the spots on which great chiefs rested during a journey became taboo and were surrounded with a fence of basket-work The head and hair, especially of a chief, were particularly taboo or sacred ; to touch a man's head was a gross insult. If a chief touched his own head with his fingers he had immediately to apply them to his nose and snuff up the sanctity which they had abstracted from his head. The cutting of a chief's hair was a solemn ceremony ; the severed locks were collected and buried in a sacred place or hung up on a tree. If a drop of a chief's blood fell upon anything, that thing became taboo to him, that is, was his property. If he breathed on a fire, it became sacred and could not be used for cooking. In his house no fire could under any circumstances be used for cooking ; no woman could enter his house before a certain service had been gone through. Whatever a new-born child touched became taboo to (that is, in favour of) the child. The law which separated tabooed persons and things from contact with food was especially strict. Hence a tabooed or sacred person ought not to leave his comb or blanket or anything which had touched his head or back (for the back was also particularly taboo) in a place where food had been cooked ; and in drinking he was careful not to touch the vessel with his hands or lips (otherwise the vessel became taboo and could not be used by anyone else), but to have the liquid shot down his throat from a distance by a second person.

There were various ceremonies by which a taboo could

be removed. In Tonga a person who had become taboo by touching a chief or anything belonging to him could not feed himself till he had got rid of the taboo by touching the soles of a superior chief's feet with his hands and then rinsing his hands in water, or (if water was scarce) rubbing them with the juice of the plantain or banana. But, if a man found that he had already (unknowingly) eaten with tabooed hands, he sat down before a chief, took up the foot of the latter, and pressed it against his stomach to counteract the effect of the food inside. In New Zealand a taboo could be taken off by a child or grandchild. The tabooed person touched the child and took drink or food from its hands ; the man was then free, but the child was tabooed for the rest of the day. A Maori chief who became taboo by touching the sacred head of his child was disinfected, so to speak, as follows. On the following day (the ceremony could not be performed sooner) he rubbed his hands over with potato or fern root which had been cooked over a sacred fire ; this food was then carried to the head of the family *in the female line*, who ate it, whereupon the hands became *noa*. The taboo was removed from a new-born child in a somewhat similar manner. The father took the child in his arms and touched its head, back, etc., with some fern root which had been roasted over a sacred fire ; next morning a similar ceremony was performed on the child by its eldest relative in the female line ; the child was then *noa*, that is, free from taboo. Another mode of removing the taboo was to pass a consecrated piece of wood over the right shoulder, round the loins, and back again over the left shoulder, after which the stick was broken in two and either buried, or burned, or cast into the sea.

Besides the taboos already described there were others which anyone could impose. In New Zealand, if a man wished to preserve his house, crop, garden, or anything else, he made it taboo ; similarly he could appropriate a forest tree or a piece of drift timber, etc., by tying a mark to it or giving it a chop with his axe. In Samoa for a similar purpose a man would set up a representation of, for example, a sea pike or a shark, believing that anyone who meddled with property thus protected would be killed by a sea pike or shark the next time he bathed. Somewhat similar to this was what may be called the village taboo. In the autumn the *kumera* (sweet potato) fields belonging to the village were taboo till the crop was gathered, so that no stranger could approach them ; and all persons engaged in getting in the crop were taboo, and could therefore for the time engage in no other occupation. Similar taboos were laid on woods during the hunting season and on rivers during the fishing season.

On looking over the various taboos mentioned above we are tempted to divide them into two general classes—taboos of privilege and taboos of disability. Thus the taboo of chiefs, priests, and temples might be described as a privilege, while the taboo imposed on the sick and on persons who had come in contact with the dead might be regarded as a disability ; and we might say accordingly that the former rendered persons and things sacred or holy, while the latter rendered them unclean or accursed. But that no such distinction ought to be drawn is clear from the fact that the rules to be observed in the one case and in the other were identical. On the other hand, it is true that the opposition of sacred and accursed, clean and unclean, which plays so important a part in the later history of religion, did in fact arise by differentiation from the single root idea of taboo, which includes and reconciles them both and by reference to which alone their history and mutual relation are intelligible.

The original character of the taboo must be looked for not in its civil but in its religious element. It was not the creation of a legislator but the gradual outgrowth of animistic beliefs, to which the ambition and avarice of chiefs and priests afterwards gave an artificial extension. But in serving the cause of avarice and ambition it subserved the progress of civilization, by fostering conceptions of the rights of property and the sanctity of the marriage tie—conceptions which in time grew strong enough to stand by themselves and to fling away the crutch of superstition which in earlier days had been their sole support. For we shall scarcely err in believing that even in advanced societies the moral sentiments, in so far as they are merely sentiments and are not based on an induction from experience, derive much of their force from an original system of taboo. Thus on the taboo were grafted the golden fruits of law and morality, while the parent stem dwindled slowly into the sour crabs and empty husks of popular superstition on which the swine of modern society are still content to feed.

It remains to indicate briefly some facts which point to a wide diffusion under various names of customs similar to the taboo. As might have been expected, the taboo is found, though in a less marked form, among the Micronesians, Malays, and Dyaks, all of whom are ethnologically connected with the Polynesians. In Micronesia both the name and the institution occur : the inhabitants of certain islands are forbidden to eat certain animals and the fruits of certain trees ; temples and great chiefs are tabooed from the people ; anyone who fishes must previously for twenty-four hours abstain from women ;[1] in conversing with women men are not allowed to use certain words, etc. Again, the Malays have the custom, though apparently not the name. In Timor and the neighbouring islands the word for taboo is *pamali* (or *pomali*) ; and during the long festival which celebrates a successful head-hunt the man who has secured the most heads is *pamali* ; he may not sleep with his wife nor eat from his own hand, but is fed by women. *Pamali* is a Javanese word, and had originally in Java and Sumatra the same meaning that it now bears in Timor. In Celebes a mother after childbirth was *pamali*. Amongst the Dyaks of Borneo the *pamali* (called by the Land Dyaks *porikh*) is regularly practised at the planting of rice, harvest home, when the cry of the gazelle is heard behind, in times of sickness, after a death, etc. At the harvest home it is observed by the whole tribe, no one being allowed to enter or leave the village. The house where a death has taken place is *pamali* for twelve days, during which no one may enter it and nothing may be taken out of it. A tabooed Dyak may not bathe, meddle with fire, follow his ordinary occupation, or leave his house. Certain families are forbidden to eat the flesh of particular animals, as cattle, goats, and snakes. The taboo is often indicated by

---

[1] For other examples of taboos (especially injunctions to continence) among various peoples in connexion with fishing, hunting, and trading, see G. Turner, *Samoa*, p. 349; E. Aymonier, *Notes sur les Laos*, pp. 21 *sq.*, 25, 26, 113, 141 ; W. Powell, *Wanderings in a Wild Country*, p. 207 ; *Report of International Expedition to Point Barrow, Alaska*, p. 39 (Washington, 1885).

a bundle of spears or a rattan. The Motu of New Guinea also have the taboo : a man is tabooed after handling a corpse. He then keeps apart from his wife ; his food is cooked for him by his sisters ; and he may not touch it with his hands. After three days he bathes and is free.[1] But the Motu appear to be Malayo-Polynesians, not Melanesians proper. However, in Melanesia also we find the taboo. It flourished in Fiji. It is observed in New Caledonia in cases of death, to preserve a crop, etc. According to the Rev. R. H. Codrington, there is this distinction between the Melanesian and the Polynesian taboo, that for the former there is no supernatural sanction : the man who breaks a taboo simply pays compensation to the person on whose tabooed property he has transgressed. But Mr. R. Parkinson states that in New Britain, a large Melanesian island, a person who violates a taboo-mark set on a plantation, tree, etc., is supposed to be " attacked by sickness and misfortune." To go through the similar customs observed by savages all over the world would be endless ; we may, however, note that a regular system of taboo is said to exist among some of the wild tribes of the Naga Hills in India,[2] and that the rules not to touch food with the hands or the head with the hands are observed by tabooed women among one of the Fraser Lake tribes in North America.[3] In fact some of the most characteristic features of taboo—the prohibition to eat certain foods and the disabilities entailed by childbirth and by contact with the dead, together with a variety of ceremonies for removing these disabilities—have been found more or less amongst all primitive races. It is more interesting to mark the traces of such customs among civilized peoples, for example, Jews, Greeks, and Romans.

Amongst the Jews—(1) the vow of the Nazarite [4] presents the closest resemblance to the Polynesian taboo. The meaning of the word Nazarite is " one separated or consecrated ", and this, as we saw (p. 80), is precisely the meaning of taboo. It is the head of the Nazarite that is especially consecrated,[5] and so it was in the taboo. The Nazarite might not partake

---

[1] *Journ. Anthrop. Inst.* viii. p. 370.

[2] *Journ. Anthrop. Inst.* xi. p. 71 ; E. T. Dalton, *Descriptive Ethnology of Bengal*, p. 43.

[3] *Journ. Anthrop. Inst.* vii. p. 206.

[4] Numbers vi. 1-21.

[5] Numbers vi. 7, " his separation unto God is upon his head " ; 9, " defile the head of his separation " ; 11, " shall hallow his head ".

of certain meats and drinks, nor shave his head, nor touch a dead body—all rules of taboo. If a person died suddenly beside him, this was said to " defile the head of his separation ", and the same effect, expressed in the same language, would apply to a tabooed Polynesian in similar circumstances. Again, the mode of terminating the vow of the Nazarite corresponds with the mode of breaking a taboo. He shaved his head at the door of the sanctuary and the priest placed food in his hands, either of which acts would have been a flagrant violation of a Polynesian taboo. (2) Some of the rules for the observance of the Sabbath are identical with rules of strict taboo ; such are the prohibitions to do any work, to kindle a fire in the house, to cook food, and to go out of doors.[1] The Essenes strictly observed the rules to cook no food and light no fires on the Sabbath.[2] (3) Anyone who touched a dead body was " unclean " for seven days ; what he touched became unclean, and could communicate its uncleanness to any other person who touched it. At the end of seven days the unclean person washed his clothes, bathed himself, and was clean.[3] In Polynesia, as we have seen, anyone who touched a dead body was taboo ; what he touched became taboo, and could communicate the infection to anyone who touched it ; and one of the ceremonies for getting rid of the taboo was washing. (4) A Jewish mother after childbirth was unclean ;[4] a Polynesian mother was taboo. (5) A great many animals were unclean, and could infect with their uncleanness whatever they touched ; earthen vessels touched by certain of them were broken. Certain animals were taboo in Polynesia, and utensils which had contracted a taint of taboo were in some cases broken.

Amongst the Greeks a survival, or at least a reminiscence, of a system of taboo is perhaps to be found in certain applications of the epithets " sacred " and " divine " in Homer. Thus a king or a chief is sacred[5] or divine ;[6] his chariot is sacred,[7] and his house is divine.[8] An army is sacred[9] and

---

[1] Exodus xxxv. 2, 3 ; xvi. 23, 29.
[2] Josephus, *Bell. Jud.* ii. 8, 9.
[3] Numbers xix. 11, 14, 19, 22.
[4] Leviticus xii.
[5] ἱερὴ ἲς Τηλεμάχοιο, *Od.* ii. 409,

xviii. 405, etc. ; ἱερὸν μένος Ἀλκινόοιο, *Od.* vii. 167, viii. 2, etc.
[6] δῖος Ὀδυσσεύς, etc.; Ὀδυσσῆος θείοιο, *Il.* ii. 335, etc. ; θείων βασιλήων, *Od.* iv. 691. [7] *Il.* xvii. 464.
[8] *Od.* iv. 43. [9] *Od.* xxiv. 81.

so are sentinels on duty.[1] This resembles the war-taboo of
the Polynesians ; on a warlike expedition all Maori warriors
are taboo, and the permanent personal taboo of the chiefs is
increased twofold : they are " tabooed an inch thick ".
The Jews also seem to have had a war-taboo, for when out on the
war-path they abstained from women [2]—a rule strictly observed by Maori warriors on a dangerous expedition. The
Dards, who with the kindred Siah Posh Kâfirs on the southern
slopes of the Hindu Kush—tribes which probably of all Aryan
peoples retain a social state most nearly approximating to
that of the primitive Aryans—abstain from sexual intercourse
during the whole of the fighting season, from May to September ; and " victory to the chastest " is said to be a maxim
of all the fighting tribes from the Hindu Kush to Albania.[3]
The same rule of continence in war is observed by some Indian
tribes of North America.[4] In Homer a fish is sacred,[5] and
Plato points out that during a campaign the Homeric warriors
never ate fish.[6] Even in time of peace the men of Homer's
day only ate fish when reduced to the verge of starvation.[7]
The Siah Posh Kâfirs refuse to eat fish, although their rivers
abound in it.[8] The Hindoos of Vedic times appear not to
have eaten fish.[9] It is probable, therefore, that among the
early Aryans, as among primitive peoples in various parts of
the world, the eating of fish was tabooed. Again, the threshing-floor, the winnowing-fan, and meal are all sacred.[10] Similarly in New Zealand a taboo was commonly laid on places
where farming operations were going on ; and among the
Basutos, before the corn on the threshing-floor can be touched,
a religious ceremony has to be performed, and all " defiled "
persons are carefully kept from seeing it.[11] Although the
Homeric folk ate swine, the epithet " divine " commonly
applied to a swineherd in Homer may point to a time when

[1] *Il.* x. 56 ; xxiv. 681.
[2] 1 Samuel xxi. 4, 5.
[3] É. Reclus, *Nouvelle Géographie Universelle*, viii. p. 126.
[4] H. R. Schoolcraft, *Indian Tribes*, iv. p. 63 ; J. Adair, *Hist. of American Indians*, p. 163. Compare Morse, *Report on Indian Affairs*, p. 130 *sq.*, and H. H. Bancroft, *Native Races of the Pacific States*, i. p. 189.

[5] *Il.* xvi. 407.   [6] *Rep.* 404 B.
[7] *Od.* iv. 363 *sq.* ; xii. 329 *sq.*
[8] Elphinstone, *Kingdom of Caubul*, ii. 379 (ed. 1839); *Journ. Ethnol. Soc.*, i. p. 192.
[9] H. Zimmer, *Altindisches Leben*, p. 271.
[10] *Il.* v. 499 ; *H. Merc*, 21, 63 ; *Il.* xi. 631.
[11] E. Casalis, *The Basutos*, p. 251 *sq.*

pigs were sacred or tabooed. In Crete pigs were certainly
sacred and not eaten,[1] and apparently at Pessinus also.[2]
Amongst the Jews and Syrians, of course, pigs were tabooed ;
and it was a moot question with the Greeks whether the Jews
abhorred or worshipped pigs.[3] The pigs kept in the great
temple at Hierapolis were neither sacrificed nor eaten ; some
people thought that they were sacred, others that they were
unclean (ἐναγέας).[4] Here we have an exact taboo, the ideas
of sacredness and uncleanness being indistinguishable. Similarly by the Ojebways the dog is regarded as " unclean and
yet as in some other respects holy ".[5] The divergence of the
two conceptions is illustrated by the history of the cow among
different branches of the Aryan race; the Hindoos regard this
animal as sacred ; the Shin caste among the Dards hold it
in abhorrence.[6] The general word for taboo in Greek is ἄγος,
which occurs in the sense both of " sacredness " and of " pollution " ; and the same is true of the adjective ἅγιος and of
the rare adjective ἀναγής, " tabooed ".[7] Usually, however,
the Greeks discriminated the two senses, ἁγνός being devoted
to the sense of " sacred " and ἐναγής to that of " unclean "
or " accursed ". " To taboo " is ἁγίζειν ; " to observe a
taboo " is ἁγνεύειν ; and the state or season of taboo is ἁγνεία
or ἁγιστεία. The rules of the Greek ἁγνεία correspond closely
to those of the Polynesian taboo, consisting in " purifications,
washings, and sprinklings, and in abstaining from mourning
for the dead, child-bed, and all pollutions, and in refraining
from certain foods ", etc.[8]

Amongst the Romans, who preserved more traces of primitive barbarism than the Greeks, the Flamen Dialis was hedged
in by a perfect network of taboos. He was not allowed to ride
or even touch a horse, nor to look at an army under arms,
nor to wear a ring which was not broken, nor to have a knot
on any part of his garments ; no fire, except a sacred fire,
could be taken out of his house ; he might not touch or even

[1] Athenaeus, 376 A.
[2] Pausanias, vii. 17. 10.
[3] Plutarch, *Quaest. Conv.* iv. 5.
[4] Lucian, *De dea Syria*, 54.
[5] J. G. Kohl, *Kitchi-Gami*, p. 38, Eng. trans.
[6] F. Drew, *The Jummoo and Kashmir Territories*, p. 428 ; J. Biddulph, *Tribes of the Hindoo Koosh*, p. 51.
[7] Bekker's *Anecdota Graeca*, 212, 32; Harpocration, *s.v.* ἀναγεῖς.
[8] Diogenes Laertius, viii. 1. 33; compare Plutarch, *Quaest. Conv.* v. 10.

name a goat, a dog, raw meat, beans, and ivy ; he might not walk under a vine ; the feet of his bed had to be daubed with mud ; his hair could be cut only by a freeman, and his hair and nails when cut had to be buried under a lucky tree ; he might not touch a corpse, etc. His wife, the flaminica, was also subject to taboos : at certain festivals she might not comb her hair ; if she heard thunder, she was taboo (*feriata*) till she had offered an expiatory sacrifice. The similarity of some of these rules to the Polynesian taboo is obvious. The Roman *feriae* were periods of taboo ; no work might be done during them except works of necessity : for example, an ox might be pulled out of a pit or a tottering roof supported. Any person who mentioned Salus, Semonia, Seia, Segetia, or Tutilina was tabooed (*ferias observabat*).[1] The Latin *sacer* is exactly " taboo " ; for it means either " sacred " or " accursed "

LITERATURE.—On the Polynesian taboo, see Cook, *Voyages*, vol. v. p. 427 *sq.*, vol. vii. p. 146 *sq:* (ed. 1809) ; G. F. Angas, *Savage Scenes in Australia and New Zealand*, passim ; W. Yate, *New Zealand*, p. 84 *sq.*; W. Ellis, *Polynesian Researches*, 2nd ed., vol. iv. p. 385 *sq.*; Langsdorff, *Reise um die Welt*, i. p. 114 *sq.*; W. Mariner, *Tonga Islands*, i. p. 141 note, ii. pp. 82, 220 *sq.* ; G. Turner, *Nineteen Years in Polynesia*, p. 294 *sq.* ; *id., Samoa*, p. 185 *sq.* ; Klemm, *Culturgeschichte*, iv. p. 372 *sq.* ; Waitz-Gerland, *Anthropologie der Naturvölker*, vi. pp. 343-363 ; Shortland, *Traditions and Superstitions of the New Zealanders*, p. 101 *sq.* ; *id., Maori Religion and Mythology*, p. 25 *sq.* ; *Old New Zealand*, by a Pakeha Maori, chapters vii.-xii. ; Polack, *Manners and Customs of the New Zealanders*, i. p. 275 *sq.* ; Dieffenbach, *Travels in New Zealand*, ii. p. 100 *sq.* ; R. Taylor, *New Zealand*, p. 163 *sq.* On the taboo in Micronesia, see Waitz-Gerland, *op. cit.* v. pt. ii. p. 147 *sq.* ; among the Dyaks and Malays, see *id.* vi. p. 354 *sq.* ; Low, *Sarawak*, pp. 260-262 ; Bock, *Head-Hunters of Borneo*, pp. 214-230 ; Spencer St. John, *Life in the Forests of the Far East*, i. p. 184 *sq.* ; A. R. Wallace, *The Malay Archipelago*, p. 196 ; in Melanesia, Williams, *Fiji and the Fijians*, i. p. 234 *sq.* (ed. 1860) ; J. E. Erskine, *The Western Pacific*, p. 254 ; Vincendon-Dumoulin et Desgraz, *Iles Marquises*, p. 259 *sq.* ; *Journ. Anthrop. Inst.* x. pp. 279, 290 ; Ch. Lemire, *Nouvelle Calédonie* (Paris, 1884), p. 117 ; R. Parkinson, *Im Bismarck-Archipel* (Leipsic, 1887), p. 144.

[1] Macrobius, *Sat.* i. 16. 8.

IV

THE LANGUAGE OF ANIMALS[1]

" Sie sprechen eine Sprache,
Die ist so reich, so schön ;
Doch keiner der Philologen
Kann diese Sprache verstehn."

HEINE.

IT is an old belief that animals, and even plants, talk to each other, and that men can freely understand and answer them. But this belief, born of that primitive communism which makes the whole world kin, is gradually dispelled by a more exact observation of Nature ; and men, beginning to draw the line more sharply between themselves and the lower creatures, are fain to confess that they understand the beast language no longer, though they cling to the idea that the faculty is still enjoyed by a few, either as a natural gift or an acquired accomplishment. Sometimes with a peculiar fitness this antique lore is the special attribute of simple folk, as fools or children, who reflect the mental state of a bygone age. A modern poet can still ask the children to

" Whisper in my ear
What the birds and the winds are singing
In your sunny atmosphere,"

as if the kingdom of Nature, like the kingdom of heaven, were hidden from the wise and prudent and revealed unto babes.[2]

Combating the practice of killing animals for food,

[1] Reprinted, with a few corrections, from *The Archaeological Review*, vol. i. Nos. 2 and 3 (April and May 1888).

[2] " *Ut non alius fere sit aditus ad regnum hominis, quod fundatur in scientiis quam ad regnum coelorum, in quod, nisi sub persona infantis, intrare non datur* " (Bacon, *Novum Organum*, i. 68).

93

Porphyry argues that they are reasonable creatures and speak
a language which differs from that of man only in this, that
whereas human language is regulated by human laws, the
language of the beasts is bound by no rules save those imposed
by Nature and the gods. " What though we do not understand the beast language ? " he asks ; " a Greek does not
understand a Hindoo ; and to a man bred in Attica, the
Syriac, Thracian, or Scythian tongue is unintelligible, and
sounds like the croaking and creaking of cranes ".[1] A belief
like Porphyry's is still held, on grounds not unlike his, by the
Indians of Guiana. " In Guiana countless Indian stories,
fully believed, introduce the sayings of animals ; and though
the individual Indian knows that he no longer understands
the language of the beasts and birds around him, yet he
attaches but little weight to this, in that he is constantly
meeting with other Indians of one or other of the many alien
tribes which surround him, who speak languages at least as
unintelligible to him as are those of birds or beasts ; and in
that, as he is fully persuaded, he constantly hears the peaiman
[medicine-man] still converse with birds and beasts."[2]

When the language of the beasts is thus a foreign tongue
to man, the ideas he has of it are naturally vague. Sometimes
he seems to think that all animals speak the same speech,
sometimes that the speech of birds differs from that of beasts,
sometimes that each species of animal has its own distinct
language. The last was perhaps Porphyry's notion, for according to him some races of men have a natural aptitude for the
language of certain animals ; the Arabs, he said, understand
crows, the Etruscans eagles.[3] A Syrian story[4] specially mentions the bear language and the lion language ; a young man
understands and converses in both, and acts as interpreter
between the lions and the daughter of the elfin-king, who,
brought to be the bride of the lion-prince, does not understand the lion language. When a bear asks the youth how
he learned the bear language, he answers " By the grace of
God ". In another Syrian tale[5] a chief's daughter has been
swallowed by a shark ; and a fish, who had been swallowed

[1] Porphyry, De abstinentia, iii. 3.
[2] E. F. Im Thurn, Among the Indians of Guiana, p. 352.
[3] De abstinentia, iii. 4.

[4] E. Prym und A. Socin, Syrische
Sagen und Maerchen (Göttingen,
1881), No. xxx.
[5] Id. No. xxiv.

by the shark at the same time, is questioned as to the girl's fate by a Mohammedan doctor of law who understands the language of fish. A Swabian story [1] tells how a man understood the language of geese, and from overhearing a conversation of these birds was able to anticipate their attack on a farmer's crop. In a modern Greek tale from Epirus [2] a poor man goes out to earn his bread. He comes to a river on whose banks the birds twitter and sing. Here he stays three years to learn their language. When he has mastered it he returns home, and hearing that a certain queen has a toad in her body and can get no help from any physician, he goes to see what he can do for her. First he speaks in the snake language, but the toad makes no answer. Next he tries the frog language ; still no response. Lastly he tries the toad language. Immediately the toad answers from the queen's body, and in the course of conversation admits that he dislikes sour things. A dose of vinegar is promptly administered to the queen, who is soon rid of the toad. The poor man receives a ducat from the grateful monarch. In this story it is implied that a knowledge of the bird language carries with it a knowledge of the languages of other animals. We shall meet the same implication again.

A knowledge of the language of animals is sometimes ascribed to particular persons, legendary or historical. Peter Petrovitch of Cracow, a hero of Russian song, talked with the fowls of the air.[3] The Indians say that Menabozho understood the languages of all animals.[4] In a fabulous life of Alexander the Great, written in French prose in the fifteenth century, Alexander is represented as borne through the air in a glass cage, yoked with eight griffins, and he is accompanied by magicians who understand the language of birds.[5]

---

[1] A. Birlinger, *Volksthümliches aus Schwaben,* i. p. 335.

[2] J. G. von Hahn, *Griechische und albanesische Märchen,* No. 33.

[3] A. Rambaud, *La Russie épique* (Paris, 1876), p. 80.

[4] A. Bastian in *Zeitschrift f. Ethnologie,* i. p. 158.

[5] John Dunlop, *History of Fiction* (2nd ed., 1816), ii. p. 127 ; *ib.* p. 184 of F. Liebrecht's German translation (Berlin, 1851) The prose romance is

based on two metrical romances, one by Lambert li Tors, the other by Thomas of Kent (Dunlop, ii. p. 124). A collection of mediaeval French metrical romances on the history of Alexander (including extracts from Thomas of Kent) was published from the MSS. by Mr. Paul Meyer, under the title *Alexandre le Grand dans la littérature Française du moyen âge* (Paris, 1886). In one of them (*MS. de la Bibl. Imp.* No. 789)

In the Koran[1] Solomon is made to say, "O ye folk! we have been taught the speech of birds"; and he is supposed to have understood more than the bird language, for, coming with his hosts to the valley of the ants, he hears an ant saying, "O ye ants! go into your dwellings, that Solomon and his hosts crush you not while they do not perceive," at which speech the king laughs.

According to an Arabic legend,[2] Solomon, reposing in the valley between Hebron and Jerusalem, is visited by the angels of the winds and the angels that bear rule over all living things; by their help he summons to his presence animals of every kind, and converses with them. Moslems still believe that "all kinds of birds, and many (if not all) beasts, have a language by which they communicate their thoughts to each other".[3] It was from the Moors of Spain that Gerbert, afterwards Pope Sylvester II., learned the meaning of the cries and the flight of birds.[4] For in the Middle Ages, Spain, so long the home of Arabian arts and learning, was a favourite abode of enchanters; magic was regularly taught at Toledo, Salamanca, and Seville.[5] To this day it is hardly possible to walk the narrow, winding, desolate streets of Toledo—perched like an eagle's eyrie in proud isolation from the modern world—without falling under the spell of the Middle Ages, and feeling that behind those white, silent walls the magician may still be working his "enchantments drear".

Grimm has conjectured[6] that the elevation of Gerbert to the Papal See may have been the origin of a German folk-tale in which a boy who had learned the language of animals rises to be Pope. The story is only one of a widespread group of similar tales, which we will now examine.

Alexander sails through the air in a griffin-car, and says (vv. 377 *sq.*):

"*Et saurai des oisiax com lor est convenant Quant il volent là sus en l'air ki est ardant.*"

[1] Ch. xxvii. (vol. ii. p. 100 *sq.*, Palmer's translation).

[2] G. Weil, *Biblische Legenden der Muselmänner* (Frankfurt, 1845), p. 225 *sqq.*

[3] Lane's *Arabian Nights' Entertainments*, i. p. 35.

[4] William of Malmesbury, *De gestis regum Anglorum*, ii. 10: "*Ibi quid cantus et volatus avium portendit, didicit*"; Vincent of Beauvais, *Speculum Historiale*, xxiv. 98 (paraphrasing William of Malmesbury): "*Ibi didicit et cantus avium et volatus mysterium.*"

[5] Sir W. Scott, note on *Lay of the Last Minstrel*, Canto ii.; Maury, *La Magie et l'Astrologie dans l'Antiquité et au moyen âge*, p. 216. Magic was even called *scientia Toletana*.

[6] Note on *Kinder- und Hausmärchen*, No. 33.

In the case of authors who wrote before the invention of printing, scholars are familiar with the process of comparing the various manuscripts of a single work, in order, from such a comparison, to reconstruct the archetype or original MS. from which the various existing MSS. are derived. Similarly in folk-lore, by comparing the different versions of a single tale, it may be possible to arrive with tolerable certainty at the original story, of which the different versions are more or less imperfect and incorrect representations. The story of " The Boy who became Pope " will furnish us with an example of this process of collation in folk-lore. Versions of the story are found in *a*, Italy,[1] *b*, Germany,[2] *c*, Normandy,[3] and *d*, Brittany ;[4] and they all belong to what a palaeographer would call the same family, being undoubtedly derived from one archetype. Other versions of the same story, differing more or less from the preceding and from each other, will be afterwards noticed.

We will first give the archetype, as restored from a comparison of the four versions belonging to the same family. Along with the text of the archetype we will give the most important variations (where they occur) in the different versions, indicating these versions by the letters I. (Italian), G. (German), N. (Norman), and B. (Breton).

The story is that of " The Boy who became Pope, or the Three Languages ". A man has a son whom he sends away to be educated. After a time the son returns and is asked what he has learned. He replies " I have learned the language of *dogs*."[5] He is sent away to school again. After a time he again comes back, and is asked what he has learned. He answers, " The language of *frogs*."[6] He is sent away to school again. He returns a third time, and is asked what he has learned. He replies, " The language of *birds*."[7]

---

[1] T. F. Crane, *Popular Italian Tales*, No. xliii.

[2] Grimm, *Kinder- und Hausmär-chen*, No. 33.

[3] J. Fleury, *Littérature orale de la Basse-Normandie* (Paris, 1883), p. 123 *sqq*.

[4] P. Sébillot, *Contes populaires de la Haute-Bretagne*, 2ème Série, No. xxv.

[5] Frogs N. ; dogs, frogs, and birds I. (this is simply an abbreviation of what follows, the three visits to school being compressed into one. But in I. the order of the archetype—viz. dogs, frogs, birds—is preserved both here and in what follows).

[6] Dogs N. ; birds G.

[7] Frogs G.

The father is angry. *He orders* [1] *a man to take the youth into a wood and murder him.* The intended assassin pities the youth and lets him go, but brings as a token to his father the heart of a deer,[2] *pretending that it is the youth's.*

In his wanderings the youth comes to a dwelling where he is received for the night. The dogs bark, and, understanding the language of dogs, the youth hears them saying that robbers are about to attack the house. He gives warning to the master of the house, and the purpose of the robbers is defeated.[3]

He comes to a house where a girl is ill. By understanding what the frogs are saying he learns that the girl is ill because she has dropped *something* [4] which a frog has got hold of. The lost object is rescued from the frog's mouth, and the girl is made well.[5]

He goes to Rome with *two* [6] companions whom he has met on the way. They hear birds singing on a tree, and the youth understands the birds to say that one of the three fellow-travellers will be made Pope.[7] At Rome they find that the Pope is dead, and by *a certain sign* [8] the youth is recognized as the future Pope and elected.

His father visits him, repents of what he had done, humbles himself before his son, receives his pardon, and lives with his son henceforward.[9]

---

[1] He orders . . . pretending that it is the youth's *omitted in* B.

[2] Heart of a dog I. ; eyes and tongue of a deer G. (For bringing back an animal's heart instead of a person's, compare Fleury, *op. cit. La Fille sans Mains*, p. 153.)

[3] In B. the incident of the dogs and the robbers follows that of the girl and the frogs, agreeably to the order in which in B. the youth learns the three languages. In G. the robbers are omitted, and the dogs bark simply because there is a great treasure in the house, and they can have no rest till it is removed.

[4] The holy wafer (host) N.B. ; a crucifix I. (which does not say that a frog had got hold of it, but simply that the girl had thrown the crucifix into a fountain).

[5] In G. the frog incident is abbre-viated to this, that the youth hears and understands the croaking of the frogs, and is saddened by what he hears.

[6] Three I. In I. he meets these companions after; in N.B. before, the adventures with the dogs and frogs. In G. the fellow-travellers do not appear.

[7] In N. it is only said that what the birds said astonished him, and that he kept the secret to himself. But the meaning is plainly as in the text.

[8] In G. two white doves alight on his shoulders ; in I. a dove alights on his head ; in B. all the people pass under the bell to see who will be Pope ; when the youth passes under it, the bell rings. In N. a portion of the sky descends on his head.

[9] His father . . . henceforward *omitted in* G. ; and lives with his son henceforward *omitted in* N.

There are two other Breton versions of the story, which differ more or less from the preceding. *e*. In one called *Pope Innocent*,[1] the son of the King of France predicts that his father will pour water for him to wash his hands, and that his mother will offer him a towel to dry them with. His parents are angry. A man is charged to kill the prince, but lets him go free. Hearing that a Pope is about to be elected, he sets out for Rome. He meets two monks who are also bound thither, and they go together. On the way they have various adventures, which have no parallel in the preceding versions. But the incidents of (1) the castle and robbers, and (2) the girl and the frogs, and (3) the prediction of the birds, all occur, though in (1) the dogs are not mentioned. At Rome the prince's candle takes fire of itself on three successive days, so he is elected Pope. His parents come to Rome to get absolution for their sin ; they fulfil their son's prediction ; he pardons them, and they live happily together.

f. In another Breton version,[2] called *The History of Christie, who became Pope at Rome*, the boy Christie makes the same prediction as in the preceding version. A servant is charged to kill him, but brings back a dog's heart instead. Christie has various adventures, of which the only one like the preceding is that of the robbers, and here the dogs reappear. The test for Pope is the same as in the foregoing tale. His parents visit Rome, and the Pope washes their feet.

In neither of these Breton versions is the language of animals distinctly mentioned, though a knowledge of it is implied in the incident of the frogs in the first and perhaps (though less clearly) in that of the dogs in the second.

Further, the general plot of the story occurs in a number of other tales. *g*. In the *History of the Seven Wise Masters of Rome*,[3] a certain knight sends his son to be educated by

[1] *Mélusine*, i. (1878), col. 374 *sqq.* For some of the parallels which follow I am indebted to Dr. Reinhold Köhler's notes in *Mélusine*, i. c. 384.
[2] *Mélusine*, i. col. 300 *sqq.*
[3] I have used the *Historia calumnie novercalis que septem sapientum inscribitur* (Antwerp, 1490) ; the English translation, reprinted at London, 1688 ; and the two old French redactions published by Mr. Gaston Paris

(*Deux Rédactions du Roman des Sept Sages de Rome*, publiées par Gaston Paris, Paris, 1876). The *Historia calumnie novercalis*, according to Mr. Paris (preface, p. xi, note) is the same text as the *Historia septem sapientum*, " *avec des changements des noms et la suppression de tout ce qui est chrétien* ". According to him, the second of the French versions is a close translation of the Latin, and the English version

a Master in a far country. After seven years the child returned and as he is sitting at table with his parents a nightingale sings sweetly. The knight marvels at the sweetness of the song and wishes that someone could interpret it. His son says he can do so but fears his father's displeasure. The knight bids him speak out. So the son says: "The bird foretells that I shall become a great lord and that my father shall bring me water to wash and that my mother shall hold the towel." His father in anger throws him into the sea, but he is picked up by a ship, taken to a distant land, and sold to a duke. The king of the country is plagued by three ravens which follow him continually, screaming loudly. He offers his daughter in marriage and the succession to the throne to anyone who shall explain the mystery and rid him of the ravens. The child explains that the ravens are a father, a mother, and a young one ; that the mother deserted the young one in a time of scarcity but now claims to exercise a mother's rights over it, while the father-raven, who fed the young one in the time of scarcity, resists the mother's claim ; the birds therefore wish the king to decide to whom the young one belongs. The king decides in favour of the father ; and the birds fly away. The youth grows up and in time weds the king's daughter. He visits his father and mother, who know him not, but do him reverence ; his father offers him water to wash with and his mother presents a towel, as he had foretold. He reveals himself to them, forgives them, and takes them to his kingdom where they dwell in honour and joy.

h. In a French version of the *Seven Wise Masters*,[1] a

is made directly or indirectly from the Latin. But the French version is certainly not a close translation of the *Historia calumnie novercalis* so far as I have compared the two, but differs from it considerably. On the other hand, the French and English translations (so far as I have compared them) agree with each other closely and differ from the Latin ; and as in some of these details, where they differ from the Latin, they agree with modern parallels, one can scarcely help concluding that the genuine folk - tale lives independently in these versions, and that the Latin is merely a transla-

tion (and an abridged translation) of a vernacular version. Hence in the story in the text I follow the French and English versions, and neglect the Latin. Mr. G. Paris himself believes that the Latin *Historia septem sapientum* is a translation of an older French version. The general question of the relation of the different versions of *The Seven Wise Masters* seems to be very complex and I do not pretend to enter on it.

[1] The version is the first of the two French versions published by Mr. G. Paris, *op. cit.* pp. 47-50.

fisherman is out fishing with his son. Hearing some birds shrieking, the father asks what it means, the son interprets their cries as the boy in the previous version interprets the nightingale. His father flings him into the sea, and the rest follows as before, except that the question between the ravens is, which of two males shall have the hen-bird to wife ; the old male had been her mate but had deserted her in a time of scarcity, when the younger male had fed and cherished her. The king decides for the younger male.

i. In a Russian version [1] which reproduces very closely the former version of the *Seven Wise Masters*, a man hears a nightingale singing a sad song and wishes that someone could interpret it. His son, a child of six, says that he knows what the nightingale is singing but fears to tell. His father bids him speak out. His son says : " The bird says that a day will come when you will serve me ; my father will pour water for me and my mother will offer the towel." His parents, enraged, set him adrift on the sea in a little boat. He is picked up by a ship and brought to a country where the king is plagued by three ravens, and the rest follows as in the *Seven Wise Masters* ; the question between the ravens being, as in the first case, whether the young one belongs to the father or mother, and the king deciding for the father. The son's visit to his parents and the fulfilment of his prediction as to the water and the towel also follow as before.

k. In a Masurian version [2] a merchant sends his son to a master to learn the language of birds. On his return his father hears him conversing with a lark. With some difficulty the son is persuaded to tell what the lark said to him, " When you come back you will be a rich man but your father will be poor ; your mother will wash your feet and your father will drink the water." His parents are angry and give him to a merchant to kill. The merchant takes the lad away in his ship but does not kill him. They come to England, where the king's son and daughter are ill of a scurf. The lad explains that at the holy communion the prince and princess had thrown on the ground the consecrated bread which had been swallowed by a toad. The toad is caught and boiled and the

[1] L. Leger, *Contes populaires slaves*, No. xxxi. (from Afanasief).

[2] M. Toeppen, *Aberglauben aus Masuren*,[2] p. 150 *sqq.*

children are cured. The king gives the lad his daughter to wife and the kingdom to boot. He now goes to visit his parents, finds them very poor, and his prediction is fulfilled.

l. In a Basque version [1] a son hears a voice saying that his parents will one day be his servants. His parents are angry and give him to two servants to kill; the servants, however, let him go and bring back a dog's heart in token that they had killed the lad. The youth sets out for Rome, meets two men also bound thither, and they all go together They lodge for the night in a house, which turns out to be an abode of robbers. The young man is warned by a voice, and the three escape from the robbers. Next they come to a house where a girl is very ill; the young man cures her.[2] As the travellers approach Rome, all the bells begin to ring of themselves; so the lad is made Pope. His father and mother come to Rome to get pardon of their sin; the son recognizes and forgives them, and they die of joy.

m. In another Basque version [3] a ship-captain asks his son what he has learned at school. The son says that he has learned to understand the songs of birds. His father takes him on a voyage. A bird perches on the ship and sings. The father asks what the bird says. The son answers: "He sings that I am now under your orders, but you shall also be under mine." The captain puts his son into a barrel and flings it into the sea. The barrel is cast up on a shore, the boy is taken out and marries the daughter of the king of that country. One day the boy's father is caught in a storm and driven on shore. He goes to the king, his son, but does not recognize him and becomes his son's servant. In time the son reveals himself and they live together happily.

n. In a Teleut version [4] a man sends his son to school. When the boy's schooling is over, his father fetches him home. On their way home they hear birds singing and the father asks his son what they are saying. The son says:

[1] Wentworth Webster, *Basque Legends*, p. 137 *sqq.*
[2] The Basque narrator forgot how the cure was effected. From a comparison of the Norman, Breton (Sébillot), Italian, and Masurian versions, we may conjecture that the girl had dropped the communion bread which had been swallowed by a toad, and that the cure was effected by recovering the bread from the toad.
[3] W. Webster, *Basque Legends*, p. 136 *sq.*
[4] W. Radloff, *Proben der Volkslitteratur der türkischen Stämme Süd-Sibiriens*, i. p. 208 *sqq.*

" If I tell you, you will be angry." But his father bids him speak out, so he says : " The birds said that I shall be emperor one day and that you will come to my castle and suffer a great indignity." His father is angry and cuts off his son's head ; also he cuts off his horse's head, wraps his son's body in the horse's hide, and throws it into the sea. The body is cast ashore ; an old woman finds it, opens the hide, and the youth comes forth alive. The king of this land is dead and has left no son. Two golden posts with a candle on the top of each are set up in the village, and everyone has to jump between them. He is to be king upon whom the two candles fall. They fall upon the youth *and take fire*,[1] so he is made king. The father comes to his son's palace and suffers the indignity his son had foretold. The son reveals himself and treats his father and mother well.

The king's decision between the ravens in *g*, *h*, *i*, occurs in a modern Indian folk-tale. Considering that this incident occurs in the *Seven Wise Masters* and in a modern Indian tale, it is remarkable that it does not appear to occur in Sindibad,[2] the oriental original of the *Seven Wise Masters*. The Indian story is as follows : Three birds came day after day to a court of justice. The Raja asked his minister what this meant. " I haven't the slightest idea," said the prime minister. " If you don't know by to-morrow," said the Raja, " I will cut off your head." The minister learned the

[1] Thus the test is the same as in the two Breton versions of " The Boy who became Pope ". The same test (candle lighting of itself) occurs in a Russian tale (Gubernatis, *Zoological Mythology*, i. p. 318). In a Swahili tale a young slave comes to a city where the sultan has just died and a new sultan is about to be elected. " They used to throw a lime, and whoever it struck three times, he was the sultan." The lime falls on the slave three times, so he is made sultan (E. Steere, *Swahili Tales*, pp. 141, 143). Dr. Krapf was told by a priest of Gurague that in the Kingdom of Senjero (south of Abyssinia) it was the custom after the death of a king " for the chief men of the kingdom to assemble outside the city, in an open field, and

wait till a vulture or an insect settled on one of the assembly ; and he to whom this happened was unanimously elected king " (J. L. Krapf, *Travels, Researches and Missionary Labours during an Eighteen Years' Residence in Eastern Africa*, p. 68). This statement, however, was contradicted by another witness whom Dr. Krapf questioned.

[2] At least I have not found it in the Greek (*Fabulae Romanenses*, ed. A. Eberhard, 1872), the Syriac (as translated by F. Baethgen, *Sindban, oder die Sieben weisen Meister, syrisch und deutsch*, 1879), nor the Arabic (as represented by the old Spanish translation appended to Comparetti's *Researches respecting the book of Sindibad*, translated for the Folk-lore Society, London, 1882).

secret from his gardener, who was a fool but understood the
bird language and had heard the dispute between the birds.
The hen-bird had seen her mate walking with another hen
and, suspecting him of bigamy, said : " Let her alone."
The cock declined to do so, and they had gone to law. The
Raja decided in favour of monogamy by holding up one
finger ; so the second hen flew away, and the old couple
departed together.[1]

So in a Kirghiz story a Khan orders his vizier under pain
of death to tell him what three geese have just said ; the vizier
cannot, but is saved by the Khan's daughter, who knows the
goose language.[2]

In the *Pentamerone* there is a story which begins somewhat like " The boy who became Pope ". A man has five
simple sons, whom he sends into the world to brighten their
wits. They come back, each with an accomplishment ; the
youngest understands the language of birds.[3]

In most stories, a knowledge of the beast language stands
its possessor in good stead. In a Kalmuck tale two dragon-
frogs dam up the source of a river and only allow it to flow
on condition of receiving annually a human victim. The
fatal lot having fallen on the Khan, his son takes his place
and goes with his devoted friend as a sacrifice to the frogs.
But the prince understands the language of all creatures and
hears the frogs saying to each other : " If they were only to
knock our heads off with a stick, and if the prince were to
eat me, the golden-yellow frog, and his friend were to eat
you, the emerald-green frog, they would spit nothing but
gold and gems, and there would be no need of victims to the
frogs hereafter." The prince takes the hint, and the result
answers to the prediction.[4] This story of the release of the
water seems to be another form of that myth of the slaying
of the frog who had swallowed the waters which Mr. Andrew
Lang has traced in North America, Australia, and the

---

[1] *Indian Antiquary*, iii. p. 320 *sq.*

[2] W. Radloff, *Proben, etc.*, iii. p. 347
sqq.

[3] Basile, *Pentamerone*, v. 7 (vol. ii.
p. 212 *sq.* Liebrecht's German translation).

[4] B. Jülg, *Kalmükische Märchen*,

die *Siddhi-Kür*, No. ii. (p. 10 *sq.*) ;
Sagas from the Far East (London,
1873), p. 18 *sqq.* In the latter version
serpents take the place of *frogs*. Jülg
translates *Drachenfrösche* in the first
instance and then *Frosch* and *Frösche*
always.

Andaman Islands.[1]   Again, in an Indian story a knowledge of the language of animals, which he has learned from the goddess Kali, saves a prince from a great crime which he was about unconsciously to commit.[2]   In other Indian stories heroes woo princesses on the strength of their knowledge of the animal language.[3]   A Zulu who understood the language of birds was able to predict the nature of the seasons through information received from a wagtail.[4]   In an old English version of the *Gesta Romanorum* three knights are sent by the Emperor Ancelmus to take a castle.   One of the knights, " a grete gever of counseille ", understands the " passing swete sonet-song " of a nightingale, which warns him that thieves are lying in wait in the wood.[5]   In a Tibetan story, " Oxen as Witnesses ", a ploughman is done a very good turn by the oxen with which he ploughs ; but it is not quite clear whether the language in which they address him is human or bovine.[6]

Sometimes, however, this gift of tongues proves dangerous or even fatal to its possessor.   A friend of Porphyry's had a slave-boy who knew the language of all birds ; but his mother, fearing lest the youthful prodigy should be sent as a present to the emperor, fouled his ears, and he never understood the bird speech again.[7]   In an Esthonian story a youth, craving after knowledge, learns the bird speech and

[1] A. Lang, *Myth, Ritual, and Religion*, i. p. 39 *sqq.* A tribe of Indians on the Orinoco is said to have kept frogs under vessels for the purpose of obtaining from them rain or fine weather, as occasion required ; if their prayers were not answered, they beat the frogs.   See *Colombia, being a geographical, etc., account of that country* (London, 1822), vol. i. p. 642 *sq.*

[2] *The Dravidian Nights Entertainments : being a translation of Madanakamarajankadai* ; by Pandit S. M. Natesi Sastri (Madras, 1886), p. 50 *sq.*

[3] *The Katha Sarit Ságara*, translated from the original Sanskrit by C. H. Tawney, i. p. 499 ; ii. p. 276.

[4] H. Callaway, *Nursery Tales of the Zulus*, p. 130 *sqq.*

[5] *Gesta Romanorum, Old English Versions*, edited by Sir Frederic Madden (London, 1838), p. 47 (p. 55 of Herrtage's edition, London, 1879).   The corresponding story in the continental Latin version of the *Gesta Romanorum* is No. 130 (p. 484 ed. Oesterley), but it does not contain the incident of the nightingale.

[6] *Tibetan Tales*, Schiefner and Ralston, No. xxx.   On p. 317 it is said that not long after the creation of the world " even brute beasts could speak ", which makes for human language ; but on p. 318 it is said that the oxen could not speak the language of men.

[7] Porphyry, *De abst.* iii. 3 καθεύδοντος εἰς τὰ ὦτα ἐνουρησάσης.   Compare the way in which swallows are thought to cause blindness (Basile's *Pentamerone* (Liebrecht), i. p. 403, ii. p. 59).

other strange lore ; but all his knowledge proves unsatisfying, and he pines away.[1] In a folk-tale of Bengal a woman enjoys " the rare faculty of understanding the language of beasts ", whereby she finds great treasure ; but neither her husband nor anyone else knows of her accomplishment, so she incurs the suspicion of being a Rakshasi, or vampire, and is knocked on the head.[2] In a Mongolian story a king sends his son to the Diamond Kingdom of Central India to be educated. The youth is accompanied by the minister's son. On their return from the Diamond Kingdom they pass through a thirsty desert, where the prince, understanding the voice of a crow, finds water. The minister's son, jealous of the prince's superior wisdom, kills him.[3]

Thus far we have had examples of the possession of the animal language. We have now to see the ways in which a knowledge of that language is acquired. Of course when a person has animal blood in him, as often happens in folk-lore, it is natural enough that he should understand the language of his kindred. Thus a child found in a wolf's den and said to be a wolf-child understands the wolves when they howl ; [4] and a Russian epic hero, whose father was a serpent, under- stands the language of birds, beasts, and fishes.[5] But the usual means of acquiring the animal language are (*a*) magic rings, (*b*) magic plants, and (*c*) serpents.

(*a*) In " the story of Cambuscan bold ", besides the present of " the wondrous horse of brass " for Cambuscan, the king of Araby and Inde sends to Canace a magic mirror and ring.

> " *The vertu of the ryng, if ye wol heere,*
> *Is this, that if hire lust it for to were*
> *Upon hir thomb, or in hir purs to bere,*
> *Ther is no fowel that fleeth under the hevene,*
> *That she ne shal wel understonde his stevene,*
> *And knowe his menyng openly and pleyn,*
> *And answere hym in his langage ageyn ;*

[1] Fr. Kreutzwald, *Ehstnische Mähr-chen, aus dem Ehstnischen übersetzt von* F. Löwe (Halle, 1869), p. 25 *sqq.*
[2] Lal Behari Day, *Folk-tales of Bengal,* No. x.
[3] B. Jülg, *Siddhi-Kür* (Innsbruck, 1868), No. xv. ; *Sagas from the Far East,* p. 157 *sqq.* ; X. Marmier, *Contes populaires de différentes pays,* 2ème Série, p. 252 *sqq.*
[4] *Sagas from the Far East* (London, 1873), p. 277 *sq.*
[5] A. Rambaud, *La Russie épique,* p. 31.

And every gras that groweth upon roote
She shal eek knowe, and whom it wol do boote,
Al be hise woundes never so depe and wyde." [1]

In a German story [2] a prince comes to a castle where all
the people are fast asleep. In a hall of the castle he finds a
table, and on the table a golden ring. A silver inscription
on the table declares that whoever puts the ring in his mouth
will understand the language of birds. Afterwards the prince
puts the ring in his mouth and thus, by understanding what
three crows are saying, he is saved from death and recovers
his eyesight.

(*b*) A Swabian legend says that three witches of Heiligen-
thal culled simples in the woods and fields, and one of these
simples imparted a knowledge of the language of animals.[3]
In an Italian story a man, plucking some grass at random,
suddenly finds that he understands what the birds are saying.
He hears one of them tell where a treasure is to be found.
He then drops the grass and immediately ceases to understand the birds ; he looks for the grass but never finds it
again. However, he finds the treasure in the place described
by the bird.[4] In an Esthonian story a girl has learned in her
youth the language of birds from an old woman, and her
eldest sister imparts a knowledge of the bird language to a
prince by giving him to eat a cake composed of meal, pork,
and certain herbs, the magic virtue residing in the herbs.[5]
In Brittany there is a plant called the golden herb (*herbe d' or*)
because it shines from afar like gold. If anyone happens to
tread on it, he at once falls asleep and understands the
language of birds, dogs, wolves, and so on. The plant is
seldom found and never but at the peep of dawn ; it can be
gathered only by holy people and with certain mystic rites.[6]

But the plant which is most commonly supposed to impart

[1] Chaucer, *Squier's Tale*, vv. 146-155.
[2] J. W. Wolf, *Deutsche Haus-märchen* (Göttingen and Leipzig, 1851), p. 148 *sqq.*
[3] A. Birlinger, *Volksthümliches aus Schwaben*, i. p. 1.
[4] Morlini, *Novellae*, No. 60.
[5] Fr. Kreutzwald, *Ehstnische Mähr-chen* (Halle, 1869), pp. i, 7, 14 *sq.* Gubernatis (*Zoological Mythology*, i. p. 152) wrongly attributes the magic influence to the pork. The words are plain : " *Mein Schweinefleischkuchen von Gestern . . . war mit Zauber-kräutern gefüllt, welche euch in den Stand setzen, Alles zu verstehen, was die klugen Vögel unter einander reden."*
[6] Laisnel de la Salle, *Croyances et légendes du centre de la France*, i. p. 233, quoting Villemarqué, *Barzaz-Breiz*, i. pp. 102, 187.

a knowledge of the language of animals is the fern.   In a German story [1] a cowherd lost his cows, and as he trudged through the grass in search of them, his great shoes (such as people wore long ago) got filled with fern seed.[2] Suddenly he heard the calf saying that a certain ale-house would sink into the ground.   The dog asked, " How long will it last ? " and the cock answered, "Till the end of the week " But the cowherd shook the fern seed out of his shoes and heard no more.   And in a week's time down sank the ale-house into an abyss.   Similar stories are told by the South Slavonians and the Wends.   In the South Slavonian version [3] a cowherd lost two of his oxen on the Eve of St. John (Midsummer Eve), which is the only time when fern seed possesses this magic power.   At last he espied his oxen lying on a bed of fern. Approaching them softly he was surprised to hear the older ox telling the younger ox that he (the elder ox) would be killed in the autumn, and that in the spring their master would be attacked by a snake, and could only be saved by the cowherd.   All came to pass as the ox had foretold, but the cowherd never knew how just at that moment he had understood the ox language.   The reason was that fern seed had fallen into his shoe without his noticing it ; for if he had seen it, he certainly would not have understood what the oxen said.   In the Wend story [4] a man was herding horses, and the bloom of the fern, which blooms only at midnight, fell into his shoe.   Next morning when he came home he told his friends what the geese had been talking about. This was noised abroad, and the squire sent for him.   To smarten himself up he took off his shoes and put on better ones, and from that moment he knew nothing of the goose language.

[1] A. Kuhn, *Märkische Sagen und Märchen*, p. 61.

[2] *Reenefare*, which (the story being given in the original dialect) Kuhn explains to be *Rainfarren*, which again Lucas in his German dictionary explains to be " common tansy ".   But Kuhn and Schwartz (*Norddeutsche Sagen, Märchen und Gebräuche*, p. 487), referring to this same story, speak of the plant in question as *Farnsame, i.e.* fern seed.   I therefore take it so in the text.   The word *Peer* which I translate " cow " seems to = *fersa*, "cow".   See G. Curtius, *Griech. Etymol.*[5] p. 282.   For in the dialect in which the story is written, " p " repeatedly takes the place of " f "; *e.g. eloopen = gelaufen, deepe = tiefe.*

[3] F. S. Krauss, *Sagen und Märchen der Südslaven*, ii. No. 159.

[4] W. von Schulenburg, *Wendische Volkssagen und Gebräuche* (Leipzig, 1880), p. 82, compare p. 269.

Of the many other mystic properties of the fern,[1] there is only one which it is desirable to mention in connexion with the language of animals. Fern seed or fern bloom is supposed to render the person who carries it invisible ; but it is found only on Midsummer Eve, when it shines like burnished gold, but quickly fades and falls, not to be found again.[2] The stories told of the invisibility conferred by fern seed resemble those told of its power of revealing the language of animals. A man was looking for a strayed foal on Midsummer Eve ; and as he went through a meadow, fern seed fell into his shoes. In the morning he came home and sat down in the parlour. But it seemed strange that neither his wife nor anybody else paid any heed to him. Then he said, " I did not find the foal after all." Everyone in the room shuddered visibly, for they heard the man's voice but did not see him. His wife shouted his name. He stood up in the middle of the room and said, " What are you shouting for ? Here I am close beside you." This only added to the general alarm. But now he felt something like sand in his shoes. Scarcely had he taken them off and shaken them, when he stood visible before the eyes of all.[3]

[1] Compare Grimm, *Deutsche Mytho-logie,*[4] p. 1012 ; Wuttke, *Der deutsche Volksaberglaube,*[2] §§ 123-125; Groh-mann, *Aberglauben und Gebräuche aus Böhmen und Mähren,* §§ 673-676; II. Friend, *Flowers and Flower Lore,*[3] pp. 60, 78, 279-283, 360-362 ; Guber-natis, *Mythologie des Plantes,* i. p. 188 *sq.,* ii. 143 *sqq.* ; Boecler-Kreutz-wald, *Der Ehsten abergläubische etc.,* pp. 2, 74, 87, 144 ; A. Kuhn, *Herabkunft des Feuers,*[2] pp. 192-197 ; I. V. Zingerle, *Sitten, Gebräuche, und Meinungen des Tiroler Volkes,*[2] §§ 882, 1573 ; Von Alpenburg, *Mythen und Sagen Tirols,* p. 407 *sq.* ; A. Bir-linger, *Volksthümliches aus Schwaben,* i. pp. 333 *sq.*, 340, ii. p. 103; E. Meier, *Deutsche Sagen, Sitten und Gebräuche aus Schwaben,* p. 243 *sq.* ; Ralston, *Songs of the Russian People,* p. 98 *sq.* ; Reinsberg-Düringsfeld, *Fest-Kalender aus Böhmen,* p. 311 *sq.*

[2] A. Wuttke, *op. cit.* § 123 ; F. J. Vonbun, *Beiträge zur deutschen Mythologie,* p. 133 *sq.* ; H. Friend, *op.*

cit. p. 362 ; A. de Gubernatis, *Myth. des Plantes,* ii. 144 *sq.* ; A. Kuhn, *Herab-kunft des Feuers,*[2] p. 196 ; Grohmann, *Aberglauben und Gebräuche aus Böh-men und Mähren,* § 675.

[3] Grimm, *D.M.* p. 1012 ; A. Kuhn, *Sagen, Gebräuche und Märchen aus Westfalen,* i. p. 276; L. Bechstein, *Thüringer Sagenbuch,*[2] No. 67. For a different story to the same effect, see A. Kuhn, *Märkische Sagen und Märchen,* p. 206 *sq.* (a peasant, driving off his wife, gets down ; fern seed falls into his shoes, he becomes invisible, and sits invisible beside his wife in the waggon ; on taking off his shoes he reappears). Again similar stories are told of how fern seed gives a knowledge of hidden treasure. In an Austrian story a man is looking for his lost cow on Mid-summer Eve ; fern seed falls into his shoes ; the existence of an under-ground treasure is revealed to him ; he hurries home to get tools with which to dig it up ; takes off his

(*c*) But most commonly it is a serpent which conveys a
knowledge of the language of animals. The ways in which
it does so are various. The application of the magic influence
may be external or internal, and the external application may
be made either to the ears or to the mouth. Applied to the
ears, the charm seems meant to impart the power of *understanding* the speech of animals ; applied to the *mouth*, it may
give the additional power of *speaking* the animal language.
But this distinction is not perhaps to be pressed.

We begin with the application of serpents to the ears.
The way in which the Greek soothsayer Melampus became
master of his art was, according to Apollodorus,[1] as follows.
He was staying in the country, and in front of the house was
an oak-tree, in which serpents had made their lair. The
servants killed the old serpents and Melampus gathered
sticks and burned their carcasses. But the young serpents
he reared. And when they were grown, one day as he slept,
they crept on his shoulders and cleansed his ears with their
tongue. He started up in a fright, and lo ! he understood
the voices of the birds as they flew overhead, and by what
he learned from them he was able to foretell events. But it
was not the birds only that he understood. For once being
caught cattle-lifting he was laid by the heels by Bias, the
owner of the cattle ; and as he lay in durance vile he heard
the worms in the roof talking to one another. One worm
said, " How much of the beam have we eaten through ? "
and the other said, " Oh ! there is only a little bit left." So
he warned Bias that the house was coming down, and scarcely
had they cleared out when sure enough down it came.[2]

The account given by the scholiast on Apollonius Rhodius[3]
of the way in which Melampus learned the language of
animals is fuller than that of Apollodorus ; and from it we

shoes, and forgets where the treasure
is (Vernaleken, *Mythen und Bräuche
des Völkes in Österreich*, p. 310).
There are similar Russian stories. In
one of them it is the man's wife, who,
seeing that his feet are wet, tells him
to change his stockings ; he does so,
with the result as before. In another,
it is the devil who persuades the man
to change shoes with him (Guber-

natis, *Mythologie des Plantes*, i. p.
189 ; Compare M. Toeppen, *Aberglaube aus Masuren*,[2] p. 72 *sq.*).

[1] Apollodorus, *Bibliotheca*, i. 9. 11 ;
Pliny, *Nat. Hist.* x. 137.

[2] Apollodorus, i. 9. 12.

[3] Scholiast on Apollonius Rhodius,
Argonautica, I. 118, vol. ii. p. 7, ed.
A. Wellauer (Leipzig, 1828).

learn that when the serpents were killed, Melampus was not in his own house but was staying with a friend, and that the killing of the serpents (or serpent) was the doing of his friend and not of Melampus, who, on the other hand, piously burned the serpent's body and reared its young. Thus the burning of the serpents in Apollodorus must have been, not a mark of contempt, but a solemn funeral rite ; and so the benefit which the young snakes afterwards conferred on Melampus may have been meant as a return quite as much for the respect he had shown to their parents as for the lives they themselves owed to him. Helenus and Cassandra acquired their prophetic power in like manner. As children they were left overnight in the temple of Apollo, and in the morning serpents were found licking their ears.[1] Porphyry says that perhaps we and all men might understand the language of all the animals if a serpent had washed our ears.[2] Tiresias received a knowledge of the language of birds from Athene, who cleansed his ears ;[3] and when we remember how closely Athene was associated with the serpent,[4] we can hardly be rash in including Tiresias among the serpent-taught seers, or rather hearers. The sacred snakes in the temple of Athene[5] may very well have done for Tiresias what the snakes did for Helenus and Cassandra in the temple of Apollo. This application of serpents to the ears seems to be exclusively classical ; at least I have found no example of it outside of Greek and Latin literature.[6] The reason why soothsayers are supposed to be specially acquainted with the language of birds is that omens are very commonly taken

---

[1] Schol. on Euripides, *Hecuba*, 86; Schol. on Homer, *Iliad*, vii. 44 ; Tzetzes, *Schol. in Lycophr.* i. p. 266 *sq.*, ed. Müller. It is implied in these passages that there were serpents in the temple of Apollo. For another example of sacred snakes in a sanctuary of Apollo, see Aelian, *De natura animalium*, xi. 2. The soothsayer Iamus was a son of Apollo and in his youth two snakes fed him with honey (Pindar, *Olymp.* vi. 45).

[2] Porphyry, *De abst.* iii. 4.

[3] Apollodorus, iii. 6. 7.

[4] See J. C. F. Baehr on Herodotus, vii. 41.

[5] Besides Baehr, *loc. cit.*, see K. Bötticher, *Die Tektonik der Hellenen*,[3] p. 389.

[6] At Woburn Abbey there is a Greek marble relief representing two ears with a serpent at each, the head of each serpent resting just above the top of each ear. The inscription is mutilated, the only word to be made out with certainty being ΕΥΧΑΡΙΣΤΗΡΙΟΝ. The tablet is probably a thank-offering for the cure of some defect of the ears. See *Archäologische Zeitung*, 1864, plate facing p. 211.

from birds. In Greek, Arabic, and Dyak the words for
" bird " are used in the sense of " omen ".[1]
    The *mouth* as the point of application of the serpent-
charm appears in a Slavonian story,[2] which runs thus. A
shepherd tending his flock heard a hissing, and perceived a
serpent in the midst of flames. He saved the serpent from
the fire, and the grateful snake led him to the abode of his [3]
father, who was king of the serpents. On the way the rescued
snake said to the shepherd, " My father will offer you silver,
gold, and gems. But don't take them. Ask only to understand
the language of animals. He will make a pother about giving
it, but in the end you will get it." But when the shepherd
asked the king of the serpents for the animal language, the
king said, " That is not for you ; if I give you it and you
tell anyone, you will die on the spot." But the shepherd
persisted, so the king spat thrice into the shepherd's mouth [4]
and the shepherd spat thrice into the king's mouth. Thus
the shepherd received the language of animals,[5] and as he

---

[1] Aristophanes, *Birds*, 720; J. Wellhausen, *Reste arabischen Heidentumes*,
p. 148 ; *Journal of the Straits Branch
of the Royal Asiatic Society*, No. 10,
p. 229.

[2] W. S. Karadschitsch, *Völks-
märchen der Serben* (Berlin, 1854),
No. 3, pp. 17 *sqq.*; *Serbian Folk-tales*,
selected and translated by Madam
Csedomille Mijatovich, edited by the
Rev. W. Denton (London, 1874), pp.
37 *sqq.*; L. Leger, *Contes populaires
slaves* (Paris, 1882), No. xi.; F. S.
Krauss, *Sagen und Märchen der
Südslaven* (Leipzig, 1883), i. No. 97.

[3] Or *her* ; the rescued snake is male
in the versions of Krauss and Leger,
female in that of Karadschitsch.

[4] In the Banks' Islands (Melanesia)
serpents are said to put their tongues
into the mouths of men who are their
familiars (*Journal of the Anthropological Institute*, x. p. 277). To spit
upon the idol's tongue is a mode of
salutation in West Africa (A. Bastian,
*Die deutsche Expedition an der
Loango-Küste*, i. p. 90).

[5] With the opening of this Slavonian
story compare the following. In a
Swahili tale a woman befriends a

snake, who in return takes her to its
parents, with whom she lives many
days. When she is coming away, the
snake whom she befriended warns her
to accept no present from the snake-
parents save the father's ring and the
mother's casket. The snake-parents
offer her wealth, but she persists in
asking for the ring and casket. The
snake-parents are very sorry and give
her the ring and casket unwillingly.
The ring has the magic virtue of
supplying clothes, food, and a house
at discretion ; the virtues of the
casket are not specified (E. Steere,
Swahili Tales, London, 1870, p. 403
sqq.). In a Tarantschi - Tartar story
a young man saves a serpent from
death. The serpent takes his benefactor to his father, the serpent-king,
and advises the young man to ask for
the serpent-king's ring. The serpent-
king in gratitude for the kindness
done to his son offers the man gold
and silver, but he refuses and asks for
the serpent-king's ring. The king is
very sorry and tries to persuade the
young man to take anything but the
ring ; at last, however, he gives it.
The ring is a wishing-ring ; whatever

went back he understood the voices of the birds, the grasses, and indeed, of everything in the world. Hearing two ravens describing a buried treasure he dug it up, became a rich man, and married a wife. Once on a time he went on a journey with his wife. He rode a horse and she rode a mare, and the mare fell behind the horse. The horse called out to the mare, " Step out faster. How you lag behind ! " But the mare answered, " It is easy for you, since you only carry one ; but I carry three, for my mistress is pregnant and so am I." The man understanding this conversation laughed. His wife asked him why he laughed, but he refused to tell her, saying that it would cost him his life to do so. But she persisted. So when they were come home, wearied with her importunity, he ordered his coffin and lay down in it, ready, as soon as the fatal words had passed his lips, to give up the ghost. Seeing his dog sitting beside the coffin, he called to his wife to throw the dog a bit of bread. The faithful dog would not look at it, but the cock came and picked at it. " Oh, you brute ! " said the dog to the cock, " to be guzzling like that when you see your master is dying." " Let him die," said the cock, " the fool ! *I* have a hundred wives and yet by a judicious system of punishment I keep them all in the most exact order ; *he* has but one and he can't make her hold her tongue." At these words the man stepped out of his coffin, took a stick, and beating his wife black and blue prevailed on her to stop.

This tale may be traced, with variations of detail, right across the old world from Italy and Finland on the one side to Annam on the other.

An Indian version of it is quoted by Adolf Bastian [1] from the *Nonthuk pakarana*, a Siamese version or imitation of the *Panchatantra*.[2] A king saves the daughter of a Naga prince

the owner of it desires, he gets (W. Radloff, *Proben der Volks-litteratur der nördlichen türkischen Stämme*, vi. p. 172 *sqq.*). In an Indian story, a young man treats a serpent kindly ; the rest follows as before, the serpent-king remarking as he gives the ring, " This ring I would not have given even to Indra if he had requested this of me" (*The Dravidian Nights Entertainments*, by

Pandit S. M. Natesi Sastri, pp. 23-27).
[1] *Zeitschrift für Ethnologie*, i. p. 152.
[2] Adolf Bastian, in *Orient und Occident*, vol. iii. (1865), p. 171 ; J. Hertel, *Das Pañcatantra* (Leipzig, 1914), p. 338. I have to thank my learned friend Professor Sylvain Lévi of the Collège de France for enabling me to identify the *Nonthuk pakarana*, which I could not do when this essay

from marrying beneath her rank ; and in gratitude the Naga prince teaches the king the language of animals. His wife asks him why he laughed, and he gives himself up for lost, till he learns a lesson from the billy-goat and his treatment of his goat-wives. In this version the Naga prince answers to the king of serpents in the Slavonian version, for the Nagas were mythical beings, half human, half serpentine in form ; indeed, Naga often stands for a common serpent.[1]

We next meet the story in the *Arabian Nights*.[2] There was a certain merchant, whom God endowed with a knowledge of the language of beasts and birds. He dwelt in the country, and in his house were an ass and a bull. Now the ass had little to do and fared sumptuously, but the bull toiled at ploughing. So when the bull bewailed his hard fate, the ass told him to feign sickness and then he would be allowed to stay at home in peace. But the merchant hearkened to these words and laid them up in his heart. And next day when the bull flopped down under the weight of the plough as though he were weak and ill, the merchant commanded and they took the ass and put him to the plough, and he drew it up and down all day long till the evening. And the next day he did likewise, and his neck was galled and raw, and he himself was reduced to an extreme state of weakness. When he came back in the evening, the bull thanked and praised him for his noble conduct. But the ass said, " Know that I am one who would give thee good advice. I heard our master say, ' If the bull rise not from his place, take him to the butcher that he may kill him.' I am therefore in fear for thee, and so I have given thee good advice, and peace be on thee." So next day when

was originally published in 1888. This Siamese collection contains between eighty and ninety stories, which seem to be translated from the Sanscrit. It takes its name from the wise ox Nonthuk which plays the chief part in the longest of the tales. The stories are woven into each other in the style of the *Panchatantra* and the *Arabian Nights*. They are put into the mouth of the princess Kankra, who entertains the King of Pataliput (Palibothra) with her story-telling in

order to save her father's life. See A. Bastian, *loc. cit.* A selection from the stories is given by Bastian in a German translation (*Orient und Occident*, iii. 479-498), but it does not include the tale about the language of animals.

[1] Monier Williams, *Religious Life and Thought in India*, p. 321 *sq.* Of course the mythical Nagas are to be distinguished from the tribes of the same name in Assam.

[2] Lane's translation, vol. i. p. 10 *sqq.* (ed. 1859).

his driver came, the bull pranced and shook his tail and
bounded about ; and the merchant beheld him and laughed
till he fell backward. Then his wife asked him why he
laughed. But he said, " Ask me not, for if I tell thee I must
surely die." But she urged him. So he sent for the kadi
that he might make his will. And he went into the stable
that he might perform his ablution before he died. There
he heard the dog reviling the cock and saying, " Art thou
happy when our master is going to die ? " But the cock
replied, " By Allah ! our master has little sense. *I* have fifty
wives ; and I please this one and provoke that ; while *he*
has but one wife and cannot manage her ; why does he not
take some twigs of the mulberry-tree and beat her till she dies
or repents ? " And the merchant did so and beat her till
she repented, and they lived together in the happiest manner
till death.

In Europe the story seems to appear first in the Latin
Novellae of Morlini, published at Naples in 1520, and reprinted by Jannet at Paris in 1855. In this Neopolitan
version[1] a man is leading his wife on a she-ass, and the
ass's foal follows lagging behind. The foal remonstrates
with its mother for going so fast, and the mother answers
much as the mare answers in the Slavonian tale. The husband who understands the speech of reptiles and quad-
rupeds (it is not said how he learned it) laughs on hearing
this conversation, and the rest follows as in the Arabian and
Slavonian stories. A few touches of local colour are put in
" to give artistic verisimilitude to a bald and unconvincing
narrative " ; thus a confessor is substituted for the kadi, and
the cock's speech is embellished with a quotation from the
Politics of Aristotle.

The story, translated from Morlini, next appears in the
second part of the Italian tales (*Piacevoli Notti*) of Straparola,
published at Venice in 1554.[2]

The Slavonian version, first published in the original by
Karadschitsch in 1852, has been already given.

[1] No. lxxi., *De Puteolano qui animalium loquelam intelligebat.*

[2] The French translation of Strapa-rola by Louveau and Larivey has been often reprinted. I have used the edition of 1857. See *Les Nuits facé-tieuses de Straparola*, traduites par J. Louveau et P. Larivey (Paris, 1857), vol. ii. pp. 326-329.

The Annamite version, differing considerably from all the foregoing, was published in 1885.[1] A man once saw two serpents in their hole. The female was casting her slough, and the male waited on her. Another time it was the male that was casting his slough ; but instead of looking after him the female went gadding about. Indignant at her misconduct the man shot her. The male serpent discovered her slayer by the arrow, and lay in wait to kill him. But the man happened to tell his wife what he had seen ; the serpent, listening in the background, recognized the justice of the man's conduct, and out of gratitude brought him his precious stone. All serpents have such a stone in their mouths, and whoever possesses it understands the language of animals. But the man durst not tell his wife of the new gift he had acquired, for if he did so the stone would vanish. One day his wife went into a corner of the house where there were some ants. The ants scrambled out of her way, and the man heard them say to each other, "Come, let us climb up to a place of safety." He laughed. His wife wished to know why he laughed, but he steadily refused to tell her, and she died of vexation.

The Tarantschi-Tartar version was published in 1886.[2] A man learns the animal speech from a man who knows the languages of all animals, and who warns his pupil that if he divulges the secret he must die. Thus warned, the man hears the dog and cat talking, and laughs, and when his wife plagues him with asking why he laughed, he beats her and she stops asking. But one day he hears the ass and the oxen talking, as in the *Arabian Nights* version ; the ass advises the oxen, who have been ploughing, to feign sickness ; one of the oxen does so ; the ass is put to the plough in his stead, and after ploughing tells the ox that their master will kill him if he continues to feign illness. Hearing this the man laughs ; his wife asks him why. In vain he tells the fatal consequences of answering her question. She persists ; so he tells her and dies.

Lastly, the Finnish version appeared, in a German transla-

[1] No. lxix. of A. Landes' "Contes et légendes annamites", in *Cochin-chine française: Excursions et Reconnaissances*, x. No. 23 (Saigon, 1885), pp. 68-69, " Le langage des animaux ".

[2] W. Radloff, *Proben der Volkslitteratur der nördlichen türkischen Stämme*, vi. p. 250 *sqq.* (St. Petersburg, 1886).

tion, in 1887.[1] A hunter saves a serpent from being burned in a stove, and the serpent out of gratitude teaches the hunter the language of birds, animals, plants, and trees ; but warns him that if he reveals the secret he must die. From hearing the fir-trees talk he finds a great treasure, becomes rich, and marries. One day he hears a mother sparrow telling her young ones to pick the seeds from the plants and not from the ground. At this he laughs ; his wife pesters him to tell her why ; he lies down to die, but hearing the cock making the usual speech (in this case not addressed to a dog but delivered as a soliloquy) about his fifty wives, he jumps up and makes a grab at his wife's head. She escapes, but troubles him no more with questions.

In a Russian story[2] a hunter saves a serpent from burning and receives from him the animal language on condition of revealing it to no one under pain of death. In a French story a shepherd carries a strayed serpent, who is the king of animals, back to the " wood of the animals ", and receives the language of animals on the usual condition.[3]

So far the animal language has been the free gift of a living serpent. But oftener it is acquired by eating a part of a dead serpent. Democritus, as reported by Pliny, said that whoever ate a serpent would understand the language of birds.[4] Philostratus thought that the Arabs gained a knowledge of the bird language by eating the heart or liver of a serpent,[5] and he says that in the same way the people of Paraka in India understood the language of animals in general.[6] Miss Gordon Cumming has been informed that " to this day both Arabs and Hindoos eat the heart and liver of serpents, hoping thereby to acquire a knowledge of the language of animals ".[7] But perhaps her informant had Philostratus in his mind. So far as the Arabs are concerned, Prof. Wellhausen[8] seems to

[1] *Finnische Märchen*, übersetzt von Emmy Schreck (Weimar, 1887), No. 6, pp. 44 *sqq.*

[2] Gubernatis, *Zoological Mythology*, ii. p. 405.

[3] E. Rolland, *Faune populaire de la France*, iii. p. 40 *sq.*

[4] Pliny, *Nat. Hist.* x. 137, compare *id.* xxix. 72. See below, note on p. 126.

[5] Philostratus, *Vit. Apoll.* i. 20.

[6] *Ib.* iii. 9.

[7] Miss C. F. Gordon Cumming, *In the Hebrides* (London, 1883), p. 54.

[8] J. Wellhausen, *Reste arabischen Heidentumes* (Berlin, 1887), p. 147. Bochart (*Hierozoicon*, p. 22, ed. 1682) quotes an Arabic writer to the same effect, but the writer seems to have copied Philostratus.

know no later authority than Philostratus. It is a German
and Bohemian superstition that whoever eats serpent's flesh
understands the language of animals.[1] The Lithuanians say
that whoever boils a white serpent and eats it with the soup
becomes omniscient.[2] The Wends tell of a man who through
eating a white serpent understood what the birds said.[3] In
a Syrian story a dervish has drunk serpent-water ; hence
serpents cannot bite him, and he talks with both serpents and
birds in their respective languages.[4] In the *Edda* Sigurd
kills the dragon Fafnir and roasts his heart on a spit. Putting
his finger to it to see if it is roasted enough he burns his
finger and sticks it in his mouth. But the moment that
Fafnir's heart's blood touches his tongue he understands the
language of birds and knows what the eagles on the branches
are saying.[5] The same story occurs in the *Volsung Saga*,
except that nuthatches take the place of eagles.[6] Saxo
Grammaticus [7] tells how Rollo, peeping through a crevice,
saw his mother Craca preparing a peculiar dish. Three
snakes hung on a rope and the juices flowing from their
mouths furnished the sauce. Two of the snakes were black ;
the third was white. The white one hung a little higher
than the other two and was fastened by a knot in its tail,
whereas the black ones had a string running through them.
When his father Regnar and his stepbrother (Craca's son)
Eric came, they all sat down to table. Craca put before Eric
and Rollo a single dish containing the flesh of the black and
white snakes. The end of the platter containing the black
snakes was put next her own son Eric ; but Rollo happening
to taste the black snake, turned round the dish and ate the
black snake, leaving the white for his brother. From eating
the black snake, Rollo acquired universal knowledge, including an understanding of the speech of animals both wild

[1] A. Wuttke, *Der deutsche Volksaberglaube*,[2] § 153; Grohmann, *Aberglauben und Gebräuche aus Böhmen
und Mähren*, No. 1658.

[2] E. Veckenstedt, *Die Mythen,
Sagen und Legenden der Zamaiten*
(Heidelberg, 1883), ii. p. 166.

[3] W. von Schulenburg, *Wendische
Volkssagen und Gebräuche aus dem
Spreewald* (Leipzig, 1880), p 96.

[4] E. Prym und A. Socin, *Syrische
Sagen und Maerchen*, p. 150 *sq.*

[5] *Die Edda*, übersetzt von K. Simrock, pp. 180, 309.

[6] *Volsunga- und Ragnars-Saga*,
übersetzt von F. H. von der Hagen[2]
(Stuttgart, 1880), p. 63 *sq.*

[7] *Historia Danica*, bk. v. p. 193 *sq.*,
ed. P. E. Müller.

and tame, much to the disappointment of his stepmother Craca, who had intended the black snake for her own son Eric. The virtue here attributed by Saxo to a black snake is unique ; in all other cases, where the colour of the serpent is mentioned, it is a *white* snake whose flesh has this magic virtue.[1] In Norway, Sweden, and Jutland down to the nineteenth century the flesh of a *white* snake was supposed to confer supernatural wisdom.[2] We are almost led to conjecture that Saxo has interchanged the rôles of the black and white serpent ; [3] this conjecture is borne out by the precedence apparently given by Craca to the white serpent in the process of cooking, as described by Saxo.

There are a number of stories in which, as in Saxo, the magic serpent is eaten by a person for whom it was not intended. In a Breton story [4] a workman, lodging with an old dame who passed for a witch, one day brought her a snake which he had killed. She cooked it ready for eating, and when she was out of the house, the man ate a bit of it. Going out of the house he was surprised to find that he understood the language of the birds. He told the dame what had happened, she breathed into his mouth, and after that he ceased to understand the bird language. The way in which Michael Scott was supposed to have become a wizard is somewhat similar. Being attacked by a white serpent he killed it by dividing it into three pieces at a blow. The landlady of the house at which he stopped for the night, hearing of this, offered a reward for the middle piece of the white serpent. It was brought to her. In the night the landlady, thinking everyone was asleep, cooked the serpent and from time to time she dipped her finger in the saucepan, upon which the cock crew. But Michael Scott was watching her and out of curiosity he too dipped his finger in the sauce and applied it to the tip of his tongue. Immediately the

---

[1] Except in X. Marmier's *Contes populaires de différentes pays*, 2ème Série, p. 56, where the serpent is blue with a green head. But in Waldau's version (of which Marmier's version appears to be an amplification) there is no mention of the snake's colour (*Böhmisches Märchenbuch*, p. 13).

[2] P. E. Müller on Saxo Gram-maticus, vol. ii. p. 146.

[3] The only example I know of virtue attributed to a *black* snake is in the *Panchatantra* (ii. p. 359, Benfey), where the steam from a black snake boiling in a pot restores the sight of a blind man.

[4] P. Sébillot, *Traditions et superstitions de la Haute-Bretagne*, ii. p. 224.

cock crew and Michael Scott's mind " received a new light
to which he was formerly a stranger ", including a "knowledge
of ' good and evil ' and all the ' second sights ' that can be
acquired ".[1]

In a German story[2] a wise king eats of a white serpent
every day after dinner. His servant, out of curiosity, one
day tastes the white serpent and immediately understands
the language of animals. In a Bohemian tale[3] an old woman
brings a serpent to a king, telling him that if he ate it he
would understand the language of all animals. He does so,
but his servant, who has strict orders not to taste the serpent,
disobeys his orders, tastes, and at once his ears are opened
and he understands the language of animals. He betrays
his knowledge by laughing at a remark made by a horse ;
but the king promises to spare his life if he will bring him
the maiden with the golden hair. In a German legend of
the origin of the Seeburger lake near Göttingen it is said that
long ago there was a wicked lord whose servant once brought
to the castle a silver-white serpent instead of a fish. The lord,
who knew a little of the beast language, was pleased, for he
was aware that whoever ate of such a serpent would attain
to a complete mastery of that language. He ate his fill of
the white serpent, and his servant, against orders, tasted the
little that was left. Soon the wicked lord heard the birds
saying that the castle was doomed to immediate destruction.
He asks his servant what the cock is saying ; the servant in
his alarm betrays his knowledge of the bird language ; his
master cleaves his skull, and rides away. At sunset the
castle sinks into the ground, and where it stood there stretches
a broad water.[4] In another German story a girl who had
eaten of a serpent foretells, from hearing what a cock says,
that an ale-house will sink into the ground that very day and
be replaced by a deep water.[5]

[1] W. Grant Stewart, *The Popular
Superstitions and Festive Amusements
of the Highlanders of Scotland* (new
ed., London, 1851), pp. 53, 56.
[2] Grimm, *Kinder- und Hausmär-
chen*, No. 17.
[3] A. Waldau, *Böhmisches Märchenbuch*, p. 13 *sqq.* ; X. Marmier,

Contes populaires de différentes pays,
2ème Série, p. 55 *sqq.*
[4] Grimm, *Deutsche Sagen*,[2] No.
132.
[5] A. Kuhn und W. Schwartz, *Norddeutsche Sagen, Märchen und Gebräuche*, p. 154. Compare the German
story above, p. 108.

In the Tyrol there are stories [1] of a Doctor Theophrastus, a marvellous physician and a master of the black art, who with great difficulty caught a *Haselwurm, i.e.* a white serpent, the taste of which imparts a knowledge of the language of all creatures and so sharpens the eyes that they can see through rocks into the veins of gold and gems deep down in the earth. When at last Dr. Theophrastus has caught the white snake, he orders his servant to boil it and to be sure not to taste it. The servant tastes it and betrays his knowledge (as in the case of the husband and wife) by laughing at the talk of two magpies, whereupon his master kills him.[2] There is a very similar story in Bohemia.[3] In a Bavarian story the servant who is charged with cooking the wonder-working serpent changes it, eats it himself, and gives his master something else ; the servant understands the language of animals and plants, and is killed by his master.[4] In an Austrian story the servant who has tasted of the white serpent betrays himself by his knowledge of the goose language, but the story has not the usual tragic end.[5] In a Highland story a drover goes to England to sell cattle with a hazel staff in his hand. He meets a doctor who asks him to go and bring him a wand from the same hazel tree from which the drover got his staff.

---

[1] J. N. Von Alpenburg, *Mythen und Sagen Tirols*, p. 302 *sqq.* Doctor Theophrastus is probably Paracelsus, whose real name was Theophrastus Bombast von Hohenheim. A Swabian legend tells how *Theophrastus Paracelsus* got fern seed (E. Meier, *Deutsche Sagen, Sitten und Gebräuche aus Schwaben*, p. 244).

[2] In another version (von Alpenburg, *loc. cit.*) the servant betrays himself by his supernatural sight ; in another by his knowledge of the language of plants. In this last version the doctor and his servant come to a meadow, and as soon as the flowers and plants see the doctor they all begin to shout out the medical properties which they respectively possess. The servant laughs at a remark of a little red flower and is killed, as before. On this plant language, acquired by tasting of the *Haselwurm*, compare Alpenburg, *op. cit.* p. 378. In a Swahili tale a man

becomes a great physician by drinking the second skimming of the cooked body of the King of the Snakes. The nature of the knowledge which he thus acquired may be inferred from the medical knowledge possessed by the King of Snakes in his lifetime ; on a certain island when the trees saw the Snake-king they each declared what they were good for ; one said : " I am medicine for the head," another " I am medicine for the feet," etc. (E. Steere, *Swahili Tales*, pp. 345, 361). Thus the Swahili doctor has an exact parallel in Dr. Theophrastus, so far as a knowledge of simples goes.

[3] J. V. Grohmann, *Aberglauben und Gebräuche aus Böhmen und Mähren*, § 1658.

[4] Sepp, *Altbayerischer Sagenschatz* (Munich, 1876), p. 615 *sq.*

[5] A. Peter, *Volksthümliches aus Österreichisch-Schlesien*, ii. p. 33 *sq.*

Also he was to watch at the foot of the hazel tree till seven
serpents came out ; he was to let the six pass but the seventh
he was to put in a bottle and bring to the doctor. The drover
went and cut some boughs from the hazel tree. Then he
watched at the hole ; six brown and barred serpents came
out ; he let them pass ; last came a white snake, which he
bottled up and carried to the doctor. The two make a fire
with the hazel sticks and put the snake in a pot to boil. The
drover is ordered not to let the steam escape, so he wraps
paper round the pot lid. But steam begins to come out at
one place, so the drover, thinking to push the paper down,
puts his finger to the place, and then his finger to his mouth,
for it was wet with the bree ; and " lo ! he knew everything,
and the eyes of his mind were opened ". Presently the doctor
came back, lifted the lid, put his finger in the steam and
sucked it. But the virtue had gone out of it, and he saw
that the drover had tasted it.   " Since you have taken the
bree of it, take the flesh too," said he in a rage, and flung
the pot at him. So the drover was allwise and became a great
doctor.[1]

The idea that the magic serpent, whose flesh imparts a
knowledge of the language of animals and plants, is to be
found under a hazel tree occurs also in Germany,[2] where
indeed, as we have seen, the serpent is often called the

[1] J. F. Campbell, *Popular Tales of
the West Highlands*, ii. p. 361 *sqq.*
In Chambers' *Popular Rhymes of
Scotland*, p. 77 *sqq.*, a similar story
(but without the hazel) is told of Sir
James Ramsay of Bamff, how by sucking his fingers, which he had burned
in cooking a white serpent for his
master, he found that his eyes were
opened and he could see through
everything ; so he became a great
doctor because " he could clearly see
what was wrang in folk's insides ".
Again Gilleadha became a famous
doctor in much the same way (Campbell, *op. cit.* ii. p. 366). Again some
giants bade Fingal roast a fish for
them, threatening to kill him if he
burned it. Seeing that one small spot
was burning he put his finger on it
and then put his burned finger in his

mouth ; a gift of omniscience was the
result (*ib.* p. 362 *sq.*). From such cases
of wisdom acquired by sucking the
fingers, Liebrecht (*Gervasius von Tilbury*, p. 156) ingeniously proposed to
explain the Egyptian Harpocrates, who
was represented sitting on a lotus
flower with his finger in his mouth.
Compare Callaway, *Religious System
of the Amazulu*, pp. 290 note, 381.

[2] Sepp. *Altbayerischer Sagenschatz*,
p. 615; compare Kuhn, *Herabkunft des
Feuers*,[2] p. 201 *sq.* In the Tyrol, on
the contrary, it is said that snakes do
not lurk under hazel bushes (Zingerle,
*Sitten, Bräuche und Meinungen des
Tiroler Volkes*,[2] No. 886). In Sweden
it is thought that snakes lose their
poison by contact with a hazel (Kuhn,
op. cit. p. 202).

" hazel-worm " (*Haselwurm*). The coincidence is not merely a verbal one, for in Gaelic (from which the Highland story is translated) the hazel is *caltuinn*. With regard to the white serpent, Miss Gordon Cumming says that " it is believed by some of the old Highlanders still to exist in the land—a faith which is occasionally confirmed by the appearance of a silvery grey specimen ".[1]

Occasionally the animal language is acquired by a combination of serpent and plant, as indeed is, to some extent, the case when the serpent is to be found under the hazel. A Bohemian receipt for learning the language of geese is to cut off a serpent's head, split it, and put a pea in the split, then bury the head in the garden ; eat the first pod of the pea-plant which grows from the pea in the serpent's head, and you will understand the language of geese.[2] In a poem of the Lebed-Tartars a young man receives from a serpent's mouth a bit of a plant, which he puts in his mouth, and immediately understands the language of serpents, and he and the serpent talk to each other.[3]

The last mode of learning the animal language which we shall notice is peculiar, though the plot of the story is closely similar to the " husband and wife " story which we have traced across the old world. The story is a Tartar one, from the village of Säit.[4] An old beggar who takes no thought for the morrow throws daily into the sea the remains of his food, and upon the bread thus cast on the waters the fish grow fat. The thing comes to the ears of the lord of the fishes, who sends for the free-handed beggar to reward him. As the fish are conducting him through the sea to their lord, they say to him, " The king of fishes will offer you gold and silver ; do not take them, but say ' Let me kiss your tongue.' " The fish-king did as the fish had foretold. The beggar refuses the proffered wealth and asks only to kiss the king's tongue. The king, after expostulating, allows the beggar to do so, but warns him that by this means he will receive a knowledge of the language of all creatures, which he must reveal to no

[1] C. F. Gordon Cumming, *In the Hebrides*, p. 54.
[2] J. V. Grohmann, *Aberglauben und Gebräuche aus Böhmen und Mähren*, § 1414.
[3] W. Radloff, *Proben der Volks-litteratur der nördlichen türkischen Stämme Süd-Sibiriens*, i. p. 322.
[4] W. Radloff, *op. cit.* iv. p. 492 *sqq.*

one under pain of death. By overhearing the talk of two birds, the beggar discovers a treasure which makes him a rich man. His sudden wealth excites the suspicions of his wife, who threatens to inform the police. The old man is in a strait. His friend, the king of the fish, discerns his embarrassment and sends two birds to give him a hint. The beggar hears the cock saying to the hen : " Eat your meat and put on your clothes, and never mind where the food and clothes come from ; that's my business, not yours." The lesson is not lost on the beggar ; he takes a whip and soon brings his wife to a better frame of mind.

In reviewing the chief means of attaining the animal language, namely, rings, fern seed, and serpents, we may notice some points of contact between them. First, as to *rings*. We have seen (p. 112, note 5) that serpents confer wishing-rings upon their benefactors just as they confer the gift of tongues. Now it is a common idea that serpents have precious stones in their heads,[1] and in the Annamite story we have seen that the gift of the animal language is a special property of these stones. We may conjecture, therefore, first, that rings bestowed by serpents contain these serpent-gems ; and second, that rings which confer the gift of animal speech are serpent-rings, that is, contain serpent-gems. This conjecture is confirmed by a second parellelism which holds between magic rings and serpent-heads (or the gems in the serpents' heads) ; both alike are capable of rendering their possessor invisible. This was the property of the magic ring of Gyges,[2] and it was equally a property of the gems found in the heads of the serpents near Paraka by the Indians, who also acquired the speech of animals by eating the heart and liver of these same serpents,[3] and it is still supposed to be a property of serpents' heads in Bohemia.[4] It is said to be a common opinion in Wales, Scotland, and Cornwall that about Midsummer Eve the snakes meet in companies and by joining heads and hissing produce a glass ring, which whoever finds shall prosper in all his undertakings ; and these rings are

[1] See Th. Benfey, *Pantschatantra*, i. p. 214, note.
[2] See Stallbaum on Plato, *Republic*, 359 D. It is a curious coincidence that both in Plato and in Chaucer the magic ring is associated with a horse of brass.
[3] Philostratus, *Vit. Apoll.* iii. 8.
[4] A. Wuttke, *Der deutsche Volksaberglaube*,[2] § 153.

called snake-stones.[1] If this idea could be proved to be wide-spread, we might perhaps suppose that this ring is the wishing-ring bestowed by serpents on their benefactors ; but in the absence of such proof it is better to suppose that these wishing-rings contain the gems from the serpents' heads.[2] However, the time when these glass rings are formed (namely, Mid-summer Eve) is remarkable, because, as we have seen, this is precisely the time when the animal language is supposed to be acquired through fern seed.

The connexion of the *fern* with serpents in folk-lore is undoubted. In Germany the fern is sometimes called the adder-plant (*Otterkraut*), and anyone who carries it is thought to be pursued by adders till he throws it away.[3] The Lithu-anians also call the fern the serpent-plant, because the king of the serpents is supposed to fetch the bloom of the fern on Midsummer Eve to be his crown.[4] In a Lithuanian legend a queen finds by night the serpents fighting with the other animals for the fern ; she plucks the fern, wounds herself in the thigh with her sword, puts the fern into the wound, the wound closes on it, and immediately the queen becomes omniscient.[5] This probably took place on Mid-summer Eve, the time when the fern possesses its magic properties. Similarly in Russia the person who catches the golden bloom of the fern on Midsummer Eve should cut his hand with his knife and insert the fern into the wound ; then all secret things become visible to him.[6] Again, the same parallelism which exists between rings and serpents exists between fern seed and serpents ; for fern seed, as we have seen (p 109), like serpents' heads, renders the wearer invisible.

[1] J. Brand, *Popular Antiquities*, i. p. 322 (Bohn's edition).

[2] We might unite the two hypo-theses by supposing that the glass ring formed by the serpents on Midsummer Eve is composed by the fusion of the gems in their heads. But this would be going too far from the facts.

[3] J. Grimm, *Deutsche Mythologie*, p. 1013 ; in Bohemia snakes are thought to lurk under ferns (Kuhn, *Herabkunft des Feuers*,[2] p. 196, note).

[4] E. Veckenstedt, *Die Mythen,*

Sagen und Legenden der Zamaiten (*Litauer*), ii. p. 180.

[5] *Id.* i. p. 116 *sq.*

[6] W. R. S. Ralston, *Songs of the Russian People*, p. 98 *sq.* For rubbing the magic substance into a wound, compare Callaway, *Religious System of the Amasulu*, pp. 313, 380 ; E. Holub, *Sieben Jahre in Süd-Afrika*, vol. ii. p. 361 ; Rochefort, *Hist. nat. et mor. des Iles Antilles*, p. 556 ; Du Tertre, *Histoire générale des Antilles*, vol. ii. p. 377.

The reason why the serpent is especially supposed to
impart a knowledge of the language of birds appears from
a folk-lore conception of the origin of serpents. According
to Democritus as reported by Pliny,[1] serpents are generated
from the mixed blood of diverse birds. This explains why
serpents should understand the language of birds ; they do
so because they are blood relations of birds, having the blood
of birds in their veins. If we ask why serpents are thought
to be formed of the blood of birds, we may conjecture that
the idea originated in the observation that serpents eat birds
and birds' eggs. Hence on the folk-lore principle that in
eating of an animal's flesh one absorbs the animal's mental
qualities, (1) the serpent acquires the bird language, (2) anyone who eats a serpent also acquires the language of birds.
From the language of birds to the language of animals in
general is not perhaps a long step in folk-lore. The idea
that birds are pre-eminently talkers appears in the practice,
observed by some Turkish tribes in Asia, of giving to children

[1] Pliny, *Nat. Hist.* x. 137. The
reader may well be startled at finding
folk-lore biology attributed to Democritus, one of the most enlightened
men of antiquity, who in his conception of physical causation stands
nearer the most modern physicists than
any other of the ancients. Some of
the ancients themselves were staggered
by the portentous absurdities fathered
on the philosopher, and justly suspected that some of the works which
passed for his were spurious. See
Aulus Gellius, x. 12 ; Pliny, *Nat. Hist.*
xxx. 10. Grounds, I believe, could be
shown for holding that some of the
worst of these absurdities are taken
from the works of Bolus the Mendesian, a nominal adherent of the
school of Democritus, especially from
his work, *On Sympathies and An-
tipathies.* It is directly stated by
Columella (vii. 5. 17) that a work of
this writer was falsely attributed to
Democritus. The *Sympathies and Anti-
pathies* of Bolus are probably the
source of the nonsense put down to
Democritus in the *Geoponica* ; and as
one of the charms there ascribed to
the philosopher (xiv. 5) consists in the

use of the name *Adam*, we may suspect
that Bolus the Mendesian was acquainted with the Jewish writings, to
which as an Egyptian he might easily
have access. He would thus belong
to the Alexandrian age. Obviously
the idea that, serpents being formed
from the blood of birds, anyone who
eats a serpent will understand the
bird language would be perfectly in
place in a folk-lore work on " sympathy and antipathy ". The passage
in Columella would seem to show that
Suidas is wrong in distinguishing
between Bolus the Democritean and
Bolus the Mendesian ; for a work of
Bolus the Mendesian could hardly
have been ascribed to Democritus if
the writer had not belonged to Democritus' school. Unless, indeed, we
suppose that Bolus the Mendesian
was confounded with Bolus the
Democritean and the latter with
Democritus. This is perhaps the
preferable hypothesis ; for Bolus the
Mendesian was (according to Suidas)
a Pythagorean philosopher, and the
Pythagorean school gave more scope
for folk-lore than the Democritean.

who are long of learning to speak the tongues of certain birds to eat.[1]

It is much less easy to say why fern seed is supposed to impart a knowledge of the language of animals. In a Thüringen story a hunter procures fern seed by shooting at the sun at noon on Midsummer Day ; three drops of blood fall down, which he catches on a white cloth, and these drops of blood are the fern seed.[2] If we could suppose that the blood thus falling from the sky was the blood of birds, all would be plain. But still this would not explain the special association of fern seed with Midsummer Day. From this association, coupled with the fact that the hunter shoots at the *sun* at noon on this day of all days in the year, it is difficult to avoid the conclusion that fern seed has a solar connexion. It would seem to be the blood of the sun rather than of birds.[3] But if this is so, why should it convey a knowledge of the language of animals ?

[1] H. Vámbéry, *Das Türkenvolk*, p. 218.

[2] L. Bechstein, *Thüringer Sagenbuch*[2] (Leipzig, 1885), No. 161 ; *Id., Deutsches Sagenbuch*, No. 500. For drawing blood by shooting at the sun, compare K. Müllenhoff, *Sagen, Märchen und Lieder der Herzogthümer Schleswig-Holstein und Lauenburg*, No. 492.

[3] Kuhn supposed that the fern is an embodiment of the lightning (*Herabkunft des Feuers*,[2] p. 194 *sqq.*). But this would leave its connexion with Midsummer Day as mysterious as ever.

V

SOME POPULAR SUPERSTITIONS OF
THE ANCIENTS[1]

A SUPERFICIAL acquaintance with classical literature is apt,
I believe, to leave on the mind an exaggerated impression
of the general level of intelligence in antiquity. The authors
commonly read are so eminently reasonable, and so little
tinctured with vulgar superstition, that we are prone to
suppose that the mass of men in the classical ages were
equally free from those gross and palpable delusions which
we designate as superstitions. The supposition is natural,
but erroneous. It is natural, because our knowledge of the
ancients is derived chiefly from literature, and literature
reflects the thoughts and beliefs of the educated few, not of
the uneducated many. Since the invention of letters the
breach between these two classes has gone on widening, till
the mental condition of the one class comes to differ nearly
as much from that of the other as if they were beings of different species. But down to the nineteenth century both sides
remained in almost total ignorance of the gulf which divided
them. Educated people, as a rule, had no inkling that the
mental state of the great majority of their fellow-countrymen
differed in scarcely any material respect from that of savages.
They did not dream that their humble neighbours had
preserved amongst themselves by oral tradition alone a set
of customs and ideas so ancient that the oldest literature of
Greece and Rome is modern by comparison. To have at
last opened the eyes of educated people to the priceless

[1] This paper was read before the
Cambridge Branch of the Hellenic
Society, and published in *Folk-lore*,
vol. i. (1890), pp. 145-171, from which
it is here reprinted.

value of popular tradition as evidence of a remote antiquity is the glory of the illustrious Grimm. When, chiefly through the influence of that great scholar, the oral tradition of the people came to be examined, the feature in it which most struck observers was the one I have just indicated, the stamp, namely, which it bears of a dateless antiquity. The reasons for assigning to it an age incomparably greater than that of the literary tradition are mainly two. In the first place, the popular tradition—and under tradition I mean to include popular customs as well as popular beliefs—the popular tradition could not have originated in historical times, because there is nothing in history to account for it. The two great historical influences that have moulded our modern civilization—the Roman empire and Christianity— have left hardly a trace in the genuine beliefs and customs of the folk. Christianity has slightly changed the nomen- clature, and that is all. But, on the other hand—and this is the second reason—if there is nothing in Roman civilization or the Christian religion to account for the origin of the popular tradition, there is in the customs and ideas of existing savages almost everything that is needed fully to explain and account for it. The resemblance, in fact, between the ideas and customs of our European peasantry and the ideas and customs of savages is so great as almost to amount to identity, and a comparison of the one set of customs with the other goes far towards explaining both. To put it metaphorically, the two sets of customs, the European and the savage, are independent copies of the same original picture ; but both copies are somewhat faded through time, and each has preserved some features which the other has lost. Thus they mutually supplement each other, and, taken together, enable us to restore the original with some completeness.

The application of all this to the subject in hand is obvious. If what I have said is true of the uneducated people, and especially of the peasantry, at the present time in Europe, must it not have been equally true of uneducated people, and especially of the peasantry, in antiquity ? If our peasants are, intellectually regarded, simply savages, could the peasantry of ancient Greece and Rome have been any better ? And if we moderns have lived so long in

K

ignorance of the mass of savagery lying at our doors, may
not the literary classes of antiquity have been equally blind
to the mental savagery of the peasants whom they saw at
work in the fields or jostled in the streets ? There are strong
grounds for answering both of these questions in the affirma-
tive. In regard to the former question, the existence of a
layer of savagery beneath the surface of ancient society is
abundantly attested by the notices of popular beliefs and
customs which are scattered up and down classical literature,
especially, as might have been anticipated, in the inferior
authors, men less elevated above vulgar prejudices than most
of the great classical writers. In regard to the second question,
the general ignorance of classical writers as to the popular
superstitions of their day is not only to be presumed from the
fact that they rarely mention them ; it is positively demonstrated by their manifest inability to understand even those
instances of popular superstition which they are occasionally
led to mention. Indeed, from the way in which they refer to
these superstitions, it is often plain that they not only did not
understand them, but that they did not even recognize them
as superstitions at all, that is, as beliefs actually current
among the vulgar. Conclusive proof of this is furnished by
the treatment which the so-called " symbols of Pythagoras "
received at the hands of the polite writers of antiquity. A
member of a modern folk-lore society has only to glance at
these " symbols " to see that they are common specimens
of folk-lore, many of which are perfectly familiar to our
European peasantry at the present day. Yet they completely posed the philosophers of antiquity, whose interpretations of them were certainly not nearer the mark than Mr.
Pickwick's reading of the famous inscription. It is almost
amusing to see the violence they did to these primitive
superstitions in order to wring some drop of moral wisdom
out of them, to wrench them into some semblance of philosophical profundity. In a paper on the popular superstitions
of the ancients I can hardly do better than begin by giving
a few specimens of these precious maxims, which have
found so much favour in the eyes of ancient philosophers
and old women.

Some of the ancients themselves remarked the striking

resemblance which the precepts of Pythagoras bore to the rules of life observed by Indian fakirs, Jewish Essenes, Egyptians, Etruscans, and Druids.[1] Thus, for example, Plutarch mentions the view that Pythagoras must have been an Etruscan born and bred, since the Etruscans were the only people known to observe literally the rules inculcated by the philosopher, such as not to step over a broom, not to leave the impress of a pot on the ashes, and other precepts of the same sort.[2] This view of the Etruscan origin of Pythagoras was countenanced by the respectable authorities of Aristotle and Theopompus.[3] Again, Plutarch expressly says that the maxims of Pythagoras were of the same sort as the rules contained in the sacred writings of the Egyptians, and he quotes as instances the Pythagorean precepts, " Do not eat in a chariot," " Do not sit upon a bushel," " Do not poke the fire with a sword." [4]

Some of the theories of physical causation traditionally ascribed to Pythagoras are entirely of a piece with the practical rules which passed under his name. Thus, according to him, the air was full of spirits, which he called demons and heroes ; the airy sounds from which men drew omens were the voices of the spirits ; [5] and he said that when people heard the wind whistle they should worship the sound of it.[6] Compare with this the view of the Esquimaux who live at Point Barrow, almost the northern extremity of the continent of America. " To them ", says an American officer who wintered among them some years ago, " to them earth and air are full of spirits. The one drags men into the earth by the feet, from which they never emerge ; the other strikes men dead, leaving no mark ; and the air is full of voices ; often while travelling they would stop and ask me to listen, and say that Tuña of the wind was passing by." [7] Again,

---

[1] Indian Fakirs, Strabo, xv. 1. 65 ; Egyptians, Eusebius, Praep. Evang. x. c. 4, §§ 9, 10, c. 8, § 8 ; Essenes, Josephus, Antiquit. xv. 10. 4 ; Druids, Hippolytus, Refut. omn. haeres. i. cc. 2, 25. On the Essenes, see also Josephus, Bell. Jud. ii. 8, §§ 2-13, xviii. 1. 5 ; Pliny, Nat. Hist v. 73.
[2] Plutarch, Quaest. Conviv. viii. 7.
[3] Clemens Alexand. Strom. i. 14, p. 352 Pott.; Aristotle, Fragm. 185, Bekker, Berlin ed. ; compare Suidas, s.v. Pythagoras, Πυθαγόρας Σάμιος, φύσει δὲ Τυρρηνός.
[4] Plutarch, Isis et Osiris, 10.
[5] Diogenes Laertius, viii. 1. 32.
[6] Jamblichus, Adhort. ad philos. 21.
[7] Report of the International Expedition to Point Barrow, Alaska (Washington, 1885), p. 42.

according to Pythagoras, the tinkling of a brass pot is the voice of a demon imprisoned in the brass.[1] A traveller in the Sahara was once informed by one of his savage escort that he had just killed a devil. It appeared that the devil was the traveller's watch, which the savage had found, and hearing it tick had concluded that there was a devil inside. Accordingly he smashed it by hurling it against a tree. This was in the desert, where it would have been unsafe to quarrel with his escort. So the traveller concealed his anguish under a smiling face till he reached the next town, where he took steps which rather damped the joy of that savage.[2] Yet the savage did no more than Pythagoras, if he had been true to his principles, might have done in the same circumstances.

Again, Pythagoras believed that an earthquake was caused by the dead men fighting with each other underground, and so shaking the earth.[3] I have collected many savage explanations of earthquakes, but none, perhaps, quite so savage as this of Pythagoras. The nearest approaches to it are the following. The Tlinkeet Indians on the north-west coast of America suppose that the earth rests upon a pillar which is guarded by a woman ; so, when the gods fight with the woman for the possession of the pillar, in order that they may destroy the earth and its inhabitants, the pillar shakes, and this produces an earthquake.[4] The Andaman islanders, who long ranked, though unjustly, amongst the lowest of savages, think that earthquakes are caused by the spirits of the dead, who, impatient at the delay of the resurrection, shake the palm-tree on which they believe the earth to rest.[5] When the people of Timor, an East Indian island, feel the shock of an earthquake, they knock on the ground and call out, " We are still here," to let the souls of the dead who are struggling to get up know that there is no room for them on the surface of the earth.[6] Even this,

[1] Porphyry, *Vit. Pythag.* 41.
[2] Mohammed Ibn - Omar El Tounsy, *Voyage au Ouaday* (Paris, 1851), p. 538 *seq.*
[3] Aelian, *Var. hist.* iv. 17.
[4] H.J.Holmberg,"Ethnographische Skizzen über die Völker des Rus-
sischen Amerika ", *Acta societatis scientiarum Fennicae,* iv. (Helsingfors, 1856), p. 346 *seq.*
[5] E. H. Man, *Aboriginal Inhabitants of the Andaman Islands,* p. 86.
[6] A. Bastian, *Indonesien,* ii. p. 3. Compare *id.,* in *Verhandl. d. Berlin.*

however, is a shade less savage than the view of Pythagoras that the dead could not even keep the peace amongst
themselves.   In Lucian's *Dialogues of the Dead* the soldier
ghost who draws near the ferry, his bright armour flashing
through the gloom, is bidden by Hermes to leave his arms
behind him on the hither side of the river, " because there is
peace in the grave ".[1] Clearly Hermes was not a Pythagorean.

But passing from Pythagoras' views of physical causation,
let us look more closely at some of the practical precepts or
symbols which he laid down for the guidance of life.

One of his precepts, as we have seen, was this : " Do not
poke the fire with a sword." [2] The precept commends itself
to us, but hardly on the grounds on which it did so to
Pythagoras.   To understand his reasons we must go to the
Tartars, who abstain from thrusting a knife into the fire on
the ground that it would cut off the fire's head.[3] The Kamchatkans also think it a sin to stick a knife into a burning
log, and so do some of the North American Indians.[4]

Again, Pythagoras told his disciples never to point the
finger at the stars.[5] This is a very common superstition in
Germany, where one reason given is that by pointing a
finger at the moon or stars one would put out the eyes of
the angels.[6] Another reason given is that one's finger would
drop off.[7] If one *has* pointed at the stars, the only way to
save one's finger from dropping off is to bite it.[8] The reason

Gesell. für Anthropol. 1881, p. 157 ;
J. G. F. Riedel, *De sluik-en kroesharige
rassen tusschen Selebes en Papua*, pp.
330, 428 *seq.*
[1] Lucian, *Dial. Mort.* x. 7.
[2] Hippolytus, *Refut. omn. haeres.*
vi. 27 ; Jamblichus, *Adhort. ad philos.*
21 ; Diogenes Laertius, viii. 1. 17 ;
Porphyry, *Vit. Pythag.* 42 ; Plutarch,
Isis et Osiris, 10 ; *id., De educ. puer.*
17 ;   Suidas, *s.v.* " Pythagoras " ;
Athenaeus, x. 77, p. 452 D.
[3] De Plano Carpini, *Historia
Mongalorum*, ed. D'Avezac (Paris,
1838), c. iii. § ii.
[4] G. W. Steller, *Beschreibung von
dem Lande Kamtschatka*, p. 274 ; H. R.
Schoolcraft, *Indian Tribes*, iii. 230.
All three passages have been already

cited in illustration of Pythagoras'
maxim by E. B. Tylor, *Researches into
the Early History of Mankind*,[2] p. 277.
[5] *Fragmenta philosoph. Graec.* ed.
Mullach, i. p. 510.
[6] J. Grimm, *Deutsche Mythologie*,
iii. p. 445 ; E. Meier, *Deutsche Sagen*,
Sitten und Gebräuche aus Schwaben,
p. 499 ; J. Haltrich, *Zur Volkskunde
der Siebenbürger Sachsen* (Wien, 1885),
p. 300.
[7] J. V. Grohmann, *Aberglauben
und Gebräuche aus Böhmen und
Mähren*, p. 32, No. 175 ; A. Kuhn
und W. Schwartz, *Norddeutsche
Sagen, Märchen und Gebräuche*, p.
458, No. 426.
[8] J. W. Wolf, *Beiträge zur deutschen Mythologie*, i. p. 235, No. 417.

for so doing is explained by the statement of an Ojebway Indian. "I well remember", says he, "when I was a little boy, being told by our aged people that I must never point my finger at the moon, for if I did she would consider it a great insult, and instantly bite it off." [1] The reason, therefore, why a German bites his finger after pointing at a star is to make the star believe that he is himself biting off the offending finger, and that thus the star is saved the trouble of doing so. Thus the Ojebway Indian is here the best commentator on Pythagoras.

Again, Pythagoras said : " Do not look at your face in a river." [2] So, too, said the old Hindoo lawgiver. " Let him not ", says Manu, " let him not look at his own image in water ; that is a settled rule." [3] Neither the Greek philosopher nor the Hindoo lawgiver assigns any reason for the rule. To ascertain it we must inquire of the Zulus and the black race of the Pacific, both of whom observe the same rule, and can give a reason for doing so. Here is the reason given by the Zulus in their own words : " It is said there is a beast in the water which can seize the shadow of a man ; when he looks into the water it takes his shadow ; the man no longer wishes to turn back, but has a great wish to enter the pool ; it seems to him that there is not death in the water ; it is as if he was going to real happiness where there is no harm ; and he dies through going into the pool, being eaten by the beast. . . . And men are forbidden to lean over and look into a dark pool, it being feared lest their shadow should be taken away." [4] So much for the Zulus. Now for the Melanesians of the Pacific. " There is a stream in Saddle Island, or, rather, a pool in a stream, into which if anyone looks he dies ; the malignant spirit takes hold upon his life by means of his reflection on the water." [5] Here, doubtless, we have the origin of the classical story of Narcissus,

[1] Peter Jones, *History of the Ojebway Indians*, p. 84 *seq.*

[2] *Fragm. Philos. Graec.*, ed. Mullach, i. p. 510.

[3] *Laws of Manu*, iv. 38, trans. by G. Bühler.

[4] H. Callaway, *Nursery Tales, Traditions, and Histories of the* *Zulus*, i. 342.

[5] R. H. Codrington, " Religious Beliefs and Practices in Melanesia ", *Journal of the Anthrop. Instit.* x. 313. This explanation of the Narcissus legend was communicated by me in a note to the *Journal of the Anthropological Institute*, xvi. 334.

who languished away in consequence of seeing his own fair image in the water.[1]

During a thunderstorm it was a Greek custom to put out the fire, and hiss and cheep with the lips. The reason for the custom was explained by the Pythagoreans to be that by acting thus you frightened the spirits in Tartarus,[2] who were doubtless supposed to make the thunder and lightning. Similarly, some of the Australian blacks, who attribute thunder to the agency of demons, and are much afraid of it, believe that they can dispel it " by chanting some particular words and breathing hard " ;[3] and it is a German superstition that the danger from a thunderstorm can be averted by putting out the fire.[4] During a thunderstorm, the Sakai of the Malay Peninsula run out of their houses and brandish their weapons to drive away the demons;[5] and the Esthonians in Russia fasten scythes, edge upward, over the door, that the demons, fleeing from the thundering god, may cut their feet if they try to seek shelter in the house. Sometimes the Esthonians, for a similar purpose, take all the edged tools in the house and throw them out into the yard. It is said that when the storm is over spots of blood are often found on the scythes and knives, showing that the demons have been wounded by them.[6] So, when the Indians of Canada were asked by the Jesuit missionaries why they planted their swords in the ground point upwards, they replied that the spirit of the thunder was sensible, and that if he saw the naked blades he would turn away and take good care not to approach their huts.[7] This is a fair sample of the close similarity of European superstitions to the superstitions of savages. In the present case the difference happens to be slightly in favour of the Indians, since they did not, like our European savages, delude themselves into seeing the blood of demons on the swords. The reason for

[1] Ovid, *Metam.* iii. 341 *seq.*

[2] Aristotle, *Analyt. Poster.* ii. p. 94 B, 33 *seq.*, Berlin ed. ; Scholiast on Aristophanes, *Wasps*, 626 ; Pliny, *Nat. Hist.* xxviii. 25.

[3] D. Collins, *Account of the English Colony in New South Wales*, p. 485 ; G. F. Angas, *Savage Scenes in Australia and New Zealand*, ii. 232.

[4] A. Wuttke, *Der deutsche Volksaberglaube*,[2] § 449.

[5] Lieut.-Col. James Low, "The Sakai", *Journal of the Indian Archipelago*, iii. 430.

[6] Boecler-Kreutzwald, *Der Ehsten abergläubische Gebräuche*, p. 110.

[7] *Relations des Jésuites*, 1637, p. 53 (Canadian reprint).

the Greek and German custom of putting out the fire during
a thunderstorm is, probably, a wish to avoid attracting the
attention of the thunder demons. From a like motive some
of the Australian blacks hide themselves during a thunderstorm, and keep absolutely silent, lest the thunder should
find them out.[1] Once during a storm a white man called
out in a loud voice to the blackfellow with whom he was
working, to put the saw under a log and seek shelter. He
found that the saw had already been put away, and the blackfellow was very indignant at his master for speaking so loud.
" What for ", said he, in great wrath, " what for speak so
loud ? Now um thunder hear, and know where um saw is."
And he went out and changed its hiding-place.[2]

One or two more classical superstitions about thunder
and lightning may here find a place, though they are not
specially Pythagorean. The skins of seals and hyenas were
believed by the Greeks to be effective protections against
lightning. Hence Greek sailors used to nail a sealskin to the
mast-head ; and the Emperor Augustus, who was nervously
afraid of thunder, never went anywhere without a sealskin.[3]
The skin of a hippopotamus buried in the middle of a field
was supposed to prevent a thunderbolt from falling on it.[4]

Another maxim of Pythagoras was this : " On setting
out from your house upon a journey, do not turn back ; for
if you do, the Furies will catch you." [5] This is a rule observed
by superstitious people everywhere, in the heart of Africa
and of India, as well as all over Europe. I will mention
only the last instance which came under my notice. A
Highland servant in our family told my mother lately that
in Sutherlandshire if anyone is going on some important
errand and has left anything behind him he would stand
and call for it for a week rather than go back to fetch it.[6]

---

[1] A. Oldfield, " The Aborigines of
Australia ", Transactions of the Ethnological Society, iii. 229 seq.
[2] Journ. and Proceed. R. Soc. N.S.
Wales, xvi. (1882), p. 171.
[3] Plutarch, Quaest. Conviv. iv. 2. 1,
compare id. v. 9; Suetonius, Augustus,
90.
[4] Geoponica, i. 16.
[5] Hippolytus, Refut. omn. haeres.

vi. 26 ; Jamblichus, Adhort. ad
philos. 21 ; Diogenes Laertius, viii.
1. 17 ; Porphyry, Vit. Pythag. 42 ;
Plutarch, De educ. puer. 17.
[6] Folk-Lore Journal, vii. 53. For
India, see Indian Antiquary, i. 170 ;
Indian Notes and Queries, iv. 270 ;
for Africa, see Felkin in Proceed. R.
Soc. Edinburgh, xiii. pp. 230, 734
seq., 759 ; for Europe, see Burne and

Once more, Pythagoras observed : " If you meet an ugly old woman at the door, do not go out."[1] Amongst the Wends, if a man going out to hunt meets an old woman, it is unlucky, and he should turn back.[2] Amongst the Esthonians, if a fisherman or anyone else going out on important business happens to meet an old woman, he will turn back.[3] A Tyrolese hunter believes that if he meets an old woman in the morning, he will have no luck.[4] In Pomerania, if a person going out of the house meets a woman he will often turn back.[5] They say in Thüringen that if you are about any weighty affair, and are interrupted by an old woman, you should not go on with it, for it could not prosper.[6] In Norway, if a man goes out to make a bargain, and an old woman is the first person he meets, he will have no luck.[7]

Another saying of Pythagoras was this : " If you stumble at the threshold in going out, you should turn back."[8] In the Highlands of Scotland and among the Saxons of Transylvania it is deemed unlucky to stumble on the threshold in going out on a journey.[9] Amongst the Malays, if a person stumbles on leaving the steps of a house on particular business, it is unlucky, and the business is abandoned for the time.[10] In Sumatra, if a Batta stumbles in leaving the house, it bodes ill-luck, and he thinks it better to abandon the journey and stay at home.[11]

Again, Pythagoras said : " If a weasel cross your path,

Jackson, *Shropshire Folk-lore*, p. 274; Grimm, *Deutsche Mythologie*,[4] iii. p. 435 ; J. A. E. Köhler, *Volksbrauch im Voigtlande*, p. 426; J. Haltrich, *Zur Volkskunde der Siebenbürger Sachsen*, p. 316; F. S. Krauss, *Sitte und Brauch der Südslaven*, p. 426.

[1] *Fragm. Philos. Graec.*, ed. Mullach, i. 510.

[2] W. von Schulenberg, *Wendische Volkssagen und Gebräuche*, p. 241 ; compare A. Bezzenberger, *Litauische Forschungen* (Göttingen, 1882), p. 85.

[3] Boecler-Kreutzwald, *Der Ehsten abergläubische Gebräuche*, p. 71.

[4] I. V. Zingerle, *Sitten, Bräuche und Meinungen des Tiroler Volkes*,[2] p. 43, No. 371.

[5] Otto Knoop, *Volkssagen, etc., aus dem östlichen Hinterpommern*, p. 163.

[6] A. Witzschel, *Sagen, Sitten und Gebräuche aus Thüringen*, p. 284.

[7] *Antananarivo Annual and Madagascar Magazine*, viii. 30.

[8] *Fragm. Phil. Gr. loc. cit.*

[9] *Scotland and Scotsmen in the Eighteenth Century*, from the MSS. of John Ramsay of Ochtertyre, edited by Alex. Allardyce (Edinburgh, 1888), ii. 456; J. Haltrich, *Zur Volkskunde der Siebenbürger Sachsen*, p. 316.

[10] *Straits Branch R. Asiatic Soc., Notes and Queries*, i. p. 18.

[11] J. B. Neumann, " Het Pane en Bila-Stroomgebied op het eiland Sumatra ", *Tijdschrift van het Nederlandsch Aardrijks. Genootschap*, 2de Ser., dl. iii. Afdeeling : Meer uitgebreide artikelen, No. 3, p. 515 *seq.*

turn back." [1]   This was a common rule in Greece.   In the
" Characters " of Theophrastus the Superstitious Man would
not go on if a weasel crossed his path ; he waited till someone else had traversed the road, or until he had thrown three
stones across it.[2]   The Zulus think that if a weasel crosses
their path they will get no food at the place whither they are
going.[3]   In Ireland, to meet a weasel under certain circumstances is unlucky.[4]   A weasel crossing the path was regarded
as an omen by the Aztecs.[5]

Further, Pythagoras warned his followers against stepping over a broom.[6]   In some parts of Bavaria, housemaids,
in sweeping out the house, are careful not to step over the
broom for fear of the witches.[7]   Again, it is a Bavarian
rule not to step over a broom while a confinement is taking
place in a house ; otherwise the birth will be tedious, and
the child will always remain small with a large head.   But
if anyone has stepped over a broom inadvertently, he can
undo the spell by stepping backwards over it again.[8]   So
in Bombay they say you should never step across a broom,
or you will cause a woman to suffer severely in child-bed.[9]

Again, it was a precept of Pythagoras not to run a nail
or a knife into a man's footprints.[10]   This, from the primitive
point of view, was really a moral, not merely a prudential
precept.   For it is a world-wide superstition that by injuring
footprints you injure the feet that made them.   Thus, in
Mecklenburg it is thought that if you thrust a nail into a
man's footprints the man will go lame.[11]   The Australian
blacks held exactly the same view.   " Seeing a Tatüngolüng
very lame," says Mr. Howitt, " I asked him what was the
matter ?   He said, ' Some fellow has put *bottle* in my foot.'
I asked him to let me see it.   I found he was probably

[1] *Fragm. Phil. Gr. loc. cit.*
[2] Theophrastus, *Characters*, p. 162, ed. R. C. Jebb.
[3] H. Callaway, *Nursery Tales, etc., of the Zulus*, p. 5.
[4] A. R. M'Mahon, *Karens of the Golden Chersonese*, p. 273.
[5] H. H. Bancroft, *Native Races of the Pacific States*, iii. 128.
[6] Hippolytus, *Refut. omn. haeres.* vi. 27.
[7] G. Lammert, *Volksmedizin und*

medizinischer Aberglaube aus Bayern, p. 38.
[8] A. Wuttke, *Der deutsche Volksaberglaube*,[2] § 574.
[9] *Indian Notes and Queries*, iv. 104.
[10] *Fragm. Phil. Gr. loc. cit.*
[11] K. Bartsch, *Sagen, Märchen und Gebräuche aus Mecklenburg*, ii. Nos. 1597, 1598; compare *id.* Nos. 1599, 1611a seq.

suffering from acute rheumatism. He explained that some enemy must have found his foot-track, and have buried in it a piece of broken bottle. The magic influence, he believed, caused it to enter his foot. When following down Cooper's Creek in search of Burke's party, we were followed one day by a large number of blackfellows, who were much interested in looking at and measuring the footprints of the horses and camels. My blackboy, from the Darling River, rode up to me, with the utmost alarm exhibited in his face, and exclaimed, ' Look at these wild blackfellows ! ' I said, ' Well, they are all right.' He replied, ' I am sure those fellows are putting poison in my footsteps ! ' " [1] Amongst the Karens of Burma, evil-disposed persons " keep poisoned fangs in their possession for the purpose of killing people. These they thrust into the footmarks of the person they wish to kill, who soon finds himself with a sore foot, and the marks on it as bitten by a dog. The sore becomes rapidly worse and worse till death ensues." [2] The Damaras of South Africa take earth from the footprints of a lion and throw it on the track of an enemy, with the wish, " May the lion kill you ".[3] This superstition is turned to account by hunters in many parts of the world for the purpose of running down the game. Thus, a German huntsman will stick a nail taken from a coffin into the fresh spoor of the animal he is hunting, believing that this will prevent the quarry from leaving the hunting-ground.[4] Australian blacks put hot embers in the tracks of the animals they are pursuing ; [5] Hottentot hunters throw into the air a handful of sand taken from the footprints of the game, believing that this will bring the animal down ; [6] and Ojebway Indians place " medicine " on the first deer's or bear's track that they meet with, supposing that even if the animal be two or three days' journey off, they will now soon sight it, the charm possessing the power of

[1] L. Fison and A. W. Howitt, *Kamilaroi and Kurnai*, p. 250. Compare R. Brough Smyth, *Aborigines of Victoria*, i. 476 *seq*.

[2] F. Mason, " The Karens ", *Journal R. Asiatic Soc.*, 1868, pt. ii. p. 149.

[3] Josaphat Hahn, " Die Ova-herero ", *Zeitschrift der Gesell. für Erdkunde zu Berlin*, iv. 503.

[4] A. Wuttke, *Der deutsche Volksaberglaube*,[2] § 186.

[5] J. Dawson, *Australian Aborigines*, p. 54.

[6] Theophilus Hahn, *Tsuni-Goam*, p. 84 *seq*

shortening the journey from two or three days to a few hours.[1]
The Zulus resort to a similar device to recover strayed cattle.
Earth taken from the footprints of the missing beasts is
placed in the chief's vessel, a magic circle is made, and the
chief's vessel is placed within it. Then the chief says, " I
have now conquered them. These cattle are now here ; I
am now sitting upon them. I do not know in what way
they will escape." [2]

We can now understand why Pythagoras said that when
you rise from bed you should efface the impression left by
your body on the bedclothes.[3] For obviously the same
magical process might be applied by an enemy to the impress of the body which we have just seen to be applied to
the impress of the foot. The aborigines of Australia cause
magical substances to enter the body of an enemy by burying
them either in his footprints or in the mark made on the
ground by his reclining body,[4] or they beat the place where
the man sat—the place must be still warm—with a pointed
stick, which is then believed to enter the victim's body and
kill him.[5] To secure the good behaviour of an ally with
whom they have just had a conference, the Basutos will cut
and preserve the grass upon which the ally sat during the
interview.[6] The grass is apparently regarded as a sort of
hostage for his good behaviour, since through it they believe
they could punish him if he proved false. Moors who write
on the sand are superstitiously careful to smooth away all
the impressions they have made, never leaving a stroke or a
dot of the finger on the sand after they have finished writing.[7]
Pythagoras also enjoined his disciples when they lifted a pot
from the ashes always to efface the mark left by the pot on
the ashes.[8] He probably feared that the persons who ate

[1] Peter Jones, *History of the Ojebway Indians*, p. 154.
[2] H. Callaway, *Religious System
of the Amazulu*, 345 *seq.*
[3] Jamblichus, *Adhort. ad philos.*
21 ; Plutarch, *Quaest. Conviv.* viii. 7 ;
Clemens Alexand. *Strom.* v. 5, p. 661,
Pott. Compare Diogenes Laert. viii.
1. 17 ; Suidas, *s.v.* " Pythagoras ".
[4] A. W. Howitt, " On Australian
Medicine Men ", *Journal of the*

Anthropological Institute, xvi. 26 *seq.*
[5] R. Brough Smyth, *Aborigines of
Victoria*, i. 475.
[6] E. Casalis, *The Basutos*, p. 273.
[7] J. Richardson, *Travels in the
Great Desert of Sahara*, ii. 65.
[8] Plutarch, *Quaest. Conviv.* viii.
7 ; Jamblichus, *Adhort. ad philos.* 21 ;
Clemens Alexand. *Strom.* vi. 5, p.
661, Pott ; Diogenes Laertius, viii. 1.
17 ; Suidas, *s.v.* " Pythagoras ".

out of the pot might be magically injured by any enemy who should tamper with the impression left on the ashes by the pot. The obligation of this Pythagorean precept is acknowledged at the other end of the world by the natives of Cambodia. They say that when you lift a pot from the fire you should be careful not to set it down on the ashes, if you can help it ; but if it is necessary to do so, you should at least be careful, in lifting it from the ashes, to obliterate the impression which it has made. The reason they give is, that to act otherwise would lead to poverty and want.[1] But this is clearly an afterthought, devised to explain a rule of which the original meaning was forgotten.

Such, then, are specimens, and only specimens, of the savage superstitions which, under the name of the symbols of Pythagoras, passed muster in antiquity as the emanations of a profound philosophy and an elevated morality.[2] The fact that they did so pass muster with the wisest of the ancients conclusively establishes the point I am concerned to prove, namely, that beneath the polished surface of classical civilization there lay a deep and solid stratum of savagery, not differing in kind from the savagery of Australian blackfellows, Zulus, and Ojebways. It lay beneath the surface, but not far beneath it. There, as everywhere, you had only to scratch civilization to find savagery. And the helpless bewilderment of classical writers in face of the few specimens of native savagery which cropped up on the surface shows how little conception they had of the depths of superstition which lay beneath their feet.

I have dwelt at some length on the symbols of Pythagoras, and their resemblance to, or rather identity with, the super-

[1] E. Aymonier, " Notes sur les coutumes et croyances superstitieuses des Cambodgiens", *Cochin-chine Française, Excursions et Reconnaissances,* No. 16, p. 163.

[2] Collections, more or less complete, of the " symbols " of Pythagoras will be found in the lives of Pythagoras by Diogenes Laertius (viii. 1), Jamblichus, and Porphyry, the *Adhortatio ad philosophiam* of Jamblichus ; Suidas, *s.v.* " Pythagoras " ; Plutarch, *Isis et Osiris,* 10 ; *id., De educat.*

puerorum, 17 ; *id., Quaest. Conviv.* viii. 7 ; Clemens Alexand. *Strom.* v. 5 ; Athenaeus, x. 77, p. 452 D E ; Hippolytus, *Refut. omn. haeres.* vi. 26 *seq.* They are given in a collected form by Mullach in his *Fragmenta Philosophorum Graecorum,* i. p. 504 *seq.,* though his references to the authorities are not always complete. On p. 510 Mullach gives, from MSS., a valuable collection of " symbols ", many of which are not found in the printed texts of classical writers.

stitions of savages at home and abroad, because they furnish a strong proof of the truth of the propositions from which I set out. But it would be unfair to Pythagoras to leave the whole burden of proof upon his shoulders. So, if I have not already taxed the reader's patience too far, I will now give a few specimens of classical superstitions drawn from other sources.

Wherever people are directly and visibly dependent for their daily bread, not on their fellow-men, but on the forces of Nature, there superstition strikes root and flourishes. It is a weed that finds a more congenial soil in the woods and fields than among city streets. The ancient Greek farmer was certainly not less superstitious than our own Hodge. Amongst the foes whom the husbandman has always to fear are the storms and hail which beat down his corn, the weeds which choke it, and the vermin which devour it. For each and all of these the ancient farmer had remedies of his own. Take hail, for example. At the town of Cleonae, in Argolis, there were watchmen maintained at the public expense to look out for hailstorms.   When they saw a hail-cloud ap- proaching they made a signal, whereupon the farmers turned out and sacrificed lambs or fowls. They believed that when the clouds had tasted the blood they would turn aside and go somewhere else. *Hoc rides ? accipe quod rideas magis.* If any man was too poor to afford a lamb or a fowl, he pricked his finger with a sharp instrument, and offered his own blood to the clouds ; and the hail, we are told, turned aside from his fields quite as readily as from those where it had been propitiated with the blood of victims. If the vines and crops suffered from a hailstorm, the watchmen were brought before the magistrates and punished for neglect of duty.[1] Apparently it formed part of their duty not only to signal the approach of a storm, but actively to assist in averting it, for Plutarch speaks of the mole's blood and bloody rags by which they sought to turn the storm away.[2] This custom of civilized Greece has its analogue among the wild tribes that lurk in the dense jungles of the Malay Peninsula. Thunder is greatly dreaded by these savages.

[1] Seneca, *Quaest. Natur.* iv. 6 *seq.*; Clemens Alexand. *Strom.* vi. § 31, p. 754 *seq.*, Pott.   [2] Plutarch, *Quaest. Conviv.* vii. 2.

Accordingly, "when it thunders the women cut their legs with knives till the blood flows, and then, catching the drops in a piece of bamboo, they cast them aloft towards the sky, to propitiate the angry deities." [1] The Aztecs, also, had sorcerers, whose special business it was to turn aside the hailstorms from the maize crops and direct them to waste lands. [2] A Roman way of averting hail was to hold up a looking-glass to the dark cloud ; seeing itself in the glass, the cloud, it was believed, would pass by. A tortoise laid on its back on the field, or the skin of a crocodile, hyena, or seal carried about the farm, and hung up at the door, was also esteemed effective for the same purpose. [3]

The little town of Methana, in Argolis, stood on a peninsula jutting out into the Saronic Gulf. It felt the full force of the south-west wind, which, sweeping over the bay, wrought havoc among the surrounding vineyards. To prevent its ravages the following plan was adopted. When dark clouds were seen rising in the south-west, and the approach of the storm was marked by a black line crawling across the smooth surface of the bay, two men took a cock with white wings (every feather of the wings had to be white) and rent it in two. Then they each took one-half of the bird and ran with it round the vineyards in opposite directions till they met at the point from which they started. There they buried the cock. This ceremony was believed to keep off the south-west wind. [4] The meaning of the ceremony is perhaps explained by the following East Indian custom. When the sky is overcast the skipper of a Malay proa takes the white or yellow feathers of a cock, fastens them to a leaf of a particular sort, and sets them in the forecastle, with a prayer to the spirits that they will cause the black clouds to pass by. Then the cock is killed. The skipper whitens his dusky hand with chalk, points thrice with his whitened finger to the black clouds, and throws the bird into the sea. [5]

[1] *Journal of the Straits Branch of the R. Asiatic Society*, No. 4, p. 48.
[2] Sahagun, *Histoire générale des choses de la Nouvelle Espagne* (Paris, 1880), p. 486. Compare *id.* p. 314 with W. Ellis, *History of Madagascar*, i. 412 (ashes thrown to the clouds to melt the clouds into rain).

[3] Palladius, *De re rust.* i. 35; *Geoponica*, i. 14. For other remedies, see *Geoponica*, *loc. cit.*; Philostratus, *Heroica*, p. 281, Didot.
[4] Pausanias, ii. 34. 1.
[5] J. G. F. Riedel, *De sluik- en kroesharige rassen tusschen Selebes en Papua*, 412 *seq.*

Clearly the idea of the Greek husbandman and the Malay skipper is that the white-winged bird will flutter against and beat away the black-winged spirit of the storm.

To rid a field of mice the Greek farmer was recommended to proceed as follows : " Take a sheet of paper, and write on it these words : ' Ye mice here present, I adjure you that ye injure me not, neither suffer another mouse to injure me. I give you yonder field ' (specifying the field) ; ' but if ever I catch you here again, by the help of the Mother of the Gods I will rend you in seven pieces.' Write this, and stick the paper on an unhewn stone in the field where the mice are, taking care to keep the written side uppermost." [1] It is fair to add that the writer in the *Geoponica* who records this receipt adds, in a saving clause, that " he does not himself believe it all, God forbid ! " To keep wolves from his beasts, a Roman farmer used to catch a wolf, break its legs, sprinkle its blood all round the farm, and bury the carcass in the middle of it ; or he took the ploughshare with which the first furrow had been traced that year and put it in the fire on the family hearth. So long as the ploughshare remained red-hot, so long no ravening wolf would harry his fold.[2]

Greek farmers were much pestered by a rank weed called the lion-weed, which infested their fields. The *Geoponica*, as usual, comes to the rescue. Here are some of its receipts : " Take five potsherds ; draw on each of them in chalk or other white substance a picture of Hercules strangling the lion. Deposit four of these potsherds at the corners of the field, and the fifth in the middle. The lion-weed will never show face in that field." Here is another receipt taken from the same golden treasury : " A lion is very much afraid of a cock, and sneaks away with his tail between his legs when he sees one. So if a man will boldly take a cock in his arms, and march with it round the field, the lion-weed will immediately disappear." [3]

It was a common superstition in ancient Italy that if a woman were found spinning on a highroad, the crops would be spoiled for that year. So general and firmly rooted was

---

[1] *Geoponica*, xiii. 5.   [2] Pliny, *Nat. Hist.* xxviii. 266 *seq.*
[3] *Geoponica*, ii. 42.

this belief, that in most parts of Italy it was forbidden by law for a woman to spin on a highway, or even to carry her spindle uncovered along it.[1]   As a last instance of these agricultural superstitions, I will mention that when a Greek sower sowed cummin he had to curse and swear all the while he did so, otherwise the crop would not turn out well.[2] Similarly, Esthonian fishermen think that they never have such good luck as when somebody is angry with them and curses them.   So, before a fisherman goes out to fish, he commonly plays a rough practical joke on some of his house-mates, such as hiding the key of the cupboard, upsetting a kettle of soup, and so on.   The more they curse and swear at him, the more fish he will catch ; every curse brings at least three fish into the net.[3]

Under the head of what may be called domestic folk-lore, I must content myself with a Greek cure for the sting of a scorpion and a couple of Roman superstitions relative to childbirth.   If a man has been stung by a scorpion, the *Geoponica* recommends that he should sit on an ass with his face to the tail, or whisper in the ass's ear, " A scorpion has stung me."   In either case, we are assured, the pain will pass from the man into the ass.[4]   The wood spirit Silvanus was believed to be very inimical to women in childbed. So, to keep him out of a house where a woman was expecting her confinement, three men used to go through the house by night armed respectively with an axe, a pestle, and a broom.   At every door they stopped, and the first man struck the threshold with his axe, the second with his pestle, and the third swept it with his broom.   This kept Silvanus from entering the house.[5]   When his wife was in hard labour, a Roman husband used to take a stone or any missile that had killed three animals—a boar, a bear, and a man.   This he threw over the roof of the house, and immediately the child was born.   A javelin which had been plucked from the body of a man, and had not since touched the ground, was the best instrument for the purpose.[6]

[1] Pliny, *Nat. Hist.* xxviii. 28.
[2] Theophrastus,   *Histor.   Plant.* viii. 3 ; Plutarch, *Quaest. Conviv.* vii. 2. 2.
[3] Boecler-Kreutzwald, *Der Ehsten*
abergläubische Gebräuche, pp. 90 *seq.*
[4] *Geoponica*, xiii. 9, xv. 1 ; Pliny, *Nat. Hist.* xxviii. 155.
[5] Augustine, *De civit. Dei*, vi. 9.
[6] Pliny, *Nat. Hist.* xxviii. 33 *seq.*

Now for war. There is a common belief in modern times that great battles bring on clouds and rain through the atmospheric disturbances set up by the rolling reverberation of the artillery. During the American Civil War it was a matter of common observation that rain followed the great battles. I have been told, by one who took part in the battle of Solferino, that the day was dull and rainy ; indeed, the Austrian commander attributed the loss of the battle to a terrific thunderstorm which burst over the field and obscured the movements of powerful masses of the enemy. The belief that heavy firing brings down rain is indeed so rooted that a civil engineer wrote a book not many years ago to prove it, and a gentleman of scientific tastes read a paper to the same effect before the British Association in 1874.[1] Perhaps they would have spared themselves the trouble if they had been aware, first, that as late as the beginning of the nineteenth century the belief was just the reverse, and batteries were regularly kept by many French Communes for the sole purpose of dispersing the clouds ;[2] and second, that the theory which connects great battles with heavy rain is very much older than the invention of gunpowder. After describing the defeat of the Teutons by the Romans under Marius, Plutarch mentions a popular saying that great battles are accompanied by heavy rain, and he suggests as possible explanations of the supposed fact, either that the atmospheric moisture is condensed by the exhalations from the slain, or that some pitying god cleanses the bloody earth with the gentle rain of heaven.[3]

When a Roman army sat down before a city to besiege it, the priests used to invite the guardian gods of the city to leave it and come over to the Roman side, assuring them that they would be treated by the Romans as well as, or better

---

[1] " On Disturbance of the Weather by Artificial Influences, especially Battles, Military Movements, Great Explosions, and Conflagrations ", by R. B. Belcher. See *Report of the meeting of the British Association for 1874, Transactions of the Sections*, p. 36.
[2] *Journal and Proceedings of the R. Society of N.S. Wales*, xvi. (1882),

p. 12. The address of the President (p. 11 *seq.*) contains a judicious discussion of the whole question. The earlier view must have been shared by Southey, for, in describing a naval action in the Mediterranean, he says " the firing made a perfect calm " (*Life of Nelson*, c. iii.).

[3] Plutarch, *Marius*, 21. 4.

than, they had ever been treated by their former worshippers. This invitation was couched in a set form of prayer or in-cantation, which was not expunged from the Pontifical liturgy even in Pliny's time. The name of the guardian god of Rome was always kept a profound secret, lest the enemies of Rome should entice him by similar means to desert the city.[1] So, when the natives of Tahiti were besieging a fortress, they used to take the finest mats, cloth, and so on, as near to the ramparts as they could with safety, and there, holding them up, offered them to the gods of the besieged, while the priests cried out, " *Tane* in the fortress, *Oro* in the fortress, etc., come to the sea ; here are your offerings." The priests of the besieged, on the other hand, endeavoured to detain the gods by exhibiting whatever property they possessed, if they feared that the god was likely to leave them.[2]

Like modern peasants, the ancients believed that the ghosts of slaughtered warriors appear by night on the battle-field, and fight their battles over again. At Marathon the neighing of horses and the noise of battle could be heard every night.[3] The sound of the sea breaking on the shore in the stillness of night may have originated or confirmed the belief. In Boeotia there was a place called " The Horses of Pyraechmes", and the local legend ran that Pyraechmes was a King of Euboea who had fought against Boeotia long ago, and, being defeated, had been bound to horses and torn in two. A river ran by the spot, and in the rush of the river people fancied that they heard the snorting of the phantom steeds.[4] Again, the whole plain of Troy was haunted ground. The shepherds and herdsmen who pastured their flocks and herds on it used to see tall and stately phantoms, from the manner of whose appearance they presaged what was about to happen. If the phantoms were white with dust, it meant a parching summer. If beads of sweat stood on their brows, it foretold heavy rains and spates on the rivers. If they came dabbled in blood, it boded pestilence.

[1] Pliny, *Nat. Hist.* xxviii. 18 ; Macrobius, *Saturn.* iii. 9. 2 *seq.* ; Servius on Virgil, *Aen.* ii. 351 ; Livy, v. 21. On the secret name of Rome itself, see Macrobius, *loc. cit.* ; Pliny, *Nat. Hist.* iii. 65 ; Joannes Lydus,

De mensibus, iv. 50.
[2] W. Ellis, *Polynesian Researches*, i. 316, compare 280 (ed. 1832).
[3] Pausanias, i. 32. 4.
[4] Plutarch, *Parallela*, 7.

But if there was neither dust nor sweat nor blood on them, the shepherds augured a fine season, and offered sacrifice from their flocks. The spectre of Achilles was always known from the rest by his height, his beauty, and his gleaming arms, and he rode on a whirlwind.[1] In the late Roman empire legend told how, after a great battle fought against Attila and the Huns under the walls of Rome, the ghosts of the slain appeared and fought for three days and nights. The phantom warriors could be seen charging each other, and the clang of their weapons was distinctly heard.[2] Stories of the same sort, which it would be needless to cite at length, are told about battlefields to this day. Terrified peasants have seen the spectral armies locked in desperate conflict, have felt the ground shake beneath their tread, and have heard the music of the fifes and drums.[3]

A word about were-wolves, and I have done. Few super-stitions are more familiar in modern times than this one. Certain men, it is believed, possess the power of turning themselves into wolves and back again at pleasure. Or they are forced to become wolves for a time, but may, under certain conditions, recover their human shape. All this was believed as firmly by superstitious people in antiquity as it has been believed by the same class of persons in modern times. There is a certain mountain in Arcadia which towers over its sister peaks, and commands from its top a prospect over a great part of the Morea. The mountain was known to the ancients as the Wolf Mountain (Mt. Lycaeus), and on its summit stood the earthen altar of the Wolf God (Zeus Lycaeus). East of the altar stood two columns, surmounted by gilt eagles. Once a year a mysterious sacrifice was offered at the altar, in the course of which a man was believed to be changed into a wolf. Accounts differ as to the way in which the were-wolf was chosen. According to one account, a human victim was sacrificed, one of his bowels was mixed with the bowels of animal victims, the whole was consumed

[1] Philostratus, *Heroica*, iii. § 18, 26.
[2] Damascius, *Vita Isidori*, 63.
[3] K. Lynker, *Deutsche Sagen und Sitten in hessischen Gauen*, pp. 11-13 ; P. Sébillot, *Traditions et Super-stitions de la Haute-Bretagne*, i. 222 ; E. Veckenstedt, *Die Mythen, Sagen und Legenden der Zamaiten (Litauer)*, ii. p. 140 ; *Indian Antiquary*, ix. (1880), p. 80. Compare F. Liebrecht, *Gervasius von Tilbury*, pp. 195 *seq.*

by the worshippers, and the man who unwittingly ate the human bowel was changed into a wolf.[1] According to another account, lots were cast among the members of a particular family, and he upon whom the lot fell was the were-wolf. Being led to the brink of a tarn, he stripped himself, hung his clothes on an oak tree, plunged into the tarn, and, swimming across it, went away into desert places. There he was changed into a wolf and herded with wolves for nine years. If he tasted human blood before the nine years were out he had to remain a wolf for ever. But if during the nine years he abstained from preying on men, then, when the tenth year came round, he recovered his human shape.[2] Similarly, there is a negro family at the mouth of the Congo who are supposed to possess the power of turning themselves into leopards in the gloomy depths of the forest. As leopards, they knock people down, but do no further harm, for they think that if, as leopards, they once lapped blood they would be leopards for ever.[3]

In the *Banquet of Trimalchio* there is a typical were-wolf story,[4] with which I will conclude this paper. Some points in it are explained by the belief of the Breton peasants, that if a were-wolf be wounded to the effusion of blood, he is thereby obliged to resume his human form, and that the man will then be found to have on his body the very same wound which was inflicted on the wolf.[5] The story is put in the mouth of one Niceros. Late at night he left the town to visit a friend of his, a widow, who lived at a farm five miles down the road. He was accompanied by a soldier, who lodged in the same house, a man of Herculean build. When they set out it was near dawn, but the moon shone as bright as day. Passing through the outskirts of the town they came amongst the tombs, which lined the highroad for some distance. There the soldier made an excuse for retiring among the monuments, and Niceros sat down to wait for him, humming a tune and

---

[1] Plato, *Repub.* viii. 16, p. 565 D E.
[2] Pliny, *Nat. Hist.* viii. 81 ; Pausanias, vi. 8, viii. 2 ; compare Augustine, *De civitate Dei,* xviii. 17. On the altar at the top of Mt. Lycaeus, see Pausanias, viii. 38. 7.

[3] A. Bastian, *Die deutsche Expedition an der Loango-Küste,* ii. 248.
[4] Petronius, *Satyricon,* 61 *seq.*
[5] P. Sébillot, *Traditions et Superstitions de la Haute-Bretagne,* i. 291 *seq.*

counting the tombstones. In a little he looked round at his
companion, and what he saw froze him with horror. The
soldier had stripped off his clothes to the last rag and laid
them at the side of the highway. Then he performed a
certain ceremony over them, and immediately was changed
into a wolf, and ran howling into the forest. When Niceros
had recovered himself a little he went to pick up the clothes,
but found that they were turned to stone. Almost dead with
fear, he drew his sword, and, striking at every shadow cast
by the tombstones on the moonlit road, tottered to his friend's
house. He entered it like a ghost, to the surprise of the
widow, who wondered to see him abroad so late. " If you
had only been here a little ago ", said she, " you might have
been of some use. For a wolf came tearing into the yard,
scaring the cattle and bleeding them like a butcher. But
he did not get off so easily, for the servant speared him in
the neck." After hearing these words, Niceros felt that he
could not close an eye, so he hurried away home again. It
was now broad daylight, but when he came to the place
where the clothes had been turned to stone, he found only a
pool of blood. He reached home, and there lay the soldier
in bed like an ox in the shambles, and the doctor was
bandaging his neck.

VI

A FOLK-LORE MEDLEY

1. Ares in the Brazen Pot[1]

HOMER (E. 385 *sqq.*) says that Otus and Ephialtes shut up
Ares for thirteen months in a brazen pot, from which he was
released by Hermes. " The traditional explanation ", says
Mr. Leaf on this passage, " makes them a personification
of the triumph of agricultural pursuits ('Αλωεύς from ἀλωή)
over warlike passions," and he quotes from Schol. D on λ
308 a statement that Otus and Ephialtes put an end to war
and made men live at peace. On this view the Aloidae shut
up the war-god in a pot to hinder him from going about
and stirring up strife, just as some New Guinea people shut
up the god of rain, thunder, and lightning, and keep him a
close prisoner in a sacred house when they wish to have
fine weather for a feast ; after the feast he is let out and
may go and rain, thunder, and lighten as much as he likes.
See Chalmers and Gill, *Work and Adventure in New Guinea*,
p. 152. A different explanation is suggested by a custom of
the Alfoors of Halmahera, a large island west of New Guinea.
Some of these people think that the war-god lives in the forest
or on a tall tree, and when they are going to war they inveigle
him into a basket, shut him up, and carry him with them in
the basket to battle. On their return, the basket, gay with
flowers, is welcomed with demonstrations of joy, but the god
is not let out of it till he has given his word of honour that
he will stand by the people in their next war. See *Tijdschrift
voor Indische Taal-, land- en volkenkunde*, dl. xxvii. p. 447
sq. ; also *Bijdragen tot de Taal-, land- en volkenkunde van*

---

[1] Reprinted from *The Classical Review*, vol. ii. No. 7 (July 1888), p. 222.

Neêrlandsch Indië. 4de volg. viii. p. 183 *sq.* Following out
the hint here given, may we not suppose that the reason
why the Aloidae kept Ares a prisoner was, not that men
might beat their spears to pruning-hooks as the scholiast
thought, but that they might have the war-god on their side
in battle ? Such a view fits far better with the known
character of the Aloidae, who appear as peaceful husbandmen nowhere but in the gentle scholiast's fancy ; in Homer
himself they are proud defiant spirits who threaten to make
their slogan heard in heaven. The story of Ares in the
brazen pot would thus be a reminiscence of a time when the
Greeks " potted " their war-god and so carried him to battle,
as the Jews took with them the Ark of God. Such a custom
would be quite in harmony with both Greek and Roman
ideas. At Sparta the statue of the war-god Enyalius was
fettered to prevent him running away, and at Athens the
goddess of Victory had no wings lest she should fly away
(Pausanias, iii. 15. 7). The reason why the gates of the temple
of Janus at Rome were shut in peace and open in war (about
which the interpreters ancient and modern have boggled so
much—*se torserunt* as they would say) was simply that the
war-god lived inside and was kept under lock and key in the
piping times of peace for exactly the same reason that the
Spartans chained up Enyalius, and the Athenians clipped
Victory's wings. But in time of war the doors were flung
open that the god might go forth to fight. This was Virgil's
explanation of the custom (*Aen.* i. 293 *sqq.*, vii. 611 *sqq.*),
and after Varro no man knew Italian antiquities better than
Virgil. It must have been a solemn moment when the great
gates swung creaking on their hinges, and the consul, amid
the blare of trumpets, called in a loud voice on the war-god
to come forth. That some such ceremony actually took place
at the opening of the gates may be inferred with certainty
from Virgil's description ; that the ceremony should be an
unfamiliar one and known only to Roman Dryasdusts was
natural, since for centuries together none but antiquaries
knew of a time when Rome had been at peace.

2. Βουλυτός, THE LOOSING OF THE OX [1]

Βουλυτός, "the hour when the ox is unyoked", is explained by Liddell and Scott to mean *evening*. But an examination of the passages adduced by L. and S. shows that βουλυτός must mean *the time immediately after noon*. Thus :
Iliad, ii. 777 *sqq.*

> ὄφρα μὲν ἠέλιος μέσον οὐρανὸν ἀμφιβεβήκει,
> τόφρα μάλ᾽ ἀμφοτέρων βέλε᾽ ἥπτετο, πῖπτε δὲ λαός·
> ἦμος δ᾽ ἠέλιος μετενίσσετο βουλυτόνδε,
> καὶ τότε δή κτλ.

Here the hour of noon is marked by the expression "when the sun bestrode the mid-heaven " ; and the beginning of the afternoon by the phrase " but when he began to cross over to βουλυτός ".
Again *Odyssey*, i. 56 *sqq.*

> ὄφρα μὲν ἠὼς ἦν καὶ ἀέξετο ἱερὸν ἦμαρ,
> τόφρα δ᾽ ἀλεξόμενοι μένομεν πλέονάς περ ἐόντας·
> ἦμος δ᾽ ἠέλιος μετενίσσετο βουλυτόνδε
> καὶ τότε δή κτλ.

Here the morning and forenoon (" the sacred day was growing ") are sharply distinguished from the passage of the sun across the meridian to βουλυτός. Eustathius on this passage defines βουλυτός as " either noon or a little after it, when the oxen are loosed from their labour ", ἢ μεσημβρία ἐστὶν ἢ ὀλίγον τι μετὰ μεσημβρίαν ὅτε βόες λύονται τοῦ κάμνειν.
The passages of Homer are not quite conclusive, for it might be said that in them βουλυτόνδε indicates not the next, but the last point, in the sun's passage from the meridian, *i.e.* sunset rather than the early afternoon. However a familiar passage in Aristophanes (*Birds*, 1498 *sqq.*) is quite decisive. Prometheus, coming on the stage under shelter of an umbrella, lest Zeus should see his traitorous correspondence

---

[1] Reprinted from *The Classical Review*, vol. ii. No. 8 (October 1888), pp. 260 *sq.*

with the enemies of the gods, asks anxiously what o'clock
it is.

ΠΡ. πηνίκ' ἐστὶν ἄρα τῆς ἡμέρας ;
ΠΕ. ὁπηνίκα ; σμικρόν τι μετὰ μεσημβρίαν.
ἀλλὰ σὺ τίς εἶ ; ΠΡ. βουλυτός, ἢ περαιτέρω ;

Here as the fun consists in Prometheus' anxiety to know
the *exact* time of day to a minute, we may be certain that
βουλυτός means the earliest time after midday which had a
designation at all.   It must have followed very closely after
noon, since Prometheus supposes that the hour may be later
(περαιτέρω) than βουλυτός, and still be only a little after
noon (σμικρόν τι μετὰ μεσημβρίαν).   Thus Eustathius'
definition of βουλυτός is correct ; it was either noon or
shortly after noon.

Horace supports this interpretation of βουλυτός by
describing the time when oxen are unyoked as the hour
when the shadows of the mountains are changing :

" *sol ubi montium*
Mutaret umbras et iuga demeret
Bobus fatigatis."   (*Carm.* iii. 6. 41 *sqq.*)

For before noon the shadows fall westward, after noon
they fall eastward, and the time when the change of shadows
takes place is just at or after noon.   This therefore is the
hour of βουλυτός.

Elsewhere than in Greece it has been the custom to stop
the day's ploughing at noon.   In ancient Wales (Seebohm's
English Village Community, p. 124 *sq.*) " it would seem
that a day's ploughing ended at midday, because in the legal
description of a complete ox it is required to plough only
to midday.   The Gallic word for the acre or strip, '*journel*',
in the Latin of the monks '*jurnalis*', and sometimes
'*diurnalis*', also points to a day's ploughing ; while the
German word '*morgen*' for the same strips in the German
open fields still more clearly points to a day's work which
ended, like the Welsh '*cyvar*', at noon." It is doubtless a
mark of primitive husbandry when the ploughing stops for
the day at noon.   At a more advanced stage of agriculture
the ploughing is resumed after the midday rest.   In Aberdeen-

shire, I am told, the horses are unyoked from the plough
about noon ; after a rest they are yoked again and plough till
toward evening. Hence in Aberdeenshire the morning and
afternoon ploughing is each called a " yoking ". Compare
jugum, jugerum. In this case there are two βουλυτοί, one
at midday and one at evening ; and writers of a later age,
familiar with the custom of ploughing till evening, might
use βουλυτός vaguely in the sense of evening, as appears to
have been done by Aratus (825 *sqq.*, with the Schol. βουλύσιος
δὲ ὥρην τὴν δύσιν κεκλῆκε) and a poet in the Anthology
(ἀστὴρ βουλυτοῖο, cited by L. and S.). But the use of βουλυτός
to mark *one* definite hour of the day could hardly have originated at a time when there were *two* separate βουλυτοί in a
day. Hence from the fact that in Greece down to the time
of Aristophanes at least, and (judging from the statement of
Eustathius) probably much later, the term βουλυτός was so
used to designate one particular hour of the day (namely
the time immediately after midday), we may infer that in
early Greece, as in Wales and Germany, ploughing regularly
stopped for the day at noon.[1]

Βουλυτός.—The note on this word in the last number awakened
old associations in my country-bred mind. When I lived in the midst
of farming, the plough-horses were commonly unyoked and taken
home in the middle of the day ; and if, at a time of pressure, the
ploughing was continued till four or five o'clock, the ploughman
called it " making two noons ". I remember thinking years ago
that Gray's reference to the ploughman returning home in the
evening was not true to nature, and the same thought struck me
in looking at F. Walker's well-known picture of ploughing in the
evening light.   S. CHEETHAM.

3. COINS ATTACHED TO THE FACE [2]

In the June number of *The Classical Review*, Mr. W. R.
Paton explained Pindar's ἀργυρωθεῖσαι πρόσωπα ἀοιδαί, no
doubt correctly, by the modern Greek custom of a musician

---

[1] The foregoing suggestion as to
βουλυτός evoked in the next number
of *The Classical Review* (vol. ii. No. 9,
November 1888, p. 291) the following
note, which, as it seems to lend some

support to my theory, I here reprint.

[2] Reprinted from *The Classical
Review*, vol. ii. No. 8 (October 1888),
p. 261.

sticking on his face the silver coins which he receives as payment. It is perhaps worth pointing out that the ancients
attached silver coins by means of wax to statues from which
they believed they had derived benefit (Lucian, *Philopseudes*,
20). This custom has also survived in modern times, for
in Rhodes Sir Charles Newton saw people sticking gold
coins with wax on the faces of saints (*Travels and Discoveries
in the Levant*, i. p. 187), and in a church in Lesbos he saw
a gold coin stuck on the face of the Panagia, and was told
that it was a native offering for recovery from sickness (*ib.*
ii. p. 4). In the distant island of Celebes when a young
man is pleased with a girl at a spinning festival, he sticks
a silver coin on her brow so that it adheres ; if it is not
returned to him, his suit is accepted (B. F. Matthes, *Einige
Eigenthümlichkeiten in den Festen und Gewohnheiten der
Makassaren und Buginesen*, p. 4, tiré du vol. II. des Travaux
de la 6ᵉ session du Congrès international des Orientalistes
à Leide).

4. HIDE-MEASURED LANDS [1]

Everyone knows how Dido bought as much land as could
be covered by an oxhide and then cutting the hide in strips
surrounded with them the site whereon she built her city
which thence received the name of Byrsa (Virgil, *Aeneid* i.
367 *sq.* ; Justin, xviii. 5). Similar stories are cited by Grimm,
Deutsche Rechtsalterthümer, p. 90 *sq.* and R. Köhler, in
Orient und Occident, iii. p. 185 *sqq.* To the parallels adduced
by them I would add the following:

(1) In a Tartar story Jermak begs a chief to give him
land to the extent of a hide. The chief grants his request.
Then Jermak cuts the hide into narrow strips, fastens a pole
in the ground, and tying one end of the thong to the pole
traces a circle, of which the full length of the thong is the
radius. He then takes possession of the land included in
this circle and dwells there (W. Radloff, *Proben der Volks-
litteratur der türkischen Stämme Süd-Sibiriens*, iv. p. 179).

(2) In a Burmese legend King Dwattabong had a
favourite female slave who asked for as much land as she

---

[1] Reprinted from *The Classical Review*, vol. ii. No. 10 (December 1888),
p. 322.

could cover with a hide. The king granted her request ;
whereupon she cut the hide in strips and with them surrounded land enough whereon to build the city of Issay-Mew.
The name of the whole kingdom, Thara-Kettara or Thaya-
kittaya, is derived by the Burmese from *Thara* or *Thá-ya,*
" a hide " (A. Bastian, *Die Voelker des oestlichen Asien,*
i. p. 25).

(3) In Cambodia Bastian was told that hundreds of years
ago the Dutch came in great ships and asked from the king
as much land as they could cover with a buffalo's hide. On
getting his leave they cut the hide in strips and enclosed a
wide space, on which they meant to build a stronghold
(Bastian, *op. cit.* iv. p. 367 *sq*).

(4) Javanese historians tell how a Dutch captain sunk
his ship off Jakatra and then requested of the prince of the
place a small piece of ground on which he might build a shed
to store the sails, etc., while he tried to raise the ship. This
request was granted. " He afterwards waited on the prince,
and requested as much more land as could be covered by a
buffalo's hide, on which he might build a small *póndok.*
This being complied with, he cut the hide into strips, and
claimed all the land he could inclose with them. To this also
the prince, after some hesitation, consented " (Sir Thomas
Stamford Raffles, *History of Java,* ii. p. 153 *sq.*, ed. 1817).

(5) According to a Balinese legend, the people of Tenganan, a district in Bali, formerly enjoyed the honour of
keeping the herds of the King of Kaloengkoeng. It befell
that the king's riding horse died at pasture. So the king
commanded that the horse should be buried on the spot and
that the land, as far as the smell of the carrion spread, should
belong to the herdsman. Thereupon the people of Tenganan
cut the carcass in pieces and each of them sticking a bit in
his girdle set off to walk. They walked and walked till they
had as much land as they knew what to do with ; and that
is why the district of Tenganan is one of the biggest in Bali
(Van Eck, " Schetsen van het eiland Bali ", in *Tijdschrift
voor Neêrlands Indië,* February 1880, p. 117).

Strictly speaking, in the last example the standard of
measurement is not the hide but the walking power of the
people of Tenganan. But the similarity to the other stories

will not be denied. The wide diffusion of such tales confirms Grimm's conjecture (*Deutsche Rechtsalterthümer*, p. 538 *sq.*) that in them we have a recollection of a mode of land measurement once actually in use and of which the designation is still retained in the English *hide*.

5. THE BEDSTEAD OF THE FLAMEN DIALIS [1]

In the curious chapter of Aulus Gellius (x. 15) which details the minute rules observed by the Flamen Dialis in his daily life, it is said the feet of his bed had always to be smeared with fine mud. The meaning of this rule becomes plain when we remember that the Σελλοί, the old priests of Zeus at Dodona, were bound to sleep on the ground (χαμαιεῦναι, *Iliad*, ii. 235), and further when we find that the priest of the old Prussian god Potrimpo was bound to sleep on the bare earth for three nights before he sacrificed to the god (Hartknoch, *Dissertationes historicae de variis rebus Prussicis*, p. 163, bound up with his edition of Dusberg's *Chronicon Prussiae*, Frankfort and Leipzig, 1679 ; Simon Grunau, *Preussischer Chronik*, ed. Perlbach, I. p. 95). Plainly the mud on the feet of the Flamen's bedstead was one of those " accommodations with heaven " which are to be found in every religion. Instead of sleeping on the ground, as his predecessors doubtless did in days of old, the modern Flamen slept in a bed, but soothed his conscience by daubing the legs of the bed with mud and thus, by a convenient ecclesiastical fiction, sleeping on the ground. A chapter on ecclesiastical fictions would be agreeable and instructive reading. The ancient Jew rent his garments in mourning ; the modern Jew (who knows the value of clothes, even of old ones) contents himself with undoing a seam for a couple of inches or so. In the second volume of Bastian's *Die Voelker des oestlichen Asien*, p. 319 *sq.*, there is a pleasant description of the way in which a Burmese monk contrives to make the best of both worlds. He may not touch a woman—but if his mother falls into a well, he may pull her out with a long pole, provided he imagines that he is pulling out a log of

---

[1] Reprinted from *The Classical Review*, vol. ii. No. 10 (December 1888), p. 322.

wood. He may not eat after noon—but he is free at any time of the afternoon or evening to ask a disciple what o'clock it is, and if the disciple says " Not noon yet " the monk may fall to. And so on *ad infinitum.*

6. OMENS FROM SNEEZING [1]

Catullus xlv. 8 *sq.*

" Hoc ut dixit, Amor sinistra ut ante
Dextram sternuit approbationem."

The passages quoted by Robinson Ellis in his Commentary prove that the ancients regarded a sneeze as ominous. They do not however show whether the omen varied according as it came from the right or left. It may therefore be of interest to note that amongst other peoples the omen did so vary. Thus in Bombay " a ˙ sneeze on the left insures success ; on the right prognosticates evil ; in front portends ruin, and at the back promises help from God " (*Indian Notes and Queries*, vol. iv. No. 611). In Fiji " some take an omen from the fact of a man's sneezing out of the right or left nostril while he holds a certain stick in his hand " (Th. Williams, *Fiji and the Fijians*, I. p. 229). It is indeed a general rule in Roman and all augury that the significance of an omen varies according to the side from which it is heard or seen, and it would be strange if sneezing were an exception to the rule. Probably the absence of classical evidence on this head is a mere accident. Considering the small chance any popular superstition had of getting into classical literature, and, if it did get in, of surviving the shipwreck of ancient books, this lack of evidence is not surprising.

7. SWALLOWS IN THE HOUSE [2]

Speaking of spring, a poet in the Anthology (*Anthol. Palat.* x. 2) says :

ἤδη δὲ πλάσσει μὲν ὑπώροφα γυρὰ χελιδών
οἰκία—

---

[1] Reprinted from *The Classical Review*, vol. iii. No. 7 (July 1889), p. 315.

[2] Reprinted from *The Classical Review*, vol. v. Nos. 1 and 2 (February 1891), pp. 1-3.

which Mr. Mackail (*Select Epigrams from the Greek Anthology*, first edition, p. 198) translates: "Now the swallow plasters her round houses under the eaves." To translate ὑπώροφα by "under the eaves" instead of "under the roof" is natural for an English scholar and cannot be incorrect, since of course the eaves are part of the roof. Still I think that ὑπώροφα may have meant a good deal more than "under the eaves". At the present day the houses of the Greek peasants have usually no glass in the windows, which are merely closed with wooden shutters at night; and the rooms are unceiled, so that one has nothing but the rafters and the roof overhead. The windows being constantly open in the daytime, the swallows fly freely in and out the house, and build their nests among the rafters. In Laconia I observed this in more than one house where I slept. I have lain abed in the early morning and heard the twittering of the swallows and the whirr of their wings as they flew about overhead in the dark, before the shutters were opened. For of course till the shutters are opened the birds cannot get out, and towards daybreak they grow restless, and flit twittering about the room. May it not have been much the same in antiquity? And does not this view sharpen the points of some references to swallows in ancient literature? Thus in another poem in the Anthology (*Anthol. Palat.* v. 237) a passionate lover tosses about on his bed all night long; at last, as the day is breaking, he drops asleep, only however to be wakened by the swallows twittering about him (ἀμφιπεριτρύζουσι χελιδόνες). He bids them cease chattering or go wail for Itylus on the mountains, that he may get a little sleep (βαιὸν ἵνα κνώσσοιμεν). The expression ἀμφιπεριτρύζουσι would hardly be appropriate if addressed to birds fluttering and twittering about the eaves outside the poet's window; but it is literally correct if the swallows were actually flying about the room. Similarly the poet who took Anacreon's name upbraids the chattering swallows for waking him from dreams of love at the peep of dawn (Anacreontea 9, Bergk's *Poetae lyrici Graeci,*[3] iii. p. 1050).

Again the expression of Aelian (*Nat. An.* x. 34) τιμᾶται δὲ ἡ χελιδὼν θεοῖς μυχίοις καὶ ᾿Αφροδίτῃ μυχίᾳ μέντοι καὶ ταύτῃ, seems to mean that the swallow is honoured by the gods of the inside of the house, which could hardly have been said if the bird only built its nest under the eaves. Once more Pythagoras said, " Do not receive a swallow in the house " (χελιδόνα οἰκίᾳ μὴ δέχου, Jamblichus, *Adhort. ad philos.* 21 ; Clemens Alexandr. *Strom.* v. 5 § 27, p. 660, ed. Potter ; Plutarch, *Quaest. Conviv.* viii. 7. 1). The words can only have had their full meaning if the birds were sometimes allowed to build their nests actually within the house.

The modern Greek peasant, I was told, is glad when the swallows build in his house, for he thinks it lucky. It is reasonable to suppose that his ancestors were of the same mind, for a like belief is still deeply rooted in the minds of European peasants and of some Asiatic peoples. In Germany and Austria the belief is very common. For example in the Tyrol the blessing of God is believed to rest on a house where swallows build their nests ; and some people leave their windows open day and night that the birds may fly freely in and out (I. V. Zingerle, *Sitten, Bräuche und Meinungen des Tiroler Volkes*,[2] § 743). In Bohemia swallows are had in high honour, and people nail boards under the eaves to tempt the birds to build there (J. V. Grohmann, *Aberglauben und Gebräuche aus Böhmen und Mähren*, § 491). Formerly in Westphalia on a day in spring when the returning swallows were looked for, the whole family, headed by the father, went to the gate to meet them, and threw wide the door of the barn that the swallows might fly in (A. Kuhn, *Sagen, Gebräuche und Meinungen aus Westfalen*, ii. p. 71). In Hesse the arrival of the first swallow was signalled by a watchman on a tower and then publicly announced by the magistrates (A. Wuttke, *Der deutsche Volksaberglaube*,[2] § 159). In some parts of Lancashire it is thought a happy omen for a house when a swallow builds its nest about the house or the barn ; and woe to the little boy who is rash enough to meddle with the birds (J. Harland and T. T. Wilkinson, *Lancashire Folk-lore*, p. 143). In Russia the same belief is current (*Archiv für wissenschaftliche Kunde von Russland*, herausgeg. von Erman, vol. i. 1848, p. 628). The Votyaks in eastern Russia think (and German peasants

M

agree with them) that if they killed a swallow their cattle would not thrive. They even build nests for the swallows (Max Buch, *Die Wotyaken*, p. 165). Evidence to the same effect might be given in handfuls ; I will content myself with mentioning that the same belief in the luckiness of a swallow building its nest under the roof is held by Chinese, Japanese, and the Minahassa of Celebes (J. Doolittle, *Social Life of the Chinese*, ed. Paxton Hood, p. 572 ; H. C. St. John, *Wild Coasts of Nipon*, p. 117 ; *Tijdschrift voor Nederlandsch Indië*, iv. July 1870, p. 11).

The famous " swallow-song ", which in ancient Rhodes children sang from door to door, seems certainly to have been meant to welcome the heralds of the spring and invite them to take up their abode in the house. The children sang (Athenaeus, viii. 60, p. 360) :

> " *He has come, he has come, the swallow !*
> *Happy seasons bringing,*
> *And happy years !*
> *Open, open the door to the swallow !* "

A similar custom is still observed in Greece. On the first of March children go through the streets singing a spring carol and carrying a wooden swallow, which they keep turning constantly on a cylinder (Grimm, *Deutsche Mythologie*,[4] ii. p. 636).

But it may be asked : If the ancients were so glad to see the swallow and so eager to welcome him to their homes, why did Pythagoras forbid him the house ?[1]

It will not do to say that Pythagoras was a philosopher who set his face against popular superstitions. On the contrary, the wise saws called " the symbols of Pythagoras " are nothing but superstitious rules of conduct such as are still quite familiar to Highland servants in Scotland, Ojebway Indians, and people of that sort.[2] May we then suppose that in regard to swallows Pythagoras for once deviated into sense ? I fear not. In popular fancy the swallow has its dark as well as its bright side, and if Pythagoras

[1] Porphyry, *De vita Pythagorae*, 42 ; Jamblichus, *Adhortatio ad Philosophiam*, 21, p. 314, ed. Kiessling ; Diogenes Laertius, viii. 1. 7 ; Plutarch, *Quaestiones Conviviales*, viii. 7. 1 ; Clemens Alexandr. *Strom.* v. 5. 27, p. 660, ed. Potter. [2] See above, pp. 130 *sqq.*

shut his door against the bird, it was probably because he deemed it a creature of ill omen. Some of the ancients certainly thought that the swallow boded untimely death (Artemidorus, *Onirocr.* 66). In some parts of Germany it is held that where swallows build new nests, someone will die in that house within the year (Grimm, *D.M.*⁴ iii. p. 446). A poor woman in England, whose young daughter had just died, remarked to a lady, " A swallow lit upon her shoulder, ma'am, a short time since, as she was walking home from church, and that is a sure sign of death " (Dyer, *English Folk-lore*, p. 69). In Yorkshire if a swallow comes down the chimney, it is an omen of death ; and in Norfolk, if the swallows gather in great numbers about a house, someone in it will die and his soul will take flight with the swallows (Swainson, *Folk-lore of British Birds*, p. 54). Archbishop Whately says that in Ireland the swallow is called " the devil's bird " by the common folk, who hold that every man has a certain hair on his head, which if a swallow can pick off, the man is certainly damned (Henderson, *Folk-lore of the Northern Counties*, p. 123). In some parts of Scotland the swallow is thought to have a drop of the deil's blood in it, and in Caithness it is called "witch hag" (Swainson, *loc. cit.*). The Chewsurs of the Caucasus are of opinion that swallows and all other migratory birds bring sickness with them, and that certain precautions are needful to avert the baleful influence. The antidote for seeing the first swallow is a glass of wine or a nip of brandy (G. Radde, *Die Chews'-uren und ihr Land*, p. 111 *sq.*).

In conclusion, it is hardly necessary to say that even if, as I have tried to show, in ancient as in modern Greece swallows may have been allowed to build their nests on the rafters inside the house, it would be absurd to suppose that they did not sometimes build them under the eaves. If any proof that they did so were needed, we might quote the lines in the Anthology (*Anthol. Palat.* x. 16. 5 *sq.*) :

καὶ φιλόπαις ὑπὸ γεῖσα δόμους τεύξασα χελιδὼν
ἔκγονα πηλοχύτοις ξεινοδοκεῖ θαλάμοις.
"*The swallow builds her nest under the eaves*," *etc.*

SWALLOWS IN THE HOUSE [1]

Since I wrote the preceding note on this subject I have received the following extract from a recent book, *Japanese Houses and their Surroundings*, by Edward S. Morse, late Professor of Zoology in the University of Tokio : " A household shrine to which the children pay voluntary and natural devotion are the birds' nests built within the house. It is a common thing, not only in the country but in large cities like Tokio, for a species of swallow, hardly to be distinguished from the European species, to build its nest in the house—not in an out-of-the-way place, but in the room where the family may be most actively engaged, or in the shop fronting the street, with all its busy traffic going on. The very common occurrence of these birds' nests in houses is another of the many evidences of the gentle ways of this people and of the kindness shown by them to animals. When a bird builds its nest in the house, a little shelf is promptly secured beneath it, so that the mats below shall not be soiled. The presence of the bird in the house is regarded as a good omen, and the children take great pleasure in watching the construction of the nest and the final rearing of the young birds. I noticed that many of the nests built within the house were much more elaborately made than those built in more exposed positions. From the symmetrical way in which many of these were constructed, one might almost imagine the birds had become imbued with some of the art instincts of the people." This passage is interesting inasmuch as it shows that the custom of allowing swallows to build their nests inside the house is not confined to the rude peasantry of remote districts but is shared by the town population of a highly refined nation. In this respect the ancient Greeks may very well have done what the Japanese still do. We are told that swallows flew freely about in the great temples at Athens, Olympia, and Epidaurus (Clemens Alex. *Protrept*. iv. 52) ; and we know that birds even built their nests in the temples, and that to meddle

---

[1] Note reprinted from *The Classical Review*, vol. v. No. 5 (May 1891), pp. 230 *sq*.

with the nests was sacrilege (Herodotus, i. 159). The Athenians actually put to death a man for killing a sacred sparrow of Aesculapius (Aelian, *Var. hist.* v. 17). If the gods welcomed birds to their temples, men may have welcomed them to their homes.

8. THE YOUTH OF ACHILLES [1]

In the last number of *The Classical Review* the story that Achilles in his youth was dressed as a girl is explained by Mr. A. E. Crawley as a reminiscence of a custom of dressing boys as girls at those initiatory ceremonies which lads in primitive society have commonly to undergo at puberty. But Mr. Crawley adduces no example of such a custom. It is perhaps more likely that the story is a reminiscence of a· custom of dressing boys as girls in infancy and for some years afterwards. Such a practice is common in some parts of India, as for example Oudh, and is not unknown in Europe. The converse custom (that of dressing little girls as boys) appears to be rarer, but examples of it are recorded both in India and Europe. The object of both customs appears to be, in general, to avert malignant influences, especially the evil eye, from the child ; this is supposed to be effected by concealing the child's sex. But in the case of girls disguised as boys another motive is sometimes at work, as will appear from one of the examples quoted below.

To give instances. " The practice of dressing boys as girls, and girls as boys, to avert the evil eye is not uncommon in the Konkan, and sometimes this superstition is carried to such an extent that in order to make the boy appear a genuine girl, even his nose is bored and a nose-ring put into it " (*Journal of the Anthropological Society of Bombay* (1886), p. 123). In Oudh " it is a common practice to dress little boys as girls to keep off the evil eye " (*Panjab Notes and Queries*, vol. i. (1883–1884), No. 869). Again, in Oudh " it is usual to bore the nose of a long-wished-for son as soon as he is born to turn him into a girl. This is done to avoid *nazar*, to which boys are more liable than girls " (*ib.* No.

---

[1] Reprinted from *The Classical Review*, vol. vii. No. 7 (July 1893), pp. 292-294.

1029). Again, in India (district not specified) " if a man has lost several male children, the nose of the next born is pierced, and a nose-ring inserted in order that he may be mistaken for a girl, and so passed over by the evil spirits " (*ib*. No. 219). Again, in India "it is a common practice in families, when a boy has been born after the death of several children or boys, to dress him up as a girl and give him an opprobrious name. . . . The reverse custom also obtains of dressing up a girl as a boy when a succession of girls have been born, in hopes that the next child may be a boy " (*Panjab Notes and Queries*, vol. ii. (1884–1885), No. 561 ; compare Nos. 344, 570). With regard to the observance of similar customs in Europe, a writer in the same journal (vol. i, No. 1007) writes : " Some years ago, when staying in the Engadine, I saw a good deal of an Italian lady, a Milanese so far as I can remember. She had a sweet little child with her, who was about five or six years old, and as it was attired in a kind of knicker-bocker suit, I naturally thought this child was a boy ; but one day to my great astonishment, it appeared dressed as a girl. On my expressing my astonishment at the transformation, the mother told me that she had only one grown up son and this little girl living ; she had lost several between—all girls. She seemed to think that by clothing this one like a boy she should in some way avert evil from it." Condorcet in his infancy was dressed as a girl for eight years or more by his superstitious mother (John Morley, *Miscellanies*, ii. p. 166).

From these instances it appears that the practice of disguising a boy as a girl is especially resorted to when several male children have already died in the family. In such a case the new-comer is regarded as exposed to the same maleficent influences which have already carried off his little brothers, and unusually stringent precautions are thought to be necessary to save him. A list of the superstitious precautions taken by fond parents in these circumstances would alone almost fill a chapter. Now it is at least remarkable that Achilles was said to be the seventh male child of Peleus and Thetis, and that all his six elder brothers had perished before him in their infancy (Tzetzes, *Schol. on Lycophron*, 178 ; Schol. on Homer, *Il*. xvi. 37 ; Schol. on Apollonius

Rhodius, iv. 816 ; Ptolemaeus Hephaestionis, vi., in Photius, *Bibliotheca*, p. 152 a 1 *sqq.*, ed. Bekker). It is true that the deaths of the first six children were attributed to the action of the mother herself, who threw them into the fire to kill them or to make them immortal, for the opinions of mythologists were divided as to her motive. Still the tradition of their premature deaths may perhaps be allowed some weight in confirmation of the view advocated above.

In regard to the story just mentioned, that Thetis killed her first six children by putting them on the fire, and that her seventh child, Achilles, was only saved by the interposition of his father Peleus, there can be little doubt that the motive originally attributed to the mother was a beneficent one (Schol. on Homer, *Il.* xvi. 37), and that the malignant motive commonly ascribed to her was a mistaken, though very natural, interpretation of this incident in the legend. This is made certain by the stories that Demeter and Isis adopted the very same expedient for rendering immortal the princely infants committed to their care (*Homeric Hymn to Demeter*, 233 *sqq.* ; Plutarch, *Isis and Osiris*, 16).

These stories probably reflect an old custom of passing a new-born child over the flames or keeping it over a smouldering fire for some time, in order to ward off evil influence.

A custom of this sort has prevailed in many parts of the world. Pennant thus describes the custom as it was observed in Scotland in the eighteenth century: " It has happened that, after baptism, the father has placed a basket filled with bread and cheese on the pot-hook that impended over the fire in the middle of the room, which the company sit around : and the child is thrice handed across the fire, with the design to frustrate all attempts of evil spirits or evil eyes " (Pinkerton's *Voyages and Travels*, iii. p. 383). This custom prevailed in Scotland down to the beginning of the nineteenth century at least ; sometimes the father leaped across the hearth with the child in his arms (Miss C. F. Gordon Cumming, *In the Hebrides*, ed. 1883, p. 101). In the Tenimber and Timorlaut islands (East Indies) " in order to prevent sickness, or rather to frighten the evil spirits, the child is, in the first few days, laid beside or over the fire " (J. G. F. Riedel, *De sluik- en*

kroesharige rassen tusschen Selebes en Papua, p. 303). The
meaning of placing the child " over the fire " in the passage
just quoted is probably explained by the practice, observed
in the neighbouring island of Timor, of keeping a smouldering
or charcoal fire (" *een kolen vuur* ") for four days under the
bed on which the new-born child is laid (*Tijdschrift voor
Neêrland's Indië*, vol. vii. (1845), p. 280). In New Britain,
after a birth has taken place, they kindle a fire of leaves and
fragrant herbs, and the mother takes the child and swings
it backwards and forwards through the smoke of the fire,
while the friends present utter good wishes. At the same
time the *Dukduk* men hold their hands in the smoke or
ashes and then lay them on the child's eyes, ears, temples,
nose, and mouth " to preserve it from the influence of evil
spirits " (R. Parkinson, *Im Bismarck-Archipel*, p. 94 *sq*.). In
ancient Mexico a young child was passed four times through
the fire (Clavigero, *History of Mexico*, trans. by Cullen, i.
p. 317) ; in Madagascar he was passed twice over the fire
before he was taken out of the house for the first time (W. Ellis,
History of Madagascar, i. p. 152). In Canton the following
ceremony is performed " at any time during the earlier years
of childhood, its object being to render the child courageous
and ward off evil. A lump of alum is taken by the mother,
and touching the child's forehead, eyes, breast, and shoulders
with it, she pronounces a certain formula. Then the alum
is put into the fire and is supposed to assume the likeness of
the creature which the child fears most. Before actually
placing the alum into the fire, the mother moves the child
several times over the glowing charcoal " (*China Review*, ix.
(1880–81), p. 303). The ancient Greek practice of running
round the hearth with a child on the fifth or seventh day after
birth (Suidas, *s.v.* ἀμφιδρόμια ; Schol. on Plato, *Theaetetus*,
p. 160 E ; Hesychius, *s.v.* δρομιάφιον ἦμαρ) may have been
a substitute for the older custom of passing the child over
the fire. But the older and ruder rite, after it had been
abandoned by the Greeks themselves, seems still to have
lingered in their legends of the gods. This was natural, since
the life of the gods is merely a reflection of the life of savage
man.

9. THE LEAFY BUST AT NEMI [1]

In *The Classical Review* for November 1907 Professor F. Granger proposed an interpretation of the remarkable double-headed bust which was found among the ruins of the temple of Diana at Nemi. The bust represents two heads turned back to back : one of the heads is that of a man of mature life with a flowing beard : the other is that of a young and beardless man. The type of face is much the same in both heads. The eyes are deep-sunk and wide open : the nose is bold and strong, but not of the Roman type : the nostrils are wide : the lips are full : the expression is wild, with a far-away look in the eyes : the whole cast of the features is neither Greek nor Roman but barbaric. The brow of the older face is wrinkled and the mouth wide open, showing the teeth. But perhaps the most singular thing about the two heads are the leaves with scalloped edges which are plastered, so to say, on the necks of both busts, and seem to appear again under the eyes of the youthful face. On either side of the mouth of this younger face there is also a curious projection, of which no certain explanation has been given.

Some years ago my friend Mr. A. B. Cook suggested that the two heads represent the double form of Dian's famous favourite, who died in Greece as the youthful Hippolytus and came to life again as the mature Virbius, with altered features, at Nemi, where he reigned as first King of the Wood.[2] That such a portrait would be eminently in place at Nemi, where the bust was found, is undeniable. This theory has been taken up and carried further by Professor Frank Granger. He suggests that the double bust is a portrait not so much of the mythical Hippolytus-Virbius as of his successor and representative the priest of Diana at Nemi, the King of the Wood (*Rex Nemorensis*), and he would explain the barbaric cast of the features by supposing that the artist copied from the life ; for since the priest of Nemi had always to be a runaway slave, it might often, perhaps

[1] Reprinted from *The Classical Review*, vol. xxii. No. 5 (August 1908), pp. 147-149.

[2] *Classical Review*, xvi. (1902) p. 373.

generally, happen that he would be a barbarian. On this hypothesis the older bearded head, with its wrinkled brow and grinning mouth, stands for the priest in possession, who would generally be the older man, while the younger beardless face would stand for his youthful and vigorous assailant. Further, Professor Granger proposes to identify the leaves on the bust as oak leaves, and he points out that one end of the moustache of the bearded figure, seen in profile, is carved in the shape of an oak leaf. This observation of Professor Granger I can confirm, for last summer I examined the cast of the bust in the Museum of Nottingham in company with the Curator, Professor Granger, and other friends, and we all agreed that, whether accidentally or not, the modelling of the moustache on one side of the face does resemble an oak leaf.

If Professor Granger's theory is right it would go a long way to confirm the view which for many years I have held that the priest of Diana at Nemi, the King of the Wood, probably personated the god of the oak ; [1] for it would be hardly possible to represent a man as a personification of an oak more graphically than by plastering oak-leaves on his body. But a crucial question remains. Are the leaves which are carved on the bust really oak-leaves ? In order to ascertain this I submitted three excellent photographs of the bust, which I received some years ago from my friend Commendatore Boni of the Roman Forum, to Mr. Francis Darwin, who very kindly examined them himself and also took the opinion of Mr. R. I. Lynch, the experienced Curator of the Botanic Garden at Cambridge. The result of their joint examination of the photographs was communicated to me by Mr. Darwin in a letter which he allows me to publish. I should add that I explained to Mr. Darwin the theories which had been put forward as to the busts and the leaves, but that he was careful not to mention these theories to Mr. Lynch, lest the knowledge of them should unconsciously

---

[1] The view was first put forward by me in *The Golden Bough* (first edition, 1890), i. 369 *sq.* It has since been maintained with fuller evidence in my *Lectures on the Early History of the Kingship*, (London 1905), pp. 281 *sqq.*, from which I will quote the conclusion (p. 284) : " On the whole, then, we conclude that at Nemi the King of the Wood personated the oak-god Jupiter and mated with the oak goddess Diana in the sacred grove."

bias his mind in the identification of the leaves. Mr. Darwin's letter, dated January 26, 1908, runs thus :

" I am sorry to say that Lynch did not suggest oak and when we got a picture of an oak-leaf and compared the two he was not much struck with the resemblance. But a Zoological friend who was with us agreed that they might be more or less conventionalised oak-leaves. I don't suppose Lynch is used to convention in art : he thought the leaves more like nettle or perhaps dead-nettle (*Lamium*). I think the scalloped edges of the leaves are, as I said, like certain leaves which are considered oak-like. The plant I was thinking of is *Teucrium chamaedrys*, and it is perhaps of interest that the name *chamaedrys* is said to have been given by Dioscorides to *Teucrium lucidum*, which has much the same leaves as *T. chamaedrys*. There is also *Veronica chamaedrys* with similar leaves; and the oak-fern *Polypodium dryopteris* in which the pinnae of the frond are less like oak and not so like the leaves on your bust. Is it possible (as my daughter suggests) that the priest is chewing leaves ? I think Miss Harrison mentions buckthorn leaves being chewed on some sacred occasion."

Thus the identification of the leaves on the bust as oak-leaves, and with it my theory of the priest as a personification of the oak, remains uncertain. I will only add that Miss Darwin's proposal to identify as leaves of some sort the things which project from the mouth of the younger face seems to me excellent. It appears that at all oracular seats of Apollo his priestess regularly chewed the laurel before she delivered her prophecies in the name of the deity.[1] By chewing the sacred plant of her god she was probably believed to fill herself with his sacred spirit. Perhaps in like manner the candidate for the priesthood at Nemi chewed oak-leaves in order to nerve his arm for the fatal stroke. It may have been with oak-leaves in his mouth, as well as with sword in hand, that he advanced upon his adversary. Can it be that in the face of the older man the artist has purposely shown us a grinning empty mouth as if to indicate that the sacred oak and with it the god had passed from him to another ?

---

[1] Lucian, *Bis accusatus*, 1 ; J. Tzetzes, *Scholia on Lycophron*, 6.

10. FOLK-LORE AT BALQUHIDDER [1]

The following scraps of folk-lore at Balquhidder were
collected by me, from personal observation and inquiry, at
Balquhidder, Perthshire, in September 1888 :

At Balquhidder, on September 25, 1888, I witnessed the
ceremony of cutting the harvest " Maiden ". The farmer,
Mr. McLaren, knowing that we were interested in the custom,
gave us notice that the cutting of the corn was almost finished
and the " Maiden " was about to be made. When we entered
the field the oats were all cut, except one small patch and a
single slender bunch or sheaf which remained standing by
itself uncut amid the cut corn. This bunch or sheaf was to
form the " Maiden ". First the standing patch was cut
down ; then an old man grasped the sheaf which was to
form the " Maiden " and gave it a twist. It was the regular
custom, he said, thus to twist it, and the sheaf should be cut
at a single stroke. The youngest girl on the field (a child
about four years old) then put her hands on the scythe and,
assisted by an unmarried lady present, cut through the sheaf.
At this point we left the field. But shortly afterwards I was
told that the " Maiden " was being carried home by a small
boy, who was hurrahing and kicking up his heels as he ran.
I hastened out, but when I met him his demonstrations of
joy had subsided, doubtless through shyness, into a very
sober walk. Mrs. McLaren kindly made a special " Maiden "
for us from part of this last sheaf cut, the remainder of the
sheaf being used to make a " Maiden " for the farm. The
head of our " Maiden " was formed of a bunch of ears of
oats ; a broad blue riband was tied in a bow under the
head, the ends of the bow projecting (to form arms ?) ; a
skirt of paper neatly made and cut out in a pattern completed
the costume of the " Maiden ". I hope to place this " Maiden "
in the Antiquarian Museum, Cambridge, and to make it
the beginning of a collection of " Maidens ", or " clyack
sheafs " (see Mr. W. Gregor, in *Revue des traditions populaires*, October 1888, p. 484, *seq.*), from all parts of the
country where the custom is still observed.

[1] Reprinted from *The Folk-Lore Journal*, vol. vi. (1888), pp. 268-271.

So much for what I saw. Now for what I ascertained about the "Maiden" by inquiry from different inhabitants, particularly Miss McColl and Miss Watt of Kirkton. At harvest the last corn cut on the farm is dressed like a doll and called "the Maiden". It is kept in the farmhouse, generally above the chimney-piece, for a good while, perhaps a year. One old woman stated that she has known people keep the old "Maiden" in the house till the new "Maiden" of the next year is brought in. It is not every house on the farm that has a "Maiden" but only the farmhouse itself. The farm on which we witnessed the cutting of the "Maiden" was a small one, and the members of the family sufficed to cut the corn without needing to hire reapers. But on large farms, where there are many reapers, a competition takes place as to who shall have the "Maiden". Each reaper is followed by a girl binding the corn as he cuts it. A reaper who wishes the girl who follows him to have the "Maiden" will sometimes leave a little corn uncut and will turn it down, and the girl who is binding the corn behind him will throw a sheaf over it to hide it. At the end of the reaping (which may not be finished for several days), when a rush has been made on the (supposed) last patch standing in order to make the "Maiden" from it, the girl who knows where the corn was turned down and hidden returns to it and cuts it after all the rest has been cut. It is for the girl who follows binding the corn that the reaper turns down the corn ; he himself takes no more concern about it. If several have thus concealed uncut corn, the girl who is cunning enough to wait till all the rest have revealed their hidden corn and cut it, is successful, for her corn is the last cut and out of it is made the "Maiden". It is supposed to be always the youngest maiden on the field who cuts the "Maiden" Mrs. Stewart, of Immercon, a farm about three miles from the Kirkton of Balquhidder, told my sister that formerly on the evening when the "Maiden" was cut they had what they called a "Kirn", that is, cream whipped up and eaten with bread or mashed potatoes ; in the potatoes were put a ring, thimble, and sixpence for the same purpose of divination as at Hallowe'en. At another farm they used to give the harvesters on this occasion a supper of curds and cream, but this is now replaced by tea. With regard to the " Kirn ", the Rev. Mr. Cameron, minister of the parish, told my sister that sometimes the cream is whipped up very stiff and mixed with oatmeal ; into this mixture the ring, thimble, and sixpence are placed. Mrs. McLaren told my mother that some people make arms of straw to the " Maiden ". Before leaving the " Maiden " I may add that my mother remembers seeing the " Maiden " at Daldouie, near Glasgow, many years ago, though she is not sure of the name by which the figure went. So far as she remembers, it had a riband tied round its head and one round its waist ; and the stalks were neatly arranged to represent the skirt of a woman's dress. It was kept hanging on the wall.

Mr. J. D. Duff, Fellow of Trinity College, Cambridge, tells me that in his part of Aberdeenshire there is a competition as to who shall have the last sheaf (the clyack sheaf) like that at Balquhidder, but with this difference, that the last corn left standing and hidden is cut by the reaper himself, not, as at Balquhidder, by the girl who followed binding. Mr. Duff adds that he was informed by a perfectly trustworthy authority that in an English county it was the custom for all the harvesters to worship the last corn in the field by bending the knee and bowing the head to it.

To return to Balquhidder. The old man who assisted at the cutting of the " Maiden " explained a mode of divination by throwing the reaping-hook over the shoulder, but as he seemed to speak English with difficulty I could not be sure that I fully understood him. He seemed to say that one man took all the reaping-hooks of the reapers in a bundle and threw them over his shoulder three times. The man whose hook stuck in the ground twice would die soon. Omens were also drawn from the direction in which the hooks fell.

At Hallowe'en each house has a bonfire. They do not dance round the fires. The custom is chiefly observed by children. The fires are lighted on any high knoll near the house.

In the churchyard at Balquhidder is a green knoll known to English-speaking people as the Angels' Mount. The Rev. Mr. Cameron told us that " Angels " is here a corruption of the Gaelic *aingeal*, the name of the knoll being *Tom-nan-*

aingeal, i.e. " the hill of the fires " (*aingeal* is genitive plural). The tradition is that the Druids kindled their fires on this knoll.

It is unlucky if a hare crosses your path. In setting out on a journey they used to regard the first person they met as ominous of good or bad luck on the journey. Some people were lucky to meet, some unlucky.

When a child was carried out of the house to be baptized, bread and cheese were given by the person who carried the child to the first person met.

In the old ruined church of Balquhidder is an ancient gravestone, said by tradition to be the grave of a Culdee saint. The Rev. Mr. Cameron informed me that formerly at marriages and baptisms the people used to stand barefoot on the gravestone as on holy ground. Some suppose it to be the tombstone of St. Angus.

The Rev. Mr. Kirk, author of *The Secret Commonwealth* (a work on fairies), and minister of Balquhidder parish about the beginning of the eighteenth century, died suddenly; it was thought by the people that he had been carried off by the fairies for revealing their secrets. Once after his death he appeared to a man and said that he (Kirk) would appear at a certain wedding, and that he might be released from fairyland if his friend would throw a knife over his shoulder. He did appear at the wedding as he had foretold, but his friend forgot to throw the knife over his shoulder ; so Mr. Kirk is still a prisoner in fairyland. This story was told me by the Rev. Mr. Cameron.

11. Notes on Harvest Customs [1]

In the following notes, where my information was derived from correspondence, I have thought it best, for the sake of accuracy, to give the writer's own words.

With regard to harvest customs in Ayrshire, I have received the following note from my sister. It is dated " Lanfine, Ayrshire, Oct. 4th, 1888 ".

" Caldwell says that in her part of the country (South Ayrshire), the last sheaf-cutting is called ' cutting the *hare*

---

[1] Reprinted from *The Folk-Lore Journal*, vol. vii. (1889), pp 47-53.

or *hair* ', she does not know which spelling is meant. In speaking of witches she says they often turn themselves into *hares*, so that perhaps it should be *hare*, as it might be a witch was in the last sheaf.[1]

" Last week here a field of corn was cut, and all the maids went up to see it done. The machine could not cut it, as the corn was much laid. Caldwell knew how to shear with the hook, so she showed the others the way to do it. They left the last sheaf standing in the middle of the field, and when all the rest was cut they went to it and *plaited* it as it stood. Then all the men in turn tried to cut it. Each went up to it in turn, then stepped backwards a good long way, and *threw* the hook at the sheaf. The hook has to be held flat by the back of the blade, *not* by the handle. No one succeeded in cutting it, so one of the maids ran in and cut it down at one blow. She held its head. The men were not very well pleased at this proceeding ; however, she carried it home in triumph, and *hung it up over the door*. The first one coming in after that was supposed to have the same name as her future husband. The sheaf is now all destroyed, as the servants began to play pranks with it, and it was torn to bits."

The Rev. W. Cunningham, rector of Great St. Mary's, Cambridge, tells me that, to the best of his memory, the custom of plaiting the last handful of standing corn, and cutting it by throwing sickles at it, was observed in his youth in Dumfriesshire ; but the introduction of scythes for cutting the corn had gone some way towards abolishing the latter part of the custom. Thus in the Ayrshire observance, already reported, the throwing the sickles would seem to be the revival of an old custom, for in Ayrshire also the scythe appears to have ousted the sickle.

The following is from a letter of Mr. Robert Matheson, addressed to a friend, the Rev. J. S. Black, of 6 Oxford

[1] The analogy of the German *Hase* which is applied to the last sheaf in some parts of Germany (see W. Mannhardt, *Die Korndämonen*, p. 3) makes it almost certain that the Ayrshire name is *hare*. Animal names for the last sheaf, though common in Germany, are not common in this country. In Hertfordshire and Shropshire the last sheaf was called the Mare (Brand, *Popular Antiquities*, ii. p. 24, Bohn's ed.). In Devon and Cornwall it was called the Craw (crow) (J. H. Dixon and R. Bell, *Ballads and Songs of the Peasantry of England*, p. 159).

Terrace, Edinburgh, who gives me leave to publish it. The letter is dated " 4 Caledonia Crescent, Edinburgh, November 12, 1888 ".

" I have been waiting for some information as to the present clyack [1] ceremonies before writing you ; but it will be better to write now the little that I know and have learned about clyack thirty to forty years ago, and I shall write again if I learn anything new.

" At Corwichen, which is a small farm of fifty to sixty acres, no great style of feasting was possible ; but a ' clyack-kebbuck ' was always produced and cut for the first time— at dinner, if clyack was got in the forenoon, and at supper, when otherwise. We called the last corn cut the ' clyack-shaif ', but it was much smaller than an ordinary sheaf ; and it was given to a favourite horse. It was made into a rude female figure, and got a drink of ale ; but I can distinctly recollect of this being done only once, and I will make enquiries. I learn from two acquaintances that in the neighbourhood of Roslin, and in the neighbourhood of Stonehaven, the last handful (or handfuls) of corn cut got the name of ' the bride ', and she was placed over the ' bress ' or chimney-piece ; she had a ribbon tied below her numerous *ears*, and another round her waist.

" Under *Kern*, in Jamieson (*Dictionary of the Scottish Language*), there is some interesting information ; and in the poem called Har'st-Rig, where a kern is described, it is said in reference to the year Aughty-Twa :

> " ' *Oh that year was a year forlorn !*
> *Lang was the har'st and little corn !*
> *And, sad mischance !* the maid *was shorn*
> *After sunset !*
> *As rank a witch as e'er was born—*
> *They'll ne'er forget !* '

" And there is the note as to the ' mischance ' : ' This is esteemed exceedingly unlucky, and carefully guarded against.' The scene of the poem is in the vicinity of Edinburgh. Clyack-shaif, kirn-cut, kirn-dollie, kirn-baby, maiden, and bride, are names given to the last handful (or handfuls)."

[1] Clyack is the name given to the last sheaf in the north-east of Scotland. See Walter Gregor, *Folk-lore of* *the North-East of Scotland*, p. 181 sq. ; *id.*, in *Revue des traditions populaires*, October, 1888.

N

The Rev. E. B. Birks, Fellow of Trinity College, Cambridge, tells me that at Orwell, in Cambridgeshire, within living memory, it was the custom to throw water on the last waggon returning from the harvest-field ; water was also carried in the waggon, and the people in the waggon threw water on those they met. The waggon was called hawkey.[1]

The Rev. J. J. C. Yarborough, of Chislehurst, Kent, informs me that in a part of Yorkshire it is still the custom for the clergyman to cut the first corn. Mr. Yarborough thinks that the first corn so cut is used to make the communion bread, but of this he is not sure. He tells me also that as the reaping-machine goes round and round the corn-field, the wild animals (hares, rabbits, etc.) retreat into the standing corn in the middle of the field, and when the last patch is to be cut down the reapers stand round it with sticks, ready to knock down and kill the animals when they dart out of the corn. A friend tells me that the same thing happens when the reaping is done by hand ; but the machine by its whirring noise seems to daze and stupefy the creatures more than does the simple reaping by hand. This fact suggests an explanation of the reason why the spirit of the corn is so often supposed (as Mannhardt has shown) to be incarnate in animal form in the last corn cut.

My friend Mr. H. E. Cameron, of Newton Leys, by Ashbourne, Derbyshire, writes me : " As a boy, I remember [2] the last bit of corn cut was taken home, and neatly tied up with a ribbon, and then stuck up on the wall above the kitchen fireplace, and there it often remained till the ' Maiden ' of the following year took its place. There was no ceremony about it, beyond often a struggle as to who would get, or cut, the last sheaf to select the ' Maiden ' from. . . . A friend from Wigtownshire was here some weeks ago, when I was away from home, and he told my wife, the only custom in that district was throwing water on the man that led the last load home, but this has been done away with, as the horses often got frightened. He did not know

[1] So I spelt the word from Mr. Birks's pronunciation ; he did not know the proper spelling. It is plainly the same word as Hawkie, Hockey, Horkey in Brand and Hone.

[2] Mr. Cameron's recollections refer not to Derbyshire, but to Invernessshire, and particularly, I believe, to Glen Moriston.

the origin of the custom, nor could he give any reason why the water was thrown."

Mr. Cameron also enclosed a letter from Horace Warner, of which the following is an extract. The letter is dated " 44 Highbury Park, N., Nov. 11th, 1888 ".

" You asked me to describe the scene of ' Harvest Home ' we witnessed in the country in Norfolk, and so I will do it to the best of my ability. The sun was setting behind the old windmill as we crossed the field of stubble, when from a little group came a woman, who with a low curtsey asked us for ' largess(e) ', the old English word for money, which is still used in parts of the country. We thence passed on to the road, where in the distance we heard merry shouts and cheering, which gradually approached, and round the corner of the road came a fine team of horses mounted by two lads dressed in the costume of women, and on the top of the corn were a merry lot. The waggon stopped, gave us three cheers, which we returned, and then on went the joyous men to the village green, where, as the children came out of the village school, they stopped, and many of the children were hoisted on to the top to join in the shouts."

In Fifeshire, the custom of the " Maiden " seems still to be regularly kept up ; for in a recent case which came before the Sheriff, the date of one of the events was fixed by the day on which the " Maiden " was cut, as if the cutting the " Maiden " was a matter of popular notoriety. This was told me by Mr. Sheriff Mackay, before whom the case was tried.

I learn on good authority that the custom of the harvest " Maiden " is practised at the end of the maize harvest in America. The ears form the " Maiden's " head and the husks her dress. A similar custom used to be observed in cutting the sugar-canes in Louisiana, as we learn from the *Journal of American Folk-Lore*. As this journal may not be in the hands of some English readers of these notes it may be worth while to transcribe the passage :

" Another custom which was quite interesting was the cutting of the last cane for grinding. When the hands had reached the last rows standing, the foreman (*commandeur*) chose the tallest cane, and the best labourer (*le meilleur couteau*) came to the cane chosen, which was the only one in the field left uncut. Then the whole gang congregated around the spot, with the overseer and foreman, and the latter, taking a blue ribbon, tied it to the cane, and brandishing his knife in the air, sang to the cane as if it were a person, and danced around it several times before cutting it. When this was done, all the labourers, men, women, and children, mounted in the empty carts, carrying the last cane in triumph, waving coloured handkerchiefs in the air, and singing as loud as they could. The procession went to the house of the master, who gave a drink to every negro, and the day ended with a ball, amid general rejoicing " ("Customs and Superstitions in Louisiana ", by Alcée Fortier, *The American Journal of Folk-Lore*, vol. i. No. ii. pp. 137 *sq.*).

The Rev. J. S. Black tells me that in the counties of Fife and Kinross it is the custom for the reapers to seize and " dump " any person who happens to pass by the harvest fields. The person is seized by his (or her) ankles and armpits, lifted up, and the lower part of his person brought into violent contact with the ground. This is called " dumping " or " benjie ". Mr. G. A. Aitken, a friend and agriculturist whom Mr. Black consulted on the subject, writes : " The only correction I can make is that it is usually administered to people *visiting* the harvest fields, not to those passing by. It is occasionally practised, in frolic, by the harvesters among themselves, but the custom is fast dying out in this quarter. ' Head-money ' is usually demanded, and if that is [1] custom is ' the fashion of the field '. How far it extends to Perth and Forfar I don't know." Mr. Black, however, has no doubt that passers-by, as well as visitors to the field, are liable to be " dumped ". He adds that the dumping was not (as someone had suggested) the exclusive function of the women reapers ; and that the custom of interposing a sheaf between the sufferer and the ground seems, where it exists, to be only a modern refinement. " Dumping " was also practised in the neighbourhood of Edinburgh, for Mrs. Nicholson, of Eden Lodge, Morningside, Edinburgh, re-

---

[1] So Mr. Aitken writes. Some words seem to have dropped out, the meaning apparently being that if head-money is refused by the victim he is dumped.

members that as a girl at Bonaly, Colinton, not many years ago, she was warned not to go into the harvest fields, as one of the servants had been " dumped ".

12. EASTER IN GREECE [1]

The Greek Easter fell this year (1890) on 13th April, and was celebrated with the usual rites at Athens. Easter candles and coloured Easter eggs were exhibited for sale in large quantities in the streets on Good Friday ; and live lambs were to be seen, which the peasants had brought in from the country to sell. Each family, as a rule, buys a lamb, kills it, and eats it on Easter Sunday. On Saturday, in various parts of Athens, I observed the gutters running with the blood of the lambs which had been thus killed to furnish the family meal on Sunday. I am told that in some country districts the blood of the lamb is sometimes smeared on the threshold of the house. On the night of Good Friday the *eikones* or holy pictures representing the dead Christ were carried in solemn procession through the streets, great crowds joining in the processions with lighted candles, or watching the processions pass. Military bands marched in the processions, playing solemn music. During Easter Saturday and Easter Sunday firing went on almost continuously all over Athens. The cartridges used were not always blank ones, for I heard the whistle of bullets, and am informed that fatal accidents on such occasions are not uncommon. The object of the firing is said to be to kill Judas. Formerly effigies of Judas used to be burned at this season, but in Athens the custom is now forbidden by the Government.

The chief ceremony of the festival takes place at midnight on Easter Saturday, that is, at the commencement of Easter Sunday, the moment when the Resurrection is believed to have taken place. In Athens a religious service, presided over by the Archbishop, is held at midnight in the square in front of the cathedral, and at the presumed moment of the Resurrection the bells ring out and the multitude who fill the square kindle the candles which they had hitherto held un-

---

[1] Reprinted from *Folk-lore*, vol. i. No. 2 (June 1890), p. 175 *sq.*

lighted in their hands. The theory is that these candles are all lighted from the sacred new Easter fire in the cathedral, but, considering the suddenness with which the square, all dark a moment before, bursts into a blaze of light, it seems hardly possible that all the candles should be lit from one source.

In the more remote districts of Greece it seems that the Easter ceremonies are of a more primitive kind than at Athens. Mr. Ernest Gardner, Director of the British School of Archaeology at Athens, witnessed the celebration of Easter at Thebes in Boeotia, and he has kindly furnished me with the following particulars : " On Good Friday the sacred picture of the dead Christ was laid on a sort of bier, or structure resembling a four-posted bed. The picture itself, the four posts, and the overhanging canopy were covered with flowers and green leaves. Every person came up to the bier, kissed the sacred picture, and carried away a flower or a leaf from it, with the intention of keeping it until the Easter of the following year. Beside the bier stood baskets of flowers and leaves, with which the bier was decked as fast as it was stripped by the worshippers. Then the bier, adorned with lighted candles, was carried in procession through the town. Similar processions started from the various churches and met at central points. While the processions were passing fireworks were let off and guns fired."

VII

A SUGGESTION AS TO THE ORIGIN OF GENDER IN LANGUAGE [1]

GRAMMARIANS and others have speculated as to the origin of gender in language. Why should lifeless things be denominated in many languages by words which seem from their form to attribute sex to them ? Formerly the answer came readily enough. If men thus personify things, it is by virtue of a personifying tendency in the human mind, just as opium sends people to sleep by virtue of its soporific qualities. This answer appears less satisfactory now than it once did, and philologers are casting about for another. A passage from the journal of an explorer, which I copied out many years ago, and had occasion to look at again lately for a different purpose, suggested to me what is, I believe, a new solution of the problem. I submitted it to friends who are better judges of such things than I am, and their approbation encourages me to lay it before the public. It is no more than a speculation, but, right or wrong, it may serve a useful purpose if it directs the attention of philologers to a neglected factor in the evolution of language.

In describing the South American tribes whom he met with on his journeys, the Spanish traveller F. de Azara remarks on what he calls an extravagant singularity in the language of the Mbayas, a tribe who inhabit the valley of the Paraguay or its tributaries. The women, he says, and boys before their marriage, give to the words a different termination from that employed by the grown men, and sometimes even use different words, so that on hearing them you would say that they speak two dialects. Something

[1] Reprinted from *The Fortnightly Review*, January 1, 1900, pp. 79-90.

similar, he goes on, might be observed in the town of Curuguaty, in Paraguay. There the women speak nothing but the Guarany language, and the men use only Guarany in talking to them, whereas among themselves the men always speak Spanish. The reason of this, he proceeds to say, was that the Spaniards who founded Curuguaty married Indian wives, who continued to speak their native Indian language and taught it to their children, whereas the men preserved the Spanish language among themselves through pride of race.[1]

Differences between the speech of the two sexes have been observed among other South American tribes. Von Martius mentions that among the Arawaks " the mode of speech of the two sexes is often enough different. The difference appears not so much in the use of quite distinct words as in the inflexions given to the same words." As instances, he says that for " yes " the Arawak men say *tase* or *hese*, the women *tara* or *kisseira* ; for " certainly " the men say *dukesse* or *hedukessi*, the women *dukara* or *hedukara*. The word *ehe*, meaning " yes " may be used both by men and women. For " no " men and women alike say *kawake* or *koake*. The men greet each other with *buili* or *büiluai*, " Are you there ? " to which the answer is *daiili* or *dailisi*, " I am there." A woman, on the other hand, is greeted with *büiru*, " Are you there ? " to which she answers, *daiiruru*.[2] So R. Schomburgk remarked that a striking peculiarity of the Arawak language consists in possessing a number of words which only the men, and others which only the women, may pronounce.[3] Among the Abipones of Paraguay the men say *héé* for " yes ", but the women say *hàà*.[4] Further, Von Martius observes that among the Guaycurus, and several other tribes of South America, " we are confronted with the strange fact that the speech of the men is wholly, or at least in certain words, different from that of the women. This peculiar condition of things, as is well known, was first remarked among the Caribs, and in

[1] F. de Azara, *Voyages dans l'Amérique Méridionale*, ii. p. 106 *sq.* (Paris, 1809).
[2] C. F. P. von Martius, *Beiträge zur Ethnographie und Sprachenkunde Amerika's und zumal Brasiliens*, i. p. 704 (Leipsic, 1867).
[3] R. Schomburgk, *Reisen in Britisch Guiana*, i. p. 227.
[4] M. Dobrizhoffer, *Historia de Abiponibus* (Vienna, 1784), ii. p. 193.

the Antilles, where they lived, it gave rise to the legend that on their arrival thither from the continent they had extirpated the male aborigines and married their women. That was said to be the reason why in the Antilles the women might never mention their husbands by their names, and never see them eating.[1] In any case the difference of speech between the sexes amongst the Brazilian tribes must also be derived from a mixed origin. The capture of women is not infrequent. The chief of the Mirambas, with whom I lodged, had captured his wife from a neighbouring tribe. Similarly it is said that the Mandrucus carried off girls and women from the Parentintins, and thus gave rise to the deadly enmity between these two tribes ; and the Tecunas capture the beauties of Marauhas, who are famed for their slender and well-proportioned figures." [2] The suggestion that the differences between the speech of the sexes in these American languages may have been due to the capture of alien women was made to me independently in conversation by my acute and learned friend, Professor W. Ridgeway, when I had the advantage of discussing with him the theory which I am about to propound, and which his suggestion materially helped to develop.

In regard to the Caribs, the first writer to note the difference of speech between the men and the women, so far as I know, was Du Tertre, who, writing in the middle of the seventeenth century, says that " the women have a language quite different from that of the men, and it would be a sort of crime to speak otherwise among themselves, when they are not obliged to converse with the men ; also they mock at the men when the latter use the feminine manner of speech ".[3] Some years later De Rochefort remarks : " Those who have long conversed with the savages of Dominique report that the inhabitants of this island believe that their

[1] Von Martius apparently makes this statement on the authority of Lafitau (*Mœurs des sauvages Ameriquains*, i. p. 54), who says merely that the women never ate with their husbands and never mentioned their husbands' names. Lafitau compares the rules observed by the descendants of the Carian women whose husbands had been massacred by the Ionian invaders (Herodotus, i. 146). The

custom which forbade the Carib women to eat with their husbands is mentioned also by Labat (*Nouveau Voyage aux isles de l'Amerique*, Paris, 1742, ii. p. 158 *sq.*).
[2] Von Martius, *op. cit.* i. p. 106 *sq.*
[3] J. B. du Tertre, *Histoire generale des Isles de S. Christophe, de la Guadeloupe, de la Martinique et autres dans l'Amerique* (Paris, 1654), p. 462.

ancestors came from the Terra Firma, from the stock of the
Calabites [Caribs], to make war on a nation of Arouagues
[Arawaks], who inhabited the islands, which nation they
entirely destroyed, with the exception of their wives, whom
they took for wives, and by this means repeopled the islands.
That is the reason why down to this day the women of the
island Caribs have a language which differs from that of the
men in several things, and agrees in some things with the
language of the Arouagues [Arawaks] of the continent." [1]
Another writer of the seventeenth century, speaking of the
origin of the Caribs of the islands, says : " Old savages have
told me that they came from the Galibis of the mainland,
neighbours of the Aloüagues [Arawaks], their enemies ;
because their language, manners, and religion have much
in common with theirs, and that they had entirely destroyed
a nation in these islands, with the exception of the women,
whom they took for themselves, and that is the reason why
the language of the men is not like that of the women in
several things." Further on, the same writer remarks :
" Although there is a difference between the language of the
men and that of the women, as I have already observed in
the chapter on their origin, they understand one another." [2]
Father Labat, who spent about twelve years in the Antilles
at the end of the seventeenth and the beginning of the
eighteenth century, writes as follows on this subject : " The
Caribs have three sorts of languages. The first, the most
usual and that which everyone speaks, is as it were the special
language of the men (est comme affecté aux hommes). The
second is so peculiar to the women that, though the men
understand it, they would think themselves dishonoured if
they had spoken it, and if they had answered their women
in case the latter had the temerity to speak to them in that
language. The women know the language of their husbands,

[1] De Rochefort, *Histoire naturelle
et morale des Antilles* (Rotterdam,
1665), p. 349 *sq.* De Rochefort was
never in America, and he copied from
Du Tertre, according to Labat (*Nouveau Voyage aux isles de l'Amerique*,
preface, p. vii. *sq.*).
[2] De la Borde, " Relation de
l'origine, mœurs, costumes, religion,

guerres et voyages des Caraibes, sauvages des Isles Antilles de l'Amerique ", printed in *Recueil de divers
voyages faits en Afrique et en l'Amerique qui n'ont point esté encore publiez
(Paris, 1684), pp. 4, 39. The memoirs
in this collection are paged separately.
There is nothing to indicate the date
when De la Borde's memoir was written.

and are bound to use it in speaking to them ; but they never use it in speaking among themselves, and employ no other idiom than their own, which is totally different from that of the men. There is a third language which is known only to the men who have been to the wars, especially the old men. It is rather a jargon which they have invented than a language. They use it in important assemblies when they wish to keep their resolutions secret. The women and the youths understand nothing of it." Labat further remarks that the language spoken by the Carib women of the Antilles closely resembled the language spoken on the larger West Indian Islands and on some parts of the mainland, whereas that language bore no resemblance to the speech of the Carib men.[1] The Jesuit Lafitau, who had visited America as a missionary, says of the Caribs : " These savages themselves relate that having vanquished their enemies and destroyed them all, they kept only the women and girls ; and they say that that is the cause of the diversity of language between the two sexes."[2] Humboldt, who travelled among the Caribs of the mainland and estimated their number at 40,000, says that the inhabitants of the islands called themselves Calinago in the men's speech and Callipinan in the women's. " This distinction ", he goes on, " between the sexes in their mode of speech is more striking among the people of the Carib stock than amongst the other American peoples (the Omaguas, Guaranis, and Chiquitos), among whom it affects only a few notions, such as the words mother and child." Then, after referring to Cicero's well-known saying, that old forms of speech are best preserved in the mouths of women, he observes that among the Caribs the distinction between the modes of speech of the two sexes is too great and striking to be explained by the mere conservatism of women in the matter of language, and he refers with approval to that traditional explanation of the discrepancy which I have already cited from earlier writers. As instances of the difference between the languages of the sexes he gives the following : " island " in the men's speech is *oubao*, in the

[1] Labat, *Nouveau Voyage aux isles de l'Amérique*, Nouvelle Edition, vi. pp. 127 *sq.*, 129 (Paris, 1742).

[2] Lafitau, *Mœurs des sauvages Ameriquains*, i. p. 55 (Paris, 1724).

women's *acaera*; "man" in the men's speech is *ouekelli*,
in the women's *eyeri*; "maize" in the men's speech is *ichen*,
in the women's *atica*.[1]   In the islands of Dominica and St.
Vincent there were, down to the last quarter of the nineteenth century, some families of Caribs who spoke their
old language.   A traveller who questioned a Carib man in
St. Vincent and a Carib woman in Dominica some fifty years
ago found that they spoke different dialects.   "For certain
things", he says, "they had two words entirely different.   In
the construction of sentences, though there would be close
analogy, there was a difference in the opening or closing words
that was at once noticeable.   In the following, for instance,
where the woman expresses a wish for a fish for dinner: *Noo-
iz, há-ma-gah, oó-do*.   And the man: *U-i-di, há-ma-ga, oo-do*.
Almost invariably a word commenced by the man with a B,
by the woman was begun with an N."[2]   More recently an excellent account of the Carib language, as spoken in Dominica,
was published by Mr. Joseph Numa Rat, of St. Kitt's, West
Indies.[3]   In regard to the question which here concerns us,
he observes that, "though the language generally speaking
is the same among both sexes, there are certain words in
it which are used by the women only".   As examples of
this difference of speech he gives the following :

	Used by Men.	Used by Women.
Moon	*Núnu*	*Káti*
Rain	*Kŭnúbui*	*Húya*
Fish-hook . .	*Kúwi*	*Búre*
Cassava root . .	*Kíere*	*Kái*
Son	*Wŭkŭri*	*Éyeri*
Daughter . .	*Wŭri*	*Yáru*
Pepper	*Bŭrmŭi*	*Ati*
Fowl	*Álira*	*Káyu*
Sea	*Bárana*	*Bárawa*

[1] A. von Humboldt's *Reise in die Aequinoctial-Gegenden des neuen Continents*, in deutscher Bearbeitung von H. Hauff, iv. p. 204 *sq.* (Stuttgart, 1874). Humboldt's statement as to the names by which the insular Caribs called themselves seems to be taken from Rochefort, who gives Calinago and Calliponan (not Callipinan) as the forms reported to be used by the men and women respectively (*Histoire naturelle et morale des Iles Antilles de l'Amérique*, p. 345). [2] F. A. Ober, *Camps in the Caribbees* (Edinburgh, 1880), p. 100 *sq.* [3] "The Carib Language as now spoken in Dominica, West Indies", *Journal of the Anthropological Institute*, xxvii. (1898), pp. 293-315.

He adds that "the resemblance between certain of these alien words and some in the Arawak language points to that tribe as the most probable source of many, if not of all the terms peculiar to the Carib women. For example the word *káti* used by Carib women for the moon is similarly employed in Arawak; while the Caribs in South America have adopted the Macusi word for one, viz. *owi*, the insular Caribs call that numeral *ába*, which is almost the same as the equivalent Arawak word *ábaro*." [1] Lastly, towards the end of the nineteenth century, some researches were made into the differences between the speech of the sexes among the Caribs, especially the Caribs who since 1796, when some of them were removed from St. Vincent by the English, have spread their settlements along the eastern coasts of Honduras and Guatemala. At Livingston, in Guatemala, the first person singular of the personal pronoun is *dü* in the men's language, but *nügüya* in the women's; the second person is *amür* in the men's language, but *buguya* in the women's. In the Carib language of the islands the word for "sun" among the men is *jüyeyü*, but *caxi* among the women; "yesterday" is *g' uñar* in the men's language, but *úrinog* in the women's; a man expresses "my heart" by *nivüäni*, a woman by *nanixi*; "my father" is *yümaan* in the men's speech, but *nücüxili* in the women's; "my mother" is *ixanüm* in the language of the men, but *nücüxürü* in the language of the women; "man" and "woman" are *vequeli* and *üele* in masculine speech, but *eyeri* and *ináru* in feminine. After giving these and a few more instances Mr. C. Sapper proceeds: "With these examples I have exhausted all the differences which I noted between the speech of the two sexes; it is obvious that they amount to very little. In all other respects, in the personal and possessive pronouns, in the conjugation, and in the translation of whole sentences, no other differences have come to light in the modes of expression employed by men and women. Thus both sexes speak, apart from comparatively few expressions, quite the same language, and hence no ground whatever remains for accepting the hypothesis of the massacre of the men and the preservation of the language in the mouth of the surviving women." [2]

[1] *Op. cit.* p. 311 *sq.*
[2] C. Sapper, "Mittelamericanische

Caraiben", *Internationales Archiv für Ethnographie*, x. (1897), p. 57 *sq.* Mr.

Mr. Sapper's conclusion appears to me not to follow very strictly from his premises. Even if the language of the women was originally, as we are assured by the earliest writer on the subject, quite different from that of the men, surely nothing could be more natural than that living together from generation to generation in the closest intimacy of family life, men and women should have borrowed something from each other's language, and that the differences between the two speeches should have progressively diminished until they nearly vanished. That this approximation between the two languages has been going on within the period open to our observation is proved by Mr. Sapper's own facts. For he shows by examples that the Carib language of Guatemala has dropped a number of the masculine terms, which were formerly in use among their ancestors of the Antilles, and has retained only the feminine equivalents, in a more or less altered form. Thus, whereas a Carib man used to call the moon *nonum*, while a woman called it *cati*, at Livingston in Guatemala both men and women now call it *hati*. Again, whereas the Carib men formerly expressed " my father " by the word *yŭmaan*, while Carib women expressed it by *nŭcŭxili*, at Livingston both men and women express it by *nŭgŭtxi*. Once more, while the masculine term for " my mother " used to be *ixanŭm*, and the feminine was *nŭcŭxŭrŭ*, at Livingston both men and women employ the one word *nŭgŭtxŭ* to express the same idea. On the other hand, in a single instance given by Mr. Sapper the masculine term for " sun " (*jŭyeyŭ*) has been retained in a modified form (*véyŭ*), while the feminine form (*caxi*) has been wholly discarded by both men and women. This mutual action of the two forms of speech upon each other, this give-and-take, and the consequent gradual obliteration of their original differences, is precisely what would naturally and almost inevitably happen under the conditions which according to tradition actually existed. Therefore the present assimilation of the two languages to each other furnishes no argument for rejecting that tradition of the massacre of men and survival

Sapper's examples of insular Carib are taken from Stoll's *Zur Ethnographie der Republik Guatemala* (Zurich, 1884), a work which I have not seen.

of women which was current, as I have shown by citations
from early writers, among the Caribs themselves in the
seventeenth century. That tradition, harmonizing as it does
with the modes of savage conquest, is not to be rejected
without grave cause. Its probability increases when we
observe the statements of these early writers that the women
used their special language only among themselves, and that
in talking to men they always employed the men's language.
For this is just what might be expected of the women of a
conquered race, who, while they cherished their old language
among themselves, might well be required to address their
lords and masters in the language of the conquerors. That
men and women of different races may, even after the fusion
of the races by intermarriage, still retain each their original
tongue, while one of the two tongues comes to serve as the
common vehicle of discourse between the sexes, is proved
by the instance of Curuguaty, in Paraguay, so aptly cited by
De Azara.

The statement that the Carib women kept their special
language to themselves, and used the language of the men
in conversing with the men, is further of great importance
as proving that the discrepancy between the speech of the
sexes did not arise, like the *hlonipa* of the Zulus, from a
superstitious avoidance by the women of certain words or
sounds, and a consequent necessity of choosing or invent-
ing others in their place. Another distinction between the
language of the Carib women and the *hlonipa* of the Zulus is
that, whereas the former is permanent and universal, in fact a
true language or dialect, the *hlonipa* of the Zulus is merely
temporary and local or personal, being based on the principle
that the names of chiefs and of certain relations, and even
the syllables composing these names, may not be mentioned.
Thus the *hlonipa* varies not merely from tribe to tribe,
according to the name of the chief, but from family to
family, and even from individual to individual, according to
the names of persons connected with the speaker by blood
or marriage ; and it is constantly producing new forms,
which are afterwards discarded when the personal names
which gave rise to them are no longer borne by chiefs or
relations. Moreover, though the custom of *hlonipa* is chiefly

observed by women, it is also obligatory to a large extent
upon men. It is, in short, a mere variable and ever-varying
fashion of speech, but in no sense a language or a dialect,
like the speech of the Carib women. The same remarks
which have just been made on the Zulu *hlonipa* apply to the
te pi of Tahiti, and to similar taboos on words imposed in
Melanesia, Madagascar, and other parts of the world.[1]
The Caribs and the Indians of South America are not
the only peoples among whom a difference has been observed
between the language of the sexes. Greenland women, we
are told, " have a particular pronunciation peculiar to themselves, and different from that of the men, making use of
the softest letters at the end of words, instead of hard ones " ;
for example, they say *am* instead of *ap* (" yes "), and *saving*
instead of *savik* (" knife ").[2] In Northern Nyassaland the
women do not employ the common names for articles of
food ; they use certain special terms peculiar to themselves,[3]
but as this custom is said to be based on superstition, it
is probably not on a line with the Carib and South American
cases which we have been considering. It is among the
savage aborigines of Australia that we find the most complete parallel to those conditions of life which seem to have
created the difference between the speech of the sexes in

---

[1] As to the Zulu *hlonipa*, see Fr.
Fleming, *Kaffraria* (London, 1853),
p. 96 *sq.*; *id.*, *Southern Africa*
(London, 1856), p. 238 *sq.*; J. Shooter,
The Kafirs of Natal (London, 1857),
pp. 219-222; Maclean, *Compendium
of Kafir Laws and Customs* (Cape
Town, 1866), pp. 92, 93; Kranz,
Natur- und Kulturleben der Zulus
(Wiesbaden, 1888), p. 114 *sq.*; Theal,
Kaffir Folk-lore (London, 1886), p.
214 *sq.*: and especially D. Leslie,
Among the Zulus, Second Edition
(London and Edinburgh, 1875), pp.
102, 141 *sq.*, 172-180. As to the
Tahitian *te pi*, see *United States
Exploring Expedition, Ethnography
and Philology*, by Horatio Hale
(Philadelphia, 1846), p. 288 *sq.* As
to the Madagascar custom, see Tyer-
man and Bennet, *Journal of Voyages
and Travels* (London, 1831), ii. p.
525 *sq.*; A. Grandidier, in *Revue*

d'Ethnographie, v. (1886), p. 224;
J. Sibree, in *Antananarivo Annual
and Madagascar Magazine*, xi. (1887),
p. 308 *sq.*; *id.*, in *Journal of the
Anthropological Institute*, xxi. (1892),
pp. 226-228; *id.*, *The Great African
Island* (London, 1880), p. 150 *sq.*
Both the *hlonipa* and the *te pi* are
noticed by F. Max Müller in his
Lectures on the Science of Language,
ii. p. 37 *sq.*, and E. B. Tylor in his
*Researches into the Early History of
Mankind*, pp. 145, 147. I may now
refer the reader to my fuller treatment
of these and similar customs in *The
Golden Bough*, Part II.; *Taboo and
the Perils of the Soul*, p. 318 *sqq.*
[2] H. Egede, *A Description of
Greenland*, New Edition (London,
1818), p. 166 *sq.*
[3] Sir H. H. Johnston, *British
Central Africa* (London, 1897), p.
452.

the Antilles and South America. In Australia the rule of exogamy appears to have been universally observed by the aboriginal population; in other words, every man was bound, if he married at all, to marry a woman of another stock from his own. This of itself would not necessarily lead to a difference of speech between husband and wife, since in Australian society the various stocks usually live more or less shuffled up among each other. But in some of the Victorian tribes the rule of exogamy was supplemented by a rule which forbade a man to marry into an adjoining tribe or into one that spoke his own dialect.[1] In these tribes husband and wife after marriage continued to speak each their own language even in talking to each other ; " so that all conversation is carried on between husband and wife in the same way as between an Englishman and a Frenchwoman, each speaking his or her own language ". Only in talking to her child the mother was bound to use her husband's language as far as she could. Otherwise, every person had to speak the language of his or her father, and might never mix it with any other. " This very remarkable law ", adds the writer whom I am quoting, " explains the preservation of so many distinct dialects within so limited a space, even where there are no physical obstacles to ready and frequent communication between the tribes." [2] On his expedition to Torres Straits, my friend Professor A. C. Haddon ascertained from some natives of Cape York, Queensland, that in their country a wife has to be taken from another district. A rule of this kind would almost certainly lead to some difference of language between husband and wife, since among savages dialects generally vary from district to district.

Thus, from the Australian and American evidence taken together, we seem to be justified in concluding that the practice of marrying women of other tribes, whether captured by force or obtained peaceably, may have often resulted in husbands and wives speaking different languages or different dialects of the same language ; and that when the women were obtained predominantly from one particular tribe and transmitted their language to their daughters, two distinct languages or dialects would come to be spoken

[1] James Dawson, *Australian Aborigines*, p. 27.   [2] *Op. cit.* p. 40.

O

within the tribe, one by the men and the other by the women. The amount of divergence between the speech of the sexes would originally depend on the greater or less divergence of the languages spoken by the tribes who thus intermarried. Where the languages of the tribes were totally distinct, the languages of the sexes within each tribe would be so also : where the tribes spoke different dialects of the same language the differences of speech between men and women would be merely dialectic ; in other words, they would affect the form of the words rather than the vocabulary. Amongst the Arawaks and Mbayas of South America, to judge from the accounts of Von Martius and De Azara, the differences of speech between the sexes seem to have been mainly of the latter sort, consisting chiefly of different inflexions given to the same words by men and women respectively. Such differences of inflexion, however their origin is to be explained, may, I conjecture, have given rise to what is called grammatical gender in language. For in time the two different modes of speech would almost inevitably tend to be confounded. It would be found both difficult and inconvenient to maintain and keep distinct a double set of grammatical forms for all or many words in the language. Each of the sexes would speak its proper dialect more and more incorrectly, dropping some of its own forms and borrowing forms from the other sex, until at last all difference of speech between them vanished, and of the original duplicated forms of words only one in each case survived. Sometimes the form which survived in the speech now common to both sexes would be the form originally employed by the men only, and this would give the masculine gender ; sometimes it would be the form originally appropriate to the women, and this would give the feminine gender. In cases where the original difference of language was due to a practice of obtaining wives from other stocks, it is obvious that the cessation of that practice, or in other words the abandonment of the rule of exogamy, would be a potent factor in hastening the assimilation of the modes of speech peculiar to the sexes. For when the language of the female sex was not constantly reinforced and refreshed by the importation of foreign women speaking that language in all its purity, it would insensibly

blend more and more with that of the men. We have seen
that this has actually happened in the Carib language spoken
in Central America, where both sexes now use the same
word for some things which they formerly designated by
two distinct sets of terms ; in some cases it is the feminine
term which has ousted its masculine rival, in one case at
least it is the masculine form which has prevailed over the
feminine.

It may perhaps be counted as some confirmation of this
theory that the Carib and Arawak languages, which seem to
have influenced each other through the capture of women,
are perhaps the only native American languages which exhibit true grammatical gender. Thus the distinguished
philologer, Mr. A. S. Gatschet, who has studied profoundly
some of the languages of the North American Indians, remarks that the class of sex-denoting languages " is rather
small upon the Western Continent. Wherever a distinction
of this sort is made in the substantives, it is made by agglu-
tinating some sexual distinction to the noun, as is done in
some Tinné and Maya languages and in the Tonica. The
Carib alone seems to have a real suffix for the feminine." [1]
On this point, however, it is important to observe what Mr.
Rat tells us of the formation of the genders in the Carib of
Dominica. He says : " The letters *l* and *t* prefixed to substantives indicate the masculine and feminine genders respectively. It should, however, be remembered that *l* and *t*
are short for *li* and *ti*, the masculine and feminine of the
third person of the personal pronoun which serve the purposes
of the definite article and the possessive pronoun. In such
expressions, therefore, as *lóaku lísibu* = ' over his face ', and
tóaku tísibu = ' over her face ', the literal translation should
be ' over the face of him ', or ' over him, his face ', and
' over the face of her ' or ' over her, her face '. Hence Carib
substantives may be grouped in two classes, the *l* class and
the *t* class ; and, as the former include all male and the
latter all female beings, the substantives of these two groups
may be described as masculine and feminine respectively

[1] A. S. Gatschet, *The Klamath Indians of South-western Oregon* (Washington, 1890), i. p. 463. Com- pare Fr. Müller, *Grundriss der Sprachwissenschaft*, ii. 1, p. 324.

with as much propriety in Carib as in any other language. A few substantives, like *duli* = ' dog ', being common to both sexes, may also be correctly described as being of a common gender. In such cases the sex is indicated by placing the word *wǔkǔri* = ' male ', or *wǔri* = ' female ', before the substantive. The majority of the substantives of the *l* or masculine class end in *i* or *e* ; and the majority of those of the *t* or feminine class in *o* or *u*." [1]

If Mr. Rat's analysis of these sex-denoting inflexions is correct, it would seem to show that the distinction drawn by Mr. Gatschet between the Carib and the other American languages in respect of gender can hardly be maintained ; and further, it would furnish a strong, if not conclusive, argument against the view that in the Carib language gender arose through the fusion of distinct dialects formerly spoken by different tribes.

Whether Mr. Rat is right or not, I am incompetent to decide ; but I wish to point out clearly that the theory which seeks the origin of gender in a difference of speech between men and women does not necessarily stand or fall with the further and quite independent theory, that such difference of speech arose through the mixture of stocks speaking distinct dialects or languages. The difference of speech between the sexes may have been due to other causes than intermarriage and the capture of women. At a certain stage of their history certain races may have found it natural and appropriate that men and women should mark their sex in their speech by the systematic use of different sets of inflexions for all, or, at any rate, many words. To take imaginary cases, it is conceivable that in speaking of a horse, a man should have said *equus*, while a woman said *equa* ; that the word for earth should be *terrus* in the mouth of a man, but *terra* in the mouth of a woman ; that when a man desired to speak of a grove he should say *lucus*, but that a woman in the same case should say *luca* ; that white should be *albus* in the speech of men, but *alba* in the speech of women. In other words, grammatical gender may have been at first purely subjective, that is, indicative only of the sex of the speaker, and not at all intended to imply, as it was afterwards under-

[1] *Journal of the Anthropological Institute*, xxvii. (1898), p. 245.

stood to imply, any sex in the thing spoken of. How the change from subjective gender to what may be called objective gender took place, if it took place at all, we can only conjecture.[1] When the different modes of speech of the sexes began to fuse into one, and the double forms of all words, the masculine and the feminine, were competing against each other for a place in the common speech, it might be felt natural that, of the duplicate forms for " man " and " woman ", those were best entitled to survive which each sex had formerly used in speaking of itself. Thus, if men had been accustomed to speak of a woman as *feminus*, while women had spoken of one of their sex as *femina*, it might be felt proper to retain the form *femina*, and discard the form *feminus*. Conversely, if men had been wont to call a man *anthropos*, while women had called him *anthropa*, the form *anthropos* would survive in the struggle for existence, and the form *anthropa* would perish. If this or something like this happened, it would naturally suggest by analogy the convenience of applying the old masculine and feminine inflexions in a new way to distinguish the sex, no longer of the speaker, but of the object spoken of. Thus the form *equus* or the form *equa* might now be used, not according as the speaker was male or female, but according as the animal designated was a horse or a mare. So, too, with adjectives. Whereas in former times everything white had been called *albus* by men, and *alba* by women, irrespective of the sex of the object, under the new system, when the two sexes spoke the same language, everything of the male sex that was white would be called *albus*, and everything of the female sex would be called *alba*, irrespective of the sex of the speaker. In short, gender from having been subjective would become objective. As to sexless objects, the question whether the masculine or the feminine form should survive would be largely decided by accident; in other words, by unknown causes which may have varied with each particular case, and about which no general principle could be laid down.

[1] In my hypothesis of the transition from subjective to objective gender, I have profited by a suggestion of K. Brugmann's which was mentioned to me in conversation by my friend Prof. J. P. Postgate. The suggestion will be found in Techmer's *Internationale Zeitschrift für allgemeine Sprachwissenschaft*, iv. (1889), pp. 104-106.

VIII

ON SOME CEREMONIES OF THE CENTRAL AUSTRALIAN TRIBES [1]

MY esteemed friend Mr. Lorimer Fison has asked me to
contribute a note on some anthropological subject which
might be read at the meeting of the Australian Association
for the Advancement of Science in 1900. I propose, therefore, to make a few remarks on some of the customs of the
Central Australian aborigines as they are described in the
recent and admirable work of Messrs. Spencer and Gillen,
a work of inestimable value to every student of the early
history of mankind, and one which does honour not merely
to the authors, but to Australia.

First, I should like to say something about the Intichiuma
ceremonies, the discovery and description of which form,
perhaps, the most novel, and certainly one of the most
important, features in the work of Messrs. Spencer and Gillen.
The general intention of these ceremonies is to increase the
supply of food by multiplying the numbers of the plants
and animals which are eaten by the natives, and, further,
to procure a sufficient supply of rain, and probably, also,
though this seems not yet to be positively made out, a supply
of wind, sunshine, fire, and of everything else that the
savage requires. The points of interest about these ceremonies are many. In the first place, they are performed
exclusively by men who have for their totem the particular
object with which the ceremony is concerned ; for example,
the ceremonies for the multiplication of kangaroos and emus
are performed by men of the kangaroo and emu totems

[1] Reprinted from *The Proceedings*   *the Advancement of Science for*   *l.e*
of the Australasian Association for   *year 1900* (Melbourne, 1901).

respectively ; ceremonies for the making of rain are performed by men of the water totem, and so on. The discovery
of these ceremonies appears to shed a new and unexpected
light on the meaning of totemism, at least among the Central
Australian tribes, by suggesting that its primary purpose is
the thoroughly practical one of satisfying the material wants
of the savage, this purpose being carried out by distributing
the various functions to be discharged among different
groups, who thereby become totem clans. On this hypothesis totemism is of high interest to the economist, since it
furnishes, perhaps, the oldest example of a systematic
division of labour among the members of a community.

In the second place, it is of great interest to observe that
these Intichiuma ceremonies are purely magical and not at
all religious. They contain no appeal by means of prayer
and sacrifice to a deity ; they are supposed to produce the
desired effect directly and immediately without the intervention or aid of any higher spiritual power. Taken together
with the apparent absence of all religious rites among the
Central Australians, who rank with the lowest races in the
scale of humanity, they tend to show that in the evolution
of thought magic has preceded religion. This is a conclusion
to which other evidence and other considerations also point,
and I venture to think that it is likely to gain ground among
students of mankind the more we know of the actual working
of the savage mind.

In the third place, it is worthy of note that the Intichiuma
ceremonies are, at least in many cases, annual, and are
generally held at the approach of what may be called the
Australian spring, at the time, that is, when animal and
vegetable life is about to burst into fresh activity through
the fall of the first heavy rains after the long season of
drought. Thus the Intichiuma ceremonies present a close
and striking analogy to the spring ceremonies of European
peasants, as these latter ceremonies have been interpreted
by the genius and insight of the German anthropologist, W.
Mannhardt. According to him the customs, of which the
Maypole, the May Queen, and the Jack-in-the-Green are
perhaps the most familiar examples to English-speaking
people, were originally charms intended to secure the revival

of vegetation in spring ; and certain other popular European customs, such as drenching mummers with water, kindling bonfires and leaping over them, and running with lighted torches about the fields, which are specially observed in spring and at midsummer, were similarly explained by Mannhardt as magical ceremonies intended to ensure that supply of rain, of sunshine, and of heat, without which neither plants nor men could exist. His interpretation of these European ceremonies was necessarily to some extent a matter of inference rather than of direct testimony, for few of the people who now practise these ceremonies in Europe could say why they do so. Australia may almost be said to have now supplied that direct testimony which was hitherto lacking, for the Arunta and other Australian tribes do consciously and avowedly practise their Intichiuma cere- monies as charms for making plants to grow, rain to fall, and so forth. The analogy thus brought to light between the modes of thought of man in Europe and Australia furnishes a striking proof of the fundamental identity of the human mind under every variety of colour and under every sky.

So much for the Intichiuma ceremonies in general. But there is one special feature in some of them to which I would direct your attention. We have long been familiar with the rule that men may not eat their totem, when their totem happens to be a plant, and that they may neither kill nor eat it when it happens to be an animal. But long ago my acute friend the late W. Robertson Smith was led by various scattered indications to conclude that among totem tribes a custom prevailed of killing and eating the totem animal on rare and solemn occasions as a form of sacrament or com- munion with the totem deity. No single instance of such a practice was known among totem tribes. Certain cases, indeed, were known in which an animal apparently regarded as divine was slain with great solemnity as a religious rite. Such, for example, were the sacrifice of the ram at Thebes in ancient Egypt, of the great buzzard among some Cali- fornian tribes, and of turtles among the Zunis ; but, in the first place, there was no positive evidence that the animals thus slain were totems, and in the second place, although they were killed, they were in many, perhaps in most, cases not eaten ; and thus essential links in the chain of Robertson Smith's argument were wanting. For, according to him, the divine animal slain was a totem, and it was slain in order that it might be eaten by the worshippers, who were thus supposed to enter into a mystic communion with the totem by partaking of his flesh and blood. Like my distinguished friend I was at one time inclined to think that some of the animals thus solemnly slain probably were or had once been totems ;[1] but as years passed, and still no evidence was forthcoming of any such practices among actual totem tribes, I became more and more sceptical as to their existence, although in the meantime the assumption of a sacramental communion with the totem by partaking of its flesh had become almost a commonplace with some writers, who had adopted Robertson Smith's conclusion without observing how extremely slight was the foundation on which it rested. Accordingly, in the year 1897, I was startled and deeply interested by reading a passage in a letter of Professor Baldwin Spencer, which Mr. Lorimer Fison kindly forwarded to me. Professor Spencer wrote from Central Australia, describing some of the ceremonies which he was then witnessing among the Arunta tribe, and at the end of the letter, which is dated Alice Springs, 21st November, 1896, he added a postscript in which he noted it as remarkable that in several of the ceremonies he had witnessed the men ate their own totems.[2] Here, then, I thought we seem to have the totem sacrament, and I communicated the information, together with my own provisional inference from it, in a letter to Mr. Andrew Lang, who made a guarded allusion to it in a book published the same year.[3] But I suspended judgment until Professor Spencer and his colleague, Mr. Gillen, should

[1] *The Golden Bough* (First Edition, 1890), ii. p. 95. In the cases to which I referred in this passage the sacred animals are killed, but not eaten. Neither in *The Golden Bough* nor in *Totemism* (First Edition, 1887) have I adduced any example of the sacramental eating of an animal which could with any show of probability be regarded as a totem. I desire to point this out expressly, as my writings have sometimes been referred to vaguely as containing evidence of this sort, though in fact they do not.

[2] " A rather curious thing is that in five of the ceremonies we have seen the performers are engaged in eating their own totem." This is all that Prof. Spencer says on the subject in the letter, which is in my possession.

[3] *Modern Mythology* (London, New York, and Bombay, 1897), p. 84.

have published their materials in full. This they have now done in their great work, *The Native Tribes of Central Australia*, which, in fact, supplies the long-sought evidence for the practice of a totem sacrament by tribes among whom totemism is a living institution. Among these Central Australian tribes the totem sacrament forms part of those Intichiuma ceremonies which are practised for the purpose of multiplying the plants and animals that are used for food ; and it is believed that the performance would fail of its purpose if the performers did not partake of the sacrament, or, in other words, if they did not eat their totem. Thus Robertson Smith's wonderful intuition—almost prevision—has been strikingly confirmed after the lapse of years. Yet what we have found is not precisely what he expected. The sacrament he had in his mind was a religious rite ; the sacrament we have found is a magical ceremony. He thought that the slain animal was regarded as divine, and never killed except to furnish the mystic meal ; as a matter of fact, the animals partaken of sacramentally by the Central Australians are in no sense treated as divine, and though they are not as a rule killed and eaten by the men and women whose totems they are, nevertheless they are habitually killed and eaten by all the other members of the community ; indeed, the evidence goes to show that at an earlier time they were commonly eaten also by the persons whose totems they were, nay, even that such persons partook of them more freely, and were supposed to have a better right to do so, than anyone else. The object of the real totem sacrament which Messrs. Spencer and Gillen have discovered is not to attain to a mystical communion with a deity, but simply to ensure a plentiful supply of food for the rest of the community by means of sorcery. In short, what we have found is not religion, but that which was first the predecessor, and afterwards the hated rival of religion ; I mean magic.

Next I venture to offer a suggestion as to the meaning of another remarkable and mysterious ceremony witnessed by Messrs. Spencer and Gillen. Near the end of the final initiation ceremony of young men a special sacred object was formed of two large wooden *churinga*, or bull-roarers, each three feet long. These were tied together with human hair-string, ornamented with rings of white down, and surmounted with a tuft of owl feathers. The object thus fashioned was called the *Ambilyerikirra*, and all night long it was lifted up and down without cessation, save for a few seconds at a time, by the master of the ceremonies, whose arms were supported in the discharge of this laborious and exhausting task by two other old men, seated one on either side of him. Meantime the men who were being initiated had to lie still and silent on the ground the whole night long without being allowed to move on any pretext; and it was believed that if the strength of the men who were lifting the *Ambilyerikirra* up and down were to fail, the young men would die. Next morning the master of the ceremonies and his two colleagues, bearing the *Ambilyerikirra* and accompanied by the novices, marched from the ground where the ceremonies were being performed to the spot where the women were grouped together to receive them. When they were within a few yards of the women, the men who bore the *Ambilyerikirra* threw themselves headlong on the ground, and the novices threw themselves on the top of them, so that only the heads of the three old men could be seen projecting beyond the pile of bodies. After remaining thus for two minutes, they all got up and returned to the ground set apart for the performance of the initiatory rites.[1]

What is the meaning of these ceremonies? Any explanation of them, as Messrs. Spencer and Gillen observe, can amount to no more than a conjecture, but I may be allowed to add my conjecture to theirs. The key to the mystery, I would suggest, is perhaps furnished by the name *Ambilyerikirra*, which, as Messrs. Spencer and Gillen inform us elsewhere, means " a newly born child ".[2] Taken in connexion with the belief that the life of the novices depends on keeping the sacred object in uninterrupted motion for a certain time, may not the name imply that at this period of their initiation the novices are undergoing a new birth? There would be nothing unusual in such a pretended new birth at initiation. Elsewhere I have shown that a pretence

[1] Spencer and Gillen, *Native Tribes of Central Australia*, pp. 363-369.
[2] *Op. cit.* p. 561.

of killing the novices and bringing them to life again is
often enacted at the initiatory rites by which boys are made
into men.[1] On this hypothesis the carrying of the *Ambilyerikirra*, " or newly born child ", towards the women, and the
falling of the novices on the top of it in their presence, would
signify that the women had also to take their part in bringing
about the new birth.

---

[1] *The Golden Bough* (First Edition, 1890), ii. pp. 342-357.

IX

THE CURSING OF VENIZELOS[1]

THE following account of a barbarous ritual, lately performed by the highest dignitaries of the Greek Church in Athens, was sent to me by Dr. R. M. Burrows, Principal of King's College, London, in a letter dated January 16, 1917, in which he says : " The enclosed is written from a cable that we received from the Venizelists at Salonica, and the accounts of the correspondents of the English papers. For some reason or other it did not appeal to the daily press and has not been widely published." The account runs thus :

" The extraordinary ceremony of ' Anathema ' against M. Venizelos performed on Christmas Day [1916] by the ecclesiastical authorities of Athens at the instigation of the League of Reservists has had its uses—besides providing anthropologists with the most remarkable instance on record of the survival in Europe amid the forms of civilisation of a magic ritual common to savages all over the world. The Metropolitan of Athens, as it was reported at the time, solemnly excommunicated a bull's head (which presumably represented the body of Venizelos), and cast the first stone ; and then each member of the crowd assembled by King Constantine's hooligans cast a stone on the pile and uttered a curse against the man who had ' plotted against the King '. But King Constantine's appearance as a Hottentot witch-doctor had unexpected results, and only served to prove even in his own stronghold that all the terrorism of German autocracy could not quench the real devotion of the Greek people to M. Venizelos. From fuller accounts of the ceremony

[1] This article was published first in *The New Europe*, vol. ii. No. 19, February 22, 1917, and afterwards in *Folk-Lore*, vol. xxviii. No. 2, June 30, 1917, from which it is here reprinted.

now received by the Anglo-Hellenic League it appears that
during the night the cairn of stones so solemnly cursed and
supposed to symbolise the ' casting out ' of the ' traitor ',
was covered with masses of flowers ; and in the morning
these bright garlands were seen to be attached to an inscription
which read ' From the Venizelists of Athens '."

This cursing and stoning of the great statesman and good
patriot Venizelos, who has been banished from Athens by
traitors, resembles the cursing and stoning of King David,
when that great monarch was banished from Jerusalem by
the treachery of his unnatural son Absalom, who had usurped
the throne. As David and the procession of loyal men who
followed their beloved king into exile were wending their way
sadly down the steep road which descends from Jerusalem
into the deep valley of the Jordan, a certain Benjamite named
Shimei kept pace with them on the hillside above, and as he
went he threw stones at the king and his escort and cursed,
saying, " Begone, begone, thou man of blood, and man of
Belial ! " This was more than one of the king's captains, a
man of hot blood, could bear, and he asked David, " Why
should this dead dog curse my lord the king ? Let me go
over, I pray thee, and take off his head." But the king
received the curses and the stones with magnanimous
patience, and rebuked the fiery Hotspur who would have
washed out the insult on the spot with the caitiff's blood.
He reminded his would-be champion that his own son
Absalom was at that moment seeking his father's life, and
" How much more ", he asked, " may this Benjamite now
do it ? Let him alone, and let him curse ; for the Lord hath
bidden him. It may be that the Lord will look on the wrong
done unto me, and that the Lord will requite me good for
his cursing of me this day." [1]

The king's trust in Providence was not misplaced. In a
short time the traitor and usurper was defeated and slain, as
he hung by the hair of his head in the forest which witnessed
the discomfiture of the rebel army. The king came to his
own again and returned in triumph to Jerusalem, the people
flocking to welcome him at the ford over the Jordan, which
he had lately crossed in haste, a fugitive and an exile. And

[1] 2 Samuel xvi. 5-13.

the first to meet him at the ford was the very man who had
so lately cursed and stoned him. There stood Shimei, the
Benjamite, waiting for him ; and when the bearer who had
carried the king through the water deposited his royal
burden respectfully on the shore, the quondam railer and
bully, now turned toady and lickspittle, fell on his face
before the king and begged for mercy, saying, " Let not my
lord impute iniquity unto me, neither do thou remember
that which thy servant did perversely the day that my lord
the king went out of Jerusalem, that the king should take
it to his heart. For thy servant doth know that I have sinned :
therefore, behold, I am come this day the first of all the
house of Joseph to go down to meet my lord the king."
The same hot-headed soldier, who would have had Shimei's
blood when he cursed and stoned the king, now earnestly
requested to be allowed to take it when the fellow fawned
and grovelled before his Majesty. But again the king calmly
checked the impetuosity of his too zealous adherent, saying
that no blood should sully the happy day of the royal restoration. So saying, he turned to Shimei and gave him his life.
" Thou shalt not die," he said, and confirmed the pardon
with an oath.[1]

The parallel is of happy augury for M. Venizelos. He,
too, we believe, will return in honour and glory to his own
in Athens, and he will doubtless complete the parallel by
treating with the same magnanimous disdain the con-
temptible ecclesiastic who has cursed and stoned him.

The ritual by which the Metropolitan of Athens has dis-
graced his cloth and his Church, without inflicting the smallest
harm on the object of his impotent wrath, is unquestionably
of heathen origin, and, set off by the gorgeous habiliments
of the officiating clergy, must have presented the same sort
of ludicrous medley which is sometimes displayed by the

---

[1] 2 Samuel xix. 15-23. In verse
18 the English version has : " And
there went over a ferry boat to bring
over the king's household." But the
true reading and translation of the
passage seems to be : " And they
passed to and fro over the ford in
order to bring the king's household
over." See S. R. Driver, *Notes on the*
Hebrew Text and the Topography of
the Books of Samuel, 2nd edition
(Oxford, 1913), p. 335. So far as I
am aware, there is no evidence of a
ferry over the Jordan in antiquity.
People had simply to splash through
the water, or to ride over it on the
backs of men or beasts.

untutored savage, who struts and flaunts in a grotesque combination of native paint and foreign velvet. In Europe such mummeries only contribute to the public hilarity, and bring the Church which parades them into contempt.

The combination of stones and curses directed at a person who, for one reason or another, is out of reach, seems to be not uncommon ; ignorance and malignity apparently trust to one or other, if not both, of these missiles hitting their mark in some manner unexplained. The poet Propertius ungallantly invited all lovers to pelt with stones and curses the grave of a certain lady whose reputation, by a stretch of charity, might perhaps be described as dubious.[1]

A writer on Syrian folk-lore has described " the customs with regard to casting curses or prayers with stones from the hand. All tourists to Jerusalem have seen Absalom's tomb, and the hole in the base of its pinnacle through which generations of Jews have conveyed thus their imprecations on an ungrateful and impious son. . . . At Biskinta, on the Lebanon, is the tomb of a Druze who, tradition says, was buried alive to obtain merit in the next stage of his existence ; for the Druzes believe in the transmigration of souls. Greek Orthodox Christians in the village—and they only—cast stones on this grave with muttered curses as they pass." [2]

A traveller in Palestine has described how between Sidon and Tyre his Mohammedan companions discharged stones and curses, with equal force and volubility, at the grave of a celebrated robber who had been knocked on the head there some fifty years before, and who still continued to receive this double testimony to his character from passers-by, whose stones remained in a heap on the spot, while their curses had melted into thin air.[3] After all a stone is perhaps a more effective missile to hurl at a man than a curse, unless, indeed, as Voltaire justly observed, the curse is accompanied with a sufficient dose of arsenic.

In view of the extraordinary persistence—we may almost say the indestructibility—of superstition, it seems likely that

[1] Propertius, v. 5. 77 sqq.
[2] Fr. Sessions, "Some Syrian Folk-lore Notes," Folk-Lore, ix. (1898), p. 15

[3] G. P. Badger, note on The Travels of Ludovico di Varthema (Hakluyt Society, London, 1863), p. 45.

the remarkable rite of cursing recently directed against
M. Venizelos has not been simply invented by his enemies,
but that it is based on a tradition which has been handed
down from antiquity, though I am not able to cite any exact
parallel in ancient Greek literature.   Euripides represents
the adulterer and murderer, Aegisthus, flushed with wine,
leaping on the grave of his victim and pelting it with stones,
but he does not say that the villain reinforced with curses
these expressions of his malignant hate.[1]   Perhaps a nearer
resemblance to the modern ecclesiastical comedy, in which
the Metropolitan of Athens took the principal part, may be
found in the treatment which Plato in his *Laws* recommended
should be meted out to the wretch who had murdered his
father or mother, his brother or sister, his son or daughter.
According to the philosopher, the criminal should be put
to death and his body cast out naked at a cross-road outside
of the city ; then the magistrates should assemble, and each
of them should cast a stone at the head of the corpse in
order to purge the city from the pollution it had contracted
by so heinous a crime.[2]   Here, again, the writer says nothing
about any curses by which the throwing of stones may possibly
have been accompanied.   But the context proves that, in
this part of his ideal legislation, Plato was less concerned
with the punishment of the criminal than with the purification
of the city, which was believed to have been defiled by his
act ; it may be, therefore, that imprecations formed no part
of the ritual of purification contemplated by the philosopher.
Whether that was so or not, we may surmise that, in pre-
scribing this form of atonement for parricide, matricide,
and similar aggravated cases of murder, Plato had his eye
on certain expiatory rites which were either actually observed
in his time or traditionally reported to have been observed
by gods or men in former ages.   For, with the growing
conservatism of age, Plato in the *Laws* clipped those wings
of his imagination which had borne him aloft in the *Republic*
into the blue.   In his later work he took a lower flight, and
hovered much nearer to Greek earth and Greek usage than
when he had surveyed the whole world from the empyreal
heights of pure idealism.   Now a ritual not unlike that which

[1] Euripides, *Electra*, 326-328.   [2] Plato, *Laws*, ix. 12, p. 873 A-B.

P

our philosopher prescribed in the case of parricide was said to have been observed at the trial of the great god Hermes for the murder of Argus. The gods, we are told, who sat in judgement on the divine prisoner at the bar, each cast a stone at him by way of purifying themselves from the pollution of his crime ; hence the origin of those heaps of stones which, in ancient Greece, were to be seen by the wayside surmounted by images of Hermes, and to which every passer-by added a stone.[1] Here, again, the casting of the stones is clearly a rite of purification rather than of commination, and it was probably not supposed to have been accompanied with curses.

The bull's head at which, in default of the head of M. Venizelos, the clerical and lay blackguards of Athens hurled their stones and curses has its parallel in the sacrificial ritual of ancient Egypt. Herodotus tells us that the Egyptians used to sacrifice black bulls, and that when they had slaughtered the victim at the altar, they skinned the carcass, cut off the head, loaded it with curses, and sold it to any Greeks who might be resident in the town ; but if there happened to be no Greek population in the place, the Egyptians carried the bull's head to the river and threw it into the water. The curses which they levelled at the bull's head consisted in an imprecation, that whatever evil was about to befall either the sacrificers themselves or the whole land of Egypt, might be diverted therefrom and concentrated on the head.[2] Naturally, no native Egyptian would purchase a head laden with malisons so dreadful ; but the Greek traders appear to have calculated, with great justice, that the curses could not affect foreigners, and as the cursed heads no doubt sold a good deal cheaper than common heads in the market, and were quite as good to eat, a shrewd Greek householder probably rather preferred to dine on a bull's head which had been blasted by the ecclesiastical thunder.

It will be observed that in this Egyptian rite the priests

[1] *Etymologicum Magnum*, *s.v.* 'Ερμαῖον, pp. 375 *sq.* ; Eustathius on Homer, *Odyssey*, xvi. 471. As to these heaps of stones, see Cornutus, *Theologiae Graecae Compendium*, 16 ; Babrius, *Fabulae*, xlviii. 1 ; Suidas, *s.v.* 'Ερμαῖον ; Scholiast on Nicander, *Ther.* 150. Of these writers Cornutus is the only one who mentions the custom of every passer-by adding to the pile.

[2] Herodotus, ii. 39.

apparently confined themselves to loading the black bull's head with curses ; they did not give point and weight to their maledictions by pelting it with stones.   In short, in ancient Egyptian ritual we have found curses without stones, and in ancient Greek ritual stones without curses.   The Metropolitan of Athens has combined both weapons, the material and the spiritual, in the assault, as futile as it was ridiculous, which he headed against the wisest and greatest of his countrymen.   By the flowers which next morning covered the shameful heap of stones, Greek patriotism converted the insult into a tribute of homage to the true leader of Greece.

X

THE KILLING OF THE KHAZAR KINGS [1]

AT a certain stage of social evolution not a few races appear
to have been in the habit of putting their kings to death,
either at the end of a fixed term, or on the failure of the
king's health and strength, or simply whenever a great public
calamity, such as drought or famine, had befallen the
country. Among the peoples who have practised this remarkable system of limited monarchy, and have elevated regicide
to the dignity of a public institution, must seemingly be
numbered the Khazars or Khozars, a nation of south-eastern
Russia, who in the Middle Ages maintained their independence for many centuries alike against Persia and the
Byzantine Empire, carried on a busy trade between the east
and the west, and repelled the wave of Mohammedan conquest, which, but for their resistance, might have deluged
Europe from the south-east. It is hardly too much to say
that during those dark ages when the power of Christendom
sank to its lowest ebb, and the power of Islam rose to its
highest pitch, Europe was protected against the swelling
tide of Moslem aggression by three great mountain barriers,
the Caucasus on the south-east, the Balkans in the centre,
and the Pyrenees on the south-west ; and that the passes
which led over these ranges into the heart of the continent
were guarded by three peoples, the Khazars, the Byzantine
Greeks, and the Spaniards. Of these three redoubtable
champions of Christendom, the Khazars have long disappeared and even their name is now hardly known but to
students of the bypaths of history.

[1] Reprinted from *Folk-Lore*, vol. xxviii. No. 4, December 31, 1917, pp.
382-407.

Yet for some nine hundred years or more (A.D. 190–1100) this almost forgotten people played a great part in history on the borderland of Europe and Asia. Their home was in the spurs of the Caucasus and along the western shore of the Caspian, which took its name (Sea of the Khazars) from them ; but at the height of their power they ruled over the whole of south-eastern Russia from the Dneiper to the middle Volga, together with the adjoining part of Asia along the eastern coast of the Caspian as far south as Astrabad. On the south their boundary never altered greatly ; at times, indeed, it extended southward as far as the Cyrus and even the Araxes, but on that side the Khazars had to face the Byzantine and Persian empires and were for the most part restrained within the passes of the Caucasus. Their capital was Itil in the delta of the Volga, but they possessed other populous and civilized cities, such as Semender (Tarkhu), which was the older capital, and Sarkel, or the White Abode, on the Don. All the Khazar cities were centres of commerce. Indeed, the Khazars have been described as " the Venetians of the Caspian and the Euxine, the organizers of the transit between the two basins ; the universal carriers between East and West ". Merchants from every nation found protection, justice, and good faith in the Khazar cities. Exiled from Constantinople, the Jews sought a home among them, developed their trade, and contended with their Mohammedan and Christian rivals for the religious allegiance of the pagan people. The reigning house accepted Judaism, apparently about the middle of the eighth century ; but all faiths were equally tolerated, and every man was held amenable to the authorized code and to the official judges of the religion which he professed. At the Byzantine court the *khakan*, or sovereign of the Khazars, was held in high honour. The Emperor Justinian Rhinotmetus took refuge with him during his banishment and married his daughter : his rival Bardanes also sought an asylum in the land of the Khazars ; and in Leo IV. the grandson of a Khazar sovereign ascended the Byzantine throne.

The origin and affinities of this interesting people appear to be still disputed. Many have assigned them to the Turkish stock ; others to the Ugrians or Eastern Finns ;

and some have even claimed them as Jews on account of their use of the Hebrew character and the profession of the Hebrew faith among them. " But their geographical position, their history, and the contemporary witness we have as to their physical character, their language, and their own national tradition, may be accepted as conclusive proof that the Khazars were an indigenous people of the Caucasus, and near akin to the Armenians and the Georgians." [1]

It is very remarkable that a custom of legalized regicide should have been practised among a people so comparatively advanced and civilized as the Khazars appear to have been, and of whom it has been said that "their government was regular, settled, and well organized. They were not wild barbarians like the Huns and the Avars." [2] Their case escaped me when I was collecting instances of such legalized regicide for *The Golden Bough*. My attention was first drawn to it in 1912 by Miss Barbara Freire-Marreco, who was so kind as to send me a long extract on the subject from the mediaeval Arab historian and geographer Abulfeda. Subsequently the Khazar practice of killing their sacred kings was described by Mr. Géza Róheim in an article contributed to *Man*.[3] But as his account seems to be based on the works of modern Hungarian historians, and the Khazar custom is probably still but little known, it may be worth while to put together those passages of mediaeval

---

[1] As to the Khazars, see C. M. Fraehn, " Veteres memoriae Chasarorum ex Ibn-Foszlano, Ibn-Haukale et Schems-ed-Dino Damasceno, Arabice et Latine ", *Mémoires de l'Académie Impériale des Sciences de St.-Pétersbourg*, viii. (1822), pp. 576-620 ; Klaproth," Mémoire sur les Khazars", *Journal Asiatique*, iii. (Paris, 1823), pp. 153-160 ; C. D'Ohsson, *Des Peuples du Caucase* (Paris, 1828), chapitres ii. et iii. pp. 30-71 ; K. F. Neumann, *Die Völker des südlichen Russlands* (Leipsic, 1847), pp. 99 *sqq.* ; P. Lyttelton Gell, *s.v.* " Khazars ", *Encyclopædia Britannica*, ninth edition, xiv. (1882), pp. 59 *sq.* ; H. Hirschfeld, *Das Buch Al-Chazari, aus dem arabischen des Abu-l-Hasan Jehuda Hallewi übersetzt* (Breslau, 1885),

pp. xi *sqq.* Mr. Lyttelton Gell's article contains a good general account of the Khazars, with references to the original authorities. The quotations in the text are made from it. The work of D'Ohsson consists of a series of extracts from the original Arab authorities, translated into French and strung together on the thread of the imaginary travels of a certain Abu-el-Cassim, whom the writer supposes to have been sent on an embassy from the Caliph to the Bulgarians of the Volga in A.D. 948.

[2] Klaproth, " Mémoire sur les Khazars ", *Journal Asiatique*, iii. (Paris, 1823), p. 153.

[3] Géza Róheim, " Killing the Divine King ", *Man*, xv. (1915), pp. 26-28.

authors which describe in some detail the Khazar kings and
their limited tenure of the crown. All the authors in question
appear to be Arabs, or at least to have written in Arabic,
but their works are accessible to the unlearned in translations, from which I borrow the following extracts. Some of
the most important passages were long ago collected and
edited in Arabic, with Latin translations, by C. M. Fraehn
in the *Memoirs* of the Academy of St. Petersburg.[1]

The earliest writer to give an account of the Khazar
kings from personal observation was Ahmed ibn Foszlan,
Fudhlan, or Fadlan, as his name is variously spelled, who
travelled through Khazaria in the year A.D. 921 or 922, at
a time when the kingdom was still at the height of its power
and glory. He was sent from Baghdad by the Caliph
Moktadir on an embassy to the king of the Bulgarians
whose dominions then lay on the Volga in central Russia,
and on his return to Baghdad he described in a book all
that he had observed worthy of note on his journey. His
work appears to be lost, but the portion of it which relates
to the Khazars was fortunately incorporated in his *Geographical Dictionary* by the Arab writer Yakut, who, after
a chequered life as a slave, commercial traveller, bookseller,
copyist, and author, died near Aleppo in the year A.D. 1229.[2]
The following are extracts from it :

" Ahmed, son of Foszlan, sent as envoy of (the Caliph)
Moktadir to the Slavs, related in a little book everything
that he saw with his own eyes in these regions, and in that
book he says that Khazar is the name of a certain country,
of which the capital is called Itil. Itil is also the name of
the river (Volga) which flows from Russia and Bulgaria to
Khazaria. Itil is the city, Khazar is the name of the kingdom, not of the city. The city is in two parts, of which
the larger is situated on the western bank of the river Itil
(Volga), while the other lies on the eastern side of the river.

[1] See above, p. 214, note 1.
[2] C. M. Fraehn, *op. cit.* p. 579 ;
C. D'Ohsson, *Des Peuples du Caucase*,
p. ix ; C. Barbier de Meynard,
*Dictionnaire géographique, historique
et littéraire de la Perse et des contrées
adjacentes, extrait du* Módjem-el-
Bouldan *de Yakout* (Paris, 1861),

pp. iv *sqq.* ; C. Brockelmann, *Geschichte der arabischen Litteratur*
(Weimar, 1898—Berlin, 1902), i.
227 *sq.*, 479 *sq.* Ibn Foszlan (Fadlan)
set out from Baghdad in June, A.D.
921, and reached the Bulgarian
kingdom on the Volga in May,
A.D. 922.

The king resides in the western part. In their tongue he is called *Ilek* and also *Bak*. This western part extends to the length of a parasang and is surrounded by a wall, but the buildings in it are few and far between. Now their edifices are huts made of felt, with a few exceptions which are made of mud. They have market-places and baths. Many Mohammedans are found there ; indeed, there are said to be more than ten thousand of them in the town, and they have thirty mosques. The king's palace is at a distance from the bank of the river and is built of baked bricks. No other person besides him is privileged to dwell in a house made of bricks, for the king will not suffer it. In the wall there are four gates, of which one leads to the river, and another to the desert, beyond the fields of the city.

" Their king is a Jew, and he is said to have four thousand retainers attached to his person. The Khazars themselves, however, are Mohammedans and Christians. Idolaters are also found among them. The fewest numerically in the country are the Jews, though the king himself is of their number. The most numerous are the Mohammedans and the Christians ; nevertheless the king and his retainers profess the Jewish religion. In the manners of the idolaters the most noticeable feature is that they prostrate themselves in token of reverence for each other, and observe certain sacred ordinances according to customs which differ from the religion of the Mohammedans, Jews, and Christians. The king's standing army consists of twelve thousand soldiers, of whom as soon as one is dead another is enlisted in his place, nor is their number ever diminished. Their pay is neither large nor frequent ; indeed, what they get is very little, and even that at long intervals, when either a war is to be waged by them or some calamity has occurred, on account of which they are mustered.

" The public revenues of the kingdom of the Khazars are derived either from the customs or from tithes levied on merchandise, and these dues, in accordance with their institutions, are levied on every highway, sea, and river. Land taxes are also collected from the inhabitants of villages and districts on every sort of food, drink, and other things, so far as is necessary.

" The king is assisted by nine judges chosen from among the Jews, Christians, Mohammedans, and idolaters. If any person takes the law of another, these judges decide his suit. Petitioners are not allowed access to the king himself ; for none but these judges are admitted to his presence. But on the day of judgement an intermediary goes backward and forward between the judges and the king, informing the king of the business in hand, and reporting to the judges the king's command, which they must carry out.

" This city (Itil) has no villages. The fields of the citizens are scattered over a space of twenty parasangs, and in summer the townspeople go forth to them, sow them, and when the crops are ripe they gather them and convey them in waggons or ships to the river or the deserts. The greater part of their food consists of rice and fish. Everything else found in their country is imported from Russia, Bulgaria, and Küjabâ. Most of the merchants dwell in the eastern part of the city ; there, too, the Mohammedans reside and the wares are stored.

" The language of the Khazars differs from the Turkish and the Persian, nor has it anything in common with the language of any people.

" The Khazars are not like the Turks. They have black hair. There are two sorts of them. The one sort are called the Kara Khazars (that is, the Black Khazars) ; they are of a dusky complexion verging on black, so that they might be taken for a species of Indians. The other sort are of a white complexion and remarkable for their beauty and symmetry. All the slaves found among the Khazars are idolaters, for the idolaters deem it lawful to sell their children and to carry off their fellows into slavery. Whereas the Jews and Christians who dwell in that country esteem it contrary to their religion to carry off people into slavery, and the Mohammedans are of the same opinion.

" Nothing is exported from the land of the Khazars to other countries, but whatever is conveyed down from it has first been imported into it, such as flour, honey, wax, and the skins of otters and other animals.

" As for the King of the Khazars, whose title is khakan, he does not show himself in public except once in every

four months, when he goes forth for his diversion to his
pleasances. He is called the Great khakan, and his viceroy
is called the khakan bh (?). It is the latter who leads and
commands the armies, administers and superintends the
affairs of state, appears in public, and conducts warlike
expeditions ; it is he whom neighbouring kings obey. Every
day he consults the sovereign khakan, with an assumed air
of modesty, respect, and gravity. Nor may he approach
him except barefoot and holding in his hand a stick, which,
after saluting him, he kindles in his presence. After that he
sits down with the king on his own throne to the right of
the monarch. After him comes a man who is called Kender
Khakan, and after him again another, who is called Chau-
shiar. It is the custom that the supreme and sovereign
king admits nobody to an interview : nobody is admitted to
him except him whom I mentioned before. The government,
the punishment of the guilty, and the administration of the
realm are presided over by the viceroy, the khakan bh.

" It has been ordained by their ancestors, that when the
sovereign king dies, a great palace (mausoleum) should be
built for him divided into twenty chambers, and that in each
chamber there should be dug a grave, the bottom of which
should be paved with stones so crushed as to present the
appearance of powdered antimony, while the whole is
covered from above with quicklime. Under the palace flows
a great river, and they make the grave above it, saying that
this is done lest Satan, or man, or worm, or other creeping
thing should approach it. When the king is buried, the
heads of those who laid him to rest are cut off, that no man
may know in which of the chambers his grave is situated.
This grave of his is called Paradise, and he himself is said to
have entered Paradise. Moreover, all the chambers are
tapestried with cloth of gold.

" It is customary for the king of the Khazars to have
twenty-five wives, all daughters of one or other of the neighbouring kings, whom he has married with or without their
consent. Further, he has sixty concubines, all remarkable
for their beauty. Each one of these women dwells in a
palace of her own, in a *kubbâ* (vaulted chamber) roofed with
the wood of the Indian plane. About each *kubbâ* a tent is

pitched. Every one of these damsels is attended by a eunuch, who guards her behind a curtain. Now when the king desires to take his pleasure with any of them, he sends to the eunuch, her guardian, by whom in less than the twinkling of an eye she is brought and placed in the king's bed. But the eunuch stands sentinel before the door of the royal chamber, and when the damsel is dismissed by the king, the eunuch takes her by the hand and leads her home, and does not thereafter leave her even for a moment.

" When the sovereign king rides on horseback in public, the whole army marches out to escort him in procession, but an interval of a mile is left between him and these cavalry. Nor does any of his subjects see him without falling on his face and humbly doing him reverence, and not raising his head until the king has passed by.

" Forty years are fixed for their king's reign. If he exceeds that term even by one day, his citizens and courtiers put him to death, alleging as the reason that his mental powers are decayed and his wisdom impaired.

" A regiment sent by him on an expedition never turns its back on the enemy ; for were it to take to flight, every soldier who should return to the king would pay for it with his head. But if the officers or the viceroy run away, the king sends for them, with their wives and children, and in their presence bestows their wives and children on others, together with their beasts of burden, furniture, weapons, and houses. It sometimes happens that he cuts them through the middle and hangs up the severed parts ; sometimes he hangs them by the neck from trees. Occasionally, when he is favourably disposed to them, he makes them his grooms." [1]

Such is the account of the Khazar kings which the Arab geographer Yakut has extracted from the original narrative of Ahmed ibn Foszlan. In the National Library at Paris there is preserved a manuscript abridgement of Yakut's work, in which his account of the Khazars and their king is condensed into a few lines, as follows :

" Country of the Khozars, a numerous race of Turks,

[1] C. M. Frachn, " Veteres Me-   *de St. - Pétersbourg*, viii. (1822),
moriae Chasarorum ", etc., *Mémoires*   pp. 589-593.
de l'Académie Impériale des Sciences

who dwell to the north of Babal abouab ; they are of two
sorts, the one white, the other blond or red. Their houses
are made of mud. They have market-places and baths.
They dwell on the banks of the river Atel. Among them
are many Mussulmans, Christians, Jews, and pagans. When
their king has reigned more than forty years, they kill him." [1]

Further, we possess accounts of the Khazars and their
kings written by two other Arab travellers and geographers
of the tenth century A.D. One of these is Abul-Hasan Ali,
commonly known as El-Mas'údy, because he was descended
in the eighth generation from Mas'úd, one of the companions
of Mohammed. Born at Baghdad towards the end of the
ninth century A.D., he spent a great part of his life in travel.
Among the countries which he visited were India, Ceylon,
China, Madagascar, and the region of the Caspian. He did
not travel for gain. His motive was scientific curiosity ; he
desired to see every land for himself and to observe and
record everything notable in the antiquities, the history, and
the manners of the peoples. His most famous book, which
bears the fanciful title, *Meadows of Gold and Mines of
Precious Stones*, was begun in the year 332 of the Hegira
(A.D. 943–4) and finished in the year 336 (A.D. 947–8). It
has survived in an abridgement, of which there are many
manuscripts in European libraries. On account of the range
of his observations and his naive uncritical honesty in recording them, he has been called the Arab Herodotus. "The
parallel, however, must be taken with great deductions. Of
the *Meadows*, the work by which Mas'údy is chiefly known,
by far the greater part is an historical compilation, enlivened
indeed in some parts by personal recollections of places and
the like, but mainly drawn from a vast mass of earlier books
which are used in the common paste-and-scissors fashion of
Eastern history. Even in the earlier cosmographical chapters
the author's vast and miscellaneous reading, which included
the Arabic translations of Ptolemy and other Greek writers,
is mingled with his original observations in that ill-digested

---

[1] M. de Guignes, "Exposition de
ce qu'il y a de plus remarquable (sur
la terre) et des Merveilles du Roi
Tout-puissant, par Abdorraschid, fils
de Saleh, fils de Nouri, surnommé
Yakouti", *Notices et Extraits des
Manuscrits de la Bibliothèque du Roi*,
iii. (Paris, 1789), p. 532.

style so often characteristic of men of prodigious acquisitive power." [1]

The following is El-Mas'údy's account of the Khazars and their kings :

" The nation nearest to Báb el-Abwáb are the Haïdan. They form one of the kingdoms of the Khazars. Next to Haïdan is the kingdom of the Khazars. Their metropolis was the city of Semender, which is eight days' journey from the town of Báb el-Abwáb. This city has a numerous population of Khazars, but it is no longer the capital, for when Solaïman Ben Rabí'ah el-Báhilí conquered Semender in the beginning of the Islám, the king transferred his residence to Itil, which is seven days' journey from Semender ; and since this time the kings of the Khazars reside there.

" This town (Itil) is divided into three parts, by a large river, which rises from the higher regions of the country of the Turks, and from which an arm branches off, somewhere near the country of the Targhiz (Bulgarians), and falls into the sea of Máyotis.[2] This town has two sides. In the middle of the river is an island, in which the king resides. The palace of the king stands on the extremity of this island, and is connected by a bridge of boats with one of the two sides of the town. In this town are many Moslims and Christians, Jews and pagans. The king, his suite [and the Khazar of his army [3]], embraced the tenets of the Jews, in the reign of er-Rashíd. To this king flock the Jews from all the Moslim districts, and from the Byzantine empire ; for the emperor forced the Jews of his dominions to turn Christians, and loaded the converts with favours. The present [332, A.H.] Byzantine emperor is Armanus (Romanus II.). . . .

" One of the various Pagan nations who live in his [the king of the Khazars] country are the Sekálibah (Sclavonians), and another the Rús (the Russians). They live in one of the two sides of this town : they burn the dead with their

---

[1] *Encyclopædia Britannica*, ninth edition, xv. (Edinburgh, 1883), pp. 623 *sq.* ; C. D'Ohsson, *Des Peuples du Caucase*, pp. iii-viii ; C. Brockelmann, *Geschichte der arabischen Litteratur* (Weimar, 1898—Berlin, 1902), i. 143-145.

[2] " The error that the Don is a branch of the Wolga is also met with in Byzantine authors (Klaproth)." (Translator's note.)

[3] " These words are left out in some copies." (Translator's note.)

cattle, utensils, arms, and ornaments. When a man dies, his
wife is burnt alive with him ; but when the wife dies, her
husband is not burnt. If a bachelor dies, he is married after
his death. Women are glad to be burnt ; for they cannot
enter into Paradise by themselves. This usage prevails also
among the Hindus, as we have said. But the Hindus never
burn a woman with her husband, unless it is her own wish.

" The majority of the population of this country are
Moslims ; for the standing army of the king consists of
Moslims. They are called al-Lárisians, and come from
Khowárezm ; whence they emigrated at an early period,
after the spreading of the Islám ; on account of drought
and plague which had visited their country. They are
brave, good soldiers, and form the strength of the king of
the Khazars in his wars. They fixed certain conditions
under which they would establish themselves in his country ;
one of these conditions was, that they should be allowed to
profess publicly the Islám ; to build mosques and call out
the prayers ; and that the vizier of the kingdom should be
a man of their religion and nation. The vizier there is
at present from amongst them ; his name is Ahmed Ben
Kuwaïh. Another condition is, that if the king of the
Khazars should have a war against the Moslims, they would
remain separate in his camp (observe neutrality), and not
fight against a nation who profess the same religion ; but
they would fight for him against any other nation. There
are, at present, seven thousand horsemen of theirs, in the
army of the king, armed with bows and equipped in
cuirasses, helmets, and coats of mail : he has also some
spearsmen. In point of arms, they are like the soldiers in
Moslim countries. Their supreme judges, in religious and
civil matters, are Moslims.

" In accordance with the constitution of the kingdom of
the Khazars, there are nine supreme judges in the country ;
two of them for the Moslims ; two for the Khazars, who
follow the laws of the Pentateuch in passing sentence ; two
for the Christians, who follow the laws of the gospel in their
decisions ; and one for the Sclavonians, Russians, and the
other pagan population. The pagan judge decides after the
heathen laws ; that is to say, the dictates of reason, (not

revelation). If any important case comes before him, he refers to the Moslim judges, and lets them decide after the law of the Islám.

" There is no other king in these parts who has *paid* troops, except the king of the Khazars. Every Moslim has there the name Lárisian, (although he may not be of this nation,) and it is even extended to such Russians and Sclavonians as serve in the (standing) army or household of the king ; although they are pagans as we have said. But there are many Moslims in this kingdom besides the Lárisians ; they are artisans, tradespeople, and merchants, who have been attracted by the justice and security (of persons and property) afforded by the government. They have a great public mosque, the Mináret of which rises above the royal palace ; and several private mosques, where children are instructed in reading the Korán. If the Moslims and Christians, who are there, agree, the king has no power over them.

" El-Mas'udi says, What we have said does not refer to the king of the Khazars himself, but we mean the Khákán (*Major domus*) ; for there is a king in the country of the Khazars, besides the Khákán. He is shut up in his palace : he never makes a public procession, nor does he show himself to the nobility or the people, and he never goes out from his palace. His person is sacred, but he has nothing to do with the affairs of the state, either to command or forbid. Everything is administered by the Khákán for the king, who lives with him in the same palace. If a drought, or any other misfortune, befalls the country of the Khazars, or if a war or any other accident happens to them, the lower and higher classes of the nation run to the king, and say, ' The administration of this Khákán brings misfortune upon us : put him to death, or deliver him to us, that we may kill him.' Sometimes he delivers him to them, and they put him to death ; at other times he takes charge himself of the execution ; and sometimes he has pity on him, protects him, and sets him free without doing him any harm, although he might have deserved it. I do not know whether this institution dates from ancient times, or whether it has been recently introduced. The Khákán is chosen from among the nobility

by their chiefs ; but I think that the royalty of the present
dynasty takes date from a remote period." [1]

Another writer of the tenth century A.D., who has described the Khazars and their kings, is the Arab traveller
and geographer Abul-Cassim Mohammed ibn Haukal or
Haukali, author of a work called *Book of the Itineraries and
of the Provinces*, in which he describes the Mohammedan
countries on the basis of his personal researches and of the
journeys which he had undertaken for the purposes of
commerce. He tells us that he began his researches and
travels in early youth, and that he set out from Baghdad in
the year 331 of the Hegira (A.D. 942–3) ; but his book was
not written till the year 366 of the Hegira (A.D 976–7). A
manuscript of the original work, in Arabic, is preserved in
the library at Leyden, but it is said to be so faulty that the
meaning is often unintelligible. The book exists also in a
Persian translation, of which an English version was published by Sir William Ouseley.[2] The portions of it which
describe the tribes of the Caucasus, including the Khazars,
are extracted and translated into French from the Arabic
manuscript at Leyden by C. D'Ohsson in his work on the
peoples of the Caucasus.[3]

The following is the account which Ibn Haukal gives of
the Khazars and their kings, as translated by Sir William
Ouseley from the Persian :

" After one passes Moukan to Derbend, for two days'
journey the country is Shirwan ; from that to Semender,
fourteen days' journey ; and from Semender to Atel. This
Atel is a certain river which comes from Rous and Bulgar.
One half of this river belongs to the western side, the other
to the eastern. The sovereign of Atel resides on the western
side : he is styled king, and surnamed Baul. Here are

[1] El-Mas'udi's *Historical Encyclopaedia, entitled " Meadows of Gold
and Mines of Gems"* : translated
from the Arabic by Aloys Sprenger,
M.D., vol. i. (London, 1841), pp. 406-
411. In transcribing this passage I
have taken the liberty of uniformly
writing Khazars instead of Khazar,
wherever the latter appears to be used
by the translator in the plural sense.

[2] Ebn Haukal, *Oriental Geography*,
translated by Sir William Ouseley
(London, 1800), pp. ii *sqq.* ; C. M.
Frachn, " Veteres Memoriae Chasa-
rorum ", *Mémoires de l'Académie des
Sciences de St.-Pétersbourg*, viii. (1822),
p. 581 ; C. D'Ohsson, *Des Peuples du
Caucase* (Paris, 1828), pp. viii *sq*.
[3] C. D'Ohsson, *Des Peuples du
Caucase*, pp. 31 *sqq.*

many tents ; and in this country there are but a few edifices
of clay, such as bazars (market-places) and bathing houses.
In these territories are about ten thousand Mussulmans. The
king's habitation is at a distance from the shore : it is constructed of burnt bricks ; and this is the only building of
such materials in all the country : they will not allow any
body but the king to erect such a dwelling. The city of Atel
has four gates. One of those gates faces the river ; another
looks towards Iran, in the direction of the desert. The king
of this country is a Jew : he has in his train four thousand
Mussulmans and Khozrians (Christians), and idolaters ; but
his principal people are Jews : and this king has twelve
thousand soldiers in his service, of whom when one dies,
another person is immediately chosen into his place ; and
they have no other commander but him. And this king has
under him nine magistrates or judges : these are Mussulmans, Jews, Christians, and Idolaters. The smallest in
number of the inhabitants of this country are the Jews ; the
greatest in number are the Mussulmans and Christians : but
the king and his chief officers are Jews. There are magistrates of each religion ; and when they sit in the tribunal
of justice, they are obliged to report to the king all that
passes, and to bring back his answer and opinion, and to
put his sentence into execution.

. " This city has not any suburbs ; but the cultivated
fields and grounds extend for nearly twenty farsang. Agriculture is much practised, and the husbandmen carry the
produce of their labour in boats and carriages to the city.
The chief diet of this people is fish and rice : they bring
honey and wax from the borders of Rous. The principal
persons of Atel are Mussulmans and merchants : their
language is like that of the Turks (or Tartars), and is not
understood by any other nation. . . . .

" The people of Khorz are near the Turks, whom they
resemble. They are of two classes ; one of blackish com-
plexions, and such dark hair that you would suppose them
to be descended from the Hindoos : the other race fair
complexioned ; these sell their children ; but it is not
allowed among the Jews and the Christians to sell, or make
one onother slaves.

Q

" They bring from other countries those commodities which Khozr does not produce, such as tapestry or curtains, honey, candles, and similar articles. The people of Khozr have not materials for making garments or clothes : they therefore import them from Gurkan, Armenia, Azerbaijan, and Roum. Their king is styled the Khacan of Khozr.

" When a prince is to be raised to the Khacanship, they bring them forth, and tie a piece of silk about his throat, so tight that he can scarcely draw his breath. At that moment they ask him, how long he will hold the sovereignty ? He answers, ' so many years '. He then is set at liberty, and becomes Khacan of Khozr. But if he should not die before the expiration of the time he mentioned, when that space is fulfilled, they put him to death.

" The Khacan must always be of the Imperial race. No one is allowed to approach him but on business of importance : then they prostrate themselves before him, and rub their faces on the ground, until he gives orders for their approaching him, and speaking. When a Khacan of Khozr dies, whoever passes near his tomb goes on foot, and pays his respects at the grave ; and when he is departing, must not mount on horseback, as long as the tomb is within view.

" So absolute is the authority of this sovereign, and so implicitly are his commands obeyed, that if it seemed expedient to him that one of his nobles should die, and if he said to him, ' Go and kill yourself ', the man would immediately go to his house, and kill himself accordingly. The succession to the Khacanship being thus established in the same family, when the turn of the inheritance arrives to any individual of it, he is confirmed in the dignity, though he possesses not a single dirhem. And I have heard from persons worthy of belief, that a certain young man used to sit in a little shop at the public market-place, selling petty articles ; and that the people used to say, ' When the present Khacan shall have departed, this man will succeed to the throne. ' But the young man was a Mussulman, and they give the Khacanship only to Jews.

" The Khacan has a throne and pavilion of gold : these are not allowed to any other person. The palace of the

Khacan is loftier than the other edifices. . . . The language of Bulgar and of Khozr is the same." [1]

In the original of Ibn Haukal's work the account of the installation of the Khozar king appears to be slightly fuller than in the Persian version. The following translation of the passage is made from Frachn's Latin version of the Arabic original :

" When the king is dead and another is to be appointed in his room, the khakan has him brought and admonishes and exhorts him ; he declares to him both what he owes to others and what others owe to him (that is to say), his royal rights and duties ; he sets before him the burdens of monarchy, and the reproach of sin and crime which he will incur if, in the discharge of his office, he should fall short of his duty in the administration which he is about to undertake, or should act rashly, or show himself corrupt and unjust in the seat of judgement. Now when he is brought to be invested with the kingdom and to receive the salutations of his subjects, the khakan puts a silken cord about his neck and begins to strangle him, and when he is almost choked, they ask him how many years he desires to reign, to which he answers, ' Such and such a number of years.' Afterwards, if he dies before the expiry of the term, it is well, but if not, whenever he attains to the appointed year, he is put to death." [2]

A similar, but briefer, report of the custom is given by the Arab cosmographer, Shems-ed-din Mohammed Dimeshky ; he seems to have derived his information about the Khazars from Ibn-el-Asir, who died in A.D. 1233. The passage relating to the appointment of the Khazar king runs as follows :

" They begin to strangle the man whom they wish to make their king. When he has thus been brought to the point of death, they ask him, how many years he wishes to reign, and he answers, ' Such and such a number of years.' His answer is written down and attested by witnesses. If

---

[1] Ebn Haukal, *Oriental Geography*, translated by Sir William Ouseley (London, 1800), pp. 185-190.

[2] C. M. Frachn, " Veteres Memoriae Chasarorum ", *Mémoires de l'Académie Impériale de St.-Pétersbourg*, viii. (1822), p. 610.

he should live till the expiry of the set term, he is put to death." [1]

It will be observed that, whereas in the Persian version of Ibn Haukal it is the new khakan who is said to have been thus forcibly interrogated as to the length of his future reign, in the Arabic original and in Dimeshky's account it is the new king who is subjected to this stringent interrogatory. The discrepancy betrays a certain confusion between the two personages who divided the Khazar sovereignty between them ; but the analogy of similar customs elsewhere renders it practically certain that it was the sacred and nominally supreme potentate, rather than his civil and nominally subordinate colleague, whose reign was limited in this peremptory fashion.

The last notice of the Khazars, or Khozars, and their kings which I shall cite is extracted from the *Geography* of the eminent Arab historian and geographer Abulfeda, who was born at Damascus in A.D. 1273 and died in A.D. 1331 at the ancient Syrian city of Hamah (the Biblical Hamath), of which he had been for many years before his death the hereditary prince and ruler. A gallant soldier and a distinguished writer, Abulfeda appears not to have travelled very widely ; hence for the materials embodied in his *Geography* he must have been in great measure dependent on the works of his predecessors.[2] The description which he gives of the Khazar kingdom is clearly based, for the most part, on the accounts of Ibn Foszlan (Fadlan) and Ibn Haukal. It runs as follows :

" The river Itil (Volga) traverses the country of the Russians and Bulgarians. The capital, also called Itil, is divided into two parts : the one is situated to the west of the river (on the right bank) and is the principal part ; the other lies to the east. The king (of the Khozars) inhabits the western part. This king is called in their language Belek ; he is also known as Bek.[3] This part is about a parasang long ; it is surrounded by a wall, but the wall is

[1] C. M. Fraehn, *op. cit.* pp. 582, 611.
[2] *Encyclopædia Britannica*, ninth edition, i. (Edinburgh 1875), pp. 60 *sq.* ; C. Brockelmann, *Geschichte der arabischen Litteratur*, ii. 44 *sq.*

[3] " Constantine Porphyrogenitus (*De administrando imperio*, part ii. cap. xlii.) employs the word πέχ ; it is evidently the common Turkish word *beg* or *bey*." (Reinaud's note.)

low.   The houses of the inhabitants consist of tents made
of felt ; only a small part is built of clay.   The town includes
market-places and baths.   Mussulmans are to be found in
it : the number of Mussulmans, they say, amounts to more
than ten thousand ; they own about thirty mosques.   The
palace of the king is built at some distance from the river ;
it is constructed of bricks.   There is no other house of bricks
in the town ; the king allows no man whatsoever the privilege (of building a brick house).   The wall which surrounds
the town is pierced by four gates, some of them facing
towards the river and the others towards the country.

   " The king of the Khozars is a Jew.   He keeps near his
person, they say, about four thousand men.   Some of the
Khozars are Mussulmans, others are Christians, a certain
number are Jews ; there are also some who worship idols.
The Jews form the smallest number ; the majority is composed of Mussulmans and Christians ; but the king and his
retinue prefer Judaism.   For the rest, the manners of the
Khozars are in general the manners of the idolaters ; when
they salute each other, they bow the head in token of respect.
The administration of the capital is based on ancient customs, contrary to the religion of the Mussulmans, the Jews,
and the Christians.   The army is composed of twelve thousand men ; when one of these men dies, he is replaced by
another.   Their pay is small and scanty.

   " The king's revenues arise from town dues and a tithe
levied on merchandise on all the roads and every sea and
river, in accordance with a system peculiar to the Khozars.
He also obliges the inhabitants of the towns and country
districts to furnish him with all the objects (in kind) which
he needs.

   " The king chooses nine judges among the Jews, Christians, Mussulmans, and idolaters.   When a suit is brought,
it is these men who judge it ; the parties do not apply to
the king, but to these men.   When the judges are sitting,
some one is charged with the duty of acting as intermediary
between the king and the judges.

   " The principal food of the Khozars consists of rice and
fish.

   " The merchants dwell by preference in the part of the

city which is situated on the eastern bank. There, too, may be found persons who profess Islam, also there are commercial establishments. As for the western part, it is the special abode of the king, his retainers, his troops, and Khozars of distinction.

" The language of the Khozars differs from all others. . . .

" The Khozars do not resemble the Turks ; they have black hair, and two sorts of them are distinguished. The one sort, called Caradjours, are brown, with a complexion so dark that it verges on black ; you might take them for an Indian race : the other sort are white and perfectly beautiful. The Khozars who, in our country, are sunk in slavery, belong to the idolaters, who, unlike the Jews, the Christians, and the Mussulmans, consider it lawful to sell their children and to sell each other.

" As to the government of the Khozars, the personage who occupies the first place bears the title of khakan of the Khozars ; he ranks above the king of the Khozars ; but it is from the latter that he receives his dignity. When they would appoint a khakan, they bring the person whom they have in view and draw a cord tightly round his neck ; when he is on the point of choking, they say to him, ' How long do you wish to keep this dignity ? ' He answers, ' So many years.' If he dies before the fixed term, they trouble themselves no more about him ; but if, when the time comes, he is not dead, they put him to death.

" The dignity of the khakan is reserved for persons of a certain birth. The khakan has no power to command or to forbid ; only they have the greatest regard for him, and when they enter his presence, they bow the head. No one but the king may enter his house, and the king does not visit him except in extraordinary cases. When the king enters the presence of the khakan, he prostrates himself on the ground and adores him. Then he rises and waits for the khakan to allow him to approach. In critical circumstances it is customary for the khakan to come forth ; but neither the Turks nor the other infidel nations of the country may see him ; they are obliged to retire and avoid meeting him, out of respect for his rank. When the khakan is dead and buried, no one may pass before his tomb, except on foot and with bowed head ; a rider may not remount his horse till the tomb is out of sight.

" One of the things which show the great respect of the Khozars for their king, is that sometimes the king desires the death of one of them, even one of the most powerful, and yet he does not wish to incur the responsibility for his death. Thereupon he orders the person to kill himself, and the man, going home, puts an end to his life.

" The dignity of khakan is reserved for certain families, which exert no authority or power. When a man has been chosen to bear this title, they install him without taking account of his former condition. None are raised to the dignity of khakan but persons who profess Judaism. The golden throne and pavilion, which are to be seen among the Khozars, are reserved for the khakan ; on the march, the tents of the khakan are placed above those of the king ; similarly in the towns, the mansion of the khakan is higher than the mansion of the king. . . .

" The language of the Bulgarians resembles that of the Khozars." [1]

From a comparison of these accounts we gather that the Khazars at the height of their power were governed by two kings, a sacred and nominally supreme king, and a civil and nominally subordinate king, and that all real power centred in the hands of the civil king, while the nominal sovereign was little more than a venerable puppet, who lived in almost absolute seclusion, seldom showing himself in public, remaining virtually invisible to the eyes of his subjects, and yet treated with marks of the most profound respect, if not of adoration, both in his lifetime and after his death. In this system of a double kingship, with its assignment of the shadow of power to one person and the substance of it to another, we trace those features of *rois fainéants* and Mayors of the Palace, which are familiar to us in Merovingian history.[2] The old line of hereditary

[1] Aboulféda, *Géographie, traduite de l'Arabe en Français*, par M. Reinaud (Paris, 1848), ii. Première Partie, pp. 301-305.
[2] Compare Klaproth, " Mémoire sur les Khazars ", *Journal Asiatique*, iii.

(Paris, 1823), p. 157 : " *Il est donc à présumer que l'autorité des Khaghans d'origine turque s'était considérablement affaiblie dans les derniers tems de la monarchie khazare. Des espèces de maires du palais, après avoir usurpé*

monarchs had fallen into a political dotage, and were practically superseded by a succession of vigorous ministers, who
were the real masters, while they professed themselves the
humble servants, of the feeble dotards on the throne. Yet
in the most stringent of the limitations imposed on the
nominal sovereigns we may detect a survival from a time
when their ancestors were men of a stronger mould and a
more masculine temper. We have seen that when a Khazar
king reigned more than forty years, even by a single day,
he was ruthlessly put to death, because his mental powers
were supposed to be decayed and his wisdom impaired. The
analogy of similar customs observed by many barbarous
tribes suggests that the reason thus assigned by the Khazars
for executing their kings after a fixed term of years was the
true original motive. In ages of ignorance men have often
believed that the welfare of the State, and even the course
of Nature, are wholly dependent on the personal qualities of
the king or chief who reigns over them, and that the decay
of his bodily or mental powers must necessarily be accompanied or followed by a corresponding decay, not only in
the commonwealth, but also in those natural resources on
which mankind is dependent for their very existence. Accordingly subjects in those days took a very short way with
superannuated sovereigns ; they put them to death, and
raised up in their stead men who were yet in the prime of
life and the full possession of all their faculties. A tightening
or a relaxation, as the case might be, of the rope thus tied
round the king's neck was introduced by the provision, that
he might reign till some public calamity, such as dearth,
drought, or defeat in war, was thought to indicate that the
dreaded enfeeblement of his majesty's powers had really set
in ; whereupon the constitutional remedy was at once resorted
to, and the king was put to death. Clearly the substitution
of this rule might tend either to lengthen or to abridge the
king's term of office according to his own natural abilities, the
vigour of his constitution, and the state of the weather ; for
the inclemency of the seasons is imputed by many races to the
defects of their rulers and is visited upon them accordingly.

le titre de roi, étaient devenus les véri-
tables souverains du pays, et tenaient

les Khaghans dans une dépendance
absolue."

In the accounts of the Khazar monarchy which I have quoted, certain discrepancies may be noted in regard to the constitutional check which regicide furnishes to the excesses or defects of kings. According to Ibn Foszlan, the king was regularly killed at the end of a reign of forty years ; according to Ibn Haukal and Abulfeda, he was put to death at the close of a period which, on being raised to the throne, he had himself determined under circumstances not altogether favourable to mature reflexion ; and according to Mas'údy, he suffered the extreme penalty of the law whenever drought or any other public misfortune had proved his unfitness to grasp the reins of power any longer. Which of these accounts is correct we have apparently no means of deciding, perhaps all of them were true at different times ; for the Khazars may have allowed themselves a certain latitude in their application of the great principle of regicide, content with putting their effete kings out of the way, without rigidly observing a pedantic uniformity in the manner and time of taking them off.

The report which Ibn Haukal and Abulfeda give of the mode of determining the length of the king's reign finds a curious parallel, and perhaps a confirmation, in the account which Chinese historians give of the manner in which the Thou khiu, or Turks, settled how long a kakhan or prince should rule over them. " When they proclaimed a kakhan, the grandees carried him on a sheet of felt nine times in a circle, following the course of the sun ; at each circuit he was saluted by everybody. On the completion of these circuits, they mounted him on horseback and threw round his neck a piece of taffeta, with which they pinched him so tight that he almost expired. Then they slackened it and immediately asked him how long he expected to reign. The confusion of his mind did not allow him to answer the question exactly. Nevertheless they regarded his answer as a prediction of the length of his reign." [1]

[1] Klaproth, " Mémoire sur l'identité des Thou khiu et des Hioung nou avec les Turcs ", *Journal Asiatique*, viii.   (Paris, 1825), p. 267. Compare W. Radloff. *Aus Sibirien* (Leipsic, 1884), i. 129.

XI

THE SCOPE AND METHOD OF MENTAL ANTHROPOLOGY [1]

THE lectures which I have the honour to deliver in this place deal with a branch of savage society and religion—the Belief in Immortality and the Worship of the Dead in Polynesia. As the subject may be novel, and the reasons for studying it obscure to some of my hearers, I propose to devote the first lecture to a general introduction, in which I will endeavour to explain why savage society is worth studying and how we should study it.

The study of savage society forms part of the general science of man or anthropology. That science is one of the latest born in the sisterhood of the sciences, being hardly older than about the middle of the nineteenth century ; in fact, the science is contemporary with not a few of its exponents who have not yet reached the extreme limit of old age. Not very many years have elapsed since two of its founders in England, Lord Avebury and Sir Edward Tylor, passed away. But, though young in years, the science has grown so rapidly that already it is hardly possible for any one man to embrace the whole of it. The principle of the division of labour, which is essential to economic progress, is no less essential to scientific progress. The time has gone by when the comprehensive intellect of an Aristotle or a Bacon could take all knowledge for its province. More and more each inquirer has to limit his investigations to a small patch of the field, to concentrate the glow-worm lamp of his intelligence

[1] An introductory lecture delivered at Trinity College, Cambridge, November 4, 1921. It was published in *Science Progress*, No. 64 (April 1922), from which it is here reprinted.

on a tiny circle, almost a speck, in the vast expanse which we dimly perceive stretching out to infinity on every side of us. Only by multiplying these glow-worm lamps, glimmering side by side, can we hope, step by step, to diffuse the light of knowledge through the boundless region of the unknown.

In our particular science the first broad and sharp division is between the study of man's body and the study of his mind. The one is known as physical anthropology ; the other is now, at least in this country, commonly called social anthropology, but I should prefer to call it by the more general name of mental anthropology. For though man is no doubt pre-eminently a social being and probably owes a large part of his superiority as an animal to the strength of his gregarious instincts, these instincts are only part of his mental endow-ment, and even when we have abstracted them from our consideration, there still remains in the human mind much that deserves to be carefully studied and that naturally falls under the science of man. It is with mental, as distinguished from physical, anthropology that I shall be exclusively occu-pied in these lectures.

But even when, in anthropology, we have limited our in-quiries to the mind of man, the subject is still so vast that, if progress is to be made, some further subdivision of it becomes necessary. For the mind of man has for ages been investi-gated by a whole series of special studies, which, under the various names of psychology, logic, metaphysics, and ethics, sometimes summed up under the general title of philosophy, have made great and noble contributions to a science of man. What place, then, is there for the new study of mental anthro-pology beside these ancient studies ? Is there room for her in the venerable college ? Can she discharge a function which was not previously performed by her older sisters ? We think that she can, and to determine what that function is, we need only perhaps consider the date at which the modern science of anthropology as a whole was first taken up seriously and systematically. The birth of anthropology followed almost immediately the promulgation of the evolution theory by Darwin and Wallace in 1859. I think I am right in saying that the foundation of anthropological societies at home and abroad has everywhere been subsequent to that date and has followed it often at very short intervals. Be that as it may, the theory of the gradual evolution of man out of a long series of inferior forms of animal life is now generally accepted, though diversity of opinion still prevails as to the precise mode in which the evolution has been brought about. It is this conception of evolution which supplies a basis for the modern science of anthropology.

On the physical side human anatomy had been studied for centuries, and was, I take it, firmly established on its main lines long before the appearance of Darwin ; the new idea imported into the science was that the human body, like the bodies of all animals, is not a finished product, a fixed type, struck out by Nature or created by God at a blow, but that it is rather a merely temporary effect, the result of a long process of what resembles growth rather than construction or creation, a growth which we have no reason to suppose has been arrested, but is probably still going on and may cause our descendants to differ as far from us as we now differ from our remotest ancestors in the scale of animated being. It is only the slowness of the process that hides the movement from our eyes and suggests the conclusion, so flattering to human vanity, that Nature has reached her consummation in us and can no farther go. An immediate result of the pro- mulgation of the evolution theory was thus to give an im- mense impulse to comparative anatomy ; for it was now recognized that man's bodily frame is not an isolated structure, but that it is closely related to that of many of the other animals, and that the one structure cannot be fully under- stood without the other. Not the least important branch of what we may call the new anatomy was the science of embry- ology, which by a comparison of the human and animal em- bryos was able to demonstrate their close resemblance for a considerable period of their development, and thus to supply a powerful argument in favour of the conclusion that man and what he calls the lower animals have had a common origin, and that for an incalculable time they probably pursued nearly parallel lines of evolution. In fact, embryology shows that the very process of evolution, which we postulate for the past history of our race, is summarily reproduced in the life-history of every man and woman who is born into the world.

Turning now from the physical to the mental side of man's nature, we may say that the evolution theory has in like manner opened up a new province of inquiry which has been left unoccupied by the older philosophy. Whenever in former days a philosopher set himself to inquire into the principles of the human mind, it was his own particular mind, or at most the minds of his civilized contemporaries, that he proceeded to investigate. When Descartes turned his eyes inwards and reflected on the operations of his own mind, he believed himself to be probing to the very deepest foundations accessible to human intelligence. It never occurred to him, I imagine, to apply for information to the mind of a Zulu or a Hottentot, still less of a baboon or a chimpanzee. Yet the doctrine of evolution has rendered it highly probable that the mind of the philosopher is indissolubly linked to the minds of these barbarous peoples and strange animals, and that, if we would fully understand it, we must not disdain to investigate the intelligence of these our humble relations.

It is a corollary of the development theory that, simultaneously with the evolution of man's body out of the bodies of lower animals, his mind has undergone a parallel evolution, gradually improving from perhaps bare sensation to the comparatively high level of intelligence to which the civilized races have at present attained. And as in the evolution of the bodily form we know that many species of lower orders have survived side by side with the higher to our own day, so in the evolution of the mind we may infer that many of the existing races of mankind have lagged behind us, and that their various degrees of mental development represent various degrees of retardation in the evolutionary process, various stages in the upward march of humanity. I say the upward march, because we have good reason to believe that most, if not all, of these laggard races are steadily, though very slowly, advancing ; or at least that they were so till they came, for their misfortune, into fatal contact with European civilization. The old theory of the progressive degeneracy of mankind in general from a primitive state of virtue and perfection is destitute of even a rag of evidence. Even the more limited and tenable view that certain races have partially degenerated, rests, I believe, on a very narrow induction. Speaking for

myself, I may say that in my reading of savage records I have
met with few or no facts which point clearly and indubitably
to racial degeneracy. Even among the Australian aborigines,
the least progressive of mankind, I have not, so far as I remember, noted the least sign that they once occupied a higher
level of culture than that at which they were discovered by
Europeans. On the contrary, many things in their customs
and beliefs appear to me to plead very strongly in favour of
the conclusion that aboriginal Australian society, so far as we
can trace it backward, has made definite progress on the
upward path from lower to higher forms of social life. That
progress appears to have been assisted, if not initiated, in
certain parts of Australia, by favourable physical conditions,
chiefly by a higher rainfall in the mountainous regions near
the coast, with its natural consequence of a greater abundance
of food, in contrast to the drought and sterility of the desert
interior.

Having said thus much, I hope I shall be acquitted of the
stale charge of treating any of the existing races of mankind
either as degenerate or as primitive in the strict sense of the
word. As to supposed degeneracy I have said enough ; but
as to the allegation that any competent anthropologist regards
even the lowest of living races as absolutely primitive, I will
add a few words, though in doing so I shall only be repeating
a protest which I have raised again and again.

Those of us who hold, as I do, that our species has been
evolved in a series of gradual stages from the lowest form of
animal life believe that the line of evolution has not been
everywhere the same nor the rate of evolution everywhere
uniform. Whether the line was single from the outset and
only divaricated later, or whether from the beginning there
were several parallel or nearly parallel lines which afterwards
diverged from each other ; in other words, whether mankind
has sprung from a single pair of progenitors or from several
pairs, is an old question which is still debated and, for aught
we can see, may continue to be debated indefinitely. The
answer to the question is of little or no practical importance,
and for my part I hold no brief either on the one side or on
the other. But whether or no human evolution started from
a single point, it has certainly run very different courses in

different ages and in different parts of the world. It is not
merely that the rate of progress has varied in time and place,
but that the products, that is, the races, have varied in kind
from each other. Hence we cannot arrange the existing
races of mankind in a progressive series, and say that in the
course of nature the lower would necessarily, though slowly,
develop into the higher. We cannot say, for instance, that if
we had spared, instead of exterminating, the Tasmanians,
they would gradually have acquired all the characteristic
features of the Australian aborigines ; that but for our inter-
ference the Australian aborigines in their turn might have
developed into negroes ; and that, given a fair chance, negroes
might change in time into Europeans. No, the march of
humanity is not in single file. We are a very awkward squad,
who are constantly breaking the ranks and are very far indeed
from keeping step with each other. We have no exact
standard whereby to measure the precise degree of evolution
attained by any one race, because the common stock or stocks
from which all have sprung are unknown to us. How then
can we single out any particular race of men, whether in the
present or in the past, and say that it is, or was, absolutely
primitive ? If we could see the whole army of our ancestors
marshalled and defiling before us, from the humblest amoebae
to the noblest specimens of mankind, could we lay our finger
on the exact spot in the long procession where mere animality
ceased and pure humanity began ? Surely the change has
been too gradual, the transitions too infinitesimal, to allow
us thus sharply to define the absolute beginning of our species,
to draw a line across our genealogical tree and to say, All our
ancestors on the hither side of the line have been men, and
all our ancestors on the farther side were beasts. Thus the
conception of an absolutely primitive human race, whether in
the present or in the past, is so far from being maintained by
the anthropologist that he even finds it difficult to attach any
precise meaning to the words. Yet he is by no means thereby
precluded from applying the adjective primitive in a relative
sense to distinguish the less from the more advanced races of
mankind. In ordinary speech the relative sense of primitive
is freely admissible. Why should it be denied to the anthropologist ?

The province, then, of mental or social anthropology may be defined as the study of the mental and social conditions of the various races of mankind, especially of the more primitive races compared to the more advanced, with a view to trace the general evolution of human thought, particularly in its earlier stages. This comparative study of the mind of man is thus analogous to the comparative study of his body which is undertaken by anatomy and physiology. But whereas comparative anatomy and physiology extend the range of their comparisons far beyond the human species so as to include the whole gamut of animated being, mental anthropology is content for the present to limit its comparisons to the members of our own kind. Yet the limitation is doubtless only temporary ; it is to be expected that in time a growing knowledge of the mental processes of the lower animals will permit of a comparison of them with the corresponding processes in the mind of man, a comparison which could hardly fail to throw light on many problems as yet unsolved.

But while in the interest of the science of man a greatly extended application of the comparative method is desirable and in the future inevitable, some well-meaning but injudicious friends of anthropology would limit the application of the method still more narrowly than I have assumed to be temporarily necessary or advisable. They would apparently refuse to allow us to compare the thoughts and institutions, the arts and crafts, of distant races with each other, and would only allow us to compare those of neighbouring races. A little reflexion may convince us that any such restriction, even if it were practicable, would be unwise ; nay, that, were it enforced, it would be disastrous. We compare things on the ground of their similarity, and similarity is not affected by distance. Radium is alike on the earth and in the sun ; it would be absurd to refuse to compare them on the ground that they are separated by many millions of miles. What would be thought of any other science which imposed on itself the restriction which some of our friends would inflict on anthropology ? Would geology prosper if it confined its investigation, say, of sedimentary rocks to those of England and refused to compare those of Asia and America ? How would zoology fare if the zoologist were forbidden to compare the animals of his own country with the animals of distant countries ? the dogs, say, of Wales with the dogs of Africa and Australia ? The futility, nay, the inherent absurdity, of the proposed restriction is so manifest that simply to state the proposal explicitly should suffice to expose it. Disguised in the fallacious form of a prudent precept, the nostrum is commonly administered to the sufferer with a trite tag from Dr. Johnson about surveying mankind from China to Peru, as if the mere idea of instituting such a survey were too preposterous for serious consideration. Yet the same men who level this taunt at anthropology would not dream of directing a similar gibe at the sciences of geology, botany, and zoology, in which the comparisons are world-wide.

To sum up : the central problem of mental anthropology is to trace that evolution of the human mind which has accompanied the evolution of the human body from the earliest times. But as the later stages of that evolution have long been studied by older sciences, it is only fair that the new science should confine itself for the most part to those earlier stages of which the older sciences had hardly taken account. That is why anthropology is commonly, and on the whole rightly, regarded as a science of origins. It is because the question of human origins was till lately a sort of no man's ground, untrodden by the foot of science but trampled by the hoofs of ignorance and superstition, that anthropology has come forward to reclaim this desert from the wild asses which roamed over it, and to turn it into a garden of knowledge. Her efforts have not been wholly in vain. Already the desert has begun to bear fruit and to blossom as the rose.

But if mental anthropology, refusing to poach on the preserves of her elder sisters, confines the scope of her inquiries mainly to the earlier phases of human thought, how is she to accomplish her object ? So far as I can see, she can accomplish it only in one of three ways—by a study of the uncivilized races, by a study of children, and by a study of mental pathology. Of the three studies the first is the only one to which I have paid any attention and on which I have the least claim to speak. But, before passing to it, I may be allowed, for the sake of completeness, to say a few words about the other two. And first in regard to the study of children. That the intelligence of children in normal cases undergoes a process of development from infancy to maturity is too obvious and notorious to need proof ; and it is a reasonable inference that, just as the development of their bodies in the womb reproduces to some extent the corporeal evolution of their remote ancestors out of lower forms of animal life, so the development of their minds from the first ·dawn of consciousness in the embryo to the full light of reason in adult life reproduces to some extent the mental evolution of their ancestors in ages far beyond the range of history. This inference is confirmed by the analogy which is often traced between the thought and conduct of children and the thought and conduct of savages ; for there are strong grounds for holding that savage modes of thinking and acting closely resemble those of the rude forefathers of the civilized races. Thus a careful study of the growth of intelligence and of the moral sense in children promises to throw much light on the intellectual and moral evolution of the race.

A study of mental pathology, under which I include all marked aberrations from the intellectual and moral standards of the community, is likely to contribute to the same end. I have been told that the wild fancies of patients in asylums sometimes resemble the superstitious notions of savages. It seems not improbable that cases of mental deficiency are often the result of arrested development or of reversion to an ancestral type ; and if that is so, the observation of them should be instructive, since on that hypothesis they reproduce for us phases of the mind which normal men and women have long transcended, and of which, but for these curious reversions, we might perhaps have no inkling.

The third of the avenues by which we may approach the childhood of humanity is the study of uncivilized races in the present and in the past. The study of uncivilized races in the present is obviously feasible, though fraught with many difficulties. But how are we to study uncivilized races in the past ? They are gone and have left no written records behind them. For we may perhaps best define an uncivilized race as one which is ignorant of the art of writing : the acquisition of the art of writing is the touchstone of civilization.

Our knowledge of uncivilized races in the past is derived from two sources : first, it is derived from the written, painted, or sculptured records of them bequeathed to us by civilized peoples who observed these vanished races ; and, second, it is derived from the skeletons or fragments of skeletons of the races themselves, together with the relics of their handiwork, whether in the form of manufactured articles or of paintings and sculptures on rocks. In regard to the former source, the ancient Egyptians have transmitted to us many graphic representations of the barbarous peoples with whom they came into contact ; and the ancient Greek, Latin, and Chinese writers have left accounts of many of the more primitive tribes lying on the outskirts of civilization ; but for the most part these accounts are very superficial and probably inaccurate.

When we come to uncivilized races which have vanished, and of which no written records survive, we depend for our knowledge of them, as I have said, on the meagre remains of their mouldering bones and on the somewhat more abundant remains of their handiwork. The task of studying these remains is the province of that branch of the science of man which is known as prehistoric archaeology or prehistoric anthropology. The study was first raised to the rank of a science about the middle of the nineteenth century. In the prosecution of it France led, and still leads, the way. Of her splendid achievements in that great work the Institute of Human Palaeontology, recently founded at Paris by the enlightened liberality of the Prince of Monaco, is a noble monument. Cambridge is to be congratulated on possessing a young and vigorous school of prehistoric archaeology under one who has had the good fortune to be a disciple and friend of the great French masters. Of its work it is not for me to speak. It lies outside the main scope of my studies, which have been directed chiefly to the still surviving savage or barbarous peoples, whom I cannot but regard as furnishing us with by far the amplest and most trustworthy materials for tracing the mental and social evolution of our species backward into regions which lie beyond the purview of history. I will conclude this introductory lecture with some observations on that subject. These observations I will comprise under two heads. First,

I will say something as to the method of the study ; and next I will mention, by way of illustration, a few of the problems which it undertakes to investigate.

First, then, as to the method. In principle it is extremely simple, however difficult it may be in the practical application. The method is neither more nor less than induction, which after all, disguise it as we may under the showy drapery of formal logic, is the only method in which men can and do acquire their knowledge. And the first condition of a sound induction is exact observation. What we want, therefore, in this branch of science is, first and foremost, full, true, and precise accounts of savage and barbarous peoples based on personal observation. Such accounts are best given by men who have lived for many years among the peoples, have won their confidence, and can converse with them familiarly in their native language ; for savages are shy and secretive towards strangers, they conceal their most cherished rites and beliefs from them, nay, they are apt wilfully to mislead an inquirer, not so much for the sake of deceiving him as with the amiable intention of gratifying him with the answers which he seems to expect. It needs a peculiar combination of intelligence, tact, and good nature to draw out a savage on subjects which he regards as sacred ; to very few men will he consent to unbosom himself.

Perhaps the class of men whose vocation affords them the best opportunities for observing and recording the habits of savage races are missionaries. They are men of education and character ; they usually live for years among the people, acquire their language, and gain their respect and confidence. Accordingly some of the very best accounts which we possess of savage and barbarous peoples have been written by missionaries, Catholic and Protestant, English, French, Dutch, German, and Spanish. At the present time one of our most valuable anthropological journals, *Anthropos*, is edited by an Austrian priest, Father W. Schmidt, and is composed mainly of articles contributed by Catholic missionaries in many parts of the world. The articles for the most part are characterized by close observation and a scientific spirit ; the theological prepossessions of the writers are not allowed to blur and distort their descriptions of native beliefs and customs. It is much to be desired that the various missionary societies of England would combine to produce a journal of the same scope and the same scientific character. Perhaps, in view of our sectarian differences, that is too much to hope for. But in any case it is highly satisfactory to know that our Protestant missionary societies are awakening more and more to the importance of anthropology in the training of missionaries, and are taking active steps to remedy what till lately was a most serious defect in their mental equipment.

Next, perhaps, to missionaries the class of men who can do most for the scientific study of native races are the Government officials who reside among them. However, this class of men labours under certain disadvantages from which missionaries are usually exempt. It is not so easy for them, without a certain loss of dignity and authority, to enter into familiar converse with the natives ; and being often transferred from district to district, they do not always gain an intimate acquaintance with the language, and are consequently obliged to trust to native interpretation, an uncertain and often tainted fount of knowledge.

Next to the information obtained by men long resident among savages may be ranked the information acquired by travellers and explorers, especially by the members of scientific expeditions sent out on purpose to investigate the habits and customs of certain tribes. The observations of an untrained traveller passing rapidly through a country are usually meagre, superficial, and untrustworthy ; in the enormous literature of travel the percentage of scientific value is exceedingly small. It is otherwise with the information collected by trained anthropologists. Though the time they spend on an expedition is sometimes comparatively short—too short to allow them to obtain a mastery of the language—yet by the application of scientific methods of inquiry they are often able to elicit important information and to make most valuable contributions to knowledge : witness the expeditions of Spencer and Gillen to Central Australia, the Cambridge expedition to Torres Strait, and the recent Mackie expedition to Central Africa.

When a large body of accurate information, based on personal observation and inquiry, has thus been collected, the task remains of examining and comparing the accounts obtained from different parts of the field, in order to see whether they throw light on each other, and whether any general conclusions can be deduced from them. Such comparisons should never be instituted by observers in the field. Hardly anything impairs the value of observations of a particular people so much as the interpolation of comparisons with other peoples, especially with the Jews, and next to them with the Greeks and Romans, these being the races who have suffered most at the hands of half-educated travellers. Every observer of a savage or barbarous people should describe it exactly as if no other people existed on the face of the earth. The business of comparison is not for him, at least not for him in the capacity of observer ; if he desires to draw comparisons with other peoples, as he is of course at liberty to do, he should keep his comparisons strictly apart from his observations : the mixture of the two is, if not absolutely fatal, at least a great impediment to the utility of both.

But while the work of comparison is entirely different from the work of observation and should always be kept separate, it is itself of high importance and is indeed essential to anthropology ; without it there could be no true science of man, and the accumulated observations, gained at the cost of great personal risks and sacrifices, would remain an undigested and disorderly heap. It is the application of the comparative method to the heap which evolves order out of chaos by eliciting the general principles or laws which underlie the mass of particulars. It is true that simple comparison is not sufficient for the discovery of the underlying law, but it is the first step towards it. If only our comparisons are just—in other words, if we have correctly sorted out the facts into their proper compartments according to their real similarities—the colligation of the similars in a general truth or law follows almost automatically. Thus everything hinges on the work of comparison. Only with its help can we rise to those generalizations which are the goal of science.

But indispensable as is the application of the comparative method to the raw materials of anthropology, it is not necessary, though it is certainly desirable, that the application should be made at once. If only the materials are collected and safely stored, the work of comparison can be done at any time hereafter ; it may even be reserved for future ages. But no doubt much might be lost by thus postponing indefinitely the examination of the facts accumulated by observers in the field. For a comparison of facts observed in different, sometimes in widely sundered, parts of the world often reveals a striking similarity between them which probably escaped the observer, because his attention was rightly concentrated on one particular part of the field, and he had neither the leisure nor the opportunity to notice similar facts elsewhere. The detection of these similarities usually suggests a question which it is desirable to put to workers in the field ; and the question in turn may direct the attention of field-workers to points which they had hitherto overlooked, but which, on investigation, may turn out to be of the utmost importance, opening up a novel and fruitful line of research of which the observer might not have dreamed before. On this ground it is very desirable that the work of sifting and comparing anthropological materials should not be deferred, but should be carried on as far as possible simultaneously with the work of observation in the field. This is possible, because the work of comparison need not be done by the same men who observe the facts ; indeed, it may often be done better by others, since it calls for the exercise of different faculties, which are not always possessed even by a keen and accurate observer. A good observer is not necessarily a good theorist, and conversely a good theorist may be a very bad observer. Here, as elsewhere in science, a division of labour and an intelligent co-operation of the labourers are the best guarantees of efficiency. Thus in anthropology at the present day, while the most urgent need is the exact observation of races as yet but little affected by European influence, there is still room for the student at home side by side with the observer in the field. They should work into each other's hands, the one observing and recording, and the other sifting and comparing the records, marking the similarities or contrasts which he detects between them, and questioning the observer accordingly. Thus labouring together in harmony, they will best contribute to the advancement of anthropology. The work of comparison and theory can be carried on with most ease and to most advantage at a great university, because there the inquirer has full access to all the apparatus of learning which few or no private students can command. As an alumnus of this ancient university, I should wish to see established in Cambridge a sort of central bureau or clearing-house, which would receive and examine anthropological reports from all parts of the world, and from which questions, hints, suggestions, and, if you please, theories, would radiate in return to observers stationed in the remotest regions of the earth. Thus a perpetual circulation of facts and ideas would be maintained between the central bureau and the outlying stations ; observation would quicken theory, and theory would stimulate observation. You would possess in the University, as it were, a lighthouse from which the rays of science would stream out to illuminate many dark corners of the earth. *Hinc lucem et pocula sacra.*

I have said so much of the method of mental anthropology that I have left myself little time to illustrate by examples the kind of problems with which the science attempts to deal. But this part of my subject is too important to be passed over altogether in silence, though in the few minutes at my disposal I can do no more than simply enumerate a few of the problems.

Mental anthropology, as I have said, is in great measure a science of human origins. It investigates, or will hereafter investigate, the origins of language, of the arts, of society, of science, of morality, of religion. To take, for example, the arts of life, it asks, How did man discover the use of fire and the modes of kindling it ? How did he become acquainted with the metals and learn to fashion them into tools and weapons ? How did he come to tame wild animals and to breed them for his comfort and convenience ? How did he first hit upon the idea of sowing seed and waiting for months till the seed should ripen and bear fruit ? In other words, how did he arrive at the conception of agriculture, a conception which has even yet not dawned on some of the rudest races of mankind ? And in regard to the origin of all the useful arts we must ask, was the origin multiple or single ? In other words, was each of the arts discovered independently

in various places and at various times ? or was each of them
discovered once for all at a single place, from which it
gradually spread, through the contact or migration of peoples,
to other parts of the world ?

Or to turn to the origin of society, we have to ask, How
did men first come to herd together ? did they do so while
they were still in the purely animal stage ? and are our gregarious instincts inherited from our bestial ancestors, who
hunted, perhaps, in packs ? Or was man, when he first
emerged from the beasts, a solitary creature, like some of
the higher apes, his near kinsfolk ? Again, when the first
social groups of men and women were formed, how were they
organized internally ? What was the relation of the sexes to
each other ? Was there a complete communism of women ?
or was marriage already instituted ? and if so, was it a
marriage of groups, or of individuals ? Again, in these
groups, what was the relation of parents to their children ?
Was the relation known or unknown ? or was it partly known
and partly unknown ? Did a man, as some people think,
know his mother but not his father ? his brothers and sisters
and his sisters' children, but not his own children or his
brothers' children ? And how did he come to refuse to marry
women who stood to him in certain definite relationships and
to regard, as he often did, any such marriage as a horror
punishable with death ? These and similar questions have
to be faced by anthropology in investigating the internal
organization of the primitive social groups. Some of them
have a more than antiquarian interest ; for, if we could solve
them, we might at the same time facilitate the work of the
modern legislator and social reformer, who has sometimes to
deal with practical problems not altogether dissimilar.

When we inquire into the government of the primitive
social groups, we have to ask, Was it despotic, or oligarchic,
or democratic ? If it was despotic, how did the despot acquire
his power ? by his prowess in war or by his pretensions as a
magician ? If the government was oligarchic, was it committed to a troop of warriors or to a junta of old men ? If it
was democratic, was it in the hands of all the adult members
of the community ? or was there a discrimination of classes,
and perhaps of sex ? Or are we wrong in postulating any

government at all in the primitive group ? May there not
have been complete anarchy, every man doing what was right
in his own eyes ?   Here, again, the questions which the
anthropologist has to ask are not altogether alien from some
which still agitate the bosoms of our civilized contemporaries.

Further, the student of social anthropology has to investigate the thorny question of the rise of private property
among men.   Is the instinct of private property, as some
think, shared by the beasts and inherited by us from our
animal ancestors ? or did it first develop in the human group ?
and was it preceded by a period of unlimited communism ?
and when, sooner or later, the institution of private property
was first recognized in a community, did the property belong
to certain social groups, say to families or clans, or to individuals ?   Once more, in investigating these and similar
questions the anthropologist can hardly exclude from his
mind the heated controversies of his own day.   He may even
be called in as witness by the disputants to say whether
gigantic measures for the confiscation—or should I say the
socialization ?—of private property may not be defended by
the practice of savages.

Then, to turn for a moment to the origin of science, it is
for mental anthropology to ask how men learned to form and
use abstract ideas, in particular the ideas of number, which
are the basis of mathematics ; how they came to note the
stars and the apparent motions of the heavenly bodies, the
observation of which laid the foundation of astronomy ; how
they arrived at the idea of measuring dimensions both in space
and time, thereby paving the way for geometry and physics ;
how by marking the annual changes of the seasons they
fashioned for themselves a rudimentary calendar ; how, perhaps, the false sequence of events assumed by magic may
have been slowly replaced in the minds of men by a truer
conception of natural law.

Lastly, the student of our science has to consider the
question of the origin of religion.   How did man come to
believe in the existence of gods and spirits ?   How did he first
suppose that he could propitiate them by prayer and sacrifice
and so induce them to direct, or alter, the course of Nature
for his benefit ?   Whatever the origin of these beliefs, it seems

certain that they are peculiar to humanity ; we have no reason to assume that they are shared by the beasts. Hence we may safely conclude that they were evolved, or revealed, at some time subsequent to the emergence of the human species from its purely animal stage.

And the conception of the human soul and its survival after death, how did man arrive at it ? Was it by meditation on the phenomena of dreams ? Was it by observation of the fluctuations and final ebbing of the breath ? by the sight of shadows on the grass or of reflections in the pool ? by the apparition of the spirits of the dead, or by the sound of their voices falling mysteriously on the ears of the living from a world beyond the grave ?

Such are, in the barest outline, a few of the problems with which mental anthropology is called upon to deal, and which she must attempt to solve. Hitherto many of them have been the favourite themes of sophists and ranters, of demagogues and dreamers, who by their visions of a Golden Age of universal equality and universal wealth in the future, modelled on the baseless fancy of a like Golden Age in the past, have too often lured the ignorant multitude to the edge of the precipice and pushed them over the brink. Hereafter it will be for anthropology to treat the same themes in a different spirit and by a different method. If she is true to her principles, she will not seek to solve, or to gloze over, the problems by rhetoric and declamation, by cheap appeals to popular sentiment and prejudice, by truckling to the passions and the cupidity of the mob. She will seek to solve them by the patient accumulation and the exact investigation of facts, by that and by nothing else, for only thus can she hope to arrive at the truth.

XII

SIR BALDWIN SPENCER [1]

THE science of man has received a heavy blow by the death of Sir Baldwin Spencer, for, in spite of his advanced years, he remained to the last in full vigour of mind and body and eager to pursue his researches in a fresh field which he had courageously undertaken to investigate. He passed the greatest part of the last two years in England, seeing through the press his two latest works *The Arunta* (1927) and *Wanderings in Wild Australia* (1928).

In the winter of 1927–28 (I think in January, 1928) he went to Paris, where I was then staying, to consult me as to his plans for future work. I gathered some of the most eminent French ethnologists, including Professor Lévy-Bruhl, Dr. P. Rivet, and M. Marcel Mauss, to meet him in the hospitable house of my friends the Comte and Comtesse Jean de Pange. Our French colleagues highly appreciated the privilege of meeting him, and he was glad to make their personal acquaintance. He was then undecided whether to return to Australia in order to investigate some unknown or little-known tribes in North-western Australia, or to set out for South America for the purpose of investigating the primitive inhabitants of Tierra del Fuego, about whom our information is far from full and satisfactory. I strongly advised him to continue his work in Australia, for which his qualifications were unique, rather than break fresh ground in the severe climate of Tierra del Fuego, where he might be exposed to hardships that would tax the strength of a much younger man.

I thought he had assented to my arguments, which, if

[1] Reprinted from *The Times*, July 27, 1929.

my memory serves me aright, were supported by the distinguished Americanist, Dr. Paul Rivet. It was, therefore,
with surprise that I learned lately from a notice in a news-
paper that he had arrived safely in Tierra del Fuego, after
a voyage in a cattle ship, in which, as the rules of the company
forbade the conveyance of passengers, he had travelled in
the capacity of purser. This news was soon followed by the
report of his death in that far and savage land. He may
truly be said to have fallen a martyr to science.

As a field anthropologist Baldwin Spencer had no
superior, perhaps no equal, in his generation. He possessed
to perfection the rare gift of the most patient and exact
observation unwarped by any theoretical bias. Hence the
works which, singly or in conjunction with his admirable
colleague, the late F. J. Gillen, he bequeathed to posterity
must remain for all time a priceless record, as immune from
error as is humanly possible, of a notable part of mankind
living in the Stone Age and as absolutely ignorant of agriculture and of cattle breeding as of metals. No such detailed
and trustworthy record of any people living under these
conditions has ever before been given to the world, or is
ever likely to be given again. Hence, so long as mankind
continues to take an intelligent interest in its own past, the
writings of Spencer and Gillen will remain documents of
the first importance for the understanding of human evolution : the facts which they record may, and probably will,
be variously interpreted : on their basis different theoretical
superstructures may be built, and after enduring for a time
may pass away ; but the foundations laid by Spencer and
Gillen must abide as a rock destined only to perish with
humanity itself. That is enough for the glory of these two
men, of whom England can claim the one and Ireland the
other.

XIII

WILLIAM WYSE [1]

WILLIAM WYSE, one of the finest Greek and Latin scholars
of his time, and a man of noble and unblemished character,
whose death was briefly announced in *The Times* of Thursday,
came of Warwickshire yeoman stock. His father, William
Wyse, owned a house and some land at Halford, a small
village situated in charming rural scenery a few miles from
Shipston-on-Stour. In his earlier life the father had been
connected with railway work, and his son was born on
March 19, 1860, at Stratford, in Essex, and went to his first
school at Walthamstow. Afterwards, his father, who had
given up his connexion with the railway before the birth of
his son, returned to the country of his forefathers and settled
at Halford, which was henceforth the beloved home of his
son William and his devoted sister, Annie Wyse. William
then went to King Edward's School at Stratford-on-Avon,
from which he got a scholarship to King's School, Canterbury.

From Canterbury he obtained a scholarship to Trinity
College, Cambridge, which he entered as an undergraduate
in 1878. He took his bachelor's degree in 1882 and his
master's degree in 1884. Meantime, after winning many
academic distinctions, including a Chancellor's Medal, he
was elected a Fellow of his college in 1883. Thenceforth
he resided regularly in college, pursuing his studies and doing
some tutorial work at Wren's " coaching " establishment in
London till 1892, when he was appointed Professor of Greek
at University College, London. This office he held for about
two years, when he was recalled to Cambridge by his college
and appointed one of the classical lecturers of Trinity. This

[1] Reprinted from *The Times*, December 9, 1929.

254

honourable duty he continued to discharge till 1904, when, in consequence of a partial failure of his bodily strength, he resigned his lectureship and retired to Halford, where he resided for the rest of his life, at first with his widowed mother and unmarried sister, and afterwards with his beloved sister alone.

Their life in the quiet village was for years very happy ; for William loved deeply the beautiful country in which he lived, and cherished the small walled garden which opened at the back of his house—a tall, plain, red-brick house facing the quiet village street. So long as his health permitted it, he worked in his garden, and in his letters to friends noted the succession of the old-fashioned flowers that bloomed in it with the change of the seasons. To his house he added a library or, as he preferred to call it, a book-room, and it was the privilege of the present writer to help him to place the books on the shelves when they arrived in cases from Cambridge. It was also the privilege of the same friend to share with him his rambles in the beautiful Warwickshire lanes and field-paths in summer days under the shade of the tall elms and through green meadows such as the patriarch Isaac might have walked in to meditate at evening. For longer excursions we drove leisurely behind a trotting horse to visit fine old manor houses that carried the mind back to the spacious days of Elizabeth, or quaint little towns nestling in the hollows of the Cotswold hills. Then in the evening, by the fireside, we renewed the Attic talks with which we had beguiled many an hour in the courts and gardens of Cambridge. Together we trod the *fallentis semita vitae*, which none loved better than he.

In his later years this quiet, happy life of commune with Nature and books was saddened and darkened by the grievous changes which the Great War and its consequences wrought on rural and village life in Warwickshire, as no doubt in many other parts of the country. The changes created domestic difficulties with which it was hard for two invalids (for his sister's health was also infirm) to struggle, and his letters to friends lost the tone of cheerful serenity and content which had marked them before. But though, to add to other trials, his strength declined and his nights in particular were much disturbed, he retained, unimpaired by bodily weakness, his admirable intellectual faculties to the end, which came after twelve days of suffering on the morning of Friday, November 29, 1929. All that was mortal of him was cremated at Birmingham.

Of his work as a classical, and especially a Greek, scholar others are better qualified to speak than the present writer. He devoted himself especially to the study of Greek history and law, and of these studies he has left a splendid record in his great edition of the speeches of the Greek orator Isaeus, which will always be the chief monument of his scholarly fame. Of the elaborate commentary in which he expounds the intricacies of the Attic laws of inheritance and lays bare the chicanery of the orator's pleadings, it is said by the latest English editor of Isaeus, Professor E. S. Forster, that it is " the most valuable and exhaustive commentary that has yet appeared ", and similar testimony is borne to it by the latest French editor of Isaeus, M. Pierre Roussel, now Director of the French School of Archaeology at Athens. Another valuable contribution by Wyse to the history of Greek law is the chapter on the subject which he wrote for the Cambridge *Companion to Greek Studies*, edited by Leonard Whibley. It contains an account of the interesting and in some ways exceptional system of law at Gortyn in Crete, which is known to us from inscriptions, and it treats at greater length of the Athenian judicial system in the fourth century B.C. In addition to these special studies Wyse paid much attention to the remains of ancient Greek writers which in our time have come to light in Egyptian papyri, and he did not a little for the correction of their texts, especially for the text of the " Constitution of Athens ", which is attributed to Aristotle. But these contributions to learning, recorded in classical periodicals, are hardly known save to professional scholars.

Apart from his classical scholarship, in which he was a master, Wyse was well read and had a fine taste in English literature, and indeed in everything that was beautiful and good. In disposition he was modest and retiring, but far from unsocial ; on the contrary, he was fond of good society in the best sense of the word, and contributed to the agree-

ableness of every social circle in which he moved by the easy
flow of his conversation, which, while it never descended to
trivialities, was always stimulating and instructive, without
the smallest tinge of pedantry. Yet he was not in manner
expansive and never carried his heart on his sleeve. But
those whom he honoured with his friendship knew that under
a somewhat reserved exterior there lay a character of the
finest temper, a solidity and sobriety of judgement, which no
sophistry could deceive, and an inflexible devotion to truth.
They will cherish his memory to the end of their days as
that of one of the best scholars and best men whom they
have ever known.

S

PART II

ADDRESSES

ADDRESS TO THE ERNEST RENAN
SOCIETY

DELIVERED AT THE ÉCOLE DU LOUVRE, PARIS,
SATURDAY, DECEMBER 11, 1920

PRÉFACE

CE petit volume [1] réunit deux discours que j'ai eu l'honneur d'offrir en hommage à la mémoire d'Ernest Renan, à Paris. L'un a été prononcé à la Société Ernest Renan, au Louvre ; l'autre, à l'assemblée qui s'est réunie pour célébrer le centenaire de l'illustre savant dans le grand amphithéâtre de la Sorbonne, le 28 février 1923. Tous deux ont été écrits en français ; parlant d'un grand Français à ses compatriotes, je n'ai pas osé me servir de ma langue maternelle. Tous deux ont été écoutés avec indulgence, ce qui m'a encouragé à les soumettre au jugement des lecteurs français.

On m'a prié d'ajouter aux discours quelques mots de préface. Que dirai-je ? Les discours, je l'espère, s'expliqueront d'eux-mêmes. Comme je l'ai déjà dit à la Sorbonne, je n'ai nullement la prétention d'analyser un génie aussi fin, aussi délicat, aussi nuancé que celui de Renan. Si pourtant j'ose revendiquer l'honneur de joindre mes hommages à ceux que le monde savant a rendus à sa mémoire, c'est peut-être en vertu de la sympathie que m'inspire une certaine communauté de race et de tempérament. Renan, en tant que Breton, était de ce vieux sang celtique qui coule aussi dans mes veines écossaises et qui comporte une façon d'envisager le monde très différente de

---

[1] The two following addresses, under the general title *Sur Ernest Renan*, were published together in a small volume at Paris in 1923. They are here reprinted from that volume, with the original preface prefixed to it.

celle qui caractérise et le génie purement français, et le génie purement anglais.

Le pur génie français est clair, logique, plein de bon sens, très porté aux abstractions, aux idées générales, mais beaucoup moins enclin aux choses de la fantaisie et de l'imagination, dont, au fond, il se méfie. Il raisonne bien, il construit facilement de grandes généralisations, mais il ne réussit pas à doter le monde de ces créations imaginatives de tout premier ordre qui font les délices de toutes les générations et de tous les pays. Il nous a donné un Descartes, un Laplace, un Pasteur, mais il lui manque un Homère, un Virgile, un Dante, un Cervantès, un Shakespeare. Au fond, c'est un esprit plutôt prosaïque que poétique, plus fait pour découvrir la vérité des choses que pour créer de nouveaux idéals de beauté et de grandeur. Voltaire lui-même, type parfait du génie français, a nettement déclaré que de toutes les nations polies la France est la moins poétique, et Renan a approuvé le mot.[1]

Un trait du génie français pur qui tient à son défaut de poésie est une indifférence marquée à l'égard des beautés de la nature, un manque de goût pour les plaisirs de la vie champêtre. Le Français de pur sang, au moins celui des classes intellectuelles, préfère la cité à la campagne ; ce qu'il lui faut, c'est surtout la société, la compagnie de gens avec lesquels il puisse échanger les idées dont pétille son esprit vif et alerte. La solitude et le silence des champs l'ennuient ; il lui tarde de les quitter pour le mouvement, le bruit, le tourbillon des grandes villes, des places publiques, des cafés, des théâtres où il peut entendre la voix de ses semblables et faire écouter la sienne. En cela, comme en beaucoup de choses (on l'a souvent remarqué), le génie français ressemble, plus que celui de n'importe quel autre peuple moderne, au génie de la Grèce antique. Si l'on en peut juger par leur littérature, telle qu'elle était à l'époque de son plein épanouissement, les Grecs avaient très peu de goût pour la contemplation des beautés de la nature. A part quelques chœurs de Sophocle et d'Euripide, la description de beaux paysages ne tient presque aucune place dans l'œuvre des

---

[1] Voir Renan : *Essais de Morale et de Critique*, deuxième édition (Paris, 1860), p. 96.

meilleurs auteurs, surtout des auteurs attiques, quoique le coup d'œil que l'on a de l'Acropole d'Athènes sur les champs gris-bleuâtres d'oliviers, les montagnes empourprées, l'azur éblouissant de la mer, soit sans doute un des plus beaux du monde. C'est seulement au temps de la décadence du génie grec que l'amour du pittoresque et le charme du monde extérieur commencent à poindre, par exemple dans les délicieuses idylles de Théocrite, dans les épigrammes exquises de l'Anthologie, dans les jolis tableaux de Philostrate. Le véritable sentiment attique à l'égard de la vie champêtre se révèle d'une façon éclatante dans les paroles que Platon prête à Socrate, en un passage célèbre du dialogue de *Phèdre*, où le philosophe avoue qu'il ne faisait pas de promenades à la campagne, mais demeurait toujours dans les murs de la cité, parce qu'il n'apprenait rien des arbres dans les champs mais beaucoup des hommes dans les rues. Néanmoins, dans ce même passage, Platon a décrit les beautés du paysage attique, vu par un jour ensoleillé d'été, d'une manière qui n'a jamais été surpassée dans aucune langue. En lisant cette immortelle description, on croit sentir la fraîcheur de l'ombre du platane qui tamise la chaleur trop ardente du soleil méridional, on croit jouir de l'odeur du thym, entendre le bruissement des feuilles dans la brise, le bourdonnement des abeilles dans les fleurs, la note aiguë des cigales qui chantent dans les buissons, et le murmure berceur de la rivière qui coule sur les cailloux. Mais c'est, je crois, le seul passage des dialogues de Platon où le philosophe se soit laissé entraîner pour quelques instants par les charmes de la nature ; dans tout le reste de ses écrits, on ne trouve que les joies austères de la dialectique variées seulement par le jeu dramatique des personnages qui prennent part aux discussions. Ces belles pages du *Phèdre* suffiraient à prouver que si le philosophe attique aux lèvres de miel a gardé un silence presque absolu sur les beautés de son pays natal, ce n'était pas assurément faute de savoir goûter leurs délices, mais parce qu'il cédait aux charmes encore plus puissants de la vie purement intellectuelle.

C'est, me semble-t-il, une preuve de cette indifférence relative pour le monde extérieur que l'absence générale de mots désignant les couleurs dans le vocabulaire des auteurs grecs de la meilleure époque. Si cette observation est juste, on peut en tirer peut-être la conclusion que le génie grec était plus sensible à la beauté des formes qu'à la beauté des couleurs, et par conséquent qu'il excellait plutôt dans la sculpture que dans la peinture. Au contraire, le génie italien, si je ne me trompe, a le goût des couleurs encore plus vif que celui des formes. Aussi, dans les poètes latins, rencontre-t-on une grande richesse d'épithètes colorées ; et dans l'art italien de la Renaissance, hors l'œuvre de Michel-Ange, la peinture l'a-t-elle de beaucoup emporté sur la sculpture.

Ces observations tendent à marquer la profonde affinité qu'on peut relever, je crois, entre le génie grec et le génie français. Tous deux sont dominés par les besoins de la raison, par leur passion pour les idées abstraites, pour la logique, bref, pour le rationalisme. Tous deux sont peu sentimentaux, et se soucient assez peu des beautés du monde extérieur. Pour tous les deux, le grand intérêt de la vie humaine, c'est l'homme lui-même.

On ne peut lire Renan sans s'apercevoir qu'à côté de cette passion pour les idées abstraites, que certes il a partagée dans une large mesure avec les vieux maîtres de la littérature française, son esprit comprenait d'autres éléments qui ont beaucoup influé sur sa pensée et coloré son style. Il n'est pas téméraire, je crois, de prétendre que ces éléments, il les a dûs en grande partie à son sang celtique. Lui-même l'avoue. On peut même dire qu'il se glorifie d'être issu de cette race ancienne qui, refoulée par des peuples plus forts ou du moins plus aptes à survivre dans la lutte pour la vie, se cramponne encore aux promontoires et aux îles de l'extrême-ouest de l'Europe, comme au dernier asile de leur langue et de leurs coutumes qui meurent.

Dans le génie celtique, on trouve la clef de maintes caractéristiques de Renan, qui, autrement, resteraient des énigmes. Ces parages bretons, un peu mornes et sombres, ce ciel couvert et brumeux, ces côtes hérissées de rochers, ces îles toujours battues par les flots d'une mer orageuse, ces grandes solitudes et ces silences de la nature se reflètent en quelque sorte dans les pages de Renan et font un contraste frappant avec le brouhaha de Paris, où l'auteur a passé la majeure partie de sa vie. Ce sont des paysages du même genre qui, pendant des siècles, ont partout nourri le génie celtique, parmi les falaises escarpées de la Cornouaille, parmi les hautes montagnes et les beaux lacs du pays de Galles, de l'Irlande et de l'Écosse. De tels pays, où la nature, une grande partie de l'année, se voile de brouillards et se trempe de pluies, ont quelque chose de mélancolique, de triste, de mystérieux, qui se prête aux rêves, au romantisme, à la religion. C'est peut-être pourquoi le Celte est toujours au fond rêveur, romantique, religieux. Un pur rationaliste est-il jamais sorti d'une souche celtique pure ? J'en doute. Laissé à lui-même, le Celte est beaucoup plus porté à créer des idoles qu'à les détruire. De ce fait témoignent les petites chapelles de saints, d'ailleurs inconnus, qu'en Bretagne on trouve parsemées partout, dans les landes, au milieu des rochers ou dans des terrains incultes et déserts. Si jamais la marée montante de scepticisme parvenait à submerger l'Europe, à étouffer le catholicisme et à chasser le pape du Vatican, je me demande si ce Saturne détrôné du Christianisme ne trouverait pas son dernier refuge dans Thulé, parmi les fidèles Celtes de Bretagne, d'Irlande, d'Écosse.

Les adversaires ecclésiastiques de Renan l'ont souvent traité comme un pur rationaliste, comme un simple iconoclaste, voire comme un Méphistophélès rusé et dissimulé qui se pare des atours d'un séraphin pour séduire les âmes simples des fidèles. Ils ont eu grand tort. De sa nature, Renan était profondément religieux ; en tant que Celte, il ne pouvait être autrement. S'il a brisé quelques-unes des images que, pendant de longs siècles, l'humanité a vénérées, il les a aimées néanmoins. Il sentait tout le charme, toute la tendresse qui s'attachent aux idoles que notre pauvre espèce humaine a si longtemps chéries comme des dieux ; il ne détruisait une vieille religion dépassée que pour rebâtir sur ses ruines une religion nouvelle plus vraie et plus belle. Ainsi s'explique ce qu'on peut appeler la double nature de Renan : son rationalisme et son romantisme. Sous la couche logique et philosophique de son être français, apparaît une couche plus profonde, la couche poétique, mystique, religieuse de son être breton. C'était, pour ainsi dire, un Janus montrant d'un côté la figure de Voltaire et de l'autre, celle de Chateaubriand. Renan a franchement reconnu la complexité, voire les contradictions de sa nature. Il nous a dit qu'il y avait en lui deux hommes : un Gascon qui riait et un Breton qui pleurait. Si la gaieté de son tempérament tenait sans doute au sang gascon qu'il hérita de sa mère, on ne se trompe guère en pensant qu'au fond du cœur il resta toujours breton. C'est comme si, au milieu du tumulte de Paris, il s'était toujours souvenu de ce soir d'automne où, quittant sa chère Bretagne pour étudier dans la grande ville, il avait entendu pour la dernière fois les pieuses sonneries de l'Angélus se répondre de paroisse en paroisse, rouler sur les collines familières, et verser dans l'air quelque chose de calme, de doux et de mélancolique, image de la vie qu'il allait laisser derrière lui pour toujours.

De cette double source, à la fois française et bretonne, découlent non seulement la variété et l'étendue de la pensée et des sympathies de Renan, mais aussi la richesse et le charme de son style. A une limpidité d'expression tout à fait française et classique, il a su joindre une douceur, une souplesse, une harmonie subtiles et indéfinissables, qui lui sont propres, et qui, réunies, lui méritent le nom de Chrysostome de la France.

Paris, le 3 mai 1923.

MONSIEUR LE PRÉSIDENT, MESDAMES ET MESSIEURS, MEMBRES DE LA SOCIÉTÉ ERNEST RENAN—Je vous remercie du grand honneur que vous m'avez fait en m'invitant à cette séance et en me permettant de vous adresser quelques mots. D'abord il faut que je vous demande pardon si j'essaye de les balbutier en français. Le but de parler étant ou devant être de se faire comprendre, il me semble que je l'atteindrais mieux en vous débitant un français quelconque qu'en me servant de ma langue maternelle.

MESDAMES ET MESSIEURS—Je suis heureux de saisir cette occasion de rendre mon hommage à la mémoire de l'illustre Ernest Renan, l'un des plus grands penseurs et des plus grands écrivains de la France. Je le fais avec d'autant plus d'empressement que depuis longtemps j'ai nourri une admiration tout à fait particulière pour lui et pour ses écrits. J'ose même dire que parmi vos grands écrivains il n'en est aucun avec lequel je me sente lié d'une sympathie aussi étroite et aussi profonde qu'avec Renan. Ce n'est pas seulement parce qu'il a traité les sujets qui m'intéressent le plus, mais parce qu'il les a traités d'une façon qui satisfait à la fois et mon esprit et mon cœur. C'est parce qu'il était de ces rares esprits qui ont su unir le génie scientifique au génie littéraire, le goût pour la vérité au goût pour la beauté. Dans presque tous les départements de la pensée humaine, la France a eu des historiens et des critiques de premier ordre ; dans l'histoire religieuse, pour ne citer que deux noms, elle a eu Voltaire et Renan. Voltaire avait une intelligence claire comme le cristal, une logique inflexible comme le fer, une passion pour la vérité et la justice ardente comme le feu. Il était en quelque sorte le rationalisme personnifié. Mais à lui, comme à la plupart des rationalistes, il manquait quelque chose ; il lui manquait cette tendresse et cette poésie qui nous charment en Renan. Il me semble que sans tendresse et sans poésie, on ne peut vraiment comprendre l'esprit humain et ses créations, soit en littérature, soit en art, soit dans toute l'étendue de ses activités multiformes et variées. C'est que l'homme n'est pas seulement une raison ambulante, un bipède calculant ; il a ses sentiments, ses émotions, ses passions et même d'ordinaire il se laisse dominer par elles beaucoup plus que par un froid calcul de ses intérêts personnels. Le grand défaut du rationalisme, c'est qu'en général il n'envisage pas ce côté de notre nature ; en s'occupant trop exclusivement de l'esprit humain, il a trop souvent oublié le cœur humain. Le rationalisme contemple la religion, pour ainsi dire, extérieurement ; Renan la sentait intérieurement ; car il a été croyant et s'il est sorti de l'Église, il est resté toujours lié à l'Église par une sympathie qui avait ses racines dans le fond même de son être. Une telle sympathie, née de sentiments et d'émotions plutôt que de pure raison, est indispensable à celui qui voudrait comprendre l'histoire non seulement de l'Église, mais de la religion en général. Sinon l'histoire religieuse reste une énigme plus insoluble que celle du Sphinx. Même pour les essors suprêmes de la pensée, il faut, en quelque sorte, l'ébranlement des émotions pour faire vibrer les cordes les plus profondes de notre être. Il me semble parfois qu'on ne se sent jamais si près des grandes vérités ou, comme dirait l'homme religieux, si près de Dieu, qu'en entendant une musique grave et solennelle, qui emporte la pensée, comme sur des ailes d'anges, vers des cimes qu'elle n'atteint pas dans la vie calme et ordinaire. Ainsi que tous les grands écrivains, Renan a souvent écrit sous l'impulsion de l'émotion. Dans sa prose harmonieuse et cadencée, on peut entendre comme les sons d'un orchestre qui joue en sourdine.

On a reproché à Renan [1] d'avoir présenté sa pensée, non pas dans une forme nette, précise, tranchée, mais toujours avec beaucoup de réserves, beaucoup de doutes, beaucoup d'hésitations, comme s'il avait de la peine à la dégager de l'amas des faits sur lesquels il l'appuyait. Mais vraiment, Messieurs, il me semble qu'un tel procédé mérite des louanges plutôt que des reproches. Rarement, peut-être jamais, la vérité est si claire, si simple, si évidente qu'on puisse la résumer dans une phrase ou la renfermer dans une formule dogmatique. C'est en vain qu'on tâche de lui poser des bornes, de lui nouer des chaînes ; elle franchira les bornes, elle rompra les chaînes. C'est en vain qu'on tâche d'explorer toutes ses profondeurs par la sonde limitée de nos moyens, d'éclairer toutes ses hauteurs à la lumière blafarde de notre faible intelligence. Non, Messieurs, la vérité est infinie, et son infinité se soustraira toujours aux plus puissants efforts du génie humain qui voudrait la saisir et la comprendre. Mieux vaut donc reconnaître que ce que nous appelons la vérité n'est qu'une partie infiniment petite de la totalité ;

---

[1] Le reproche a été fait par Brunetière ; voir Rémy de Gourmont : *Promenades littéraires*, septième édition (Paris, 1916), p. 19. Comparer au contraire Renan : *Études d'histoire religieuse*, septième édition (Paris, 1864), pp. iii. *sq.* "Le dogmatisme théologique nous a conduits à une idée si étroite de la vérité, que quiconque ne se pose pas en docteur irréfragable, risque de s'ôter à lui-même toute créance auprès des lecteurs." L'esprit scientifique, procédant par de délicates approximations, serrant peu à peu la vérité, modifiant sans cesse ses formules pour les amener à une expression de plus en plus rigoureuse, variant ses points de vue pour ne rien négliger dans l'infinie complexité des problèmes que présente cet univers, est en général peu compris et passe pour un aveu d'impuissance ou de versatilité."

mieux vaut avouer nos doutes, notre incertitude, notre ignorance, que de les cacher sous le manteau trompeur d'affirma-
tions positives, d'assurances absolues. Non, Messieurs, le
scepticisme a toujours raison, le dogmatisme a toujours tort ;
car toujours les vérités humaines d'aujourd'hui deviennent
les erreurs de demain. Donc, c'est une des gloires de Renan
d'avoir pleinement reconnu ce qu'il y a d'incertain et de
douteux même dans les choses qui, au vulgaire, paraissent
des plus sûres, et des plus évidentes ; d'avoir saisi toutes
ces nuances, toutes ces délicatesses, toutes ces pénombres,
qui encadrent comme un nimbe la vérité, et qui se manifestent
aux yeux du génie, mais se cachent et se dérobent aux sens
obtus et émoussés de la grande foule. Le prophète voit
les chariots et les chevaux de l'armée angélique dans le ciel
où son serviteur ne voit que les nuages.

Renan a consacré sa vie à l'étude de cette partie de
l'histoire religieuse qui, pour nous tous, possède le plus vif
intérêt, je veux dire l'étude de cette grande religion israélite,
qui, renouvelée et transformée par le dernier et le plus
illustre des prophètes, par Jésus-Christ, a conquis d'abord
l'empire romain et ensuite toutes les nations civilisées de
l'Europe et de l'Amérique. Cette histoire, pleine des épisodes
les plus émouvants et des conséquences les plus graves, Renan
l'a tracée à grands traits et de main de maître, depuis l'origine
de la nation israélite jusqu'à l'époque où, sous le règne de
Marc-Aurèle, le christianisme s'empara fermement de
l'empire romain et commença à l'étrangler Mais même
les admirateurs les plus convaincus de Renan, parmi lesquels
je me range, admettront volontiers que dans cette histoire
magnifique et magistrale, le grand maître a commis quelques
erreurs et a laissé quelques lacunes, et qu'il nous incombe à
nous autres, ses élèves, de tâcher de corriger ces erreurs et
de combler ces lacunes. La tâche nous est à la fois imposée
et aisée, et cela d'autant plus que, dans les années écoulées
depuis la mort de Renan, la science a fait de grands progrès,
non seulement dans les études religieuses en général, mais
particulièrement dans l'étude des antiquités sémitiques. Les
grandes fouilles babyloniennes, par exemple, pour ne parler
que d'elles, ont déjà retracé l'histoire de la race et de la

civilisation sémitiques jusqu'à une époque si reculée que, comparé à elle, le peuple d'Israël semble presque moderne. Mais ce n'est pas à moi, qui ne suis pas assyriologue, de vous parler de ces découvertes, si grandes et si imposantes qu'elles soient. Dans les quelques minutes que j'ai encore à ma disposition, je voudrais, avec votre permission, vous entretenir d'une autre discipline qui, si je ne me trompe, a fait, elle aussi, quelque progrès depuis la mort de Renan et qui peut combler les quelques lacunes qu'on peut remarquer dans son œuvre historique. Je parle de la méthode comparative, appliquée à l'étude des religions. Je sais bien, Mesdames et Messieurs, qu'il n'est nul besoin, à Paris, de prôner cette méthode comme si elle formait un évangile nouveau : ici, au Louvre, au Collège de France, à la Sorbonne, à l'École des Hautes Études, à l'École des Langues Orientales, au Musée Guimet, au Musée de Saint-Germain, vous avez des maîtres qui apprécient la haute importance de cette méthode et qui ont donné de beaux exemples de son application. Ce serait de ma part à la fois superflu et impertinent, que de désigner ces grands savants français. Leurs noms sont connus partout où l'on s'intéresse à ces études. Je n'ai donc nullement la présomption de prétendre que j'aie quelque chose de nouveau à vous apprendre. C'est en simple témoignage de mon profond respect pour la mémoire de Renan, que je vais vous offrir quelques remarques, comme une gerbe de fleurs éphémères déposée par la main d'un passant sur le tombeau de votre grand savant immortel.

Renan lui-même a bien compris la portée et la valeur de la méthode comparative, et il l'a appliquée à la linguistique dans son beau livre : *Histoire générale et système comparé des langues sémitiques*, qui reste malheureusement inachevé ; mais il n'a pas essayé d'appliquer cette méthode d'une façon systématique à l'étude de l'histoire religieuse. La grande impulsion donnée à l'emploi de cette méthode dans l'histoire est venue de la biologie. La théorie de l'évolution animale, proposée par Darwin et appuyée sur une vaste étendue de connaissances et de comparaisons tirées de tous les départements des sciences naturelles, a démontré quel puissant instrument pour la découverte de la vérité peut être fourni à la science par la méthode comparative. Encouragés par son exemple, d'autres savants se sont hâtés d'appliquer à l'étude de l'homme intellectuel, moral, social, la même méthode que Darwin a appliquée principalement, mais non exclusivement, à l'étude de l'homme en tant qu'animal ; et ils étaient d'autant plus autorisés à faire ainsi, qu'en somme la méthode comparative ne diffère pas, en principe, de la méthode par laquelle l'homme a acquis toutes ses connaissances. Le véritable fondement de cette méthode appliquée à l'étude de l'homme a été signalé par Renan avec l'instinct du génie dans une phrase significative, quand il a dit que, dans le grande marche de l'humanité, les hommes avancent, non pas tous de front mais en échelons. En d'autres termes, l'évolution de notre espèce n'a pas été accomplie parallèlement, c'est-à-dire au même degré de vitesse dans toutes les races humaines. Il est vrai que toutes les races qui existent de nos jours, même les plus sauvages, ont fait d'immenses progrès, en comparaison de l'état purement animal d'où, d'après les théories les plus probables, sont sortis leurs ancêtres reculés. Mais tandis que chez quelques races le progrès a été relativement rapide, chez d'autres il a été plus ou moins lent et tardif. Les premières, nous les appelons races civilisées ; les dernières, nous les appelons races non civilisées ou barbares ou sauvages. Mais il faut bien se garder, soit de traiter toutes les races non civilisées comme demeurant au même niveau de barbarie ou de sauvagerie, soit de considérer même les plus sauvages d'entre elles comme représentatives de l'humanité absolument primitives. Dans la longue échelle évolutionnaire qui s'élève du commencement de notre espèce jusqu'à notre époque, il est probable que les sauvages les plus arriérés de nos jours occupent une place plus proche du sommet que du pied de l'échelle. En effet, les diverses races humaines existantes sont échelonnées sur diverses étapes du grand progrès qui a amené l'humanité de ses origines les plus humbles jusqu'aux hauteurs les plus éminentes de la civilisation. De plus il est probable que les races les plus civilisées ont parcouru à peu près toutes les étapes auxquelles les races arriérées sont restées jusqu'ici. D'où il découle qu'en rangeant les races d'après l'état plus ou moins évolué de leurs connaissances et de leurs mœurs, on obtient un tableau de l'évolution humaine en général. Ce tableau ne sera jamais tout à fait complet, parce que l'état vraiment primitif de notre espèce nous est inconnu et nous restera inconnu probablement pour toujours. Car les hommes vraiment primitifs ont disparu de la terre il y a longtemps, et les races même les plus sauvages qui existent à présent sont toutes très éloignées de l'état absolument primitif de l'humanité. J'insiste sur ce point, parce que souvent on reproche aux anthropologues de traiter tous les sauvages sans distinction comme de vrais primitifs, et d'en tirer des conclusions très hasardées sur les origines de l'homme et de la société. Ce reproche, croyez-moi, est foncièrement injuste. Les anthropologues en général ne sont pas assez peu éclairés pour commettre une telle absurdité. S'ils désignent, comme ils en ont le droit, les sauvages sous le nom de primitifs, c'est qu'ils emploient le mot primitif dans un sens relatif et non pas absolu, par comparaison avec les races plus avancées. Quant à moi, j'ai formellement déclaré que sur l'homme absolument primitif je ne sais rien, et que je ne compte rien apprendre sur ce sujet de mon vivant. Les idées, les croyances et les institutions que j'appelle primitives, sont rudimentaires si nous les mettons en parallèle avec celles de l'homme civilisé ; tandis que si nous les comparons à celles de l'homme primordial, elles indiquent sans exception un développement plus ou moins grand.

Avec cette réserve importante, nous pouvons dire que d'après les données de la méthode comparative, on peut suivre en ses grandes lignes l'évolution de la race humaine, non pas certes depuis son berceau, mais de son enfance jusqu'à son âge adulte. C'est en appliquant ces données à l'étude de la religion qu'on peut combler certaines lacunes et résoudre certains problèmes de l'histoire des grandes religions, qui, sans cette aide, resteraient toujours à combler et à résoudre. Car dans toutes les grandes religions, on trouve des survivances de croyances et de rites, qui ne s'expliquent que par comparaison avec les croyances et les rites plus rudimentaires, et qui, contrastées avec le caractère général de ces autres religions, nous frappent comme des reliques de la barbarie ou même de la sauvagerie. De telles survivances servent comme de bornes milliaires pour marquer des étapes intellectuelles et morales que les civilisés ont depuis longtemps dépassées.

Si l'on demande comment il se fait que ces survivances de barbarie aient persisté si longtemps au milieu de la civilisation, il ne suffit pas d'expliquer cette persistance par un simple instinct conservateur de la nature humaine. Il faut avouer que ces restes de sauvagerie persistent parce qu'ils répondent aux besoins intellectuels et moraux d'une grande partie des hommes, même dans les sociétés les plus civilisées. Car la loi du progrès formulée par Renan, d'après laquelle l'humanité avance, non pas de front mais en échelons, s'applique non seulement aux différentes races comparées les unes aux autres, mais également aux hommes de n'importe quelle race, à n'importe quelle époque. En dépit des formules égalitaires que les démocrates se piquent de prôner et de faire circuler de par le monde, les hommes ne sont pas égaux, ils ne l'ont jamais été, et ils ne le seront jamais. Seuls les petits esprits se croient les égaux de tout le monde ; il faut de la grandeur d'esprit pour reconnaître la supériorité des autres. S'il reste donc de la sauvagerie dans nos mœurs, dans nos idées, dans nos religions, c'est tout simplement parce qu'il reste des sauvages parmi nous, c'est-à-dire des gens qui, bien qu'ils s'efforcent de maintenir une apparence de civilisation, gardent néanmoins dans leur for intérieur des façons de penser et de sentir qui sont de tout point semblables à celles des sauvages. L'étude approfondie de ces survivances a démontré que sous la surface du monde civilisé, il subsiste une couche profonde de sauvagerie, une sauvagerie non pas morte, mais vivante et vivace, toujours en ébullition, toujours prête à crever l'écorce mince et fragile de la civilisation qui la réprime. Ce danger pour la civilisation est permanent, car il est fondé sur l'inégalité radicale et irréductible de la nature humaine. Renan lui-même l'aperçut et la signala. Ayant vu les magnifiques restes des temples grecs à Paestum, il a montré le contraste entre ces belles reliques d'une civilisation éteinte et la sauvagerie des paysans italiens modernes ; et il a ajouté qu'il tremblait pour la civilisation, en voyant qu'elle reposait sur si peu de gens,

T

même dans les pays où elle a le plus longtemps existé.[1] Hélas ! depuis que Renan a écrit ces mots, les évènements de notre temps n'ont que trop confirmé son sinistre présage. Si la civilisation reste encore debout dans l'Ouest de l'Europe, elle a été bouleversée par une éruption de sauvagerie dans l'Est. Heureusement, de tels bouleversements ne peuvent pas durer. Par sa supériorité intellectuelle et morale, l'homme civilisé a dompté les sauvages du dehors ; par sa supériorité intellectuelle et morale, il saura dompter les sauvages de l'intérieur.

Par ce que j'ai dit, vous pouvez comprendre, Mesdames et Messieurs, la grande importance que j'attache à l'étude des sauvages de toutes sortes, soit du dehors, soit de l'intérieur. Mais dans les temps où nous vivons, l'étude des sauvages du dehors est d'une importance encore plus haute et plus urgente que l'étude des sauvages vivants au sein de nos sociétés civilisées, parce qu'alors que nous aurons toujours, sans doute, de ces gens-là parmi nous, les vrais sauvages, refoulés par l'avance de notre civilisation, tendent de plus en plus à disparaître et à périr, voire à perdre toutes leurs anciennes croyances et habitudes, qui seules ont de la valeur pour l'histoire de l'humanité. Comme je l'ai exprimé ailleurs, les sauvages d'aujourd'hui sont comme des monuments historiques qui se délabrent et s'écroulent de jour en jour, et qui dans peu d'années ou bien n'existeront plus, ou du moins auront cessé de porter inscrite sur leur face une grande partie de l'histoire humaine. Hâtons-nous donc, Messieurs, d'étudier ces monuments, de copier ces inscriptions pendant qu'elles sont encore lisibles : la postérité nous accuserait de négligence coupable, si nous omettions de sauver pour ceux qui nous suivront ces archives si précieuses de notre commun passé.

Pour l'étude exacte et sérieuse des tribus sauvages qui gardent encore leurs mœurs peu entamées par la civilisation, il nous faut deux classes d'étudiants. D'abord, des observateurs, qui vivront parmi les sauvages, approfondiront leur pensée, observeront leurs coutumes avec soin, et enregistreront avec exactitude les résultats de leurs observations et de leurs recherches. Pour que de telles observations aient

---

[1] Renan et Berthelot : *Correspondance* (Paris, 1898), pp. 15 *sq.*

leur plus grande valeur scientifique, il faut que l'observateur
connaisse le langage des indigènes parmi lesquels il vit, et
qu'il puisse parler avec eux couramment dans leur propre
langue, sans l'aide d'un interprète. Mais une telle connaissance des langues sauvages présuppose un assez long
séjour parmi les tribus. C'est pourquoi les observations
faites par de simples voyageurs ont en général très peu de
valeur scientifique ; ne connaissant pas les langues et ne
s'entretenant avec les indigènes que par l'intermédiaire d'un
interprète, ils ne peuvent vraiment ni pénétrer l'âme de ces
gens ni gagner leur confiance, de sorte qu'ils courent grand
risque de se tromper et d'être trompés sur les questions les
plus intimes et les plus importantes ; car le sauvage se méfie
de tous les étrangers et n'ouvre pas son cœur au premier
venu. Pour ces raisons, même les expéditions scientifiques
envoyées exprès pour étudier des sauvages n'obtiennent pas
toujours les meilleurs résultats, car rarement elles demeurent
assez longuement parmi les tribus pour acquérir à la fois la
confiance des indigènes et une connaissance exacte de leur
langue. En général, les gens qui ont les plus grandes
facilités pour étudier les sauvages sont les missionnaires,
parce qu'ils consacrent souvent la meilleure partie de leur
vie à cette œuvre et se donnent pour devoir d'apprendre la
langue de leurs ouailles et de gagner leur confiance. Je suis
heureux de constater que dans la littérature qui décrit la vie
et la pensée des sauvages, nous devons un assez grand
nombre de livres de premier ordre aux travaux soigneux et
dévoués des missionnaires, soit catholiques, soit protestants.

Mais pour comprendre la vie et la pensée des tribus
sauvages éparses dans le monde, il ne suffit pas de faire de
simples observations, fussent-elles très soigneuses et très
exactes. Il nous faut des étudiants qui recueilleront les
observations envoyées de toutes les parties du monde, qui
les compareront, et en tireront les conclusions qui s'imposent.
Cette œuvre de comparaison, distincte de l'œuvre d'observation, constitue une partie essentielle des études anthropo-
logiques ; sans elle, notre connaissance de l'homme primitif
resterait toujours fragmentaire et imparfaite. Même l'œuvre
d'observation ne peut s'accomplir pleinement sans l'aide de
l'œuvre de comparaison, qui dirigera ses efforts, attirera son

attention sur des points nouveaux ou insuffisamment décrits, et expliquera beaucoup de choses qui autrement resteraient peut-être toujours obscures ou mal comprises. Car l'œuvre de comparaison doit être en même temps une œuvre d'interprétation, puisque beaucoup de faits qui, considérés en eux-mêmes, ne s'expliquent pas, admettent une explication facile du moment qu'on les compare à des faits analogues. Il faut ajouter que cette œuvre de comparaison et d'interprétation comporte toujours un élément de théorie et même de conjecture, parce que rarement nos interprétations de faits de ce genre atteignent un degré de certitude démonstrative. D'où il s'ensuit que cette œuvre exige des qualités d'esprit assez différentes de celles qui suffisent pour une simple œuvre d'observation. Un bon observateur est parfois mauvais interprète et méchant théoricien ; et, d'autre part, un bon théoricien est souvent très mauvais observateur. La science de l'homme a besoin de tous les deux : pour la construction de son grand édifice, il faut des architectes aussi bien que des maçons ; ici comme ailleurs, le progrès se fait par une division de travail.

J'ai achevé ces quelques remarques sur la méthode comparative dans l'étude des phénomènes religieux. En vous les soumettant, j'ose espérer que dans la poursuite de la tâche que la Société Ernest Renan s'est donnée, elle usera quelquefois de cette méthode féconde et encore assez nouvelle, qu'elle ne se limitera pas à l'étude des grandes religions historiques, mais qu'elle étendra ses recherches jusqu'aux religions les plus humbles et les plus rudimentaires, parce que chez celles-ci on trouve pour ainsi dire le germe de ces systèmes grandioses de croyances et de rites qui ont si longtemps soutenu et si souvent égaré notre pauvre humanité dans son pénible progrès vers le bien et le vrai. Quoiqu'il en soit, je ne doute pas, Messieurs, que vous ne poursuiviez votre but dans l'esprit de votre grand maître, un esprit non pas de dédain, mais de tendresse pour ces faiblesses humaines que nous partageons tous, un esprit plein d'admiration généreuse pour tout ce qu'il y a de bon et de beau même dans les systèmes que nous n'acceptons pas, et surtout en vous souvenant toujours de cette ignorance profonde et illimitée, qui nous impose le double devoir d'humilité et de charité.

En vous remerciant, Mesdames et Messieurs, pour la patience avec laquelle vous m'avez écouté, je veux en même temps m'acquitter d'une dette que depuis longtemps je dois à la mémoire de Renan. Dans ses belles *Études d'Histoire Religieuse*, il a consacré une étude spéciale à M. Feuerbach, un théologien allemand assez célèbre de son temps. Je dois vous avouer, Mesdames et Messieurs, que je n'ai pas lu les livres de M. Feuerbach et que je n'ai nulle intention de les lire. Les malheurs du jour me suffisent sans y ajouter la lecture d'une théologie allemande surannée. Mais voici en quels termes émouvants Renan s'exprime à l'égard de ce théologien aride et un peu revêche.

" Plût à Dieu que M. Feuerbach se fût plongé à des sources plus riches de vie que celles de son germanisme exclusif et hautain ! Ah ! si, assis sur les ruines du mont Palatin ou du mont Cœlius, il eût entendu le son des cloches éternelles se prolonger et mourir sur les collines désertes où fut Rome autrefois ; ou si, de la plage solitaire du Lido, il eût entendu le carillon de Saint-Marc expirer sur les lagunes ; s'il eût vu Assise et ses mystiques merveilles, sa double basilique et la grande légende du second Christ du moyen-âge tracée par le pinceau de Cimabue et de Giotto ; s'il se fût rassasié du regard long et doux des vierges du Pérugin, ou qu'à San-Domenico de Sienne il eût vu Sainte Catherine en extase, non, M. Feuerbach ne jetterait pas ainsi l'opprobre à une moitié de la poésie humaine, et ne s'exclamerait pas comme s'il voulait repousser loin de lui le fantôme d'Iscarioth!"

Je ne sais, Mesdames et Messieurs, si ces belles paroles ont touché l'âme et attendri le cœur de feu M. Feuerbach ; mais elles m'ont suggéré l'idée de faire sonner les cloches éternelles de Rome à la fin de mon livre *Le Rameau d'Or*. En effet, j'ai fait entendre leurs pieuses sonneries à Némi à la tombée du soir comme le dernier soupir du jour et du dieu qui meurt. Malheureusement un ami très savant et un peu méticuleux m'a fait observer que vraiment à Némi on ne peut pas entendre les cloches de Rome, parce qu'elles sont trop éloignées. La vérité était indiscutable, et à regret, dans la dernière édition de mon livre, j'ai remplacé les cloches de Rome par les cloches d'Aricie. Mais le son de ces cloches se prolongeant et mourant à travers l'étendue vaste et morne de la Campagne, cela m'a été inspiré par Renan. Je voulais, il y a trente ans, lui écrire et lui rendre grâce de cette inspiration. Mais on m'a déconseillé de le faire, en disant que j'étais alors un jeune homme inconnu et que Renan était un grand homme au sommet de sa renommée littéraire. Je me suis donc abstenu, et parfois je l'ai regretté. C'est pourquoi, Mesdames et Messieurs, disciples et en quelque sorte héritiers de Renan, je vous ai fait cet aveu tardif ; et si vous me permettiez un peu de fantaisie, j'oserais rendre ensemble mes grâces et mes hommages à son ombre auguste, qui, sortie pour quelques brefs instants du royaume des esprits et de la gloire, semble planer sur nous dans cette salle.

II

ADDRESS ON THE CENTENARY OF ERNEST RENAN

DELIVERED IN THE AMPHITHEATRE OF THE SORBONNE,
PARIS, WEDNESDAY, 28TH FEBRUARY 1923[1]

MONSIEUR LE PRÉSIDENT DE LA RÉPUBLIQUE, MONSIEUR
L'ADMINISTRATEUR DU COLLÈGE DE FRANCE, MONSIEUR
LE RECTEUR DE L'UNIVERSITÉ, MESDAMES ET MESSIEURS—
Je suis profondément touché de l'honneur qu'on m'a fait en
m'invitant à prendre la parole en cette occasion solennelle
et dans cette auguste assemblée, où se trouvent réunis les
plus éminents représentants de la France.

Il ne m'appartient pas, à moi, étranger, devant un tel
auditoire, de tâcher d'analyser et d'apprécier le génie de
votre illustre savant Ernest Renan dans toutes ses mani-
festations si multiples, si variées, si saisissantes, si belles.
Je ne prétends que joindre mes hommages personnels
d'admiration et, j'ose dire, d'affection à ceux qu'aujourd'hui
la France et le monde des savants apportent de partout à
sa tombe.

S'il m'est permis de signaler un seul trait parmi tant
d'autres, qui réunis caractérisaient ce génie si merveilleuse-
ment doué, ce serait la combinaison si complète, si harmonieuse de l'esprit littéraire avec l'esprit scientifique. Avec
une clarté philosophique et une logique vraiment françaises,
que ni la passion, ni le préjugé, ni l'amertume des contro-
verses n'a jamais troublées, il possédait toute la sensibilité

---

[1] In the absence of the writer the
Address was read by Monsieur
    Maurice Croiset, Administrateur du
    Collège de France.

279

délicate, toute l'imagination chaude et tendre, toute la grâce exquise d'un grand écrivain ; et ces qualités, si belles et si rarement associées dans le même individu, comblées d'une sérénité de tempérament et d'une douceur de caractère sans pareilles, se reflétaient dans un style pur, limpide, harmonieux, qui coule comme une rivière, dont le courant paisible et miroitant offre les images les plus vraies, les plus variées et les plus ravissantes : tantôt de grandes cités et des fourmilières d'hommes affairés, tantôt des prés fleuris, des solitudes pastorales, des troupeaux broutant l'herbage sur les bords verdoyants, bref, les scènes les plus mouvementées et les plus tranquilles, les plus gaies et les plus tristes de cette grande tragi-comédie que nous appelons la vie humaine.

Grâce à cette combinaison de talents incomparable, Renan a su tracer pour nous et pour la postérité l'histoire de notre religion depuis ses humbles semences dans les déserts de l'Arabie jusqu'à la superbe éclosion de sa fleur dans les deux premiers siècles de notre ère. C'est un panorama et en quelque sorte une épopée qui se déroule devant nos yeux, une épopée infiniment plus grandiose et plus attachante que l'Iliade et que l'Odyssée, parce qu'il ne s'agit pas ici des destinées d'une seule cité ou d'un seul individu ; il s'agit des destinées d'une grande partie de l'humanité, voire la partie la plus progressive et la plus civilisée. Car on peut dire que notre civilisation dérive de trois sources primaires : de la religion de la Judée, de la philosophie de la Grèce, de la législation de Rome.

Du premier de ces trois grands éléments, qui composent encore aujourd'hui le fond de notre vie, Renan a voulu être l'historien et, j'ose dire, le poète ; sa grande histoire, sa grande épopée religieuse restera immortelle parmi les grandes créations du génie humain ; elle brillera comme une des plus pures étoiles de ce ciel où brillent et brilleront, tant que durera l'humanité sur la terre, toutes les gloires de la France.

III

ADDRESS AT
THE SORBONNE ON THE RECEPTION
OF AN HONORARY DOCTORATE

PARIS, 19TH NOVEMBER 1921

MONSIEUR LE PRÉSIDENT DE LA RÉPUBLIQUE, MONSIEUR
LE MINISTRE, MONSIEUR LE RECTEUR DE L'UNIVERSITÉ,
MESDAMES ET MESSIEURS—Le grand honneur que votre
ancienne Université, la plus célèbre de toutes, vient de me
conférer me touche infiniment et c'est avec reconnaissance
respectueuse que j'accepte l'honneur en tant qu'il témoigne
votre approbation de mes travaux littéraires. Je l'accepte
encore plus chaleureusement en signe de votre amitié pour
mon pays et pour ma nation, en signe que vous me regardez
comme ami de la France. Pour ma part, ce n'est pas
d'aujourd'hui que je suis pénétré d'une admiration profonde
pour le génie français et pour l'esprit français ; et cette
admiration n'a fait que grandir à mesure que j'ai acquis une
connaissance plus intime de votre noble nation, et qu'à
l'admiration est venue s'ajouter l'affection. Veuillez croire,
Messieurs, que cette admiration et cette affection sont
partagées partout par mes compatriotes. Nous admirons,
nous aimons la France. Nos penseurs révèrent vos grands
penseurs : nos soldats ne tarissent pas en éloges de vos
soldats glorieux, à côté desquels ils sont fiers d'avoir com-
battu. De tous les pays du monde des étudiants viennent
apprendre les principes de leur science chez vos grands
maîtres. Je suis heureux et fier d'être devenu en quelque
sorte le collègue de ces grands maîtres français par le doctorat
que l'Université de Paris a daigné m'accorder. Le souvenir

281

de cet honneur demeurera parmi les plus précieux de ma vie, et s'il me reste encore, comme je l'espère, quelques années pour le travail, je les consacrerai à mes études avec d'autant plus d'ardeur grâce à l'encouragement que votre approbation et votre sympathie m'ont inspiré.

IV

ADDRESS ON A VISIT OF MONSIEUR PAINLEVÉ, FRENCH MINISTER OF WAR, TO THE INSTITUT FRANÇAIS DU ROYAUME UNI, LONDON

17TH NOVEMBER 1927

Au nom de l'Institut français et de ses amis, au nombre desquels je suis fier de me compter, nous remercions Monsieur le Ministre du grand honneur qu'il nous a fait en venant nous donner ce beau discours plein d'instruction et de science exacte.

C'est un grand homme qui est venu nous parler ce soir. La France, qui connaît sa valeur, lui a confié la première nécessité de l'État, la défense nationale, et nous savons, comme tout le monde le sait, qu'en lui la défense nationale est ainsi en mains sûres.

Mais M. Painlevé est plus qu'un homme d'État. Il est orateur. Dans les temps les plus critiques de la guerre il est venu à Londres, et nous qui l'avons écouté parler à la Mansion House et à Queen's Hall, nous savons avec quelle ardeur, quelle éloquence, quel feu il a su transporter son auditoire à l'enthousiasme.

Mais M. Painlevé est plus qu'orateur. C'est un savant de premier ordre dans les sciences les plus abstraites et les plus difficiles, les sciences mathématiques et physiques. Hier à Cambridge il a parlé de ses recherches à un auditoire qui comptait quelques-uns des plus grands savants du monde, et même parmi eux ce ne furent pas tous qui surent s'élever à la hauteur de sa pensée.

Mais M. Painlevé est plus qu'un savant. C'est un

philosophe qui s'intéresse à toutes les grandes questions qui touchent l'humanité. Nous avons lu avec émotion son magnifique discours sur Pascal, discours écrit dans un style littéraire digne de Renan, discours qui révèle l'esprit non seulement d'un penseur mais d'un poète.

Monsieur le Ministre,

En vous nous saluons un grand homme d'État, un grand orateur, un grand savant, un grand penseur, et ce qui est encore plus beau, un grand fils de la France.

Daignez, Monsieur le Ministre, agréer ce petit témoignage de notre profonde admiration et de notre profonde reconnaissance.

(Sir James Frazer remet à M. Painlevé une édition française reliée à Londres des *Œuvres de Pascal*.)

V

ADDRESS TO THE SOCIETY OF FRENCH FOLK-LORE

THE SORBONNE, PARIS, 14TH FEBRUARY 1929[1]

MONSIEUR LE DOYEN, MESDAMES ET MESSIEURS—C'est une grande joie pour lady Frazer et pour moi que d'assister à la naissance de la *Société du Folklore français*, et si nous ne sommes pas les auteurs de cet enfant, nous prétendons en être en quelque sorte les parrains. Et j'espère qu'avec l'indulgence qu'accorde toujours un auditoire français vous m'excuserez si, en ma qualité de parrain, je ne suis qu'un Écossais. Mais si à coup sûr le sang de France ne coule pas dans mes veines, je puis vous assurer en toute sincérité que l'amour de la France m'emplit le cœur.

M. le Doyen, notre président, vous a déjà indiqué avec une éloquence et une clarté parfaite le but que se propose la nouvelle Société, soit de recueillir et de décrire dans une revue les restes de ce qu'on appelle le folklore de France, c'est-à-dire les anciennes coutumes, les anciennes croyances et superstitions, les anciens contes, les anciennes légendes, les anciennes fêtes, les vieilles chansons et leurs vieilles mélodies belles et touchantes, en un mot, tout ce qu'on peut encore retroüver, comme on nous l'assure, de la vieille vie populaire dans toutes les provinces de France.

Ainsi c'est surtout du passé que s'occuperont nos recherches, ou, pour mieux dire, ce sera du présent qu'on s'occupera, car le présent sera pour nous un miroir du passé. C'est donc une science très pacifique dont nous

[1] Reprinted from the *Revue de Folklore Français, Organe de la Société du Folklore Français*, i. No. 1 (Janvier-février, 1930).

espérons favoriser l'essor.   Les brûlantes questions de politique, de nationalité, de religion, qui divisent encore aujourd'hui les hommes en camps opposés, n'entreront jamais dans notre paisible province et ne troubleront jamais notre repos.   Même sur les problèmes si compliqués et si difficiles des origines nous comptons garder une réserve, voire un silence prudent.   Il suffira pour nous de constater les faits en laissant à d'autres plus clairvoyants que nous la tâche d'enchaîner ces faits particuliers aux principes généraux qui ont dirigé la grande marche de l'humanité à travers les brumes et les tempêtes des siècles.

Le charme de ces vieilles coutumes et de ces vieilles croyances, c'est qu'elles sont à la fois très vieilles et très jeunes ; c'est la jeunesse du monde qui a survécu dans un monde déjà vieux.   Mais elles sont en voie de périr, ces fleurs d'un passé éloigné.   Les roses de la fantaisie se fanent trop vite comme se fanent toutes les belles choses ; gardons au moins quelques feuilles desséchées et le parfum de ces printemps évanouis ; et alors même que les feuilles mortes seront tombées en poussière, gardons-en, et toujours, précieusement le souvenir, qui est immortel comme l'esprit humain.

Voilà ce que nous vous invitons à faire, Français et Françaises, pour le folklore de France.   Vous êtes les héritiers d'un passé riche en souvenirs qui remontent aux temps de l'antiquité classique ; vous êtes plus rapprochés que nous des sources logées sous le beau ciel de l'Italie et de la Grèce dont a découlé la meilleure partie de notre civilisation moderne.   Le fleuve de la vie d'aujourd'hui nous entraîne de plus en plus loin de ces sources, mais il est bon d'y remonter parfois pour nous rafraîchir en trempant nos lèvres dans ces eaux d'une jeunesse éternelle.   Or, en étudiant le folklore français, vous toucherez à ce passé éloigné et auguste, car la vie romaine n'a pas disparu comme un nuage avec la ruine de ses beaux temples, de ses grands amphithéâtres, de ses aqueducs prolongés à perte de vue : elle existe encore dans les croyances et les coutumes de vos paysans : elle s'accroche aux flancs de vos hautes montagnes, elle s'étiole dans les solitudes de vos forêts verdoyantes, elle surnage sur le courant tranquille de vos rivières lentes et sinueuses.   Et

aux restes de l'antiquité romaine se mêlent dans votre pays
les restes d'une antiquité encore plus ancienne et plus mysté-
rieuse, l'antiquité celtique entourée comme d'une auréole de
tous ses enchantements poétiques.   Car la France était un
pays celtique longtemps avant qu'elle fut devenue une province romaine, et encore aujourd'hui des milliers de Français
parlent une langue celtique.   Mais pour trouver des vestiges
de cette antiquité celtique nous n'avons pas besoin d'aller
jusqu'aux mornes bruyères, aux falaises escarpées, aux mers
brumeuses et orageuses de la Bretagne, nous les retrouvons
dans cette salle même.   Regardez le gui que plusieurs de
vous portent déjà à la boutonnière comme emblème de la
Société qui vient de naître dans cette ancienne Université,
mère de tant d'autres Universités, de tant d'autres institutions
savantes et illustres consacrées à la recherche du vrai et du
beau.   Or le gui que vous voyez parmi nous était au temps
jadis la plante la plus sacrée de la religion celtique ; les
Druides le coupaient avec une faucille d'or sur un chêne
séculaire et adoré.   Agréez donc, Mesdames et Messieurs,
le gui en symbole des recherches que nous voulons pousser
dans toutes les provinces de France afin de récolter les dernières gerbes d'une moisson qui, flétrie par un souffle
d'automne, languit et meurt sous nos yeux.   C'est une belle
œuvre à laquelle nous vous convions, une œuvre qui, en
rattachant le présent de votre grande nation à son passé
reculé, peut servir à la fois à l'histoire et à la gloire de la
France.

VI

ADDRESS
TO THE INTERNATIONAL ASSOCIATION
OF ANTIQUARIAN BOOKSELLERS

LONDON, 26TH JANUARY 1927

MR. CHAIRMAN, LADIES, AND GENTLEMEN—This has been a memorable, I may say a unique, day for my wife and me; for in the middle of the day we lunched with the Individualistic Bookshop Society, and to-night we are entertained by the International Association of Antiquarian Booksellers. I trust that there is no radical opposition between an Individualistic Bookshop and an Antiquarian Bookshop, otherwise I should have come here in fear and trembling, for I confess to being a convinced partisan of individualistic enterprise, at least in authorship, the only subject about which I profess to know anything. I cannot conceive of a book, at any rate of a good book, being written by a syndicate. I think I have read that in Russia of late, where everything is now done, or supposed to be done, on co-operative principles, they tried to compose poetry in this fashion by a number of people laying their heads together in committee, but the result of their lucubrations, so far as I know, has not been given to the world, and, if it were, I imagine that it would not be worth much. A syndicalist epic would hardly rival Homer, though to be sure some eminent critics, with whom I do not agree, have held that Homer himself was a syndicate or something of that sort.

No doubt much good work has been done by co-operation, not only in business and industry, but also in matters of learning, as we may see, for example, by the admirable dictionaries, encyclopaedias, and even histories produced in our own time by the united labours of bands of scholars. I should be the last to decry such works, which are in fact indispensable to the advancement of learning. I only mean to say that what we may call the higher literature must always be the product of individual genius and can gain little or nothing by co-operation. We have all heard, I think, of the line of poetry composed by the joint efforts of Tennyson, FitzGerald, and, I think, another poet whose name I have forgotten. The line runs :

A Mr. Wilkinson, a clergyman.

Yet this verse is hardly characterized by that flight of imagination, that outburst of lyrical rapture, which we associate with the highest poetry.

But to leave this controversial subject and come to one on which we are all agreed—I mean the value of antiquarian books—I think that without any disrespect for modern authors, some of whom are now sitting round your hospitable table— and far be it from me to disparage their works, all the more because I may myself perhaps still claim to be a modern author, though I fear that I am fast approaching, if I have not already passed, the line which divides the modern from the ancient world—I was about to observe, when I lost my way in this parenthesis, that much might be said for the view that the oldest books are the best, witness, for example, the Bible and Homer. And why should the oldest books be the best ? The reason, I take it, is simple. The principle of the survival of the fittest applies to books as well as to men. Bad books perish, but good books survive, because the world will not willingly let them die. Therefore the older a book, the stronger the testimony of humanity to its excellence. If men have taken the trouble to reproduce a book again and again and to hand it on from generation to generation, depend upon it there is something in that book that deserves to live and be remembered even when the name of the author, as sometimes happens, is forgotten. " A good book ", Milton says, " is the precious life-blood of a master-spirit embalmed and treasured up on purpose to a life beyond life." It is your business, gentlemen, thus to hand on to future ages these precious monuments of the past, to give them, in Milton's phrase, a life beyond life. It is a high calling, a noble vocation. The greatest force in the world is thought : the best thought of humanity is enshrined in books ; and you are the agents to disseminate that thought in the world and to preserve it for posterity.

Gentlemen, in the name of the guests whom you have invited to your hospitable table to-night, I thank you for your generous hospitality, and I feel sure that I speak for all your guests in wishing the International Association of Antiquarian Booksellers every possible success in their honourable, their beneficent mission of diffusing among men the best and most enduring monuments of human genius.

VII

ADDRESS AT THE JUBILEE OF THE SOCIETY FOR THE PROMOTION OF HELLENIC STUDIES

LONDON, 24TH JUNE 1929[1]

MR. PRESIDENT, MY LORD, LADIES, AND GENTLEMEN—I
could have wished that the honour of seconding this toast had
been entrusted to someone more intimately associated than
myself with the work of the Hellenic Society or more conversant with the recent developments of Greek studies. In
this learned gathering there are doubtless many better
qualified than I in both respects to do justice to the toast ;
but at least I yield to no one in my conviction of the excellence
and utility of the object which the Hellenic Society has set
itself to accomplish, and which it has consistently and successfully pursued for half a century. That object I take to
be the maintenance of the Greek tradition in England and
wherever the English language is spoken or understood. And
why do we wish to maintain the Greek tradition ? Because
we believe Greece to be the true mother of our modern
civilization. From her we derive the tradition of political
liberty, of intellectual freedom, of the disinterested search
for truth untrammelled by dogma and prejudice, of the love
of beauty in all its forms, whether in Nature, in literature, or
in art. It is a noble heritage : we have received it from our
fathers, and we mean to hand it on intact and, if possible,
enriched to our descendants. In doing so we believe that we
are following the traditional policy and the soundest instincts
of the English race, the policy of preserving in the present

[1] Reprinted from *The Journal of Hellenic Studies*, vol. xlix. part ii. (1929).

and carrying on into the future whatever has been found to be good and useful in the past. Hence we hold that in promoting Greek studies and maintaining the Greek tradition as an integral and important part of our national education the Hellenic Society is serving the best interests, not only of scholarship and learning, but of culture and humanity.

If we would picture to ourselves the immense loss which humanity would suffer by the extinction of the Greek tradition, we need only perhaps reflect on what happened in Europe during the Middle Ages, when the illumination of the Greek genius had died out, except for the solitary candle glimmering at Byzantium. It was a time of political and intellectual servitude, stagnation, and slumber, the long hibernation of the European spirit. The revival of Greek literature at the Renaissance was not merely a symptom, it was a powerful instrument of that awakening of the European mind to fresh life and activity which since then has proceeded with ever-increasing energy down to our own time. The fifty years during which the Hellenic Society has existed have witnessed a great advance in our knowledge of ancient Greece and of classical antiquity in general. The epoch-making discoveries, first of Schliemann and afterwards of Sir Arthur Evans, to name no others, have opened up a new vista into the Hellenic past, while at the same time excavations in Egypt, Babylonia, and Asia Minor have carried back the history of civilization in the near East to still remoter ages. But I think we may say with confidence that these wonderful discoveries in Egypt and Babylonia have done nothing to lessen or impair our estimate of the debt we owe to Greece ; if anything they tend rather to enhance it by contrasting the material wealth and technical perfection of these Oriental nations with the poverty and rudimentary nature of their thought compared with the richness, the range, the variety of thought which ancient Greece enshrined in its matchless literature.

In the progress of Greek studies during the last fifty years the Hellenic Society has borne an honourable part. The best record of its activity is contained in the long series of volumes of its *Journal*, comprising an immense variety of

valuable articles on every aspect of Greek culture contributed by many of the best scholars of our time both
English and foreign. And by its steady support of the
British School at Athens the Hellenic Society has directly
contributed to the exploration and excavation of many
ancient sites which have yielded much precious material for
the enlargement and enrichment of our knowledge of Greek
history and life. It is a record of which the founders and
friends of the Society may well be proud.

Of the founders of the Society, two, and the two principal, are happily still with us. They are Mr. George
Macmillan and Mr. Gennadius. Together they had the
happy thought, I may almost call it the inspiration, of
founding a Society for the promotion of Greek studies in
England and among English-speaking peoples all over the
world. They communicated the idea to some of the leading
scholars of the day, who took it up warmly, and in concert
they drew up the scheme of the Society and laid down the
lines on which, with little variation, it has run ever since.
The ever-increasing success of the Society, as attested by the
increasing number of its members, the great increase of its
library, and the extension of its activities in other directions,
is the best proof of the wisdom and foresight of its founders.
Of these founders, Mr. George Macmillan has been a main
prop and support of the Society from its foundation down
to this day. By his constant devotion to its best interests,
by his sober enthusiasm, calm wisdom, and sound good
sense, he has contributed, more perhaps than anyone else,
not only to launch the ship but to steer it on its long and
prosperous voyage of half a century. The members of the
Hellenic Society desire to take this opportunity of thanking
Mr. Macmillan for the eminent service he has thereby
rendered to the cause of learning in England and throughout
the world ; they congratulate him on the conspicuous success
of his achievement, and they hope that for many years to
come the Society may continue to benefit by his wise counsels
and wide experience.

My Lord, Ladies, and Gentlemen, I ask you to drink to
the prosperity of the Hellenic Society, coupled with the name
of Mr. George Macmillan, our Founder.

PART III

REVIEWS

I

A LIBERIAN TRIBE *

SHORTLY before the war the Royal Academy of Science at Göttingen appointed a Commission charged with the duty of collecting and publishing a series of documents on the history of religion which should render to students, especially in Germany, the same sort of service that is rendered to students among English-speaking peoples by the well-known *Sacred Books of the East*. But the scope of the German series (*Quellen der Religions-Geschichte*) is much wider than that of the corresponding English series, for it embraces all the religions of the world, with the exception of the Bible and Christianity, which are sufficiently provided for by other institutions. The character of the works published or contemplated by the Commission is purely scientific; all apologetic, philosophical, and aesthetic considerations are rigorously excluded. The aim of the series is to furnish the student of the history of religion with comprehensive and trustworthy materials for carrying out his inquiries.

The book under review is the ninth of the series. It deals with the religion and social life of the Kpelle, a tribe of the negro republic of Liberia, and is all the more welcome because exact information as to the half-wild tribes of that little-known region has hitherto been extremely scanty. The author is a German Protestant pastor, who is already favourably known to anthropologists by a good book on the Shillook tribe of the Upper Nile, whom he studied on the spot. He prepared himself for his work in Liberia by a long preliminary study of the

---

* *Die Kpelle, ein Negerstamm in Liberia.* By Diedrich Westermann. (Göttingen, Vandenhoeck & Ruprecht, 1921.) (*The Times Literary Supplement*, May 25, 1922.)

languages, so that three days after landing he was able to begin taking down texts in them. The four months which he spent in the Kpelle and Gola tribes enabled him thus to collect a large body of materials at first hand. These materials form the basis of the present work. They are given in the form of close translations of the reports which Mr. Westermann took down from the lips of the natives in their own languages ; he hopes to publish the original texts with the help of the University of Hamburg. The texts deal not merely with the religion but with the economic condition, the family and social life of the people, their political institutions, their mythology and folk-tales. Mr. Westermann has devoted his attention chiefly to the intellectual and spiritual life of the natives, which is pre-dominantly religious. We have detected no trace of theoretical bias, of theological or national prejudice, in the book. The tone throughout is clear, calm, impartial—in a word, scientific.

The Kpelle inhabit a dense forest region in the northern part of Liberia ; they differ little in bodily characteristics and general culture from the other forest tribes of the country. Linguistically they belong to the great Mandingo or Mande family. The economic basis of life is agriculture ; the staple food is rice. Most of the people are pagans, but there are some traces of Mohammedan influence among them. Thus the diviners, who profess to divine by figures drawn on the sand, and who occupy an important place in the religious life of the people, are always Moslems ; and this particular mode of divination, though it is widespread in other pagan tribes of West Africa, appears to be of Mohammedan origin. Again, if a European asks a native about the numerous offerings which may be seen everywhere near houses, at the entrances of villages, on graves, and so forth, the native will usually tell him that they are made " to God " ; but this is an answer which he has learned from the Moslems and thinks will be satisfactory to a white man ; in reality most of these offerings are made to the spirits of the dead. The worship of the dead occupies a foremost place in the religion of the Kpelle. To their thinking there is no essential difference between the living and the dead. The dead, like the living, have need of nourish-ment, and like the living they hear and see what goes on around them ; they are sensible of the good or evil that is done them, and have it in their power to benefit or injure the survivors. Hence when a bad man dies, who in his lifetime dabbled in black magic or was believed to be possessed by an evil spirit, he is buried outside the village and magical fences are erected and other defensive measures adopted to prevent his ghost from returning and troubling the inhabitants. But when a good man dies, especially an aged head of a family, his ghost is expected to be a public benefactor to the village ; so to keep him in good humour food and drink are regularly offered at his grave.

The dead are supposed to dwell in the neighbourhood of the village and often in tall trees, especially the great silk-cotton trees. These trees, accordingly, are never felled, and the ground about them is cleared of grass and shrubs ; here offerings are made monthly, often by the head of the clan. Sometimes the dead are believed to be born again in the person of infants. This takes place especially when a death is quickly followed by a birth in the family, particularly when the deceased was an old and honourable man ; the return of such a one is welcomed and the new-born child is identified with him.

The Kpelle stand in fear of demons, which take possession of men in their lifetime and are mischievous also in their dis-embodied state after death. Regular societies exist for the purpose of catching demons and rendering them harmless ; and when a village is infested by swarms of fiends the help of one or other of these societies is called in by the authorities to abate the nuisance. The business of demon-catching is hereditary in many families from father to son. By the use of incantations and certain herbs with which he fumigates the patient, the exorcist can catch the foul fiend and shut him up in a calabash or a bag ; after that it is open to him either to destroy the demon outright by burning him or to retain his services for the purpose of injuring his enemies. But the retention of such a familiar spirit is dangerous, not only because the demon may turn on his master and rend him, but because all intercourse with evil spirits is a crime punishable with death by fire.

Like many West African tribes, the Kpelle have a conception of a high God, who seems to be a personification of the sky. He is said to have created the earth and all that on it is, including

men and animals, though Mr. Westermann was not able to
hear of any creation myths. This great God is good ; He is
the source of happiness and prosperity to mankind. When a
man dies in old age, it is said that he has gone to " God's
village " ; that " God has fetched him," or that " God has
come to meet him." Yet God is too great, too good, and too
far away to need to be appeased by offerings of food and drink ;
and though most of the public sacrifices and prayers are now
addressed to Him, Mr. Westermann is inclined to see in this
custom another effect of Moslem influence.

　　Mr. Westermann has a good deal to tell us about totemism
and taboo among the Kpelle ; but he confessedly uses the
words totem and totemism in a loose sense to cover all superstitious relations into which a person may enter with animals,
plants, and other natural phenomena ; and many of the facts
which he classes under this head do not fall within the ordinary
definitions of totemism. In this connexion it is well to bear in
mind the caution which M. Delafosse, one of our best authorities
on the natives of West Africa, has given as to the danger of
regarding as totemic all the numerous and complex systems of
taboo which prevail in this part of the continent from Sierra
Leone to Angola. These systems no doubt present certain
analogies to totemism, but at the same time they differ from it
in so many points that they ought not to be classed as totemic
without qualification. Mr. Westermann distinguishes animal
totems and plant totems. Animal totems, he tells us, are
inherited by sons from their fathers and by daughters from
their mothers. This distinction of inheritance according to sex
is most unusual ; elsewhere, in the great majority of cases, all
the children of a family inherit their totem either from their
father or from their mother. A man may not eat the flesh
of his totem animal, and he respects the whole species. These
are normal rules of totemism. Among the totemic animals are
leopards, elephants, wild pigs, chimpanzees, porcupines, tor-
toises, water-snakes, dogs, and several sorts of antelopes ;
among the totemic plants are banana trees, oil palms, raphia
palms, and manioc. But what Mr. Westermann calls totem
plants appear to be, as indeed he himself remarks, rather life-
trees than totems. The plant to which an individual, whether
man or woman, is intimately related is always one particular

plant, not a whole species : it need not be inherited either from father or mother : it may be planted at any time of a person's life ; and his or her welfare is thenceforth supposed to be bound up with it.

Among the Kpelle, as among many West African tribes, secret societies play a very important part ; according to Mr. Westermann they form the dominant factor in the life of the people. Among them is the notorious Leopard Society, the members of which, disguised as leopards, perpetrate, or used to perpetrate, many atrocious murders. But the most important of these societies is the Poro, which is also found, under the same name, in many tribes of Sierra Leone as well as of Liberia. According to Mr. Westermann, it dominates the whole social life of the tribes as the Catholic Church dominated the life of Western Europe in the Middle Ages. It is for men only, but there is a corresponding society for women called the Sande Society. At the head of the Poro is the Grand Master, a mysterious personage, who is believed to be himself immortal, and to possess the power both of killing and of bringing to life again. He is popularly supposed to kill the novices at initiation and four years afterwards to resuscitate them. In the interval they live strictly secluded in the forest. It is given out that the Grand Master has swallowed them, that he keeps them in his stomach all the time of their seclusion, and that he gives birth to them when they are at last restored as full-grown men to their families. This restoration is a great occasion and is attended by some quaint ceremonies. As the procession issues from the forest the shrill notes of a flute are heard to sound, signifying the pangs which the Grand Master suffers at bringing the young men to the birth ; and for some time afterwards the newly initiated youths behave like newly born children, professing to know nobody, not even their own relations, and to be complete strangers in their native village. Curiously enough, similar rites are practised far away among some tribes of Northern New Guinea, where in like manner youths at initiation are supposed to be swallowed by a monster and afterwards disgorged as full-grown men.

Among the Kpelle, children belong to the clan of their mother, not to that of their father ; and in conformity with this rule the mother's eldest brother possesses a certain authority over his sister's children ; for example, he can pledge them as security for a debt contracted by his clan, and the father of the children has no right to interfere. Yet, on the other hand, children inherit their father's property and have no legal claim to the inheritance of their mother's brother. These facts, as Mr. Westermann points out, seem to show that the Kpelle are in a transitional stage between mother-kin and father-kin ; and here, as usual, the change is proceeding from matrilineal to patrilineal descent, and not in the reverse direction.

These few facts may serve to indicate the interesting ethnological matter collected by the author in this valuable book. It may be confidently recommended to the attention of all serious students of anthropology.

II

NEGROES OF THE IVORY COAST *

THE Ivory Coast forms part of the French Possessions in West Africa ; on the east it is bounded by the British Possession of the Gold Coast. A province (*cercle*) of the Ivory Coast takes its name from the large city of Bondoukou, the capital. It stretches for nearly two hundred miles from north to south, beginning towards the south in dense tropical forest and ending towards the north in the park-like savannahs of the Sudan. The climate is equatorial in character, being marked by two rainy and two dry seasons, of unequal length, in the course of the year. The population is sparse, numbering in all only some 64,000, so that there is abundance of unreclaimed land, where fresh clearings can be made for cultivation in the forest. Yet, small as is the total population, it comprises a considerable number of different races, which have become partly mixed by inter-breeding. These various races have been carefully studied and described by a French Colonial administrator, M. Tauxier, who has already published at least two similar monographs on tribes of the French Sudan. In the present work he devotes his attention chiefly to the three principal tribes of the region, the Koulangos, the Abrons, and the Dyoulas. After giving an account of the country, its climate, fauna, and flora, he narrates the history of the inhabitants, so far as it can be ascertained ; then describes in detail each of the principal tribes, next passes more summarily in review the smaller tribes, and ends

* *Études Soudanaises.* Le Noir de Bondoukou ; Koulangos, Dyoulas, Abrons, etc. Par L. Tauxier, Administrateur des Colonies. (Paris : Ernest Leroux, 1921.) (*The Times Literary Supplement, October* 12, 1922.)

303

with a series of appendices which include ample vocabularies of the various languages. The book is thus a thorough monograph based on exact personal knowledge of the people. From the rich ethnographical materials collected by the author we may select a few points for notice.

Of the three principal tribes, the Dyoulas, who belong to the well-known and widely spread race of the Mandingos, profess Islam, but the other two, the Koulangos and Abrons, are mostly pagans. In their religion the two great deities are the Earth and the Sky, or, as M. Tauxier prefers to describe it, the Atmosphere ; for he tells us that the celestial deity worshipped by the people is not so much the blue vault, which they believe to be solid, as the clouds, thunder, lightning, and rain, which they personify as a single powerful divinity. But apparently both Earth and Sky are conceived as masculine beings, not as husband and wife. However, on the question of their sex the writer is not explicit. Of the two, the Earth seems to rank as superior, for it is by the Earth rather than by the Sky that the worshippers swear. But sacrifices are offered to both. For example, the Abrons sacrifice a chicken to the Earth when they clear a patch for cultivation in the forest, and they promise the same deity a chicken or a goat if he grants them a good crop. Thus the Earth is naturally enough supposed to be endowed with a fertilizing virtue. But it is also viewed as a moral power, for we are told that this great divinity hates murderers, thieves, sorcerers, and all evil-doers. In the opinion of the Nafanas, one of the minor tribes, any act of unchastity committed in the forest is very offensive to Earth, who manifests his or her displeasure by withholding the rain. The Koulangos often represent this deity in the form of a tree with great spreading roots, at the foot of which they lay a large red block of ferruginous stone. The water-spirits of pools and lakes are also commonly revered by the pagans. Once a year the Nafanas sacrifice an ass to the spirit of a certain pool by drowning the animal in the water.

But besides the personified powers of Nature the spirits of their ancestors are also worshipped by the heathen and receive sacrifices at their hands. For example, when several deaths have taken place one after the other in one of the

large communal households which are characteristic of
Koulango society, the head of the household sacrifices a goat
in the hut of the oldest woman (the huts of the various
families which compose the household being grouped together round one or more courts) ; and before the animal's
throat is cut he prays, saying in substance, " O Ancestors,
I offer you this goat in order that you may not draw away
to you any more people of this house "   In every village
there is an old woman who particularly represents the
ancestors of the village ; and at the Festival of Ancestors,
held in the dry season, the head of the household who is
lucky enough to have this particular old woman in his family
digs a hole in front of her hut and sacrifices a goat over it,
so that the blood runs into the hole, while he prays to the
ancestors to grant offspring, a good crop, plenty, and everything else that the heart of man can desire. For the spirits
of the ancestors are believed to dwell underground, though
sometimes they issue from their subterranean abode and
appear to their descendants in dreams. But they also come
forth to be born again in human form ; for the Koulangos,
like many other Sudanese peoples, believe that new-born
infants are nothing but ancestors come to life again ; and
they identify the particular person thus born again by the
resemblance which the baby bears to him or her. When
two children of a woman have died, and she gives birth to
a third, the newcomer is supposed to be the same child that
died come to life again, and to prevent it from dying a third
time they score the infant with three lines on each side of
its mouth ; though how these marks serve as a life-preserver
is not clear to the ordinary European mind. The Koulangos
also attribute souls to animals, and even to vegetables and
minerals ; in particular, hunters often allege that they are
haunted by the souls of animals which they have killed.
Among the Abrons, at the death of a king or great chief it
used to be customary to sacrifice all his wives and slaves
who did not save themselves by flight ; as many as a hundred
persons were commonly put to death on such occasions.
Moreover, every year, on the anniversary of the late king's
death, his successor was wont to sacrifice a slave, an ox, and
a sheep at the grave. All these human butcheries have been

X

rigorously suppressed since the French occupation of the country.

In regard to the family life of the natives, M. Tauxier remarks that, like the negroes of West Africa in general, they have a more or less pronounced system of communism, which is of the patriarchal type in the regions of the Sudan, but of the matriarchal type in the regions bordering on the Coast. Of this matriarchal type a characteristic feature is the descent of property, not to a man's own children, but to his nephews, the children of his sisters, and in particular to the eldest son of his eldest sister. This, for example, is the rule of succession among the Koulangos. Among them, when the head of a household dies, his own son counts for nothing in the house ; it is the eldest son of the eldest sister of the deceased who succeeds, not only to the dignity and the property of his uncle, but also to his widows, and in the capacity of heir comes and takes up his abode in the house. However, though the dead man's son gets nothing at the death of his father, his turn comes when his maternal uncle goes the way of all flesh ; for then he steps into his uncle's shoes and enters into possession of his uncle's house, goods, and widows. Thus it comes about that there is a perpetual circulation of nephews from house to house when death has removed the head of a family. It is another symptom of matriarchal institutions that among the Koulangos a man has the right to pledge his sisters' sons, but not his own sons, as security for his debts ; and yet another is the custom which permits a woman after marriage to continue to reside with her parents instead of going to live with her husband. In the same tribe cross-cousins (the children of a brother and a sister respectively) are allowed to marry each other, but ortho-cousins (the children of two brothers or of two sisters) are forbidden to do so. This distinction between cousins of different sorts in respect of marriageability is very widespread among the lower races, though it is completely ignored among most of the higher.

While the Koulangos and the Abrons subsist mainly by agriculture and arboriculture, the Dyoulas are, above all, a tribe of traders, and by the adoption of Mohammedanism have risen to a higher religious level than the pagan tribes among

whom they live. Yet they retain not a few marks of a lower
stage of barbarism or savagery which they have left behind
them. Thus, for example, they are divided into clans, at
least ten in number, which appear to have been originally
totemic, if indeed they have even now ceased to be so. The
members of each clan regard as sacred the animals of a
particular species, it may be lions, leopards, pythons, elephants, crocodiles, or hippopotami ; they will not kill and
eat, nor even touch the sacred animals, and they explain the
sanctity of the creatures by saying that their ancestors were
leopards, and so forth, or that they possessed the power of
turning themselves into the animals. Another explanation
which they give is that the souls of their ancestors trans-
migrated at death into the bodies of leopards. Some of the
Koulango clans have a pair of totems apiece ; for example,
one clan has the leopard and the hare for its totems ; another
has a species of serpent and the palm-rat ; a third has the
leopard and the hippopotamus ; and a fourth has the python
and the elephant. In such cases the relation to the second
totem seems commonly to be explained in some other way
—for example, by a service which an animal of the species
rendered to an ancestor of the clan in days of old. Another
possible relic of totemism among the Koulangos consists in
the masked dances that are performed at the Festival of the
New Moon which succeeds the Fast of Ramadan. It is true
that the masks now worn at the dances are more or less
fantastic representations of human faces, but in the Sudan
the dance-masks generally represent animals, such as antelopes, crocodiles, and apes. Masked dances are characteristic
features of the secret societies which existed among the
Dyoulas before their conversion to Islam, and which are still
found among the Huelas, one of the minor tribes of the same
province. The general function of the societies is to protect
the village against sorcery and to detect the sorcerers, or
" eaters-of-souls ", of whom the natives, like almost all
negroes, stand in very great dread. Death is commonly
ascribed by them to the machination of a wizard or witch ;
the corpse, or some portion of it, such as a packet of the hair
and nails, is interrogated to discover the culprit ; and
according to the answer, which is signified by the motions of

the bearers of the body or of the relics, the criminal is arrested and, if he denies his guilt, is subjected to an ordeal of one sort or another, such as drinking a decoction of the poisonous bark of the *Erythrophlaeum guineense*. If the accused succeeds in vomiting the poison, he escapes with his life and without a stain on his character ; but if he succumbs, his guilt is taken to be established beyond the reach of doubt, and his body is thrown away in the forest without receiving the ordinary rites of burial—at least this used to be the custom before the French took over the government of the country.

III

LIFE IN SOUTHERN NIGERIA*

THIS is a very interesting and valuable account of the Ibibio, a negro people inhabiting the district of Eket in Southern Nigeria. The author, Mr. P. Amaury Talbot, already well known to ethnologists by his former volume, *In the Shadow of the Bush*, has made excellent use of his opportunities as District Commissioner to collect a large body of information on the beliefs, customs, and traditions of the people. In spite of the revolting cruelty of some of their religious customs, which appear to be hardly yet completely suppressed under British rule, Mr. Talbot writes with obvious sympathy for the people whom he has been called upon to govern, and this sympathy has given him an insight into their character and ways of thought which otherwise must have remained a sealed book for him. The result is a volume which will not only be welcomed by anthropologists as a contribution to their science, but should serve as a manual for future administrators of the district. Mr. Talbot is deeply convinced that no British official charged with the government of native races can adequately and wisely perform his duty without an understanding of the beliefs and customs of the people who are entrusted to his care.

" I would venture, moreover [he says], to point out here how important to officials is the study of what one of my kind critics lately styled ' the infant science of anthropology '. Without the guidance of such a mistress it is impossible even for the best intentioned to avoid the many pitfalls spread

* *Life in Southern Nigeria : The Magic, Beliefs, and Customs of the Ibibio Tribe.* By P. Amaury Talbot. (London : Macmillan, 1923.) (*The Times Literary Supplement*, April 10, 1924.)

round the feet of the ignorant in a state of affairs so different
from that to which most white men are accustomed. . . .
With every month spent among people such as these, the
importance of anthropological study for all whose lot is cast
among primitive tribes is more and more strongly borne in
upon me."

Fortunately for his readers, Mr. Talbot is no dry-as-dust
chronicler of the facts which he has laboriously collected.   He
is master of a clear, graceful, and graphic style, and succeeds
in conveying a vivid impression of the scenes and the people
among whom he has lived.   The gloomy mangrove swamps,
with their black mud and crocodile-haunted ooze, the winding
creeks and waterways, cumbered with snags and fallen tree-
trunks, the dense and tangled forests, choked and darkened
with the rank luxuriance of tropical vegetation, but lit up
every here and there by a blaze of colour, where flowers of
every imaginable hue and almost unimaginable splendour
refresh the eye and excite the curiosity of the weary and
footsore traveller—all this seems to pass before the reader in
a succession of pictures as varied as they are entrancing.
From the preface we learn that these descriptions of scenery
are due to the author's brave and devoted wife, a lady whose
scientific enthusiasm and energy won the admiration of all
who knew her.   A skilful draughtswoman as well as a keen
ethnologist, she co-operated with her husband in his botanical
labours by recording in a series of beautiful coloured draw-
ings the many plants, including not a few hitherto unknown
genera and species, which together they collected in the
forests and swamps of Nigeria.   She fell a victim to the
deadly climate, but her work lives after her in the produc-
tions of her pen as well as of her pencil, and in the books of
her husband.

In a volume which offers so much of interest it is difficult
to select points for special notice.   The author pays great
attention to what used to be called fetishes, but what are
now usually known by the native name of jujus.   He has
much to tell us of witchcraft, of magical plays, of were-beasts,
and of secret societies.   But among the most interesting
passages of the book are those which throw light on the
Ibibio doctrine of the soul.   In this connexion the author

rightly emphasizes the importance of ancestor worship as one of the chief factors in the life of the people. " The dead and the jujus ", he tells us, " are almost equally revered ; in fact, they are deemed to work together in helping mankind, and the two cults therefore partly coincide." But the spirits of the dead are not always propitiated with prayer and sacrifice ; when they prove troublesome, as they often do, they may be enticed into pots and buried in a deep hole, or swept out of the house with a broom. If a manslayer is haunted, by the ghost of his victim, he will offer him a dog ; and if that sacrifice proves unavailing, he will catch a lizard and hang it on a little gallows, crying out to the ghost, " Here I give you a man instead of me. Take him and leave me free." It might be difficult to find a better illustration of the theory of vicarious atonement. Among the Ibibio, persons who, for one reason or another, have rendered themselves unpleasant in life are buried face downward in the grave to prevent their ghosts from returning to trouble the living ; and with a similar intention the earth is stamped down very hard in the grave, on the principle " *Sit tibi terra gravis* ". The dead bodies of witches and wizards and mothers of twins, who are looked upon with great horror, may not be carried out of the house by the door ; a hole is knocked in the wall to admit of their passage and is afterwards filled up to prevent the return of the ghost ; for, as usual, the feeble-minded ghost knows no way back to the house except that by which he quitted it ; and if that is stopped up, how is he to get in ? The problem is too much for the reduced intelligence of departed spirits. Sometimes very old people are killed from a curious notion that the years which they have added to the normal span of life are subtracted from the life of younger people, who in consequence are cut off in the flower of their age. Again, old women are strictly forbidden to eat food cooked on wood in which any sap is left, lest the sap should pass through the food into their withered limbs and so renew their youth like the eagle's. The people believe that, were an aged crone to break the rule, her ghost would not welcome their ghosts when they came to deadland, but would drive them away with harsh words and force them to dwell, lonely and friendless, among outcast spirits.

As usual, the popular superstitions of civilized Europe have their counterparts in the superstitions of savage Africa ; for after all civilization is only a veneer on the deep-seated savagery of our species.   Thus in Nigeria, as in Europe, sick people creep through a hole in a tree to rid them of their sickness :   in Nigeria, as in Europe down to recent times, people annually drive their cattle, sheep, and goats between two great fires to protect them against evil influences throughout the year ;   and in Nigeria, when a man was wounded the doctor used to cut a stick and wash and tend it, leaving the wound to take care of itself.   This is only one step more absurd than the practice which still prevails in some English counties of anointing the weapon instead of the wound which it inflicted, so little difference is there between the rustic and the savage intelligence.

IV

ON THE TRAIL OF THE BUSHONGO*

THE author of this book, Mr. E. Torday, is well known to anthropologists by the excellent accounts he has published of his travels and researches among various tribes in the basin of the Congo, to our knowledge of which he has added very materially. In the present volume he deals mainly with the Bushongo, or Bakuba, as they are called by their neighbours, a tribe whose home is in the valley of the Sankuru River, one of the southern tributaries of the Congo. His visit to that tribe was paid a good many years ago, and, in conjunction with Mr. T. A. Joyce, of the British Museum, he published a full and valuable account of the people in a Belgian series of ethnographical works. But that somewhat expensive and finely illustrated work, published at Brussels and written in the French language, is probably accessible to comparatively few people in this country, and for the sake of English readers Mr. Torday has done well to compress his description of this interesting people by omitting many details which find an appropriate place in his scientific report, and by lightening it with narratives of his personal experiences and adventures, spiced with humour, and told in a pleasant vein which wins the reader's sympathy and carries him along without fatigue.

Though the Bushongo live surrounded by Bantu tribes, it appears from Mr. Torday's inquiries that they do not belong to that great African family, but are akin to the Azande and have made their way southward from the edge of the Sahara, somewhere in the neighbourhood of Lake Tchad, to

* On the Trail of the Bushongo. By E. Torday. (London: Seeley, Service, 1925.) (The Times Literary Supplement, May 7, 1925.)

their present home in the southern basin of the Congo. They retain some relics of an ancient language which, according to Sir Harry Johnston, is related to languages spoken near Lake Tchad. The people have many traditions concerning one of their kings, called Shamba Bolongongo, whose name is often in their mouths, and who appears to have been a wise, humane, and far-seeing legislator. From the tradition of a total eclipse of the sun which is said to have occurred in the Bushongo country at an interval of three reigns from the time of Shamba, Mr. Torday calculates that the African Solon or Lycurgus reigned somewhere about A.D. 1600.

Like not a few other African monarchs, the King of the Bushongo is not only an absolute monarch, but is deemed entitled to divine honours and is styled " God on Earth." Formerly he was not allowed to set foot on the ground, but the present enlightened and very humane King has relaxed the strictness of the rule. The spirit of the founder of the dynasty, whose name was Bumba, is supposed to have been incarnate in every one of his successors down to and including the reigning monarch.

" It is his spirit that makes the moon wane and increase, that makes the sun shine ; it is his spirit that in shape of rain quenches the thirst of the soil after the months of drought ; it is his spirit that makes the seeds germinate and presides over the reproduction of all that lives. This spirit is incarnate in the Chembe Kunji [' God on Earth '], and Kwete [the King of Bushongo] is Chembe Kunji [' God on Earth '] ; any weakening of his power, every affront to his dignity sends a tremor through all and everything that shares his spirit and pushes it towards the abyss of annihilation."

The tribe has an official historian, who must be the' son of a king, and who takes precedence over all other descendants of Royalty. His duty is to preserve the ancient tribal legends and to hand them down by oral tradition. The town-crier of the capital must always be a twin. The King is assisted by a council which includes representatives of provinces, representatives of trades, and representatives of the fathers of twins. The reason for the special distinction thus conferred on the fathers of twins in a representative body is not manifest to the European mind. Among other odd customs the

Bushongo practise the couvade. When a woman has been delivered of a child, her husband has to go to bed and be nursed ; even before the birth he is obliged to stay at home, and to prevent him from stirring abroad his belt is cut, so that if he walked about, or even stood up, his clothes would fall off. So all he can do is to sit in front of his house and make the best of it. At initiation the youth receive some sound moral instruction, and their courage is tested in various ways, as by being invited or forced to go through a tunnel, in which men disguised in the skins of leopards and monkeys, and others armed with a naked sword and red-hot irons, are stationed in niches at intervals to frighten the candidates as they pass. Another ordeal consists in leaping from a tree, round which arrows are stuck in the ground with the points upwards. Bull-roarers are also sounded to frighten the lads ; their noise is supposed to be the voice of ghosts.

But perhaps the most interesting feature in the life of the Bushongo is their artistic talent, which is especially displayed in wood-carving. In Mr. Torday's opinion, they are the greatest artists of black Africa ; he tells us that as weavers, embroiderers, carvers in wood, and workers of metal they have not their equals in the whole continent, unless for metal work we except the people of Benin, who, however, were taught by Europeans. No boy may be initiated who has not learned how to make their artistic mats, and every scion of the Royal House must become a trained smith. Even the kings of old loved to show their skill in welding iron, and one of them, who lived early in the sixteenth century, is still remembered as a great smith. But the most remarkable products of the native art are the wooden portrait statues of their kings. The oldest and finest is that of the great King and legislator Shamba Bolongongo. Mr. Torday was fortunate enough to procure many specimens of Bushongo art, which are now exhibited in the British Museum.

Mr. Torday also gives us some account of the Baluba, a widespread Bantu people in the southern basin of the Congo. The ordeals undergone by lads at initiation among them resemble those of the Bushongo. The tribe is also the possessor of a Secret Society, the members of which devour the bodies of slaves and malefactors in order to prevent the

ghosts of these wretches from returning to torment the survivors. The remedy is completely effective ; at least, no
authentic case of the return of a ghost appears to be on record
in the tribe.

On his return from the Bushongo the author passed
through the territory of the Bakongo, a tribe not far distant
from the Bushongo and not to be confounded with the much
better known people of the same name in the lower valley of
the Congo. Like most Bantu peoples, these Bakongo worship
their ancestors and offer the first-fruits of the harvest to them.
Like many other Bantu tribes, also, they test accusations of
witchcraft by compelling the suspected witch or wizard to
submit to the poison ordeal ; if he vomits the poison, he is
innocent ; if he dies, he was guilty. In either case, truth is
vindicated and the demands of justice rigorously satisfied.

V

IN WITCH-BOUND AFRICA*

In this work the author, Mr. F. H. Melland, gives us an account of the Bakaonde, a Bantu tribe of Northern Rhodesia, among whom he has resided as District Magistrate for eleven years. Regarding the British people as trustees for the native races which acknowledge their sway in many parts of the world, Mr. Melland deemed it his duty to acquaint himself with the customs and beliefs of the tribe committed to his charge, and the results of his inquiries, or some of them, are embodied in this book ; and students of man will be grateful to Mr. Melland for having written it, though they may wish that he had entered into fuller details on various topics, such as the physical type of the people, their social organization, folk-tales, and arts and crafts. The subjects to which he has paid most attention are religion and witch-craft, and considering the dominating influence which these systems of belief exercise on the life and thought of the natives, he has done well to give them a foremost place in his book.

From his account we gather that the Bakaonde are a typical Bantu tribe, with little to distinguish them from their fellows. They are organized in totemic clans, with the usual rule of exogamy forbidding a man to marry a woman who has the same totem as himself. But among them totemism has clearly fallen into the sere and yellow leaf ; for apparently a man pays no respect to his totem animal, but will kill and

* In Witch-bound Africa : An Account of the Primitive Kaonde Tribe and their Beliefs. By Frank H. Melland. (London : Seeley, Service, 1923.) (The Times Literary Supplement, November 29, 1923.)

eat it freely when he gets the chance ; and though he will
show hospitality to a stranger of his own totem, to knock a
fellow totemite on the head is no more and no less of a
crime than to do the same to anybody else.   Descent is
traced and property descends exclusively in the female line ;
a man's heirs are first his brothers, and next the sons of his
sisters ; his own children inherit nothing from him, since
they belong not to him, but to his wife's family.   Consistently with this rule a man at marriage takes up his abode
with his wife's family and works for her parents, his services
being accepted as payment for his wife, for he does not pay
a regular bride-price for her.   The favourite marriage would
seem to be with a cousin, the daughter of the mother's
brother ; yet marriage with any other cousin (the daughter
of the mother's sister, or of the father's brother, or of the
father's sister) is forbidden and regarded as incest.   This
sharp distinction between different kinds of cousins, favour-
ing marriage with some and absolutely prohibiting marriage
with others, is eminently characteristic of savage society and
probably goes back to a very early stage of social evolution.
In general the savage, contrary to what an untrained
European would expect, is far more scrupulous than his
civilized brother as to the prohibited degrees of kinship,
and often multiplies these obstacles to marriage to an extent
undreamed of among more advanced races.

A very peculiar feature of the Kaonde marriage system
is that girls are generally married and sometimes bear
children, before they have attained to puberty ; but children
born in these circumstances are thrown away, because it is
believed that, were such infants allowed to live, all the elders
in the village would die.   Similarly, in accordance with a
very widespread African custom, all children that cut their
upper incisor teeth before the lower are drowned.   The
reason which the Bakaonde assign for this barbarous custom
is that, if the child lived, every time it cut a milk tooth somebody would die.   Hence a mother who should refrain from
drowning such a child would be deemed constructively
guilty of murdering many people ; and to escape this fearful
imputation she hardens her heart and sacrifices her offspring.
As in many African tribes, a miscarriage at birth is thought

to entail a dangerous pollution on the mother, who has, therefore, to be secluded for a time in a shelter on the out- skirts of the village ; and on her return she and her husband have to tattoo all the people of the village, men, women and children, with small parallel lines between the breasts, as a means of guarding them against the evil that might otherwise befall them in consequence of the miscarriage.

The religion of the Bakaonde, as of other Bantu tribes, is in the main a worship of the spirits of the dead, who rule the living with a rod of iron. The intense conservatism of the people and their dread of innovation have their deepest roots in religion ; for they believe that the souls of the dead insist upon the strict maintenance of ancestral customs and resent any deviation from them. When the Balunda, a kindred tribe and neighbours of the Bakaonde, were shown an improved type of bellows to be used in smithcraft, they admitted the superiority of the new model, but refused to adopt it, because they said the spirits would be angry at the innovation. The spirits of the dead are divided into two classes—the spirits of dead friends and the spirits of dead foes ; the former are naturally friendly and the latter un- friendly ; a man's aim is to secure the help of the one and to avoid exciting the active hostility of the other. In the spirits of dead enemies we may perhaps detect a system of demonology in embryo. The fear of these dangerous beings appears often to act as a powerful and wholesome moral restraint on the people ; for a man will refrain from many acts of injustice against his fellow lest, when the man whom he had wronged dies, his angry ghost should haunt him. On the other hand, Mr. Melland traces the inveterate native habit of lying to the supposed necessity of deceiving the hostile spirits who are all around and within hearing ; for the native believes that, in spite of their power, the spirits can be easily outwitted. There is apparently no notion that the souls of the dead depart to a distant country to receive there the reward of their deeds, whether good or evil ; on the contrary, the dead seem to be conceived as surrounding the living invisibly, waiting to be born again into the world. For all the living are supposed to be reincarnations of the dead ; when a baby is born, divination is resorted to for the purpose of ascertaining whose soul has been reborn in him or her, and the child accordingly takes the name of the deceased relation who is thought to have again appeared in the flesh. Grandparents are often reincarnated in their grandchildren, and uncles and aunts in their nephews and nieces. This belief in reincarnation is, indeed, according to Mr. Melland, the basis of the native religion : " The dead are the real rulers of the country, for the souls of the living come from the dead."

The soul is conceived as a shadow, and a man who desires to live long will sometimes detach his soul from his body and bottle it up in an antelope horn, which he hides somewhere, for example in a hole in the ground, believing that, so long as his shadow-soul is safe in its hiding-place, he cannot die. But should the horn with its precious contents be destroyed, lost, or stolen, the owner of the soul will die within the year. Thus the belief and practice of the Bakaonde conform to a widespread type of folk-tale of which the Norse story of the " Giant who had no heart in his body " is perhaps the best-known instance. Doubtless that tale originated in, and reflects, a corresponding belief and custom. A similar practice of stowing the soul away for safety outside of the body prevails among the Balunda, and had previously been reported among the neighbouring Ila-speaking tribes by Messrs. Smith and Dale.

But the belief in the spirits of the dead, though the most important, is not the only element in the religion of the Bakaonde. According to them, the Supreme Being, whom they call Lesa, created the first man and woman and now lives in the sky, where He manifests His power in thunder, lightning, rain, and the rainbow. Some of them hold that Lesa is married, and that His wife lives underground, where she causes the earth tremors which are common in this part of Africa. In time of drought the Bakaonde pray to Lesa for rain, sitting in a circle round a tall white pole erected for the purpose on the outskirts of the village. This is the only occasion on which prayers are offered to Lesa. There are no professional rain-makers in the tribe, nor do the chiefs claim to possess power over the waters of heaven.

VI

PYGMIES AND BUSHMEN*

THE title of this book is apt to be misleading, for there are
no pygmies in the strict sense of the word in the Kalahari
desert or in any other part of South Africa. But the Bushmen, who form an important element of the population, are
believed by the author to be closely related to, and indeed substantially identical with, the true pygmies of the Ituri forest
in Central Africa, and on this ground the introduction of
the term pygmies into the title of the book may be justified,
though as it stands it suggests rather the distinction than the
identity of the two peoples.

The Kalahari desert is part of the great arid plateau of
South Africa, which, beginning well to the south of the
Orange River, extends as far north as the Zambezi. The
general characteristics of this vast area are shared by the
Kalahari. It is an arid country, scored by the dry beds of
former rivers ; for, like other portions of the globe, such as
Central Asia and Australia, South Africa would seem to be
undergoing a process of gradual desiccation. At the present
time the rivers of the Kalahari have seldom any running
water even in the wet season ; their beds contain only a
succession of pools ; along their banks stretch great flats of
mud and sand which the rains convert into salt pans of
shallow water. The drainage of the rivers is into Lake
Ngami, which, at the date of its discovery by Livingstone in
1849, appears to have been much more extensive than at
present ; it is now nothing more than an immense reedy

* *Pygmies and Bushmen of the Kalahari.* By S. S. Dornan. (London:
Seeley, Service, 1925.) (*The Times Literary Supplement,* January 15,
1925.)

marsh, with patches of open water here and there. A great portion of the country is covered by sand dunes rising in regular succession like waves of the sea, their crests rippled by the wind and their troughs filled, on the leeward side, with deep sand in which the traveller sinks half up to the knees. Yet the wilderness is not without vegetation. Along the river beds are dense, almost impenetrable, thickets of acacias, the haunts of wild beasts. In places there are large forest trees ; and the great level plains, especially in the south, are covered with tall grasses, so as to give the country the appearance of a vast cornfield. It is especially after the bursting of the rains in October or November that a marvellous transformation of the landscape takes place and the desert blooms with an exuberance of verdure which a short time before might have seemed impossible. The heat in the long summer months is excessive, almost unbearable ; the frequent whirlwinds, laden with fine sand and dust, are like the breath of an oven ; the traveller caught in them feels half smothered in the storm. As might be expected in a country so vast and so thinly peopled, wild animals abound ; indeed, the Kalahari is still a sportsman's paradise, though year by year the quantity of game is lessened, and its ultimate extinction is only a question of time.

Of this interesting but not altogether attractive country Mr. Dornan gives a clear and graphic account as an introduction to his book, the bulk of which is occupied by a description of the native inhabitants. These belong to three different races, the Bushmen, the Hottentots, and the Bantus. The greater part of the work is devoted to the Bushmen, and for this the ethnologist may be thankful, as the Bushmen are amongst the most primitive races of men, and full and trustworthy accounts of them have hitherto been lacking. The present book should go some way to fill a large gap in the literature of ethnology, for Mr. Dornan appears to be intimately acquainted with the people and their language, though he omits to tell us how long and in what capacity he has lived among them. He regards the Bushmen and Hottentots as belonging to the same stock and their language as originally one, though in course of time it has developed into two distinct forms, in consequence partly of the local separation of the two peoples and partly of the divergence of their habits ; for, while the Bushmen have always remained hunters pure and simple, the Hottentots have acquired cattle and adopted the pastoral mode of life. Mr. Dornan supposes with some probability that the Bushman-Hottentot race represents the aboriginal inhabitants of the whole of Africa from the great lakes southward, and that their ancestors were gradually driven, by the pressure of the Bantu tribes, from the equatorial regions into the restricted area which they now occupy towards the southern extremity of the continent. The Bushmen are known to have been formerly much more numerous to the south of the Orange River ; but the great bulk of the survivors have now found a refuge in the Kalahari desert, though there can be little doubt that their race is doomed to extinction at no very distant period. Some of them have accepted the position of menial or servile herdsmen to Bechuana masters ; but for the most part they continue to roam the wilderness in pursuit of game, seemingly incapable of accommodating themselves to the routine of a pastoral or agricultural existence.

In respect of their culture Mr. Dornan inclines to the view that they correspond to the Aurignacians of the Palaeolithic Age in Western Europe. According to him, the rock paintings and engravings of the two peoples resemble each other so closely that they would be indistinguishable if it were not for the differences in the fauna depicted. The scenes represented are usually incidents of the chase, more rarely of war and domestic life. As usual, the figures of wild animals are well executed, but the human figures much less so. These paintings and sculptures are not confined to the Kalahari desert, they are found all over South Africa ; some of the best occur in Southern Rhodesia. Archaeologists are now inclined to explain the cave paintings of prehistoric man as based in large measure on the principles of sympathetic magic ; they suppose that by depicting himself in the act of killing game or dispatching his foes the primitive hunter and warrior hoped to ensure corresponding success in the chase and in war. Mr. Dornan questioned the Bushmen as to this interpretation of their paintings, but he could elicit from them no confirmation of the theory. But he is careful to add that this negative result of his inquiries cannot be regarded as decisive evidence against the views in question, since the Bushmen are usually unwilling to give any information about the pictures.

There is little or no tribal organization among the Bushmen. They are, or were, divided into totemic clans, and in former times the nearest clans or families would combine to resist a common foe, but as soon as the danger was over the alliance was dissolved. The totemism of the Bushmen would also seem to have been of an elementary sort, though apparently they generally complied with the two fundamental principles of the system in refusing to marry a woman of their own totemic clan and in abstaining from eating their totem animal except in cases of extreme hunger. This abstinence is all the more remarkable because otherwise the Bushmen are omnivorous and voracious : no animal, bird, insect, or plant comes amiss to them. Thus the Bushmen stand at a much lower social level than the Australian aborigines, who have developed elaborate systems of totemism and of tribal organization. Like most African races, the Bushmen have a story of the Origin of Death, which conforms to the common type of the Two Messengers. In this case the messengers are the tortoise and the hare, both of which the Moon dispatched to men with tidings that after death they would come to life again like the new moon after an interval of absence and darkness. But the glad tidings were perverted by the haste or carelessness of the hare, and death has consequently been irreparable ever since.

Of the Hottentots our author has not much to say, and his notice of their customs is to some extent borrowed from the racy description of the old Dutch writer Kolben, who wrote some two centuries ago. Of the Bechuanas, a Bantu tribe who give their name to Bechuanaland, in which the Kalahari desert is situated, Mr. Dornan has a good deal more to tell us from personal observation. They are divided into totemic clans, and some of the clans take their names from their totems. Thus the Bakwena take their name from their totem, the crocodile (*bakuena*) ; the Baphuti take their name from their totem, the duiker (*phuti*). Another clan has for its totem the baboon (*tsuene*) ; hence the people are sometimes called the Batsuene. Among the other totems are the elephant, the lion, the wild cat, the hyena, the wild vine, the sun, the rain, and iron. Mr. Dornan discusses, but rejects, the view of the late Dr. Theal, that Bantu totemism is a form of ancestor worship, the souls of the dead being supposed to be incarnate in the totemic animals.

A valuable chapter is devoted by Mr. Dornan to an account of witch-doctors among the Bechuanas. Like many savages, the Bechuanas disbelieve in death from natural causes, and imagine that nobody would die if he were not killed by witchcraft. Therefore after the death of any important man it was deemed necessary to discover the guilty witch and to execute him or her. Hence a considerable part of the population, some say as many as thirty per cent, used to suffer death on accusations of witchcraft. It was the business of the witch-doctor to detect and bring to condign punishment these imaginary miscreants. Of course the British Government lends no countenance to this devastating superstition, and one enlightened Bechuana chief, by name Khama, had the courage and energy to forbid and suppress the profession of witch-doctor in his country. But besides detecting witches, the witch-doctor had many other functions to discharge, such as healing the sick, procuring rain, averting hail, and casting enchantments over armies and parties of hunters in order to achieve success in war and the chase. To ensure that an army would be invisible to the foe, they took a black ox, sewed up its eyelids, then killed it, and gave its flesh to the soldiers to eat. By partaking of an animal whose eyes had been sewed up the warriors would effectually blind the enemy to their movements. But of all the duties incumbent on the witch-doctors none perhaps was more important in the dry and thirsty land than that of rain-making. There were regular guilds of rain-makers, and in the old days the chief was the great rain-maker of the tribe ; indeed, in Mr. Dornan's opinion, there is little doubt that the office of chief was evolved out of the office of rain-maker. A man who was successful in this line of business was likely to become not only wealthy and powerful, but eventually a chief. One way in which the rain-maker sought to draw showers from the sky was by anointing his body with the gall of a black sheep mixed with other ingredients. By thus blackening his body he imagined, on the principles of sympathetic magic, that he blackened the clouds and compelled them to rain.

Like the Bushmen, the Bechuanas have a story of the Origin of Death, modelled on the ordinary pattern of the Two Messengers. In this Bechuana version of the far-spread tale the messengers are a lizard and a chameleon, which are the regular messengers in what we may call the orthodox African version of the myth. We have said enough to indicate our opinion that in this volume Mr. Dornan has made a useful addition to the ethnological literature of South Africa, especially to the portion of it concerned with the Bushmen.

VII

THE MACKIE EXPEDITION TO CENTRAL AFRICA—THE BAKITARA OR BANYORO*

THE author of this book, the Rev. John Roscoe, is well known to anthropologists as one of our best authorities on the tribes of the Uganda Protectorate, to which he devoted close attention during his residence of many years among them. Since the Great War he has been enabled, through the enlightened munificence of Sir Peter Mackie and under the auspices of the Royal Society, to make an expedition to Central Africa for the purpose of investigating a number of tribes about which it was desirable to obtain fuller and more accurate information. The enterprise was successfully accomplished, and in this volume we have the first part of the scientific report of the results obtained by the expedition. It deals exclusively with the important tribe, or rather nation, of the Bakitara, more commonly known as the Banyoro, among whom the author spent several months, collecting information as to the customs and beliefs of the people. In this inquiry he enjoyed the great advantage of the co-operation of the native King of Kitara (Bunyoro), who personally interested himself in the investigation and supplied Mr. Roscoe with ample means of prosecuting his researches. Through his knowledge of the native dialects the author was able to obtain the whole of his information without the use of an English interpreter ; hence the record which he has given us comes directly from native sources, uninfluenced by contact with the European mind. As such it possesses a

---

* *The Bakitara or Banyoro : The First Part of the Report of the Mackie Ethnological Expedition to Central Africa.* By John Roscoe. (Cambridge : at The University Press, 1923.) (*The Times Literary Supplement*, May 24, 1923.)

high degree of scientific value, all the more so because many of the customs and beliefs which it describes are passing away under European influence, and will probably before long have vanished more or less completely.

The country of Kitara (generally known as Bunyoro) was at one time the largest and most powerful of all the autocratic kingdoms in the lake region of Central Africa ; but three or four generations ago the kingdom began to diminish in size and power, chiefly through the encroachments of its great enemies, the Baganda. In the heyday of their prosperity the kings of Kitara may have ruled over some two millions of people, though at present the population of their shrunken territory numbers little over one hundred thousand. The population is composed of two entirely different racial elements —to wit, an aboriginal negro people, called Bahero, who cultivate the soil, and a pastoral people of the Hamitic stock, who at some early time invaded the country and conquered the negro aborigines, whom they still dominate and treat as serfs. These Hamitic invaders, who are known as Bahuma, would seem to have entered the country from the north-east and to be an offshoot from the Gallas. To this day they remain a tribe of nomadic herdsmen, devotedly attached to their cattle and looking down on the agricultural tribes as their natural inferiors. For long the two races kept entirely distinct, the invaders forbidding all intermarriage with the conquered aborigines ; but the rule is now to a certain extent relaxed, wealthy peasants being sometimes allowed to marry daughters of poor herdsmen. The effect of these mixed marriages shows itself in a certain blending of the two racial types in some members of the nation, as well as in a mixture of customs. Thus, for example, the pastoral people of old confined themselves to a diet of milk and flesh, strictly abstaining from vegetable food, because they believed that, were they to partake of such food, it would injure the cows through sympathetic magic. However, nowadays the severity of this regimen is less rigidly observed, and a vegetable diet has been to a certain extent introduced among the pastoral people. On the other hand, the agricultural people for many generations were not expected to keep cows, and they were liable to be plundered if they did so, but in later times this restriction has been set aside, and the peasants may now acquire cows like their lords and masters.

Both peoples, the pastoral and the agricultural, are divided into a large number of totemic clans, which are exogamous—that is, no man is allowed to marry a woman of his own clan. In general they can give no account of the origin of their totemic system, which is marked by some peculiar features. Thus, many clans possess the same totem ; for example, the bush-buck, which is the totem of the royal clan, is also the totem of many clans which are not royal. In such cases, it is obvious that the totem has ceased to be the touchstone of exogamy, since apparently a man is free to marry a woman of the same totem, provided that she is of a different clan. Another remarkable feature of Bakitara totemism is that some of the pastoral clans have what we may call temporary totems : for example, when a cow has drunk salt water, she is a totem to a certain clan during that day, and her milk may not be drunk by any member of that clan, but the next day she ceases to be a totem, and members of the clan may freely drink her milk. Similarly, a cow which has mated with a bull is for five days a totem to certain clans, who may not drink her milk nor eat her flesh during that period, but who may do so without scruple after the five days have elapsed.

At the head of the nation is the King, who in the old days was an absolute monarch and ranked, in the opinion of his people, almost as a god. Yet, whenever he fell seriously ill or was wounded in battle, he was formerly obliged to take poison and die ; he might not continue in office after he had ceased to be able to discharge his important duties. When, for lesser ailments, he was cupped or blistered, all his numerous wives had to submit to be cupped or blistered in the same manner and on the same part of the body. On the death of the King two of his widows used to be buried with him in the grave. And every year, about the time when the last King had died, a poor man of a certain clan was appointed to im-personate the deceased monarch ; in that character he lived in regal state at the King's tomb for eight days, and was called by the name of the monarch he represented, for he was said to be the old King come to life again. During his brief reign he used as his wives the widows of the dead King, distributed gifts of cows from the royal herds, and sent his blessing to the reigning King, the country, and the cattle. But on the ninth day he was taken away to the back of the tomb and strangled. This was an annual ceremony. It presents a striking analogy to the custom of the temporary King who, at the annual festival of the Sacaea in Babylon, enjoyed similar privileges and was similarly put to death after a reign of a few days.

A remarkable feature in the social system of the Kitara is what we may call the sexual communism which prevails, or used to prevail, between members of the same clan ; a man's wife was common to him with all the other members of his clan, any of whom might have intercourse with her. " No husband ", we are told, " would think of making any complaint on the subject, and no one would think of blaming a woman for allowing her husband's clan-brothers to share her bed any more than for allowing her husband to do so. No Judge would condemn such a woman for adultery, for the act was perfectly legal." In the controversy over the question of a primitive sexual communism this case of the Bakitara deserves to be considered. On the other hand, while the sexual relations of the married women among the Bakitara were, from our point of view, very loose, the conduct of unmarried women was comparatively strict, and, as a rule, a girl was pure at marriage. A girl who had a child by an unknown father used to be banished from the kraal, because it was believed that her presence would bring ill-luck to her home ; the children would die, or the cows cast their calves.

In the religion of the people the elaborate ceremonies observed at the new moon occupied a conspicuous place. They lasted for nine days, during which dancing and rejoicing went on in the royal enclosure, and the royal bands had to play night and day continuously except for a short rest between 6 and 7 o'clock in the morning, when they snatched a little sleep. No sooner was the appearance of the new moon announced by the watch set for the purpose than a man was taken away secretly and killed and his blood used to smear the royal fetishes. Again, in the religion of the Bakitara, as of most African tribes, the fear of the dead played a large part. But as a rule it was only the ghosts of rich or powerful men who were dreaded ; hence no special attention was paid to the burial of poor men, for their ghosts would not be powerful and, therefore, inspired no terror. So, too, when a woman died " no attention was paid to the ghost, for a woman had no property, and her ghost was not dangerous ". However, a woman who had been wrongfully accused of adultery might take her revenge after death, for sometimes she would hang herself, and then her ghost would be a malignant influence ; hence, to disarm or destroy the unquiet spirit, or at all events to confine it within narrow bounds, it was customary to bury the body near the place of death, and to cut down and burn the fatal tree from which the poor wretch had hung. On the other hand, when a man of property died his heir had to build him a shrine in the house near his own bed ; and he generally dedicated to him some cows, whose milk was daily offered at the shrine, that being the place where the ghost came to visit his family and to take his meal. If a ghost were displeased at anything, he was supposed to manifest his displeasure by causing illness or death among the people or the cattle. When the ghost of a deceased relative was believed to be causing sickness by taking possession of a man or woman, a medicine-man would sometimes induce the ghost to quit the body of the sufferer and enter into a goat. After that the animal, thus tenanted by a family spirit, was sacred ; it lived in the house and was treated with respect, and should it die the owner must at once replace it with another. If it had kids, they were regarded as belonging to the ghost, and the owner must ask the ghost's permission before he could use the animals for any purpose. When illness was caused, as it often was, not by a ghost but by magic, a goat might still be used to cure it ; but in this case the animal was employed as a scapegoat in the strict sense of the word. The medicine man rubbed a bunch of herbs over the patient, then tied them to the neck of the goat and drove the animal away into the wilds. Sometimes in the wilderness the legs of the goat were broken and it was left to die and be devoured by wild beasts.

Iron is found in the country, and the natives have been in the habit of extracting and smelting it from time immemorial. It is even possible, as the author seems to imply, that Kitara was one of the centres from which in prehistoric times a knowledge of iron spread throughout the world. In this book the writer has given a full account of the primitive methods employed by the Bakitara in mining, smelting, and working the metal. A curious custom was observed when the block of stone which was to serve a smith as an anvil was brought from the quarry to the house. It was called a bride and was treated as such by the smith and his wife. It was veiled as a bride and brought in with singing and dancing as in a marriage procession ; the husband told his wife that he had brought a second wife home to help her in the house and with the family, and he sprinkled the stone with grain and water that it might bear many children.

VIII

THE MACKIE EXPEDITION TO CENTRAL AFRICA—THE BANYANKOLE*

UNDER this title Canon Roscoe publishes the second part of the report on the ethnological expedition to Central Africa which, through the munificence of Sir Peter Mackie, he was enabled to carry out in the years 1919 and 1920 under the auspices of the Royal Society. The first part of the report, dealing with the Bakitara or Banyoro, has been already reviewed in these pages. In the present part the author deals with a different tribe, the Banyankole or Bahuma, whose country is situated in the south-western part of the Uganda Protectorate. Like the ruling class of the Bakitara, to whom they are akin, the Bahuma are a pastoral tribe who have at some time, probably not very remote, invaded the country and conquered the agricultural aborigines. But the conquerors were not a fierce, bloodthirsty race ; their rule was mild ; they allowed the aboriginal inhabitants to retain their lands and to pursue their customary mode of life. Accordingly in Ankole, as in Bunyoro, we have the interesting and instructive case of two distinct races, the one pastoral and the other agricultural, existing side by side in the same country, each preserving its ancient institutions hardly modified by those of the other. Thus, in the tribes admirably described by Canon Roscoe in this and the preceding volume, we have ample materials for the study of that cultural contact of races which at present has attracted much attention

* *The Banyankole: The Second Part of the Report of the Mackie Ethnological Expedition to Central Africa.* By John Roscoe. (Cambridge : at The University Press, 1923.) (*The Times Literary Supplement*, April 3, 1924.)

among ethnologists. One result of the author's investigations is to prove that two different races may exist side by side in the same country for considerable periods without modifying very materially their respective cultures. The pastoral conquerors are devoted to the care of their herds, on which all their interest is concentrated; they set no value on land, except so far as it serves to pasture their cattle, and they despise the agricultural people and treat them as serfs. But these conquered aborigines are not slaves, for they are free to move about the country at will, to cultivate new land, and to serve new masters. Of this freedom, however, they make little use; generally they are attached to certain districts, which they seldom care to leave.

The pastoral people, the Bahuma, are divided into totemic clans with the usual rule of exogamy, which forbids a man to marry a woman of the same clan as himself. But among these Bahuma the rule is subject to large exceptions, for the three principal clans are subdivided into many sections, each with its own secondary totem, and a man of any one of these three great clans may marry a woman of his own clan, provided that she belongs to a different section and has a different secondary totem.

The government of the country is monarchical, and the King's power in the old days was absolute. Yet no King ever allowed himself to grow old; he had to put an end to his life by poison before his powers, whether physical or mental, began to deteriorate. Even the appearance of old age must be avoided; to prevent his hair from growing grey a magical mixture was smeared on his head in the darkest hour of the night before the new moon appeared. At his death the King's soul was believed to pass into a lion. The King's mother always held an important position in the kingdom; but when she fell seriously ill she also, like the King, had to drink poison and die. At her death she was thought to be transformed into a leopard. The early Kings of the dynasty were deified; they had no temples, but there were certain men and women who claimed to be their mediums, and thereby professed to heal sickness and to help the people. In the King's kraal there was a place devoted to the shrines of past rulers, and there offerings were made and milk from dedicated cows was placed daily. For the main element in the religion of the Banyankole, as of many African tribes, was the worship of the dead. All classes of the people, from the King downward, had shrines for the family ghosts, and dedicated cows to them. The milk from these cows was placed daily on a special stand for the ghost, and after he had partaken of the essence of the milk the gross material substance was drunk by the owner of the house and his children. The ghost might also intimate his wish to eat meat, whereupon a fat cow or bull was killed, and its flesh eaten by the worshippers near the shrine, the ghost having presumably to content himself with the essence of beef. The shrine of a ghost stood regularly at the gate of the kraal. As many as forty such shrines might sometimes be seen at the gate of a single kraal. Many illnesses were attributed to the anger of ghosts, who were very touchy and apt to deem themselves defrauded of their dues ; or their displeasure might be roused by some breach of the traditionary laws—for example, by a marriage within the forbidden degrees. When it had been ascertained by divination that a sickness was caused by a ghost who had taken possession of the patient, efforts were made to expel the ghost from the body of the sufferer by massage, by administering bitter medicines to him, and by scratching him and rubbing a powder into the scratches till he writhed with pain. Driven out by these forcible measures, the ghost was caught in a pot, and either drowned or burned. Sometimes the ghost which infested a sick man was transferred to a goat and ultimately to a fowl, which was buried alive in the gateway to prevent the ghost from returning.

A very peculiar feature of the religion was the worship of certain royal drums, or rather of the spirits which were supposed to animate the drums. A sacred herd of cows yielded a supply of milk, which was daily offered in pots to the drums ; when the spirits of the drums had partaken of the essence of the milk, the remainder was drunk by the guardians of the drums. A woman, who looked after the milk, was called the Wife of the Drums, and a fire had always to be kept burning in the drum-house, because the drum-spirits required warmth. When the guardian of the drums declared that they were hungry, a cow was killed and its blood smeared on the drums. And when it was necessary to cover the drums with new skins a fat boy was killed and his blood, mixed with the blood of a cow and with ashes, was applied to the drums. In sacrificing a cow to the drums the guardian prayed to them for the health and prosperity of the King. The worship of these royal drums was all the more remarkable because they were the only drums in the country; for, unlike most African tribes, the Bahuma did not constantly use drums as musical instruments, but elicited their music from a primitive harp, shaped like a tortoiseshell, which was played by women.

Like the ancient Greeks and Romans, the Banyankole made much use in ritual of boys whose parents were both alive. For example, a boy whose parents were alive and well slept with the bride and bridegroom at marriage for a few nights " to ensure that the bride would bear healthy children ". Similarly, as we learn from some verses of Callimachus discovered in Egypt not many years ago, ancient Greek ritual ordained that before marriage the bride should sleep with a boy whose parents were both alive. The poet omits to mention the reason of the custom, or rather he was about to assign a mythical one for it in the conduct of the goddess Hera, but he refrained for fear of impiety. The true original motive of the custom—namely, the desire to procure healthy offspring by means of sympathetic magic—is assigned by the Banyankole. It is thus that modern Central Africa can throw light on ancient Greece.

IX

THE MACKIE EXPEDITION TO CENTRAL AFRICA—THE BAGESU AND OTHER TRIBES OF THE UGANDA PROTECTORATE*

THIS volume forms the third part of the Report on the Mackie Ethnological Expedition to Central Africa. The two former parts of the report have already been noticed in these pages. Whereas the first two volumes dealt in detail each with a single tribe, this third and last volume treats more summarily of several tribes which the writer encountered in his expedition, but to which he was unable to devote so much time as to the others. Yet in spite of the comparative brevity of his stay in most of these tribes, Canon Roscoe has collected a large amount of very valuable information concerning their customs and beliefs; and if the book loses somewhat in detailed investigation, it gains in the extent of ground covered and the variety of interest raised by the many different tribes passed in review. Taken together with his previous writings, particularly *The Baganda* and *The Northern Bantu*, the three volumes of the Report on the Mackie Expedition constitute by far the fullest and most accurate record which we possess of the tribes of the Uganda Protectorate, and they will probably always remain the standard authority on the subject.

The tribes described in the present volume belong for

---

* *The Bagesu and other Tribes of the Uganda Protectorate : The Third Part of the Report of the Mackie Ethnological Expedition to Central Africa.* By John Roscoe. (Cambridge : at The University Press, 1924.) (*The Times Literary Supplement*, June 19, 1924.)

the most part to the Bantu race, and depend for their sub-
sistence mainly on agriculture, thus contrasting with the
tribes of Hamitic origin and pastoral pursuits who formed
the principal theme of the author's first two volumes. The
Bagesu, who give their name to the volume, are one of the
most primitive of the negro tribes of Africa. They occupy
the well-watered slopes of the lofty Mount Elgon, to which
they were driven by the attacks of their enemies in the
plains below. They are divided into many clans and sub-
divisions of clans, each occupying its own territory. Constant hostility used to prevail between the clans, so that it
was unsafe even for an armed man to wander alone into
the territory of another division. Yet the clans were exogamous ; in other words, every man was forbidden to marry
a woman of his own clan and consequently obliged to seek
his wife among the women of another and almost always
hostile clan. This was not so difficult as might at first
appear, for every year, after harvest, there was observed a
truce, during which the people went about in safety from
village to village. At such times the members of the various
clans met together in the villages to dance, to drink themselves drunk on millet beer, and to indulge in sexual orgies
in which all regard to marriage relationship was thrown aside.
These saturnalia were the more remarkable because at other
times the women were strictly chaste and the men guarded
their wives with jealous care. It was at these harvest festivals that marriages were usually arranged.

The Bagesu are, or used to be, cannibals. They did not
bury their dead, but carried them out to waste land. Then,
when darkness had fallen, elderly women went out, cut up
the bodies, and carried back the flesh to be eaten by the
relatives, leaving the mangled remains of the corpses to be
devoured by wild beasts. The reason they gave for not
burying their dead was that if they allowed the body to
decay the ghost would haunt the place of death and cause
illness in the family. Among the Bagesu all males are
obliged to undergo the rite of circumcision, or rather an
operation much more radical and severe than ordinary
circumcision, before they are considered fit to marry and to
take part in the councils of the men. The Bagesu appear

to be without totemism, but most of the other tribes described
by the writer are divided into clans which are both exogamous
and totemic.   Canon Roscoe omits to say whether descent
of the clans is reckoned in the paternal or in the maternal
line ; but from his silence we may perhaps infer that children
belong to the clan of their father rather than to that of their
mother.   The inference is all the more probable because in
most of the tribes the principal heir is the eldest son, who
usually inherits his father's widows as well as his property,
which he could not do under a system of exogamy with
maternal descent of the clan, since in that case he would
belong to the same clan as the widows, and therefore could
not marry them.

The birth of twins is the occasion of many curious
ceremonies and regulations among several of the tribes.
Contrary to the customs which prevail in West Africa, where
the birth of twins is commonly regarded as a monstrosity
only to be expiated by the death, or at least the banishment,
of both mother and twins, the advent of twins in these Central
African tribes appears to be hailed as a happy occurrence
which may prove a source of blessing not only to the parents
but to people in general, and even to cattle and the crops.
Hence, in Busoga, the parents of twins go about the country
for weeks, dancing and paying visits, and are everywhere
welcomed on account of the prosperity which they are
believed to diffuse around them.   The Basabei imagine that,
if the mother of twins did not sprinkle beer with a cow's tail
in the direction of the herds and the rivers, the cows would
cast their calves, and the rivers would dry up.

Some of the tribes believe in a Creator god ; but except
in Busoga, where he had many shrines, at which people
prayed and sacrificed, he seems to have been seldom appealed
to for help in ordinary life.   The practical religion of these
tribes, like that of most African tribes, consists mainly in the
propitiation of the spirits of the human dead, especially the
ghosts of departed relatives.   Not that ghosts are supposed
to be always kindly and helpful.   Far from it.   Illness, at
least serious illness, is commonly attributed to the agency of
ghosts, whose anger has been excited by some misdeed or
negligence either of the sufferer or of his friends.   Accordingly

a medicine-man is called in and an offering is presented to the offended spirit as an inducement to allow the patient to recover. In this respect the Bambwa draw a sharp distinction between the ghosts of a man's own family and the ghosts of his foes. If the sage decides that the sickness is caused by a ghost of the patient's own family, the perturbed spirit is appeased by the sacrifice of a goat, whose blood is poured out at the shrine of the ghost. But if, on the other hand, the doctor pronounces that the ghost of an enemy has taken possession of the sick man, stronger measures have to be resorted to for the purpose of ejecting him from his temporary domicile. Accordingly the unfortunate sufferer is scarified all over his body, and a pungent powder is rubbed into the wounds to make them smart, by way of making things unpleasant for the ghost. As if this were not enough, the sufferer is transported to a small temporary hut which is thereupon set on fire, and the sufferer is snatched from the flames like a brand from the burning. This is the last stroke at the ghost. The fire has proved too much for him ; he has now quitted the body of the sufferer, and a dish of savoury meat is offered to him with a prayer that he will be pleased to molest the patient no more.

The same dread of ghosts influences the life of these people in many ways. If they avenge the murder of a kinsman by killing the murderer, it is because they fear the ghost of the victim, who might punish their heartless neglect by sickness or death ; if the Bakyiga strictly guard the chastity of maidens before marriage and banish from the clan all girls who have lost their virginity, it is still because they dread the anger of the ancestral ghosts at the crime of fornication. The man who has slain a foe in battle is honoured for the deed, but for a time he has to be severely secluded and to undergo a ceremony of purification in order to rid him of his victim's ghost, who would otherwise follow him into his house and do him a mischief. In Busoga mourners have to be very abstemious in diet and to subject themselves to various other restrictions for a period varying from four days to three months after the death ; all this time the ghost is supposed to keep watch on them from a tree and to visit an infraction of the rules with dire consequences. Hence any mourner guilty of a breach of propriety is fined, and the others flee the place in terror lest the ghost should overtake them and wreak his vengeance on their devoted heads. Yet, on the other hand, ghosts, if respectfully treated, can be helpful. A child is usually named after some dead relative or ancestor, whose ghost thereupon becomes the guardian spirit of the infant. In time of drought, again, the Basoga sacrifice a bull to the ghosts, and these powerful spirits are believed to send the needed rain in return for the delicate attention.

In this, as in the former volumes, Canon Roscoe wisely confines himself to describing in clear and simple language the results of his personal observations and inquiries, without attempting either to co-ordinate these results with those of other observers or to institute comparisons with the customs and beliefs of other tribes in Africa or elsewhere. For this prudent abstention the anthropologist at home can hardly be too grateful to him. In anthropology the work of description should always be kept strictly apart from the work of comparison ; and while description is the function of the worker in the field, the task of comparison should be reserved for students at home, who in their libraries alone possess the means of profitably comparing the institutions, customs, laws, and religions of the various races of man.

X

THE LANGO*

THE author of this book, Mr. J. H. Driberg, lived as an administrator for about seven years among the people whom he describes, and his book is the fruit of long and patient observation and inquiry. It is marked throughout by the true scientific spirit, and will unquestionably rank among the very best monographs which we possess on African tribes. The writer has wisely confined himself to recording the results of his personal observations, and has abstained alike from speculating on the origin and meaning of the institutions which he describes and from instituting far-reaching comparisons between them and those of other peoples in distant parts of the earth. Within these self-imposed limits Mr. Driberg has given us an excellent and very complete account of a tribe about which hitherto very little had been known. The account comprises the history of the tribe, so far as it can be ascertained, its natural environment, physical and mental characteristics, mode of life, social organization, and system of religion and magic. The ethnographical part of the book is followed by a linguistic part, which embraces a detailed grammar and full vocabularies, both Lango-English and English-Lango, concluding with twelve fables in the Lango language with parallel English translation.

The Lango belong to the group of tribes which from its habitat in the valley of the Nile is commonly described as Nilotic, and of which the Shilluk are probably the best-known members. They number some quarter of a million, and now

* *The Lango : A Nilotic Tribe of Uganda.* By J. H. Driberg. With a Foreword by Sir Robert Thorne Coryndon. (London : Fisher Unwin, 1923.) (*The Times Literary Supplement*, August 9, 1923.)

occupy an extensive territory of Uganda on the upper waters of the Nile ; but it appears that their original home lay at a considerable distance to the north-east, and that they have been gradually driven southward under pressure partly of Hamitic tribes and partly of drought and famine. Their present country is a savannah-like flat, intersected by in-numerable swamps and marshy rivers, whose sluggish current is almost blocked by dense vegetation. It is covered for the most part with coarse spear-grass some eight or ten feet high. Woods are scarce, though here and there a grove breaks the monotony of the scenery, and in one part of the country the gullies are fringed with magnificent trees draped with convolvulaceae and lianae. It is remarkable that the Lango make little use of the waterways which abound in their country and offer easy means of communication between the villages. They possess but few canoes, and these of poor construction, and they are unskilful watermen.

The Lango are physically a handsome race. They are well-built and tall, the men averaging as much as 5 ft. 11 in. Their complexion is dark, but their lips are much thinner and their noses better formed than those of the true negroes. They are strong and capable of great endurance ; in contrast with the practice of the Bantu tribes, the men do all the hard work of cultivation, for they till the ground as well as keep cattle. They knock out the two central incisors of their children at the age of about thirteen, believing that if the teeth were not thus removed the children would not grow up. Men and women ornament, or disfigure, their bodies with raised scars cut in the flesh. The patterns thus formed vary with the taste of the individual, and have no special meaning. But a man who has killed an enemy cuts rows of scars on his shoulder and upper arm, not so much as a badge of his prowess as (so we are told) for the purpose of appeasing the spirit of the slain foe by the emission of some of the slayer's blood ; and Mr. Driberg thinks it probable that " all cicatrisation should be traced back to this ceremonial prac-tice, the system having been extended for effect and by degeneration having lost all religious significance ".

In character the Lango are an estimable people. Brave and warlike, they have earned the respect and fear of their neighbours. Unlike many Nilotic tribes, they disdain to protect their villages by stockades or walls, trusting for their protection only to their own courage and valour. Their family relations are pleasing. The love of parents for their children is particularly noticeable ; the little ones are well cared for and kindly treated. Ideas of sexual morality are high, and as a consequence the tribe is singularly free from disease. Marriage is the result of individual choice on both sides ; prostitution is unknown. The aged are respected and are maintained by their families when they have ceased to be able to work for themselves.

The Lango are divided into many clans, which are exogamous ; no man may marry a woman of either his father's or mother's clan ; children belong to the clan of their father. Every clan observes very strictly one or more taboos ; some of these taboos are clearly totemic. For example, the Patas Monkey clan regard that species of monkey as members of their clan ; they will not hunt nor injure the animals, and if they find one of them dead they mourn for it as for a human being. The behaviour of members of the Leopard clan towards leopards is exactly the same ; in the old days, it is said, women of the clan used to place their babies in a leopard's mouth, and the children were thenceforth safe from leopards for the rest of their life. Again, members of the Duiker clan may not hunt a duiker nor injure it in any way ; and if one of the animals should be accidentally killed, they bury it and cover its grave with leaves. With these examples before us, we may reasonably suppose that the other Lango clans had formerly in like manner their totems, though in many cases these seem to be now forgotten.

The author's account of Lango religion is particularly interesting and instructive. He tells us that Lango religion is compounded of two separate elements : on the one hand the worship of ancestral spirits, and on the other hand a sort of monotheism, which has now in large measure broken down but which was formerly observed in the person of the high god Jok, who appears to be conceived as a great invisible and all-pervading deity of the air, the creator of heaven and earth, and the author of all life, since the birth of animals as well as of human beings is referred to his agency. Of a woman with child it is said that " God who is within her causes her to bear " ; or again, " God visited So-and-so ; she has borne twins " ; for, unlike many African tribes, the Lango look upon the birth of twins as the highest manifestation of divine favour and celebrate the auspicious event with public dances and rejoicings. It is significant of the monotheistic conception of Jok that there is no plural form of his name. On the whole, he is deemed benevolent ; yet at the same time he is a jealous god, who demands his meed of sacrifice and observance, and who punishes neglect with severity. But he has his limitations, and his votaries imagine that they can circumvent him in various ways, especially by calling in magic to their aid.

The human soul is identified by the Lango with the shadow ; it departs from the body in dreams and at death. The soul of a dead man is apt to be very dangerous to the living, especially if he died a violent death ; in that case the ghost is always malevolent and must be propitiated by many ceremonies and sacrifices ; if these ceremonies were omitted, the ghost would drive the slayer mad. Even after a natural death, we are told, the funeral rites and sacrifices are all directed towards the pacification of the soul of the deceased. Some souls of ancestors have shrines built for them, where from time to time they receive offerings of food, beer, and so forth. In return for these attentions the ghost will communicate with his descendants and advise them oracularly in the various contingencies of life. But if a ghost prove to be incorrigibly malignant by haunting his relations, causing sickness, and destroying the crops, it becomes necessary to lay him once for all. For that purpose he is lured into a pot baited with savoury food such as his soul loved in life, and while he is licking his lips over these dainties the lid is clapped down on him, and in spite of his struggles and remonstrances he is hurried away in the pot and buried in a swamp, from which it is physically impossible for him to escape. Sometimes, however, on a promise of amendment the ghost is released from the pot and honoured with a shrine in the village. It is said that such a repentant sinner has never been known to relapse into sin. Ghosts of lepers and of persons afflicted with cancer are particularly dreaded

If it becomes necessary to kill such persons, they are driven into a hut and burnt alive ; for then, we are informed, " the fire will be a barrier which the spirit of the leprous or cancerous will not be able to pass to afflict the slayer ". Some animals, such as elephants, rhinoceroses, and giraffes, are also believed by the Lango to possess souls, which survive their death and are dangerous to their slayers. So a hunter who has killed one of these animals has to propitiate its ghost by offerings, and especially by the sacrifice of a black ram at his own door, before he is free to cut up the carcass.

The Lango abhor witchcraft and punish it with death. Among the practices which adepts in the black art resort to for the injury of others is the familiar one of bewitching people by means of some relics of their person, such as cut hair and nails and earth from their footprints. A convicted wizard is clubbed to death and his body is burnt in a great fire, while all the people run away, lest his dangerous ghost should overtake them. On the other hand, magic is publicly practised for certain useful ends, such as the procuring of rain and of good harvests. The ceremonies at rain-making are elaborate and last for several days. They are performed annually at any time from April till July, but usually in April. Songs and dances under trees form conspicuous features of the rites, which consequently are sometimes designated by a phrase which means " to dance the rain ". Water is also thrown into the air and upon the leaves of trees with a prayer for rain and a good harvest. That this latter proceeding is an imitation of rain is proved by the words of the prayer with which the old men accompany the action. They say : " May rain fall as this water falls ; may it fall on our grain and fructify it exceedingly, bringing joy and increase to our wives and children." Sometimes, besides dancing under trees, the people rush at them with much noise and shouting to drive out the rain which they fancy has taken shelter in their trunks ; and having thus expelled it they tie ropes of plaited grass round the boles to prevent the wind from blowing. If in spite of their ceremonies no rain falls and the drought is prolonged, they think that somebody is holding up or, as they put it, concealing the rain by his magic. The old men, who take the lead in the ceremonies, seek for the culprit, and if they find him they beat him severely to make him undo his magic.   But if they fail to detect him, the young men fall upon the old men and thrash them all mercilessly in the hope of inducing them to give up the offender to public justice.   One section of the tribe goes so far as to put to death one of the old men if they persist in withholding the rain.

When a village or any of its inhabitants has been struck by lightning, the people collect all the spears in the village and thrust them through the roofs of the houses with the blades upwards in order to frighten the lightning and to prevent it from striking the houses again.   Apparently they think that the lightning is not such a fool as to fall down and hurt himself on the naked blades.   A rationalist might suggest that the spears may serve as lightning-conductors.

XI

VANISHING TRIBES OF KENYA*

MOUNT KENYA is the huge mountain, crowned with perpetual ice and snow, that rises about the centre of the province of East Africa which now takes its name from the
great peak. Below the snowline on the south-eastern side a
stretch of moorland, usually enveloped in damp mists,
gradually merges into a belt of bamboos, which in turn
yields to the dense virgin forest that covers the lower slopes
down to the limit where human inhabitation is gradually
encroaching on the primeval shade. Deep, rocky gorges,
their sides mantled with timber and swept by torrents of rain
in the wet season, divide these lower declivities into a series
of ridges radiating like the sticks of a fan from the towering
mass of the mountain. This broken and difficult country,
hemmed in between the plains below and the hanging woods
above, is the home of a number of small and little-known
tribes, which for the most part seem to have been driven up
into these fastnesses by the pressure of larger and more
powerful tribes from below. The deep valleys, furrowed by
river-beds and crossed only by difficult and precarious foot-
paths, isolate the ridges from each other, and with them the
communities which have settled on them. The large tongues
of forest that clothe some of the ridges raise yet another
barrier to the intercourse of the tribes. The great expanse
of virgin forest contributes to maintain a regular rainfall and
with it an equable climate, though the range of temperature
is great, from the tropical heat of the lowlands to the Arctic

---

* *The Vanishing Tribes of Kenya*. By Major G. St. J. Orde Browne.
(London : Seeley, Service, 1925.) (*The Times Literary Supplement*,
April 23, 1925.)

cold of the ice-bound summit. The wide variation in altitude, and consequently in climate, has favoured the growth and multiplication of an exceedingly rich and varied fauna and flora ; the number of different species of plants and animals is almost incredible, and offers to the naturalist a paradise in which he could labour for years. Only the rocks are monotonous, for the mountain is an extinct volcano and the country is almost entirely volcanic.

Such is the home of the tribes described by Major Orde Browne in the present volume. As a district officer he has been called on to administer the country for years, and he has wisely devoted the somewhat scanty leisure of his office to studying the people whom he ruled. The results of his inquiries are embodied in this valuable volume; they include interesting observations on the fauna and flora, for the author appears to be a keen naturalist as well as a magistrate and a soldier. It would seem to have been with regret that the gallant and learned Major interrupted some entomological experiments which he was conducting to command a battery in action under the shadow of Mount Kilimanjaro; and we have no doubt that the enemy on whom his guns were turned had even better reason to regret his change of occupation.

The small tribes described by the author are the Chuka, the Embu, the Emberre, and the Mwimbe. Of these the Chuka represent the original stock, which in the others has been modified by contact with the larger neighbouring tribes —the Akikuyu on the west, the Akamba on the south-east, and the Meru on the north. All four of the minor tribes have remained in a comparatively backward condition, chiefly by reason of the inaccessible nature of the country ; isolated among their forests and gorges, they have kept their freedom and with it their primitive customs. This renders them all the more interesting to the student of early humanity. All the tribes are divided into exogamous clans—in other words, no man may marry a woman of his own clan ; marriage within the clan is regarded as incestuous. Some at least of the clans appear to be totemic, being associated with various animals and insects, which are regarded as their emblems or representatives. Among the totems are the frog and the ostrich. However, totemism would seem to be in a state of decay ; many a man knows his clan but not his totem. In the Chuka Major Orde Browne found many clans but no traces of totemism. Besides the organization in clans the people are divided into age-grades, which seem to be determined by the time at which the youths are circumcised. For boys and girls alike at puberty have to undergo a sort of circumcision as an introduction to manhood and womanhood respectively. At the same time they are instructed in the rules of tribal morality ; in particular, they are taught the complicated customs of ceremonial uncleanness (*thahu*) and purification which permeate the whole social life of the people. Under native rule sexual intercourse before circumcision was a very grave offence ; the offspring of such intercourse was destroyed, and the parents were killed by having a stake thrust through their bodies.

In early infancy, or at a somewhat later period, every boy and girl has to submit to the curious ceremony known as " Goat Birth ", which seems to be neither more nor less than a pretence that the child is born again from a goat. A goat is killed and skinned, and the skin is spread on the mother's lap. The child is seated on the skin, facing its mother, then the skin is wrapped round the infant. Old women next snatch the child from the skin and utter the trilling cry which is customarily raised at a birth. Sometimes, to complete the resemblance to a birth, an intestine of the goat is tied round the mother's waist and is cut at the moment when the child is snatched from the goat-skin. This imitation of severing the navel-string at birth is unmistakable. An exactly similar pretence of being born again from a goat is observed among the neighbouring Akikuyu, and has been repeatedly described. But among the Chuka and kindred tribes goats are also killed both before and after circumcision, and the young people of both sexes have to wear strips of the skins of the slain animals according to certain prescribed rules. Curiously enough, both these rites observed before and after circumcision are associated with the wild fig-tree : the first of the rites is called " the Goat of the Wild Fig-Tree " ; and in the second the carcass of the goat is placed on sticks of the wild fig-tree, and the circumcised lad or girl steps over it backward. It is remarkable that the same association between goats and wild fig-trees meets us in classical antiquity, for the Romans called the wild fig-tree the " goat fig-tree " (*caprificus*), and the Messenians called it simply the " he-goat ".

The ceremonial uncleanness, to which the people attach great importance, may arise from a variety of causes, among which are the killing of a human being or of a hyena, the touching of a corpse, the collapse of a hut, the breaking of the marriage bed, or the mounting of a child upon it. A person who has become thus unclean is secluded from society until he or she has been purified by a medicine-man or doctor, the ceremony varying in elaboration with the degree of uncleanness incurred ; the more serious cases involve the killing of a goat. The medicine-man or doctor, who exercises the beneficent function of cleansing the unclean and readmitting them to the society of their fellows, is quite a different personage from the sinister witch-doctor (*mganga*), who practises black magic and dispenses charms and curses for the undoing of enemies. Divination by a variety of hocus-pocus is part of the business of these rascals. Their influence is evil and they are greatly dreaded ; but sometimes the patience of the people is exhausted by their knaveries—they rise up in their wrath and expel the knave or drown him.

The dead are not buried but carried out into the forest and left there to be devoured by hyenas. The house in which a death takes place is destroyed ; hence it is usual to build a small temporary hut just outside the village, into which a person whose life is despaired of is conveyed, in order that his death may not involve the destruction of his house. The natives seem to have no idea of the return of a dead man's spirit ; the whole theory of ghosts is alien to their minds. Indeed, they are said to have very little notion of a life after death, and flatly deny the activity of the human spirit in a world hereafter. This incredulity is a great stumbling-block to missionaries, both of Christianity and Islam, who are taken aback by encountering a people who have seemingly no particular need of heaven or fear of hell. The glowing accounts which the missionary furnishes of the former of these abodes attract and fascinate the simple-minded native for a time, " but the lack of obvious and verifiable communication between the living and dead soon makes him return to an attitude of scepticism towards the theory of human immortality ".

Yet, if the natives are sceptical as to the survival of the human soul under the present dispensation, they have a tradition of a time when immortality was almost within reach of mankind, who were only deprived of the inestimable boon by the misconduct of a hyena. The story runs thus. Long ago the Sun made some medicine that should raise all dead people to life again ; all that was needful was to smear some of it on the lips of the corpse, which would immediately start up alive and well. Having compounded this valuable medicine, the Sun made it up in a packet and gave it to the mole to distribute to all men, for in those days the mole used to run about on the surface of the ground. So off the mole set with the packet of immortality. On his way he met the hyena, who stopped and asked him what errand he was running. The mole told him all about the new medicine, and showed him the precious packet. The hyena was dumbfounded by the intelligence : " What am I to eat ", said he, " if there are no more nice fresh corpses for me to live on ? You, mole, have always been a friend of mine, so do me one favour : take this packet of medicine from me, and give me the packet that the Sun gave to you." Now the medicine of the hyena was meant to kill all men, so that there might be many corpses for the hyena to devour. The mole did not altogether like the proposal, but to oblige an old friend he agreed to the exchange, which was accordingly effected, and the hyena departed well pleased with the bargain. The mole returned to the Sun, told him what had happened, and showed him the medicine he had received from the hyena. But the Sun was very angry and said, " You have lost the medicine which I had made with so much trouble, and now I cannot make any more ; I trusted you to take my message, and you have failed ; henceforth you shall fear my face, and hide when you see me". The mole went away much ashamed, and ever since he has lived beneath the earth ; if he sees the face of the Sun he dies.

In this story we have only a duplicate with variations of the story current among many African tribes which professes to explain the origin of death, or at all events the loss of immortality, by the mistake or misconduct of a messenger whom a great deity had sent with the glad tidings to mankind. In the other versions the deity who sends the gospel of immortality is often the moon ; and among the animals which the moon employs as his messengers the most frequently mentioned are the chameleon, the lizard, and the hare. The story of the Fall of Man in Genesis belongs to the same type of folk-tale, which is nowhere so common as among the black races of Africa.

XII

KILIMANJARO AND ITS PEOPLE*

KILIMANJARO is the highest mountain in Africa and apparently in the British Empire. Though it is situated near the Equator, the summit of the mountain for thousands of feet is encased in perennial glaciers, which render it absolutely inaccessible to the natives and very difficult of ascension even for expert European climbers. Indeed, very few have reached the top. The writer of this book, who is Senior Commissioner of the Tanganyika Territory (formerly German East Africa), has painted a very attractive picture of the scenery, which appears to be extremely beautiful. But his main interest is with the people, with whom, as representative of the British Government, he has been brought into intimate contact. He has used his opportunities to good purpose, and his book must have permanent value as a record of the primitive customs and beliefs of a people who, perched on their mountain heights, remained absolutely unknown to Europe down to the middle of the nineteenth century.

The people belong to the Bantu stock, and have been formed by the union of clans which, from time to time, have split off from various tribes in the lowlands and have moved up the mountain either in search of better land or under the pressure of enemies. All are purely agricultural, except in one district, which alone affords grazing land for large herds. Under European government, which put a stop to wars, the population has rapidly increased and now numbers about 125,000. Originating from different tribes, and even different races, they settled in separate communities, which were usually divided from each other by deep river valleys, and

* *Kilimanjaro and its People.* By the Hon. Charles Dundas. (London: Witherby, 1924.) (*The Times Literary Supplement*, May 22, 1924.)

each community took its name from the ridge which it occupied. They had no general name for themselves, but the name Wachagga, or Chagga, the origin of which is unknown, has been applied to the people as a whole and is now generally accepted by them. The German missionaries were active among them, and one of them, Mr. B. Gutmann, has published some interesting accounts of the tribe.

They worship a high god, Ruwa, whose name means " the Sun " ; he created men, he lives in the Sun, his wife is the Moon, and his children are the stars. In praying to him the people look up to the sky, spit thrice, and pronounce his name. But, like the supreme god of many Bantu tribes, Ruwa plays little part in the practical religion of the people ; he is supposed to have ceased long ago to mingle with and to care for his creatures, and they on their side appeal to him only in extreme distress, sacrificing to him at rare intervals. The real workaday religion of the Wachagga, as of all Bantu tribes, is the worship of ancestral spirits. As a rule, people only worship the spirits of their own family and ancestry. The only general exception to this rule is formed by the ancestors of the chief, who are worshipped by all the people and receive public sacrifices ; even in the spirit land they rule and must be served by the spirits of their dead subjects. Any general calamity, such as an epidemic, famine, or drought, may be attributed to the anger of the chief's dead ancestors, and their wrath must be appeased by prayer and the sacrifice of goats. Sometimes, however, the elders decide that these public disasters are caused, not by the ancestors of the chief, but by the spirits of chiefs who were conquered, killed, and despoiled of their lands, and who, resenting the wrongs done them, have appealed to the great god Ruwa for redress. In that case they have to be appeased by prayer and the sacrifice of a bull and a goat.

But the spirits of the dead are not the only spirits recognized by the Wachagga. They have an elaborate system of irrigation to promote the growth of their crops, especially of the Eleusine, from which they brew a favourite beverage ; and to the spirits of the water thus conducted to their fields they used to sacrifice children by drowning them in the water-channels. They also believe that trees are inhabited by spirits ; and when one of them has to be cut down to make beehives, an elaborate ritual has to be performed to placate the spirit who is thus rudely deprived of his abode. A pretence is made that the tree is a bride whom the owner of the tree is giving away in marriage : he presents the supposed bride with a dower consisting of milk, honey, beer, and beans : the man who lays the first axe to the tree apologizes for his act, explaining that he has been driven to it by poverty ; and when the tree has been felled, the owner, who has decently absented himself in the meantime, reappears lamenting and expressing his sorrow that he has arrived too late to prevent the deed.

The legends of the tribe, like some of those recorded among the neighbouring Masai, bear a striking resemblance to some of those recorded in the early chapters of Genesis ; and it seems doubtful whether these can be traced to missionary influence in modern times. In one of their stories of the origin of death, human mortality is the consequence of eating a certain yam which the great god Ruwa had forbidden the people to eat, while he permitted them to eat all the bananas and potatoes of the grove. In another version of the story, men were told by Ruwa's messenger that when they were old they would cast their skins and so renew their youth perpetually, on condition that nobody should see them in the act of sloughing off their old skin. But an old man was unfortunately seen by his granddaughter in the very act of transformation, when he had cast off half his skin ; and the natural consequence has been that nobody has ever since been able to renew his youth and live for ever. A very similar story of the origin of death is widely diffused in the islands of Melanesia, and has been reported also in New Guinea and Celebes. Among the legends of the Wachagga is one of a great flood, which the supreme god Ruwa sent on earth to punish men for their unkindness and inhospitality to his disguised messenger. But from the flood one righteous man, with his family, was saved, because he had been kind and hospitable to the god's messenger on earth

Besides the religion and legends of the people, Mr. Dundas has treated fully of such subjects as marriage, initiation, burial, occupations and industries, law and constitution. His book is a storehouse of information, well arranged and lucidly set forth.

XIII

BANTU BELIEFS AND MAGIC*

THE author of this book, Mr. C. W. Hobley, has long been known to anthropologists as one of our best authorities on the native races of British East Africa, or Kenya Colony, as it is now called, where he resided as Provincial Commissioner for many years. The time he could spare from his official duties he wisely devoted to studying the customs and beliefs of the tribes whom he was appointed to govern, and through the knowledge and experience thus acquired he was able to make a valuable series of contributions to ethnography. In the present work he has resumed and largely supplemented his former studies of two important tribes, the Kikuyu and Kamba, enriching his previous accounts with many fresh details and fruitful observations.

The result is a monograph replete with information of great variety and of the highest interest for the student of savage thought and institutions. But the book has a practical as well as a scientific value. Placed in the hands of British officials engaged in the maintenance of order and the administration of justice among the natives, it must prove of real service to them in their task by affording them an insight into the habits and ideas of the people, and thus greatly facilitating the work of government. Indeed, without some such knowledge of the native's point of view it is impossible to govern him wisely and well. The savage way of thinking

* The following article was contributed as an introduction to the book of which the title is *Bantu Beliefs and Magic, with particular reference to the Kikuyu and Kamba tribes of Kenya Colony ; together with some reflections on East Africa after the War.* By C. W. Hobley, C.M.G. (Late Senior Commissioner, Kenya Colony). London : H. F. and G. Witherby. 1922.

is very different from ours, and Mr. Hobley is right in insisting that it is by no means simple, but, on the contrary, highly complex, and that, consequently, it cannot be understood without long and patient study. To legislate for savages on European principles of law and morality, even when the legislator is inspired by none but the most benevolent intentions, is always dangerous and not seldom disastrous ; for it is too often forgotten that native customs have grown up through a long course of experience and adaptation to natural surroundings, that they correspond to notions and beliefs which, whether ill or well founded, are deeply rooted in the native mind, and that the attempt to discard them for others which have been developed under totally different conditions may injure instead of benefiting the people. Even when the new rules and habits which Government seeks to force upon the tribes are in themselves, abstractly considered, better than the old, they may not be so well adapted to the mental framework of the governed, and the consequence may be that the old moral restraints are abolished without the substitution of any equally effective in their room. To this danger Mr. Hobley is fully alive, and he gives a timely warning on the subject to those well-meaning but ill-informed persons at home who would treat the native African in accordance with the latest political shibboleths of democratic Europe. Such treatment, which its ignorant advocates seem to regard as a panacea for all human ills, would almost inevitably produce an effect precisely the opposite of that intended : instead of accelerating the progress of the natives, it would probably precipitate their moral, social, and even physical decline. In practical life few things are so dangerous as abstract ideas, and the indiscriminate application of them to concrete realities is one of the most fatal weapons in the hands of the moral or political revolutionary.

Among the mass of interesting topics dealt with in Mr. Hobley's book it is difficult to single out any for special mention in an introduction. The subjects to which, on the whole, he has paid closest attention are natural religion and magic. In respect of religion, the author again and again notes the remarkable similarities which may be traced between East African and Semitic beliefs and rites, and he raises the question how these similarities are to be explained. Are they due to parallel and independent development in the African and the Semitic races ? Or are they the consequence of the invasion of Africa either by a Semitic people or, at all events, by a people imbued with the principles of Semitic religion? In my book, *Folk-lore in the Old Testament*,[1] I had been similarly struck by some of these resemblances, and, while abstaining from speculation on their origin, had remarked that the hypothesis of derivation from a common source was not to be lightly rejected. On the other hand, Mr. Hobley thinks it safer, in the present state of our knowledge, to assume that the resemblances in question have arisen independently, through parallel development, in the African and Semitic areas. He dismisses as highly improbable the idea that the ancient Semitic beliefs should have originated in East Africa and spread from there to Arabia. Yet recent investigations in this part of Africa, particularly with regard to the native veins of iron and gold, tend in the opinion of some competent inquirers to show that East Central Africa, including the region of the great lakes, was an extremely ancient seat of a rudimentary civilization, the seeds of which may have been carried, whether by migration or the contact of peoples, to remote parts of Europe and Asia. In regard to iron, which has been wrought in Central Africa from time immemorial, Mr. Hobley quotes Professor Gregory, who thinks it probable that the art of forging the metal was invented in tropical Africa at a date before Europe had attained to the discovery and manufacture of bronze ; he even suggests that the ingenious smith who first fused tin and copper into bronze may have borrowed the hint from the process of working iron which he had learned in Africa.

Among the many curious superstitions recorded by Mr. Hobley, none is perhaps more interesting and suggestive than that which is known by the name of *thahu* or *thabu*, and which presents points of similarity to the Polynesian taboo. Mr. Hobley thinks that the idea involved in it is best expressed by the English term "curse". But to this it may be objected that a curse implies a personal agent, human or divine, who has called down some evil on the sufferer ; whereas in many, indeed

[1] Vol. ii. pp. 4 *sq.*

in most, of the cases enumerated by Mr. Hobley there is no suggestion of such an agent, and the evil which befalls the sufferer is the direct consequence of his own action or of a simple accident. Thus it would seem that "ceremonial uncleanness" answers better to the meaning of *thahu* than "curse". Be that as it may, deliberate cursing apparently plays a prominent part in the superstition of the Kikuyu and Kamba ; but it is significant that they give it a different name (*kirume, kiume*) from that which they apply to ceremonial uncleanness. Great faith is put in the effectiveness of curses, especially the curses of dying persons ; and as these latter curses often refer to the disposal of the dying man's property after his death, and are intended to prevent the alienation of land from the family, Mr. Hobley is led to make the ingenious suggestion that in some curses we may detect the origin of entail and of testamentary dispositions in general.

Not a few of the customs and beliefs described by Mr. Hobley remind us of similar practices and ideas in the religion and mythology of classical antiquity. Thus the warriors who, armed with swords and clubs, dance or hop from foot to foot at the time when the *mawele* grain is reaped, are curiously reminiscent of the Roman Salii, the dancing or leaping priests of the war-god Mars, who, similarly accoutred with swords and staves, danced or leaped while they invoked Saturn, the God of Sowing. Again, the strange sort of madness which from time to time seizes on Kamba women, and under the influence of which, wrought up to a state of frenzy, they caper about with cow's tails suspended from their arms, offers a parallel to the Greek legend of the daughters of Proetus and the other Argive women, who, oddly enough, were said, like their African sisters, to have been healed of their infirmity by dances and the sacrifice of cattle.[1] The study of such hysterical and infectious manias among primitive peoples opens up an interesting field of inquiry to the psychologist.

Such are a few specimens culled from the rich collection of East African folk-lore and religion which the author has presented to his readers in this volume. The facts recorded by him provide much food for thought, and suggest many lines of investigation for inquiries in the future. For, as he

---

[1] Apollodorus, *The Library*, ii. 2. 2, with my notes.

reminds us, with equal truth and modesty, the field of inquiry is far from being exhausted. Let us hope that it will yet yield an abundant harvest to others, who will follow in Mr. Hobley's footsteps and imitate the example he has set them of patient and open-minded research.

XIV

THE FOLK-LORE OF BOMBAY*

THE author of this work, Mr. R. E. Enthoven, is already
known to folk-lorists by his two volumes on the folk-lore of
Gujarat and the Konkan, two districts included in the Bombay
Presidency. More recently he has published in three volumes
a treatise on the tribes and castes of Bombay, which ranges
with the corresponding works of Risley, Crooke, Thurston,
and Russel on other regions of India, the whole forming a
fairly complete survey of Indian ethnology, with the exception
of Assam, of which the tribes are described separately in a
series of valuable monographs published under the auspices
of the Assam Government. In the present work Mr. Enthoven
has given us an account of the popular religion and superstitions of the various races included in the Bombay Presidency.
A residence of some thirty years as a magistrate in the Presidency
has afforded him ample means for the collection of material,
and he has made excellent use of his opportunities. In the
large store of facts accumulated, the orderliness of their
arrangement, and the clearness of their description the book
is a model of what such a work should be. It is a further
merit of the writer that he strictly abstains from speculation
and from far-reaching comparisons, which only tend to impair
the value of a descriptive work on a definite ethnical area.
Yet the very severity of Mr. Enthoven's treatment makes the
book not easy reading to the ordinary Englishman. The
serried array of facts, joined to the multitude of strange and
seemingly barbarous names of deities, spirits, and places,

---

* *The Folklore of Bombay*. By R. E. Enthoven. (Oxford: at The
Clarendon Press, 1924.) (*The Times Literary Supplement*, February
12, 1925.)

presents to the English reader a series of difficulties and obstacles which might to some extent have been lightened by a fuller index and the addition of a glossary. Perhaps these may be supplied in a subsequent edition, which is likely to be called for, since the book promises to be the standard work on the subject for a long time to come.

Mr. Enthoven rightly recognizes the fusion, or at all events the mixture, of Aryan with non-Aryan elements in the population of the Bombay Presidency. Characteristic of the non-Aryan element is the practice of totemism, which survives in full vigour in the southern or Kanarese regions of the province. The usual totemic rules, which command respect towards the totem and forbid intermarriage between persons of the same totem, appear to be generally observed ; and, further, the totem, whether it be an animal, a plant, or an inanimate object, is worshipped on important occasions, such as marriage, the occupation of a new house, and the setting up of a threshing-floor at the beginning of harvest. The number of totems hitherto identified appears to amount to about one hundred and sixty ; and it is significant that they include some (such as the tiger, snake, tortoise, and horse) which are identical with the totems of the primitive tribes of Bengal and the Central Provinces. It is a probable inference that totemism of a uniform pattern was widely spread among the aboriginal inhabitants of India before the advent of the Aryans.

Another test which enables us to discriminate between the Aryan and non-Aryan elements of the population is furnished by the distinction between the great Hindoo deities, such as Brahma, Vishnu, and Shiva, on the one hand, and the minor local deities or godlings on the other. For while the worship of the great gods is, of course, of Aryan origin and is maintained by Brahman priests, who represent the purest Aryan type, many or, perhaps, most of the lesser deities, such as the monkey-faced Maruti and the smallpox goddess Shitala, are probably of indigenous origin.; for many of them may only be propitiated by priests or exorcists of low castes who have no drop of Aryan blood in their veins. Indeed, Brahmans for the most part do not worship those minor deities, and will not partake of food offered to them. One reason which they allege for this refusal is that once an image is consecrated it should be worshipped uninterruptedly every day, and that he who neglects to worship such an image daily incurs the sin of Brahman murder, the most heinous of all crimes. But the number of the lesser gods is legion, and if a Brahman were to pay his respects to them all daily, the day would not be long enough for him to complete the round of them. For not only are they innumerable, but they are constantly on the increase, and there is absolutely no limit to their pullulation. Any new disease or untoward incident is liable to create a new deity out of hand. Nowhere, accordingly, is the observer in a better position to follow the progress of a god from the incubatory stage upward ; and he may be pardoned if he ends by suspecting that some of the great gods of Hindooism may have sprung from the same humble germs as the lesser fry of divinities which he sees swarming under his eyes to this day.

The many superstitious beliefs and customs recorded by our author on the whole conform to types which are now familiar to students of folk-lore and primitive religion. We hear, for example, of water-spirits who demand a human victim every year, and who resent any attempt to snatch their prey from them by rescuing a drowning person. We have examples of the curious pretence of marrying persons to trees before they engage in a real marriage which happens to be deemed dangerous or unlucky, as when a man marries a third wife or a widow. In the case of widow marriages, as Mr. Enthoven observes, the source of danger which is apprehended appears to be the ghost of the widow's late husband, who is naturally jealous of his successor, and may almost be excused for troubling his connubial bliss. So, in order either to deceive or to pacify him, the bold man who weds the widow is first united in holy matrimony to a tree, which is afterwards cut down ; 'and the ghost of the man is left to console himself with the ghost of the tree-bride. Again, when a girl born under an unlucky star is about to be married, she is first wedded to a tree or an earthen pot before being married to a man ; in this way the ill-luck attaching to her is communicated to the tree or the pot instead of to her husband. Again, we meet with the familiar belief that the souls of the dead are reborn in their descendants, particularly the soul of a grandfather in the body of his grandson, who accordingly takes the name of his grandfather, since in point of fact he is merely his grandfather come to life again. Again, ghosts are as much dreaded in Bombay as elsewhere, and many are the precautions taken against them. For example, among the lower castes the hands or feet of second wives are tattooed, in the belief that this prevents the ghost of the first wife from attacking her successor.

But in Bombay, as everywhere else, there are ghosts and ghosts ; for some are more mischievous and malignant than others, such, for example, as the ghosts of persons who have been devoured by tigers or other wild beasts. As usual, one of the most dangerous of all ghosts is believed to be that of a woman who died in childbed, and various devices are resorted to for the purpose of preventing her from returning to annoy her kinsfolk. One way is to scatter cotton-wool over the bier and all along the road to the cemetery, for it is believed that the ghost cannot make her way back to the house unless she succeeds in picking up all the wool in one night. This she cannot do ; the sun rises on her while she is still wool-gathering, so her relations at home feel perfectly safe. Further, the fear of the Evil Eye is as rampant in Bombay as in some parts of Christian Europe, and many are the quaint means adopted to counteract its baneful influence. Among these one of the most approved would seem to be old shoes, which are tied, for example, to fruit-trees to protect them against the Evil Eye. This perhaps explains our European custom of throwing old shoes after a bride and bridegroom at marriage, for it is notorious that a bridal pair are more exposed than ordinary folk to the unwelcome attention of bogeys of all sorts. Other persons of whom the same melancholy truth may be predicated are infants at birth ; accordingly they are subjected to many kinds of ignominious treatment in order to impress the bogeys with the belief that the children are beneath their notice. Thus, all kinds of opprobrious names are applied to the little ones : for example, a child will be thrown away on a dunghill and named Dunghill, or rolled in the dust and named Dust. Witches, again, are still as rife in India as they used to be here in Europe, and they are still at their old tricks, for example, that of stealing milk from a neighbour's cow, which they do by milking an earthen image of the animal. Lastly, we have

the old, old notion that disease is caused by the entrance into
the patient of an evil spirit or devil, who can be exorcized from
the sufferer's body into that of an animal, as in the celebrated
case of the Gadarene swine. Sometimes in India the animal
into which a devil has been thus transplanted is tied up to a
post for the term of its natural life, and with it the disease is
supposed to be chained up also, and thereby disabled from
doing any more mischief. Sometimes the devil who has taken
possession of a sick man is transferred, not to an animal, but
to a bottle, which is carried out of the village and buried in
the ground or thrown into the sea. This answers all the
purposes of a perfect cure ; the devil has received his quietus,
and the patient is hopeful of recovery.

The conclusion which a philosophic student of mankind
draws from such a work as this is that, while the range of
human folly is unlimited, it everywhere tends to run into
similar moulds, so that whereas the number of its instances
is incalculable, its patterns are comparatively few and repeat
themselves with a monotonous iteration. This is perhaps well
for humanity, which might soon be strangled if only the brood
of Folly were as manifold in kind as it is countless in number.

XV

THE PALAUNGS OF BURMA*

MRS. LESLIE MILNE is already well known to ethnologists by her excellent book on the Shans of Burma. She has now given us a similar study of the Palaungs, another people of the same district who are scattered over various regions of the Shan States. They belong to the Môn-Khmer family, a people whose language is now spoken in Cambodia and by the Khasis of Assam. Their ancestors appear to have been early immigrants into Burma and to have been afterwards driven up into the hills, which their descendants still occupy, by later swarms of invaders from Central Asia. Secure on their hill-tops, they have been hardly touched by the tide of battle which surged to and fro in the valleys below, where Shans, Burmans, and Chinese contended for the mastery. But, as the Shans settled permanently in the lowlands, the various Palaung clans have been separated from each other by wedges of an alien race ; and thus in their isolation they have developed different dialects and, to a certain extent, different customs. They are a pacific, unwarlike people, chiefly occupied in the cultivation of tea. In their gentle character and peaceful pursuits they contrast strongly with the Wild Wahs, who speak a kindred language, but are the only barbarous tribe now left in Burma ; for it seems that these fierce mountaineers still justify their evil reputation by indulging in the practice of head-hunting.

The author deals chiefly with the Katur tribe of the Palaungs, who live in or near Namhsan, the capital of Tawng-

* *The Home of an Eastern Clan : A Study of the Palaungs of the Shan States.* By Mrs. Leslie Milne. (Oxford : at The Clarendon Press, 1924.) (*The Times Literary Supplement*, September 4, 1924.)

peng, which, though nominally a Shan State, is governed
by a Palaung Chief and is inhabited almost entirely by
Palaungs. Mrs. Leslie Milne has lived among the people
and learned their language, and she writes of them with
much sympathy and insight. Almost everything which she
sets down about the customs of the people has been told her
by the Palaungs themselves. The book is therefore a record
of high ethnological value. In it we find a full account of
the life of the individual from the cradle to the grave. The
long and elaborate ceremonies of courtship and marriage are
described in detail. In many clans a form of elopement,
strictly regulated by custom, is an invariable preliminary to
marriage. But we miss information on some important
aspects of social life, such as the organization of the clans, the
system of relationship, the prohibited degrees of marriage,
the criminal code (if crimes are committed in this Burman
Arcady), and the rules of inheritance. Perhaps on these and
kindred topics Mrs. Leslie Milne will in future supplement
her otherwise admirable account of the people whom she has
studied with loving care. But where so much has been given
it seems almost ungrateful to ask for more.

Perhaps the most interesting part of a very interesting
and well-written volume is that which treats of Palaung
religion. The Palaungs profess Buddhism of an orthodox
pattern. The Buddhist temples or image-houses and the
Buddhist monasteries occupy conspicuous sites in the villages.
As a rule, the villages are built on the ridges and slopes of
the hills, and the summits are often levelled to admit of being
crowned by these religious edifices. There, too, on the tran-
quil hill-top, stand rest-houses to which pious people retire
from time to time for the sake of religious meditation and
prayer. Buddhist monks and nuns, in their gay robes of
yellow, orange, or apricot colour, figure prominently in village
life. Buddhist festivals are celebrated throughout the year
at the regular seasons and in the regular way. The people go
on pilgrimage to famous Buddhist shrines in distant parts of
Burma, even as far as Mandalay and Rangoon. Yet is
Buddhism after all little more than a veneer which overlies,
without concealing, the ancient faith of the people in the
spirits of Nature and of the dead.

" Their belief in spirits " [says Mrs. Leslie Milne] " is the real though not the acknowledged basis of the popular religion, which has even transformed the Buddha into a beneficent spirit, who, contrary to all the teaching of the monks, may be appealed to in prayer."

The worship of the spirits is regularly organized and presided over by a High Priest (*Ta Pleng*), who in the State of Tawngpeng used always to be an elder brother or an elderly relative of the ruling chief. The relation of the Buddhist monks to him is one of mutual tolerance. They wink at him, and he winks back at them. Perhaps the monks themselves do not wholly renounce the inherited faith in spirits when they put on the yellow robe. Certainly they attend the great festival in September at which all the spirits in the State of Tawngpeng are solemnly summoned by the High Priest to come and partake of the offerings of the people.

Among the spirits to whom prayers are put up and sacrifices offered are the spirits of trees and of water. At the end of the dry season freshly picked tea leaves are offered to the spirit of a stream or spring in order that plentiful rains may fall on the tea-gardens. But if the water-spirits give no help, and the drought obstinately continues, the villagers resort to a quaint mode of eliciting showers from the brazen heaven. On a moonlight night they go to a graveyard, strip themselves naked, streak their bodies with charcoal to imitate the stripes of a tiger, and thus disguised crawl thrice round a newly made grave on their hands and knees, scratching the ground and growling like tigers. Afterwards they sit astride a pole taken from a bier, and, mounted on it, ride from one end of the village to the other. How these proceedings tend to procure the fall of rain is no doubt clear to the native mind, but it is less obvious to the benighted European.

The graveyard also witnesses a more gruesome ceremony for the making of an amulet. The Palaungs believe that the little finger of an unborn babe is an irresistible love-charm. Accordingly, when a woman has died in childbed without bringing her child to the birth, a lover will sometimes repair to her grave, cut open her body, and bite off the little finger of the unborn infant. Armed with it, he believes himself to be invincible in love. But the ghost of the child pursues him to demand the restoration of its finger. Accordingly, on returning to the house, he assumes the posture and the air of a woman who has just given birth to a child, in order to deceive the infant ghost into the belief that he is its mother ; and to appease its natural indignation he offers it rice and bananas for seven successive nights, after which he hopes that the ghost has gone away for good and all. The ghost of a woman who has died in childbed is deemed the most terrifying of unhappy spirits. Her body is taken out of the house by a hole cut in the floor for the purpose (Palaung houses are raised above the ground), and afterwards the hole is closed with new boards to prevent the return of her dangerous ghost. Moreover, her body, like that of a man killed by lightning, is buried upright in a well-like grave with a large earthenware pot, turned upside down, resting on her head and shoulders. The reason for this curious mode of burial is not mentioned, but the intention probably is to render it more difficult for the ghost to extricate himself or herself from the grave and return, a very unwelcome guest, to the old home. On the other hand, steps are taken to prevent persons from dying, either by impeding the departure of the soul from the body or by recalling it while it is supposed to be still within hearing. For the former purpose white threads are tied round the wrists of the dying, and the friends say, " We shall not let thee fly away, we would tie thy spirit here." To recall the departing soul of her dying child a mother will appeal to it in pathetic language not to wander away into the dark, cold night, but to come back to the home where the fire burns brightly on the hearth. At the same time she holds a bag with its mouth wide open, apparently for the reception of the returning spirit. A small silver coin is sometimes, but not always, placed on the tongue of the corpse to pay the ghost's passage to the other world, or to defray his expenses when he arrives there ; but whether the ghost pays it out as toll at a turnpike gate, or at a bridge across a river, or as a fee to the aged couple who guard that Fruit of Forget-fulness which corresponds to the Water of Lethe in Greek mythology, is a point on which Palaung opinion is not agreed.

Prayers and offerings to the spirits who inhabit trees appear to be not uncommon. Thus the first leaves picked

from a tea-tree are offered to the guardian spirit of the tea ;
and a sick person will hang a basketful of flowers, rice, and
curry on a branch of a banyan tree as an offering to the tree-
spirit, who is supposed to be causing the sickness, while at
the same time the sufferer prays the spirit to pardon his
offence and to heal his disease.   But to make a barren tree
bear fruit stronger measures are employed.   The owner gets
a friend to climb up into the branches, while he himself
takes up his post with a sword or spear at the foot of the tree.
Then, resting the point of the weapon against the trunk, he
sternly demands of the tree, " Wilt thou bear fruit ? "   To
this the man in the tree, acting as mouthpiece of the tree-
spirit, answers, " I shall bear fruit."   The owner then threatens
to kill the tree if it does not keep its word by bearing fruit ;
and again the pretended tree-spirit among the boughs gives
an earnest promise of bearing a plentiful crop, and entreats
the irate owner not to cut him down.   Similar modes of inducing barren trees to do their duty are not unknown in
Europe.   And corresponding to the European ritual of the
last sheaf of corn is the ritual of the last sheaf of rice among
the Palaungs.   The last sheaf left standing on the rice-field is
cut by the oldest man living in the house of the owner of the
field ;   and having been made up in the figure of a man, it is
placed on the threshing-floor, where the harvesters kneel
before it and return thanks for the harvest.   It is then carried
to the house and placed beside the images of Buddha in the
domestic shrine.   There, if it remains in good condition, it is
kept till next harvest, when it may again be carried to the
threshing-floor to receive again the homage of the harvesters.
In this ritual of the harvest-field and the threshing-floor it
is not rash to discern a worship of the rice-spirit, which is
probably far older than Buddhism.   Here, as elsewhere, a
simple religion of Nature has preceded, and may yet survive,
a great historical religion, the fruit of profound philosophical
thought and of lofty moral aspiration.

XVI

THE SEA GIPSIES OF MALAYA*

THE Mergui Archipelago is a group of small islands in the Bay of Bengal, lying off the coast of Tenasserim, the extreme southern province of Burma. The inhabitants are commonly known as Salons, Selons, Selongs, or Selungs, which are various forms of the name applied to them by the Burmese. But they call themselves Maw-ken, which is said to mean " Sea-drowned ". They say that formerly their ancestors lived on the mainland, where they had settlements, with houses and cultivated lands. But living at the point where two different and more numerous races meet, the Burmese on the north and the Malays on the south, they suffered from the encroachments of these more powerful and warlike neighbours, till they were finally compelled to abandon their homes on the mainland and to take refuge on the islands, or, rather, on the sea ; for most of them live regularly in their boats, cruising about the archipelago in search of fish and pearl oysters, though a certain number possess camps or settlements, consisting of a few rude shelters on the islands, where they cultivate coco-nuts, bananas, pineapples, breadfruit, and so forth. Very little has hitherto been known about these people ; hence the account which Mr. White gives of them in this book is all the more welcome. The author was chaplain of Tenasserim for some years, and his quarterly visits to Mergui led to his making the acquaintance of the Mawken and interesting

* *The Sea Gypsies of Malaya : An Account of the Nomadic Mawken People of the Mergui Archipelago.* By W. G. White. With a Foreword by R. R. Marett. (London : Seeley, Service, 1922.) (*The Times Literary Supplement*, October 19, 1922.)

himself in them and their ways.   He acquired a knowledge
of their language, and was able to converse with them
in it.

The racial and linguistic affinities of the Mawken appear
to be doubtful, and on these questions the writer does not
venture to pronounce a decided opinion.   The common
view seems to be that the language belongs to the Malay
family ; but Sir George Grierson, our highest authority on
such points, considers that it is " probably the residuum of
a tongue spoken at an extremely remote period by a prehistoric race on the continent of Farther India ".   With
this view the character and history of the Mawken would
seem to harmonize very well ; for they are just such a simple
and peaceful folk as are apt to be driven, step by step, from
their old homes on land by the pressure of more vigorous
races, till they are forced to betake themselves to a last
refuge on the sea or islands.   The simplicity of the Mawken
is attested by the rudimentary state of the arts among them ;
though tin and silver exist in the islands, the natives appear
to have known nothing of metals till they procured them
from members of the more advanced races ; they have no
bows and arrows and are ignorant of the art of weaving,
though the women plait mats and construct plain earthen pots
without any decoration.   The pacific character of these sea
gipsies, as Mr. White calls them, is tacitly implied in his
description of them, for he nowhere alludes to war or warlike
weapons among them ; it is true that they possess spears, but
these they apparently employ only for harpooning the larger
fish and hunting wild animals.   The heads of these spears
are sometimes made of hard fish-bones, like the spear with
which Ulysses is said to have been killed by his son ; though
nowadays most of them are made of iron or steel procured
from foreigners.

Of the social relations of the people Mr. White has not
much to say ; he tells us that they practise monogamy, that
prostitution is unknown among them, and that parents are
careful to safeguard the virtue of their unmarried daughters.
He gives no hint of the existence of exogamous clans.   From
his account of the terms of relationship we learn that they
employ different terms for brothers according as they are older

or younger than the speaker ; and that they similarly differentiate between sisters, father's brothers, father's sisters, mother's brothers, mother's sisters, between the wives of elder and younger brothers, and between the husbands of elder and younger sisters. Such differentiations of kinsfolk according to age with reference to the speaker point to the existence of the classificatory system of relationship among the Mawken, though the author does not expressly refer to it. On the subject of the religion and folk-lore of the people the writer was seemingly able to acquire but little exact information ; indeed, in the matter of folk-lore he candidly confesses the scantiness of his knowledge. According to him, " in religion the Mawken had no conception of God. Their language has no word for God, the Ultimate Source, the Creator. The word *Thida*, now used for God, has come to them from the Siamese, and it has come within comparatively recent times." However, they believe in spirits, who can help or hurt, and they have wizards or medicine-men who recite prayers or incantations addressed to these powerful beings. They are also acquainted with the malignant art of black magic. Thus we read of a dreaded sorcerer, who was supposed to do his victims to death by various applications of the principle of sympathetic magic. For example, he would take a pair of jaws of a fish and snap them together at a man, threatening him at the same time that soon in like manner he would be snapped up by a crocodile. Or, again, he would take up sand from a man's footsteps and insert it into a ball of beeswax, which he afterwards moulded into an image of the man, and taking it to an island would place it on the ground between two candles of beeswax, while he prayed the spirit of the island to cause his victim to fall ill. The Mawken believe that the human soul survives the death of the body ; but, like many other peoples, they fancy that the ghost becomes an agent of evil when once he or she has shuffled off the mortal coil. They used to expose their dead on scaffolds in certain islands ; but more recently they have adopted the custom of burying them in the ground, to preserve the bodies from the depredations of Malays, who used to rob them, and of crocodiles, which used to devour them.

Mr. White's book, meritorious as it is, serves rather to whet than to satisfy the curiosity of the student of man. It is to be hoped that some other inquirer will resume the investigation and give us a fuller and more detailed account of these interesting people.

XVII

THE ANDAMAN ISLANDERS*

THE Andaman Islanders possess great interest for the student of primitive man, since they rank among the very lowest of existing savage races. Not only did they never attempt to till the ground or own any domestic animals until dogs were introduced among them in 1858, but they were unacquainted with the almost universal art of working stone, except in the rudimentary form of flaking quartz for the purpose of shaving and scarifying themselves; the adzes which they employed as cutting tools were made of shell, not of stone. It is true that they obtained some iron from vessels wrecked on their coasts, but they never learned to work the metal by heat. More than that, alone of all known races of men, they were not acquainted with any means of kindling fire, whether by friction or percussion, though they were in possession of fire and carefully preserved it for use in daily life. In their legend of the origin of fire the king-fisher plays much the same part as the wren and the robin redbreast in the corresponding European stories, which relate how the bird stole the first fire for men and was burnt for his pains, the red plumage on the neck or breast of the bird, where the flame scorched it, serving as proof indubitable of the truth of the tale. Yet, while the Andaman Islanders were destitute of the elementary art of making fire, they practised certain other crafts, particularly pottery and archery, to which some savages at higher levels of culture were strangers. For example, the Polynesians, who rank far

* *The Andaman Islanders: A Study in Social Anthropology.* By A. R. Brown. (Cambridge: at The University Press, 1922.) (*The Times Literary Supplement*, August 24, 1922.)

above the Andaman Islanders in their general culture, nevertheless knew nothing of pottery and made no use of archery in war, though some, but not all, of them were acquainted with bows and arrows, which they employed in hunting rats or as simple playthings.

The Andaman Islands are divided into two very unequal portions, known as the Great and the Little Andaman respectively. They are hilly and covered with dense tropical forest. There are no streams of any size, but the coast is broken by many fine harbours. The climate is warm, moist, and fairly uniform throughout the year. The isolation of the islands in the centre of the Gulf of Bengal, by cutting off the inhabitants from intercourse with other people, has doubtless contributed in great measure to retain them in their very backward condition. There is nothing whatever to suggest that they have ever been influenced by contact with any other race since the time, many centuries ago, when they first reached the islands. They belong to what is called the Negrito race, a primitive stock totally different, except in its black colour, from the African negroes. At a remote time the Negritos probably occupied large areas of south-eastern Asia and the Indian Archipelago, for branches of the stock, akin to the Andamanese in physique and culture, are still to be found in the interior of the Malay Peninsula and of the Philippine Islands. In 1788, on account of the menace to shipping constituted by the islanders, who murdered all sailors wrecked on their shores, the East India Company established a settlement in the Great Andaman, but after some years the scheme was abandoned. In 1858, the Indian Government established a penal settlement at Port Blair, which has existed ever since, to the great misfortune of the natives, who, ravaged by European diseases, were reduced in less than fifty years to about 27 per cent of their former population, and seem now to be in process of rapid extinction ; a birth among them is a rare event, and of the children born very few survive infancy. Only the inhabitants of the Little Andaman, protected by their isolation from the European virus, continue to flourish, comparatively speaking, in their pristine state. But very little is known of them. Their language is so different from that of the Great

Andaman Islanders that the natives cannot make themselves
understood by each other ; and the Little Andaman Islanders,
and that portion of them which has settled at the southern
end of the Great Andaman, have wisely maintained a settled
policy of hostility to Europeans and their ways.

The penal settlement at Port Blair has enabled British
officers to observe the natives of the Great Andaman, and
two of them, Mr. E. H. Man and Mr. M. V. Portman, have
used their opportunities to good purpose. The very valuable
observations of Mr. Man on the manners and customs of
the people have hitherto been our principal source of information on the subject ; to them must now be added, as worthy
to rank with them, the book by Mr. A. R. Brown under
review. His work serves to complete and, to some extent, to
correct the works of his predecessors, his criticisms of whom
are always courteous, never carping or censorious. Throughout he is most careful to define precisely the sources of his
information, always warning his readers when these sources
were doubtful, defective, or inconsistent. He never attempts
to weave a number of contradictory native reports into a
single consistent and readable narrative ; he simply sets such
reports side by side in their bald opposition, though he is
often able to suggest probable explanations of their real or
apparent discrepancies. In a word, his procedure from first
to last is strictly scientific. He makes no concession to mere
popularity, beyond writing in a clear and simple style which
anybody can understand. In particular, he is commendably
free from the use of a technical jargon, which imposes on
the simple without enlightening the wise. Unfortunately his
researches were confined almost entirely to the tribes of the
Great Andaman. He spent nearly three months encamped
with the less known, wilder, and therefore scientifically more
interesting natives of the Little Andaman ; but the difficulty
of their language, which is but little related to that of the
Great Andaman tribes, proved an insuperable obstacle to
the prosecution of inquiries among them.

Nevertheless, from the tribes of the Great Andaman,
particularly from those of the North Andaman, among whom
Mr. Man had not worked, Mr. Brown succeeded in eliciting
a large body of new and interesting facts, many of which he

has elucidated in convincing fashion. Of these only a very few can be mentioned in a brief review like the present. Thus, for example, Mr. Brown seems to have rendered it practically certain that the circular communal hut, which is or was in use in some of the tribes, has been developed out of a village in which the huts are ranged in a circle round a central dancing place, the development having been effected by placing the huts in contiguity to each other and joining the roofs together. Again, Mr. Brown's investigation of the spiritual beliefs of the natives renders it highly probable that the spirits of the sea and the jungle, of which they stand greatly in dread, and to which they ascribe the cause of all sickness and death from natural causes, are no other than the souls of the human dead. Yet this fear of ghosts appears not to have led to a practice of propitiating them by prayer and sacrifice—in short, to a worship of the dead, unless indeed their custom of treasuring the skulls of their relatives and carrying the smaller bones about with them can be regarded as a form of propitiation. In favour of this interpretation it may be observed that strings of these bones are worn by the natives for the avowed purpose of curing or preventing sickness, and as sickness seems to be invariably traced to the anger of the spirits of the forest and sea, which are identical with the spirits of the dead, we seem left to infer that the presence of the bones serves somehow to disarm the anger or satisfy the pride of these spirits, and so to ensure the health or recovery of the patient. It is notable that the belief in evil magic, which has wrought havoc among so many backward peoples in many parts of the world, is not highly developed among the Andamanese, who accordingly do not in general attribute death to the machinations of sorcerers, and consequently do not avenge it by killing the real or imaginary culprit. Nevertheless they have their magicians or medicine-men, but these seem to lay themselves out rather for the healing than the infliction of diseases, and for the control of the weather in the interest of their fellows. By the exercise of these useful arts they acquire not only reputation and respect, but a certain degree of wealth, if we may speak of wealth among savages so destitute of material comforts ; at least they receive a good share of the game caught by others, and presents of all kinds from such as seek their goodwill. They appear to be the only professional class among the islanders, for in all the ordinary affairs of life every man is his own hunter, fisher, and artisan ; in short, every individual is a jack-of-all-trades, and therefore master of none ; the division of labour, which is essential for economic progress, has hardly begun among them. Yet in this differentiation of a class of men distinguished from their fellows by a higher degree of real or imaginary knowledge, and enjoying a more than common influence, we may discern the incipient rise towards power of chiefs, who can hardly be said to exist at present in the very democratic society of these islanders.

But Mr. Brown, not content with accurately observing and carefully recording the customs and beliefs of the Andamanese, has set himself to interpret them, and it is to his interpretations of them that the author himself attaches most weight. He is careful to explain that his aim is not to discover or conjecture the historical origin, but to reveal the meaning and function, of the ceremonies and legends which he has recorded. The search for the origins of institutions among peoples who have no history he regards as at once vain and unscientific ; whereas he deems it possible, by personal inquiry and the application of psychological analysis, to ascertain the motives and sentiments which established and still maintain the institutions in question, and to discover the uses which they subserve. To do this effectively, he tells us, it is not enough to take each institution separately, to detach it from its surroundings, and to compare it with the corresponding institutions of other peoples ; it is necessary to study all the institutions of a single society or social type together, so as to exhibit their intimate mutual relations as parts of one coherent and organic system. This new or analytic method, as we may call it, of studying the customs of primitive peoples he contrasts with the old comparative method, and contends that in such inquiries it is necessary to substitute analysis for comparison. Even where we may hesitate to accept the results of his analysis, we cannot but admire its philosophic depth and subtlety. If anything, Mr. Brown is perhaps over-subtle, too much inclined to search for recondite and hidden motives where simpler and more probable ones lie on the surface. Further, we are disposed to think that he has been biassed unduly by the sociological speculations of Durkheim and his French followers, and that, preoccupied—we had almost said obsessed—by their theories, he is too apt to explain everything in terms of what he calls social value, and to use that conception as a key to open all the locks in the rich treasury of Andaman lore which he has garnered for us. In the science of man, as in all other sciences, there is always a risk and a temptation of pushing too far, in the first ardour of discovery, a new method which, within proper limits, is both legitimate and fruitful ; and we do not feel sure that Mr. Brown has everywhere escaped the risk and resisted the temptation. But in saying this we would not be thought to condemn, but only at the most to suspend judgement on, the conclusions at which he has arrived by a patient and scientific investigation of the facts.

XVIII

AMONG THE HEAD-HUNTERS OF FORMOSA *

FORMOSA is a large island off the coast of China, lying half within and half without the Tropic of Cancer. After remaining in possession of the Chinese for over two centuries, it was wrested from them in 1895 by the Japanese, who have remained masters of the island. In the seventeenth century the Dutch, then at the height of their maritime power, built forts in Formosa and controlled the island for thirty-seven years before they were compelled to cede it to the Chinese. The memory of their government survives to this day as a sacred tradition among the aborigines, who look back to the too brief period of Dutch supremacy as a Golden Age of peace and prosperity, when they were treated by their foreign rulers with a benevolence, sagacity, and sympathy which have been sadly lacking in the conduct of their later masters. The great bulk of the existing population is of Chinese descent ; the aboriginal tribes, which no doubt once occupied the whole island, have under foreign pressure been gradually driven from the fertile western lowlands into the lofty and rugged mountains, which extend throughout the whole of the eastern part of the island, and which for many miles together fall sheer into the sea in tremendous precipices thousands of feet high. It was this mountain scenery which won for the island the name of Beautiful (Formosa) from its early Portuguese discoverers.

The number of the aborigines is steadily diminishing, and

* *Among the Head-hunters of Formosa.* By Janet B. Montgomery McGovern. With a Preface by R. R. Marett. (London : Fisher Unwin, 1922.) (*The Times Literary Supplement*, March 8, 1923.)

at the present time can hardly exceed 105,000. Very little
has hitherto been known about them. Perhaps the fullest
account hitherto accessible is that by a Japanese writer, which
was published by the American writer, Mr. J. Davidson,
in his general work on Formosa.[1] In subsequent years a
Japanese gentleman, Mr. Shinji Ishii, resided for some time
among the aborigines and acquired a considerable knowledge of their customs and traditions. He published a few
articles on the subject in the journals of English learned
societies, but unfortunately he could not find an English
publisher willing to undertake the complete publication of
the valuable materials he had collected. In this dearth of
information the work of Mrs. McGovern is all the more
welcome ; it sheds a great deal of new light on these interesting people. The authoress spent two years in Formosa as
teacher of English in a Japanese Government school ; and
as her duties were not very onerous, she was able to devote
a considerable amount of leisure time to travelling among
the aborigines and studying their ways. She tells her story
and sets forth the results of her inquiries in a plain, straight-
forward way which wins the reader's confidence.

Physical and linguistic evidence combine to prove that
the aborigines of Formosa belong to the Indonesian or
Malay stock ; and at least one tribe (the Ami, of the east
coast) has a tradition, probably trustworthy, that their
ancestors crossed a great sea in boats from an island somewhere in the south. But they have ceased entirely to be a
seafaring people ; and boat-building seems to be a lost art
among them, though it survives to a certain extent among
the Yami, the natives of the tiny island of Botel Tobago,
off the south-east coast of Formosa. The aborigines are
divided into a number of independent tribes, of which the
Taiyal in the north is the largest and most powerful. In its
mountain fastnesses this tribe retains to some extent the
custom of head-hunting, which has died out among most of
the other tribes, though it was universal among all the tribes
within living memory. To cut off and bring home the head
of an enemy is, or used to be, an indispensable preliminary
to marriage—no head, no wife, was a rigid rule. But in

[1] J. Davidson, *The Island of Formosa* (London and New York, 1903).

these degenerate days the rule is relaxed, so that boys who have merely carried heads on their back, or placed their hands on heads decapitated by their fathers, are allowed to rank as homicides in full and to wear the honourable badge of manslaughter, which among the Taiyal consists of a series of straight lines tattooed on the chin. Among the Paiwan, another large tribe which keeps up the practice of head-hunting, the badge of the successful head-hunter is a kind of cap made by the women of the tribe. A captured head is received with great demonstrations of joy by the people at home Food and wine are set before it, or even thrust into its mouth, and the chief or the high-priestess of the village addresses it as follows : " O warrior, you are welcome to our village and to our feast ! Eat and drink, and ask your brothers to come and join you, and to eat and drink with us also." This invocation is supposed to have a magical effect in procuring more victories and thereby more heads for the shelves, where these grinning trophies are preserved in long rows.

With regard to the social organization of the tribes, Mrs. McGovern failed to find clear evidence either of totemism or of exogamy. On the other hand, she believes that the matriarchate, in the strict sense of the word, exists among these tribes ; but the evidence she adduces hardly suffices to establish this conclusion, though the chief appears to be often a woman, and among the Paiwan " chieftainship seems to be hereditary, usually descending from mother to daughter, although over some groups male chiefs rule, this apparently being usual when the old queen has died without leaving a daughter ". In the religious life of the people priestesses play an important part. They engage in frenzied dances till they fall exhausted in a swoon, and on recovering they deliver oracles which they profess to have derived from spirits. Among the Taiyal, when rain is heavy and persistent the priestesses also dance, slashing the air with long knives and chanting in a threatening manner till they swoon with excitement and fatigue. In this way they are supposed to cut with their knives the god or devil of the rain, who flees and is drowned in one of the pools of his own making. At marriages, also, the priestesses dance and cut the air with their knives to repel the evil spirits, which otherwise would attack the newly wedded pair. A curious feature of the marriage ceremony is that the priestess mingles the blood of bride and bridegroom, which she has drawn from cuts in their legs. This may be regarded as a form of blood-covenant.

Among the Taiyal, religion consists almost entirely in a reverence for ancestral spirits. These spirits are fed twice a year at the great festivals of seedtime and harvest, both of which are timed so as to coincide with the night of the full moon. Balls of boiled millet are hung from the branches of trees in or near the village, and the spirits descend from the high mountains, where they usually reside, to partake of this food by night. To light them on the way a new fire is ceremonially kindled by the friction of two pieces of bamboo. It is the priestess who kindles the new fire, and she does so by the method known as the " stick and groove ", drawing a sort of bamboo saw rapidly to and fro in a shallow groove cut in another piece of bamboo. This custom of kindling a new fire at seedtime and harvest is practised also by the Bunun, another tribe of these aborigines ; but among them the fire is kindled, not by a priestess, but by a chief, and the method he employs is the commoner process of the " fire-drill ", which consists in twirling the point of a piece of hard wood in a hole made in a piece of soft wood till the powder produced by the friction bursts into a glow. From the flame thus kindled all the fires in the village are relit. It is interesting to meet with the two distinct methods of kindling fire practised by two tribes of the same people.

Among the Taiyal the dead are left in the houses where they die ; a little food, wine, and tobacco, together with some of the weapons or tools which belonged to them in life, are deposited beside the corpses, and the houses are abandoned, after the roof has been broken in. As Taiyal houses are built only of bamboo and grass, the erection of a new house for the family of the deceased is not a serious matter, and is often accomplished in a single day. On the other hand, among the Paiwan and the eastern Bunun, whose houses are substantially built of slate, the dead are buried in a crouching posture under the hearthstone of the

2 C

house, and the family continues to inhabit the house as if nothing had happened. In this case the fear of the ghost, which undoubtedly underlies the custom of abandoning a house to the dead, is clearly restrained by economic considerations ; a man may sacrifice a house of bamboo to the spirit of his dead relative, but he cannot afford to lose a house of slate. Thus the style of architecture adopted may have its influence on the religion even of savages.

XIX

IN PRIMITIVE NEW GUINEA*

THIS is an account of the Ipi and Namau, two groups of tribes living side by side on the southern coast of British New Guinea, or Papua, as it is now officially called. The district occupied by the tribes is a stretch of coastland on the Gulf of Papua from the delta of the Purari River on the west to Cape Possession on the east. The author, Mr. J. H. Holmes, is a missionary in the service of the London Missionary Society, who lived among these tribes for twenty-five years and is intimately acquainted with the people and their language. As a correspondent of the Royal Anthropological Institute he had published some interesting information concerning some of the customs and beliefs of the tribes in the *Journal* of that society. In the present work he gives a general account of the people based on the knowledge acquired during his long residence among them. His work is all the more welcome because, apart from the writings of his predecessor, the Rev. James Chalmers, published many years ago, very little accurate information concerning these particular tribes had been accessible to students.

Both groups of tribes described by him, the Ipi and the Namau, belong to the Papuan stock and speak Papuan languages, being thus distinguished from the people of the Melanesian stock, speaking Melanesian languages, who occupy the south-eastern part of New Guinea and have been described by Dr. C. G. Seligman in his standard work, *The Melanesians of British New Guinea*. Yet, in spite of their affinity and local proximity, the two sets of people are very different from each

* *In Primitive New Guinea.* By J. H. Holmes. (London : Seeley, Service, 1924.) (*The Times Literary Supplement,* April 17, 1924.)

other in speech, appearance, character, and customs. The Ipi are physically fine people, of prepossessing appearance, with faces expressive of intelligence ; the Namau are short and sturdy, with flat faces, sunken eyes, snub noses, and an expression of sullenness and moroseness, which, however, is said to do their real disposition less than justice. The Ipi are strict monogamists ; among them bigamy is an unpardonable offence: in one case known to Mr. Holmes a man who married a second wife was so ostracized by the tribe that he died of a broken heart, though he was a comparatively young man, strong and of exceptionally fine physique, who had been highly respected by all the people of his tribe till he committed the inexpiable sin of bigamy. In the same tribe adultery is, or used to be, punished with death ; indeed, Mr. Holmes assures us that " the standard of sexual morality of these barbarian monogamists was infinitely higher than is known in any civilized land to-day ". On the other hand, their neighbours, the Namau, practised polygamy, and among them the relations between the sexes were of the loosest and, judged by European standards, the most immoral sort ; concubinage was rampant, and the common decencies of life ignored. Again, the Namau were cannibals, while the Ipi were not. The reason alleged by the Namau for their cannibalism was that by eating the bodies of the foes whom they had slain they acquired the courage of their victims, thereby enhancing their own fighting qualities.

Among the topics on which the author dwells at some length are totemism, initiation, and the ceremonial use of masks. On the subject of totemism the information which he gives is not so clear and full as might be desired. We gather that the system existed fully developed among the Ipi, but not among the Namau. Totem kinship, the author tells us, was more sacred and binding than blood kinship. A man might not marry a woman of the same totem as himself, nor kill and eat his totemic animal ; if he saw anyone else killing it, he was bound to express his sorrow and sympathy with the creature. This so far is totemism of the most regular pattern. But Mr. Holmes distinguishes totems of different sorts, and it is not always clear to which sort he is referring. Thus, he speaks of tribal totems, communal totems, and individual totems ; also of name totems, dream totems, and parental totems. Every legitimate child, he tells us, was provided at birth with a totem by his or her parents ; and the males, when old enough to do so, were allowed to choose an additional totem. Every man of the tribe possessed as his individual totem an animal or a tree, and in addition always a species of fish as his second totem. Thus, the Ipi had that system of linked totems which has been recorded elsewhere in British New Guinea.

The initiation of young men was practised by both groups of tribes : among the Ipi the youths were presented to Kovave, the god of the mountains ; among the Namau they were presented to Kaia Imunu, the god of the sky, who was believed to enter into them through the sap of a cane which they had sucked. The initiation rites were divided into several successive stages : during their performance the youths were secluded in the sacred club-houses of the men, which Mr. Holmes repeatedly describes as totem-temples. At the first stage of initiation among the Ipi the novices were shown a long mask hanging from the roof of the temple (*eravo*) ; this mask, they were told, represented the god Kovave, whom they would meet at a later stage of initiation. As usual, the humming sound of bull-roarers played a conspicuous part in the ceremonies, being supposed to be the voice of the god to whom the novices were introduced. Among the Ipi an interesting feature at the final stage of initiation was the discharge of a cloud of arrows in the direction of the novices, who thereupon dropped to the ground as if they had been mortally wounded. Mr. Holmes does not explain this particular ceremony, but we may conjecture that it formed part of that pretence of death and resurrection which has been a conspicuous feature of initiatory rites in many regions of the world.

Important objects in the social and religious life of the people were the large carved wooden masks which are amongst the most remarkable products of their native art. These masks were sacred, and as such they were burnt at the conclusion of the religious ceremonies at which they had figured ; it would have been thought sacrilege to keep them or to dispose of them in any other way. Young men wearing a particular type of mask, and clad in grass petticoats that reached to the knees, were deemed by the vulgar to be god-men, messengers of the god Kovave come down to tell the people that the deity would soon visit the village. Again, the taboos annually imposed on certain pieces of land and water for the sake of the coco-nuts and fish were maintained by young men wearing masks and carrying bows and arrows, with which they were at liberty to shoot anyone who dared to break the taboo.

On the theology, the myths, and legends of the people Mr. Holmes does not tell us much. While we are grateful to him for what he has given us, we cannot but wish that he had given us a good deal more. The loss of some of his notes, to which he refers, may perhaps be partly responsible for a certain meagreness in the treatment of some topics about which, after his long experience, the author might have been expected to furnish us with more ample details. It is to be hoped that future inquiries on the spot may yet fill up some of the gaps in Mr Holmes's otherwise valuable record of these interesting tribes.

XX

ARGONAUTS OF THE WESTERN PACIFIC*

MY esteemed friend, Dr. B. Malinowski, has asked me to write a preface to his book, and I willingly comply with his request, though I can hardly think that any words of mine will add to the value of the remarkable record of anthropological research which he has given us in this volume. My observations, such as they are, will deal partly with the writer's method and partly with the matter of his book.

In regard to method, Dr. Malinowski has done his work, as it appears to me, under the best conditions and in the manner calculated to secure the best possible results. Both by theoretical training and by practical experience he was well equipped for the task which he undertook. Of his theoretical training he had given proof in his learned and thoughtful treatise on the family among the aborigines of Australia ; [1] of his practical experience he had produced no less satisfactory evidence in his account of the natives of Mailu in New Guinea, based on a residence of six months among them.[2] In the Trobriand Islands, to the east of New Guinea, to which he next turned his attention, Dr. Malin-

* The following article was contributed as a preface to the book of which the title is *Argonauts of the Western Pacific. An Account of Native Enterprise and Adventure in the Archipelagoes of Melanesian New Guinea.* By Bronislaw Malinowski, Ph.D. (Cracow), D.Sc. (London). London: George Routledge and Sons, Ltd., 1922.

[1] *The Family among the Australian Aborigines : A Sociological Study.* London : University of London Press, 1913.
[2] " The Natives of Mailu : Pre- liminary Results of the Robert Mond Research Work in British New Guinea " (*Transactions of the Royal Society of South Australia*, vol. xxxix., 1915).

owski lived as a native among the natives for many months together, watching them daily at work and at play, conversing with them in their own tongue, and deriving all his information from the surest sources—personal observation and statements made to him directly by the natives in their own language without the intervention of an interpreter. In this way he has accumulated a large mass of materials, of high scientific value, bearing on the social, religious, and economic or industrial life of the Trobriand Islanders. These he hopes and intends to publish hereafter in full ; meantime he has given us in the present volume a preliminary study of an interesting and peculiar feature in Trobriand society, the remarkable system of exchange, only in part economic or commercial, which the islanders maintain among themselves and with the inhabitants of neighbouring islands.

Little reflection is needed to convince us of the fundamental importance of economic forces at all stages of man's career from the humblest to the highest. After all, the human species is part of the animal creation, and as such, like the rest of the animals, it reposes on a material foundation ; on which a higher life, intellectual, moral, social, may be built, but without which no such superstructure is possible. That material foundation, consisting in the necessity of food and of a certain degree of warmth and shelter from the elements, forms the economic or industrial basis and prime condition of human life. If anthropologists have hitherto unduly neglected it, we may suppose that it was rather because they were attracted to the higher side of man's nature than because they deliberately ignored and undervalued the importance and indeed necessity of the lower. In excuse for their neglect we may also remember that anthropology is still a young science, and that the multitude of problems which await the student cannot all be attacked at once, but must be grappled with one by one. Be that as it may, Dr. Malinowski has done well to emphasize the great significance of primitive economics by singling out the notable exchange system of the Trobriand Islanders for special consideration.

Further, he has wisely refused to limit himself to a mere description of the processes of the exchange, and has set himself to penetrate the motives which underlie it and the feelings which it excites in the minds of the natives. It appears to be sometimes held that pure sociology should confine itself to the description of acts and should leave the problems of motives and feelings to psychology. Doubtless it is true that the analysis of motives and feelings is logically distinguishable from the description of acts, and that it falls, strictly speaking, within the sphere of psychology ; but in practice an act has no meaning for an observer unless he knows or infers the thoughts and emotions of the agent ; hence to describe a series of acts without any reference to the state of mind of the agent would not answer the purpose of sociology, the aim of which is not merely to register but to understand the actions of men in society. Thus sociology cannot fulfil its task without calling in at every turn the aid of psychology.

It is characteristic of Dr. Malinowski's method that he takes full account of the complexity of human nature. He sees man, so to say, in the round and not in the flat. He remembers that man is a creature of emotion at least as much as of reason, and he is constantly at pains to discover the emotional as well as the rational basis of human action. The man of science, like the man of letters, is too apt to view mankind only in the abstract, selecting for his consideration a single side of our complex and many-sided being. Of this one-sided treatment Molière is a conspicuous example among great writers. All his characters are seen only in the flat : one of them is a miser, another a hypocrite, another a cox-comb, and so on ; but not one of them is a man. All are dummies dressed up to look very like human beings ; but the likeness is only on the surface, all within is hollow and empty, because truth to nature has been sacrificed to literary effect. Very different is the presentation of human nature in the greater artists, such as Cervantes and Shakespeare : their characters are solid, being drawn not from one side only but from many. No doubt in science a certain ab-stractness of treatment is not merely legitimate, but necessary, since science is nothing but knowledge raised to the highest power, and all knowledge implies a process of abstraction and generalization : even the recognition of an individual whom we see every day is only possible as the result of an

abstract idea of him formed by generalization from his
appearances in the past. Thus the science of man is forced
to abstract certain aspects of human nature and to consider
them apart from the concrete reality ; or rather it falls into
a number of sciences, each of which considers a single part
of man's complex organism, it may be the physical, the
intellectual, the moral, or the social side of his being ; and
the general conclusions which it draws will present a more or
less incomplete picture of man as a whole, because the lines
which compose it are necessarily but a few picked out of a
multitude.

In the present treatise Dr. Malinowski is mainly concerned with what at first sight might seem a purely economic
activity of the Trobriand Islanders ; but, with his usual
width of outlook and fineness of perception, he is careful to
point out that the curious circulation of valuables which
takes place between the inhabitants of the Trobriand and
other islands, while it is accompanied by ordinary trade, is
by no means itself a purely commercial transaction ; he shows
that it is not based on a simple calculation of utility, of
profit and loss, but that it satisfies emotional and aesthetic
needs of a higher order than the mere gratification of animal
wants. This leads Dr. Malinowski to pass some severe
strictures on the conception of the Primitive Economic Man
as a kind of bogey who, it appears, still haunts economic
text-books and even extends his blighting influence to the
minds of certain anthropologists. Rigged out in cast-off
garments of Mr. Jeremy Bentham and Mr. Gradgrind, this
horrible phantom is apparently actuated by no other motive
than that of filthy lucre, which he pursues relentlessly, on
Spencerian principles, along the line of least resistance. If
such a dismal fiction is really regarded by serious inquirers
as having any counterpart in savage society, and not simply
as a useful abstraction, Dr. Malinowski's account of the
Kula in this book should help to lay the phantom by the
heels ; for he proves that the trade in useful objects which
forms part of the *Kula* system is in the minds of the natives
entirely subordinate in importance to the exchange of other
objects which serve no utilitarian purpose whatever. In its
combination of commercial enterprise, social organization,

mythical background, and magical ritual, to say nothing of the wide geographical range of its operations, this singular institution appears to have no exact parallel in the existing anthropological record ; but its discoverer, Dr. Malinowski, may very well be right in surmising that it is probably a type of institution of which analogous, if not precisely similar, instances will hereafter be brought to light by further research among savage and barbarous peoples.

Not the least interesting and instructive feature of the *Kula*, as it is described for us by Dr. Malinowski, is the extremely important part which magic is seen to play in the institution. From his description it appears that in the minds of the natives the performance of magical rites and the utterance of magical words are indispensable for the success of the enterprise in all its phases, from the felling of the trees out of which the canoes are to be hollowed down to the moment when, the expedition successfully accomplished, the argosy with its precious cargo is about to start on its homeward voyage. And incidentally we learn that magical ceremonies and spells are deemed no less necessary for the cultivation of gardens and for success in fishing, the two forms of industrial enterprise which furnish the islanders with their principal means of support ; hence the garden magician, whose business it is to promote the growth of the garden produce by his hocus-pocus, is one of the most important men in the village, ranking next after the chief and the sorcerer. In short, magic is believed to be an absolutely essential adjunct of every industrial undertaking, being just as requisite for its success as the mechanical operations involved in it, such as the caulking, painting, and launching of a canoe, the planting of a garden, and the setting of a fish-trap. " A belief in magic ", says Dr. Malinowski, " is one of the main psychological forces which allow for organisation and systematisation of economic effort in the Trobriands."

This valuable account of magic as a factor of fundamental economic importance for the welfare and indeed for the very existence of the community should suffice to dispel the erroneous view that magic, as opposed to religion, is in its nature essentially maleficent and anti-social, being always used by an individual for the promotion of his own selfish ends and the

injury of his enemies, quite regardless of its effect on the
common weal. No doubt magic may be so employed, and
has in fact probably been so employed, in every part of the
world ; in the Trobriand Islands themselves it is believed to
be similarly practised for nefarious purposes by sorcerers,
who inspire the natives with the deepest dread and the most
constant concern. But in itself magic is neither beneficent
nor maleficent ; it is simply an imaginary power of controlling
the forces of Nature, and this control may be exercised by
the magician for good or evil, for the benefit or injury of
individuals and of the community. In this respect, magic is
exactly on the same footing with the sciences, of which it is
the bastard sister. They, too, in themselves, are neither good
nor evil, though they become the source of one or other
according to their application. It would be absurd, for
example, to stigmatize pharmacy as anti-social, because a
knowledge of the properties of drugs is often employed to
destroy men as well as to heal them. It is equally absurd to
neglect the beneficent application of magic and to single out
its maleficent use as the characteristic property by which to
define it. The processes of Nature, over which science exercises a real and magic an imaginary control, are not affected
by the moral disposition, the good or bad intention, of the
individual who uses his knowledge to set them in motion.
The action of drugs on the human body is precisely the same
whether they are administered by a physician or by a poisoner.
Nature and her handmaid Science are neither friendly nor
hostile to morality ; they are simply indifferent to it and
equally ready to do the bidding of the saint and of the sinner,
provided only that he gives them the proper word of command.
If the guns are well loaded and well aimed, the fire of the
battery will be equally destructive whether the gunners are
patriots fighting in defence of their country or invaders
waging a war of unjust aggression. The fallacy of differ-
entiating a science or an art according to its application and
the moral intention of the agent is obvious enough with
regard to pharmacy and artillery ; it is equally real, though
to many people apparently it is less obvious, with regard to
magic.

The immense influence wielded by magic over the whole

life and thought of the Trobriand Islanders is perhaps the feature of Dr. Malinowski's book which makes the most abiding impression on the mind of the reader. He tells us that " magic, the attempt of man to govern the forces of nature directly by means of a special lore, is all-pervading and all-important in the Trobriands " ; it is " interwoven into all the many industrial and communal activities " ; " all the data which have been so far mustered disclose the extreme importance of magic in the Kula. But if it were a question of treating of any other aspect of the tribal life of these natives, it would also be found that, whenever they approach any concern of vital importance, they summon magic to their aid. It can be said without exaggeration that magic, according to their ideas, governs human destinies ; that it supplies man with the power of mastering the forces of Nature; and that it is his weapon and armour against the many dangers which crowd in upon him on every side."

Thus, in the view of the Trobriand Islanders, magic is a power of supreme importance either for good or evil : it can make or mar the life of man : it can sustain and protect the individual and the community, or it can injure and destroy them. Compared to this universal and deep-rooted conviction, the belief in the existence of the spirits of the dead would seem to exercise but little influence on the life of these people. Contrary to the general attitude of savages towards the souls of the departed, they are reported to be almost completely devoid of any fear of ghosts. They believe, indeed, that the ghosts return to their villages once a year to partake of the great annual feast ; but " in general the spirits do not influence human beings very much, for better or worse " ; " there is nothing of the mutual interaction, of the intimate collaboration between man and spirit which are the essence of religious cult ". This conspicuous predominance of magic over religion, at least over the worship of the dead, is a very notable feature in the culture of a people so comparatively high in the scale of savagery as the Trobriand Islanders. It furnishes a fresh proof of the extraordinary strength and tenacity of the hold which this world-wide delusion has had, and still has, upon the human mind.

We shall doubtless learn much as to the relation of magic

and religion among the Trobrianders from the full report of Dr. Malinowski's researches in the islands. From the patient observation which he has devoted to a single institution, and from the wealth of details with which he has illustrated it, we may judge of the extent and value of the larger work which he has in preparation. It promises to be one of the completest and most scientific accounts ever given of a savage people.

XXI

SAVAGE LIFE IN CENTRAL AUSTRALIA*

THIS work describes the country, the habits, customs, and beliefs of the Wonkonguru and their neighbours, tribes of South Australia whose territory lies immediately to the east of Lake Eyre. The principal author of the work, Dr. Horne, tells us that the book is the result of a visit which he paid to the district ; but when the visit was paid, and how long it lasted, he omits to say. The other author, Mr. Aiston, of the Mounted Police, has lived for many years among the natives, and has consequently enjoyed ample opportunities of collecting information concerning them. The book is therefore a very welcome addition to our knowledge of the Central Australian natives, all the more so because the tribes with which it deals are not included in the great ethnographical survey which Spencer and Gillen have given of Central Australia in books which have long been anthropological classics. The present book may be regarded in some sort as a supplement or appendix to these great works, and to that of Dr. A. W. Howitt on the tribes of South-Eastern Australia ; for Dr. Howitt deals to some extent with the tribes described by Dr. Horne and Mr. Aiston, particularly with the Dieri tribe, who are the neighbours of the Wonkonguru on the south.

The general effect of the inquiries of Dr. Horne and Mr. Aiston is not so much to add to our knowledge of the Central Australian aborigines as to confirm in all respects the evidence of their eminent predecessors, even on points which have been

---

* *Savage Life in Central Australia.* By G. Horne and G. Aiston, Mounted Police of South Australia. (London : Macmillan, 1924.) (*The Times Literary Supplement*, October 9, 1924.)

vehemently disputed by writers whose ignorance of the Australian facts has proved no impediment to their dogmatizing confidently about them. Thus the present writers inform us that physical paternity is absolutely unknown to the aborigines (" that the father has anything to do with conception is absolutely foreign to the native mind "). Corresponding to this ignorance of the process of propagation in the human sexes is their ignorance of the process of propagation in plants. Though these savages have been in contact with white people for many years and have enjoyed the advantages of missionary teaching, they have not yet learned that seeds sown in the ground will spring up and produce fruit after their kind. It is true that they perform ceremonies to promote the growth of those plants which furnish them with food ; but what they scatter about in these ceremonies on these occasions are not seeds, but stones ; or, if they do throw seed about broadcast, they are at pains to crush it between stones before sowing it, so that fertilization is rendered impossible. They also perform ceremonies of the familiar type to ensure a fall of rain, which is much wanted in their arid and sun-scorched country ; in these ceremonies they throw water about, doubtless in imitation of rain, and with bunches of feathers they make a swishing sound to mimic the plash of falling rain. A more singular, but no doubt equally effectual, way of drawing down showers is for a number of performers to pierce the skin of their arms, thighs, and other parts of their bodies with sharp bones, collect the flowing blood in a vessel, and drink it. How this is supposed to ensure a fall of rain is not clear to the European mind. The appearance of the Aurora Australis in the sky excites great alarm in the minds of these savages, and to avert the threatened danger they resort to indiscriminate sexual intercourse. How such intercourse affects the Aurora remains a mystery ; but as it is invariably followed by the disappearance of the alarming celestial phenomenon, the native is no doubt perfectly satisfied of the causal connexion between the two, and goes to sleep with the calm conviction that he has adopted the right remedy in the emergency.

The natives, like many other savages, never ascribe death to natural causes, except when somebody has been knocked on the head in a fight. The principal, if not the only other, cause of death, in their opinion, appears to be magic. The commonest mode of doing a man to death by magic is, seemingly, for his enemy to point a bone at him from any distance, while at the same time the foe chants an incantation appropriate to the sort of disease by which he desires the other to be afflicted. Afterwards the enchanter buries the bone in the ground, digs it up from time to time, and burns a piece off the end. Meantime the victim is supposed to grow worse and worse, and if the bone that is doing the mischief is not found and dipped in water it is believed that the patient will die. Children are instructed almost from infancy in this unamiable art, which is responsible for countless deaths ; not, of course, that it really kills anybody, but that the unquestioning faith of the blacks in its efficacy induces them to put to death many innocent persons who are accused of having practised it with fatal effect on the sick and dying.

The tribes in question, like many others of the same region, believe in the existence of ancestral spirits called *mooras* or *moora-mooras*, about whom they tell many tales and legends. This belief and the practices based on it are described by Dr. Horne as " a sort of ancestor worship " ; but the term seems too strong in view of the writer's own statement that " no ceremonies seem to have been performed to propitiate the *mooras* ". However, some of the ceremonies, if not propitiatory, appear to be dramatic. At a ceremony witnessed by the authors, two men, with bunches of box-tree leaves tied to their ankles, represented ancestral spirits ; and at other ceremonies emblems (*waninga*) of the ancestors are carried about and in some sort venerated.

Like most Australian tribes, the Wonkonguru believe in the resurrection of the body ; and in that belief they considerately leave a supply of wood and sticks at the grave, in order that, when the dead man " jumps up", he may be able to build a hut and light a fire to warm himself, in case he should feel chilly. At the same time, not very consistently, all the personal belongings of the deceased are broken at the grave, " so that his spirit will not come back and use them ". Perhaps, while they are willing to contribute to the personal comfort of the departed brother, they fear that, if they left

2 D

him his weapons whole, his ghost might swarm down on them in the hours of slumber and dispatch them with his boomerang or other lethal implement. In favour of this hypothesis may be alleged the circumstance that women's belongings are not broken at the grave, probably because their ghosts are less truculent than those of men.

On the important subject of totemism and the complex rules of marriage connected with it the authors tell us almost nothing, except that a man must always marry a woman of another totem, and that the children take the totem of their mother, not that of their father. On the question of the system of relationships, which is doubtless classificatory, Dr. Horne and Mr. Aiston are silent. In fact, while we are grateful to them for what they have given us, we wish that they had given us much more ; for on many topics their information is disappointingly scanty. One of the subjects on which they dwell at comparative length is the making and use of stone implements ; for the natives, in spite of their intercourse with white people, are still in the Stone Age. This section of the book should prove useful to antiquaries who study the palæolithic and neolithic remains of prehistoric peoples in other parts of the world.

The account of the natives, which occupies the greater part of the book, is appropriately preceded by an interesting and vivid description of their country, which is for the most part an arid and a dreary expanse of low sandhills and stony flats, where the river-beds are generally dry and water can only be found by digging. But after a heavy rain a wonderful change comes over the landscape, and the whole country bursts into blossom as by magic. But the beauty is transient ; the bloom soon fades. In a few weeks the scorching heat of the sun has withered up the vegetation, and nothing remains but dry stems and blackened seeds to tell where gorgeous masses of flowers had lately spangled the desert with a blaze of colour and filled the air with their sweet perfume. The book is well illustrated by photographs which convey to the reader clear ideas both of the country and the people, and there is an excellent map.

XXII

A YEAR AMONG THE MAORIS*

THE author of this work, Miss Frances Del Mar, is an artist who has collected and described ethnological materials for American museums in the course of her travels in Polynesia and elsewhere. In the present book she gives us the results of a visit to New Zealand. From the title we are left to infer that the visit lasted a year, and from incidental references we gather that it fell during the Great War and was confined to the North Island ; for the authoress vouchsafes no dates and hardly any particulars of her travels beyond the statement that she " set out by train from Wellington one evening ".

The bulk of the text deals with the past history and mode of life of the Maoris, the information being largely drawn, often in the form of quotations, from well-known printed sources. But on some subjects, such as weaving, carving, and the use of weapons of war, Miss Del Mar has made personal inquiries among the Maoris and has embodied the results of her investigations in her book. In her researches she has had the benefit of the advice and assistance of Mr. Elsdon Best, the eminent authority on the Maoris, and of Mr. T. F. Cheeseman, late Director of the Auckland Museum. But the value of the book consists chiefly in the numerous photographs and sketches with which the authoress has illustrated various aspects of Maori life, art, and architecture. Among the subjects which she describes and illustrates are tatooing, weaving, fire-making, dancing, fortification, and carving. The old Maori mode of kindling fire was by the method of the stick-

---

* *A Year among the Maoris : A Study of their Arts and Customs.* By Frances Del Mar. (London : Benn, 1924.) (*The Times Literary Supplement*, January 8, 1925.)

and-groove, which was universally employed in Polynesia, but rarely in other parts of the world, though in recent years it has been found in use among a few African tribes of the Congo Valley. Miss Del Mar thinks that the stick-and-groove was probably the oldest mode of making fire ; but it is doubtful whether priority should not rather be assigned to the fire-drill, which has prevailed far more widely throughout the world, not only among savages, but also among the civilized peoples of antiquity Miss Del Mar adds the interesting particular that " a custom of the old days in fire-making was for a woman to place her foot upon the soft wood as it lay on the ground while a man worked the hard stick in the groove ". Of this custom Miss Del Mar quotes a fanciful explanation by a modern writer, but the true one was given her by the Maoris themselves, who told her " that as male and female were essential to all creation, so in the creation of fire the joint action of the sexes was symbolized " For in the kindling of fire by the friction of wood savages often see an analogy to the union of the sexes, and they frequently give the names of " male " and " female " to the upright and the horizontal firesticks respectively.

The authoress refers to the well-known practice of willing a person to death, which was frequently attended with fatal results in New Zealand. The victim so denounced, she tells us, " rarely survived two days, and frequently expired at the appointed time ". The statement could doubtless be supported by a large body of evidence, which demonstrates that faith can kill quite as readily as cure. However, Miss Del Mar was informed by a Maori woman of a way in which the fatal effects of the ill-wish can be averted. If a man had been willed to death, and was fortunate enough to discover his ill-wisher, he consulted a priest (tohunga), who could not only save him but turn the tables on his foe by causing him to die. For this purpose the priest and the patient entered the water naked and faced the east ; then the priest sprayed the water towards the abode of the original ill-wisher, who naturally succumbed sooner or later. From Miss Del Mar's account of Maori games we learn that the grinning match, immortalized by Addison in the *Spectator*, has not been peculiar to English bumpkins, but has been shared independently by the

Maoris, who enriched the most hideous grimaces and con-
tortions of the human frame with a melodious accompaniment
of groans and sneezes. Further, she tells us that at the mourning for a chief bull-roarers were swung to drive off evil spirits,
and that on the same sad occasion tops were spun, apparently
because their humming sound was felt to chime in with the
general gloom of the mourners.

XXIII
RELIGION AND MYTHOLOGY OF THE UITOTO*

THE Uitoto are a tribe or nation of Indians settled on one of the northern tributaries of the Amazon. Their number is estimated at about 25,000. The author of the present work, Dr. K. Th. Preuss, Director of the Berlin Ethnological Museum, and well known as a writer on the religion of the American Indians, spent some four months in 1914 among an outlying branch of the tribe in Columbia, and has here given us the first-fruits of his labours among them. Unfortunately he did not penetrate to the main body of the nation, which appears to dwell a good deal farther south on the Caraparana River, a tributary of the Amazon. The Uitoto studied by Dr. Preuss numbered no more than 131 individuals all told, distributed in two villages on the Niña Maria, a tributary of the Orteguasa, which is itself a tributary of the Amazon. It was not, therefore, to be expected that the author could collect much information concerning the social life and tribal organization of these Indians, and his account of these subjects is very meagre. We learn that the inhabitants of the two small villages included representatives of no fewer than thirty-one tribes or clans (*Stämme*); that the names of these tribes or clans are mostly derived from animals or plants, more rarely from other natural objects; and that the law of exogamy is strictly observed, no man

---

* *Religion und Mythologie der Uitoto.* Textaufnahmen und Beobachtungen bei einem Indianerstamm in Kolumbien, Südamerika. Von Professor Dr. K. Th. Preuss. Vol. I. (Göttingen : Vandenhoeck and Ruprecht, 1921.) (*The Times Literary Supplement,* January 18, 1923.)

marrying a woman of his tribe or clan. These facts point to the existence of totemism among the Uitoto, though on the subject of totemism Dr. Preuss is silent. With regard to their system of relationship, the writer tells us that they have no terms for the remoter degrees of kinship ; but he explains that some of the terms, such as those for brother and sister, are employed in a widely extended sense so as to include cousins and others whom we should not call brothers and sisters, and this generalization in the use of kinship terms introduces much uncertainty. All this is suggestive of the classificatory system of relationship, about which also Dr. Preuss is silent.

Although the inhabitants of the larger village visited live in a large communal house divided into chambers for the accommodation of separate families, the system of property appears not to be communal : every grown person in both villages owns his own field, which he cultivates at his discretion. The men clear the forest for cultivation ; the women help at clearing the underwood, plant, hoe, and bring home the produce of the fields ; they are also the potters. The men, besides hunting and fishing, occupy themselves with the making of baskets and wooden implements for household use. The staple food is cassava, a species of bread baked from the roots of manioc. The social position of women is not high : they must wait hand and foot on the men when they are not at work in the fields. Their degradation is marked by the rule that when the house has two doors, as it used always to have, the women may enter it only by the back door. Hence a suitor used only to apply to the father for the hand of his daughter ; and in the stories there are traces of the custom which obliged a man to work for his father-in-law either during a residence with the parents of his wife or on subsequent visits to them. After a birth the father abstains from work for five days and the mother for fourteen days ; during this time they eat no flesh, and paint their hands and feet red. They believe that if they did not observe these rules the child would die. Thus they practise the couvade, and assign for it what is probably always the true reason for that curious custom—namely, a belief that even after birth the infant is united to its parents by so close a tie of sympathy that whatever they do affects the child physically for good or evil. The dead were buried under the pile-supported platform on which the village is built.

But it is to the religious ideas and customs of the Uitoto that Dr. Preuss has paid most attention, and his account of them forms the most valuable part of his work. He applied himself especially to taking down the myths and legends of the people in the native language, and these he has printed with parallel translations in German. We possess so little detailed information concerning the religion of the South American Indians that the large collection of religious or mythical tales brought back by Dr. Preuss possesses a particular interest and value for the anthropologist. Among the tales are versions of the widespread legends of a great flood and the origin of fire. In one of these versions the great flood is said to have been caused by somebody's belabouring a parrot with a stick and knocking out the shining red feathers of its tail. This so enraged the owner of the parrot, a certain Dyaere by name, that he called down a heavy rain, which drowned all the tribes of men who then lived on earth ; the existing race of men came subsequently. Another version traces the great flood to the killing of a fish, the offspring of a woman who had married a fish. This excited the sorrow of the fish-father ; as he wept, the rain fell ; the fish lashed the water to fury, and, pursuing the guilty people from river to river, dragged them all under water. The legend of the origin of fire forms part of the story which relates to the origin of manioc. Of old the people had no fire and no manioc ; they ate white earth and the decayed trunks of trees. But in time a woman, im-pregnated without her knowledge, gave birth to offspring which mysteriously turned into manioc and grew up into a stately tree. After that the people ceased to eat earth and rotten tree trunks, and subsisted on the bread which they made from the roots of the manioc. But they could only bake the bread in the sun, for as yet they knew not fire. At last the Fire-woman, or Wife of the Fire, came to some children as they sat alone in the house, and drawing fire from her mouth baked their cassava bread for them. Having done so, she departed, but not before she had effaced all

traces of the fire and strictly enjoined the children to keep
the secret from their parents.   On their return the parents
were astonished to find the cassava better baked than it had
ever been in the sun, and after a good deal of questioning
they contrived to elicit the truth from the children, whom
they thereupon charged to steal the fire from the Fire-woman.
So the next time she came and was busy roasting the cassava,
the children managed to conceal some of the fire in a pot ;
and when she had gone away all the people procured fire
from the portion of it which the children had stolen and
hidden.   Next day the Fire-woman came again and re-
proached the children with the theft ;   but she was not
seriously angry and bade them bake the bread for themselves
in a pan which she left for their use.   So saying she went
away and cowered down beside the open space, which, we
are told, means that she sank down in the fire, since she was
herself nothing but the fire.

Curiously enough, the Fire-woman is also spoken of as
a *dormilon*, which is a species of bird that flies by night and
sleeps by day.   In many legends scattered over the world
the first fire is thus associated with an animal, and especially
a bird, often on the ground of some red feathers which are
traditionally said to have been burnt or scorched by the fire.
In the myths of the Uitoto, says Dr. Preuss, " it is a quite
common incident for animals or plants to appear as men.
Indeed, one often does not know whether the tribes with the
names of animals or plants represent human tribes or not,
for there is no distinction made between them and men, and
they are sometimes actually described as ancestors ".   More
than that, the apparently human actors in the stories frequently turn into animals.   In Indian, as in other folk-tales,
such metamorphoses as Ovid describes in his poem of
that name are everyday occurrences.   Our kinship with the
beasts is recognized by the Uitoto in their creation myth,
which relates how in the beginning all creatures had tails,
until the wasp gnawed off the tails, first of toads and afterwards of human beings.   The confusion between beasts and
men comes out, for example, in a striking and dramatic tale
entitled " The Wanderings of Fuyedamona and his Combat
with the Bat ", for in the story it is by no means clear whether

the Bat, who devours tribe after tribe of Indians and is finally killed by the hero and eaten by the people, was the mammal of that name or a ferocious but human savage.

From incidental references we gather that the Uitoto Indians studied by Dr. Preuss are nominal Christians, or at all events baptized. But they are said to have kept their old customs and dances, and some of these are described by Dr. Preuss. Amongst them are the Festival of Manioc or of the Ancestors (*okima*), which, as witnessed by Dr. Preuss, included flute-playing, dances, and a sham fight with spears between the inhabitants of the two villages. Another is a festival of ball-playing (*uike*), in which an india-rubber ball is thrown between the players, who strike it with their knees and keep it as long in the air as possible. This festival is celebrated every second year in the dry season, either in March or September, when fruits are plentiful ; it lasts for some time, with intervals of four days, during which stories are told by night. Another festival, called *dyadiko*, has for its main feature a dance of men on the hollowed-out trunk of a tree, which has been felled for the purpose and painted on the outer side with the devices of an alligator, a woman's face, and a water-snake, on which many butterflies are perched. Another festival, also characterized by dances, is celebrated at the making of a pair of drums (*huare*) ; another used to be held on the return of warriors from battle, after they had partaken of the flesh of slain foes or prisoners, whose skulls were hung from the beams of the roof and their teeth worn as necklaces. Many stories were told in the nights preceding this festival. Another festival, called *meni*, is or used to be held by the medicine-men, when they caught in the air the fluttering spirits of the dead, who cause sickness and death. Having captured these vagabond and dangerous spirits, the medicine-men shut them up in nuts, which they sealed with wax and buried in the ground, thus disposing of the cause of sickness and ensuring the recovery of the sick. When caught and rubbed between the hands of the wizards, the souls of the dead presented the appearance of small pebbles.

Myths and festivals are explained by Dr. Preuss as all alike referring to the phases of the moon. Thus, in regard to the Manioc Festival, he observes that " in fact all the proceedings of the festival, including the combat as well as the dances, are to be referred to the processes of the moon. The combat signifies the conquest of the old moon by the new one, as is often described in the myths ". In the festival of ball-play the ball is the new moon, which, we are informed, knocked off the head of the old moon. The object of the festival of dancing on the painted tree trunk, as we learn on the same authority, is the killing of the old moon, whereby the road is cleared for the renewal of the new moon. In the festival of the making of drums the drum is naturally the dark moon, while an axe, which figures in the festival, represents the new moon ; so does a squirrel, and likewise an effigy of an ape, while the men who carry the effigy are " lunar beings, representatives of the new moon ". Even in the war-dance, which to a superficial observer might seem to celebrate a victory over human foes, the vanquished party is really the moon, for Dr. Preuss assures us that in it the central idea is " the destruction of the moon ".

Similarly in dealing with the myths Dr. Preuss unmasks the moon under all the disguises under which the cunning luminary might hope to evade detection by a less instructed European observer. It is, indeed, suprising to see how often the moon turns up in the most unexpected places. To take the first instances that come to hand in turning over the pages, we are apprised that a burst water-ball is the dark moon, who has had his head knocked off in the manner so characteristic of moons (" *eine Todesakt, die bezeichnend für Monde ist* ") : the breaking of a staff signifies the waning of the moon : the adversaries of the lunar being are themselves nothing but new moons ; nay, the sun himself is the moon, for can anything be more obvious than that the expression " the pointed sun " is merely a circumlocution for " the sickle of the moon " ? When a child is born and put in a pot, we learn, no longer with surprise, that the child is the new moon, which at first is invisible, while the mother, equally as a matter of course, becomes the dark moon. A serpent in a myth is not a serpent but the moon, the resemblance of which to the reptile is too patent to require justification. After this it is needless to observe that the parrot who lost his fine feathers in the story of the great flood is our old friend the new moon, who, " like many lunar beings, is very greedy " ; so when the parrot eats till he is like to burst, this cannot possibly have any other signification than that the moon is waxing to the full, and so on and so on. Nothing escapes the lunar net in which Dr. Preuss catches all the beings that figure in the myths and folk-tales of the Uitoto. In one form or another everybody and everything is the moon : the changes may be rung on the new moon and the old moon, the bright moon and the dark moon, the waxing moon, the full moon, and the waning moon ; a character may disguise himself as he pleases and make a bolt for freedom, but Dr. Preuss is on his track and will sooner or later catch him up, tear the mask from his face, and reveal to us the moon, the moon, and nothing but the moon. In short, the moon is to Dr. Preuss what King Charles's head was to Mr. Dick : it amounts to an obsession, which seriously detracts from the value of an otherwise meritorious work. Dr. Preuss promises to complete the book by a second volume, which will contain myths, songs, and a lexicon of the language. We hope in the interest of science that he will carry out his intention, and that in the interval he will seriously reconsider his lunar theory and reduce it within more reasonable limits.

XXIV

PRIMITIVE MENTALITY*

In this book the author, Professor Lévy-Bruhl, of the Sorbonne, takes up again and develops the subject treated by him in a former work, *Les Fonctions mentales dans les sociétés inférieures*. That subject is the modes of thought current among savage or, as he prefers to call them, " primitive " peoples. He admits that the term " primitive " applied to uncivilized races is very improper, since even the rudest of these races, as known to us, is very far from being primitive in the strict sense of the word. But, understood in a relative sense as indicating a lower stage of mental and social evolution than that attained to by the civilized races, the term is convenient.

The main theme of the author in both his books is the essential difference which he believes he can trace between primitive and advanced mentality, between the thought of the savage and the thought of the civilized man. According to him, primitive thought is essentially prelogical and mystic. It is prelogical because, failing to recognize the law of contradiction, it can entertain two contradictory ideas at the same time without perceiving their inconsistency ; it is mystic because it explains a great, if not the greater, part of experience by supernatural, instead of by natural, causes. In his former work Professor Lévy-Bruhl laid stress mainly on the illogical or, as he prefers to call it, prelogical character of primitive thought ; in the present work he dwells chiefly on its mysti-

---

* *Primitive Mentality.* By Lucien Lévy-Bruhl, Professor at the Sorbonne. Authorized Translation by Lilian A. Clare. (London : Allen and Unwin, 1923.) (*The Times Literary Supplement*, September 13, 1923.)

cism, its readiness to resort to invisible and supernatural agency for the explanation of natural phenomena. Primitive man, he tells us, believes himself to be surrounded by a host of invisible beings, which exert a constant and, indeed, preponderant influence on the course of Nature and of human life. For the most part these unseen agents are personal beings or spirits, either the spirits of the human dead or the spirits of natural objects, whether animate or inanimate. But among them must be reckoned the invisible force of sorcery or witchcraft, the dread of which acts like an obsession on the minds of many savages, notably in Africa. Believing that his life is at the mercy of spirits and sorcerers, the savage devotes an infinity of thought and trouble to propitiating the one and combating, or at least neutralizing, the other. These futile, yet often pathetic and tragic, endeavours are admirably illustrated by the author in a series of chapters in which he deals with such topics as the primitive conception of death, of dreams, of omens, of the causes of accident and misfortune, or of success and prosperity, the practice of divination, the use of ordeals, and so forth.

Many of the themes are familiar, but the author's treatment of them is always instructive; for the examples are apt, well arranged, and accompanied by acute and suggestive comments. From the wealth of materials collected in the volume it is difficult, without doing injustice to the author, to select specimens for special mention ; but we may refer to the interesting evidence adduced to prove that primitive peoples do not regard omens as simple predictions of coming events, but that they deem it possible, by manipulating the omens, to alter the events in a sense favourable to themselves ; for example, they think that before a sacrificial victim is killed to furnish omens from its entrails, they can induce the animal to modify its internal structure in accordance with their wishes. Similarly in Borneo it seems to be thought that the omen birds are causes as well as signs of the events which they foretell ; hence the natives adore and thank the birds as the dispensers of gifts as well as the bearers of good tidings. Again, Professor Lévy-Bruhl brings out very clearly the need which the primitive mind feels of accompanying all the ordinary business of life, such as hunting, fishing, agriculture,

and so forth, by appeals to those mystic and invisible powers
on which success or failure is believed to depend far more
than upon the merely material instruments and physical processes employed in these various operations.

In short, the author demonstrates, by an abundance of
excellent evidence, the great extent to which primitive thought
is dominated by belief in the supernatural. Yet we may
doubt whether he is right in treating the supernaturalism of
savages as constituting a fundamental difference between
them and civilized men as a whole. It is true that civilized
men generally pay much more attention to material or natural
causes than do savages ; yet in civilized society religious
people believe that the forces which ultimately control the
world are spiritual and supernatural ; the Christian, as well
as the savage, holds that the unseen powers are as real as,
and far more potent than, the visible powers which seem to
regulate mundane affairs. The missionary who traces the
hand of Providence and the intervention of saints, angels, or
devils in the incidents of his daily life, as well as in the handiwork of Nature, is hardly less of a mystic than the savage who
refers the same things to the agency of ghosts, goblins, and
sorcerers. Nor is the savage so wholly wrapt up in the search
for mystical or supernatural causes as entirely to ignore the
actual relations of cause and effect in the physical world.
This is expressly recognized by Professor Lévy-Bruhl. He
rightly observes that savages " attain their ends by means of
instruments, the use of which involves the actual connexion
between cause and effect, and if they did not conform to this
objective connexion they, like ourselves (and like the animals)
would immediately perish ". To say this is to admit that
savages and even animals recognize the sequence of cause
and effect in Nature, and that without such recognition they
could not continue to exist. What, for example, would become of the man or the animal which did not perceive that
fire burns and water drowns ? The elaborate traps constructed by savages for the catching of fish or game imply a
much higher perception of the causal relation than is attained
by any animal. No doubt the savage cannot define, probably
he cannot even frame for himself, the abstract conception of
causality ; but even philosophers find it difficult to do so,

and are very far from being in agreement with each other on the subject. Again, it would be a mistake to regard all savages as equally ready to accept the mystical explanation of phenomena, to refer all events to the agency of invisible and supernatural powers. In savage as in civilized society there are sceptics as well as mystics, and for proof of it we need go no farther than the pages of Professor Lévy-Bruhl's book. On this point he quotes the evidence of missionaries :

" In the midst of the laughter and applause of the populace the heathen inquirer is heard saying : ' Can the God of the white men be seen by our eyes ? and if God is absolutely invisible, how can a reasonable being worship a hidden thing ? ' ' I will go up to the sky first,' said a Mosuto, ' and see if there really is a God, and when I have seen him I'll believe in him.' "

Again, when a missionary was preaching the Gospel to some heathen he pointed to the New Testament in his hand, and observed that he was only repeating what the Word of God said. On that one of his hearers snatched the book from the missionary's hand and, putting it to his ear, exclaimed, " It is a lie ; I am listening carefully, and the book is not saying anything at all ", at which there were roars of laughter and mocking gibes.

And if the savage sometimes argues illogically and believes, or fancies he believes, two contradictory propositions at the same time, is it for the civilized man to throw stones at him ? Do not our books on formal logic set forth the multitude of pitfalls, in the shape of fallacies, that beset the path of reasoners among ourselves ? And in regard to the law of contradiction, is it not directly violated by some of the highest doctrines of Christian, and especially Catholic, theology, which are yet accepted implicitly as true by millions of educated and intelligent men and women ? Judged by this test, Pascal and Newton were " primitives ". Has not Pascal said that " *Quand la parole de Dieu, qui est véritable, est fausse littéralement, elle est vraie spirituellement* " ? And is not this a perfect example of the method in which, according to Professor Lévy-Bruhl, the savage contrives to reconcile contradictory notions by virtue of what our author calls " the law of participation " ? Hegel himself spent a world of energy in reconciling contradictions in " a higher unity ". Are we, therefore, to number Hegel also among the " primitives " ?

On the other hand, if savages often, like civilized men, argue illogically, they often, like civilized men, argue quite correctly, nor is this denied by Professor Lévy-Bruhl. " It is not to be doubted ", he says, " that the Greenlanders, when following the avocations necessary to their existence, do reason, and that they employ means which are sometimes complicated in order to arrive at the ends they are seeking." And in regard to the Hottentots he quotes the testimony of the experienced missionary, Dr. Moffat :

" It is extremely difficult adequately to conceive of the extent of the ignorance, even of their wise men, on subjects with which infants are conversant in this country. Yet it cannot be denied, in spite of general appearances, that they are acute reasoners, and observers of men and manners."

No doubt the savage in general is much less capable than the civilized man of reasoning on abstract questions ; but the cause is not so much a defect in his logical apparatus as an incapacity of forming ideas that involve a high degree of abstraction. In that, as in many other respects, the savage adult is on an intellectual level with the civilized child ; the analogy between the two should never be forgotten. And if the savage cannot explain his reasoning process, that is no argument for denying him the power of reasoning ; for in that respect he resembles a large part of civilized mankind at the present hour, nay, the whole of mankind down to the days of Aristotle. Yet nobody on that account would dream of maintaining that mankind was incapable of reasoning until the hour when Aristotle discovered the laws of the syllogism

To sum up, we think that Professor Lévy-Bruhl is quite right in emphasizing the illogical and mystical elements in " primitive " or savage thought, but he seems to err in regarding these elements as constituting a difference of kind between " primitive " and civilized mentality ; for the same logical defect, and the same tendency to fall back on mystical or supernatural causes for the explanation of natural processes, are characteristic of a large portion of civilized humanity at this day ; so far as a difference in these respects exists between savagery and civilization, it is a difference

2 E

rather of degree than of kind. If the civilized man does not reason more logically than the savage, at least he oftener arrives at sound conclusions, since through the advance of knowledge he oftener starts from true premises ; and if he is still to a great extent a mystic, at least he commonly relegates the mystic or supernatural powers to a much greater distance, interposing between himself and them a very considerable interval in which there is free play for the natural forces of the physical world.

With this reserve, which hardly affects its scientific value, Professor Lévy-Bruhl's book may be warmly recommended as a thoughtful, learned, and valuable contribution to the psychology of the savage. The translation appears to be excellent : it possesses one of the highest qualities of a translation, that of reading like an original work.

XXV

A HISTORY OF GREEK RELIGION *

THE author of this book, Professor Martin P. Nilsson, of the University of Lund, has long been known to scholars as one of the most learned and sagacious exponents of ancient Greek life and thought. In his volume on Greek religious festivals, outside of Attica,[1] he has collected all the available evidence, both literary and inscriptional, and discussed it with a rare combination of learning, acumen, and good sense. But in his researches he is far from limiting the range of his inquiries to the Greek field in the narrower sense of the word. It is one of the discoveries of our age that the wonderful civilization of ancient Greece cannot be fully understood so long as it is contemplated merely in itself and without reference to the culture of other lands and of other peoples. Within our lifetime the intellectual horizon of scholars has been widened enormously. Apart from the flood of light which excavations have shed on the past history of the Aegean area and its relations to the older civilizations of the East, the comparative study of man has done much to reveal the links that bind together the different races of our species. The multitudinous similarities in the stages of their mental and moral evolution are more and more clearly discerned : the unity and interdependence of humanity in the past, as in the present, stand out ever more prominently : less and less

* The following article was contributed as a preface to the book of which the title is: *A History of Greek Religion*. By Martin P. Nilsson Professor of Classical Archaeology and Ancient History in the University of Lund. Translated from the Swedish by F. J. Fielden. (Oxford: at The Clarendon Press, 1925.)

[1] *Griechische Feste von religiöser Bedeutung mit Ausschluss der attischen* (B. G. Teubner, Leipzig, 1906).

is it possible or legitimate to isolate a single people and treat
it as a unique phenomenon in history, as a flower that
bloomed solitary in some divine or magic garden, without
striking roots in the common earth, without breathing the
common air, without expanding in the common sunshine.

Of this truth, which is fast becoming a truism, Professor
Nilsson is well aware, and he has amply proved it in his
writings. He has given us a popular, but scientific, sketch
of primitive religion [1] which shows that he has thoroughly
mastered the method and principles of the modern science
of comparative religion in its widest application to the be-
ginnings of man's religious consciousness. Again, having
undertaken to write on the religious element in the ancient
Greek calendar, he quickly perceived that he could not treat
of it successfully without first studying the calendars of
primitive peoples all the world over ; and he has published
the results of his inquiries in a book,[2] of which it is saying
little to say that it is incomparably the most complete and
valuable treatise hitherto written on the subject. Among the
fruits of his researches in this wide but neglected field are a
memoir on the origin and religious significance of the Greek
calendar,[3] and another on the history of Christmas.[4] In
addition, Professor Nilsson has contributed many articles on
various points of Greek religious antiquities to a number of
learned journals. In the interest of Greek scholarship it is
much to be desired that these scattered writings should be
collected and published in a form in which they would be
more accessible to students.

In the present work Professor Nilsson has traced in outline,
but with the sure touch of a master, the history of ancient
Greek religion from the cradle to the grave, if, indeed, we
can speak of the grave of a religion which, as the author
points out, survives in certain primitive forms under all the

[1] *Primitiv Religion* (H. Geber, Stockholm, 2nd edition, 1923; German translation, J. C. B. Mohr, Tübingen, 1911).
[2] *Primitive Time-reckoning* (*Acta Societatis Humaniorum Litterarum Lundensis*, vol. i.), C. W. K. Gleerup, Lund, and Oxford University Press, 1920.
[3] *Die Entstehung und religiöse Bedeutung des griechischen Kalenders* (*Lunds Universitets Årsskrift*, N.F., Avd. I. vol. xiv. No. 21), C. W. K. Gleerup, Lund, 1918.
[4] " Studien zur Vorgeschichte des Weihnachtsfestes ", *Archiv für Religionswissenschaft*, vol. xix. pp. 50-150.

weight of an alien faith and ritual. He shows how the seeds
of its gorgeous efflorescence were planted deep in the fruitful
soil prepared for it by a people of another race and another
tongue, the possessors of a far more ancient civilization, the
builders of those frowning fortresses and splendid palaces
whose ruins, cleared of the dust and mould of ages, have risen
up as by magic in our own day to reveal the glories of a
vanished and almost forgotten world. Not the least interesting and original part of Professor Nilsson's book is that in
which he indicates how all the familiar cycles of Greek myth
and legend, which have long been deemed the peculiar creation of the Hellenic genius, cluster round the great centres
of Minoan and Mycenaean culture in Crete and on the
mainland, and therefore presumably drew much of their
inspiration from these seats of a civilization which, by its
antiquity and its splendour, must have cast a glamour on the
eyes of the still barbarous Greeks when they emerged from
the gloom of their native forests into the sunlight of the
South and voyaged, as in fairyland, from island to island of
the blue Aegean.

A striking confirmation of Professor Nilsson's views on
this point is furnished by a discovery recently announced
by Sir Arthur Evans to the Hellenic Society. During the
late war a royal Minoan or Mycenaean tomb was unearthed
at Thisbe, in Boeotia, the port of Thebes, on the Gulf of
Corinth. In the tomb was found a treasure of gold signet-
rings and bead-seals. On one of the engraved beads is seen
a youthful hero attacking a sphinx of Egyptian-Minoan type
with a dagger or short sword. On another we see a man in
a chariot, whose high rank is indicated by the triple helmet
which he wears. He carries a bow, and he is attacked by
a bareheaded youth, who is similarly armed with a bow.
The scene of the encounter is a rocky defile. We can hardly
doubt that these engravings, found on Boeotian soil and
dating, according to Sir Arthur Evans, from about 1450 B.C.,
represent scenes from the legend of Oedipus. If that is so,
it seems to follow that the Oedipus saga is of Minoan or
Mycenaean rather than of purely Greek origin. In the same
treasure another intaglio appears to figure the crowning
tragedy of the house of Atreus, the murder of Clytaemnestra

and her paramour Aegisthus by her son Orestes. In the
scene there appear to be two princes and a richly dressed
queen. The young champion has surprised the guilty couple,
and after dispatching the adulterer turns his fury on the
adultress, whom he pursues dagger in hand. If Sir Arthur
Evans is right in his interpretation and dating, we must
apparently conclude that the tragedy, and with it the Trojan
war, must be dated earlier by several centuries than is allowed
for by our traditional chronology.[1]

But if Greek mythic and legendary lore thus sprang from
the contact of two alien races, a race of barbarous invaders
and a race of civilized aborigines, it becomes probable that
the contact was not one of ideas alone, but that it involved
in some measure a fusion of blood. If that was so, we seem
driven to surmise that the magnificent growth of Greek
thought and art, which hitherto we have regarded as a pure
product of the Aryan mind, may have owed not a little of its
luxuriance to this grafting of the Aryan scion on a foreign stock.
The extent of the debt it is no longer possible to measure,
but, if we recognize the existence of the debt, it appears to
follow that for the pure, the unmixed offspring of the Aryan
intellect we must look elsewhere than to Greece, perhaps to
the less varied, the less artistic, the less beautiful literature of
ancient India and the Scandinavian North. The conclusion
is humbling to our pride of race. Yet if we have borrowed
the whole of our religion from the Semites, why should we
not have borrowed a part of our civilization from the Minoans?

In following the history of Greek religion from its
splendid dawn to its splendid sunset, Professor Nilsson dis-
plays throughout that sobriety of judgement, combined with
freshness and originality, which is characteristic of all his
work. He bestrides no mythological hobby-horse, he tilts
at no windmills which a fevered imagination mistakes for
men-at-arms. While he is ready to apply the approved
results of the comparative method to Greek religion, for
example in his sharp distinction of magic from religion and

[1] In *The Times* and the *Manchester
Guardian* of the 5th November 1924
Sir Arthur Evans published a short
account of his communication to the
Hellenic Society. He has favoured me
with a copy of this account, and has
kindly supplemented it with some
further details in a letter, upon which
I have drawn in the text.

in his recognition of the great part which magic, masquerad-
ing as religion, played in Greek ritual, he is far too cautious
to push the comparisons to extremes, to discover a totem
under every bush and a ghost under every god. To take a
single instance, his treatment of the worship of heroes as
essentially a special development of the worship of the dead,
is, so far as I can judge, thoroughly sound, and contrasts
very favourably with the theories of " faded gods " which
have been much ventilated on this subject in recent years.
And the same happy union of exact scholarship, wide intellectual outlook, and sober sense never fails him in the
difficult and delicate task which he has set himself and has
successfully accomplished in the present volume. The book
presents an excellent view of Greek religion in its growth,
maturity, and decay as seen by the light of the latest researches and discoveries. It is written throughout in a style
of perfect lucidity without a tinge of pedantry. Such a work
is sure to commend itself to the reader who desires to acquaint
himself with the best and most recent results of inquiry in
this fascinating department of history ; it will also be welcomed by scholars, not only for the details of myth and
ritual which it has gathered from many quarters and brought
to a focus, but also for the thoughtfulness and suggestiveness
of its exposition, the fruit of ripe learning and mature
reflection.

To many readers these prefatory words will seem, as they
seem to me, to be superfluous. So good a wine needs no
bush to recommend it. Yet in acceding to the author's
request I was glad to have the honour and the privilege of
introducing so eminent and admirable a scholar to English
readers, some of whom may still be unacquainted with the
nature and the extent of his contributions to classical learning.

PART IV

NOTES

NOTES

VESTA AND THE VESTALS

P. 65, note 2. That the daughter who acts as priestess is unmarried is not stated by my authorities, but seems a natural inference from the nature of her duties.—In the text I have compared the actual fire-worship of the Damaras or Herero of South Africa with what I conceive to have been the original form of the Roman worship of Vesta, the goddess of the fire on the hearth. On my hypothesis the original Vestals were the unmarried daughters of the chief or king, who tended the fire in their father's house, whether hut or palace, which formed the central ·point of the community. I have shown that among the Damaras the priestess, as she is called, who tends the sacred fire, which burns in or outside of the chief's hut, is the chief's daughter, but the authorities whom I consulted in writing my original paper did not say that she was an *unmarried* daughter, and thus a link was wanting to complete the analogy between modern Damaraland and ancient Rome, where the Vestals were always unmarried. I am now able to supply the missing link by quoting good authorities, who definitely state that the fire-priestess of the Damaras is the chief's eldest *unmarried* daughter, and as two of these authorities wrote long before my theory was published they cannot have been influenced by it.

Thus, in describing the customs observed by the Ovaherero (that is, the Herero or Damaras) at the birth of a child, the Rev. E. Dannert says : " The woman now remains, according to necessity, a longer or shorter time in her temporary house, and, during this time, the child also remains without a name. When the time of her confinement comes to an end, she goes for the first time out through the front door, in order to carry her child to the sacred fire, to be named. It sits in the *otyevereko*, that is, in a skin tied to the back [of the mother]. On the way [to the *okuruo*] she is followed by *omuatye ondangere*, that is, the eldest un-married daughter of the Chief, who has charge of the sacred fire, since this must never be allowed to go out. This maiden priestess or vestal, however she may be called, sprinkles, on the way to the *okuruo*, with water which she carries in a dish, the back of the mother and the child." [1] Elsewhere Mr. Dannert defines the *okuruo* as the " [place of] the sacred fire ", and tells us that it is always towards the west of the chief's house.[2] From his account we learn that the Damara Vestal not only tends the sacred fire but assists at the purifica-tion of a woman after childbirth by sprinkling the mother and her child with water. We are not told that the Roman Vestals discharged any such function, though the standing epithet of " Mother " applied to Vesta might suggest that she was a patróness of women in childbed.

Again, speaking of the Herero or Damaras, another writer, the Rev. H. Beiderbecke, tells us that " the eldest unmarried daughter of a Chief is called ' The big girl ', and ' Favourite ', occupying also a ' privileged ' position. She is the guardian and carrier of the sacred fire." [3] Again, Dr. Hans Schinz, who travelled in what was then German South-West Africa between 1884 and 1887, describes the *okuruo* of the Herero as the place in a Herero kraal where is the ash-heap with the sacred fire, " the care of which is committed to the eldest unmarried daughter of the (chief's) Great Wife. The fire ", he says, " must be kept up con-tinuously ; at night it is brought into the hut of the (chief's) Great Wife and is there carefully preserved from extinction. But should it go out, which is always interpreted as an evil omen, it must be relit by the friction of the two fire-sticks." [4] Once more, the German missionary, J. Irle, who has given us a full and excellent account of the Herero, informs us

[1] Rev. E. Dannert, " Customs of the Ovaherero at the birth of a child ", (*South African*) *Folk-lore Journal*, vol. ii. part iv. (July 1880), Capetown and London, 1880, p. 66.
[2] Rev. E. Dannert, *op. cit.* p. 63.
[3] Rev. H. Beiderbecke, " The Flee-ing Girls and the Rock, a Herero Legend ", (*South African*) *Folk-lore Journal*, vol. ii. part v. (September 1880), Capetown and London, 1880, p. 83, note (4).
[4] Dr. Hans Schinz, *Deutsch-Sud-west-Afrika* (Oldenburg and Leipzig, N.D., Preface dated April 1891), p. 165.

that " every morning and evening, at the time of the milking,
the sacred fire is kindled on the *okuruo*, which (sacred fire)
the *ondangere*, the chief's eldest unmarried daughter, keeps
perpetually glowing in his hut (*pontok*) ".[1] Thus it appears
that the sacred fire, tended by the chief's eldest unmarried
daughter, is kept perpetually aglow in the hut of his principal
wife, from which a brand is brought out morning and evening
to kindle a holy flame on the ash-heap (*okuruo*) when the
cattle are being milked ; for the fresh milk must be consecrated by the chief at the sacred fire before it can be used
for common purposes.[2]

But, while in a Damara or Herero kraal the chief's fire,
maintained perpetually in the hut of his principal wife, is
always the most sacred, it is not the only holy fire in the
village, as appears from the following account : " It will be
of interest, to students of native customs, to add here that
a missionary from one of the most northern stations in
Damaraland informs us that there is *more than one holy fire*
(*okuruo*) to be met with in an Ovaherero village. That one
which is the most highly thought of belongs to the *omurangere*, or priest of the village ; and to this fire are his own
children, as well as certain members of his own family,
taken to be there named by himself. Each head of a family
(that is to say here of a household), however, possesses an
okuruo of his own ; considered to be inferior in importance
to that of the priest ; and here it is that the children, with
the exception of those already mentioned above, receive
their names, from the respective fathers, each at his own
okuruo."[3] In this account the native word *omurangere* is
explained as " priest of the village ", but it is employed by
another good authority on the Herero in the sense of " chief
of the village ".[4] However, there is no inconsistency, for
the Herero chief is at the same time the priest of the village,
and his eldest unmarried daughter is the priestess of his
sacred fire. But the account which I have just quoted is of
interest as showing that in a Herero village every head of a

[1] J. Irle, *Die Herero* (Gütersloh,
1906), pp. 78 *sq.*
[2] J. Irle, *op. cit.* p. 79.
[3] (*South African*) *Folk-lore Journal*,
vol. ii. part v. (September 1880), p. 113,
note of the editor on an article of the
Rev. E. Dannert, entitled " The Customs and Ceremonies of the Ovaherero
at the Birth of Twins ".
[4] J. Irle, *Die Herero*, p. 79.

family has a fire which is deemed sacred, though doubtless less so than the fire of the chief. So in ancient Rome, no doubt, every head of a household regarded the fire on the domestic hearth as sacred to Vesta, though the fire on the King's hearth took precedence of all others in respect of sanctity and was, after the deposition of the kings, if not before, lodged in a separate house of its own, which we commonly speak of as the temple of Vesta, although, as we have seen, the shrine of the sacred fire never ranked as a temple in the strict sense of the term.[1]

The worship of a sacred fire, closely resembling that of the Damaras or Herero, is practised by their neighbours, the Berg-Damaras or Berg-Damas, a people of an entirely different stock and at a much lower level of culture ; indeed, they are said by one who knows them well to be the most primitive folk in South Africa, more primitive even than the Bushmen.[2] Where they have not been altered by mixture with other races, or improved by a better diet and more favourable conditions of life, they appear to be a dwarfish race, with a bluish-black complexion and negro-like features, upturned lips, and broad flat noses. They are migratory, subsisting mainly by the chase and by the collection of edible roots and fruits, but those of them who dwell in the valleys, instead of on the tops of the hills, have got possession of goats and so have attained to a somewhat higher standard of life.[3] Their kraals, like those of the Herero, consist of round huts arranged in a circle, and, as among the Herero, the sacred fire burns normally at a point within the circle of the huts.[4] But, unlike the Herero custom, it is not the daughter but the principal wife of the chief who is the guardian of the sacred fire and responsible for its mainten-ance, and she it is who carries it to the new home when the tribe is on the march. Yet neither she nor any other woman may approach the sacred fire where it burns on the holy

[1] See above, p. 58. The fire-worship of the Herero has been fully described and discussed from the comparative standpoint, and its analogy to the wor-ship of Vesta duly recognized, by Dr. Erich Brauer in his learned and judi-cious work, *Züge aus der Religion der* *Herero* (Leipzig, 1925), to which I would refer the reader for more de-tailed information on the subject.
[2] H. Vedder, *Die Berg-Dama* (Ham-burg, 1923), i. 4.
[3] H. Vedder, *op. cit.* i. 1-3.
[4] H. Vedder, *op. cit.* i. 11-17.

hearth within the circle of the huts ; her duty is limited to maintaining a perpetual fire on her own hearth, from which a brand may be taken at any time to maintain or rekindle the sacred fire on what we may call the common hearth, though only the elders and men of a certain rank have the right of access to it.[1] The reverence for the sacred fire appears to be real and deep : the prosperity of the community is believed to depend on it ; and when things go ill with the people and the supply of food runs low, the sacred fire is allowed to die out and is solemnly relit by the friction of two sticks worked by the chief and his principal assistant.[2] As usual, the two fire-sticks employed for this purpose are regarded as male and female : the flat stick, which is laid on the ground, is called the female ; and the upright stick, which is twirled between the hands of the operator with the point resting on the flat stick, is called the male.[3] Yet the operation of fire-making, at least on these solemn occasions, is performed by two men alone, not by a man and a woman.

THE LANGUAGE OF ANIMALS

P. 101. In a Russian version, which reproduces very closely the former version of the Seven Wise Masters.—A full English translation of this Russian version, of which I have only given a summary in the text, has now been published by Mr. C. Fillingham Coxwell in his copious and valuable selection of Siberian and other folk-tales.[4]

P. 110. But most commonly it is a serpent which conveys a knowledge of the language of animals.—Among the Roumanians of Transylvania there is a popular belief that, if a man will lie on his belly beside a pool or on the bank of a river on St. George's Day (April 23), he will see in the water a white snake, by means of which he can acquire the gift of conversing with every living thing that God has

---

[1] H. Vedder, *Die Berg-Dama*, i. 25, 32, 33, 34-36.
[2] H. Vedder, *op. cit.* i. 25-28.
[3] H. Vedder, *op. cit.* i. 21 *sq.* As to the sacred fire of the Berg-Damas, compare E. Brauer, *Züge aus der Religion der Herero* (Leipzig, 1925), pp. 95 *sqq.* His account is based on

that of Vedder.
[4] C. Fillingham Coxwell, *Siberian and Other Folk-tales, Primitive Literature of the Empire of the Tsars*, collected and translated, with an Introduction and Notes (London: the C. W. Daniel Company, N.D.), pp. 726 *sq.* The original is Afanasief, No. 138.

created. All that he has to do is to catch the snake, knock
off its head with a silver coin, cover the head up with earth,
and plant garlic in the earth. Then, if before next St.
George's Day he eats of the garlic which has thus been
fertilized by the serpent's head, he will be able not merely
to talk with every living creature but even to hear the grass
growing.[1] In the *Gesta Romanorum* we read how a knight
learned to understand the speech of all animals by swallowing
a certain root which a serpent had put into his mouth.[2] In
a Greek story the hero learns the language of all animals in
the belly of a dragon which, as a particular favour, had
swallowed him on purpose to endow him with this precious
accomplishment.[3] In Chinese and Malay stories, derived
from India, it is the Serpent-King who imparts a knowledge
of the language of animals,[4] and the same is true of an
Armenian version of the tale ;[5] but in a Turkish version of
the same story it is a simple snake who bestows the wondrous
gift.[6] In a South African version of the story a mythical
serpent teaches a lad the language of animals by writing on
the boy's tongue.[7] But in a Magyar version of the story it
is the daughter of the Serpent-King who, out of gratitude,
imparts a knowledge of the language of animals to the
shepherd who has saved her life.[8] A Walloon story relates
how a young man brought back the son whom the Father
Serpent had lost, and how to reward his benefactor the Father
Serpent breathed and spat into his mouth, after which the
young man understood the language of birds.[9] In a French
story a man acquires the language of animals accidentally
by eating a piece of a snake which a fairy or a witch had
cooked, but he loses the knowledge when the fairy has breathed
into his mouth.[10]

P. 113. **This tale may be traced, with variations of detail,
right across the old world from Italy and Finland on the one side**

[1] W. Schmidt, *Das Jahr und seine
Tage in Meinung und Brauch der
Romänen Siebenbürgens* (Hermann-
stadt, 1866), p. 10.
[2] See below, pp. 466 *sq.*
[3] J. G. von Hahn, *Griechische und
Albanesische Märchen* (Leipzig, 1864),
vol. i. p. 236.
[4] Below, pp. 441 *sq.*, 443.

[5] Below, p. 453.
[6] Below, p. 449.
[7] Below, pp. 464 *sq.*
[8] Below, p. 469.
[9] P. Sebillot, *Le Folk-lore de France*,
iii. (Paris, 1906), p. 293.
[10] P. Sebillot, *Le Folk-lore de France*,
iii. 293 *sq.*

to **Annam on the other.**—The wide diffusion of this particular story of the *Language of Animals* in Asia, Europe and Africa was long ago pointed out by Theodor Benfey,[1] and in more recent years it has been much more fully, almost exhaustively, demonstrated by a Finnish scholar, Antti Aarne, in a learned dissertation.[2] It may be well to supply some of the gaps in my former treatment of the subject by drawing on the stores amassed by these writers, eked out in places by my own reading.

In the first place, then, the oldest known versions of the story are found in the literature of ancient India, which of itself may be thought to point to India as the original home of the story, whence it may have spread, through oral transmission or literary influence, to all the remote corners of the world, where it has been recorded. Of these old Indian versions there are at least five.

1. Thus, in a Jain-Prakrit version of the *Munipaticaritram*, it is said that King Brahmadatta of Kampilya was once carried away by his horse into a forest, but his servants, following up his horse's tracks, found him there and brought him back. At home the Queen asked him what he had seen in the wood. He told her how he had seen a woman in the form of a Nâginî (a mythical snake) holding dalliance with a Gonasa snake. Indignant at the lewd behaviour of the pair he lashed them with his whip, whereupon they disappeared. After thus unbosoming himself the King stepped out of his palace, and whom should he light on there but a God. The deity informed him that he was the husband of the lady whom the King had seen misbehaving in the wood ; that his wife had told him that the King had tried to seduce her and that she had spurned his advances ; wherefore the God had come to kill the royal seducer, but having learned the truth from the King's talk with his wife, which he (the deity) had overheard, he was perfectly satisfied of the King's irreproachable conduct and was ready to reward it by

[1] Theodor Benfey, "Ein Märchen von der Thiersprache, Quelle und Verbreitung", *Orient und Occident*, ii. (Göttingen, 1864), pp. 133-171.
[2] Antti Aarne, *Der Tiersprachenkundige Mann und seine neugierige Frau*, Hamina, 1914 (FF Communications, No. 15). This valuable work is now, I believe, out of print. For a copy of it I am indebted to the kindness of Professor Kaarle Krohn of Helsingfors.

granting the King a wish. Thereupon the King expressed
a desire to understand the language of all living things.
The God granted his wish, but on condition that, if he ever
revealed the secret to anybody, he should die on the spot
with a cloven skull.

Now one day, when the King was at his toilet, he heard
the tame hen-cuckoo say to the cock-cuckoo, " Bring me
the King's pomade." The cock refused to do so from fear
of the King, whereat the hen said that, if he did not do as
she bade him, as sure as death she would die. At that the
King burst into a loud guffaw. His wife desired to know
the cause of his laughter. He declared that he could not
tell her, for if he did so he would die on the spot. But she
persisted, saying that die she would if he did not tell her.
So he promised to reveal to her the fatal secret so soon as he
had mounted the funeral pyre. So the two repaired together
to the burial-ground, and the news of the thing got wind
among the folk.

A she-goat begged of the he-goat, her mate, that he
would give her a bunch of barley from a heap that lay to
hand, but he refused because the barley was meant for the
King's horse—anybody else who should take of it would be
put to death. The she-goat protested that if he did not do
as she wished she would die. The he-goat answered, " Die
then ! I'll find other mates." The she-goat cast in his
teeth the example of the mighty King who, for his wife's
sake, was ready even to die. " But as for you," she went on,
" you're a brute ! " The he-goat was not to be moved ; he
answered, " It is true that I am only a brute by birth, but if
the King has made up his mind to die for his wife's sake he
must be a brute by nature." The King, who was passing
by at the moment, heard all that was said. He gave the he-
goat a golden crown and told the Queen that, if she was
weary of her life, she might die and be done with it, but as
for himself he would find other wives just as good as her.[1]

2. A somewhat abridged version of the story occurs in
the *Harivamça*, a supplement of the great Indian epic, the

---

[1] Theodor Benfey, *Kleinere Schrif-*
ten, ausgewählt und herausgegeben
von Adalbert Bezzenberger, ii. (Berlin,
1892), Dritte Abtheilung, pp. 234-
236.

Mahabharata, to which it has been added as a nineteenth book. The *Mahabharata* appears to have existed in its complete form about A.D. 400.[1] In the *Harivamça* the tale runs as follows :

King Brahmadatta knew the language of all animals. Once he walked with his wife Sannati, daughter of Devala, in the wood. There he heard a male ant lovingly beseeching his mate, the female ant, who was angry with him. At that Brahmadatta suddenly burst into a loud laugh. His poor wife was filled with shame, and for many days she refrained from all food. When her husband spoke to her gently, she said, " Thou didst laugh at me, O King, wherefore I can no longer live." He told her what he had laughed at, but she did not believe him, and she said to him angrily, " No man ever possesses such a gift. For what man can understand the ants save by the favour of a God or as the meed of merit in a former life ? But if thou dost really possess this knowledge of all languages, impart it to me that I also may know them. Else will I resign my life, I swear it to thee." When the King heard this cruel saying of the Queen, he was very sorrowful and prayed for help to the Supreme God, the Lord of all beings, Narayana ; six nights long he prayed and fasted. Then the King saw visibly the God Narayana, the Lord. And the All-merciful spake to him, " O Brahmadatta, to-morrow morning shalt thou see great salvation." Thus favoured by the deity, the King, after washing his head, drove joyfully to the city, seated in his golden chariot. Next morning Brahmadatta with his wife walked to the same wood. Then, full of joy at the religious meditation (*yoga*), his wife Sannati, the wise daughter of Devala, said to the King, as he went to the wood, " Well aware was I, great King, that thou knowest the speech of the ants, but I wished to exhort thee by the semblance of anger, which now is vanished into air. Henceforth we will walk the highest, the happy way ; for I have wakened in thee the memory of that religious meditation of which the thought had grown dim in thy mind." The King was exceedingly glad to hear the words of his wife ; he discovered the life of religious

[1] A. A. Macdonell, *India's Past History of Sanskrit Literature* (Lon-
(Oxford, 1927), p. 88 ; compare *id.*, don, 1900), p. 287.

meditation and attained to the way that is hard of attainment.[1]

In this version the merry old tale has been converted, for the sake of religious edification, into a sort of pious tract. The hard-hearted wife, who prizes the satisfaction of her own idle curiosity above the life of her husband, has been transformed into a devout dame, who only feigns curiosity in order to recall her backsliding spouse to that higher life of religious meditation which he had for a time forsaken. Henceforth the two will walk hand in hand as pilgrims seeking a celestial city by the practice of those religious austerities on which so many people in India and elsewhere have pinned their hope of eternal happiness.[2]

3. The story meets us again in the other great Indian epic, the *Ramayana*, and here the shrewish wife reappears in all her shrewishness to receive her just reward in what we may call the Indian version of the Taming of the Shrew. In the epic the stepmother of Rama, the hero, forces her husband to drive her stepson into banishment, thus drawing down on herself the ill will of the whole kingdom. Sumitra, the charioteer, gives tongue to the popular feeling and loads the Queen with the bitterest reproaches (Book II., chapter 35). Amongst other things he casts up to her a painful episode in the life of her mother :

'I believe it runs in your blood ; you are just what your mother was before you.
For, as the proverb has it, honey flows not from a nimba *tree.*[3]

[1] Theodor Benfey, " Ein Märchen von der Thiersprache, Quelle und Verbreitung", *Orient und Occident*, ii. (Göttingen, 1864), pp. 135, 140, 147-150.

[2] As to the practice of *yoga*, or pious seclusion and meditation, in Indian religions, see A. A. Macdonell, *India's Past*, p. 153 : " The primary meaning is the ' yoking ' of the mind with a view to concentrate thought on a single point ; for these exercises aim at the regulation of breathing, sitting, and restraining the senses for the purpose of exclusive concentration on a single supernatural object, in order to obtain as a result supernatural knowledge and

supernatural powers. Such practices are prehistoric, going back to a time when there was no essential difference between a saint and a magician. That they were pre-Buddhistic in India appears from the great part these exercises play in ancient Buddhism. As restraint of the senses forms part of them, they evidently include morality. In this aspect, Yoga could be combined with any philosophical system. In one form or another Yoga is to be found among all Indian ascetics, including Buddhists and Jains."

[3] The *nimba* tree is the *Melia azidaracta*. Trees of this sort have bitter astringent qualities ; their exudations

A Gracious One gave your father a splendid gift,
Whereby he bridled your mother's stubbornness.
Thereby the King understood the speech of every creature,
And so every word of crawling things was known to him.
Then your father, lying in bed, understood by its whimpering
The love-making of an insect, and long he laughed at it.
Your mother at that was wroth and spoke of hanging herself.
But the King answered her, ' If I tell you the cause of my laughter,
I must die the same moment ; there is no help for it.'
' Live or die ! ' says she, ' it is all one to me. Tell me, and mock me not.'
Thus adjured by his wife the monarch
Related the whole business, word for word, to the Gracious One.
The brave Gracious One gave the King this answer :
' Let her die and be hanged to her, O King. On no account do what she
wants.'
When the King heard this speech he was brimful of glee ; he drove
Your mother out of the house with all speed and lived as happy as a God." [1]

4. The same story occurs, with variations, in a Tamul translation of the *Vetāla-pañcaviṃsātikā*, or ' Twenty-five (tales) of the Vetāla ', a collection of Indian stories associated with a Vetāla, or ghost that infests cemeteries. Magic plays an important part in these tales, and like the *Panchatantra* the collection has furnished many stories to the literature of the world.[2] The Tamul version is known as the *Vedala Cadai*. In it the *Language of Animals* is the ninth story, and runs as follows :

" In a city called Ubastipuram, there was a king named Grahabujan, and he had a daughter whose name was Saundari. Whilst he was thinking of forming a suitable match for her with someone of high scientific attainment, a Raja presented himself, of profound knowledge, wisdom, and prudence, to whom, after a due investigation of his merits, he gave his daughter in marriage.

" After the celebration of the nuptials, the young man took his bride, and returned to his own city. On their arrival, whilst the husband and wife were reposing together on a raised bedstead, some little ants were proceeding to pass in a line under the bed, upon which those that walked

are used for lamp oil (Th. Benfey's note, referring to Roxburgh, *Flora Indica*, ii. 394 ; J. Lindley, *Vegetable Kingdom*, Ed. 2, London, 1847, p. 394.)
[1] Theodor Benfey, " Ein Märchen

von der Thiersprache, Quelle und Verbreitung ", *Orient und Occident*, ii. (Göttingen, 1864), pp. 151 *sq.*
[2] A. A. Macdonell, *History of San-krit Literature* (London, 1900), p. 375 ; *id., India's Past*, p. 127.

first suddenly halted. The ants that were coming up in the rear demanded on what account they were stopped ; to which they replied that there was no room to pass under the bed. The ants that stood behind rejoined, ' Can you not take up the bedstead, and throw it on one side ? ' to which the others answered, ' It would be a heinous sin to do so whilst a husband and wife are sleeping together upon it.'

" The Raja, hearing the conversation which the ants held, was struck with the oddity of their remarks, and began to laugh. The wife seeing this, asked him what was the cause of his mirth. The ants, on hearing the sounds of their voices, cried out in their language to the Raja, ' If you tell anyone what we have been saying, may your head be split asunder.' The Raja being thus threatened with a curse became afflicted with grief, while his spouse demanded why he did not open his mouth in reply to what she had asked. ' Since I find no favour in your sight,' said she, ' I will put a period to my existence by a violent death.' On hearing these words, the Raja commanded that a pile of wood should be raised in the burning-ground, and stretching himself upon it, was on the point of calling his wife to share his fate, when it chanced that a ewe and a ram came that way, and as they were standing together the ram went to pay his addresses to the ewe, when the ewe turning to the ram said, ' I will not receive your attentions, unless you will gather for me some grass which is hanging in this well.' The ram, on hearing this, was much afflicted, and thus replied, ' If in stretching out to gather that grass I should fall and be killed, whom will you then have to bear you company ? If you do not choose to associate with me, it is of no great consequence, you may go about your business.' The Raja, having witnessed this scene, instantly rose up, and returning to the city, made another marriage, and lived happily." [1]

5. The same story occurs in a Marathi version of the *Panchatantra*, where it runs as follows :

In the city of Kimkalapura, in the Deccan, reigned King

[1] *The Vedala Cadai*, translated by B. G. Babington, M.D., F.R.S., in *Miscellaneous Translations from Oriental Languages*, vol. i. (London, 1831), pp. 55-57. Compare Th. Ben- fey, " Ein Märchen von der Thiersprache, Quelle und Verbreitung ", *Orient und Occident*, ii. (Göttingen, 1864), pp. 154 *sq.*

Mayoradhvaja, who was over head and ears in love with his wife Prabhavati. One day, night overtook him in a wild wood, and he passed it under a sandal-wood tree. Under the tree he met an aged hermit, who reproved the King's passion for hunting and taught him the language of all animals, warning him at the same time that he would lose the knowledge and must go to hell if ever he came hunting again, and that he must infallibly die if ever he revealed his secret to anybody.

Now the King was once sitting with his wife at table and saw a female ant, big with young, dragging laboriously a single grain of rice. On her path she met a male ant, who took the grain of rice from her. For that the female up-braided him in very bitter terms, referring pointedly to her own delicate situation and reminding him that it is the husband's duty to provide for his wife. At that the King laughed. The Queen, thinking that he laughed at the meal which she had dressed for him, insisted on learning the reason of his laughter, and threatened to starve herself to death if he did not comply with her wish. At last he con-sented to do so, but first he went with his suite on a pil-grimage to holy places. While he rested under a tree he heard a she-goat asking a he-goat to carry her across a river, since she was with young and had a longing to browse on the grass that grew on the other bank. The he-goat answered that he was not a doting fool like the King to die for the sake of a woman, adding that if the King had only given his wife a good hiding he would not be in the plight in which he found himself that day. The King took the lesson to heart, returned to his palace, and when the Queen again pestered him with questions he did unto her what he had omitted to do before, and with the happiest results.[1]

In modern India the story of the *Language of Animals* with which we are here concerned has been recorded among the Santals, an aboriginal people of the Munda stock inhabit-ing the eastern outskirts of the Chota Nagpur tableland in the Province of Bengal. The Santals are great story-tellers.

[1] J. Hertel, *Das Pañcatantra, seine Geschichte und seine Verbreitung* (Leipzig und Berlin, 1914), pp. 284 *sq.*   In the Marathi version the story is numbered iv. 10.

Their stories and legends have been collected and published by the Rev. O. Bodding, D.D., of the Scandinavian Mission to the Santals, and many of them have been translated by Mr. C. H. Bompas of the Indian Civil Service. The following is the Santal version of the story we are discussing :

Once upon a time a brownie (*bonga*) haunted the house of a certain man and gave so much trouble that the man had him exorcized and safely pegged down to the ground, and they fenced in with thorns the place where the brownie lay, and they put a big stone on the top of him. Just at the spot was a clump of the bushes called Kite's claws, and one day, when the berries on the bushes were ripe, a certain cowherd named Ramai went to pick the berries. When he came round to the stone which covered the brownie he stood on it to pick the fruit, and the brownie called to him to get off the stone. Ramai looked about and seeing nobody said, " Who is that speaking ? " The brownie answered, " I am buried under the stone ; if you will take it off me I will give you whatever boon you ask." The man said he was afraid the brownie would eat him up, but the brownie swore to do him no harm. So Ramai lifted up the stone, and the brownie came out, thanked him, and told him to ask a boon.

The man asked for the power to see brownies and to understand the language of ants. " I will give you the power," said the brownie, " but you must tell no one about it, not even your wife ; if you do you will lose the power, and in that case you must not blame me." Then the brownie blew into his ear, and he heard the speech of ants ; and the brownie scratched the film of his eyeballs with a thorn, and he saw the brownies ; and there were crowds of them living in the village like men. In December, when we thresh the rice, the brownies carry off half of it ; but Ramai could see them and would drive them away, and so was able to save his rice.

But he soon lost his useful power. One day, as he was eating his dinner, he dropped some grains of rice, and two ants fell to quarrelling over one grain, and Ramai heard them railing at each other, and he was so tickled that he laughed out loud.

His wife asked him why he laughed, and he said that he

laughed at nothing in particular. But she insisted on knowing, so he said that it was at some scandal he had heard in the village. Still she would not believe him, and worried him till he told her that he had laughed at the quarrel of the ants. Then she made him tell her how he had gained the power to understand what they said. But from that hour he lost the powers which the brownie had bestowed on him.[1]

Outside of India the same story of the *Language of Animals* meets us in many other parts of Asia, though we may surmise that in all such cases the story has been borrowed directly or indirectly from an Indian original. In the text I have cited Siamese, Annamite, and Tartar versions, in addition to the better-known version in the *Arabian Nights.*[2] A Chinese version of it, translated from the *Tripiṭaka*, was made by a Buddhist monk and missionary, Seng-houei, at Nanking about the middle of the third century A.D. It runs as follows :

In time gone by the daughter of a Serpent-king (Nâgarâja), having gone out for a walk, was clapped into bonds and beaten by a cowherd. The King of the country, going forth to visit his lands, perceived the damsel, delivered her, and let her go. The Serpent-king asked his daughter, " Why have you been weeping ? " His daughter answered him, " The King of the country beat me wrongfully." The Serpent-king said, " The King is generally good and gentle ; how could he beat people unreasonably ? " When it grew dark the Serpent-king turned himself into a serpent, and hidden under the bed he heard what the King was saying to his wife. He said, " On my walk I saw a little girl beaten by a cowherd ; I delivered her and let her go."

Next day the Serpent-king in human form presented himself to the King and said to him, " You have rendered me a great service. Yesterday I allowed my daughter to take a walk ; she was beaten by a man, but luckily for her you, O King, came and delivered her. I am a Serpent-king ; whatever you may wish, you shall have." The King said,

[1] Cecil Henry Bompas, *Folklore of the Santal Parganas* (London, 1909), No. clvii., " Ramai and the Bonga ", pp. 393-395.

[2] Above, pp. 113-115, 116. The Tartar version is now accessible in an English translation. See C. Fillingham Coxwell, *Siberian and other Folktales* (London, N.D.), pp. 319-321.

" Of precious things I have plenty. I desire to understand
the language of all animals." The Serpent-king said to him,
" You must purify yourself for seven days ; when these
seven days are over, come and speak to me. But take great
care that nobody knows of it." [1]

This being so, the King was eating with his wife when he
saw a pair of butterflies, of which the female told the male
to get her some food ; the male answered that everybody
should get food for himself, to which the female replied that
being with young she could not. The King burst out laughing. His wife asked him, " O King, why do you laugh ? "
The King kept silence. Another time, sitting with his wife,
the King saw a pair of butterflies who met on the wall,
quarrelled, and fell fighting to the ground. Again the King
burst out laughing. His wife said to him, " Why do you
laugh ? " So it happened thrice, the King always making
answer, " I will not tell you." Then his wife declared to
him, " O King, if you do not tell me I will kill myself." The
King answered her, " Wait till I have taken a walk, and I will
come back and tell you." Then he went out to take a walk.

The Serpent-king produced by magic a flock of some
hundreds of sheep which were crossing a stream. One
sheep, which was with young, cried out to the ram, " Come
back and fetch me." The ram answered, " I could by no
means carry you across the stream." The sheep replied,
" If you do not carry me across the river, I will kill myself.
Do not you see that the King of the country is about to die
for the sake of his wife ? " The ram answered her, " The
King is a fool to die for his wife. You may die. Does that
mean that I shall have no more sheep ? " At hearing these
words the King thought to himself, " King as I am of the
whole realm I am not as wise as that ram." When he returned home his wife said to him, " If you do not explain
to me why you laughed, I will kill myself." The King
answered her, " You are at perfect liberty to kill yourself ;
it will be a very good job if you do ; I have plenty of wives
in my harem ; what need have I of you ? "

[1] We must understand that the King
is in danger of death if ever he reveals
to anybody that he understands the
language of animals. (Note of E.
Chavannes.)

The Master said, " The man who would kill himself for the sake of a woman is a great fool." [1]

A Malay version of the story runs as follows :

The King of Hindoostan had a very beautiful wife of whom he was very fond. He was also devoted to the chase, and one day he saw a very pretty female snake toying with a very ugly male snake. He drew his sword and killed the male snake. The female snake was wounded, but escaped. She hastened to her husband, and when he asked her why she was wounded, she said that the King had tried to seize her, and that, failing in the attempt on her virtue, he had struck at her with his sword. So her husband, the King of Snakes, resolved to kill the King of Hindoostan for having made love to his wife. But in the King of Hindoostan's palace he heard the King relating the affair of the snakes to his wife, and so he learned the truth of the matter. He thereupon showed himself to the King, and told him that he had come to kill him, but that now he would reward him by teaching him to understand all languages, including the language of animals. At the same time he warned the King that only one man could possess this knowledge at a time, and that if he imparted the knowledge to another he would die. Then he took his leave, went home, and slew his false and faithless wife, the female snake.

Some time afterwards the King of Hindoostan, on his return from hunting, was being refreshed by his wife with perfumes. At the same time he heard two cockroaches on his pillow talking to each other. The female cockroach asked the male cockroach to steal some of the perfume which the Queen had let fall in order that she (the female cockroach) might in like manner apply it to her husband (the male cockroach), but the latter replied that the Queen would be much frightened. This caused the King to burst out laughing. When the Queen asked him why he laughed, he told her that he had learned the language of animals, and how he had done so. Thenceforth the Queen was always coaxing him to teach her to understand the language of animals,

---

[1] E. Chavannes, *Cinq Cents Contes et Apologues extraits du Tripiṭaka Chinois et traduits en français*, i. (Paris, 1910), No. 112 (*Trip.*, xix. 7, p. 21 v°), pp. 382-383. As to the collection of stories and its author, or rather translator, Seng-houei, see Chavannes' Introduction, pp. i *sqq.*

although she knew that it would entail his death if he complied. She threatened to kill herself if he did not tell her.
As he could not bear to see her die or to live without her,
he had resolved to impart the secret to her, and only asked
for a respite of seven days, during which he made merry.
On the seventh day he was sitting with his wife on a beautiful
green islet in a little lake in his garden, and there he heard
a conversation between a pair of goats. The she-goat was
far gone with young, and asked the he-goat to fetch her
some of the fine grass of the islet. The he-goat plunged
into the water, but finding he could not reach the island he
turned back. However, the she-goat persisted in her demand,
and said she could never get over it if she did not obtain her
wish. " Do as you like," replied her mate ; " if I perish, you
can get another husband, and if you perish I can get another
wife. For I am not as the King of Hindoostan, who does
all that his wife tells him to do." The King of Hindoostan
took the hint, and when his wife again asked him to teach
her the language of animals, and again threatened to kill
herself if he refused, he gave her the same answer that the
he-goat gave the she-goat. And the Queen did not kill herself after all.[1]

As we shall see presently, this Malay version of the story
agrees closely with a Turkish version, from which it may be
derived directly or indirectly.

A Mongolian version of the story is contained in the
twenty-fifth chapter of the *Kasna Chan*. It runs thus :

Bikarmatshita had returned home with his wife Nargi to
his royal parents. While the pair were eating sweetmeats, a
morsel of the pastry fell on the ground. An animal [2] came,
picked up the pastry, and carried it off to its hole. Another
animal of the same sort came out and said, " Comrade, if
you do not give me a bit of the pastry you have picked up,
I will eat you and the pastry to boot." The other animal
said, " Much of the pastry has fallen to the ground beside
Bikarmatshita, go and eat it." Bikarmatshita heard that

---

[1] J. Brandes, " Iets over de Pape-
gaai-boek, zooals het bij de Maleiers
voorkomt ", *Tijdschrift voor Indische
Taal- Land- en Volkenkunde*, xli.
(1899), pp. 460 *sq.*

[2] In German, *ein Schiragoldschin*.
I do not know what kind of creature
this is.

and laughed. Then said Nargi, " Bikarmatshita, tell me at what you are laughing." He answered, " I laughed involuntarily." Thereupon Nargi said, " O King, since we are after all one body, why will you not tell me ? If you will not tell me, I will not stay with you." When she moved away from him, Bikarmatshita took her by the hand and said, " Nargi, the teacher who taught me the speech of these animals [1] forbade me to reveal the speech to anybody. Were I to reveal it, I should die and my soul would go to hell. Therefore I have not told it." Nargi in a passion said, " You may die a thousand deaths, but I will not again sit down beside you." Bikarmatshita answered, " Wife, look at me, I will tell it to you. Nargi, stay quietly here ; when I shall have found a place for my burial I will come back and tell you."

In order that he might not hurt the feelings of any living creature, he spared the feelings of his wife and was ready to sacrifice his own life. So he looked about for a burial place for himself, marked it out, and then turned to go home. On the way he saw many goats near a well. An old she-goat said to her kid, " Are you not ashamed to lie all day long on the ground sucking at my teats ? For once in a way jump over that well ; come and play with me ! Quick, quick ! " But the kid said, " Would you have me fall into the well and be drowned ? Am I such a fool as Bikarmatshita ? I am not the sort of person to go at a woman's word and look out for a place to die in." When Bikarmatshita heard that, he went home in great haste, gave his wife a sound drubbing, and cast her out of the house. While he was engaged in chastizing her, the Bodhisattvas (the future Buddhas) and everybody else rejoiced, and a rain of flowers fell down from heaven.[2]

A Persian version of the story runs as follows :

Once upon a time there was a hunter whose name was Adagar. One day, when he was out hunting with his brothers on the mountains, he saw a black snake and a white

---

[1] The *Schiragoldschin.*

[2] B. Laufer, " Fünf indische Fabeln aus dem Mongolischen von Hans Conon von der Gabelentz ", *Zeitschrift* *der Deutschen Morgenländischen Gesellschaft*, lii. (1898), pp. 287 *sq.* The stories in question are translated from an unpublished manuscript in the Royal Library at Berlin.

snake fighting. The Black Snake prevailed and gave chase to the White Snake. The hunter's heart was grieved, and he placed an arrow on the string of his bow and shot at the Black Snake. But the arrow hit the tail of the White Snake and knocked it off. Deeply grieved, he called to his brothers and said, " Come on and let us go home." And home he went inconsolable, and though his wife tried to cheer him, and baked a cake for him, he would not eat it, and refused to be comforted.

Now the White Snake was the daughter of the King of the Fairies (*Perīs*), and she went to her father and said to him, " O King, a human being has shot off my tail." " Very good," said the King, " do you know what you must do ? " " No, I don't," said she. " Well," said he, " go to where the man is sitting ; then if he is cheerful and in good spirits, creep into his shoe, and as soon as ever he puts his foot in it, bite his ankle. But if he is sad and sorrowful, do nothing to him, but come back here quickly."

" Good," said she, and she went and crept into the man's shoe. There she saw that he was so distressed that he would not even eat his dinner, but sat with folded hands and his head bowed down on his knees. So she came back and told her father, the King of the Fairies. " Ah, now I know," said he.

Next morning the Fairy King sent a messenger to the hunter to say that the King had a piece of business with him. So the hunter went to the King, and the King asked him, " Why did you shoot off the White Snake's tail ? " Thereupon the hunter began to weep, and said, " O King, I shot at the Black Snake, but by chance the arrow hit the White one, and so grieved am I for the White Snake that now my heart is become like roasted meat."

The King began to laugh and said, " O man-born, tell me now whatever you would like to have as a gift." " I want no gift," replied the hunter, " except that I may understand the speech of every created thing." Now, since these people were not really snakes but fairies (*perīs*), whatever they willed came to pass with them. So the Fairy King granted to the hunter the power to understand the language of all created things. " Now go," said he, " but tell your secret to no one, otherwise you will die." The hunter then took his leave and departed.

Time passed, and through his knowledge of the language of dogs Adagar had acquired a flock of sheep. One day it chanced that one of his ewes had lambed, and he was holding its head while his wife was milking it. Just then a lamb came up and said, " Give me a little milk, Mamma." [1] " You are perfectly shameless," replied the ewe. " Can't you see that my master is holding my head and my master's wife is milking me ? Leave me alone till I am free. When I'm at liberty I'll give you all you want." Adagar laughed. His wife adjured him, saying, " You must tell me what you are laughing at." " What business is that of yours ? " said he. " If I tell you, I shall die." However, he went on, " Do you know what you must do ? " " No," said she. " Well," said he, " first have four sheep killed, and cook freshly a lot of rice, and collect a great deal of ghee, and cook my funeral alms. [2] After that, assemble all my relations and all your relations, and then I will tell you what I was laughing at." The wife agreed, and collected all their relations and set the broth to cook on the fire.

Now Adagar the Hunter had a dog and a cock and a cat. The dog put its head down on its paws and sat in dejection, but the cock pecked at the dough and dipped his beak into the broth. The dog looked up and said to him, " You are perfectly shameless ; this is the funeral alms of your master that is standing on the fireplace." " You are a great fool," retorted the cock, " our master is a miserable hen-pecked creature." " How so ? " asked the dog. " I'll tell you," said the cock ; " our mistress is a mischievous woman. She asks her husband his secret, and he loves her very much and will tell her, but when he tells her he will die. As soon as ever he is dead his wife will grab all the gear, marry some blackguard or other, and kick her first husband's grave. Why should anyone give himself a headache over what a couple of words in black and white could set right ? "

[1] In the original " it is not a lamb who interrupts to ask its mother for milk but a ram who comes to claim the ewe for intercourse " (Major Lori-mer, in a letter to J. G. F.).

[2] When a person has died, food is distributed as alms by his family to his relations and others.

" The cock speaks truly," said Adagar to himself, and
he got up and went into the assembly. " Brothers of my
wife, and my own brothers," said he, " my wife has been
nagging at me in this way to tell her my secret, and if I do
tell her I shall die that very instant. That being so, I have
decided not to tell her, but to give her a bill of divorce."
They all said, " Very well. We certainly will not make ourselves responsible for driving you to your death. Divorce
her."

Then he quickly instructed a mullah to make out a bill of
divorce, and he handed it to her, and she took her departure.
But some time later she stole a hundred tumans from her
brothers and brought them as a bribe to her husband, and
he married her again, and they minded their own business
and lived at ease.[1]

The story of the *Language of Animals*, with which we
are here concerned, occurs in a Turkish version of the *Tuti-
Nameh*, or *Parrot-book*, a Persian collection of popular tales
which is itself a translation of an Indian original, the *Suka-
saptati*, or ' Seventy Tales of a Parrot ', written partly in
Sanskrit and partly in Prakrit. Nothing is known about the
author of the *Suka-saptati* or *Parrot-book*, nor about the time
when it was composed. The Persian translation of it, under
the title of *Tuti-Nameh*, was made early in the fourteenth
century A.D. The uncouth quality of this rendering induced
Nachshabi, a contemporary of Hafiz and Sadi, to remould its
matter in an artistic poem. A Turkish translation, based on
Nachshabi's work, was executed about a century after his
time.[2] In it the story of the *Language of Animals*, stript of
some of the flowers of rhetoric with which Nachshabi or
another had tricked it out, runs as follows :

[1] D. L. R. Lorimer and E. O.
Lorimer, *Persian Tales written down
for the first time in the original Ker-
māni and Bakhitāri* (London, 1919),
No. xxxiv., " The Story of the Hunter
and the White Snake", pp. 225-231.
I have shortened the story.

[2] Theodor Benfey, " Ein Märchen
von der Thiersprache, Quelle und Verbreitung", *Orient und Occident*, ii.
(Göttingen, 1864), p. 157 ; A. A. Macdonell, *India's Past*, p. 128 ; *id., History of Sanskrit Literature*, pp. 375 *sq.*
There is a German translation of the
Suka-saptati. See *Sukasaptati, das
Indische Papageienbuch, aus dem Sanskrit übersetzt* von Richardt Schmidt
(München, 1913). But the story of
the *Language of Animals*, with which
we are here concerned, does not occur,
so far as I see, in this version of the
Suka-saptati.

In the history books it is written that an Indian Sultan once went out to hunt. Coming to a lonely place he saw a female snake wantoning with a male snake of another sort. Indignant at their unnatural union he drew his sword and struck at the female snake, but only succeeded in cutting off a piece of her tail. She glided away and disappeared into her hole. There her husband, the male snake, found her and questioned her about her hurt. She told him that the Sultan of the city had seen her and, falling in love with her gay colours, had attempted to seduce her, but strong in her virtue she had withstood him, whereupon he fell into a rage and wounded her.

Fired with jealousy her mate crept into the Sultan's palace and hid under the monarch's bed, intending to sting him to death as soon as he should have fallen asleep. Presently the Sultan's wife came and would have lain down beside him on the bed, but he repulsed her and drove her away. When she wept and asked him why he did so, he told her what he had seen of the behaviour of the two snakes, adding that the sight had so convinced him of the lewdness and lechery of the female sex that he was resolved to have nothing more to do with women for the rest of his life.

Listening under the bed to the conversation of the royal pair the male snake was now fully convinced of the Sultan's innocence ; so crawling to the monarch's feet he acknowledged himself to be the husband of the wanton, craved the Sultan's pardon for his former intention of murdering him, and begged to know what he could do for him, assuring him that any wish he might express would be granted. The Sultan said, " It is my dearest wish to learn the language of animals." The snake replied, " O Sultan, your wish is possible, but you must promise me not to reveal the secret to any woman, for if you do you will infallibly die on the spot." After giving the Sultan this solemn warning, the snake instructed him in the language of animals and took his departure.

Next morning the Sultan's banished wife, losing patience, came to her husband's bed and began to soft-sawder him with rose-water and sandal-wood oil, which she poured on his feet, intending thereafter to rub her face on them. It chanced that in the room there was a cage with a pair of turtle-doves in it. The hen bird said to the cock bird, " O that I had rose-water and sandal-wood oil to pour on your feet and then to rub my face on them ! " When the Sultan heard that, he began to laugh. His wife thought he was mocking her. She flew into a rage and said with an oath, " You must tell me why you laughed. If you do not, I will kill myself."

The Sultan tried to soothe her, saying, " I did not laugh at you. If I were to tell you, I would surely die. Do not press me, else you will be the cause of my death." But she insisted, and when he could no longer withstand her importunity he said, " I will tell you it in a lonely place, for when I have told it I must die." So he gave orders that every one should quit the palace garden where he proposed to reveal the fatal secret. This quieted his wife.

When day broke and not a soul was in the garden, the Sultan and his wife entered it. They came to a well where, by the providence of God, two sheep were feeding. The ewe went to the edge of the well, and seeing some fresh green grass in it she said to the ram, " If you do not fetch that grass for me to eat, I will throw myself into the well." The ram looked at the grass and said that he could not fetch it. " Were I to grant your wish," said he, " I should lose my life, and it would be folly in me to kill myself lest you should commit suicide. I am not like the Sultan to throw away my life for the sake of a woman. If you wish to make an end of yourself, pray do so. It is perfectly indifferent to me whether you do so or not. There you are and there is the well ! If you are bent on dying you could never do it easier than now."

The Sultan laid to heart the sage speech of the ram. He took back his word, and all the prayers and entreaties of his wife could not wring his secret from him. So he continued to live and reign.[1]

A version of the story occurs in a Georgian collection of

[1] *Tuti-Nameh, Das Papageienbuch, eine Sammlung orientalischen Erzählungen, nach der türkischen Bearbeitung zum ersten Male übersetzt* von Georg Rosen, ii. (Leipzig, 1858), pp. 236-241. Compare Th. Benfey, " Ein Märchen von der Thiersprache, Quelle und Verbreitung ", *Orient und Occident*, ii. (Göttingen, 1864), pp. 157 *sq.*

stories which was made by a certain Orbeliani about the year 1700. The work exists in a Russian translation by Tsagareli. The sources from which Orbeliani drew the stories are uncertain ; the Russian translator thinks that they were mainly derived from oral tradition. This Georgian version runs as follows :

The hero of the tale is a righteous man who has a volatile wife. One day, as he sat eating on the bank of a river, he threw some of his food into the water. A man rose from the river and in return for the food cast upon the water he taught the generous giver the language of all animals by putting his tongue into the other's mouth. A young crow attempted to peck out the hero's eyes, but the hero let the bird escape, and for this good deed he was rewarded by the mother crow with the revelation of a buried treasure. Then follows a conversation between a foal and its mother, a pregnant mare, like the similar dialogue between a horse and a mare in the Slavonian version, to which the Georgian version bears a close resemblance.[1] The man laughs at the talk of the mare and foal, and is about to tell his wife the reason of his laughter when he hears a little dog, with tears in its eyes, lamenting to a cock that his master must die, all for the sake of his wife. Thereupon the cock summons all the hens of the village, struts round them, and says to the man, " I have sixty wives and not one of them durst pick up a grain of corn without my leave. And you are dying all through a woman ! Go and thrash her within an inch of her life." The man does so and thus escapes death. This story is said to be known all over Georgia.[2]

An Armenian version of the story runs as follows :

In autumn, when the weather grows cold, the serpents gather before the gate of the greatest and richest of their number. He usually has his abode in a high place, in a cleft of the rocks facing the sun. They bring him presents of all sorts, all that has fallen into their hands, royal jewels and diamonds. Then each relates the adventures that have befallen him. A scribe writes down everything that is worth recording, and this writing is sent by two royal serpents to

---

[1] See above, pp. 112 *sq.*
[2] Antti Aarne, " Zum Märchen von der Tiersprache ", *Zeitschrift des Vereins für Volkskunde*, xix. (1900), p. 303.

their Great King, who dwells at Baghdad and Bassora, and who governs the whole nation of serpents both on land and sea. Thus he receives presents of great value and takes note of the letters that come to him from the four quarters of the world. He administers justice, punishing and rewarding each according to his deserts.

The son of the King of the Serpents, being vizier of the country of Diarbekir, wrote to his father : " O King, live for ever ! May God increase thy greatness ! But know that this year thy daughter-in-law and thy grandchildren have been sick, and that the doctors ordered them to go for a cure to the waters of Bingeul, there to take the baths and to eat a petal of the flower *hamaspiur* (*Lychnis orientalis*). So we bestirred ourselves and sent them with a numerous suite. We wrote to the governor to pay them the honours due to their rank and to facilitate their journey. When they reached Bingeul they sent a letter to the general in command at Mouch in Daron. He came with many serpents and ordered thy daughter-in-law to be put to the torture.

" The serpents who escorted the lady exerted themselves valiantly to defend her. There was a great battle on the top of Bingeul. There chanced to be there one Semon, who kept the flocks of a merchant in order to send them to Scham (Damascus) and Aleppo. Semon took a cudgel and rushed into the thick of the serpents of Daron ; he slew them and scattered them, and thy daughter-in-law was saved, with her children and servants. So there are good folk even among men. O Great King, I will punish them of Daron. But it is for thee to reward, in a manner befitting thy Greatness, the man who saved thy daughter-in-law."

The King of the Serpents took store of precious stones and came in great state to his palace on the road to Aleppo. He posted sentinels, and lo ! one came to tell him that Semon had passed by. The serpents performed some magic rites, and Semon thought he saw the world turned upside down. His companions had left him, and he found himself alone with thousands of serpents in front of him.

One of the serpents took a paper in which the noble deed done by Semon was recorded in complimentary terms, and this report he read out before the King and the princes.

They decided that Semon might take as much gold and diamonds as he pleased, and that, if he had a desire in his heart, it should be granted him.

" I should like ", said he, " to understand the language of all animals, reptiles, and birds." " Be it so," said the King, " but if you tell anybody whatever what you shall have seen and heard of the animals, you shall die."

Semon went home. He understood the words of animals, reptiles, and birds. He perceived that they knew all the secrets of men, and that they told one to another the things that should come to pass. His hair stood up on his head, and what between laughter and fright he found himself at Death's door. He retraced his steps and came to the village. He heard the cats, the dogs, the cocks and the hens telling that Semon's pockets and the breast of his coat were full of gold and precious stones. He went into his house and threw all the treasures he was carrying at the feet of his wife.

" Where does all that come from ? " she persisted in asking.

" Enjoy it and ask no questions," said Semon. He heard the house-dog and the fowls talking of all that was happening in the house. He laughed, and sometimes too he was angry. His wife noticed it and would know what it was all about. She besought him, she wept, she fumed. At last one day Semon promised to tell her on the morrow all about it.

But the dog heard him. The same evening the cock was driving his hens before him, with a sound like *cluck, cluck, cluck*; he entered by the door. The dog said to him, " Why are you clucking like that ? Our master has promised his wife to tell her everything to-morrow evening, and he will die. They will come and cut your throat and kill me, and rob and demolish our master's house."

" Since everything must come to an end some day," answered the cock, " it may just as well come at once. As for me, I have forty hens, and they all obey me. If our master spoiled his wife a little less, it would be better for her ; he himself would not die, and none of these troubles would come upon us."

Semon heard this talk and took a lesson from it. He

got up, grasped a hazel rod, went to his wife, and thrashed her within an inch of her life.[1]

A Syrian version of the story runs thus :

Once on a time, near Damascus, there was a peasant who understood the language of animals. He had an ox, with which he tilled the soil, and an ass which he used to ride. One day, when the ox was ploughing the fields, while the ass was browsing on the grass, the peasant left off his work and lay down under a tree. The ass went up to the ox, and the ox said to him, " Curse you ! You eat grass and barley the whole blessed day without doing anything at all, whereas I work from morning to evening, and all the night you will not let me sleep for your roaring and braying." " My dear fellow," answered the ass, " this evening you will make believe to be ill, not touching your fodder, and when your master comes and sees you in that state, he will give you two or three days' rest." " Yes, by Gad," said the ox, " that is what I will do."

However, the master had heard their talk and thought to himself, " Cursed be the father of the ass ! I will make him work instead of the ox." He got up and returned to the house, riding the ass and followed by the ox. Then he brought barley for them both ; but when he went at midnight and opened the door of the cattle-stall he saw that the ox was asleep and had eaten none of its fodder. He shut the door and went and slept till morning. Then he returned to the stall and said to the ox, " You are sick to-day ; I will leave you here, and the ass shall do your work." So he took the yoke and put it on the neck of the ass, who thought, " Curse the scoundrel ! It was a devilish bad idea of mine to advise the ox to feign sickness."

The peasant went with the ass to his field and ploughed with him till set of sun. When the ass came back worn out with weariness, he said to the ox, " Your master said to-day that he will slaughter you to-morrow, because he thinks you will die at any rate." At that the ox woke up and began to kick the crib till it fell down. The peasant came, saying, " Ah, there you are all right again, old boy ! " So he gave

[1] Fr. Macler, *Contes Arméniens* (Paris, 1905), No. xiii., " Semôn ", pp 103-109.

him a lot of oats and a sack of chopped straw to boot. The ox devoured it all and lowed to show that he wanted more. The peasant gave it tó him and laughed.

Then his wife said to him, " Why do you laugh ? " He said, " Something happened to me that made me laugh." " No," said she, " you are making fun of me." He denied it, but when she demanded the cause of his laughter, he said, " I cannot tell you. If I were to tell you, I should die." She insisted, and on his refusal she said, " If you do not tell me I will return to my family." The peasant was very fond of his wife and said to her, " I will tell you to-morrow morning, but after that I shall die." " That is all one to me," said she, " you must relate it to me." They went to bed, but while his wife slept the peasant lay awake.

Suddenly he heard one of the hens saying to the cock, " Our master is going to die to-morrow." " Why so ? " asked the cock. " Because he is about to tell his wife the trick of the ass and the ox," said the hen. " On my word," said the cock, " our master is a fool. I have twenty wives, and they are all afraid of me, and he, who has only one wife, does not know how to manage her." " What would you have him do ? " asked the hen. " He should take a stick," replied the cock, " and give her fifty blows on the back every day till she says, ' Forgive me ! I no longer ask you to tell it me.' "

On hearing these words the peasant said to himself, " Egad, the cock has more sense than me." He got up, and taking a stick said to his wife, " Well, do you want to know ? " " I want you to tell me why you laughed," replied she. " Look here," said he, " I am the husband and you are the wife. Would you order me about ? May God curse your father and mother ! " So saying he whacked her with the stick till she cried, " Forgive me ! I no longer want you to tell it me ! " So he let her be, and from that time she never asked anything of him, and the peasant thought, " God bless the cock which gave such good advice ! But for it I must have died." [1]

This Syrian story, as the editor of it remarks, is clearly a variant of the version in the *Arabian Nights*, which has

[1] J. Oestrup, *Contes de Damas* (Leyde, 1897), No. vii., " Le paysan, le bœuf et l'âne ", pp. 97, 99, 101. The intermediate pages contain the Syrian text.

already been laid before the reader.[1] The same is true of two Jewish stories, except that in one of them the hero has obtained a knowledge of the language of animals as a gift from the wise King Solomon.[2] In the other version, taken down in Palestine, it is merely said that " there was once a merchant who understood the language of beasts ".[3] But both these Jewish versions follow the story in the *Arabian Nights* so closely that it would be at once needless and tedious to repeat them. Their text is given in the Appendix (pp. 505 *sqq.*).

In our survey of the geographical diffusion of the tale we may now turn from Asia to Africa, where the story has been recorded at various points from the north to the south of the continent.

A Berber version of the story runs as follows :

Long ago there was a man who had much gear. One day he went into a butcher's shop. A greyhound came and gnawed some bones. The butcher struck him, and the dog yelped. At the sight the man was touched with pity. He bought of the butcher a bit of meat and threw it to the dog, who took it and went away. But the dog was really the son of a king who dwelt under ground.

Fortune changed with our man ; he lost all his gear and betook himself to washing people's clothes for a livelihood. One day he went to wash something ; he spread it out on the white sand to dry. A jerboa appeared with a golden ring in its ear. The man ran after it, killed it, hid the ring, kindled a fire, cooked the animal and ate it. A woman came out of the earth, laid hold of him, and asked him, " Did you not see my son, who has a ring in his ear ? " " I saw no boy," replied he, " but I saw a jerboa that had a ring in its ear." " It was my son," quoth she. She drew him under ground and said to him, " You have eaten my son. You have parted me from him. I will part you from your children ; you shall serve me in his stead."

That day he who had been changed into a greyhound saw the man there and said to him, " It was you who bought

---

[1] Above, pp. 114 *sq.*

[2] L. Ginzberg, *The Legends of the Jews*, vol. iv. (Philadelphia, 1913), pp. 138-141.

[3] J. E. Hanauer, *Folk-lore of the Holy Land, Moslem, Christian and Jewish*, edited by M. Pickthall (London, 1910), pp. 258-260.

meat for a greyhound and threw it to him." "It was I,"
said the man. "I am that greyhound," replied the other;
"who brought you here?" "A woman," answered the
other, and he related the whole of his adventure. "Go and
complain to the king," said his friend; "I am his son. I
will go and tell him, ' This man has done me a kindness.'
When he shall say to you, ' Go to the treasury and take as
much money as you can,' answer, ' I don't want any, I
want you to spit the blessing into my mouth.' If he asks you,
' Who told you to say that?' reply, ' Nobody.' "

The man went to the king and complained of the woman.
The king sent for her and said to her, "Why did you take
this man captive?" "He ate my son," said she. "Why
did your son turn himself into a jerboa?" asked the king;
"when men see one of them, they catch it and eat it." Then,
addressing the man, he said, "Give her back the ear-ring."
He gave it back to her. "Go," continued the king, "take
back this man to the place whence you brought him." The
king's son then said to his father, "This man has done me a
kindness. He must be rewarded for it." The king said to
him, "Go to the treasury and take as much money as you
can." "I do not want money," answered he, "I wish you
to spit the blessing into my mouth." "Who has told you
that?" asked the king. "Nobody," said the man. "You
will not be able to bear it," said the king. "I shall be able,"
said the man. "When I shall have spat into your mouth,"
said the king, "you will understand the language of beasts
and birds; you will know what they say when they talk, but
if you reveal it to people, you will die." "I will not reveal
it," said the man. The king spat into his mouth and sent
him away, saying to the woman, "Go, take him to the place
where you found him." She went and took him to the place.

He mounted his ass and returned to his house. He
tethered his beast and took back the washing to the people.
Then he mounted his ass again to go and look for some
fuller's earth. He was in the act of digging when he heard
a raven in the air saying, "Dig down. Thou wilt sing when
God shall enrich thee." He understood what the bird said,
dug down, and found a treasure. He filled a panier with it,
put a little earth on the top, and returned home. Then he

came back to the spot several times. On one of these occasions his ass met a mule, who said to her, " Still working away ! " She answered, " My master has found riches and is carrying them off." The mule replied, " When you come among people, do you just jib and drop the panier on the ground. The folk will see it, the murder will be out, and your master will leave you in peace." The man had heard their talk and he filled the panier with nothing but earth. When they came among people, the ass backed and dropped the panier to the ground, and her master beat her to his heart's content. Then he resumed the business of carrying off the treasure and became a merchant of good standing.

Now in his house he had fowls and a bitch. One day he went into his barn ; a hen followed him and ate some grains of corn. A cock said to her, " Bring me a little." The hen answered him, " Eat for yourself." At that their master fell a-laughing. His wife asked him, " What makes you laugh ? " " Nothing," says he. " You are laughing at me," says she. " Not a bit of it," says he. " You must tell me what you are laughing at," says she. " If I tell you, I shall die," says he. " You shall tell me and die to-night," says she. He brought forth corn and said to his wife, " Give alms." He asked people in and made them eat, and when they went forth he set food before the bitch, but she would not touch it. The neighbour's dog came, as he did every day, to eat with the bitch. That day he found the food untouched. " Come, eat," says he. " No," says she. " Why ? " says he. She told him : " On hearing the fowls talk, my master fell a-laughing ; his wife asked him, ' Why do you laugh ? ' ' If I tell you,' says he, ' I shall die.' ' Tell me and die,' says she. That," added the hen, " is why he has given alms, for when he has revealed the secret he will die, and I shall find nobody like him." The dog answered, " Since he understands the language of animals, let him take a stick and lay on to her till she has had her fill of it, and as he beats he shall say, ' That was why I laughed ! That was why I laughed ! That was why I laughed ! ' till she says, ' Reveal nothing to me.' "

The man heard the talk of the dogs ; he went and took a stick. When his wife and he went to bed, " Tell it to me," quoth she. Then he drew out the stick and hit her, saying

NOTES 459

to her, " That is why I laughed ! " till she began to cry out,
" Don't tell it me ! Don't tell it me ! " So he let her be.
When the dogs heard that, they were glad, ran on the terrace
of the house, gambolled and ate their food. From that day on
the wife never said to her husband, " Tell me." They lived in
peace. May God forgive me for what I have left undone.[1]

In Bornu, formerly a powerful independent kingdom of
Central Africa, the story has been recorded in the native
Bornu or Kanuri language. Translated into English it runs
as follows :

" There was a Servant of God who had one wife and one
horse ; but his wife was one-eyed : and they lived in their
house. Now, this Servant of God understood the language of
the beasts of the forest, when they spoke, and of the birds
of the air, when they talked, as they flew by ; this Servant
of God also understood the cry of the hyena, when it arose
at night in the forest, and came to the houses, and cried near
them ; so, likewise, when his horse was hungry, and neighed,
he understood what it neighed, rose up, brought the horse
grass, and then returned and sat down.

" It happened one day, that birds had their talk, as they
were flying by above, and the Servant of God understood
what they talked. This caused him to laugh, whereupon his
wife said to him, ' What dost thou hear that thou laughest ? '
He replied to his wife, ' I shall not tell thee what I hear, and
why I laugh.' The woman said to her husband, ' I know
why thou laughest : thou laughest at me, because I am one-
eyed.' The man then said to his wife, ' I saw that thou wast
one-eyed before I loved thee, and before we married and sat
down together in our house.' When the woman heard her
husband's word, she was quiet.

" But on one occasion, at night, as they were lying on
their bed, and it was past midnight, it happened that a rat
played with his wife at the top of the house, and that both
fell to the ground, whereupon the wife of the rat said to her
husband, ' Thy sport is bad : thou saidst to me that thou
wouldst play, but when we came together, we fell to the
ground so that I broke my back.' When the Servant of God

[1] R. Basset, *Nouveaux Contes Berbères* (Paris, 1897), No. 108, " Le Langage des Bêtes ", pp. 119-124.

heard the talk of the rat's wife, as he was lying on his bed, he laughed. Now as soon as he laughed, his wife arose, seized him, and said to him, as she held him fast, ' Now this time I will not let thee go out of this house, except thou tell me what thou hearest, and why thou laughest.' The man begged the woman, saying, ' Let me go I ' but the woman would not listen to her husband's entreaty, and said to him again, ' I shall not let thee go, except thou tell me what thou heardest to-night, and why thou didst laugh.'

" When the man had heard the word of his wife, he said to her, ' I am God's : let me go and I will let thee know why I was laughing.' The woman then relaxing her hold, her husband said to her, ' The reason why I laugh, is this, that I understand the language of the beasts of the field, as they talk, and what the birds of the air say, as they fly past, and that I understand the cry of the hyena, when it gets up in the forest and cries near the town in order to carry off people's goats ; also that I understand the neighing of our horse in the stable, as it neighs when it is hungry, so that I may arise and go to give it grass.' Then he and his wife were at peace with each other, and slept on their bed.

When they had slept, and it was day, the Servant of God arose, and went to his horse ; but when it neighed, he did no longer understand it ; so as to the birds of the air, which talk, when they see that it is day, he did no longer understand their talk, on listening ; neither did he any longer understand the cry of the beasts of the field, when they cried, nor the cry of the hyena, when it came near the town and cried. So he went, sat down in his house, hung down his head, and said to himself, ' If a man opens and tells his inward thoughts to a woman, God will punish him for it : formerly I understood the language of all the beasts of the field, when they talked, and of the birds of the air, and of the rats in the house, and the neighing of my horse ; but to-day Satan has taken me out of the (right) way : when I told my secret to a woman, our Lord shut mine ears ; therefore, henceforth let no man tell all his secrets to a woman ! ' " [1]

[1] Rev. S. W. Koelle, *African Native Literature, or Proverbs, Tales, Fables, and Historical Fragments in the Kanuri or Bornu Language, to which are* added a *Translation of the above and a Kanuri-English Vocabulary* (London, 1854), pp. 143-145, "Story of a Servant of God ".

An Abyssinian version, taken down in the Tigrē dialect, runs as follows :

" God gave a man knowledge of the language of [all] the wild and domestic animals. But he said to him : ' Whatever thou mayest hear of the language of all the animals, do not tell it to men ; when thou hast heard it thyself keep silent ; if thou tellest it, then thou shalt die.' And the man said : ' Very well.' And the man knew the language of all the animals, domestic and wild ; and whenever he heard it, although he knew the meaning, he kept silent.

" Then one day the man said to his wife : ' Let us lie down that we may rest a little ! ' And when they had lain down two kids that were in the house said to each other : ' Let us lie down too ; our masters are also lying down.' When the man heard their talk he smiled. And his wife said to him : ' Why doest thou smile ? What hast thou perhaps done unto me that thou hast smiled ? ' He answered : ' I have smiled at myself, not at thee.' His wife said : ' Tell me then why thou hast smiled.' Now the man feared death if he should tell her ; so he said to her : ' I have smiled for nothing.'

" But his wife continued : ' Either tell me about what thou hast laughed, or leave me ! ' The man, however, did not know divorce, and he wanted to tell her. But he said to her : ' Wait that I tell it to thee ! ' Then he prepared himself for his death : he shaved and bathed ; and he brought the cows for his funeral sacrifice and tied them. But one cow of them he killed, that he might himself taste the meat of the cows of his funeral.

" And when the cow was skinned, the dog of the man took a piece of the vertebrae and ran with it into the side-room to gnaw it. Thereupon another dog came to that dog to gnaw the vertebrae with him. But the dog drove him off from the bone and snarled at him to scare him away. And the other dog said to him : ' Of [all] the masters thy master is most despicable who ties the cows of his funeral sacrifice instead of divorcing his wife. And of [all] the dogs thou art most despicable, who keepest away thy brother from the bone ! ' And after he had spoken thus he went off.

" The man heard the words which the dog said, and he knew that it was easier for him to divorce his wife than to

die ; before that, he had not known much of divorce and had
chosen death instead. So the man divorced his wife and was
saved from death. And from this time onward divorce
became customary. [This is what] they say." [1]

Another Abyssinian version of the story, taken down in
the Saho dialect, runs in an abridged form as follows :

A man who, on account of a quarrel with his brother, had
fallen out with all the world, set out one day to kill God. He
met God, and God asked him, " Whither away ? " The
man answered, " I am out to kill God." God made Himself
known to the man, and asked him what he wanted. Then
the man answered, " I want nothing for myself but to understand every language which Thou hast created." God bestowed on him the gift of understanding every language.

On the way the man lay down to sleep under a tree, and
he heard two eagles speaking which had hidden a chest full
of gold. He demanded and received from them the chest
and the gold, and so he became a rich man and married a
beautiful wife. By night he heard the he-goat saying to the
she-goat, " Our master is now sleeping with his wife, so
come thou that I may sleep with thee." The man understood
the talk and laughed. His wife insisted on knowing why he
had laughed. Then he said, " Since I must die as soon as
I have told thee, make ready my death-feast." The man's
dog heard that and told it to his friend. But his friend said,
" Thy master is a fool ; he should let his wife go hang and
not reveal the secret to her."

This story is clearly a variant of the tale in the *Arabian
Nights*.[2]

In East Africa the story has been recorded in the Swahili
language. In an abridged form it runs as follows :

God gave the Sultan Seliman bin Daud (that is, King
Solomon, son of David) the power of understanding the language of birds and of all animals both on land and in the
sea, also the language of the winds and of the trees. So the

[1] Eno Littmann, *Publications of the Princeton Expedition to Abyssinia*, vol. ii.; *Tales, Customs, Names, and Dirges of the Tigrē Tribes, English Translation* (Leyden, 1910), No. 76, " The Tale of a Man who knew the Language of Animals ", pp. 95 *sq.*
[2] D. H. Müller, in *Zeitschrift der Deutschen Morgenländischen Gesellschaft*, xlvi. (1892), pp. 401 *sq.*, review-ing *Die Sahosprache von Leo Reinisch*, 2 Bände (Wien, 1889–1890).

Sultan appointed the animals their various tasks, and they obeyed him. Among other things he ordered the asses to carry stones and clay. The asses did so, and when they were very tired they consulted the ox, who advised them to pretend to be sick next morning. The asses did as he advised, and the servants, on finding the asses apparently sick, reported it to the Sultan, who ordered that all the oxen should be set to carry stones and clay. After toiling thus for many days the ox said to the ass, " I have heard that the Sultan will slaughter you to-morrow if you do not get up." Sitting with his wife, the Sultan heard these words of the ox and laughed. His wife asked him why he laughed. He said, " At nothing." But she insisted and said she would leave him if he did not tell her. Now the Sultan loved his wife and promised to let her know in seven days. But God had told the Sultan that if he revealed his knowledge of the language of birds and beasts to anyone he must die.

So all men and animals mourned that the Sultan must die. On the morning when he was to reveal the fatal secret the cocks crowed. The Sultan's dog went and seized the cocks. When the Sultan asked the dog why he did so, the dog answered, " These cocks are shameless. Every creature in the world mourns that thou must die, but the cock crows ; he loves thee not." The cock said, " The Sultan has no sense. I have many wives ; if one of them grows too proud, I beat her. But the Sultan has only one wife and is about to die on her account. If he took a stick and thrashed her, she would repent, and not wish to know why he laughed." When the Sultan heard that, he took a stick and struck his wife, and she said, " I repent ; I do not wish to know why you laughed." Everybody rejoiced that the Sultan had recovered his life and health through the good sense of the cock.[1]

In South Africa the story has been recorded among the Ba-Ronga, a Bantu tribe of Delagoa Bay in Portuguese East Africa. Their version of it, translated into English, runs thus :

---

[1] G. Lademann, *Tierfabeln und andere Erzählungen in Suaheli* (Berlin, 1910), No. 5, " Geschichte von Seliman bin Daud ", pp. 63-65 (*Archiv für das Studium deutscher Kolonialsprachen*, vol. xii., Berlin, 1910).

Once on a time there was a king who was so poor that he had to gain a livelihood by fishing. He caught little fishes and went and sold them. One day he saw a great serpent with seven heads. The monster said to him, " What are you doing here ? " " I come a-fishing," said the king, " to gain my living, for I have nothing at all." " Very well," said the serpent, " I will give you much gold on condition that you give up to me the first thing you meet on going home." The king accepted all that wealth and went home.

On coming to his house he met his wife, who was with child. " Alas ! " said he to himself, " I shall have to give to the serpent the child that will be born to me." The child was born ; it was a boy. He grew and grew. One fine day the serpent came to claim him. The father called his son into the house and said to him, " My child, to-morrow I must go and throw you into the water in order to give you to the Great Serpent." " All right," replied the boy, " do as you think best."

That night the young lad sang the whole time. Two men clad in white came to him who said, " How can you sing ? Don't you know that your father is going to give you up to the Great Serpent with seven heads ? " " I know it very well," said he, " but what is the use ? Since I shall be dead to-morrow, I must sing to-day." They said to him, " Do what we are about to bid you do. Ask your father for seven pitchers of milk and place them one at each of the doors of the rooms. You will see what will happen."

The young lad asked his father for seven pitchers, filled them with milk, and set them at the doors. Then, when night fell, he set himself to sing again the whole night long.

The Great Serpent came crawling and said, " I am hungry." The boy showed him a pitcher ; the serpent drank the milk with one of his heads. He cried, " I am still hungry." The lad showed him the second pitcher, and so on with the rest till the serpent's seven heads had finished drinking.

Then the serpent said to him, " Very good, I have drunk my fill. Now put out your tongue, and I will write something on it. But you must not tell it to your father nor your mother nor your brothers, and when you are married you must not say a word of it to your wife." The serpent did as he had said, and so departed. But the young man thereby acquired the gift of understanding what the animals said. He heard them talking; he laughed, but he spoke of it to nobody.

One day he went to his fields, riding on his ass, while the ox drew the plough. The ox looked disdainfully at the ass and said to him, "As for you, you are naught but an idler; you walk about, whereas I am yoked to this heavy plough." At that the lad burst out laughing.

The time came for him to marry; a wife was found for him, and the pair lived together.

One day some birds came and perched on the trees of the yard while the fowls were pecking at the corn on the ground. "The fowls are lucky," said the birds; "people set food out for them, whereas when we go to eat in the fields, they drive us away." At hearing that, the man laughed. Then his wife grew angry and said to him, "You are always mocking me because you find me ugly." "Not at all," said he, "I am not mocking you, I am only laughing." She would not listen to him and went into the house. He followed her. The cat was there at the time.

A cock came and began to peck at the crumbs on the floor. The cat said to him, "Are you not ashamed to come into the room and gobble while the master is having a tiff with his wife?" "Not a bit," replied the cock, "I am not at all ashamed. Why should I bother? What are they wrangling about?" "O, she is vexed," said the cat, "because he is always laughing. He understands what we say, and she thinks that he is laughing at her. It is in vain that he defends himself. She is nettled at him." On hearing this talk the husband began to laugh. His wife burst into tears, saying, "Why do you think me such a silly? There you are, laughing at me again!" "Not at all," said he; "when I married you, did not I choose you just because you are pretty and clever?"

The cock said to the cat, "Among us, when a couple fall out, the husband takes a stick and brings his wife into a better frame of mind." Hearing these words the man went to look for a rod, and as his wife continued to taunt him with mocking her, he beat her soundly. "Pray forgive me,"

2 H

said she, " I will never again say that you are laughing at me." And she held her tongue.[1]

In Europe the particular story of the *Language of Animals*, with which we are here concerned, is widely spread, and many examples of it have been recorded in many languages. A long list of them, some still in manuscript, has been given by Mr. Antti Aarne in his learned dissertation on the subject.[2] In the text, besides the old versions of Morlini and Straparola, I have cited a Slavonian and a Finnish version.[3]

The oldest European version of the story appears to be one which occurs in the popular mediaeval story-book, the *Gesta Romanorum*. It runs thus :

Honorius once reigned mightily at Rome. In his kingdom there was a knight, who upon a day rode from one city to another and came by chance to a village which was all on fire. There he spied in a house an adder which whined and whimpered because it was surrounded by the flames. He took pity on it and ordered his servant to help the adder out of the fire. But the servant dissuaded him and refused to comply. Thereupon the knight took the fellow's pike, lifted the adder out of the fire, and went on his way. Now the knight was weary, so he halted in a meadow beside a cool spring and rested there. When they had sat there a short while, they saw the adder, which the knight had helped out of the fire, come hurrying after them. The servants would have hindered it, but the knight forbade them, and when the adder made up to them it ran to the knight and put a root into his mouth. No sooner was that done than he thought he heard someone saying to him, " Swallow it down, but tell nobody." As he understood what was said, he swallowed the root, and so the adder went on its way.

[1] Henri A. Junod, *Chants et Contes des Ba-Ronga* (Lausanne, 1897), No. xxix., " Le jeune garçon et le Grand Serpent ", pp. 314-317.

[2] Antti Aarne, *Der tiersprachen-kundige Mann und seine neugierige Frau* (Hamina, 1914), pp. 3-24 (*FF Communications*, No. 15).

[3] Above, pp. 112 *sqq.* What I have called a Slavonian is really a Bulgarian version. See L. Leger, *Recueil de* *Contes populaires Slaves* (Paris, 1882), pp. 109-116 ; A. H. Wratislaw, *Sixty Folk-tales from exclusively Slavonic Sources* (London, 1889), pp. 199-203, where the tale is included among Bulgarian stories. For another translation of the Finnish version, besides the one I have quoted in the text (pp. 116 *sq.*), see E. Beauvois, *Contes populaires de la Norvège, de la Finlande, et de la Bourgogne* (Paris, 1862), pp. 171-179.

The knight did not think much about it, and rode home to his own house. But it chanced one evening that he supped for his pleasure with his wife in the garden, and as he sat there he heard a great twittering of sparrows, which had quarrelled and were making it up again among themselves; it was all about a heap of threshed millet in a barn which some of the sparrows had devoured against the will of the others, and in the squabble one sparrow had been pecked to death. All this the knight understood through the virtue of the root which he had swallowed; and his wife was surprised at the close attention he paid to the dispute, and she desired that he would tell her what the sparrows had said, since he had listened so attentively to their chatter. The knight answered, " I only looked at the sparrow which has now been worried to death by the others, but what they meant by that is more than I know." But the lady persisted in her inquiries even more eagerly than before, and when she saw that he would not confess the truth, she swore that she would not eat or drink till he told her, and soon she fell sick and asked for the last sacraments. At that the knight was much troubled.

Now it fell on a day that he sauntered dolefully in his yard, and there he heard one cock say to another cock, " I thought that we had a master, but now I see clearly that we have none, for my master lets himself be bullied by his wife to the top of her bent. As for her sickness, I know all about it; for she devours two of my hens daily, and should her sickness last only ten days more there will not be one solitary hen left on the roost. If only my master were a man, he would take a pair of stout cudgels and break them over her back; that would cure her, I warrant you." The knight understood every word, and thinks he to himself, " Egad, I'll take your advice." With that he rode out into the country, and when he came into the wood he hews him two stout cudgels and hies him home at evening, and goes to his wife and begs her to get out of bed and sup with him. She refused, and said testily that she would not eat. Then the knight fairly lost his temper and whacked her without mercy till he had broken the two cudgels across her back, but still she would not sup with him. And when the cock heard her shrieks, he came flying and looked on, and when he saw that his master had broken both the cudgels, he screamed, " Give it her with the stumps ! " Hearing these words the knight took the hint and gave it her with the stumps till the blood ran, and when the knight's wife saw that he was in earnest she got up out of bed and supped with him. Thus the knight took a leaf out of the cock's book ; and as for you, my brethren, beware how you let yourselves be hoodwinked by your wives.[1]

A German version of it, recorded orally at Gross-Kreutz, near Brandenburg, about 1842, runs as follows :

Once upon a time there was a man who was very clever, for he understood the language of all animals, but for all his cleverness he could not keep his wicked wife within bounds. It happened one day that he sat in his yard and listened to the talk of the beasts, but as their talk fell on a merry topic he laughed aloud, and his wife saw it. Thereupon she pressed him with great vehemence (for she was very curious) to tell her what he had laughed at ; but though he would gladly have contented her, yet durst he not, for it would have cost him his life. So he refused, but that only made his wife the more impatient and angry, and she heaped taunts and reproaches on him, saying that he always kept secrets from her.

So it went on from day to day, till the man at last grew sad and moody, and went about with hanging head, thinking how he could mend matters. Well, one day he went into the yard and saw how the cock strutted about and crowed loudly. But the dog kept quite still and said to the cock, " How can you be so gay when our master is so sad on account of his wicked wife who gives him no peace ? " " I think," answered the cock, " that he will change his tune. He has only to take an example from me. I have more than a hundred wives, but woe to the one that would dare to disobey me, I would peck the eyes out of her head in a moment ; and yet he has only one wife and cannot manage her ! " The master heard this discourse with pleasure, for he saw that the cock was right ; so he went into his house on the instant, took a

[1] *Gesta Romanorum, das älteste Märchen- und Legendenbuch des christlichen Mittelalters, zum ersten Male vollständig aus dem Lateinischen ins* *Deutsche übertragen* von Dr. Johann Georg Theodore Grässe, 3. Ausgabe (Leipzig, 1905), vol. ii. pp. 182-184.

whip and laid on lustily to his wife, asking if she still wished
to know why he had laughed. She at once knocked under
and never again in her life desired to know her husband's
secrets. And from that moment they lived happy and content to the end.[1]

A Magyar version of the story runs thus :

A shepherd saved the life of the daughter of the King of
Snakes, the princess narrowly escaping death by fire. To
show her gratitude to her deliverer she taught him the
language of animals, and he was able to understand them.
One day his donkey said something that made him smile ;
whereupon his wife began to tease him, wishing to know the
joke, but the shepherd could not gratify her wish, because
he knew that the penalty of betraying the secret would be
his own sudden death.

However, his wife would not give in and leave him in
peace, but continued to badger him with so many questions
that he at last made up his mind to die rather than bear his
wife's nagging any longer. So he had his coffin made and
brought to his house, and he lay down in it, ready to divulge
the secret and die on the spot. His faithful dog sat mourn-
fully by his side watching, while the house-cock hopped
merrily about the room. The dog expostulated with the
cock, saying that this was not the time for merriment when
their master was so near to death. But the cock took him
up very short. " It's master's own fault," said he, " why is
he such a great fool and coward ? Look at me ! I have fifty
wives, and they all do as I tell them to do. If I can manage
so many, surely he ought to be able to manage one ! "

Hearing that, the shepherd jumped out of the coffin, seized
a wet rope-end, and gave his wife a sound thrashing. Peace
was thus restored, and they lived happily together ever after.[2]

A Roumanian version of the story runs, in an abridged
form, to the following effect :

Once upon a time there was a rich man who had an only
child, a daughter, named Marie. The girl was loved by a

[1] Adalbert Kuhn, *Märkische Sagen
und Märchen* (Berlin, 1843), pp. 268-
270, " Die böse Frau ".

[2] *The Folk-tales of the Magyars,*

collected by Kriza, Erdélyi, and others,
translated and edited, with comparative notes, by the Rev. W. Henry Jones
and Lewis L. Kropf (London, 1889),
pp. 301 *sq.*

poor young man named John, who offered to marry her. But
her father was proud as well as rich and would bestow his
daughter's hand on none but a wealthy suitor ; so he rejected
John's suit on account of his poverty.

Now it happened that the rich man had two goldfinches
which he kept in a cage. The birds sang ravishingly, and
their owner used to listen to them with rapture till the tears
came into his eyes for very joy. But one day the birds fell
silent and nothing seemingly could induce them to tune up
their melody again. The master was distressed, for he loved
the birds and sorely missed their music. In his distress he
even declared that he would give his daughter in marriage
to any man who should induce the birds to sing again. When
John heard this he resolved to learn the language of birds,
in order that he might question the two goldfinches and find
out why they had fallen suddenly and obstinately silent.

One day, on his wanderings, John saw a white snake in a
well and saved it from drowning by drawing it out of the
water. The grateful snake requested John to carry him to
his mother, the Queen of Snakes, assuring him that his mother
would offer his deliverer a rich reward, but warning him to
accept no gift save a knowledge of the language of animals.
It turned out as the white snake had foretold. The Queen
of Snakes offered him bronze, silver, or gold, but John refused
them all, saying that he would accept no reward but a knowledge of the language of animals. The Queen of Snakes at
first objected to granting the request, but at last she brought
him the head of a white snake, telling him that if he roasted
and ate it he would understand the language of flowers and
birds and all animals, but warning him at the same time that
he must not reveal his knowledge to any one or he must die
at once.

Armed with this secret knowledge, John now returned to
the house of the rich man and questioned the two goldfinches
as to the reason of their silence. To his joy he discovered
that their silence was caused by their master's refusal to give
his daughter in marriage to John, and that nothing but the
union of the young pair would induce them to resume their
melodious minstrelsy. So the girl's father was obliged to
consent to their marriage, and married they were.

One day, as he and his wife were out riding, the horse on which he was mounted fell behind the horse on which his wife rode. The horse on which his wife rode thereupon asked the other horse, " Why do you lag behind ? " The other horse replied, " Because you carry the mistress, who is slim and light, while I carry the master, who is big and heavy." John understood this talk of the horses, but his wife did not.

Another time, when he was out hunting with his wife in the wood he heard the talk of two dogs. One of the dogs said to the other that he would run home and look after the house, lest in the absence of the master and mistress it should be robbed by thieves. So saying, the dog ran away and made for home. John understood what the dog had said, but his wife did not.

Another day John stood at the window looking out into the garden. There some sparrows were busy pecking at the seeds on a row of hemp stalks. In doing so they let fall some of the seeds, which were picked up by the barndoor fowls. But one of the sparrows flew down to the ground and began picking up the fallen seeds among the fowls. On that the cock remonstrated with the sparrow, saying, " You have enough seeds up there among the stalks, leave the seeds on the ground to us." On hearing this remark of the cock John laughed. His wife asked him why he laughed, adding that she had long suspected him of keeping a secret from her. John said that if he told her he must die. But she insisted on knowing, so her husband prepared to die and ordered his coffin.

But on his way home from ordering the coffin he heard the cock crowing, and saying, "Our master is a fool; he has only one wife and cannot manage her. I have a whole troop of wives and they must obey me. In his place I would buy a rope and give her a good hiding. She would soon drop her curiosity and forget to ask questions." The man thought to himself, " What a stupid fellow am I, to need to have my eyes opened by the cock ! " So he went and bought a rope of the rope-maker, and with it he gave his wife such a drubbing that she lost all her curiosity and taste for asking questions. She never again inquired of her husband why he laughed, and if he did not die of sickness or old age he must be alive to this day.[1]

An Albanian version of the story runs as follows :

" A certain man was gifted with the power to understand the talk of beasts and birds, but on condition only that, should he ever tell that which he heard, he would drop down dead.

" One day he heard the donkey talking to the horse. The donkey's remarks were very funny, and, as he came from the stable, he laughed. ' Why are you laughing ? ' asked his wife. 'At something the donkey said.' ' What did the donkey say?' 'You know I cannot tell you. I should drop down dead.' But she was wicked, as all women are, and she only answered, 'What did the donkey say?' And all day long and all night she gave him no peace, and he had neither sleep nor rest, for still she asked, ' What did the donkey say ? '

" Worn out at last, he could bear no more : ' To-morrow I will tell you,' he said. He called his little children and said good-bye to them, and told them he must die to-morrow. They cried bitterly and begged, ' Oh, mother, do not kill our dear father ! ' But she answered only, ' I want to know what the donkey said.'

" So the poor man went out to take a last look at the yard, and there he saw the cock standing on tiptoe, flapping his wings and crowing as loud as he could. ' Oh, you wicked bird!' cried the dog, 'How can you laugh and sing when our dear master, who is so kind to us, must die to-morrow?' But the cock only crowed the more. ' Laugh ! ' said he, ' I shall die of laughing ! Look at him—the silly fool ! He has only one wife, and cannot manage her ; while I have fifty, and keep them all in order ! '

" The man heard this. He picked up a large stick, and went back into the house. ' Do you want to know what the donkey said ? ' he asked. ' Yes,' said his wife. Then he gave her a good beating. ' Do you want to know what the donkey said ? ' he asked. ' Yes,' said she. So he beat her again. ' Do you want to know what the donkey said ? ' ' Yes,' said she. So a third time he beat her till he was quite

tired. ' Do you still want to know what the donkey said ? '
' No,' said she. And they lived very happily ever afterwards." [1]

A Greek version of the story, taken down in the island
of Lesbos, runs thus :

There was a young man who had not all his wits about
him. Every day he walked in the streets and everybody
made fun of him. " Go, then, and give alms to the sea ! "
they said to him. So he used to buy a loaf, go down to the
shore, and, crumbling the bread, throw the crumbs into the
water. A fish used to come and eat them.

Once the young man went to the edge of the sea with
empty hands ; when he saw the fish drawing near as usual
he began to weep. " Poor fish," said he to it, " I have no
more money to buy you bread." " It is my turn," answered
the fish, " I will now repay the kindness you did to me. Put
your finger to my mouth." And he gave him a little shining
stone and said to him, " When anybody has this stone in his
mouth, he understands the language of animals. Such is
its worth. But beware of speaking about it to anyone under
pain of losing your life."

Endowed with this wonderful stone the young man went
into a valley and there lay down on the ground with the stone
in his mouth. A raven came flying over him, accompanied
by its young one. The young one, thinking that the man
was dead, swooped down to devour his flesh. The man
caught it. By virtue of the stone he could talk with the mother
raven, who begged him to let go her young one, promising
to show him a hidden treasure. So the young man grew rich
and married a wife.

One day he went to a fair with his wife. He had the
stone in his mouth. His wife, who was with child, rode a
mare, which was also pregnant. The mare was followed by
her little foal. Now the foal was hard put to it to keep pace
and always lagged behind. Then it said to its mother, " Stop
a bit that I may catch you up." " But as for me," replied
the mare, " I carry three and yet I walk fast, whereas you are
free. So make haste ! "

Hearing this talk, the man began to laugh. His wife asked

[1] M. Edith Durham, *High Albania* (London, 1909), pp. 187-189.

GARNERED SHEAVES

him why he laughed. "It is nothing," answered the man, "it was something I remembered that made me laugh." But his wife insisted, so he said to her, "I will confide it to you when we have returned to the house."

When they were at home, his wife reminded him of his promise. Seeing there was no help for it the poor man resolved to make a clean breast of it and die. He went down into the yard to feed the fowls for the last time. He saw the cock make up to a hen. The hen fought shy and said to the cock, "Our master will soon die, and yet you think of nothing but your pleasure!" "Let him die!" answered the cock, "he is a fool." "But what is he to do with the nagging of his wife?" replied the hen. "He has only to take a stick and beat her till she stops nagging," said the cock. At that the good man said, "The cock is not such an ass as I am." He followed the cock's advice, and his wife left him in peace.[1]

An Italian version of the story, recorded in the Abruzzi, runs as follows :

When Jesus Christ and his apostles were on earth they lodged one day in the house of a rich man. In return for the hospitality which he showed them the host begged of Jesus Christ as a favour that he might learn the language of animals. Jesus Christ granted his request, but warned him that he must not reveal the secret to anyone, not even to his wife.

After the august guests had departed, the man said to his wife, "Let us go and see how the cattle are faring." So they went to the cattle-stall and found the animals wrangling. The ox was saying to the ass, "It is all very fine for you. You have nothing to do but to carry your mistress on the saddle ; you have fresh grass to eat, and fresh water to drink, and no beating to fear." The ass said, "Have you no sense? Has God given you such weapons and yet you do not know how to use them in your own defence? When next they come to yoke you to the plough, do you just kick with your hoofs and butt with your horns." The ox replied, "Tell that to the asses. If I did that, they would carry me off to the

[1] G. Georgeakis et Léon Pineau, *Le Folk-lore de Lesbos* (Paris, 1894), Conte No. viii. " Le Langage des Animaux ", pp. 46-49.

slaughter-yard the very next day." The ass answered, "Well, when you wish to rest, flop down as if you were ill." The ox was delighted with the sly advice, but the master was still more astute, for he had heard and understood everything.

Next morning early, when the servant went to fetch the ox, he found him stretched at full length on the ground. So he ran to tell the master. But the master, aware of the trick, said to the servant, "Yoke the ass and the sick ox to the plough, and let the other oxen rest." The servant thought it a crazy order, but he obeyed.

That evening the ass and the ox returned to the stall dead with fatigue. The master set himself to listen to what they said to each other. The ox said, "You see what has happened to me all through you!" The ass answered, "Thank God for it! What if the master had sent you to the shambles?" At that the master burst out laughing. His wife wished to know why he laughed. But he made an excuse. "An odd thing came into my head," said he. His wife would not believe him, she insisted on his revealing the secret, but he remained firm. So she went away in a fury and shut herself up in her room. Her husband also went into the house. In a melancholy mood he looked out of the window. Meanwhile the cock was crowing and strutting about among the hens. But the dog said to the cock, "Are you not ashamed? The master is downcast and the mistress is enraged, and you sing and are merry!" The cock answered, "It serves master right. Look at me! I have more than twenty wives, and no sooner do I call them than they all run to me and always obey me. Let the laggard beware of my beak! But the master would always be good-natured. Why doesn't he take a mallet and break the woman's ribs?"

The master knocked at the door of his wife's room. She opened it, but was still on her high horse. He said to her, "Well, have you come round?" "No, no," said she, "you're a brute. Who knows what you were thinking? And you would not tell me. Why? why?" "Would you like to know why?" he asked, "then this mallet will tell you." With that he began to hammer her in good earnest.

She cried, " Beat me no more ! I no longer wish to know your doings. I am quite content." From that day she never played the grumbler again.[1]

The story with which we are dealing appears to be particularly common in Central and especially in Eastern Europe. Mr. Antti Aarne has noted six Esthonian and no less than sixty-two Finnish versions.[2] On the other hand, it is seemingly absent in the west ; not a single example of it has been recorded from oral tradition in Spain, France, and the British Islands.[3] This remarkable contrast in respect of distribution suggests that the story is of Oriental origin and has passed into Europe from the East.

The question of the origin of the story has been carefully investigated by Mr. Antti Aarne. He distinguishes two forms of it, an Eastern and a Western, but comes to the conclusion that both forms had a common origin in India.[4] Yet he holds it unlikely that any of the ancient literary versions is the origin of the story ; probably they are all derived either from a still older literary version, now lost, or from popular oral tradition.[5] Further, he is of opinion that the story was invented at a stroke by a single individual, and not gradually elaborated by a succession of story-tellers, who added one feature after another to the tale.[6] On such a subject demonstration is impossible and we are confined to a weighing of probabilities. So far as I can judge, all the evidence and all the probabilities favour the conclusions reached by Mr. Aarne in his learned and judicious monograph. His views are in substantial agreement with those of the great scholar, Theodor Benfey, who first called attention to the story and illustrated its wide geographical diffusion. Benfey held that the tale originated in India and spread thence through Western Asia to Europe and Africa, being one of the few products of Indian fancy which have made their way over the whole of the Old World.[7]

[1] Antonio de Nino, *Usi e Costumi Abruzzesi*, iv. (Firenze, 1887), pp. 51-54.

[2] Antti Aarne, *Der tiersprachenkundige Mann und seine neugierige Frau*, pp. 4-20 (*FF Communications*, No. 15).

[3] Antti Aarne, *op. cit.* p. 68.

[4] Antti Aarne, *op. cit.* pp. 55 *sqq.*

[5] Antti Aarne, *op. cit.* p. 70.

[6] Antti Aarne, *op. cit.* pp. 80 *sq.*

[7] Theodor Benfey, " Ein Märchen von der Thiersprache, Quelle und Verbreitung", *Orient und Occident*, ii. (Göttingen, 1864), p. 135.

To consider the question of origin for a moment from a more general point of view, in endeavouring to trace the history of any invention or institution we must always bear in mind, as I have pointed out elsewhere,[1] a twofold possibility; either, on the one hand, the invention may have originated once for all in a single place, from which it has gradually spread over a greater or lesser area of the earth's surface; or, on the other hand, it may have originated independently several times over in various places, from which it may in like manner have been gradually diffused over a greater or lesser portion of the globe. Of the institutions which have originated once for all in a single place, the great historical religions, Buddhism, Confucianism, Christianity, and Mohammedanism, are among the most conspicuous and the most indubitable instances, for few can doubt that these great systems took their rise in the religious genius of individuals in India, China, Palestine, and Arabia. But on a lesser scale folk-tales of a certain degree of complexity furnish almost equally sure examples of inventions which have had their origin once for all in a single place; for while similar stories of a very simple type may conceivably have been invented independently several times over, it is difficult to imagine that complex narratives, involving a series of connected incidents, can have ever been invented more than once in the history of humanity. Who could think that the *Pilgrim's Progress* or *Vanity Fair* could ever be conceived and written twice or thrice over by authors wholly independent of each other ? Among such fictions as have been invented once for all may safely be reckoned the story of the Man who understood the Language of Animals and his Curious Wife.

P. 116. The Tarantschi-Tartar version was published in 1886. —This Tartar version is now accessible in an English translation.[2]

P. 120. In a Bohemian tale an old woman brings a serpent to a king, telling him that if he ate it he would understand the language of all animals.

---

[1] *Folk-lore in the Old Testament,* vol. i. pp. 106 *sq.* ; *The Gorgon's Head,* pp. 348 *sqq.*

[2] C. Fillingham Coxwell, *Siberian and other Folk-tales* (London, N.D), pp. 319-321.

This Bohemian story is now accessible in an English translation.[1]

P. 122. The idea that the magic serpent, whose flesh imparts a knowledge of the language of animals and plants, is to be found under a hazel tree, occurs also in Germany.

In Lechrain, the country on both sides of the river Lech which from time immemorial has formed the boundary between Bavaria and Swabia, " adders are very plentiful on the Lech ; they are of all sizes and colours. Many of them have their lair particularly at wells. There are even white adders, and where these are, the King is never wanting. He has a golden crown, but is extremely seldom seen. Such white adders are also to be found under hazel bushes which have mistletoe growing on them and are therefore very old ; it is there that the white adders can most easily be caught. If a man catches one of them, strips the skin off, extracts the tongue, and eats a good piece of the flesh, he has all the luck in the world ; also he can make himself invisible, and all doors and bolts open before him ; also he knows all herbs on earth, and understands the language of birds." [2]

P. 124. It is said to be a common belief in Wales, Scotland, and Cornwall that about Midsummer Eve the snakes meet in companies and by joining heads and hissing produce a glass ring, which whoever finds shall prosper in all his undertakings ; and these rings are called snake stones.—This belief in serpent-stones appears undoubtedly to be a relic of Druidism in the Celtic countries where it exists, or at all events existed down to modern times. Pliny calls them a sort of eggs, and says that they were very famous in Gaul, though unknown to the Greeks. They were believed to be produced by the slaver and foam of serpents coiling and writhing together. According to the Druids, as reported by Pliny, the egg thus produced by the hissing serpents was shot up by them into the air, and he who would possess himself of the treasure must catch it in a cloak, lest it should touch the ground, and having caught it he must gallop away, for the serpents would pursue him

[1] A. H. Wratislaw, *Sixty Folk-tales from exclusively Slavonic Sources* (London, 1889), pp. 25 *sqq.*, " Golden-hair ".

[2] Karl Freiherr von Leoprechting, *Aus dem Lechrain. Zur deutschen Sitten- und Sagenkunde* (München, 1855), p. 77.

till they were stopped by the interposition of a river. The proof of the genuineness of one of these serpent-eggs was if it floated against the stream, even when it was set in gold. The Druids thought that the precious egg could only be got on a certain day of the moon. Pliny had himself seen one of these serpent eggs. He describes it as of the bigness of an ordinary apple encrusted in a cartilaginous skin like the prickly shell of a sea-urchin. The Druids set a high value on such an egg as a talisman to ensure success in lawsuits and access to kings. The Emperor Claudius put to death a knight of the Vocontian Gauls for carrying in his bosom a serpent-egg when he was engaged in a lawsuit.[1]

In Scotland the stone is called in Gaelic *Clach Nathrach*, that is, Serpent Stone, or *Glaine Nathair*, that is, Serpent Bead or Glass. "The ordinary *Glaine Nathair* (Serpent Glass) is of smaller size than is indicated by Pliny. The one which the writer saw was about the size of a gun bullet, and about $1\frac{1}{4}$ in. long. There was a hole through from end to end, and depressions on its sides, as if it had once been soft, and had been taken up gently between the finger and thumb. It is of transparent glass, but glass unlike that of the present day. There are extremely brilliant and curious streaks of colour in it. It is now merely a family heirloom, but in olden times was in great demand for dipping in water to be given to bewitched persons or beasts. The sloughed skin (*cochull*) of the serpent itself was used for the same purpose. Water in which it was dipped was given to sick beasts. The tale as to the manner in which it was originally got is the same as is told of other beads of the same kind. The serpents are assembled in a coiling mass, with their heads in the air hissing horribly, slavering, and out of their slaver making the serpent stone. The spittle, in course of becoming solid, was known as *meall èochd*. That the story was not implicitly believed is shown by the addition that, when the bead is finished, one of the serpents puts its tail through it. Thus the hole by which it is perforated is made.

" In the case of the bead which the writer saw, the person who came upon the serpents at their work is said to have waited till the reptiles slept. He then worked the bead out

[1] Pliny, *Nat. Hist.* xxix. 52-54.

of their circle with a straw or twig of heather. As he took it
up between his finger and thumb, and made off with it, he
observed that the pressure of his fingers marked it, it being
still soft, and this made him put a straw through it to carry
it home. This story fairly accounts for the shape of the bead
and the marks upon it. The marks look as if they were so
made when the stone was soft. Another account says that
the finder came on a rock above where the serpents were at
work, and, rolling his plaid into a ball, threw it down the
rock near them. Instantly the serpents made a dash at the
plaid, and while they were reducing it to shreds he made off
with the Adder Stone. By means of a sharp-pointed stick,
prepared for the purpose, and thrust through the soft bead,
he raised it to the top of the rock, and taking it between his
finger and thumb, ran home.

" Similar legends of the Adder Stone were current in the
Lowlands. Scott says the name is applied ' to celts and other
perforated stones '. In the Highlands the name is not applied
to stones. In Wales and Ireland the bead is known as
' Druid's Glass '." [1]

With regard to Adder or Serpent Stones, an English
visitor to Scotland in 1699 reported that " not only the vulgar,
but even gentlemen of good education, throughout Scotland,
were fully persuaded that snakes made them ". He had seen
at least fifty different kinds of these amulets between Wales
and the Highlands of Scotland. The Adder Stone was hung
from the neck as a cure for whooping cough and other ailments of children. It was esteemed a charm to ensure prosperity and repel evil spirits. The owner kept it in an iron box
as a security from fairies, who are believed to have a peculiar
aversion to that metal.[2]

On this subject an eminent Scottish antiquary speaks of
" the large beads of glass or vitreous paste and amber, so
well known among the contents of British tumuli, and associated, even in our own day, with the same superstitious virtues
ascribed to them in the writings of the philosophic but credu-

[1] John Gregorson Campbell, *Witchcraft and Second Sight in the Highlands and Islands of Scotland* (Glasgow, 1902), pp. 84, 85-87.
[2] John Graham Dalyell, *The Darker*

Superstitions of Scotland (Glasgow,
1835), p. 141, referring to *Llwyd*,
Letter from Linlithgow, ap. *Philosophical Transactions*, vol. xxviii. No. 9,
p. 98.

lous Pliny. The very same story, in fact, is told of the *Adder-stane* in the popular legends of the Scottish Lowlands as Pliny records of the origin of the *Ovum Anguinum*. . . . They are variously known as Adder Beads, Serpent Stones, Druidical Beads, and among the Welsh and Irish by the synonymous terms of *Gleini na Droedh* and *Glaine nan Druidhe*, signifying the Magician's or Druid's glass. Many of them are exceedingly beautiful, and are characterized by considerable ingenuity in the variations of style. Among those in the Museum of the Scottish Antiquaries there is one of red glass, spotted with white; another of dark brown glass, streaked with yellow; others of pale green and blue glass, plain and ribbed; and two of curiously figured pattern, wrought with various colours interwoven on their surface." [1] Among the magical virtues which these ancient glass beads are believed to possess is that of a preservative against the bite of a serpent. [2]

SOME POPULAR SUPERSTITIONS OF THE ANCIENTS

P. 130. the so-called " symbols of Pythagoras ".—In the text I have argued that many of these so-called " symbols ", which passed muster in antiquity for profound moral or philosophical maxims, are nothing but popular superstitions, which survive to this day among the uneducated classes of Europe and among many uncivilized peoples in many parts of the world. The same view of them has since been adopted and amply demonstrated by a German scholar, Dr. Friederich Boehm, in a learned and judicious dissertation. [3] It is no longer possible for any well-informed student to mistake the majority of these " symbols " for anything else than curious and instructive examples of primitive ignorance and error persisting even in the midst of a civilized and cultured society.

P. 132. Pythagoras believed that an earthquake was caused by the dead men fighting with each other under ground, and so shaking the earth.—So the Baluba, a large tribe in the upper

[1] Daniel Wilson, *The Archaeology and Prehistoric Annals of Scotland* (Edinburgh, 1851), pp. 303 *sq.*

[2] J. A. MacCulloch, *The Religion*

of the Ancient Celts (Edinburgh, 1911), pp. 328 *sq.*

[3] Fridericus Boehm, *De symbolis Pythagoreis, Dissertatio Inauguralis* (Berolinum, 1905).

2 I

valley of the Congo, think that an earthquake is caused by the spirits of the dead fighting among themselves after the fashion of human beings.[1] As the spirits of the dead are supposed to dwell just under the surface of the ground, below the feet of the living,[2] it is perfectly natural that when they fight a battle they should cause that disturbance which we call an earthquake. Thus on the question of the cause of earthquakes these black people of the Congo are perfectly at one with Pythagoras, or rather with the simple-minded folk who cloaked their crude superstition under the flowing mantle of the philosopher.

In the Province of Bombay there is a belief " that deities of some strange species reside in the nether regions, and the earth is shaken whenever these beings fight among themselves ".[3]

P. 133. Again, Pythagoras told his disciples never to point the finger at the stars.—It is an Esthonian notion that you ought not to point the finger at the moon or a star, else your finger will rot off or (according to others) be drawn up to the moon or the star.[4] " No Teton dare look at the stars and count even ' one ' mentally. For one is sure to die if he begin to count the stars and desist before finishing. They are also afraid to point at a rainbow with the index finger, though they can point at it with the lips or elbow. Should one forget and point with the index finger, the bystanders laugh at him, saying, ' By and by, O friend, when your finger becomes large and round, let us have it for a ball bat.' "[5] Apparently they think that by pointing at the rainbow a finger will become bent into a semicircle, like the rainbow, through sympathetic magic. This conjecture is confirmed by the reason which the Galelareeze of Halmahera, a large island to the west of New Guinea, assign for their observance of the very same rule : they say that if you point your fingers at the rainbow, they will become bent like the rainbow ; you should

---

[1] Le R. P. Colle, *Les Baluba* (*Congo Belge*), ii. (Bruxelles, 1913), p. 428.

[2] Le R. P. Colle, *op. cit.* ii. 720.

[3] R. E. Enthoven, *The Folk-lore of Bombay* (Oxford, 1924), p. 80.

[4] F. J. Wiedemann, *Aus dem inneren und äusseren Leben der Ehsten* (St. Petersburg, 1876), p. 458.

[5] James Owen Dorsey, " A Study of Siouan Cults ", *Eleventh Annual Report of the Bureau of Ethnology* (Washington, 1894), p. 467.

point at it with your elbow,[1] which, being already bent, need not fear distortion through the bending influence of the rainbow. The Bukaua of Northern New Guinea believe that if a man points with his finger at a rainbow, he will get ulcers in his armpits. For according to them the rainbow is composed of the blood of murdered men, and the spirits of these unfortunates are angry at the pointer and punish him in the painful manner aforesaid.[2]

P. 135. During a thunderstorm it was a Greek custom to put out the fire, and hiss and cheep with the lips.—In antiquity the custom of cheeping with the lips at a thunderstorm was not confined to the Greeks, for Pliny says that it was observed by all nations.[3] It is expressly mentioned by Aristophanes.[4] In Lesbos the custom is still kept up : when it thunders people twitch the tip of their ears and make with the lips a sound like that of a kiss.[5] When the Annamites see a flash of lightning, they make with their lips a cheeping sound as if they were calling fowls, and this they do in order to drive away the thunderstorm. The explanation which they give is this. Thunder is produced by a spirit or demon called Ông lôi who is terribly afraid of cocks, because once on a time, being transformed by the deity into a slice of meat, he received in that shape such a dreadful pecking from the beaks of cocks that he has lived in terror of these birds ever since. So when it thunders and people cheep with their lips, the demon thinks they are really summoning the fowls to attack him, and he flees accordingly, and with him the thundercloud rolls away.[6] The Jehehr of the Malay Peninsula sometimes try to drive away a threatening storm by blowing through the teeth with a hissing sound like " Hish ".[7]

P. 135. the Esthonians in Russia fasten scythes, edge upward,

[1] M. J. van Baarda, " Fabelen, Verhalen en Overleveringen der Galelareezen ", *Bijdragen tot de Taal- Land- en Volkenkunde van Nederlandsch-Indie*, xlv. (1895), p. 513.
[2] Stefan Lehner, " Bukaua ", in R. Neuhauss, *Deutsch Neu-Guinea*, iii. (Berlin, 1911), p. 466.
[3] Pliny, *Nat. Hist.* xxviii. 25, "*Fulgetras poppysmis adorare consensus gentium est*".

[4] Aristophanes, *Wasps*, 626, κἂν ἀστράψω, ποππύζουσιν.
[5] G. Georgeakis et L. Pineau, *Le Folk-lore de Lesbos* (Paris, 1894), p. 341.
[6] Paul Giran, *Magie et Religion Annamite* (Paris, 1912), p. 129.
[7] Ivor H. N. Evans, *Studies in Religion, Folk-lore and Custom in British North Borneo and the Malay Peninsula* (Cambridge, 1923), p. 153.

over the door, that the demons, fleeing from the thundering god,
may cut their feet if they try to seek shelter in the house.—The
custom of placing edged tools, edge upward, in the open air
for the purpose of wounding demons or witches in a storm
of thunder or hail appears to be widespread, not only in
Europe but in other parts of the world. In antiquity
it was thought that hail could be averted from a field by
brandishing bloody axes threateningly towards the sky,[1]
no doubt to let the hail know what it might expect if it
were rash enough to fall down on a field thus protected. In
modern times Southern Slav peasants commonly believe that
hailstorms are caused by witches, and they take their precautions against these maleficent beings accordingly. One
approved method of doing so is to fire at the clouds with
consecrated powder and old nails extracted from horse-shoes.
The witch then falls down dead from the clouds or is choked
by the fumes of the holy powder and rusty nails. But the
more usual practice, which is said to prevail universally among
the Southern Slavs as well as among German peasants, is to
carry all large cutting and chopping instruments, such as
scythes and axes, out into the open air, in order that the
witches may wound themselves thereon and so be induced to
stop the hail. A more humane mode of effecting the same
desirable end is to bring out the chairs from the house and
set them upside down in the yard, that the witches may break
their bones or necks by falling on the upturned legs of the
chairs.[2] Customs of the same sort are known in Italy ; for
we are told that in the Romagna, when a dark thundercloud
is threatening, the peasants resort to the following remedy :
they hastily carry out to the yard or threshing-floor all the
iron implements they possess, such as scythes, shovels, and
mattocks, believing that they thus avert from their fields the
hail which otherwise might ruin the corn and the vines.[3]

Similar devices to stop the fall of hail are resorted to in
India. At Naini Tal it happened that a gardener had trans-

[1] Palladius, *De re rustica*, i. 35. 1,
" *Contra grandinem multa dicuntur.
Panno roseo mola cooperitur : item
cruentae secures contra caelum mina-
citer levantur."*
[2] F. S. Krauss, *Volksglaube und*

religiöser Brauch der Südslaven (Mün-
ster i. W., 1890), pp. 118 *sq.*

[3] Michele Placucci, *Usi e Pregiudisi
dei Contadini della Romagna* (Palermo,
1885), pp. 135 *sq.*

planted some pot plants into the garden in the belief that hail was over for the season. But a few hours later a storm came on and hail began to fall. The gardener at once dived into the kitchen and came out with the cook's chopper, with which he made some strokes on the ground outside where the hail was falling. Having done so, he deposited the chopper on the ground with the edge uppermost and explained his behaviour to his mistress by saying that if you brought out the *hatyár* (implements) the hail would pass over.[1] In Kumaun, where hail is much dreaded, some people put an axe in the open air with the edge turned up, so that the hailstones may be cut in pieces and cease falling. In Multan it is believed that if you can catch a hailstone in the air, before it reaches the ground, and cut it in two with a pair of scissors, the hail will abate.[2]

In thunderstorms the Bukaua of Northern New Guinea stick their spears, point upward, in the roofs of their houses that the lightning may spike himself on them when he falls, and they lay three sorts of sharp-edged grasses on the roof that he may cut himself on them in case he should miss being spiked on the spears.[3] Thus they make sure of catching him one way or another. Among the Nandi, a tribe of Kenya in East Africa, there is a clan called Toiyoi which has for its totem the soldier ant and rain. During a heavy thunderstorm the Toiyoi seize an axe and, after rubbing it in the ashes of the fire, throw it outside the hut, exclaiming at the same time, " Thunder, be silent in our town." [4] On the same principle the ancient Thracians used to shoot arrows at the sky when it thundered and lightened, while at the same time they threatened the god who was flashing and roaring in the clouds.[5] The modern peasant of South-eastern Europe, who fires rusty nails at the hail-clouds and sets out scythes and axes to wound the witches riding in the storm, is no wiser than his predecessor the old Thracian archer ; the advance

---

[1] *North Indian Notes and Queries*, vol. i. (Allahabad, 1891), p. 13, No. 81.

[2] W. Crooke, *The Popular Religion and Folk-lore of Northern India* (Westminster, 1896), i. 79. Compare *id.*, *Religion and Folklore of Northern India*, edited by R. E. Enthoven (Oxford University Press, 1926), pp. 78 *sq.*

[3] Stefan Lehner, " Bukaua ", in R. Neuhauss, *Deutsch Neu-Guinea*, iii. (Berlin, 1911), pp. 430 *sq.*

[4] A. C. Hollis, *The Nandi* (Oxford, 1909), p. 9.

[5] Herodotus, iv. 94.

of knowledge has not touched him ; he remains at heart a barbarian.

P. 142. At the town of Cleonae, in Argolis, there were watchmen maintained at the public expense to look out for hailstorms. . . . If the vines and crops suffered from a hailstorm, the watchmen were brought before the magistrates and punished for neglect of duty.—A precisely similar institution exists, or existed down to recent times, in Eastern Bengal. We are told that *Ṣilārí* is the title of " a magician employed in Eastern Bengal to protect crops from hailstones. Formerly the Silárí, like the Gárapagárí of the Central Provinces, was a paid village servant, and officiated as priest at an annual festival performed for the benefit of the crops. Now the festival has fallen into disuse, and a member of any caste may become a Ṣilárí, being remunerated in kind—it is unlucky to give him money—according to the success of his enchantments. . . . ' At the present day', says Dr. Wise, ' this magical art is falling into disrepute, and it is no unusual thing for the peasantry to punish a Ṣilárí who fails to protect their fields. The Ṣilárís confess that their skill is inadequate to call down a storm on a neighbour's crop, as was formerly done ; but they still profess ability to drive away a cloud threatening any tract of country. As hailstorms in Bengal occur usually in March and April, when the *Boro-dhán*, or spring rice, is in the ear, the services of the magician are called for in low lands, where this crop is cultivated. When a storm is impending the Ṣilárí, summoned by the peasantry, rushes, almost naked, from his hut, with a rattan wand in his right hand. Invoking Parameṣwara, the supreme god, he ascends a mound, where spreading abroad his hands, and waving his rod to indicate the direction the storm-cloud is to take, he recites one or other of the following doggerel incantations in the vernacular,' " in which, amid other gibberish, he bids the storm-clouds begone to the mountains of the north.[1]

In the Central Provinces of India there is a regular caste whose function it is to avert hailstorms from the crops. Their name, as we have just seen, is Garpagari, which is derived

[1] (Sir) H. H. Risley, *The Tribes and Castes of Bengal. Ethnographic Glossary*, ii. (Calcutta, 1892), p. 251.

from *gār*, the Marathi word for hail. They worship Mahadeo or Siva and Mahabir, but usual they do not distinguish between the deities. Their principal festival takes place on the first day of December, that being the day from which hailstorms may be expected to occur. These it is the duty of the Garpagari to ward off, and for discharging this duty he was formerly remunerated by a customary contribution of rice from each cultivator in the village. It is melancholy to relate that, with the spread of a barren and paralysing scepticism, the earnings of the Garpagari have fallen off, and farmers now often refuse to give him anything at all, or at most only a single sheaf at harvest.[1] Yet the personal sacrifices which the Garpagari is prepared to make in the discharge of his public duty are very heavy, as will appear from the following account of his proceedings :

" When the sky is of mixed red and black at night like smoke and flame the Gārpagāri knows that a hailstorm is coming. Then, taking a sword in his hand, he goes and stands before Mahābīr, and begs him to disperse the clouds. When entreaties fail, he proceeds to threats, saying that he will kill himself, and throws off his clothes. Sometimes his wife and children go and stand with him before Mahābīr's shrine and he threatens to kill them. Formerly he would cut and slash himself, so it is said, if Mahābīr was obdurate, but now the utmost he does is to draw some blood from a finger. He would also threaten to sacrifice his son, and instances are known of his actually having done so." [2]

Thus the parallel between ancient Greece and modern India is fairly close. In both we see men regularly paid to look out for approaching hailstorms, and in both we see an attempt to avert the descent of the hail by a sacrifice of blood, if it be only the blood of a finger. So like are the forms which human folly assumes in distant countries and distant ages.

P. 143. **when it thunders the women cut their legs with knives till the blood flows, and then, catching the drops in a piece of bamboo, they cast them aloft towards the sky, to propitiate the angry deities.**—This custom, observed by the Negrito tribes

[1] R. V. Russell, *The Tribes and Castes of the Central Provinces of India* (London, 1916), iii. 19, 20 *sq.*, 23 *sq.*

[2] R. V. Russell, *The Tribes and Castes of the Central Provinces of India*, iii. 21.

of the Malay Peninsula for the purpose of stopping a thunderstorm, has often been described by subsequent inquirers.
Thus Mr. W. W. Skeat says : " During a storm of thunder
and lightning the Semang draw a few drops of blood from
the region of the shin-bone, mix it with a little water in a
bamboo receptacle, and throw it up to the angry skies
(according to the East Semang or Pangan, once up to the
sky and once on the ground, saying ' bö ', *i.e.* ' stop '). On
my inquiring further, one of the women offered to show me
how to do this, and drawing off a drop or two of blood into
a bamboo vessel by tapping with a stick the point of a
jungle-knife pressed against her shin-bone, she proceeded to
perform this strange ' libation ' ceremony in the manner thus
described." [1]

On this subject Mr. Ivor H. N. Evans writes : " Thunder
and lightning, being, according to Negrito ideas, caused by
the powers above, are much feared. The Menik Kaien and
Kintag Bong, I was told by Tōkeh, draw blood from the
outer side of the right leg near the shin-bone when a bad
thunderstorm comes on, and throw it up towards the sky
saying, *'Loim mahum pek keping !'* (*i.e.* ' Throw the blood
aloft ! '). Měmpělam, in 1921, supplemented my information with regard to the blood-offering made by Kintak Bong
when a bad storm arises, stating that before the blood is
thrown upward, as described above, a little is poured downwards to the earth for the benefit of the ' grandmothers ',
the person who makes the offering saying, '*Un Yak Kalcheng,
Yak Manoid, tembun ajer nteng chuchok Chapor, Chalog
chigiog nteng Tapern pi-weg kaii pek kid beteu !* ' This is, I
think, fairly correctly translated as follows : ' Yak Kalcheng,
Yak Manoid, come up *and* give advice *to the* ears *of your*
grandchildren Chapor *and* Chalog *to* relate *to the* ears *of*
Tapern *that he should make* go back *the* thunder to *the* roots
of the waters.'

" The Jehehr, cutting the leg in the same manner, take
a few drops of blood from the wound on the blade of the

---

[1] W. W. Skeat and C. O. Blagden,
Pagan Races of the Malay Peninsula
(London, 1906), ii. 204. Mr. Skeat
also quotes (p. 205, note [1]) a more detailed description of the same custom
by the German traveller Vaughan-
Stevens, according to whom the ceremony of cutting the skin is performed
both by men and women of all ages.

knife, and putting them into the palm of the left hand, throw them up into the air saying, '*Haroidh ! Saidth !*' ('Throw it away ! Sleep !' (?)). A man of the group which lives in the neighbourhood of Grik informed me that his people also perform the blood-throwing ceremony when frightened by thunder, saying as they do so, '*Daiah hog di-baling*', which seems to mean, 'Take up the blood (*darah* in Malay) that is thrown'."[1]

The blood sacrifice offered by these Negritos during thunderstorms was repeatedly witnessed by Mr. Paul Schebasta, who travelled among them in 1924 and 1925. On the first occasion, after an appalling crash of thunder and in a cascade of rain, he watched a woman, "who, with a splinter of bamboo (*abag*), was stabbing her shin until the blood poured from it. In her left hand she held a bamboo filled with water, into which she wiped off the blood. She then poured the mixture into a split bamboo and sprinkled a little of it upon the ground. Then she raised herself and began to scatter the blood and water in the air, once in the direction from which the thunder came, and then towards every quarter of the heavens, crying as she did so : '*Chub ! Chub !*' (Go ! Go !). . . . As I learned the following morning, the blood sacrifice is always consummated when the thunder crashes directly over the encampment. First the women draw blood from their calves with a bamboo, or with the knife used for rattan-splitting. Some of the mixture is then poured on the ground ; this is dedicated to Manoid, Karei's wife. That which is scattered in the air is for Karei, the thunder-god, himself."[2]

According to another account, it is a certain Pedn or Ta Pedn who lives up aloft and causes the thunder (*karei*) and hurls the lightning. But one of his informants informed Mr. Schebasta that Ta Pedn and Karei are one and the same person.[3]

[1] Ivor H. N. Evans, *Studies in Religion, Folk-lore, and Custom in British North Borneo and the Malay Peninsula* (Cambridge, 1923), pp. 151 *sq.*
[2] Paul Schebesta, *Among the Forest Dwarfs of Malaya* (London, N.D.), pp. 87 *sq.*

[3] P. Schebesta, *op. cit.* pp. 250-252. But according to another account Ta Pedn is a son of Karei, the thunder-god. Manoid is the wife of Karei and lives in the earth, while Karei dwells in the sky. See P. Schebesta, *op. cit.* pp. 185 *sq.*

Among the Kĕnsiu, one of the Negrito tribes, Mr. Schebesta had many opportunities of witnessing the blood ceremony and of acquainting himself with the details of the ritual and the accompanying prayers. The Kĕnsiu " believe that the thunder is Pedn's warning to sinners to expiate their transgressions. Should they hesitate to perform the blood ceremony, even only up to the fourth or fifth peal of thunder heard above the camp, they would incur the greatest danger of floods rising from the earth and trees falling upon men. This fear causes the Kĕnsiu at once to snatch up the knife and stab his leg." [1]

On one occasion, among the Kĕnsiu, Mr. Schebesta witnessed the sacrifice of blood accompanied by the confession of sins. " The storm came quickly up. Although it was not particularly heavy, Ramlei's wife at once prepared to carry out the blood sacrifice. She beat her shin with the flat handle of a cocoanut spoon, and then placed the blade of a pocket-knife I had given to Ramlei against her calf and struck it with a piece of wood until the blood flowed. With the knife she scraped off the blood into a bamboo that was standing ready filled with water. She poured some of the contents into the spoon and then threw it on the ground, saying : ' Grandmother, down there, I throw my guilt to Pedn ; I pay, I am not wanton.' Then she shouted aloud : ' *Od, od !* ' and threw the blood mixture repeatedly towards the sky, saying : ' I pay for my guilt. Pedn, accept my guilt ! I pay for it.' Then she poured the rest on the ground for Manoid, saying : ' Thou there, grandmother ! thou below there ! Go and tell Pedn to hear that I pay.' . . .

" Some days later, when the men had lain down to sleep after a long talk, distant thunder was repeatedly heard. Though the approaching storm was only slight, after the second peal the same woman was again preparing for the sacrifice. From my bed I watched her strike both shins with a bamboo and then draw off the blood with a knife in the way described. I asked my neighbour, Ramlei, who was busy with the camp fire, why it was again his wife who was performing the rite. The man replied that she had again committed a *telaidn* (sin), as that same day on an expedition in

[1] P. Schebesta, *Among the Forest Dwarfs of Malaya,* p. 252.

the forest she had caused pain to a leech. But Ramlei also prepared himself for the sacrifice, the reason for this being that in the morning he had laughed at a dog. His dog had crept up under my shelter looking for something to pick up and an ant had crept into his nose. The animal sneezed and shook its head desperately to get rid of the ant. Ramlei had laughed at this and now had to atone with his own blood. There was nothing unusual about the way he performed the ceremony, except that he called his sin *dusa les* (guilt connected with the ant), which expression he included in his formula." [1]

Thus it appears that among these tribes thunder is regarded as the sign of God's wrath at a sinner, and the sacrifice of blood is viewed as an atonement for sin, the consequent cessation of the thunder being taken as a token that the deity has accepted the sacrifice. This view is confirmed by what Mr. Schebesta tells us of the similar views about thunder which are held by the Kenta-Bogn, another Negrito tribe of the Malay Peninsula. With them " Kaei is the thunder, and at the same time the thunder-god, just as he is among the Jahai. When Kaei thunders, he is angry ; some one has assuredly transgressed one of his commandments, and in his wrath he demands atonement. As with all other Semang tribes, expiation takes the form of the blood sacrifice." [2] The transgression of one of Kaei's laws is called *telaidn* ; for each of them the transgressor must make atonement with his own blood. Among the sins which must be expiated with the sinner's blood are the killing of certain animals and the mocking or laughing at certain others, particularly the leech, a certain kind of serpent, butterflies, and various species of apes.[3] We can now understand why a woman had to atone with her blood for hurting a leech, and why her husband was obliged to submit to a similar punishment for laughing at a dog. Truly these forest dwarfs appear to have tender consciences.

P. 144. It was a common superstition in ancient Italy that if a woman were found spinning on a highroad, the crops would be spoiled for that year.—Some light is thrown on this curious

[1] P. Schebesta, *Among the Forest Dwarfs of Malaya*, pp. 252 *sq.*

[2] P. Schebesta, *op. cit.* p. 221.

[3] P. Schebesta, *op. cit.* pp. 222 *sq.*

belief by a parallel superstition of the Huzuls of the Carpathian mountains, who think that a hunter's wife should not spin while her husband is at his meal, else the game would turn and twist about like the spindle, and so the hunter would not be able to hit it.[1]   In like manner it may have been thought in ancient Italy that, if a woman were to spin beside a corn-field, the circular motion of the spindle would, by sympathetic magic, communicate such a circular motion to the cornstalks as would twist off the ears and so spoil the crop.

P. 145. The wood spirit Silvanus was believed to be very inimical to women in childbed.—With the precautions which the ancient Romans took to prevent this dangerous spirit from entering a house where there was a woman in travail we may compare the similar measures adopted by some of the Philippine Islanders in similar circumstances to exclude the dangerous ghost of a woman who has died in childbed (pontianak).   " The pontianak was an evil spirit which prevented women in travail from bringing forth. Hence, in order to exorcize it, still at the present day, when a woman begins to feel the pangs of labour, her husband cleans up the space in front of the house-door and kindles a great fire there ; after which he takes up his post on the ground floor, stark naked, with a sword in his hand, with which he cleaves the air, stabbing and cutting to prevent the demon from approaching until after his wife has been delivered."[2]   The particular people of the Philippines who practise this custom are the Tagalogs, as we learn from the account of a Spanish priest, Padre Tomas Ortiz, which was published at Manila in 1713.   He says that " to hinder the evil work of the patianak (sic), they make themselves naked, and arm themselves with cuirass, bolo, lance, and other arms, and in this manner place themselves on the ridge-pole of the roof, and also under the house, where they give many blows and thrusts with the bolo, and make many gestures and motions ordered to the same intent ".[3]

[1] Dr. R. F. Kaindl, " Zauberglaube bei den Huzulen ", Globus, lxxvi. (Brunswick, 1899), p. 273.
[2] J. Mallat, Les Philippines (Paris, 1846), i. 65.

[3] Fletcher   Gardner,   " Philippine (Tagalog) Superstitions ", Journal of American Folk-lore, xix. (1906), pp. 192 sq.   The bolo is a broad-bladed knife or sword.   See A. E. Jenks, The

P. 149. In the "Banquet of Trimalchio" there is a typical were-wolf story.

There is a Chinese story like the were-wolf story in Petronius, but in it the were-animal is not a wolf but a tiger. It runs as follows :

" A certain man in Sung-yang entered the mountain to gather fuel. Overtaken by the dark, he was pursued by two tigers. As quickly as he could he climbed a tree, which was, however, not very high, so that the tigers sprang up against it, but without reaching him. Suddenly they said to one another : ' If we can find Chu Tu-shi, we are sure to get this man.' One tiger then remained to keep watch at the tree, while the other went away, and on a sudden there appeared another tiger, leaner and longer, and consequently peculiarly fitted to catch prey. The moon was shining brightly that night, so that our hero distinctly discerned how the small tiger frequently stretched out its paws at his coat ; but his fuel-axe was still at his waist, and just when the brute grabbed at him again, he dealt it a blow and hacked off its fore-claw With loud roars the tigers ran off one after the other, and not until the morning the man went home.

" The assembled villagers asked him what had happened, and when he had related his adventure, one of them said : ' There lives one Chu Tu-shi in the east of this district ; let us go and visit him, to see whether it is he or not.' Some men went and asked about him. ' Last night ', they were told, ' he went out for some moments and wounded his hand ; hence he is now in bed.' Having thus attested that he was the tiger, they denounced him to the prefect of the district. This grandee ordered his underlings to arm themselves with swords, to besiege his dwelling, and set fire to it. Chu Tu-shi suddenly rose from his bed, ran about, changed into a tiger, and charging upon the men escaped ; and it is unknown whither he went." [1]

Bontoc Igorot (Manila, 1905), p. 130. For another account of the custom described in the text see Ferd. Blumentritt, " Der Ahnencultus und die religiösen Anschauungen der Malaien des Philippinen-Archipels", *Mittheilungen der Wiener Geographischen Gesellschaft* (1882), p. 178; *id.*, *Versuch einer Ethno-* *graphie der Philippinen* (Gotha, 1882), p. 14 (*Petermann's Mittheilungen, Ergänsungsheft*, No. 67). I have cited these authorities in my Commentary on the *Fasti* of Ovid (vol. iii. pp. 215 *sq.*).

[1] J. J. M. de Groot, *The Religious System of China*, v. (Leyden, 1907), p. 548.

An African parallel to the were-wolf story in Petronius may also be quoted, though in it the were-animal is neither a wolf nor a tiger but a hyena. In the district of Gesireh Sennar, a province of the Egyptian Sudan, the Hammeg and Fungi have the reputation of being powerful magicians. It is said that they can turn themselves into hyenas and in that guise scour the country at night, howling and gorging themselves on the flesh of their prey. By day they are men again ; but even by day they can by their mere look bewitch your bowels, heart, hand, or foot, so that these parts of your body wither up. It is dangerous to shoot at such were-hyenas by night. Once a soldier shot at one of these creatures and wounded it. The animal dragged itself away, but next morning, when the soldier followed up the blood tracks, they led him straight to the house of a man who was a notorious magician. Of the hyena nothing was to be seen, but the man of the house was suffering from a fresh wound, of which he died soon afterwards, and the soldier did not long survive him.[1] Which seems to show, as I have said, how dangerous it is to fire at a were-hyena ; in hitting the brute you may be signing your own death-warrant.

A FOLK-LORE MEDLEY

P. 153. βουλυτός, the Loosing of the Ox.—Lucian seems to employ βουλυτός in the sense of "evening"; for he represents Charon, the infernal ferryman, grumbling at Hermes for his delay in bringing the souls of the dead to the ferry. "The ferry-boat", he says, " is quite ready ; the bilge-water has been pumped out ; the mast is stepped, the sail spread, the oars are in the rowlocks ; so far as I am concerned, nothing remains but to haul up the anchor and set sail. But Hermes tarries, though he should have been here long ago. As you see, there is not a single passenger on board the boat, though she might have made three voyages to-day already, and it is now almost βουλυτός, and I have not taken so much as a penny fare yet."[2] As the joke here consists in the length of

[1] Ernst Marno, *Reisen im Gebiete des blauen und weissen Nil, im Egyptischen Sudan und den angrenzenden* *Negerländern, in den Jahren 1869 bis 1873* (Wien, 1874), pp. 239 *sq.*
[2] Lucian, *Cataplus*, 1.

time which Charon has been kept waiting for Hermes, it is probable that by βουλυτός Lucian meant us to understand "late evening" rather than a time soon after noon. Cicero also appears to use βουλυτός in the sense of "evening", for he speaks of a friend arriving "just at βουλυτός, while we were at dinner".[1] Virgil speaks of the oxen drawing home the upturned plough in the lengthening shadows cast by the descending sun,[2] and the picture of the ploughman's return is repeated by Horace and Ovid[3] in contexts which imply that the time was evening, not midday. In their age and country, accordingly, we must apparently suppose that βουλυτός was evening.

P. 155. Coins attached to the Face.—A Moorish marriage custom is thus described by Lancelot Addison, the father of the famous essayist : " In the interim of this entertainment, the bachelors make a kind of offering to their wedded companion ; in which they observe this method : the bridegroom placeth himself upon a little low seat, behind him stand two Negroes bending his head moderately back ; then come the bachelors, who cover the bridegroom's forehead and brow with metacales (or single coins of gold) and blankéles, according to their affection and ability : and as they lay them on, the Negroes stroke them off into a basin set for that purpose in the bridegroom's lap, who all the while shuts his eyes."[4] Among the Ruâfa of Morocco the bride's father presents her with an ornament consisting of dollar or half-dollar pieces threaded on a string of horsehair. This ornament the bride binds round her forehead on the morning after her marriage, and she wears it for a week. Afterwards she adorns herself with it only on special occasions, such as religious feasts, weddings, and visits to shrines. The ornament is purchased by the bride's father out of the dowry which he receives for her.[5]

In Cambodia there are idols inhabited by spirits who are

[1] Cicero, *Ad Atticum*, xv. 27, "*O turpem sororis tuae filium ! Cum haec scriberem, adventabat αὐτῇ βουλύσει cenantibus nobis.*"

[2] Virgil, *Ecl.* ii. 66.

[3] Horace, *Epodes*, ii. 63 *sq.* ; Ovid, *Fasti*, v. 497.

[4] Lancelot Addison, "An Account of West Barbary", in John Pinkerton's *General Collection of Voyages and Travels*, vol. xv. (London, 1814), p. 430.

[5] Edward Westermarck, *Marriage Ceremonies in Morocco* (London, 1914), pp. 72 *sq.*

ever ready to heal such as do them homage. It is particularly agreeable to these spirits to have their images regilt in whole or in part. So when suffering pilgrims come to be made whole they always bring with them gilt paper which they stick on that part of the idol which corresponds to the sick or injured part of their own body. They may accompany this act of devotion with prayers for success in business and the acquisition of a large fortune. In such cases the devotee may gild afresh the whole image from top to toe. Hence traces of gilding are to be seen almost everywhere on statues and the principal figures of bas-reliefs, and have led some people to suppose that originally all these sculptures were completely gilded.[1]

P. 156. Hide-Measured Lands.—To the examples of the widespread Dido story which I have cited in the text may be added the following :

Among the Jews, " according to a narrative mentioned by Samuel in his *Itinerary* (seventeenth century) a Keraïte of Egypt, named Samuel, had obtained, several generations before, from the queen regent of the country a grant of as much land outside of the town as could be enclosed within a bull's hide. He cut the hide into thin strips, out of which he made thongs as fine as hairs ; he then measured (with the thongs) a space of ground outside the town and appointed it to be used as a cemetery by the Jews." [2]

The Indians of Pennsylvania used to tell a similar tale of the arrival of the first Dutch colonists at New York Island. " They took every white man they saw for an inferior Mannitto (spirit) attendant on the supreme Deity, who shone superior in the red and laced clothes. As the whites became daily more familiar with the Indians, they at last proposed to stay with them, and asked only for so much ground for a garden spot as, they said, the hide of a bullock would cover or encompass, which hide was spread before them. The Indians readily granted this apparently reasonable request ; but the whites then took a knife and, beginning at one end of the hide, cut it up to a long rope, not thicker than a child's

---

[1] J. Moura, *Le Royaume de Cambodge* (Paris, 1883), i. 179.
[2] R. Basset, " La peau coupée en lanières ", *Revue des Traditions populaires*, vii. (1892), p. 551.

finger, so that by the time the whole was cut up, it made a great heap ; they then took the rope at one end, and drew it gently along, carefully avoiding its breaking. It was drawn out into a circular form, and being closed at its ends, encompassed a large piece of ground. The Indians were surprised at the superior wit of the whites, but did not wish to contend with them about a little land, as they had still enough themselves." [1]

The Burmese story of this type, which I have cited in the text, is told by Sir J. George Scott (Shway Yoe) in a slightly different form, which may be quoted here for comparison with Bastian's version :

" The chronicles of Prome relate the well-known world-story of the bullock's hide of ground. A tribe came from the East under the command of an Amazon. She obtained from the aborigines—probably now some of the hill-tribes in Arakan—a grant of as much land as could be enclosed within an ox-hide, and, following the example of Dido, cut the hide into strips. She got into difficulties, however, and would probably have been driven out had she not married a neighbouring king. A stepson of hers founded the ancient town of Tharekattara (Prome)." [2]

P. 158. a pleasant description of the way in which a Burmese monk contrives to make the best of both worlds.—Custom is found to wink at, if not to consecrate, many evasions of the strict Buddhistic rules of monastic life in Burma. Thus a monk is forbidden to touch gold and silver, but he is free to receive both in his hands if his hands are covered with a handkerchief. He may not ask for anything, not even for food to save his life from death by hunger ; but he may say, " Such and such a thing is useless to me ; but what is the value of that ? Thrice blessed is he that giveth alms, his merit will wax great." By such indirect requests he often

[1] The Rev. John Heckewelder, " An Account of the History, Manners, and Customs of the Indian Nations, who once inhabited Pennsylvania and the neighbouring States", *Transactions of the Historical and Literary Committee of the American Philosophical Society,* held at *Philadelphia, for promoting useful Knowledge,* vol. i. (Philadelphia, 1819), p. 58.

[2] Shway Yoe (Sir J. G. Scott), *The Burman, his Life and Notions* (London, 1910), p. 442.

2 K

gets the thing he wants without having to part with anything which he had previously received as alms.[1]

P. 159. Omens from Sneezing.—A passage of Plutarch shows clearly that an omen from sneezing varied according as the sneeze was heard on the right or on the left. In an imaginary dialogue on the subject of the famous familiar spirit, as we may call it, of Socrates, one of the speakers says he has heard that the spirit in question was simply a sneeze, either of the philosopher himself or of somebody near him; if somebody near him on the right sneezed, it was an intimation to Socrates that he was to go on with the thing he had in hand; but if somebody near him on the left sneezed, it was a sign to Socrates that he was to refrain.[2] On this interpretation a sneeze on the right was a good omen, a sneeze on the left was an evil omen; which agrees with the usual Greek view that the right was the lucky quarter, and the left the unlucky.

P. 163. Some of the ancients certainly thought that the swallow boded untimely death.—However, this view of the ill-omened character of the swallow is warmly disputed by the very writer who records it, to wit, Artemidorus, who in antiquity devoted as much misapplied labour to extracting sense from the nonsense of dreams as many modern psychologists.[3] Yet there seems to be some ground for thinking that, in certain circumstances, the ancient Greeks looked on the swallow with fear and aversion, and that consequently, far from welcoming the visit of a swallow, they tried to send the bird away to other people. For in speaking of poets Plato says that, if one of them were to come to his ideal city and propose to read his poems in public, the citizens should treat him with the utmost respect but should tell him that they have no occasion for

---

[1] Shway Yoe (Sir J. G. Scott), *The Burman, his Life and Notions* (London, 1910), p. 121, compare p. 136. As to the strict rules of monastic life in Burma and the conventional evasions of them, see further Father Sangermano, *The Burmese Empire a Hundred Years Ago* (Westminster, 1893), pp. 114 *sqq.*; Capt. C. J. F. S. Forbes, *British Burma and its People*

(London, 1878), pp. 330 *sqq.*

[2] Plutarch, *De genio Socratis*, xi. p. 581 A B. (Plutarch, *Moralia*, ed. Bernardakis, vol. iii. p: 502).

[3] Artemidorus, *Onirocriton libri V*, ed. R. Hercher (Lipsiae, 1864), ii. 66, pp. 157 *sq.* The reference to Artemidorus in the text (p. 163) should be corrected accordingly.

his services, and that they should send him away to another city, after pouring scented oil on his head and crowning him with fillets of wool.[1] Now we are informed by Dio Chrysostom that what Plato here playfully proposes to do to the poets is just what women actually did to the swallows,[2] from which we may infer that it was a custom of Greek women to catch a swallow, pour scented oil on its head, crown it with a fillet of wool, and let it fly away, hoping that it would not come back. Such a custom implies a mixture of respect and fear ; the respect is displayed by the anointing and crowning of the bird, the fear is indicated by sending it away. With such mixed feelings the ancient Greeks appear to have regarded swallows. We can therefore understand both why some people welcomed them to their houses and why other people respectfully banished them.

P. 165. a custom of dressing boys as girls . . . to avert malignant influences, especially the evil eye, from the child.—In the North-West Provinces of India, " a woman whose sons have died, gets the nose of her new-born son bored and puts on it a nose-ring, indicative of the fact that the child is not a boy but a girl. The nose-ring is worn till marriage, when it is removed by the bride's mother, or in her absence by some elderly female relative. . . . The idea, of course, is to avoid the evil eye." [3] Similarly in India " change of sex is often simulated in marriage rites, when it is not uncommon to dress the bridegroom as a girl, or vice versa, apparently with the object of avoiding fascination. Gaoli herdsmen in the Central Provinces dress the bridegroom in women's clothes when he goes to fetch his bride, and as an additional protection he carries a dagger or a nut-cracker, and the girl wears an iron bangle. Abhīras, who follow the same occupation in Khāndesh, dress the bride in a man's turban and coat, seat her on a horse and parade her through the village ; and at a Brahman wedding in Kanara the bride hides in the house and the groom has to find her, her place in the wedding hall being taken by a boy in female dress." [4]

[1] Plato, *Republic*, iii. 9, p. 398 A.

[2] Dio Chrysostom, *Or.* liii., vol. ii. pp. 164 *sq.*, ed. L. Dindorf.

[3] *North Indian Notes and Queries*, vol. iii. No. 99, p. 46.

[4] W. Crooke, *Religion and Folklore of Northern India*, edited by R. E. Enthoven (Oxford University Press, 1926), pp. 279 *sq.*

500 GARNERED SHEAVES

A SUGGESTION AS TO THE ORIGIN OF GENDER IN LANGUAGE

P. 184. Differences between the speech of the two sexes have been observed among other South American tribes.—On this subject the eminent French ethnologist, Alcide d'Orbigny, who spent about eight years with a scientific expedition exploring a great part of the interior of South America, expresses himself as follows :

" Another sort of exception has given rise to much speculation. In certain languages the words employed by the man are different from those employed by the woman, every word, in passing through a woman's mouth, taking a distinct termination. The language of the Chiquitos presents this characteristic in the highest degree ; but in the others, where it is found, it is limited to terms of relationship. For a very long time this anomaly has been explained by the habit of certain conquering peoples (especially the Guaranis) to kill the men and keep the women—a supposition which seems to me fairly probable." [1] Again, speaking specially of the Chiquitos, a numerous nation which inhabits the dense forests of Eastern Bolivia, the same writer observes : " A singular anomaly meets us in the Chiquitan language, in which for many things the man uses different words from those employed by the woman ; while for other things the woman uses the same words as the man, contenting herself with changing the terminations." [2] " A particularity of this language is the difference in the expressions employed by the two sexes to designate the same objects. Not only have the names of objects in the speech of women different terminations from those employed in the speech of the men, but in addition the words are often quite unlike ; thus the man expresses ' father ' by *Iyài*, and the woman expresses it by *Yxupu* (pronounced *Ychoupou*)." [3]

[1] Alcide d'Orbigny, *L'Homme Américain (de l'Amérique Méridionale)* (Paris, 1839), i. 153.

[2] A. d'Orbigny, *L'Homme Américain*, ii. 135.

[3] A. d'Orbigny, *L'Homme Américain*, ii. 163. I cited d'Orbigny's evidence on this subject many years ago. See my article, " Men's Language and Women's Language ", *Man*, i. (1901), No. 129, pp. 154 *sq.*

Again, speaking of the language of the Caraya tribes on the Rio Araguaya in Brazil, the German ethnologist Dr. P. Ehrenreich, who visited the tribes in 1888, observes that " its most remarkable peculiarity is the existence of a special speech for men and a special speech for women, just as occurs among the Guaycurus and the Chiquitanos (Chiquitos). However, only a few words are quite different; in most words the form is only slightly modified. Where, for example, in the men's dialect two vowels follow each other, in the women's dialect the vowels are separated by a *k*. Thus, for instance, ' rain ' is *biū* in the men's dialect, but *bikū* in the women's dialect; ' maize ' is *mahī* in the men's dialect, but *makī* in the women's dialect. Sometimes the woman's word has only an additional syllable at the end, etc. Probably the women have only retained an older form of the language." [1]

Elsewhere Dr. Ehrenreich has published a long list of words which differ more or less in the speech of Caraya men and women.[2] Here it may suffice to give some specimens from the list :

	WOMEN'S SPEECH	MEN'S SPEECH
my shoulder	*wasikotă*	*wasiotă*
nail	*desikä*	*desiä*
girl	*yadokoma*	*yadŏma*
upper arm	*wa-anthika*	*wa-anthia*
tongue	*toroto*	*wa-daratŏ*
mouth	*rŭŭ*	*wa-ru*
sole of the foot	*wa-wakubĕ*	*wa-waubĕ*
brain	*i-raokunĕ*	*i-raonĕ*
bone	*i-ti*	*wa-ti*
liver of fish	*i-tari*	*wa-tari*
fire	*hekautŏ*	*he-autŏ*
sky	*bikuätĕkĕ*	*biuätekĕ*
house	*hetŏkŭ*	*hetŏ*
hammock	*riakŭ*	*riiŏ*
son (small child)	*warikorĕ*	*wariorĕ*
chief	*hauatŏ*	*isandenŏdŏ*
coco-nut	*hĕĕrŭ*	*uoŏ*
to eat	*rokusi*	*rŏsi*
to weep	*i-berŏ*	*ro-bŭ-rere*
to hunt, seek	*ditiüänanderi*	*iramdănrăkrĕ*

[1] P. Ehrenreich, *Beiträge zur Völkerkunde Brasiliens* (Berlin, 1891), p. 9.
[2] P. Ehrenreich, " Materialien zur Sprachenkunde Brasiliens ", *Zeitschrift für Ethnologie*, xxvi. (1894), pp. 20-37, 49-60.

Another eminent German ethnologist, the late Theodor Koch, remarks that the differences between the speech of men and women in the Mbaya language have been attested by many inquirers, and he collects from earlier authorities a number of examples, among which may be noted the following : [1]

	MEN'S SPEECH	WOMEN'S SPEECH
to die	*aleo*	*gemá*
dead	*alco*	*ghema*
I go to the house	*saragigo oypilo*	*saragigo yoi*
to drink	*jaguipá*	*jaucá*
man	*houlegre*	*agouina*
water	*nógodi*	*niðgo*
now	*anaga leegi*	*aca*
late evening	*coquidi*	*aguy*
quickly	*ale*	*otegĕ*

Among the Indian tribes of North America there appears to be very little evidence of a difference of speech between men and women. However, in regard to the Hitchiti, a Muskhogean tribe, we are told that their language, " like the Creek, has an archaic form called ' women's talk ', or female language ".[2] And in regard to the languages of the North American Indians in general we read that " one of the frequent types of differences is that between the language of men and that of women. This difference may be one of pronunciation, as among some Eskimo tribes, or may consist in the use of different sets of imperative and declarative particles, as among the Sioux, or in other differences of vocabulary ; or it may be more fundamental, due to the foreign origin of the women of the tribe." [3]

In regard to the language spoken by the natives of the Aleutian Islands, off the north-western coast of North America, it is said that in it, " as in the Greenland language, there is a marked difference between the speech of men and the speech of women ".[4]

Still rarer, apparently, are traces of a difference of speech

[1] Theodor Koch, " Die Guaikuru-Gruppe ", *Mittheilungen der Anthropologischen Gesellschaft in Wien*, xxxiii. (1903), p. 16

[2] *Handbook of American Indians*, edited by F. W. Hodge, Part I. (Washington, 1907), p. 551.

[3] *Handbook of American Indians*, edited by F. W. Hodge, Part I. p. 759, *s.v.* " Languages ".

[4] Adelbert von Chamisso, *Reise um die Welt mit der Romanzoffischen*

between men and women in other parts of the world. However, in regard to the Jadam, a caste of Rajput descent in the Central Provinces of India, it has been stated that " both sexes have a peculiarity in their speech, men using the feminine form of verbs and women the masculine form ".[1] However, the statement seems to lack confirmation.[2]

P. 195. the Carib and Arawak languages . . . are perhaps the only native American languages which exhibit true grammatical gender.—On this subject the eminent American philologist, A. S. Gatschet, whose evidence I have quoted in the text, says in another place : " What seems to be a genuine sex-denoting affix to the noun appears in one of the South American linguistic families of the northern part of that continent. This stock is commonly designated as *Carib*." [3] And in regard to the Tonika language the same authority says : " The only sex-denoting language which I have had the opportunity to study is the Tonika or Toniχka of Eastern Louisiana, discovered by me in the autumn of 1886. It proved to be a language heretofore unknown to science, and by its strange peculiarities deserves to be carefully studied and compared with other languages, especially with those spoken in its nearest vicinity." [4]

Entdeckungs-Expedition in den Jahren 1815-1818 (Leipzig, 1836), vol. ii. p. 379, " *Im Aleutischen wie im Grönlandischen findet zwischen der Rede der Männer und der der Frauen ein ausgezeichneter Unterschied statt*".

[1] *Central Provinces, Ethnographic Survey*, vi. Draft Articles (Allahabad, 1911), p. 59.

[2] It is omitted in the account of the Jadam which is given in R. V. Russell's

Tribes and Castes of the Central Provinces of India (London, 1916), iii. 217-219, which is based upon the *Ethnographic Survey*.

[3] Albert S. Gatschet, "Sex-denoting Nouns in American Languages" *Transactions of the American Philological Association*, xx. (Boston, 1889), p. 161.

[4] Albert S. Gatschet, *op. cit.* p. 163.

APPENDIX

FOR the sake of completeness it may be well to give here the text of the two Jewish versions of the story of *The Language of Animals* to which reference has been made above.[1] One of them runs as follows :

" Annually a man came from a great distance to pay a visit to the wise king, and when he departed Solomon was in the habit of bestowing a gift upon him. Once the guest refused the gift, and asked the king to teach him the language of the birds and the animals instead. The king was ready to grant his request, but did not fail to warn him first of the great danger connected with such knowledge. ' If thou tellest others a word of what thou hearest from an animal,' he said, ' thou wilt surely suffer death ; thy destruction is inevitable.' Nothing daunted, the visitor persisted in his wish, and the king instructed him in the secret art.

" Returned home, he overheard a conversation between his ox and his ass. The ass said : ' Brother, how farest thou with these people ? '

" The ox : ' As thou livest, brother, I pass day and night in hard and painful toil.'

" The ass : ' I can give thee relief, brother. If thou wilt follow my advice, thou shalt live in comfort, and shalt rid thyself of all thy hard work.'

" The ass : ' O brother, may thy heart be inclined toward me, to take pity on me and help me. I promise not to depart from thy advice to the right or the left.'

" The ass : ' God knows, I am speaking to thee in the uprightness of my heart and the purity of my thoughts. My advice to thee is not to eat either straw or fodder this night. When our master notices it, he will suppose that thou art sick. He will put no burdensome work upon thee, and thou canst take a good rest. That is the way I did to-day.'

" The ox followed the advice of his companion. He touched none of the food thrown to him. The master, suspecting a ruse on the part of the ass, arose during the night, went to the stable, and watched the ass eat his fill from the manger belonging to the ox. He could not help laughing out loud, which greatly amazed his wife, who, of course, had noticed nothing out of the way. The master evaded her questions. Something ludicrous had just occurred to him, he said by way of explanation.

" For the sly trick played upon the ox, he determined to punish the ass. He ordered the servant to let the ox rest for the day, and make the ass do the work of both animals. At evening the ass trudged into the stable tired and exhausted. The ox greeted him with the words : ' Brother, hast thou heard aught of what our heartless masters purpose ? ' ' Yes,' replied the ass, ' I heard them speak of having thee slaughtered, if thou shouldst refuse to eat this night, too. They want to make sure of thy flesh at least.' Scarcely had the ox heard the words of the ass when he threw himself upon his food like a ravenous lion upon his prey. Not a speck did he leave behind, and the master was suddenly moved to uproarious laughter. This time his wife insisted upon knowing the cause. In vain she entreated and supplicated. She swore not to live with him any more if he did not tell her why he laughed. The man loved her so devotedly that he was ready to sacrifice his life to satisfy her whim, but before taking leave of this world he desired to see his friends and relations once more, and he invited them all to his house.

" Meantime his dog was made aware of the master's approaching end, and such sadness took possession of the faithful beast that he touched neither food nor drink. The cock, on the other hand, gaily appropriated the food intended for the dog, and he and his wives enjoyed a banquet. Outraged by such unfeeling behaviour, the dog said to the cock : ' How great is thy impudence, and how insignificant thy modesty ! Thy master is but a step from the grave, and thou eatest and makest merry.' The cock's reply was : ' Is

it my fault if our master is a fool and an idiot ?   I have ten
wives, and I rule them as I will.   Not one dares oppose me
and my commands.   Our master has a single wife, and this
one he cannot control and manage.'   ' What ought our
master to do ? ' asked the dog.   ' Let him take a heavy stick
and belabour his wife's back thoroughly,' advised the cock,
' and I warrant thee, she won't plague him any more to reveal
his secrets.'

" The husband had overheard this conversation, too, and
the cock's advice seemed good.   He followed it and death
was averted." [1]

This version of the story reveals the interested motive
which the ass had in tendering his apparently disinterested
advice to the ox ; he calculated on himself devouring the
fodder left untouched by his bovine brother, but though he
succeeded in doing so he was outwitted by the superior
cunning of his master.

The other Jewish, or possibly Moslem, version of the
story, taken down from oral tradition in Palestine, runs
thus :

" There was once a merchant who knew the language of
beasts.   But this knowledge had been granted him only
upon condition that, if he told the secrets learnt by its means,
he should die instantly.   No one, not even his wife, was
aware that he was gifted beyond the common.

" One evening, standing near his stables, he heard an ox,
which had just returned from ploughing, complaining bitterly
of his hard labour, and asking the ass on which the merchant
rode to business how he might lighten it.   The ass advised
him to be very ill, to leave his food untouched and roll on
the ground in pain, when the ploughman came to take him
to the field.   The ox took this advice, and next day his master
was told he was too ill to work.   The merchant prescribed
rest and extra food for the ox, and ordered that the donkey,
which was strong and fat, should be yoked to the plough in
his place.

" That evening the merchant stood again by the stable,
listening.   When the ass came in from ploughing, the ox
thanked him for his advice, and expressed the intention to

[1] L. Ginzberg, *The Legends of the Jews*, iv. (Philadelphia, 1913), pp. 138-141.

act upon it again next morning. ' I don't advise you to do that,' said the ass, ' if you value your life. To-day, while I was ploughing, our master came into the field and told the ploughman to take you to the butcher's to-morrow, as you seemed ailing, and have you killed to save your life ; for should you sicken and die, he would lose the value of your carcase.' ' What shall I do ? ' cried the ox in terror. ' Be well and strong to-morrow morning,' said the ass. At that the merchant, unaware that his wife stood near him, laughed aloud, and excited her curiosity. His evasive answers only made her more inquisitive ; and when he absolutely refused to satisfy her, she lost her temper, and went to complain of him to her relations, who soon threatened him with a divorce. The poor man, who really loved his wife, in despair resolved to tell her all and die·; so he put his affairs in order, made his will, and promised to content her on the morrow.

" Next morning, at a window overlooking the stable yard, where a cock was gallanting with a number of hens, he heard his watch-dog reprove the bird for such light conduct on a day of grief. ' Why l what is the matter ? ' inquired the cock. The dog told the story of their master's trouble, when the cock exclaimed : ' Our master is a fool. He cannot keep one wife in order, while I have no trouble with twenty. He has only to take a stick and give the mistress a sound thrashing to make her amiable.' These words came as light to the merchant's gloom. Forthwith he called his wife into an inner room, and there chastised her within an inch of her life. And from that hour she gave him no more trouble." [1]

Both these Jewish versions are clearly duplicates of the corresponding story in *The Arabian Nights*,[2] and may be borrowed from it.

[1] J. E. Hanauer, *Folk-lore of the Holy Land, Moslem, Christian and Jewish*, edited by M. Pickthall (London, 1910), pp. 258-260.

[2] See above, pp. 114 *sq.*

INDEX

The numbers refer to the pages

Classificatory system of relationship, 374, 407

Claudius, the Emperor, 479

Clavie at Burghead, 62 *n.*

Cleonae, in Argolis, mode of averting hail at, 142, 486

Clothes as bait to soul of the dying, 28

Clyack sheaf, 172, 174, 177

Clytaemnestra murdered by Orestes, 421 *sq.*

Cock in the Language of Animals, speech of the, 113, 115, 447, 451, 453, 455, 463, 465, 467, 468, 469, 471, 472, 475; sacrificed to avert wind or clouds, 143

Codrington, R. H., on taboo, 88

Coins in mouth of the dead, 19 *n.*[2], 370; attached to the face, 155 *sq.*, 495

Colour, adjectives of, their absence in Greek literature, 263 *sq.*

Colours in mourning, 45 *sq.*

Columbia, the Uitoto of, 406

Communal house, 407

Communism, sexual, 330

Comanche Indians, mourning custom of, 44

Comparative method in anthropology, 240 *sq.*, 246 *sq.*, 270 *sq.*, 275 *sq.*; applied to the history of religion, 272

—— study of man, 419

Compluvium, 42 *n.*, 50, 75 *n.*[1], 78

Conclamatio, 47

Condorcet dressed as a girl in childhood, 166

Confucianism, origin of, 477

Congo, the basin of the, 313; the Baluba of the, 481 *sq.*

—— negroes, their custom after a death, 31

Continence in war, rule of, 90

Contradiction, the law of, 413, 416

Cook, A. B., on the leafy bust at Nemi, 169

Corea, death customs in, 9, 12, 20 *n.*; funeral custom in, 29, 43; corpse candles in, 34 *n.*; fasting after a death in, 35; mourning costume in, 45, 46; recall of the soul in, 46 *sq.*; king of, his avoidance of iron, 63 *n.*; perpetual house-fires in, 73

Cornutus as to piles of stones, 210 *n.*[1]

Cornwall, belief as to serpent-rings in, 124, 478; the last sheaf called the Craw (crow) in, 176 *n.*[1]

Corwichen, clyack sheaf at, 177

Cousins, marriage of, 306, 318

Couvade, 407 *sq.*; among the Bushongo, 315

Coxwell, C. Fillingham, his *Siberian and other Folk-tales*, 431

Crawley, A. E., on the youth of Achilles, 165

Creator god, 339

Crete, burial customs in, 18, 21; pigs sacred in, 91

Crooke, W., on marriage customs in India, 499

Cross-cousins, marriage of, 306

Crow reveals a buried treasure, 451

Crows, language of, 94, 106, 107

Cumming, Miss Gordon, 117, 123

Cunningham, R. W., on cutting the last corn, 176

Curcho, a Lithuanian deity, 74 *n.*[1]

Curses, benefits expected from, 145; combined with stones, 205, 206, 208

Curtius, E., on the prytaneum at Athens, 54 *n.*[7]

Curuguaty in Paraguay, 184

Cuzco, sacred fire at, 68

Cyclades, custom at childbirth in the, 27 *n.*[1]; mourning custom in the, 36

Cyprus, burial custom in, 18

Daldouie, near Glasgow, the harvest " Maiden " at, 174

Damaraland and ancient Italy, parallel between, 65 *sq.*, 427 *sqq.*

Damaras, burial customs of, 5, 6, 8; purification of Damara hunters, 22 *sq.*; their perpetual fire, 64 *sq.*, 427 *sqq.*; their superstition about footprints, 139 *See* Herero

Damascus, 452, 454

Dances, to expel ghosts, 7; masked, to heal the sick, 43; of the Salii, 360; frenzied, of priestesses, 384 *sq.*

Dannert, Rev. E., on birth customs and sacred fire of the Ovaherero, 427 *sq.*

Dards observe continence in war, 90; Shin caste of the, 91

Darien, custom as to the sick at, 9

Darwin, Charles, and the theory of evolution, 235, 271

——, Francis, on leafy bust at Nemi, 170 *sq.*; Miss Darwin (Mrs. Cornford), on *id.*, 171

David, King, his fast for Abner, 35 *sq.*; cursed by Shimei, 206 *sq.*

Davidson, J., on Formosa, 383

De Coulanges, Fustel, 74 *n.*[5]

Kaffir customs at sickness and death, 8
—— hunters, purification of, 22 ;
treatment of the sick, 26 ; of widows,
27
Kaffirs fast after a death, 35 ; birth
custom of, 43
Kaia Imunu, god of the sky, 389
Kakhyens, their burial customs, 7, 11,
20 *n.*, 30 ; their idea about women
dying in childbed, 10 *sq.*
Kalahari desert, 321 *sq.*, 323
Kali, the goddess, imparts a know-
ledge of the language of animals,
105
Kalmuck story of the language of
animals, 104
Kalmucks, their custom at a death,
25 *n.*
Kamba, tribe of Kenya Colony, 357,
360
Kamchatkans, their rule about knives
and fire, 133
Kampilya, in India, 433
Kanarese regions of Bombay, 363
Kanikars of Travancore, their practice
at a death, 25 *n.*
Kanuri language, story of the Lan-
guage of Animals in the, 459
Karei, thunder-god, 489
Karens of Burma, their superstition
about footprints, 139
Kasi Indians, funeral custom of the,
19 *n.*²
Kasna Chan, 444
Kattadias in Ceylon, masked dances
of, 43
Katur tribe of Palaungs, 367
Kĕnsiu, a Negrito tribe, their custom
in regard to thunder, 490
Kenta-Bogn, a Negrito tribe, their
notions about thunder, 491
Kenya, vanishing tribes of, 348 *sqq.* ;
Mount Kenya, 348 ; the Nandi of,
485
Khakan, title of the Khazar kings,
213, 217, 218, 223, 226, 227, 228,
230, 231 ; title of Turkish prince,
233
Khasis of Assam, their language, 367
Khazar Kings, the killing of the,
212 *sqq.* ; their kingdom, 212 *sq.* ;
accepted Judaism, 213
Khazaria, the kingdom of the Khazars,
215
Khozars or Khazars, 213, 228, 229,
230, 231. *See* Khazars

Kikuyu, tribe of Kenya Colony, 357,
360
Kildare, perpetual fire of St. Bridget
at, 67
Kilimanjaro and its people, 354 *sqq.*
King, temporary, put to death after
short reign, 329 *sq.* ; not allowed to
grow old, 334 ; his soul trans-
migrates into a lion, 336
—— of Kitara, 327, 329 ; obliged to
take poison in case of serious illness,
329
—— of the Snakes, 121 *n.*², 469 ; of
the Fishes, 123 ; of the Serpents,
125, 452 ; of the Wood at Nemi,
169, 170 ; of the Fairies, 446 ; of
Adders, 478
King's mother obliged to take poison
in serious illness, 334
—— palace at Athens, 56, 57 ; at
Rome (the Regia), 58, 60
Kingfisher stole the first fire for man,
376
Kings as priests, 59 *n.*¹ ; put to death
on failure of their health, on occasion of public calamities, or at end
of fixed period, 212, 219, 223, 226,
227, 230, 232 *sq.* ; early, deified,
334 *sq.*
Kinross, " dumping " at harvest in,
180
Kinship, scrupulosity of the savage as
to prohibited degrees of, 318
Kintag Bong, a Negrito people, 488
Kirghiz story of language of geese,
104
Kirk, Rev. Mr., on the fairies, 175
Kirn, coagulated cream eaten at
harvest, 173 *sq.*
Kirn-dollie, kirn baby, names of last
corn cut, 177
Kitara or Bunyoro, a country of Central
Africa, 328
Knives not to be left edge upwards, 31
Koch, Theodor, on differences of speech
between the sexes in the Mbaya lan-
guage, 502
Köhler, Reinhold, 99 *n.*¹
Kolben on the Hottentots, 324
Koossa Kaffirs. *See* Kaffirs
—— widow, mourning custom of, 45
Koosas, their treatment of the sick, 26
Koulangos, a tribe of the Ivory Coast,
303, 304, 305, 306, 307
Kovave, god of the mountains, 389,
390

2 M

THE END

For Product Safety Concerns and Information please contact our EU
representative GPSR@taylorandfrancis.com
Taylor & Francis Verlag GmbH, Kaufingerstraße 24, 80331 München, Germany

www.ingramcontent.com/pod-product-compliance
Lightning Source LLC
Chambersburg PA
CBHW070622270326
41926CB00011B/1786